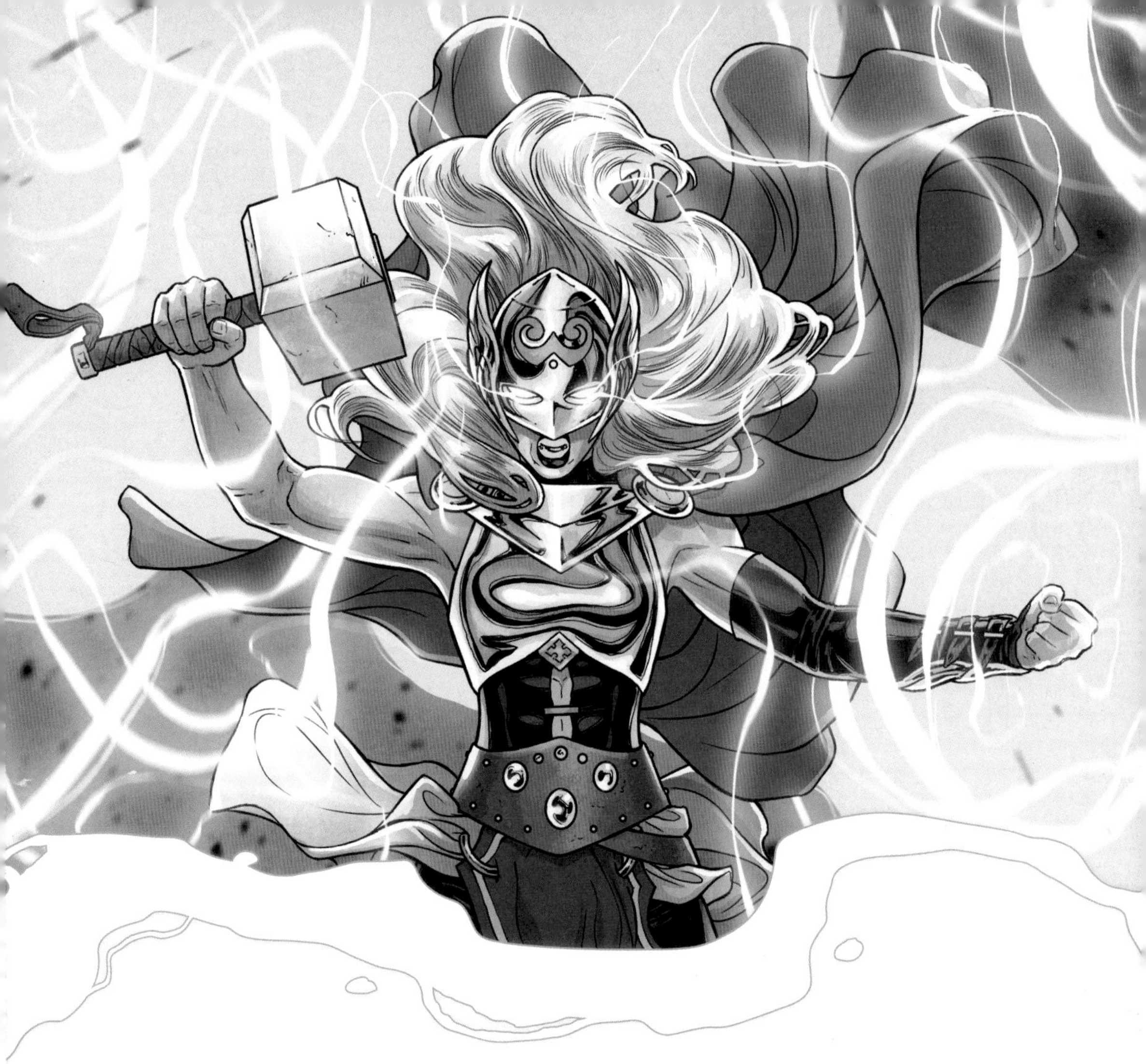

MALEKITH AND HIS ALLIES ARE WAGING WAR ACROSS THE TEN REALMS. TO STOP HIM, VOLSTAGG PICKED UP THE HAMMER OF THE ULTIMATE THOR AND BECAME THE WAR THOR — BUT ITS POWER DROVE HIM INTO A MAD BLOODLUST. THOR COULD NOT CALM HIM, BUT JANE FOSTER REMINDED HIM OF HIS HUMANITY, AND HE GAVE UP THE HAMMER.

AND SO THE WAR — AGAINST MALEKITH, AND AGAINST JANE'S CANCER — CONTINUES. SO, TOO, DOES THE LEGACY OF THOR, AND OF THE ODINSON WHO HAS LONG CARRIED THAT NAME. THIS IS A STORY OF THE ANCIENT, THE PRESENT AND THE FORETOLD…

DEDICATED TO MICHAEL W. WILSON

**THOR** CREATED BY **STAN LEE, LARRY LIEBER** & **JACK KIRBY**

COLLECTION EDITOR: **JENNIFER GRÜNWALD**
ASSISTANT EDITOR: **CAITLIN O'CONNELL**
ASSOCIATE MANAGING EDITOR: **KATERI WOODY**
EDITOR, SPECIAL PROJECTS: **MARK D. BEAZLEY**

VP, PRODUCTION & SPECIAL PROJECTS: **JEFF YOUNGQUIST**
SVP PRINT, SALES & MARKETING: **DAVID GABRIEL**
BOOK DESIGNER: **ADAM DEL RE**

EDITOR IN CHIEF: **C.B. CEBULSKI**
CHIEF CREATIVE OFFICER: **JOE QUESADA**
PRESIDENT: **DAN BUCKLEY**
EXECUTIVE PRODUCER: **ALAN FINE**

**MIGHTY THOR VOL. 5: THE DEATH OF THE MIGHTY THOR.** Contains material originally published in magazine form as MIGHTY THOR #700-706 and MIGHTY THOR: AT THE GATES OF VALHALLA #1. First printing 2018. ISBN 978-1-302-90660-3. Published by MARVEL WORLDWIDE, INC., a subsidiary of MARVEL ENTERTAINMENT, LLC. OFFICE OF PUBLICATION: 135 West 50th Street, New York, NY 10020. Copyright © 2018 MARVEL No similarity between any of the names, characters, persons, and/or institutions in this magazine with those of any living or dead person or institution is intended, and any such similarity which may exist is purely coincidental. **Printed in the U.S.A.** DAN BUCKLEY, President, Marvel Entertainment; JOHN NEE, Publisher; JOE QUESADA, Chief Creative Officer; TOM BREVOORT, SVP of Publishing; DAVID BOGART, SVP of Business Affairs & Operations, Publishing & Partnership; DAVID GABRIEL, SVP of Sales & Marketing, Publishing; JEFF YOUNGQUIST, VP of Production & Special Projects; DAN CARR, Executive Director of Publishing Technology; ALEX MORALES, Director of Publishing Operations; DAN EDINGTON, Managing Editor; SUSAN CRESPI, Production Manager; STAN LEE, Chairman Emeritus. For information regarding advertising in Marvel Comics or on Marvel.com, please contact Vit DeBellis, Custom Solutions & Integrated Advertising Manager, at vdebellis@marvel.com. For Marvel subscription inquiries, please call 888-511-5480. **Manufactured between 4/20/2018 and 5/22/2018 by LSC COMMUNICATIONS INC., KENDALLVILLE, IN, USA.**

10 9 8 7 6 5 4 3 2 1

# THE MIGHTY THOR

## THE DEATH OF THE MIGHTY THOR

WRITER
**JASON AARON**

---

MIGHTY THOR #700

ARTISTS
**WALTER SIMONSON & MATTHEW WILSON, RUSSELL
DAUTERMAN & WILSON, DANIEL ACUÑA, JAMES HARREN &
DAVE STEWART, BECKY CLOONAN & STEWART, DAS PASTORAS,
CHRIS BURNHAM & IVE SVORCINA, ANDREW MACLEAN &
STEWART, JILL THOMPSON, MIKE DEL MUNDO**
AND **OLIVIER COIPEL & STEWART**

---

MIGHTY THOR #701

ARTIST
**JAMES HARREN**

COLOR ARTIST
**DAVE STEWART**

---

MIGHTY THOR #702-706

ARTIST
**RUSSELL DAUTERMAN**

COLOR ARTIST
**MATTHEW WILSON**

---

MIGHTY THOR: AT THE GATES OF VALHALLA

ARTISTS
**JEN BARTEL
& RAMÓN PÉREZ**

COLOR ARTIST
**MATTHEW WILSON**

---

COVER ART
**RUSSELL DAUTERMAN & MATTHEW WILSON** (#700-705),
**RUSSELL DAUTERMAN** (#706) AND **NICK DERINGTON** (AT THE GATES OF VALHALLA)

LETTERER
**VC's JOE SABINO**

ASSOCIATE EDITOR
**SARAH BRUNSTAD**

EDITOR
**WIL MOSS**

## 700

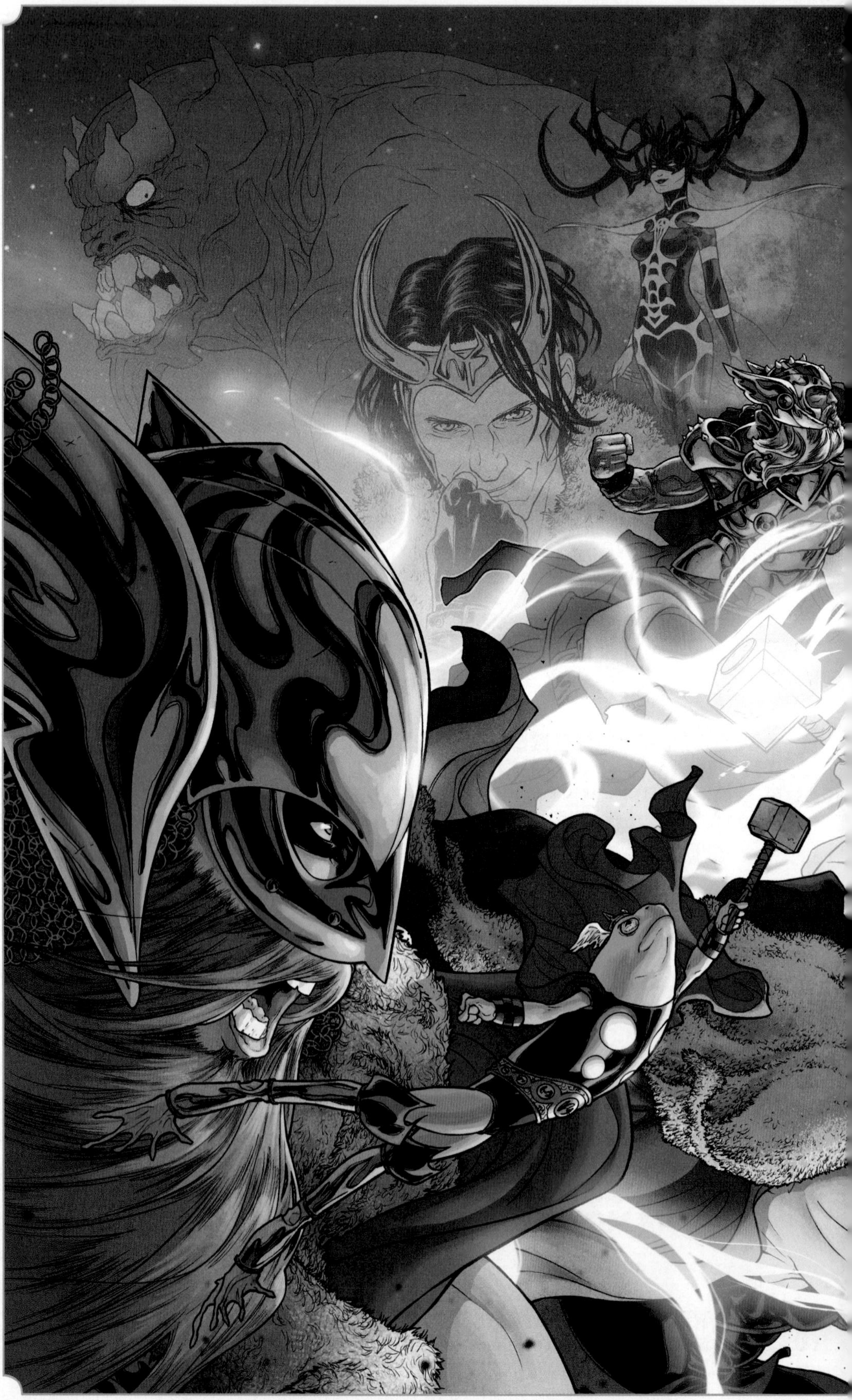

# THE BLOOD OF THE NORNS

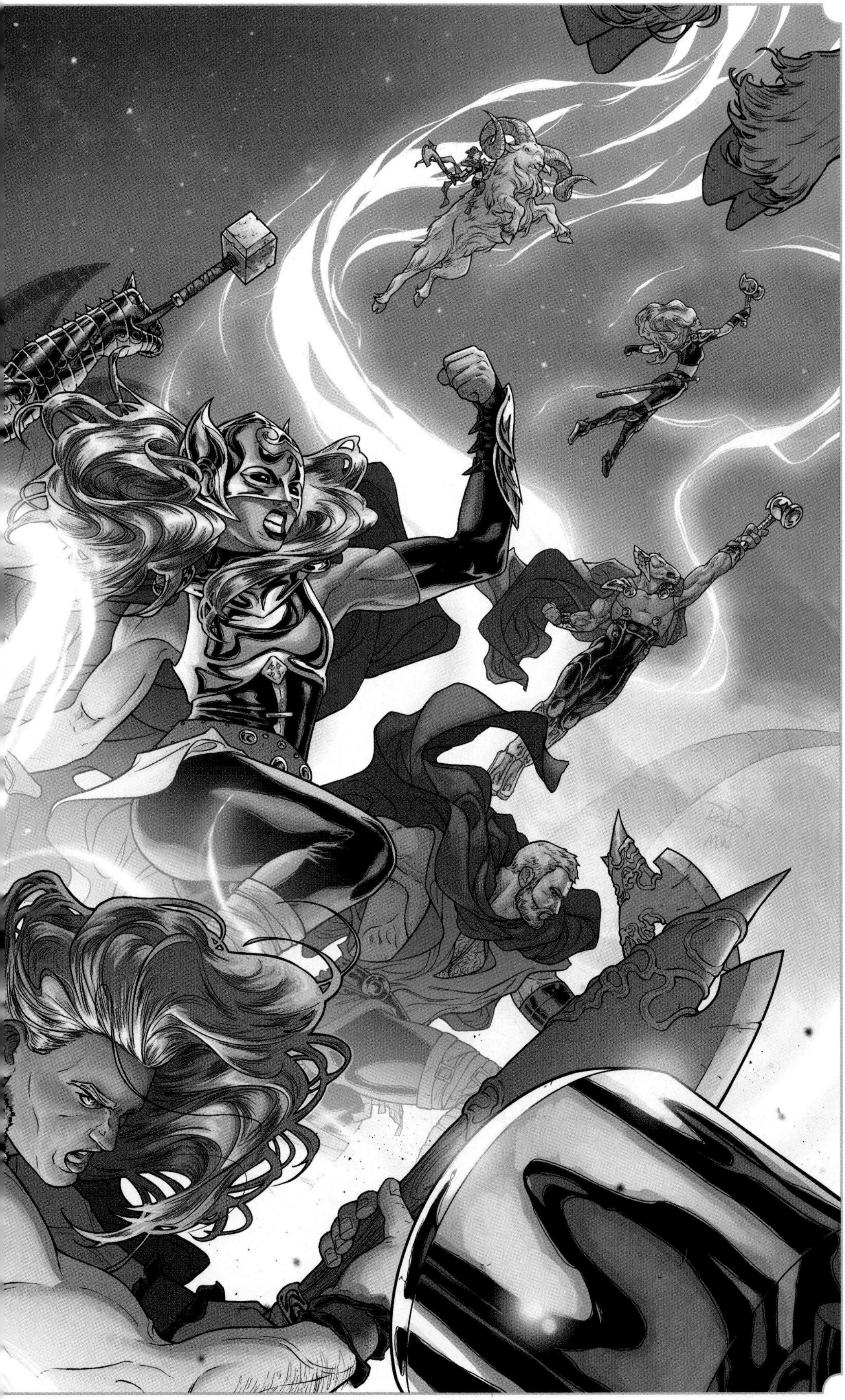

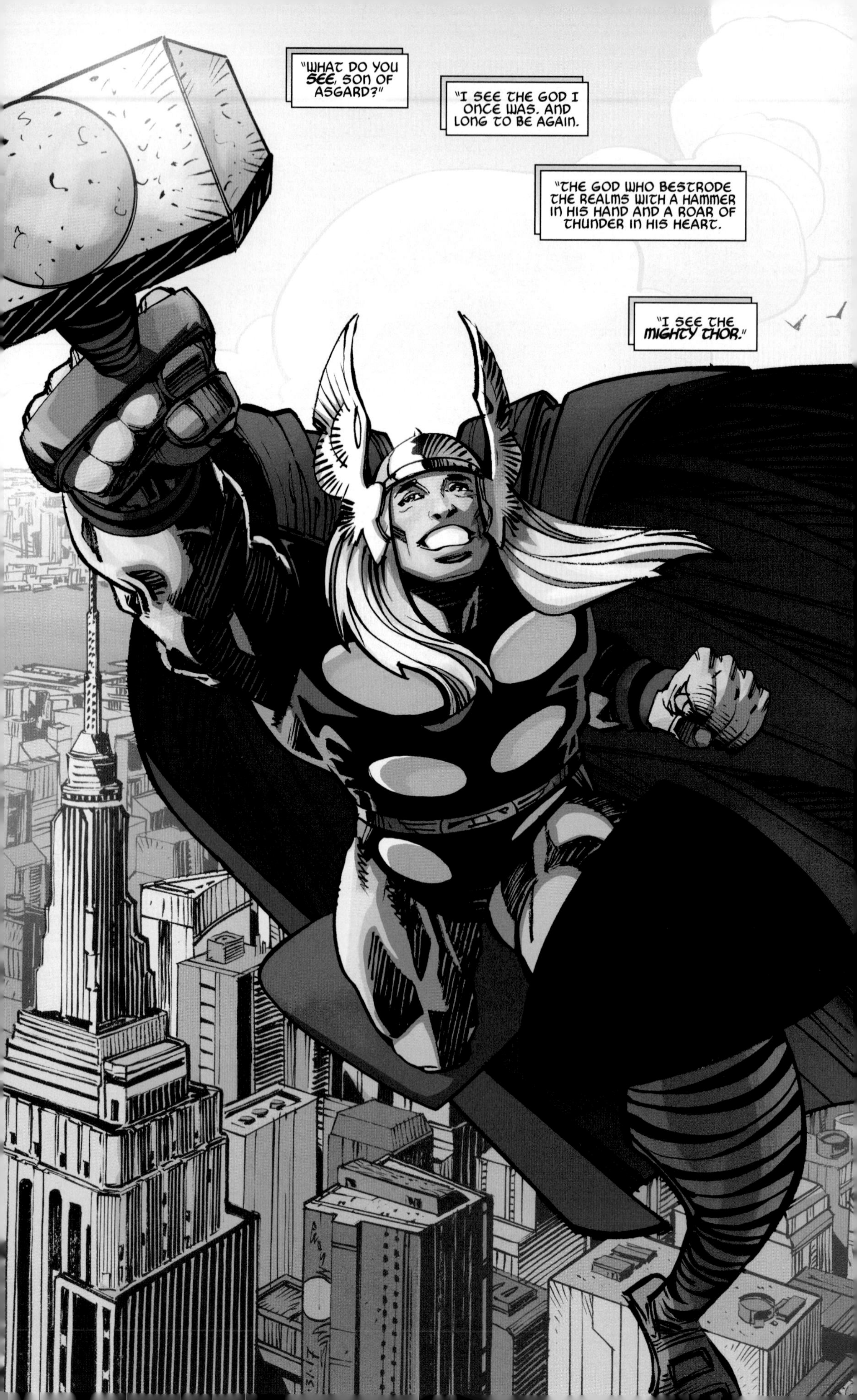
"WHAT DO YOU SEE, SON OF ASGARD?"
"I SEE THE GOD I ONCE WAS. AND LONG TO BE AGAIN.
"THE GOD WHO BESTRODE THE REALMS WITH A HAMMER IN HIS HAND AND A ROAR OF THUNDER IN HIS HEART.
"I SEE THE MIGHTY THOR."

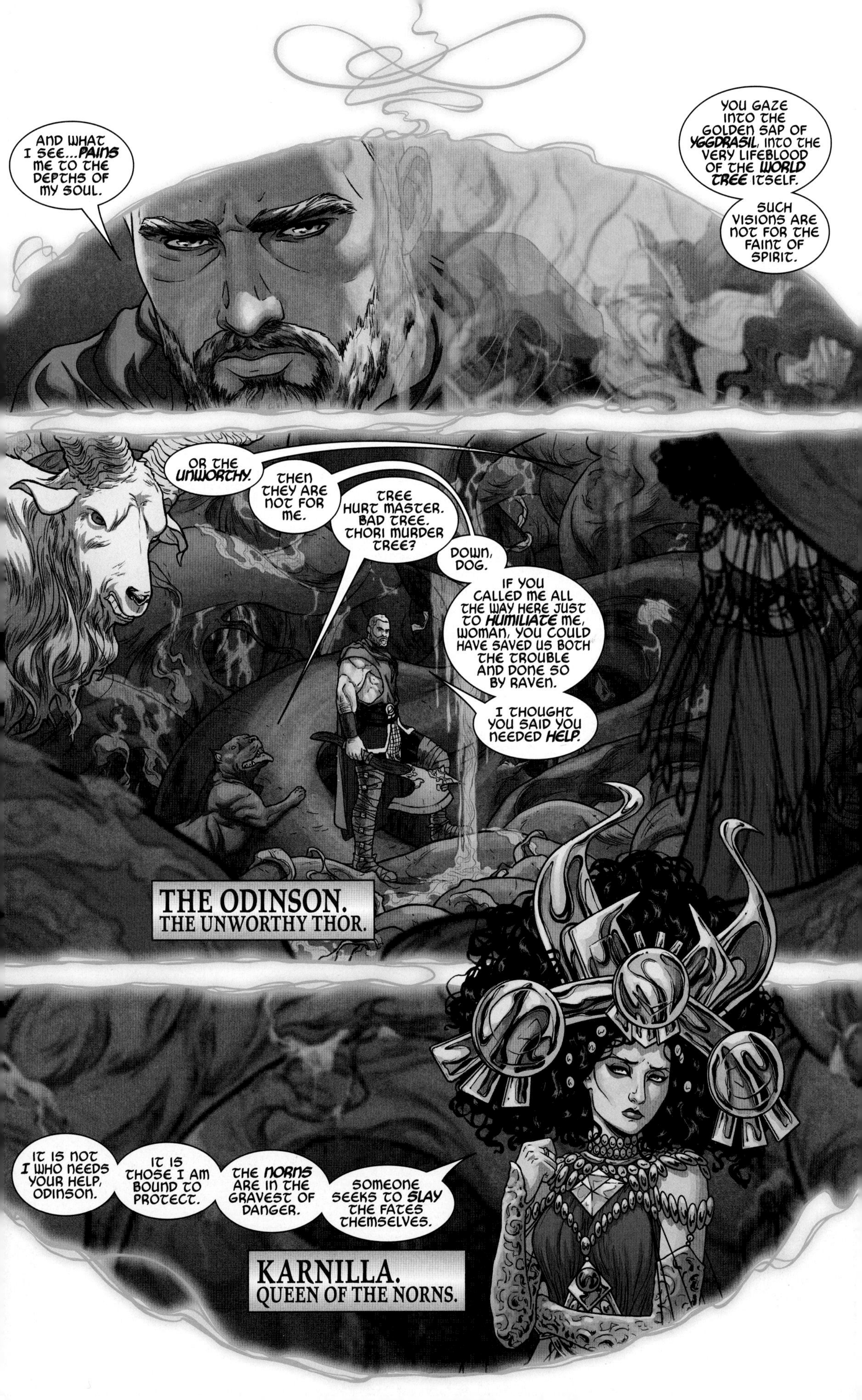
AND WHAT I SEE...PAINS ME TO THE DEPTHS OF MY SOUL.
YOU GAZE INTO THE GOLDEN SAP OF YGGDRASIL, INTO THE VERY LIFEBLOOD OF THE WORLD TREE ITSELF.
SUCH VISIONS ARE NOT FOR THE FAINT OF SPIRIT.
OR THE UNWORTHY.
THEN THEY ARE NOT FOR ME.
TREE HURT MASTER. BAD TREE. THORI MURDER TREE?
DOWN, DOG.
IF YOU CALLED ME ALL THE WAY HERE JUST TO HUMILIATE ME, WOMAN, YOU COULD HAVE SAVED US BOTH THE TROUBLE AND DONE SO BY RAVEN.
I THOUGHT YOU SAID YOU NEEDED HELP.
THE ODINSON. THE UNWORTHY THOR.
IT IS NOT I WHO NEEDS YOUR HELP, ODINSON.
IT IS THOSE I AM BOUND TO PROTECT.
THE NORNS ARE IN THE GRAVEST OF DANGER.
SOMEONE SEEKS TO SLAY THE FATES THEMSELVES.
KARNILLA. QUEEN OF THE NORNS.

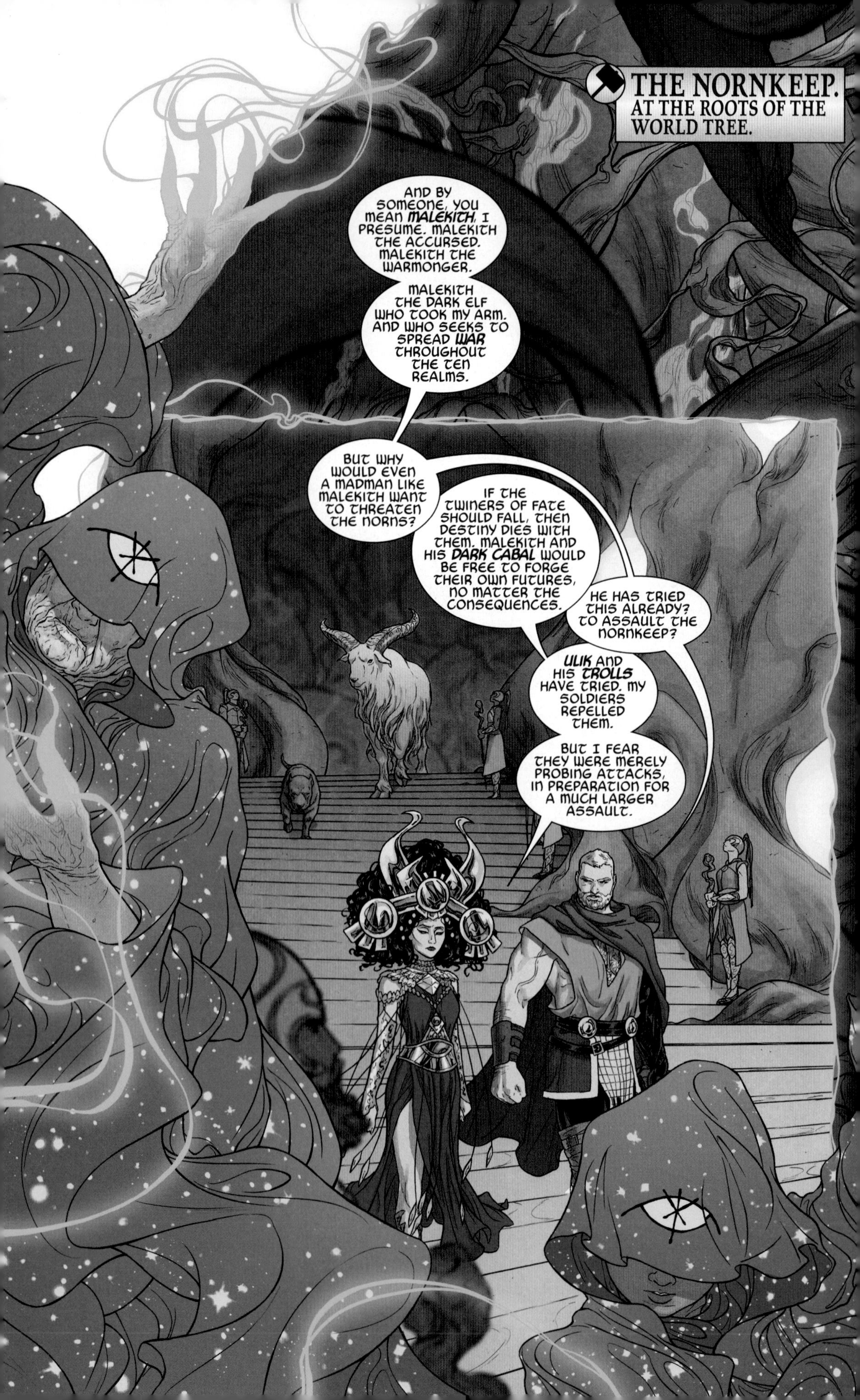
THE NORNKEEP.
AT THE ROOTS OF THE WORLD TREE.
AND BY SOMEONE, YOU MEAN MALEKITH, I PRESUME. MALEKITH THE ACCURSED. MALEKITH THE WARMONGER.
MALEKITH THE DARK ELF WHO TOOK MY ARM. AND WHO SEEKS TO SPREAD WAR THROUGHOUT THE TEN REALMS.
BUT WHY WOULD EVEN A MADMAN LIKE MALEKITH WANT TO THREATEN THE NORNS?
IF THE TWINERS OF FATE SHOULD FALL, THEN DESTINY DIES WITH THEM. MALEKITH AND HIS DARK CABAL WOULD BE FREE TO FORGE THEIR OWN FUTURES, NO MATTER THE CONSEQUENCES.
HE HAS TRIED THIS ALREADY? TO ASSAULT THE NORNKEEP?
ULIK AND HIS TROLLS HAVE TRIED. MY SOLDIERS REPELLED THEM.
BUT I FEAR THEY WERE MERELY PROBING ATTACKS, IN PREPARATION FOR A MUCH LARGER ASSAULT.

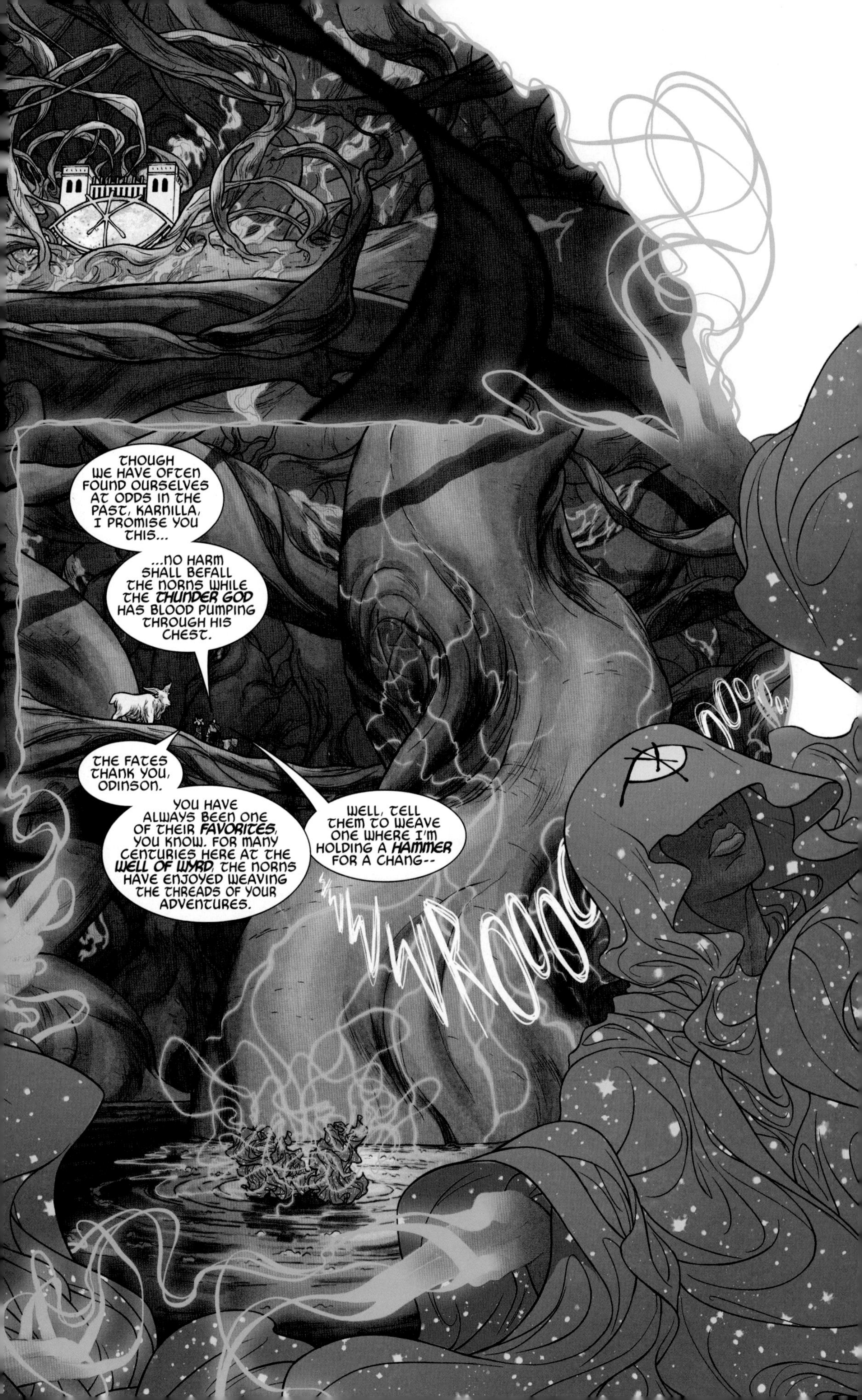
THOUGH WE HAVE OFTEN FOUND OURSELVES AT ODDS IN THE PAST, KARNILLA, I PROMISE YOU THIS...
...NO HARM SHALL BEFALL THE NORNS WHILE THE THUNDER GOD HAS BLOOD PUMPING THROUGH HIS CHEST.
THE FATES THANK YOU, ODINSON.
YOU HAVE ALWAYS BEEN ONE OF THEIR FAVORITES, YOU KNOW. FOR MANY CENTURIES HERE AT THE WELL OF WYRD, THE NORNS HAVE ENJOYED WEAVING THE THREADS OF YOUR ADVENTURES.
WELL, TELL THEM TO WEAVE ONE WHERE I'M HOLDING A HAMMER FOR A CHANG--
WHROOOOOOOOM

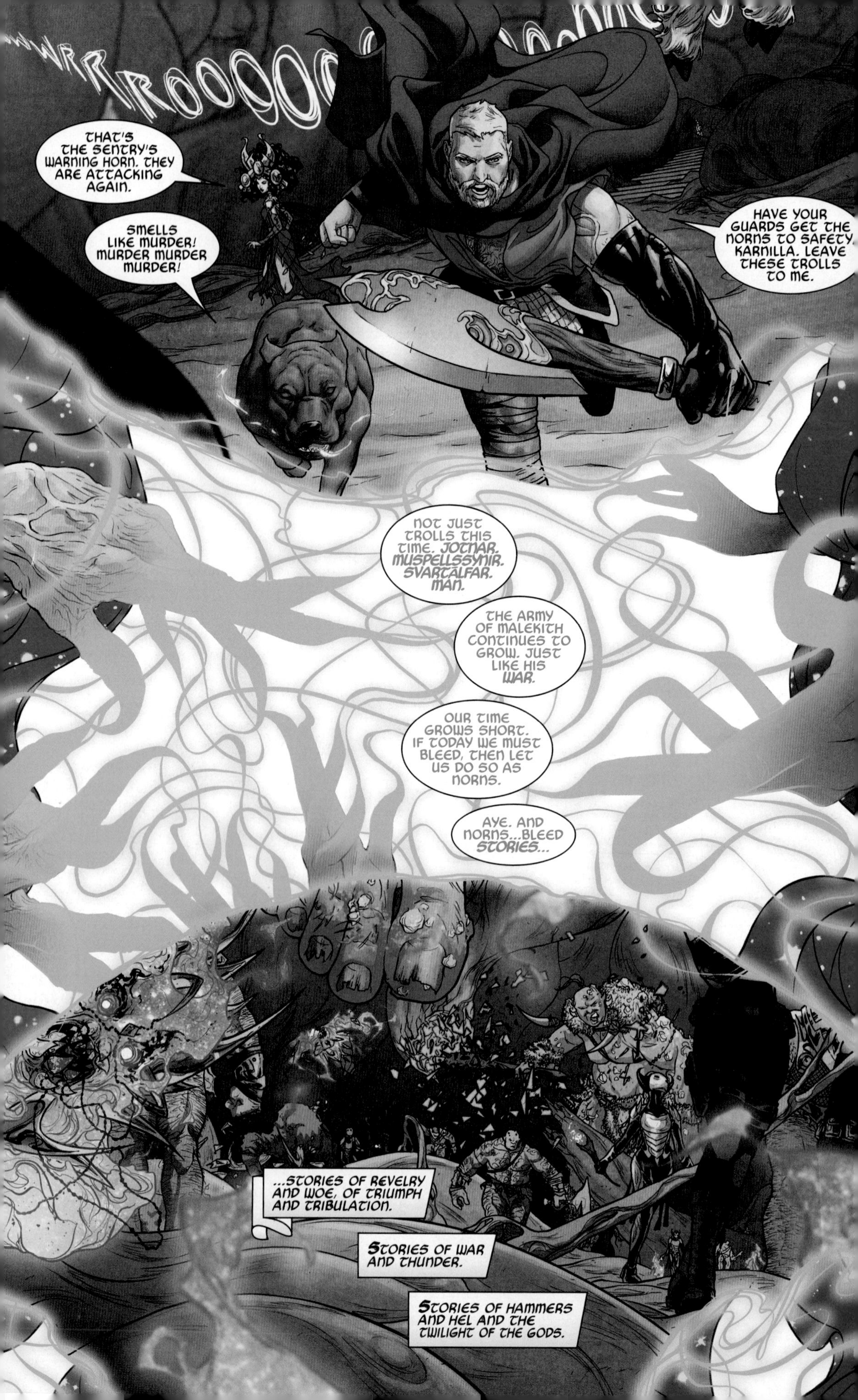
WWRRRROOOOOOOOOOOO
THAT'S THE SENTRY'S WARNING HORN. THEY ARE ATTACKING AGAIN.
SMELLS LIKE MURDER! MURDER MURDER MURDER!
HAVE YOUR GUARDS GET THE NORNS TO SAFETY, KARNILLA. LEAVE THESE TROLLS TO ME.
NOT JUST TROLLS THIS TIME. JOTNAR. MUSPELLSSYNIR. SVARTALFAR. MAN.
THE ARMY OF MALEKITH CONTINUES TO GROW. JUST LIKE HIS WAR.
OUR TIME GROWS SHORT. IF TODAY WE MUST BLEED, THEN LET US DO SO AS NORNS.
AYE. AND NORNS...BLEED STORIES...
...STORIES OF REVELRY AND WOE, OF TRIUMPH AND TRIBULATION.
STORIES OF WAR AND THUNDER.
STORIES OF HAMMERS AND HEL AND THE TWILIGHT OF THE GODS.

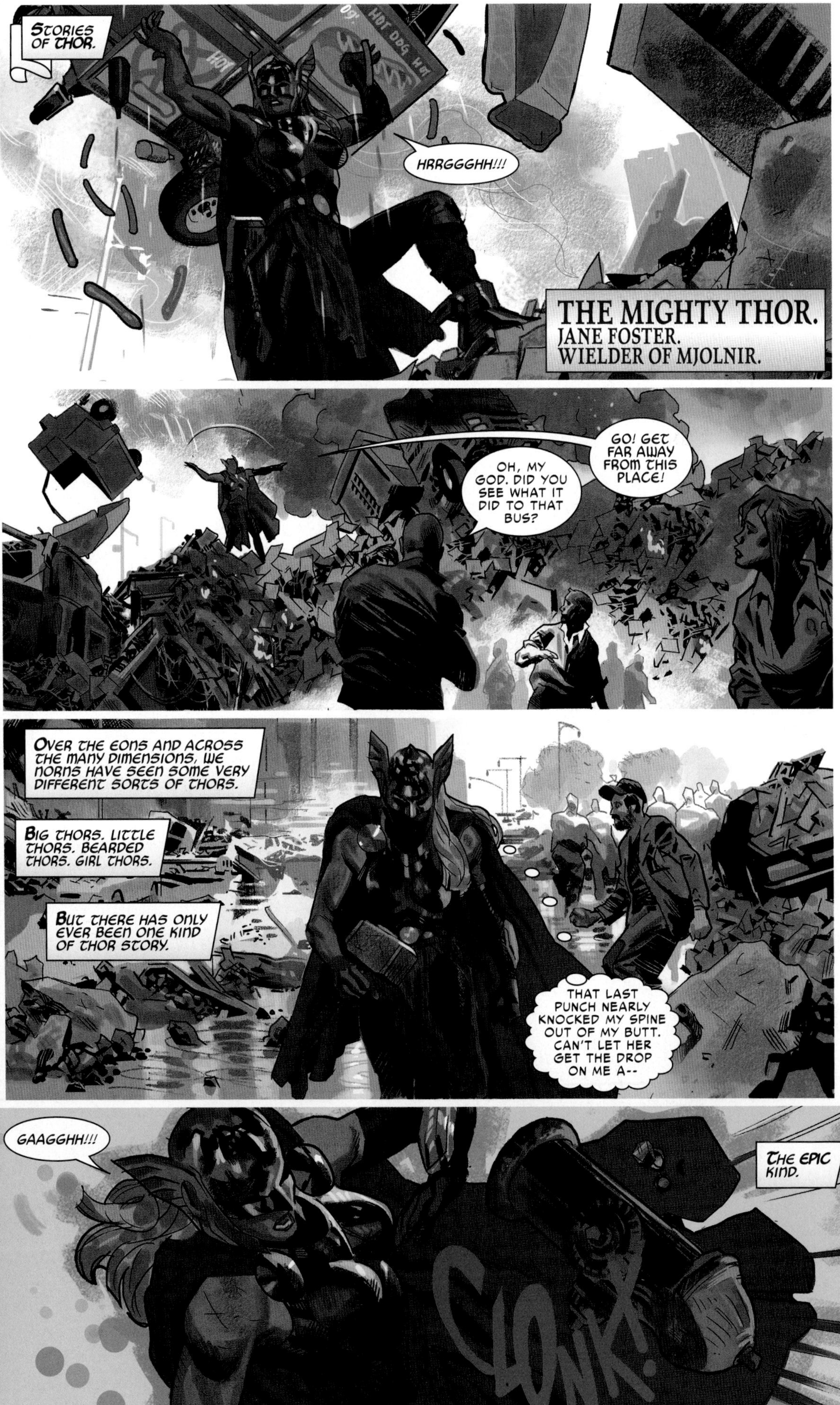

STORIES OF THOR.
HRRGGGHH!!!
THE MIGHTY THOR.
JANE FOSTER.
WIELDER OF MJOLNIR.
GO! GET FAR AWAY FROM THIS PLACE!
OH, MY GOD. DID YOU SEE WHAT IT DID TO THAT BUS?
OVER THE EONS AND ACROSS THE MANY DIMENSIONS, WE NORNS HAVE SEEN SOME VERY DIFFERENT SORTS OF THORS.
BIG THORS. LITTLE THORS. BEARDED THORS. GIRL THORS.
BUT THERE HAS ONLY EVER BEEN ONE KIND OF THOR STORY.
THAT LAST PUNCH NEARLY KNOCKED MY SPINE OUT OF MY BUTT. CAN'T LET HER GET THE DROP ON ME A--
GAAGGHH!!!
THE EPIC KIND.
CLONK!

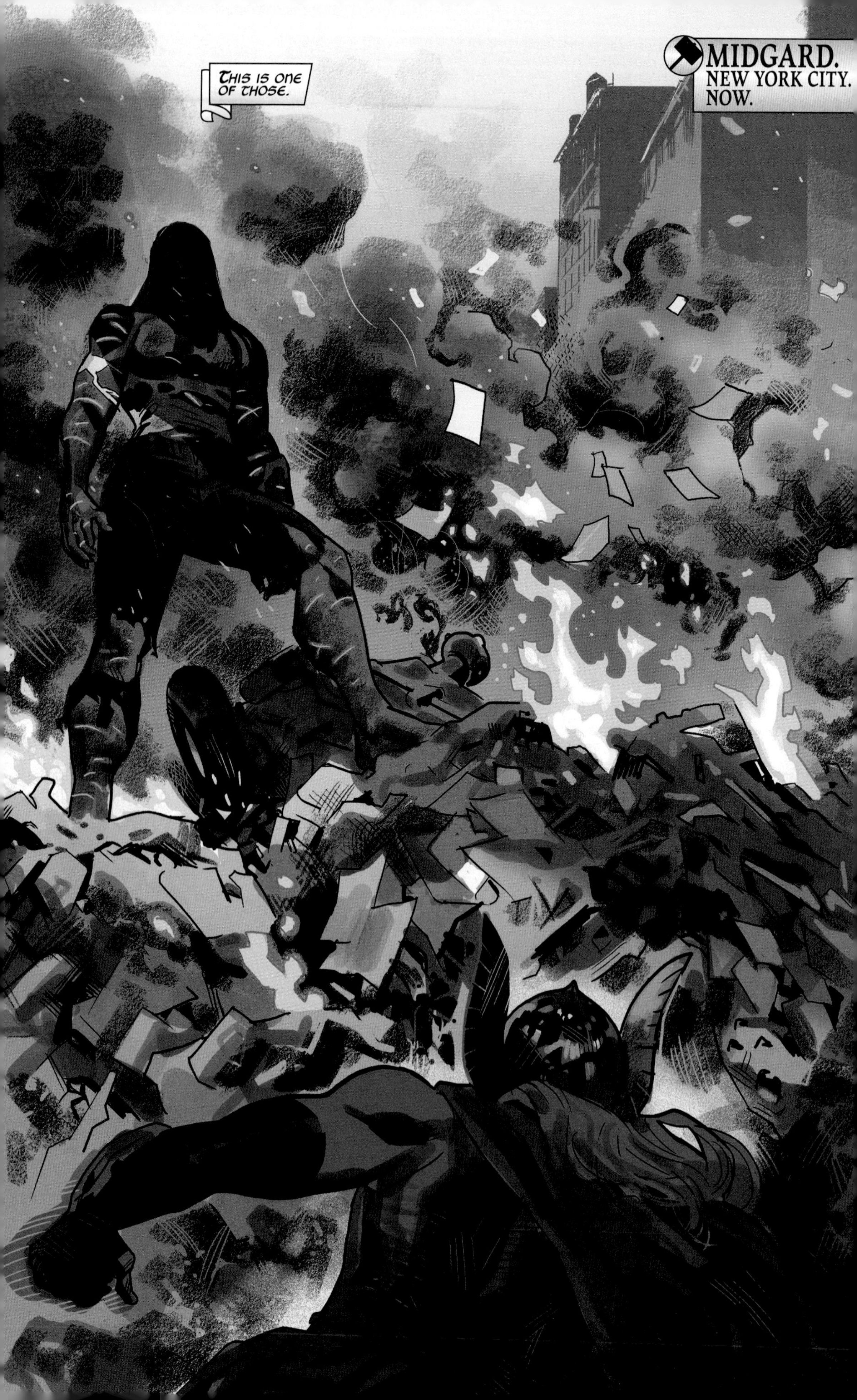
THIS IS ONE OF THOSE.
MIDGARD.
NEW YORK CITY.
NOW.

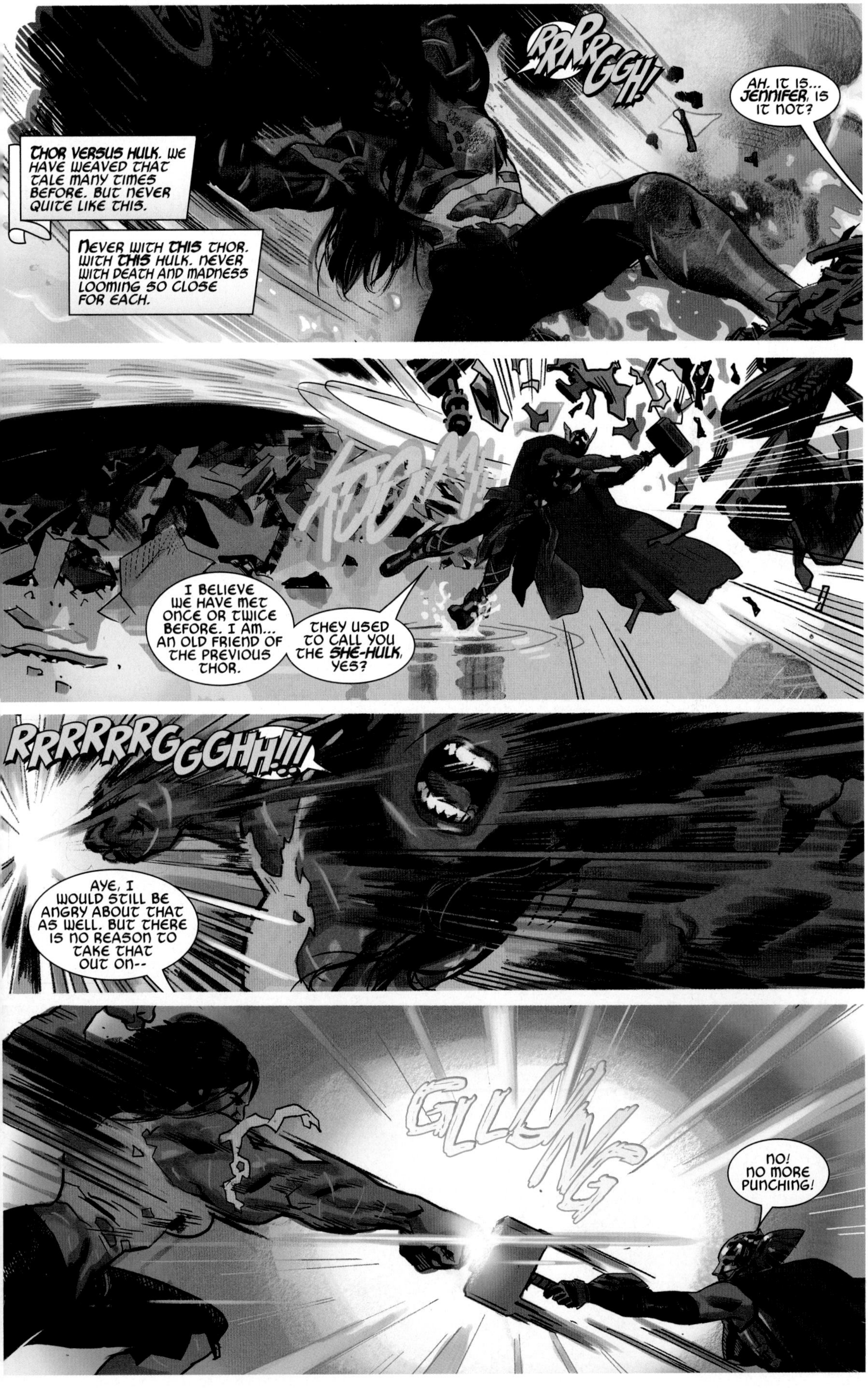
RRRRRGGH!
AH. IT IS... JENNIFER, IS IT NOT?
THOR VERSUS HULK. WE HAVE WEAVED THAT TALE MANY TIMES BEFORE. BUT NEVER QUITE LIKE THIS.
NEVER WITH THIS THOR. WITH THIS HULK. NEVER WITH DEATH AND MADNESS LOOMING SO CLOSE FOR EACH.
KOOM!
I BELIEVE WE HAVE MET ONCE OR TWICE BEFORE. I AM... AN OLD FRIEND OF THE PREVIOUS THOR.
THEY USED TO CALL YOU THE SHE-HULK, YES?
RRRRRRGGGHH!!!
AYE, I WOULD STILL BE ANGRY ABOUT THAT AS WELL. BUT THERE IS NO REASON TO TAKE THAT OUT ON--
GLLONG
NO! NO MORE PUNCHING!

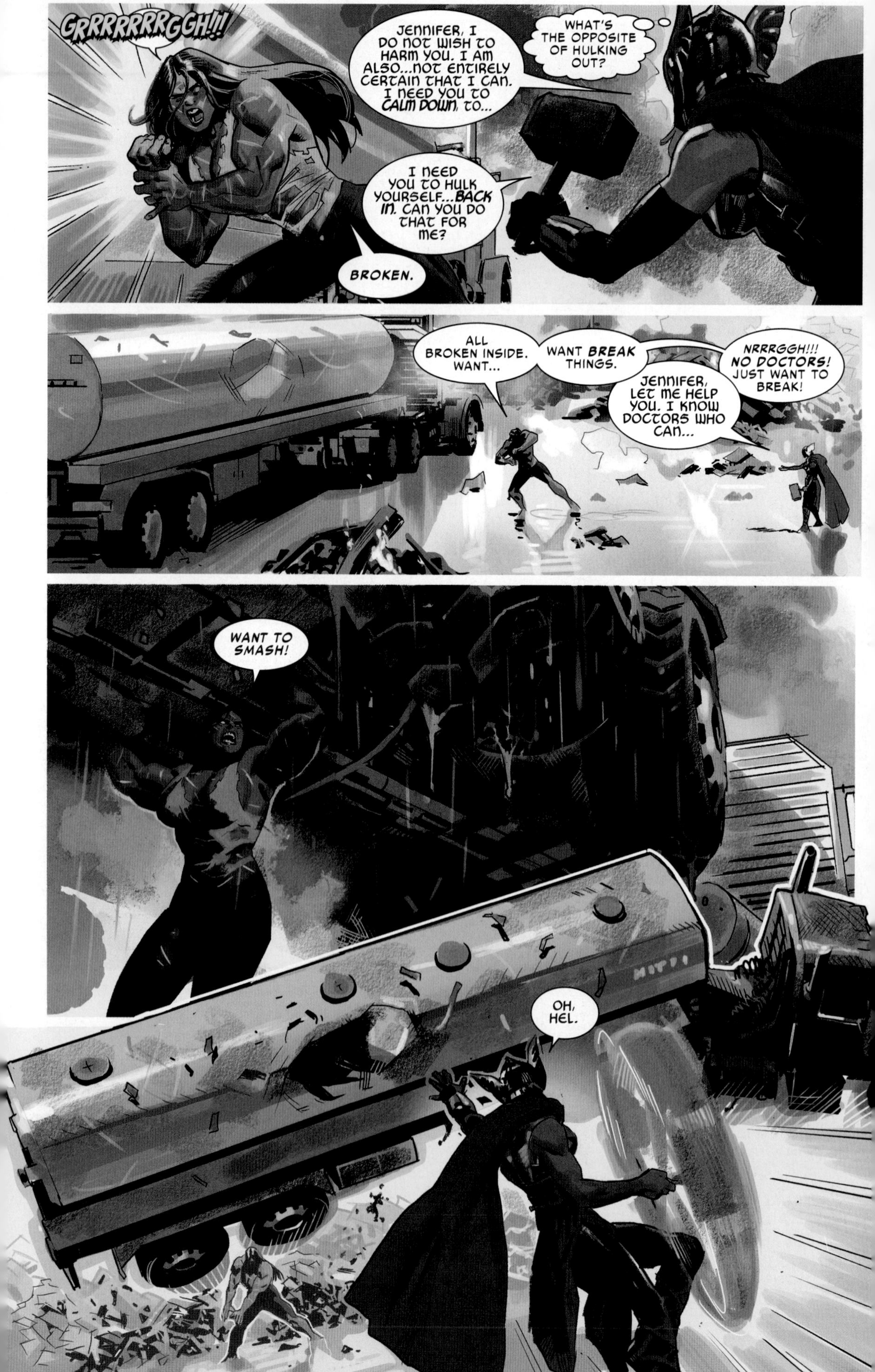
GRRRRRRRGGH!!!
JENNIFER, I DO NOT WISH TO HARM YOU. I AM ALSO...NOT ENTIRELY CERTAIN THAT I CAN. I NEED YOU TO CALM DOWN, TO...
WHAT'S THE OPPOSITE OF HULKING OUT?
I NEED YOU TO HULK YOURSELF...BACK IN. CAN YOU DO THAT FOR ME?
BROKEN.
ALL BROKEN INSIDE. WANT...
WANT BREAK THINGS.
JENNIFER, LET ME HELP YOU. I KNOW DOCTORS WHO CAN...
NRRRGGH!!! NO DOCTORS! JUST WANT TO BREAK!
WANT TO SMASH!
OH, HEL.

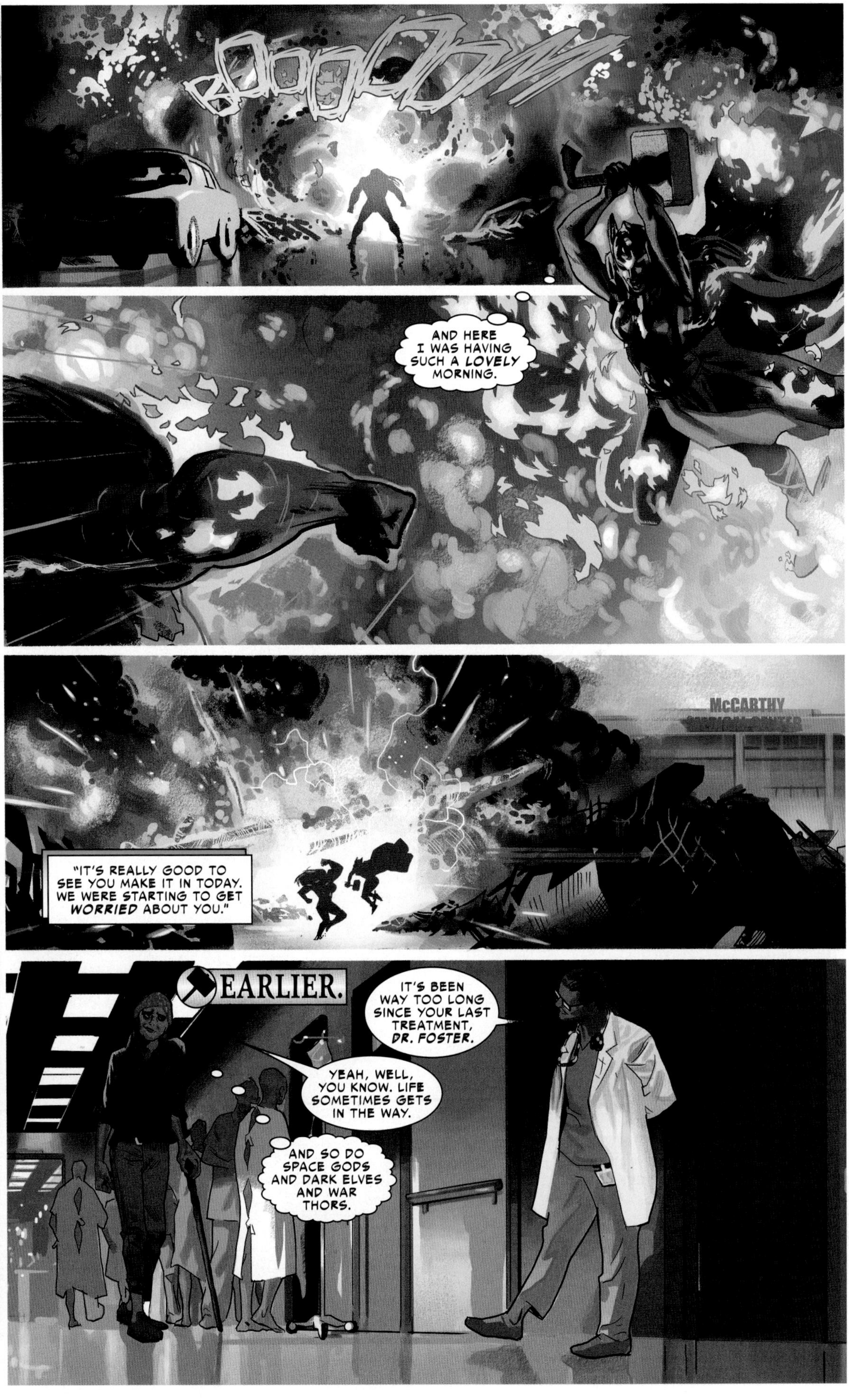
AND HERE I WAS HAVING SUCH A *LOVELY* MORNING.
McCARTHY
"IT'S REALLY GOOD TO SEE YOU MAKE IT IN TODAY. WE WERE STARTING TO GET *WORRIED* ABOUT YOU."
EARLIER.
IT'S BEEN WAY TOO LONG SINCE YOUR LAST TREATMENT, *DR. FOSTER.*
YEAH, WELL, YOU KNOW. LIFE SOMETIMES GETS IN THE WAY.
AND SO DO SPACE GODS AND DARK ELVES AND WAR THORS.

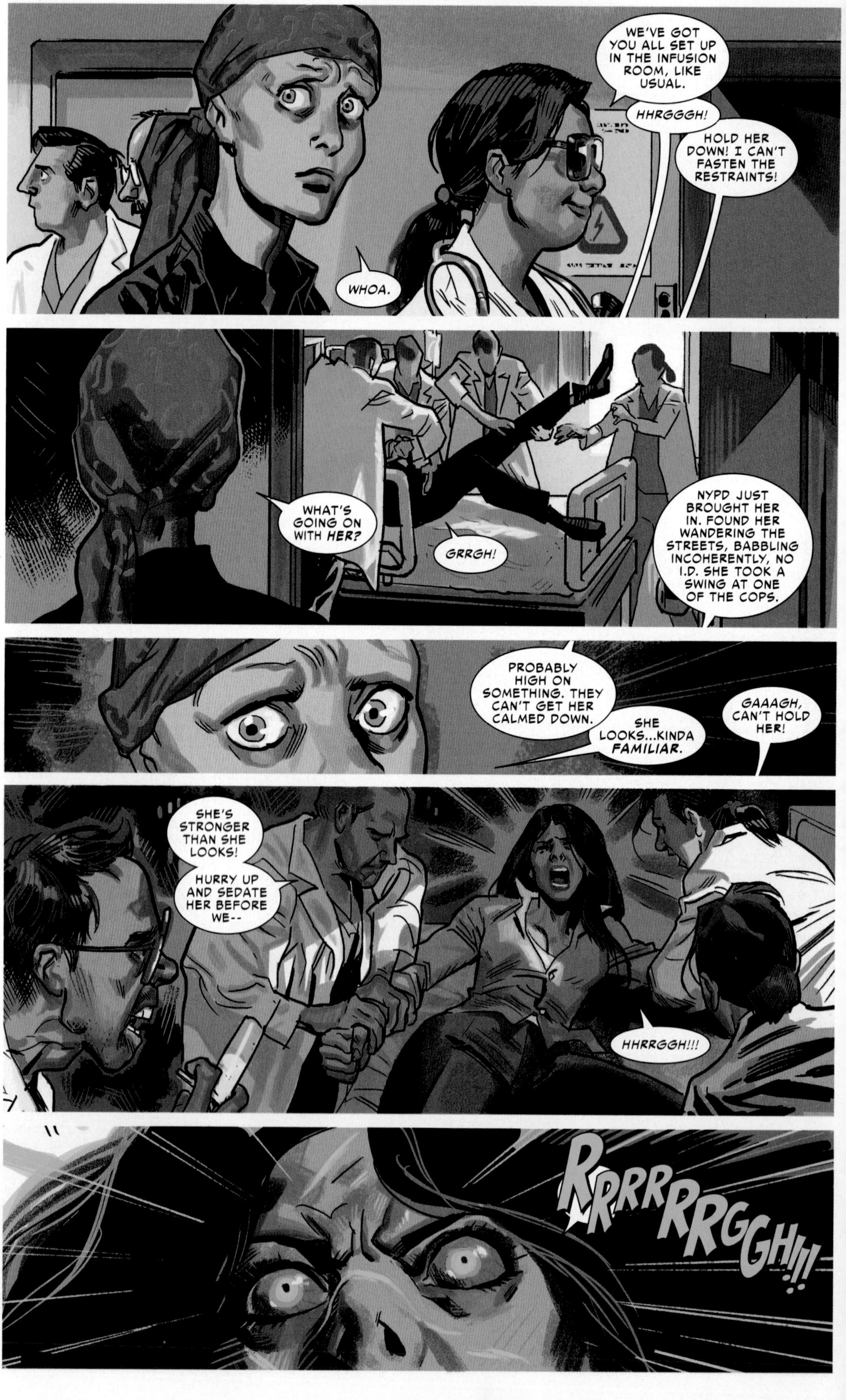
WE'VE GOT YOU ALL SET UP IN THE INFUSION ROOM, LIKE USUAL.
HHRGGGH!
HOLD HER DOWN! I CAN'T FASTEN THE RESTRAINTS!
WHOA.
WHAT'S GOING ON WITH HER?
GRRGH!
NYPD JUST BROUGHT HER IN. FOUND HER WANDERING THE STREETS, BABBLING INCOHERENTLY, NO I.D. SHE TOOK A SWING AT ONE OF THE COPS.
PROBABLY HIGH ON SOMETHING. THEY CAN'T GET HER CALMED DOWN.
SHE LOOKS...KINDA FAMILIAR.
GAAAGH, CAN'T HOLD HER!
SHE'S STRONGER THAN SHE LOOKS!
HURRY UP AND SEDATE HER BEFORE WE--
HHRRGGH!!!
RRRRRRGGH!!!

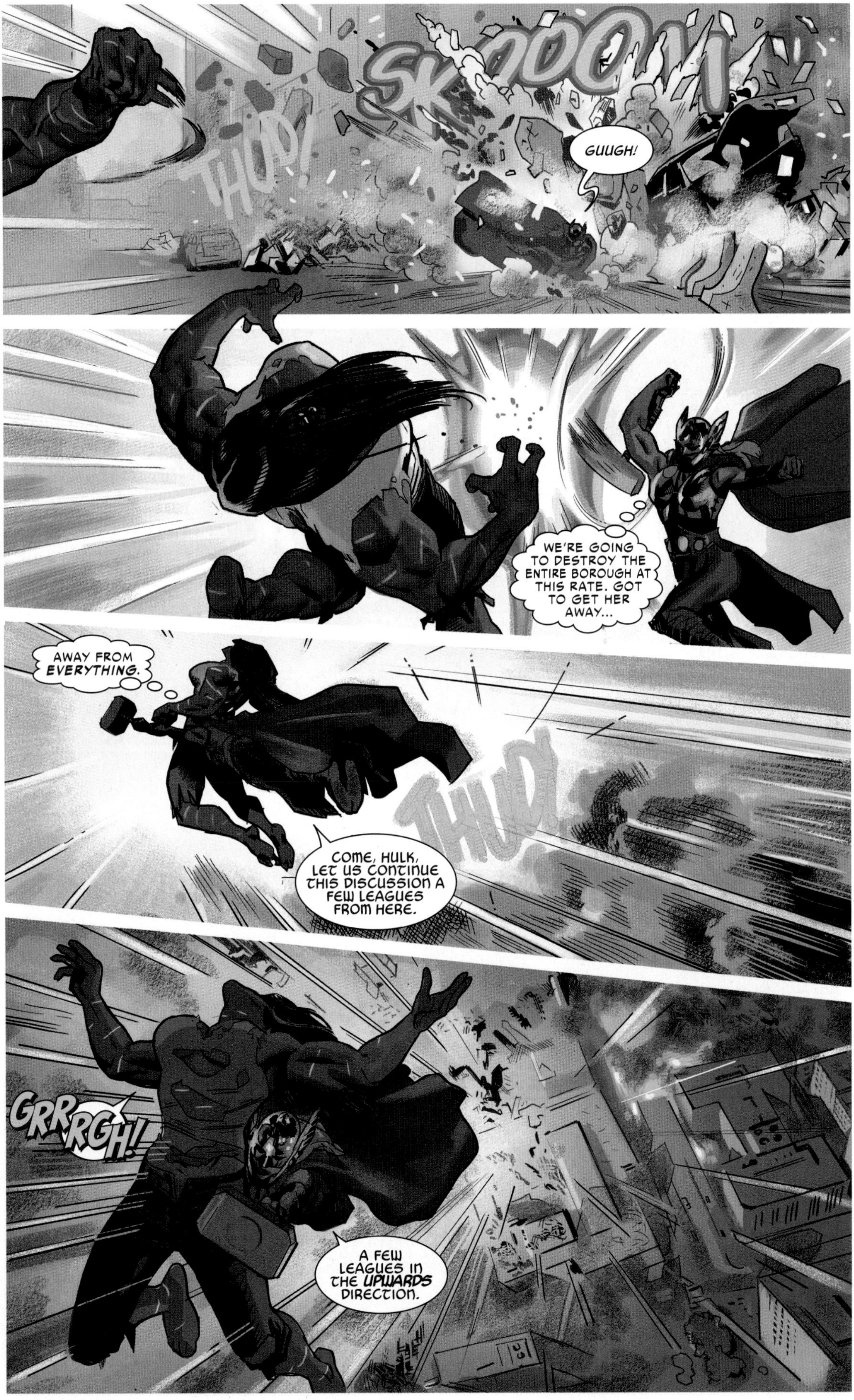
SKOOOM
THUD!
GUUGH!
WE'RE GOING TO DESTROY THE ENTIRE BOROUGH AT THIS RATE. GOT TO GET HER AWAY...
AWAY FROM EVERYTHING.
THUD!
COME, HULK, LET US CONTINUE THIS DISCUSSION A FEW LEAGUES FROM HERE.
GRRRGH!!
A FEW LEAGUES IN THE UPWARDS DIRECTION.

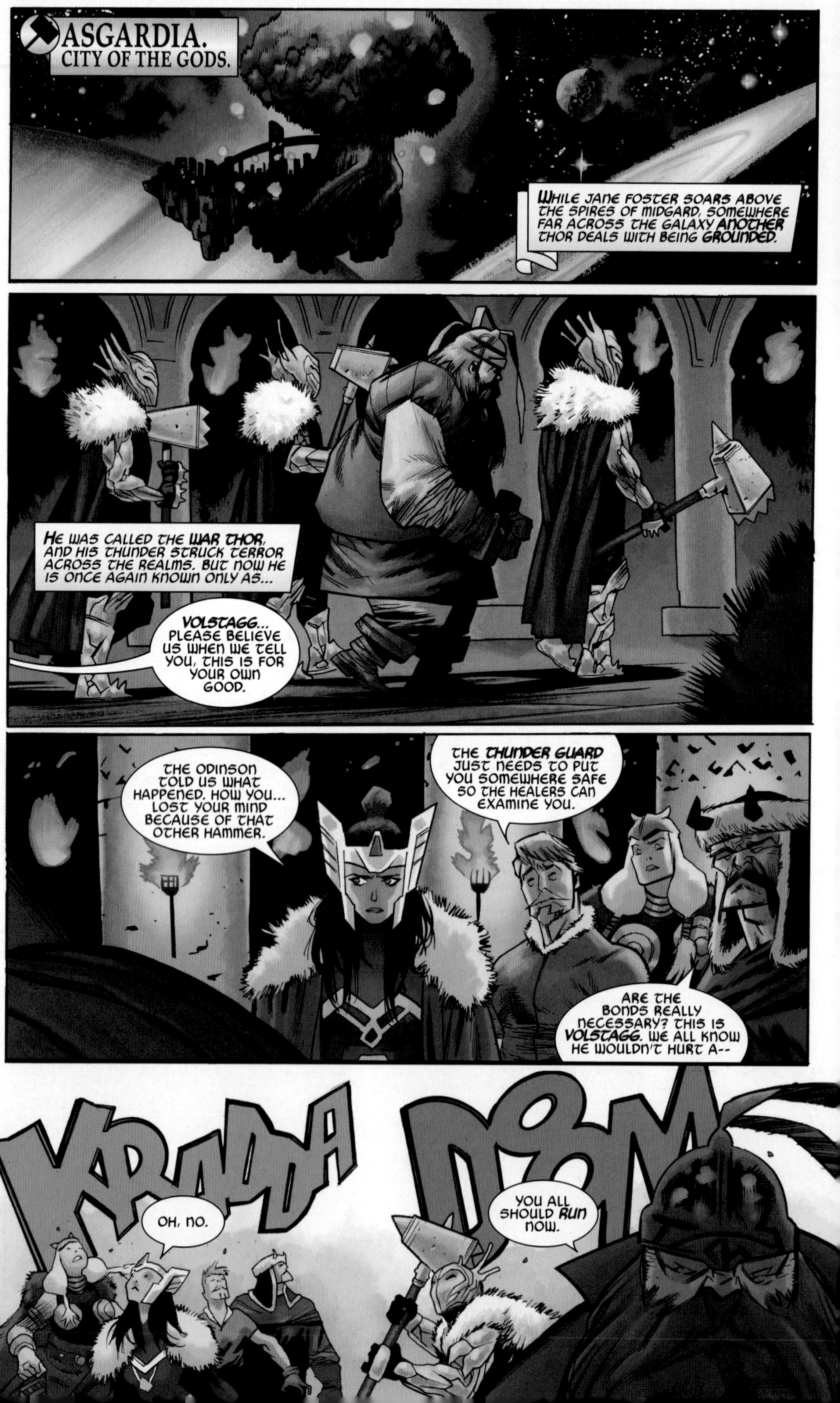
ASGARDIA. CITY OF THE GODS.
WHILE JANE FOSTER SOARS ABOVE THE SPIRES OF MIDGARD, SOMEWHERE FAR ACROSS THE GALAXY ANOTHER THOR DEALS WITH BEING GROUNDED.
HE WAS CALLED THE WAR THOR, AND HIS THUNDER STRUCK TERROR ACROSS THE REALMS. BUT NOW HE IS ONCE AGAIN KNOWN ONLY AS...
VOLSTAGG... PLEASE BELIEVE US WHEN WE TELL YOU, THIS IS FOR YOUR OWN GOOD.
THE ODINSON TOLD US WHAT HAPPENED. HOW YOU... LOST YOUR MIND BECAUSE OF THAT OTHER HAMMER.
THE THUNDER GUARD JUST NEEDS TO PUT YOU SOMEWHERE SAFE SO THE HEALERS CAN EXAMINE YOU.
ARE THE BONDS REALLY NECESSARY? THIS IS VOLSTAGG. WE ALL KNOW HE WOULDN'T HURT A--
KRADDA DOOM
OH, NO.
YOU ALL SHOULD RUN NOW.

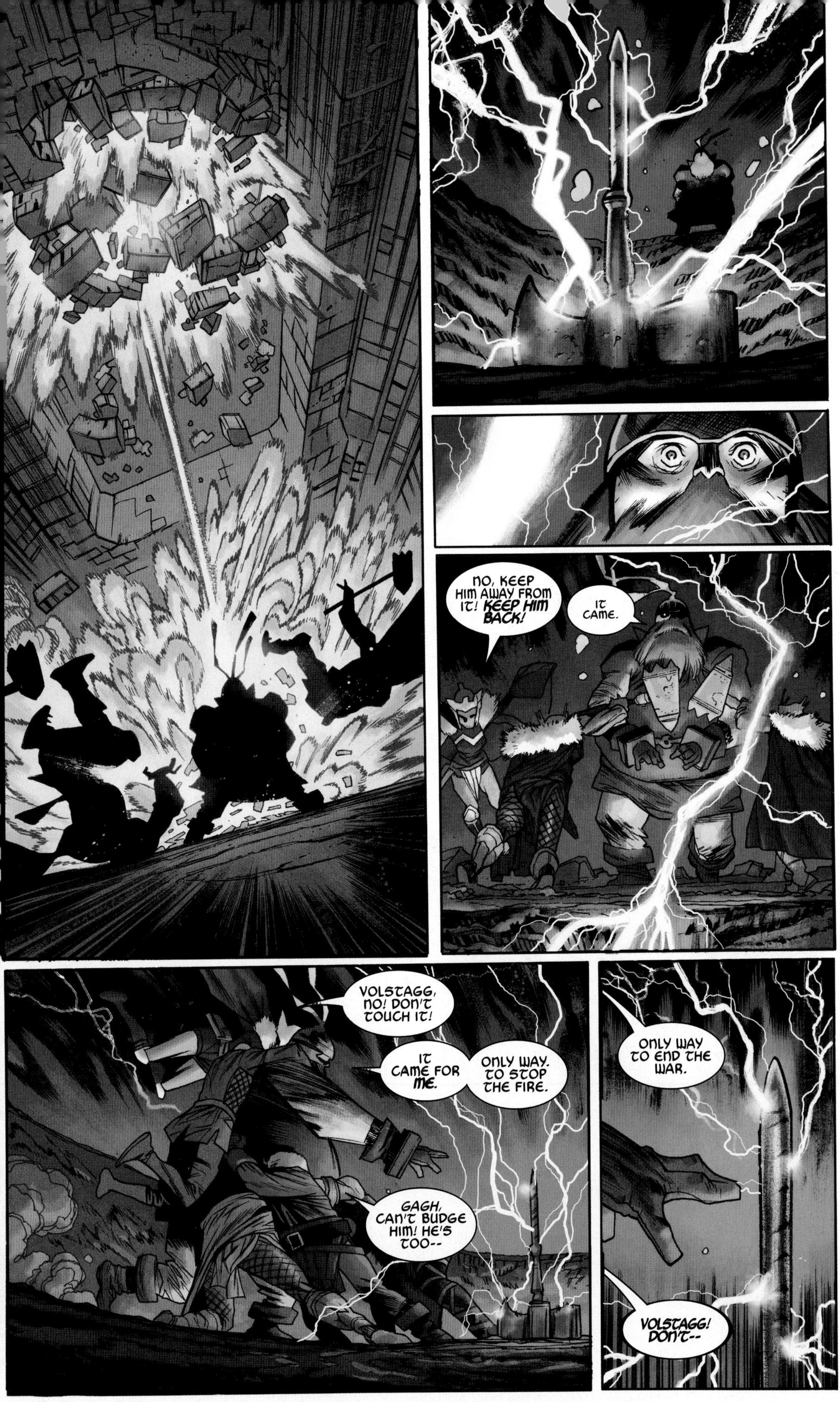
NO, KEEP HIM AWAY FROM IT! KEEP HIM BACK!
IT CAME.
VOLSTAGG, NO! DON'T TOUCH IT!
IT CAME FOR ME.
ONLY WAY. TO STOP THE FIRE.
GAGH, CAN'T BUDGE HIM! HE'S TOO--
ONLY WAY TO END THE WAR.
VOLSTAGG! DON'T--

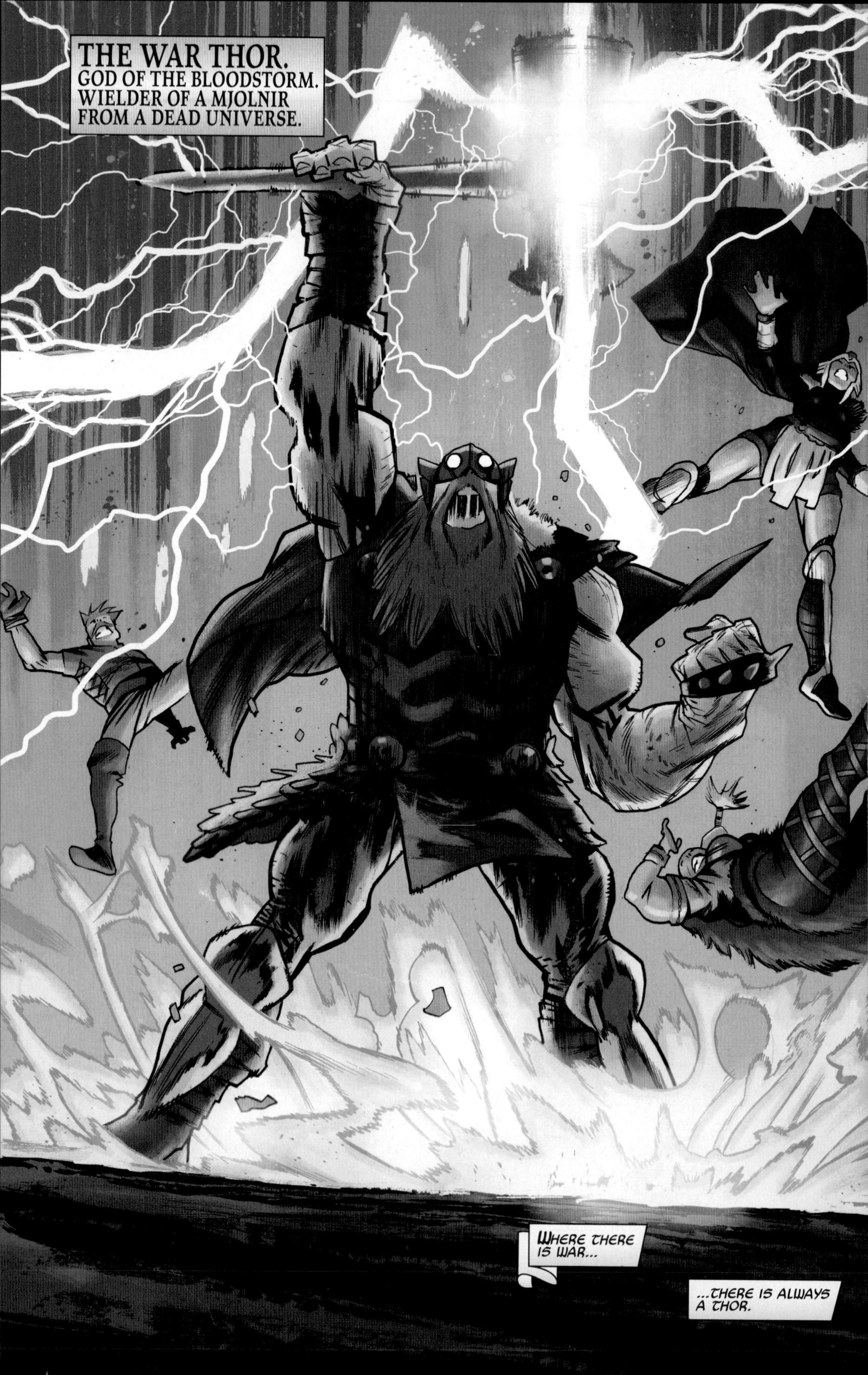
THE WAR THOR.
GOD OF THE BLOODSTORM.
WIELDER OF A MJOLNIR
FROM A DEAD UNIVERSE.
WHERE THERE IS WAR...
...THERE IS ALWAYS A THOR.

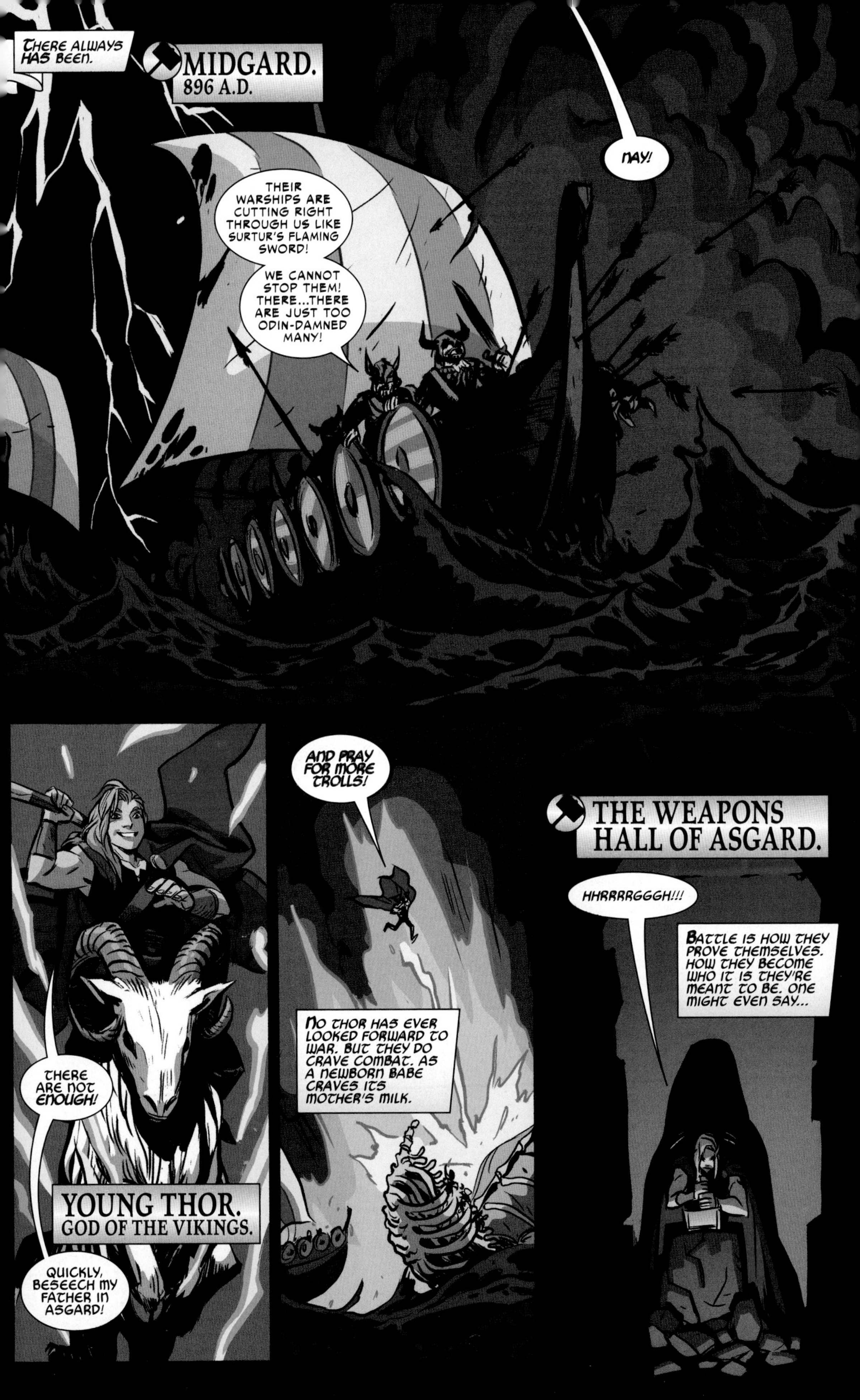
THERE ALWAYS HAS BEEN.
MIDGARD. 896 A.D.
NAY!
THEIR WARSHIPS ARE CUTTING RIGHT THROUGH US LIKE SURTUR'S FLAMING SWORD!
WE CANNOT STOP THEM! THERE...THERE ARE JUST TOO ODIN-DAMNED MANY!
THERE ARE NOT ENOUGH!
YOUNG THOR. GOD OF THE VIKINGS.
QUICKLY, BESEECH MY FATHER IN ASGARD!
AND PRAY FOR MORE TROLLS!
NO THOR HAS EVER LOOKED FORWARD TO WAR. BUT THEY DO CRAVE COMBAT. AS A NEWBORN BABE CRAVES ITS MOTHER'S MILK.
THE WEAPONS HALL OF ASGARD.
HHRRRRGGGH!!!
BATTLE IS HOW THEY PROVE THEMSELVES. HOW THEY BECOME WHO IT IS THEY'RE MEANT TO BE. ONE MIGHT EVEN SAY...

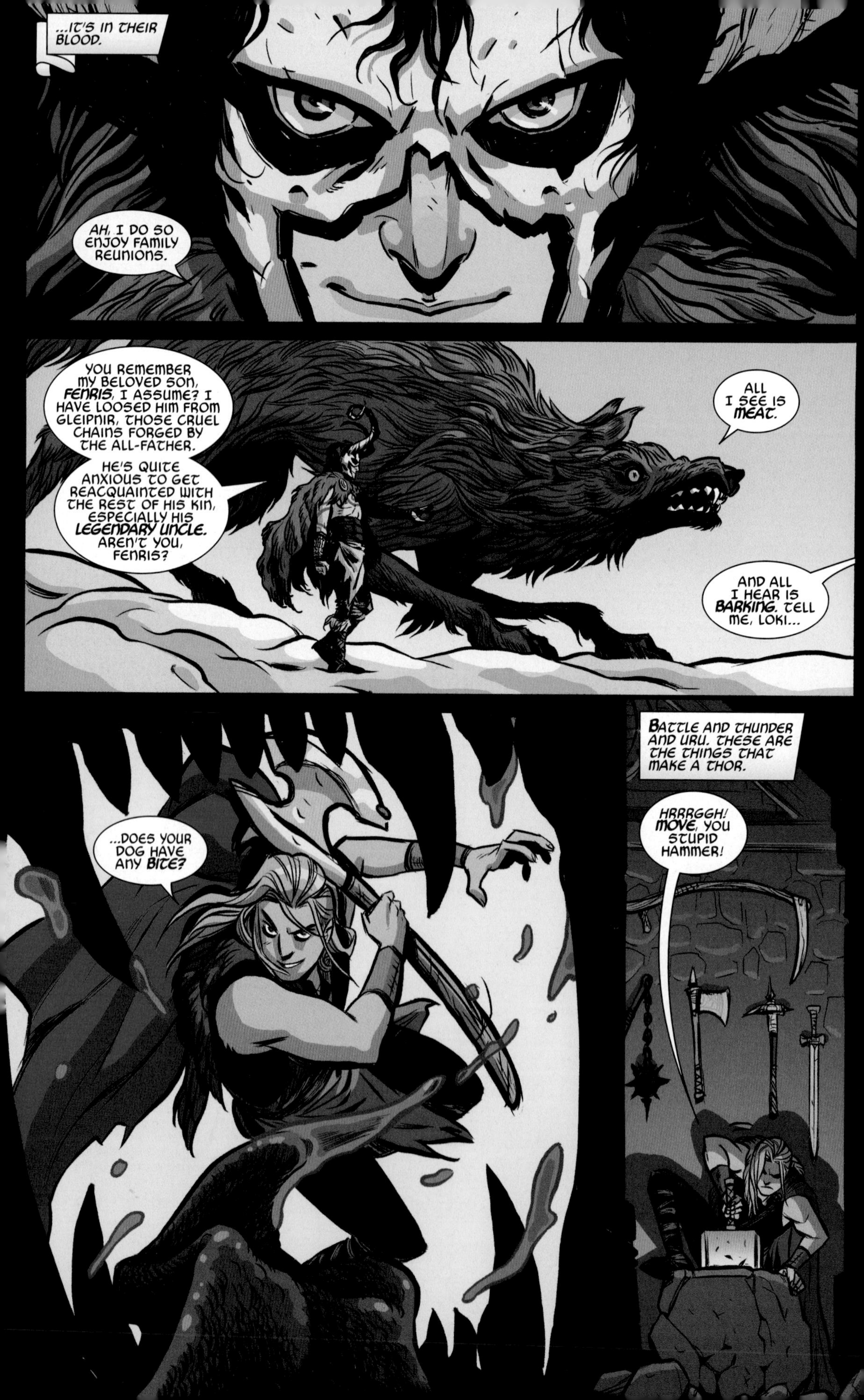
...IT'S IN THEIR BLOOD.
AH, I DO SO ENJOY FAMILY REUNIONS.
YOU REMEMBER MY BELOVED SON, FENRIS, I ASSUME? I HAVE LOOSED HIM FROM GLEIPNIR, THOSE CRUEL CHAINS FORGED BY THE ALL-FATHER.
HE'S QUITE ANXIOUS TO GET REACQUAINTED WITH THE REST OF HIS KIN, ESPECIALLY HIS LEGENDARY UNCLE. AREN'T YOU, FENRIS?
ALL I SEE IS MEAT.
AND ALL I HEAR IS BARKING. TELL ME, LOKI...
...DOES YOUR DOG HAVE ANY BITE?
BATTLE AND THUNDER AND URU. THESE ARE THE THINGS THAT MAKE A THOR.
HRRRGGH! MOVE, YOU STUPID HAMMER!

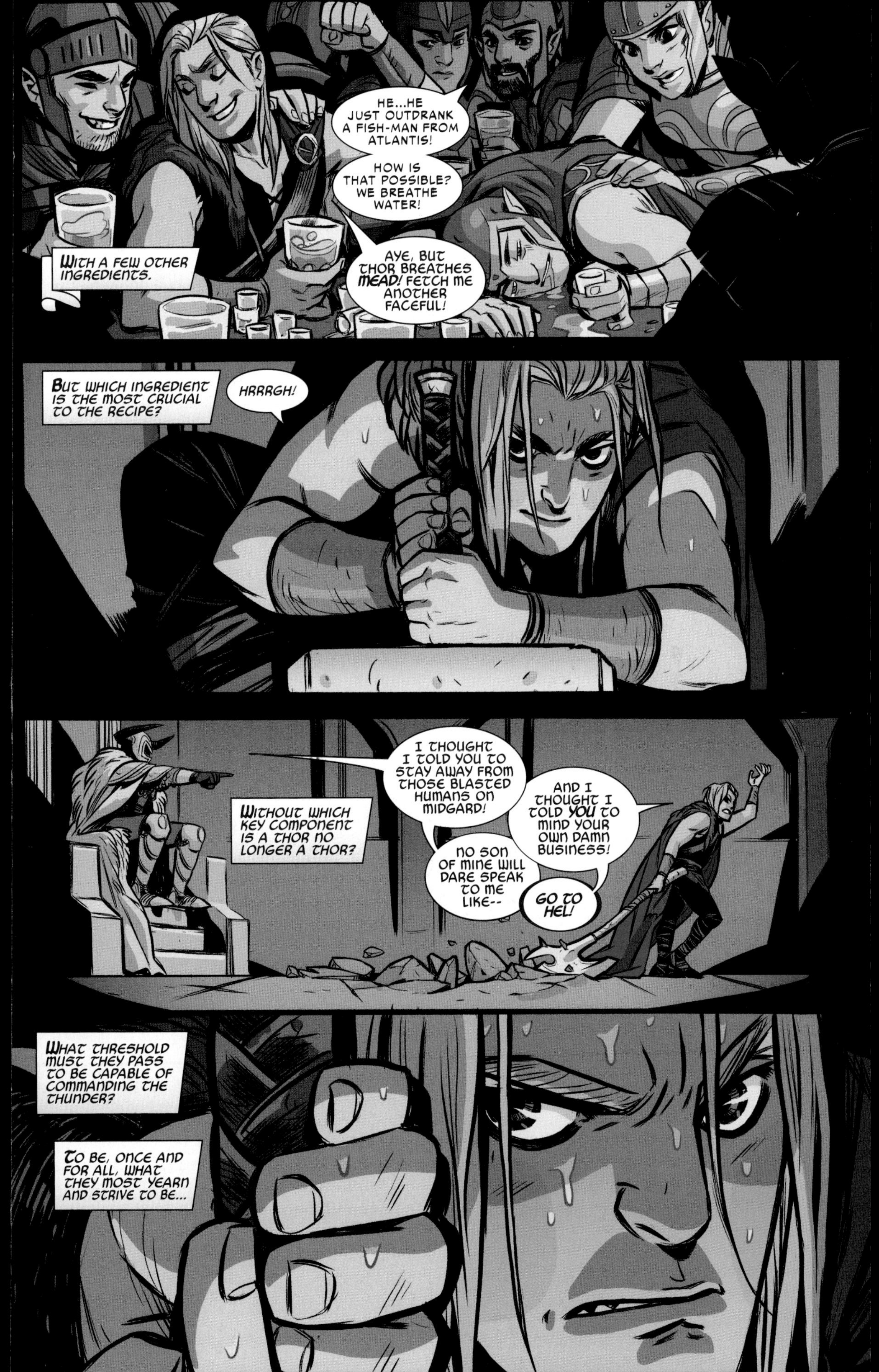
HE...HE JUST OUTDRANK A FISH-MAN FROM ATLANTIS!
HOW IS THAT POSSIBLE? WE BREATHE WATER!
WITH A FEW OTHER INGREDIENTS.
AYE, BUT THOR BREATHES MEAD! FETCH ME ANOTHER FACEFUL!
BUT WHICH INGREDIENT IS THE MOST CRUCIAL TO THE RECIPE?
HRRRGH!
WITHOUT WHICH KEY COMPONENT IS A THOR NO LONGER A THOR?
I THOUGHT I TOLD YOU TO STAY AWAY FROM THOSE BLASTED HUMANS ON MIDGARD!
AND I THOUGHT I TOLD YOU TO MIND YOUR OWN DAMN BUSINESS!
NO SON OF MINE WILL DARE SPEAK TO ME LIKE--
GO TO HEL!
WHAT THRESHOLD MUST THEY PASS TO BE CAPABLE OF COMMANDING THE THUNDER?
TO BE, ONCE AND FOR ALL, WHAT THEY MOST YEARN AND STRIVE TO BE...

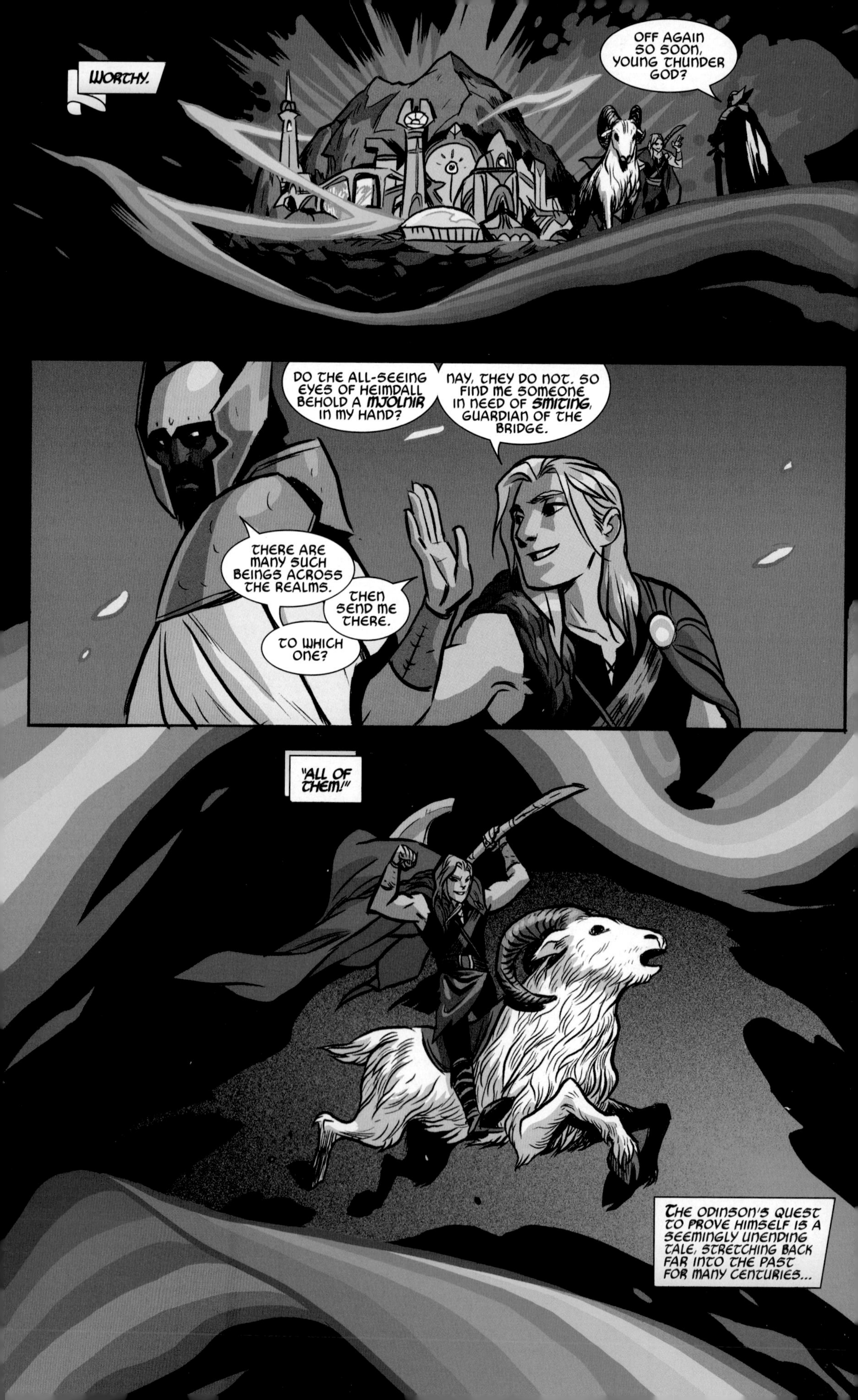
WORTHY.
OFF AGAIN SO SOON, YOUNG THUNDER GOD?
DO THE ALL-SEEING EYES OF HEIMDALL BEHOLD A MJOLNIR IN MY HAND?
NAY, THEY DO NOT. SO FIND ME SOMEONE IN NEED OF SMITING, GUARDIAN OF THE BRIDGE.
THERE ARE MANY SUCH BEINGS ACROSS THE REALMS.
THEN SEND ME THERE.
TO WHICH ONE?
"ALL OF THEM!"
THE ODINSON'S QUEST TO PROVE HIMSELF IS A SEEMINGLY UNENDING TALE, STRETCHING BACK FAR INTO THE PAST FOR MANY CENTURIES...

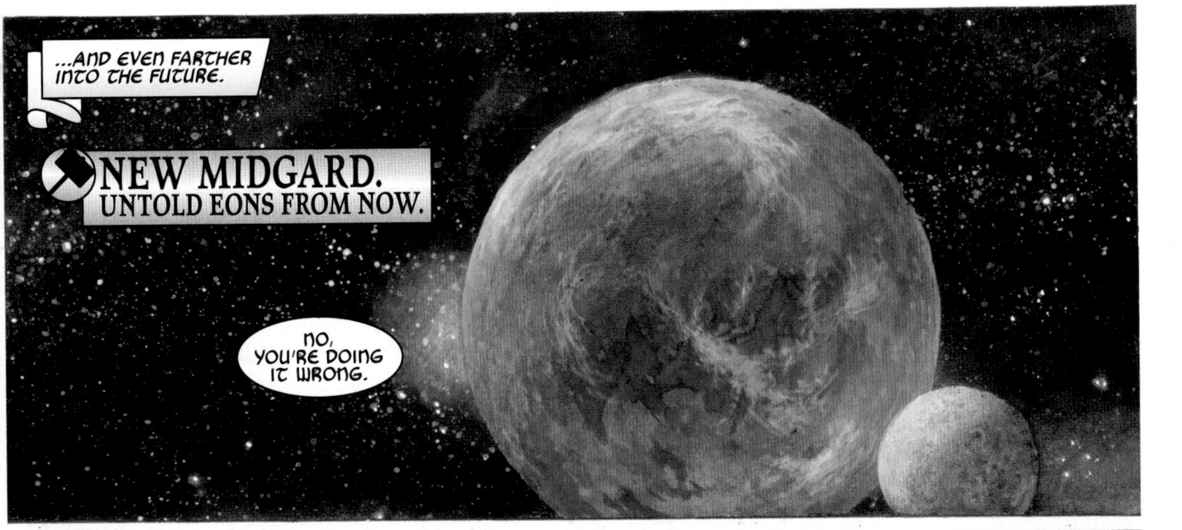
...AND EVEN FARTHER INTO THE FUTURE.
NEW MIDGARD. UNTOLD EONS FROM NOW.
NO, YOU'RE DOING IT WRONG.

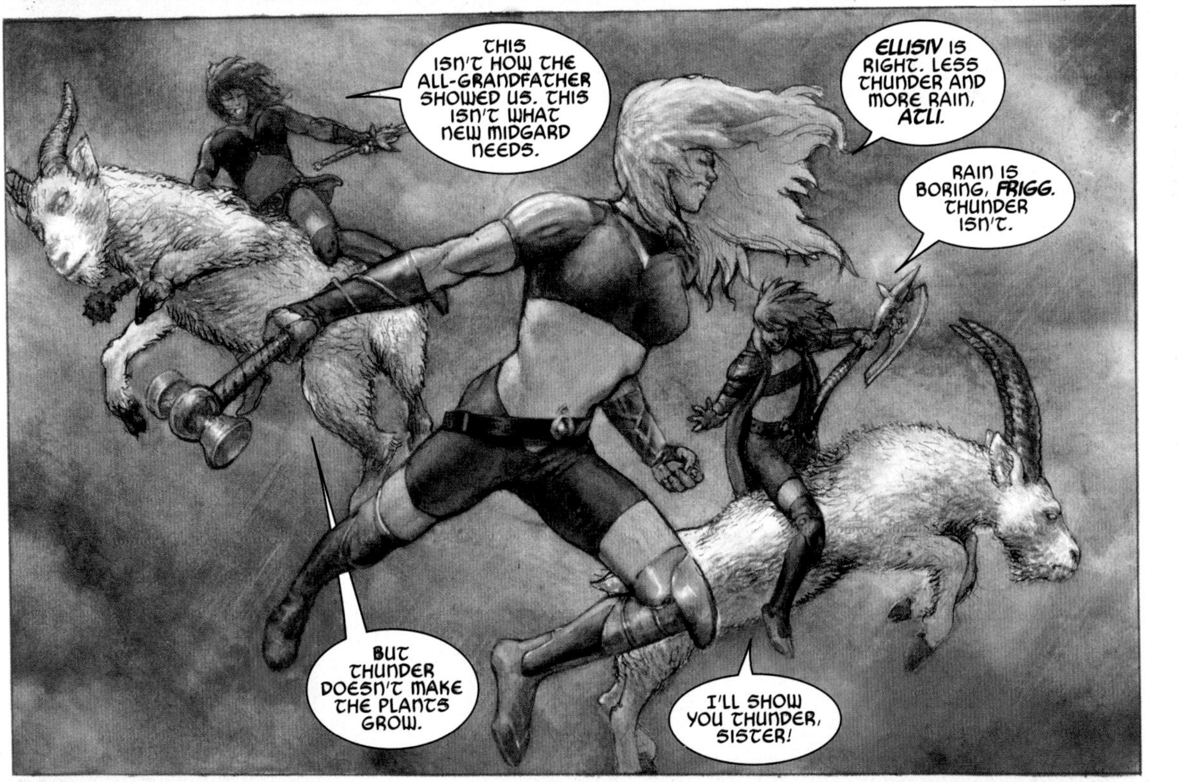
THIS ISN'T HOW THE ALL-GRANDFATHER SHOWED US. THIS ISN'T WHAT NEW MIDGARD NEEDS.
ELLISIV IS RIGHT. LESS THUNDER AND MORE RAIN, ATLI.
RAIN IS BORING, FRIGG. THUNDER ISN'T.
BUT THUNDER DOESN'T MAKE THE PLANTS GROW.
I'LL SHOW YOU THUNDER, SISTER!

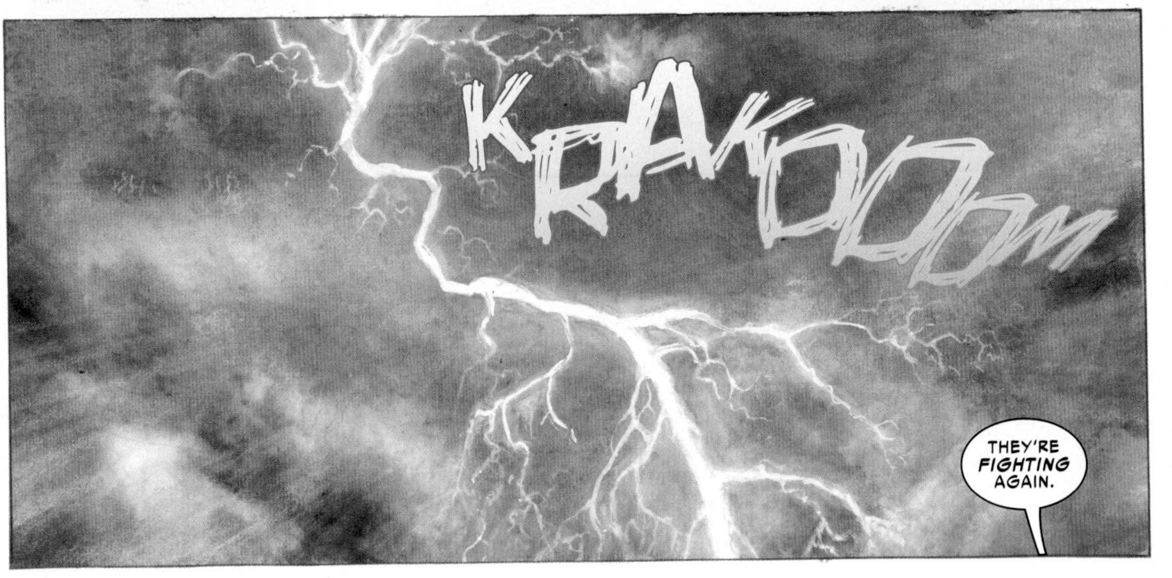
KRAKOOOM
THEY'RE FIGHTING AGAIN.

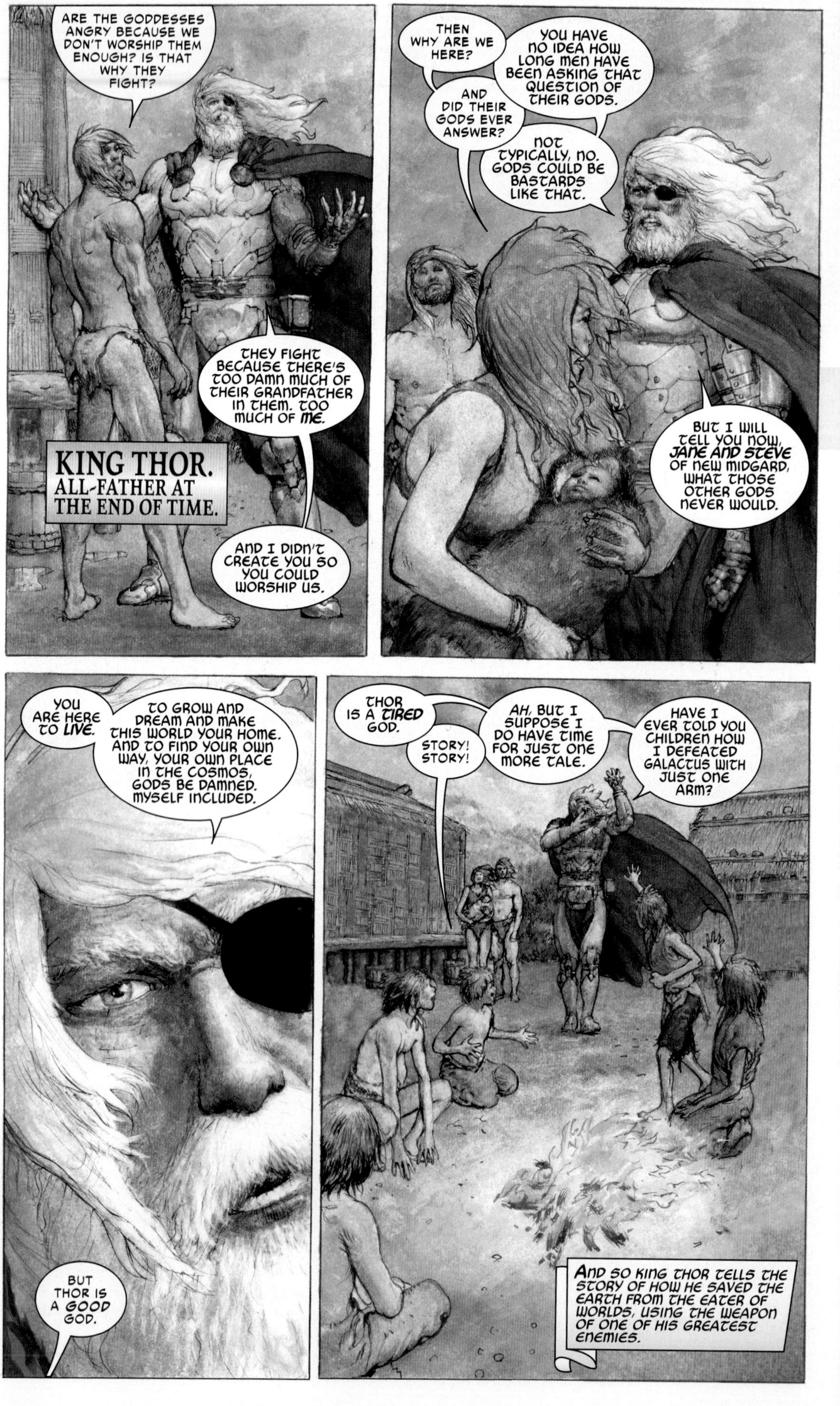
ARE THE GODDESSES ANGRY BECAUSE WE DON'T WORSHIP THEM ENOUGH? IS THAT WHY THEY FIGHT?
THEY FIGHT BECAUSE THERE'S TOO DAMN MUCH OF THEIR GRANDFATHER IN THEM. TOO MUCH OF ME.
KING THOR. ALL-FATHER AT THE END OF TIME.
AND I DIDN'T CREATE YOU SO YOU COULD WORSHIP US.
THEN WHY ARE WE HERE?
YOU HAVE NO IDEA HOW LONG MEN HAVE BEEN ASKING THAT QUESTION OF THEIR GODS.
AND DID THEIR GODS EVER ANSWER?
NOT TYPICALLY, NO. GODS COULD BE BASTARDS LIKE THAT.
BUT I WILL TELL YOU NOW, JANE AND STEVE OF NEW MIDGARD, WHAT THOSE OTHER GODS NEVER WOULD.
YOU ARE HERE TO LIVE.
TO GROW AND DREAM AND MAKE THIS WORLD YOUR HOME. AND TO FIND YOUR OWN WAY, YOUR OWN PLACE IN THE COSMOS, GODS BE DAMNED. MYSELF INCLUDED.
BUT THOR IS A GOOD GOD.
THOR IS A TIRED GOD.
STORY! STORY!
AH, BUT I SUPPOSE I DO HAVE TIME FOR JUST ONE MORE TALE.
HAVE I EVER TOLD YOU CHILDREN HOW I DEFEATED GALACTUS WITH JUST ONE ARM?
AND SO KING THOR TELLS THE STORY OF HOW HE SAVED THE EARTH FROM THE EATER OF WORLDS, USING THE WEAPON OF ONE OF HIS GREATEST ENEMIES.

THE WEAPON OF GORR THE GOD BUTCHER.

BUT WHAT KING THOR DOES NOT KNOW IS THAT THE STORY OF ALL-BLACK THE NECROSWORD DID NOT END.

THAT IT CONTINUES ON, ELSEWHERE AT THE END OF TIME, IN THE DEEPEST REACHES OF SPACE...

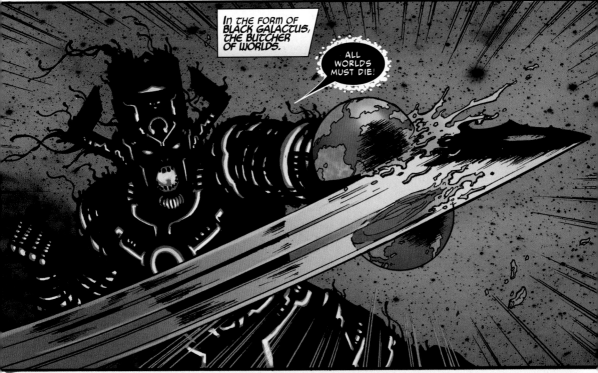

IN THE FORM OF BLACK GALACTUS, THE BUTCHER OF WORLDS.

ALL WORLDS MUST DIE!

THE NECROSWORD HAD NOT BEEN DESTROYED, BUT INSTEAD WAS ABSORBED BY GALACTUS. OR PERHAPS...

...GALACTUS HAD BEEN ABSORBED BY IT.

MURDERER!

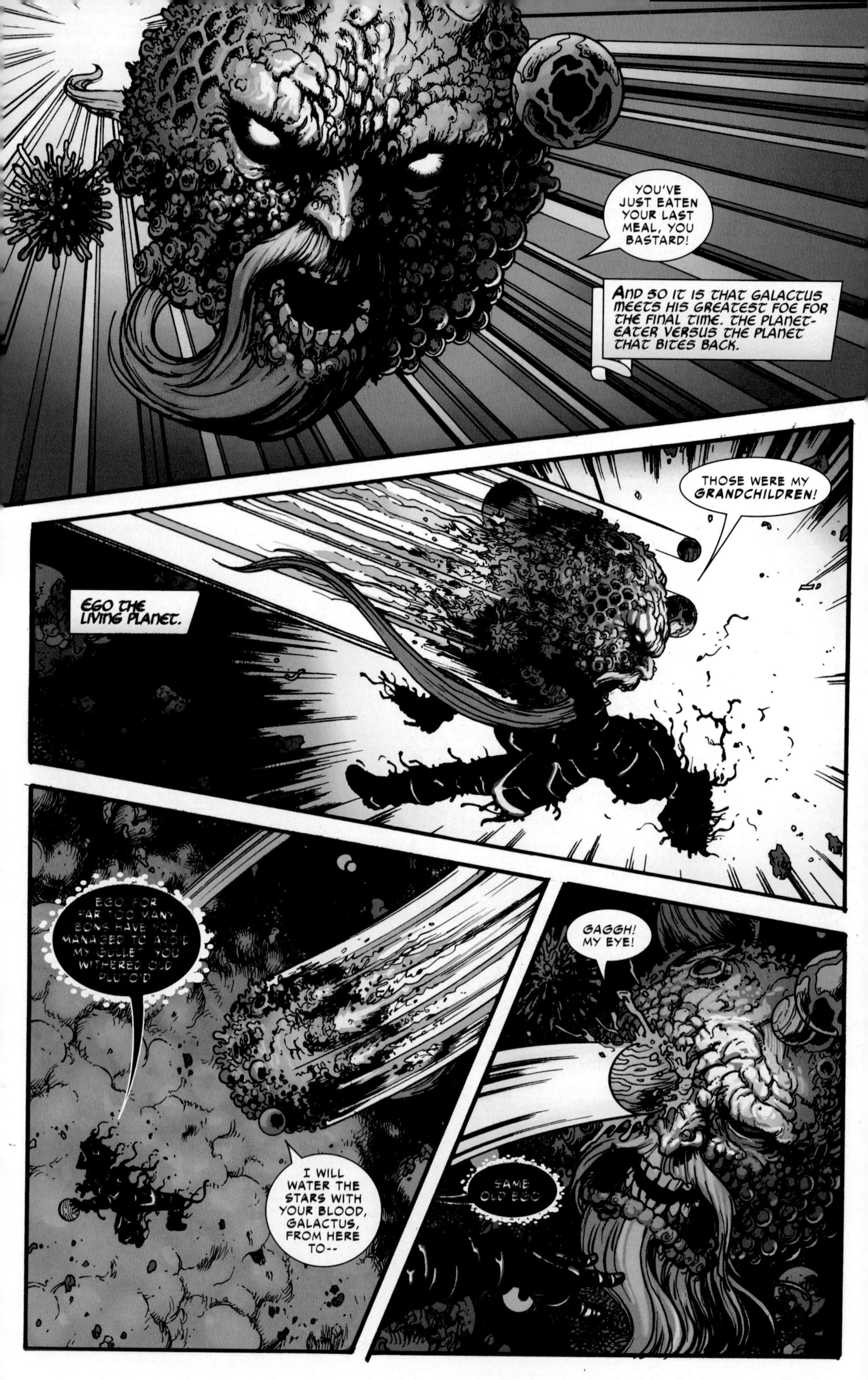
YOU'VE JUST EATEN YOUR LAST MEAL, YOU BASTARD!
AND SO IT IS THAT GALACTUS MEETS HIS GREATEST FOE FOR THE FINAL TIME. THE PLANET-EATER VERSUS THE PLANET THAT BITES BACK.
THOSE WERE MY GRANDCHILDREN!
EGO THE LIVING PLANET.
EGO FOR FAR TOO MANY EONS HAVE YOU MANAGED TO AVOID MY GULLET YOU WITHERED OLD PLUTOID
I WILL WATER THE STARS WITH YOUR BLOOD, GALACTUS, FROM HERE TO--
GAGGH! MY EYE!
SAME OLD EGO

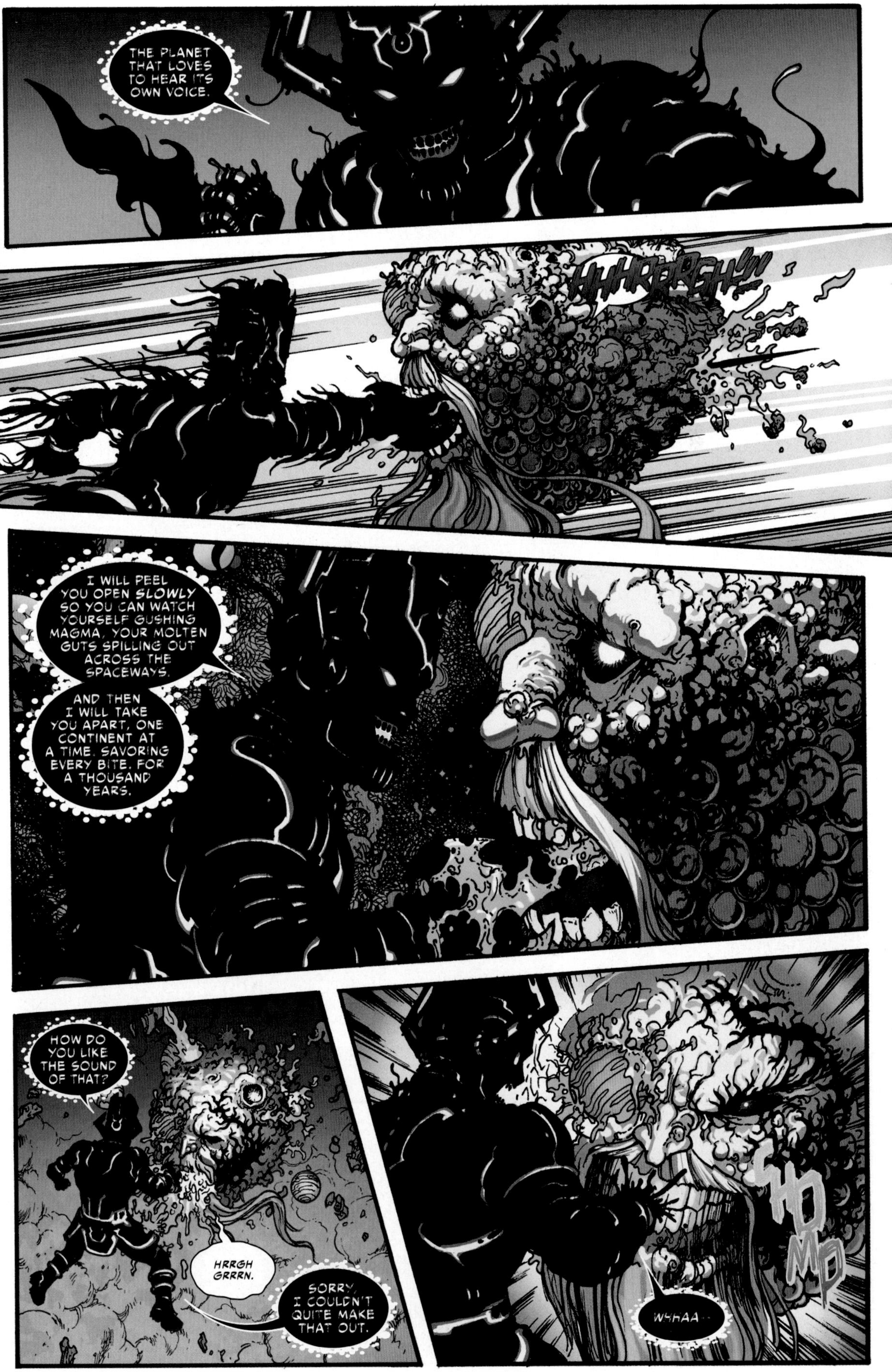
THE PLANET THAT LOVES TO HEAR ITS OWN VOICE.
HHHRRRGH!!!
I WILL PEEL YOU OPEN SLOWLY SO YOU CAN WATCH YOURSELF GUSHING MAGMA, YOUR MOLTEN GUTS SPILLING OUT ACROSS THE SPACEWAYS.
AND THEN I WILL TAKE YOU APART, ONE CONTINENT AT A TIME. SAVORING EVERY BITE. FOR A THOUSAND YEARS.
HOW DO YOU LIKE THE SOUND OF THAT?
HRRGH GRRRN.
SORRY, I COULDN'T QUITE MAKE THAT OUT.
CHOMP
WYHAA...

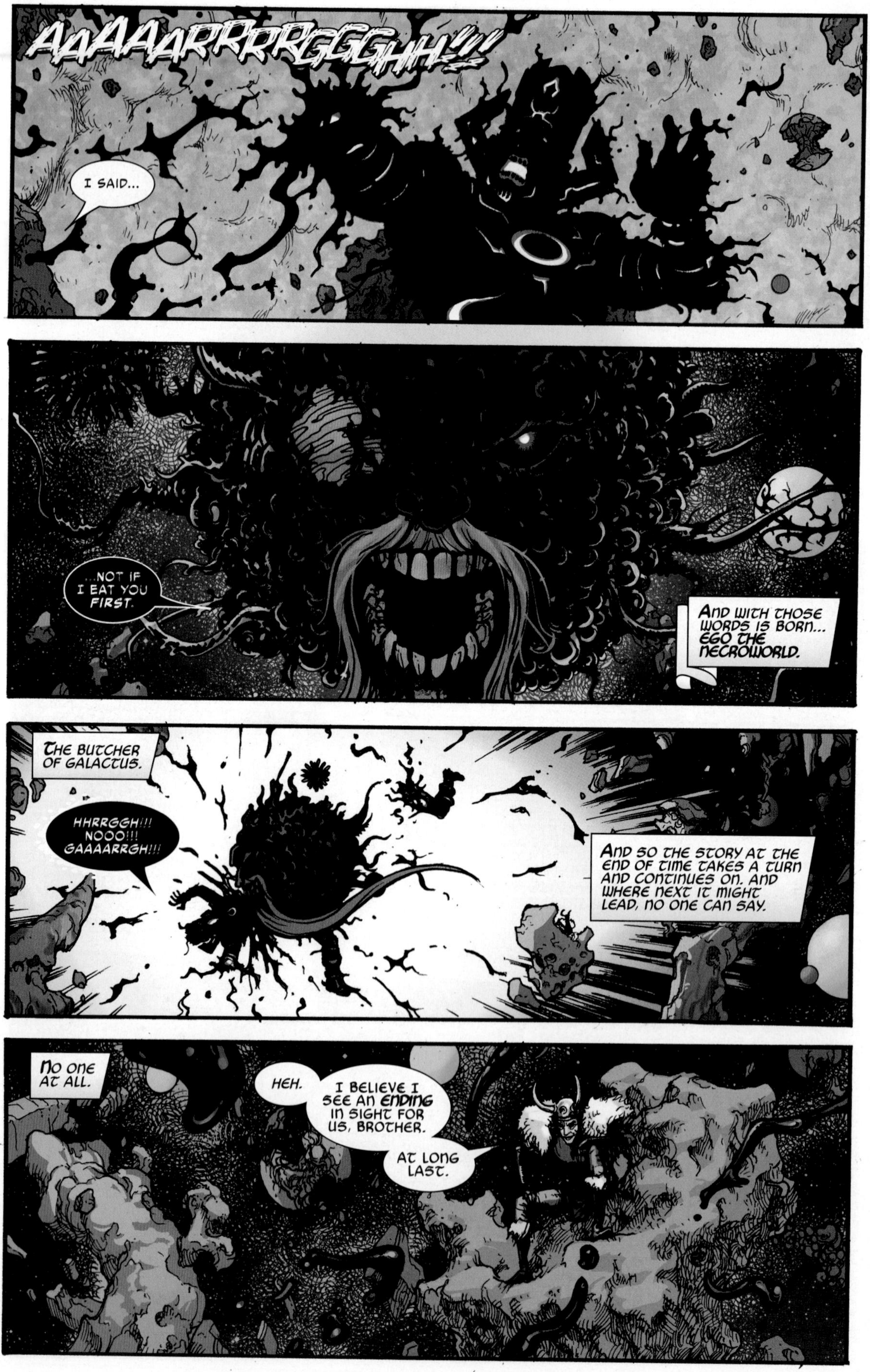
AAAAARRRRGGGHH!!!
I SAID...
...NOT IF I EAT YOU FIRST.
AND WITH THOSE WORDS IS BORN... EGO THE NECROWORLD.
THE BUTCHER OF GALACTUS.
HHRRGGH!!! NOOO!!! GAAAARRGH!!!
AND SO THE STORY AT THE END OF TIME TAKES A TURN AND CONTINUES ON. AND WHERE NEXT IT MIGHT LEAD, NO ONE CAN SAY.
NO ONE AT ALL.
HEH.
I BELIEVE I SEE AN ENDING IN SIGHT FOR US, BROTHER.
AT LONG LAST.

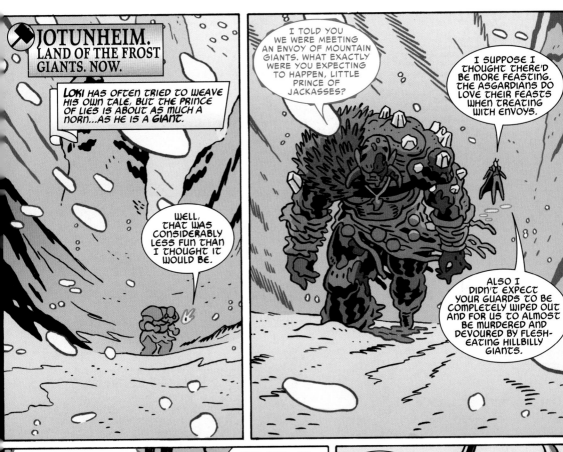

**JOTUNHEIM.** LAND OF THE FROST GIANTS. NOW.

*LOKI HAS OFTEN TRIED TO WEAVE HIS OWN TALE, BUT THE PRINCE OF LIES IS ABOUT AS MUCH A NORN...AS HE IS A GIANT.*

WELL, THAT WAS CONSIDERABLY LESS FUN THAN I THOUGHT IT WOULD BE.

I TOLD YOU WE WERE MEETING AN ENVOY OF MOUNTAIN GIANTS. WHAT EXACTLY WERE YOU EXPECTING TO HAPPEN, LITTLE PRINCE OF JACKASSES?

I SUPPOSE I THOUGHT THERE'D BE MORE FEASTING. THE ASGARDIANS DO LOVE THEIR FEASTS WHEN TREATING WITH ENVOYS.

ALSO I DIDN'T EXPECT YOUR GUARDS TO BE COMPLETELY WIPED OUT AND FOR US TO ALMOST BE MURDERED AND DEVOURED BY FLESH-EATING HILLBILLY GIANTS.

COWARDS AMBUSHED US. *REAL* GIANTS FIGHT FACE-TO-FACE. YOU'D KNOW THAT, BOY, IF YOU WERE MY SON IN MORE THAN NAME.

YES, WELL, AT LEAST THIS FINALLY AFFORDS US SOME TIME ALONE.

THERE ARE SO MANY QUESTIONS I'VE WANTED TO ASK YOU SINCE YOU CAME BACK TO LIFE, FATHER.

LIKE... OH, I DON'T KNOW...

IS IT TRUE MY MOTHER FARBAUTI BURIED AN ICE DAGGER IN HER OWN HEART THE NIGHT I WAS BORN?

OR... OR DID YOU...

UM, KING LAUFEY?

THIS DOESN'T STRIKE ME AS A PARTICULARLY GOOD PLACE FOR A NAP.

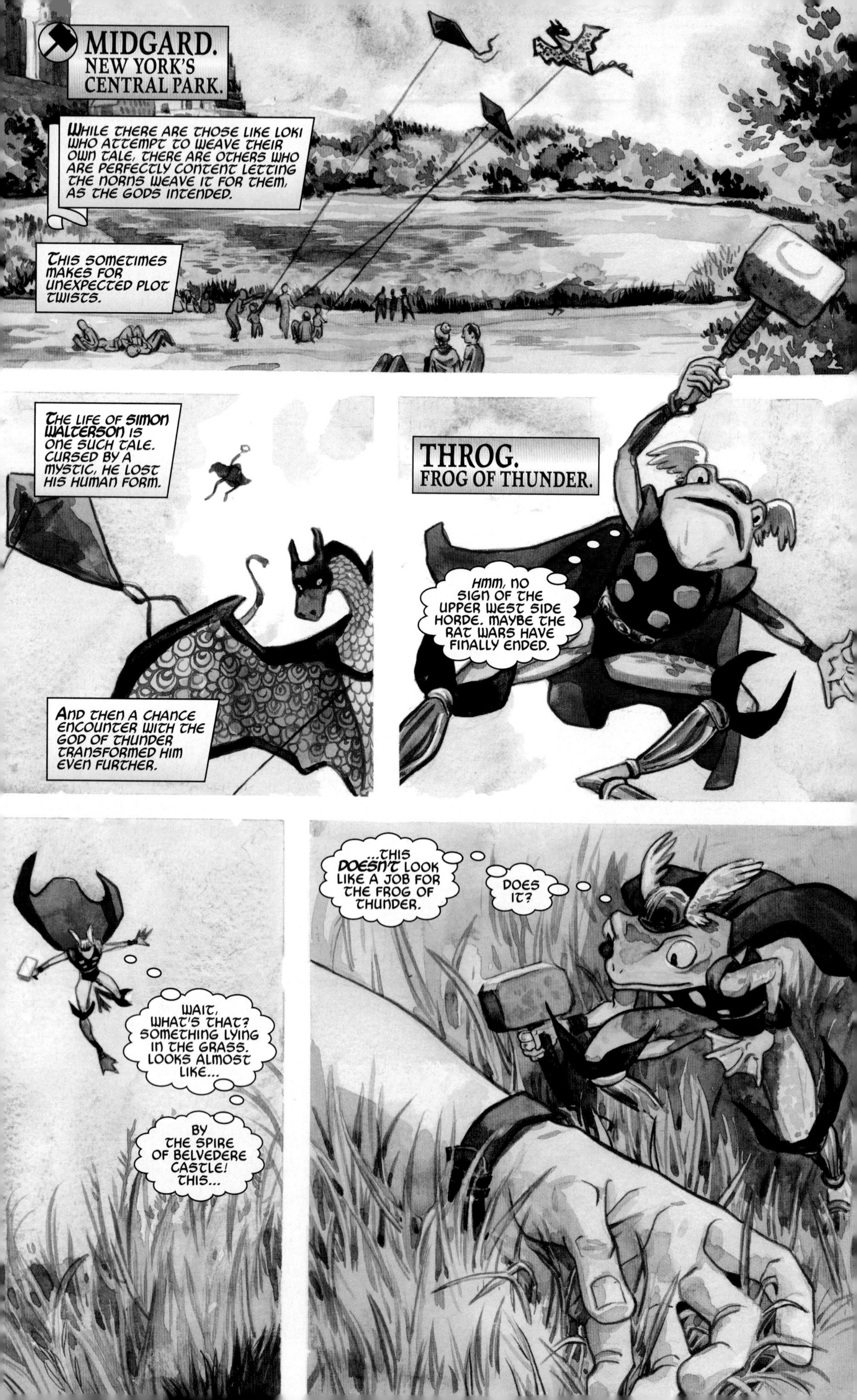
MIDGARD. NEW YORK'S CENTRAL PARK.
WHILE THERE ARE THOSE LIKE LOKI WHO ATTEMPT TO WEAVE THEIR OWN TALE, THERE ARE OTHERS WHO ARE PERFECTLY CONTENT LETTING THE NORNS WEAVE IT FOR THEM, AS THE GODS INTENDED.
THIS SOMETIMES MAKES FOR UNEXPECTED PLOT TWISTS.
THE LIFE OF SIMON WALTERSON IS ONE SUCH TALE. CURSED BY A MYSTIC, HE LOST HIS HUMAN FORM.
AND THEN A CHANCE ENCOUNTER WITH THE GOD OF THUNDER TRANSFORMED HIM EVEN FURTHER.
THROG. FROG OF THUNDER.
HMM, NO SIGN OF THE UPPER WEST SIDE HORDE. MAYBE THE RAT WARS HAVE FINALLY ENDED.
WAIT, WHAT'S THAT? SOMETHING LYING IN THE GRASS. LOOKS ALMOST LIKE...
BY THE SPIRE OF BELVEDERE CASTLE! THIS...
...THIS DOESN'T LOOK LIKE A JOB FOR THE FROG OF THUNDER.
DOES IT?

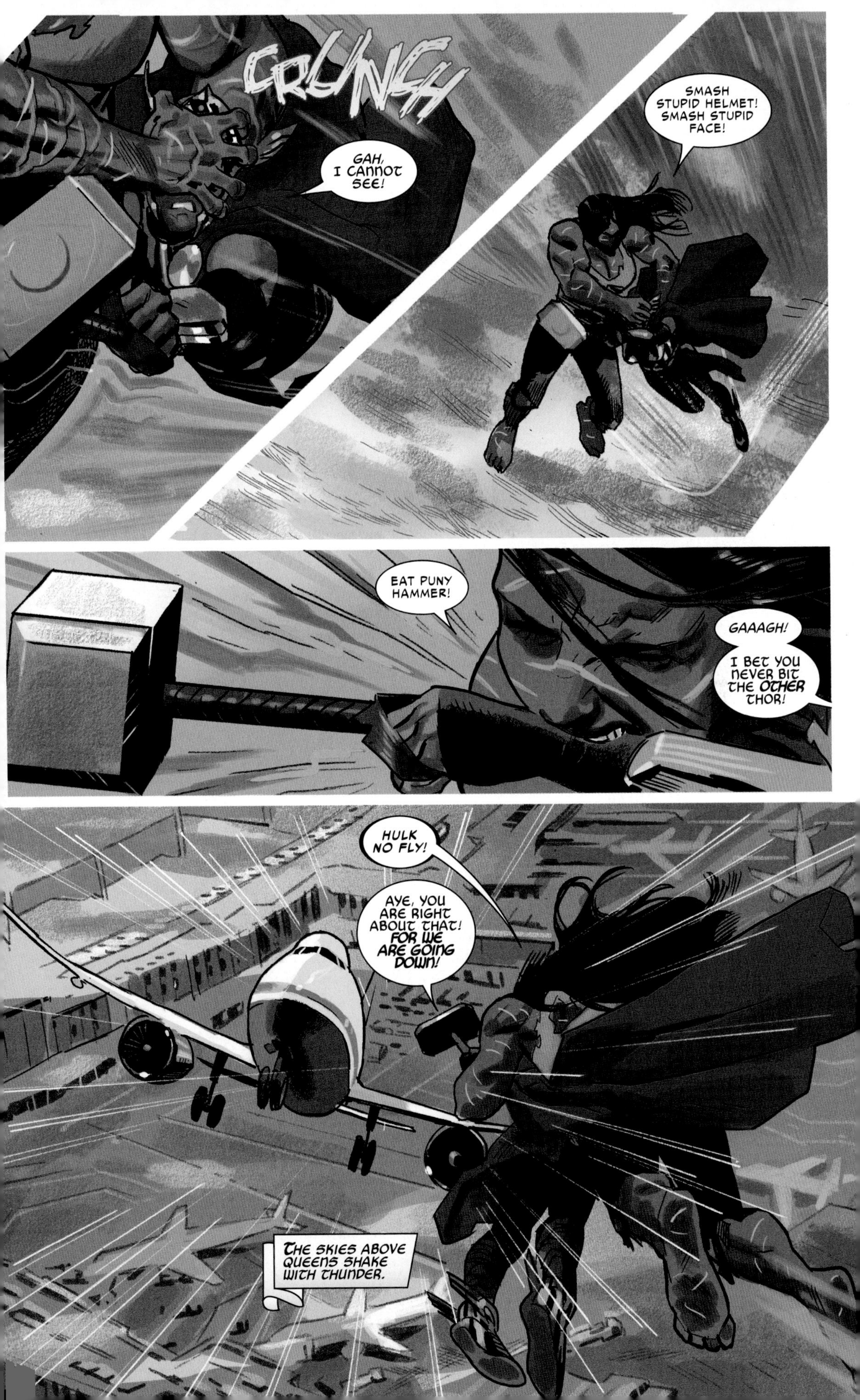
CRUNCH
GAH, I CANNOT SEE!
SMASH STUPID HELMET! SMASH STUPID FACE!
EAT PUNY HAMMER!
GAAAGH!
I BET YOU NEVER BIT THE *OTHER* THOR!
HULK NO FLY!
AYE, YOU ARE RIGHT ABOUT THAT! **FOR WE ARE GOING DOWN!**
THE SKIES ABOVE QUEENS SHAKE WITH THUNDER.

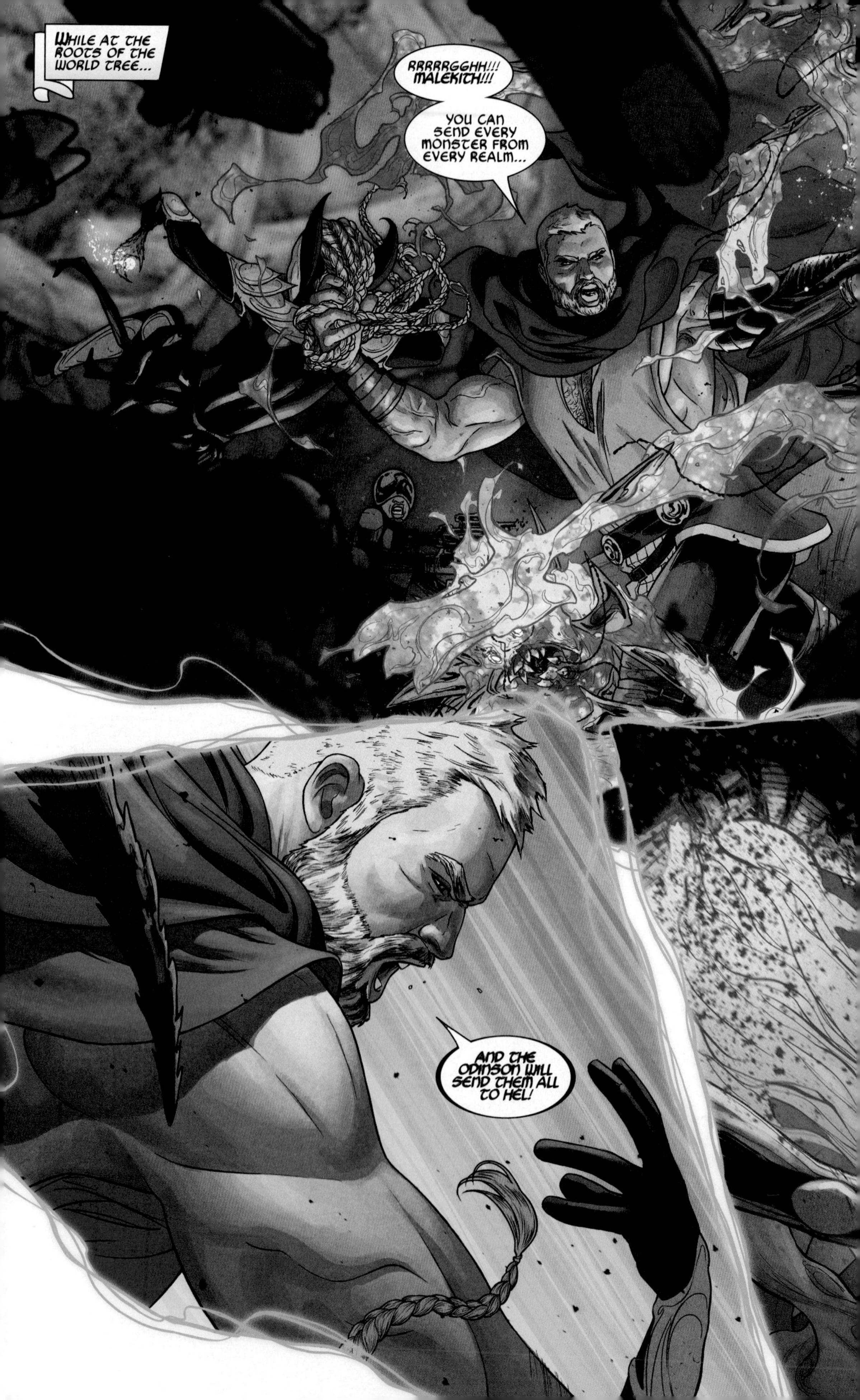
WHILE AT THE ROOTS OF THE WORLD TREE...
RRRRRGGHH!!! MALEKITH!!!
YOU CAN SEND EVERY MONSTER FROM EVERY REALM...
AND THE ODINSON WILL SEND THEM ALL TO HEL!

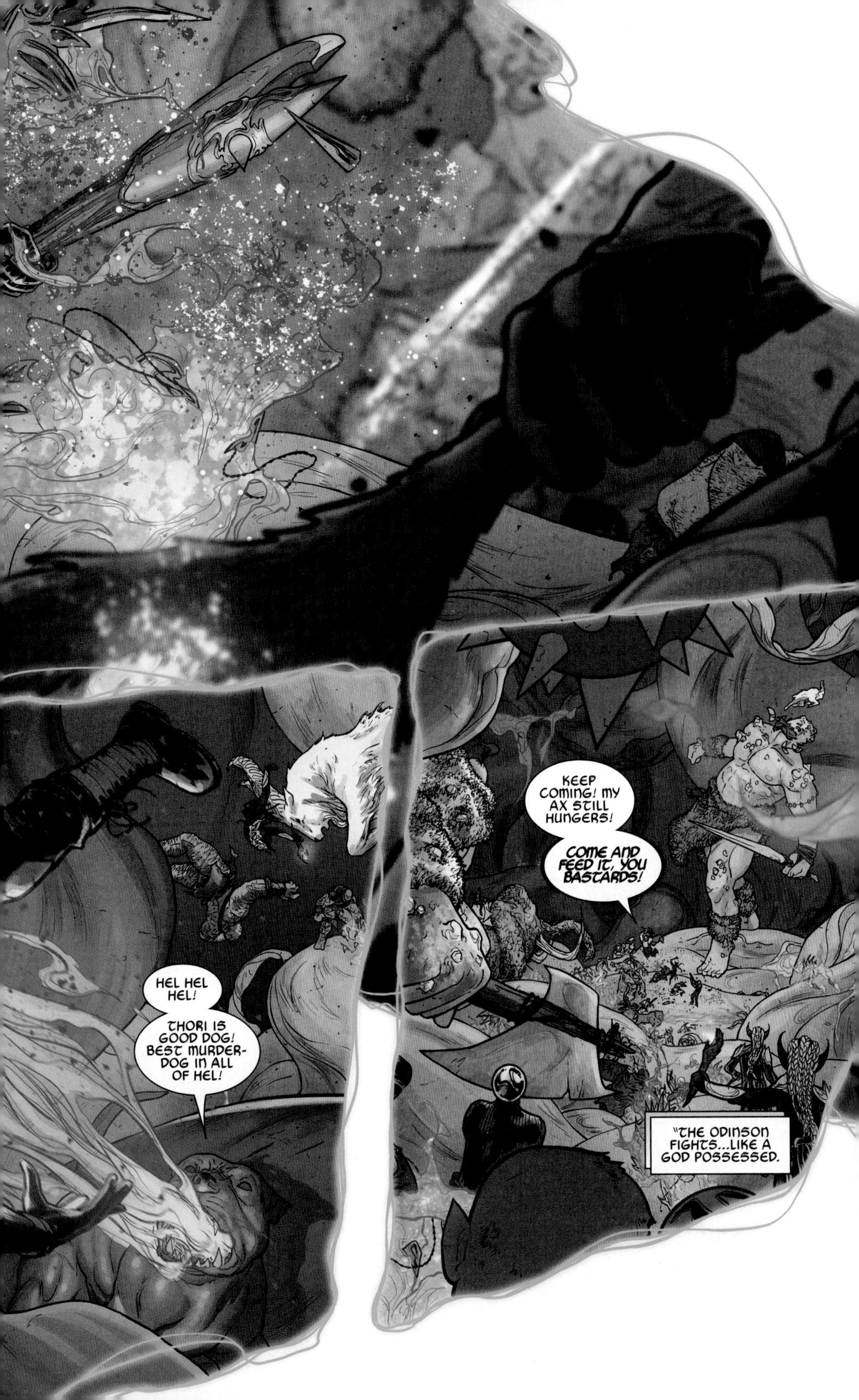
HEL HEL HEL!
THORI IS GOOD DOG! BEST MURDER-DOG IN ALL OF HEL!
KEEP COMING! MY AX STILL HUNGERS!
COME AND FEED IT, YOU BASTARDS!
"THE ODINSON FIGHTS...LIKE A GOD POSSESSED.

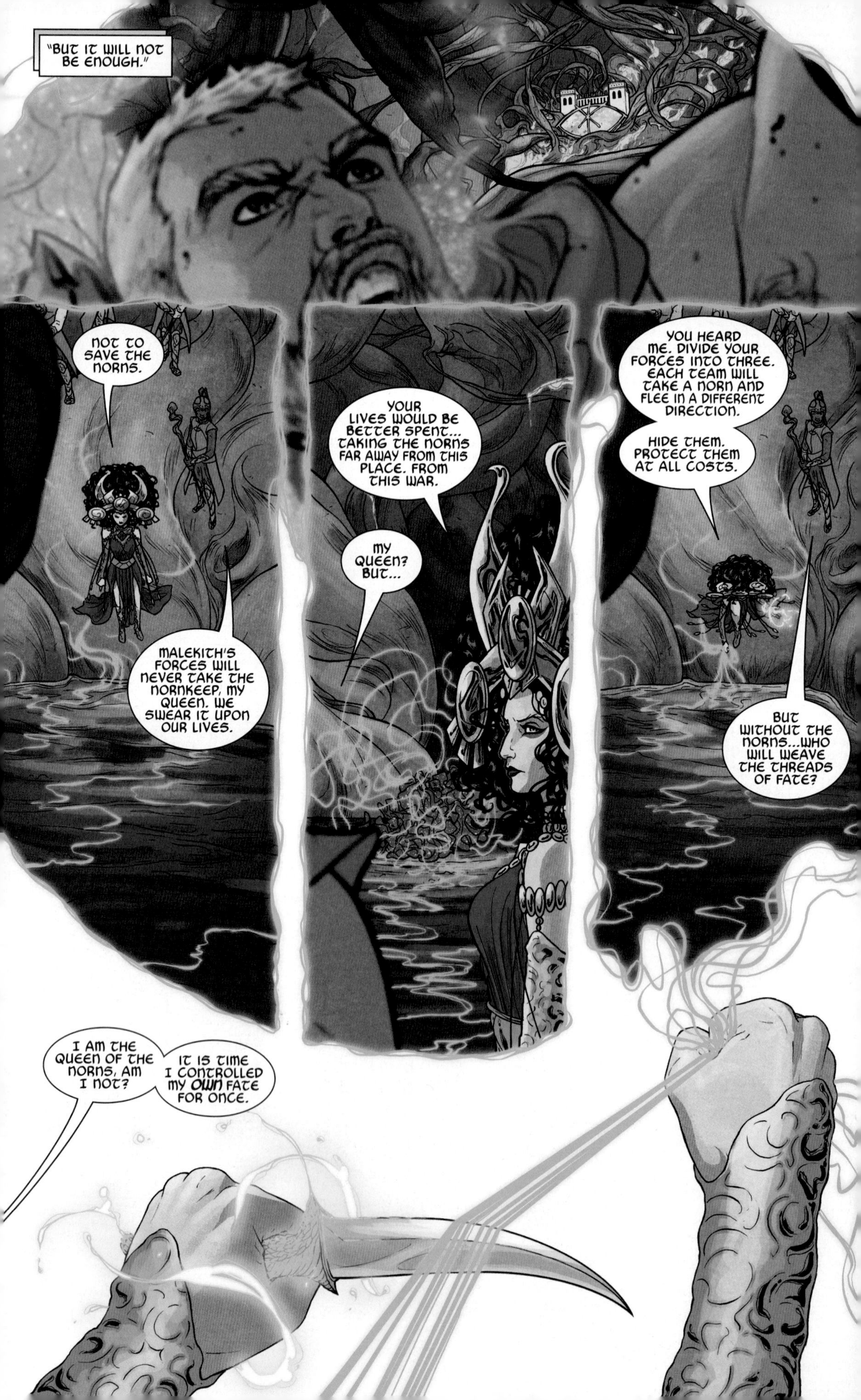
"BUT IT WILL NOT BE ENOUGH."
NOT TO SAVE THE NORNS.
MALEKITH'S FORCES WILL NEVER TAKE THE NORNKEEP, MY QUEEN. WE SWEAR IT UPON OUR LIVES.
YOUR LIVES WOULD BE BETTER SPENT... TAKING THE NORNS FAR AWAY FROM THIS PLACE. FROM THIS WAR.
MY QUEEN? BUT...
YOU HEARD ME. DIVIDE YOUR FORCES INTO THREE. EACH TEAM WILL TAKE A NORN AND FLEE IN A DIFFERENT DIRECTION.
HIDE THEM. PROTECT THEM AT ALL COSTS.
BUT WITHOUT THE NORNS...WHO WILL WEAVE THE THREADS OF FATE?
I AM THE QUEEN OF THE NORNS, AM I NOT?
IT IS TIME I CONTROLLED MY *OWN* FATE FOR ONCE.

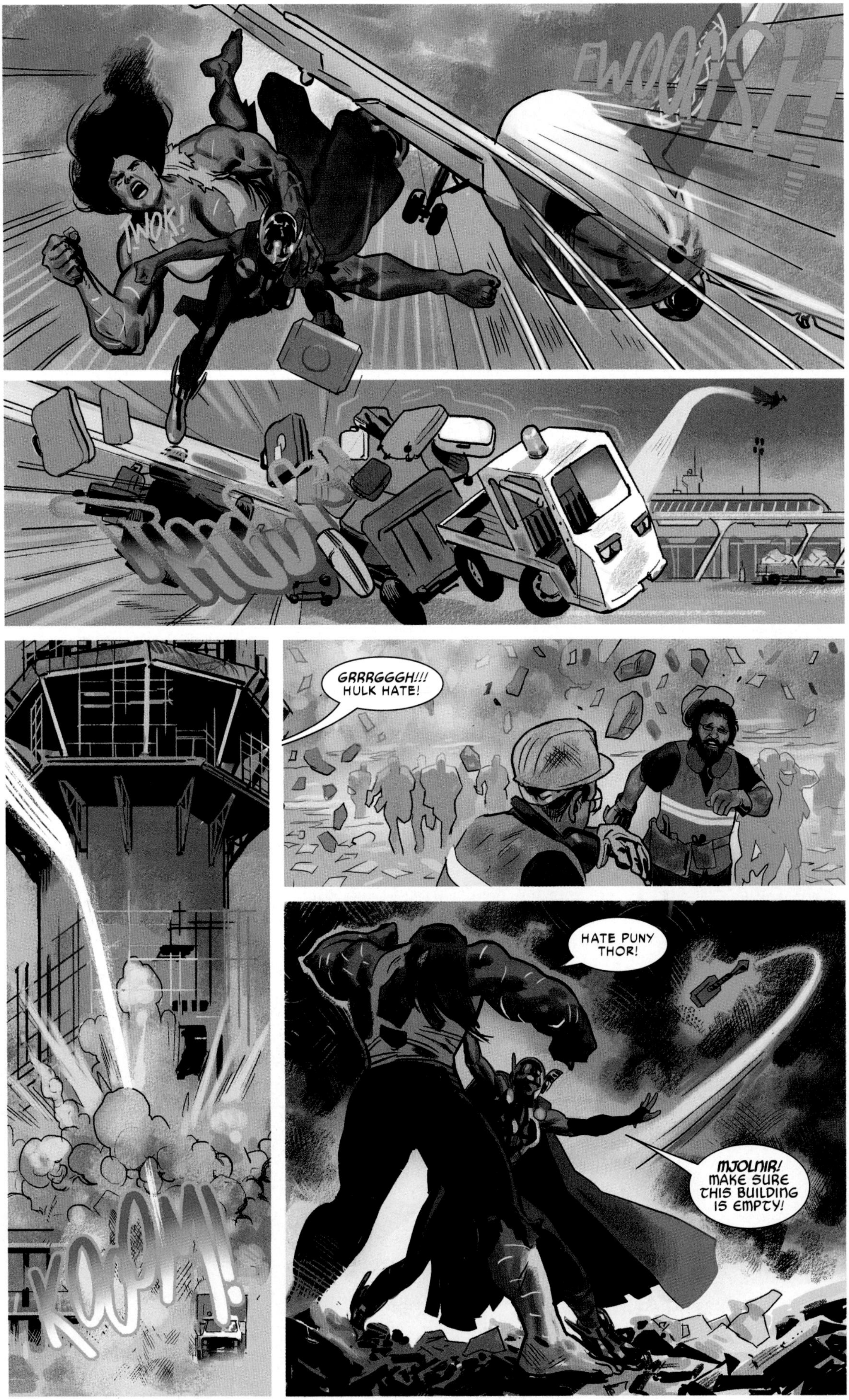
FWOOSH
TWOK!
GRRRGGGH!!!
HULK HATE!
KOOM!
HATE PUNY
THOR!
MJOLNIR!
MAKE SURE
THIS BUILDING
IS EMPTY!

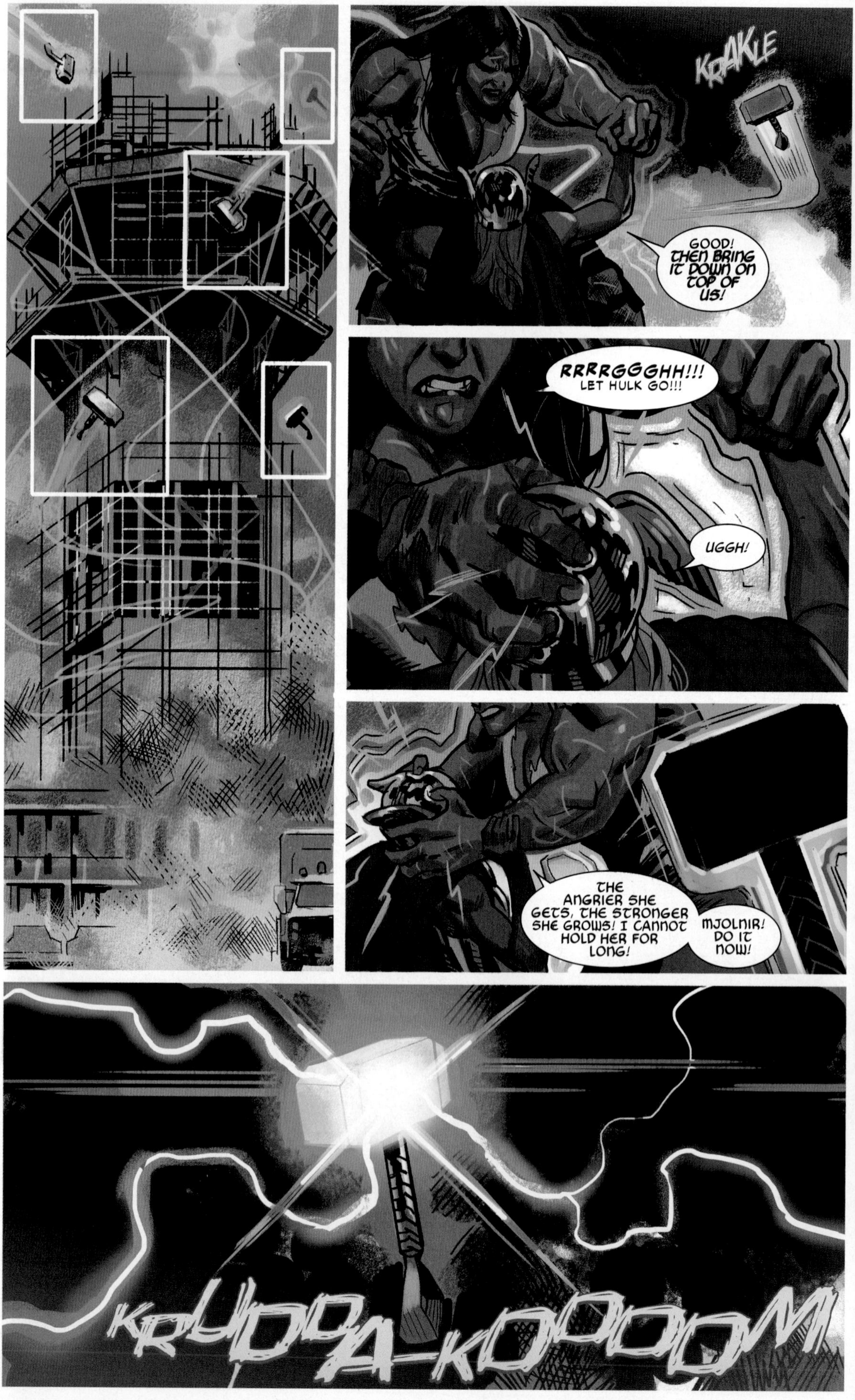
KRAKLE
GOOD! THEN BRING IT DOWN ON TOP OF US!
RRRRGGGHH!!! LET HULK GO!!!
UGGH!
THE ANGRIER SHE GETS, THE STRONGER SHE GROWS! I CANNOT HOLD HER FOR LONG!
MJOLNIR! DO IT NOW!
KRUDDA-KOOOOOM

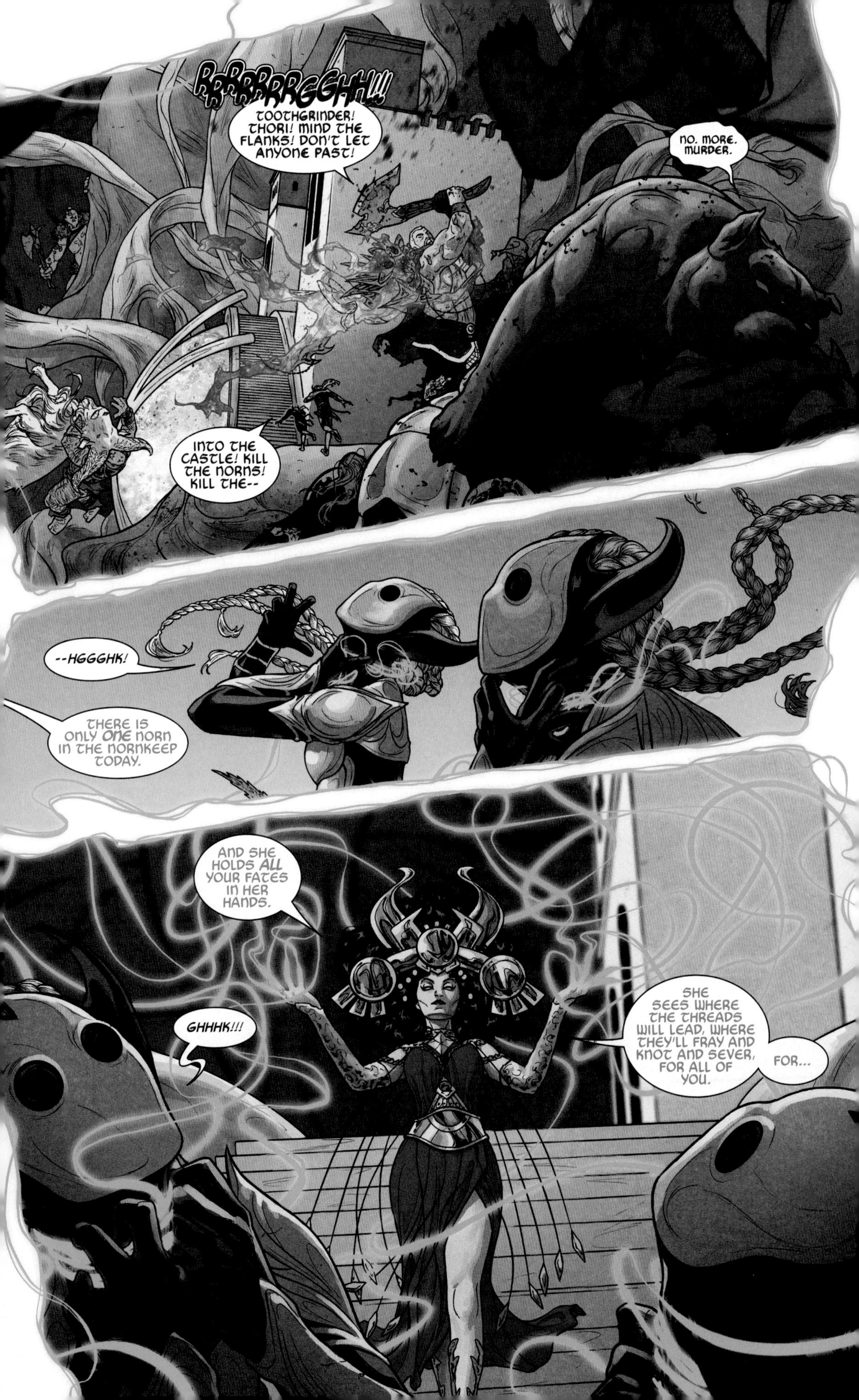
RRRRRRRGGHH!!!
TOOTHGRINDER! THORI! MIND THE FLANKS! DON'T LET ANYONE PAST!
NO. MORE. MURDER.
INTO THE CASTLE! KILL THE NORNS! KILL THE--
--HGGGHK!
THERE IS ONLY ONE NORN IN THE NORNKEEP TODAY.
AND SHE HOLDS ALL YOUR FATES IN HER HANDS.
GHHHK!!!
SHE SEES WHERE THE THREADS WILL LEAD, WHERE THEY'LL FRAY AND KNOT AND SEVER, FOR ALL OF YOU.
FOR...

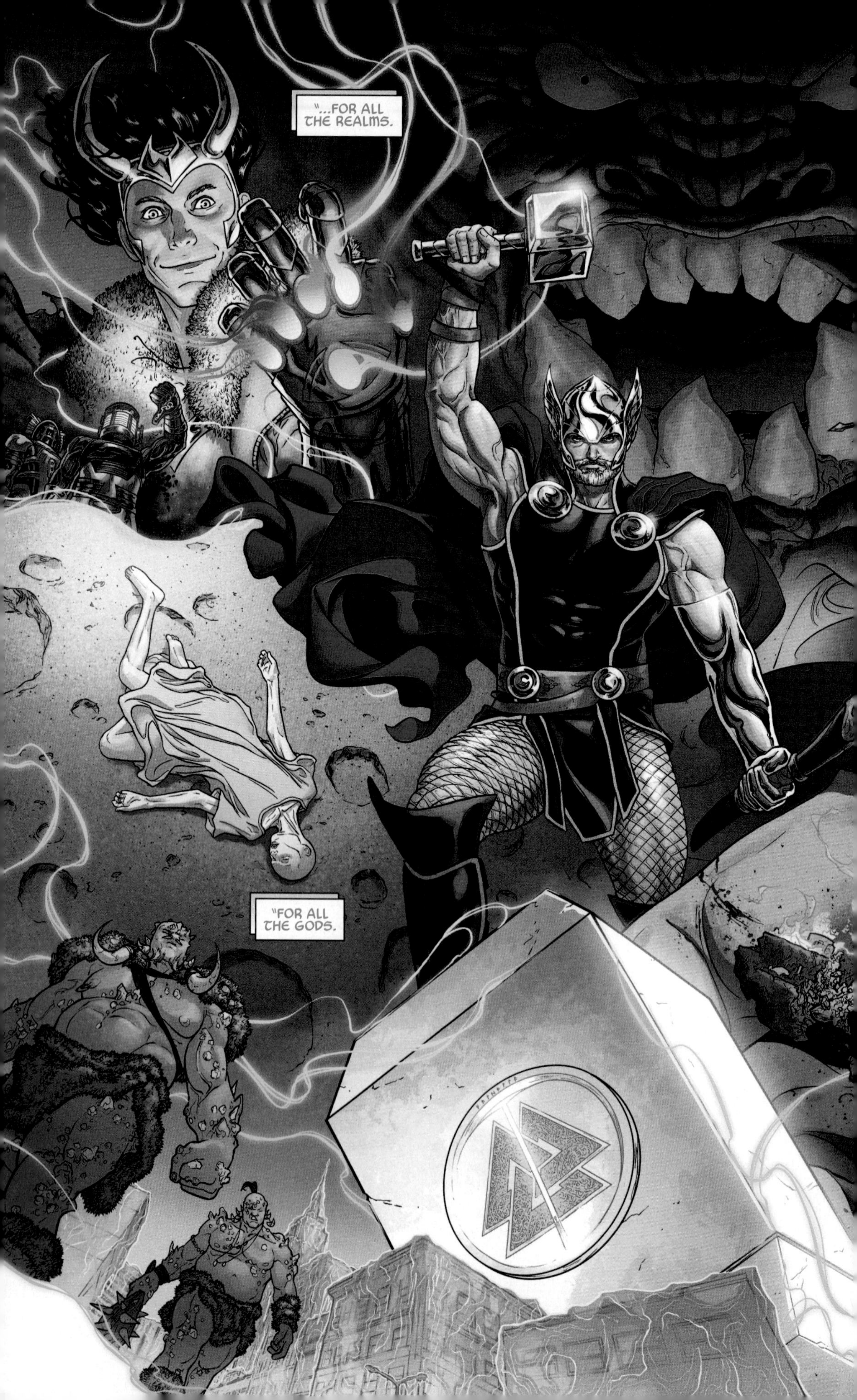
"...FOR ALL THE REALMS.
"FOR ALL THE GODS.

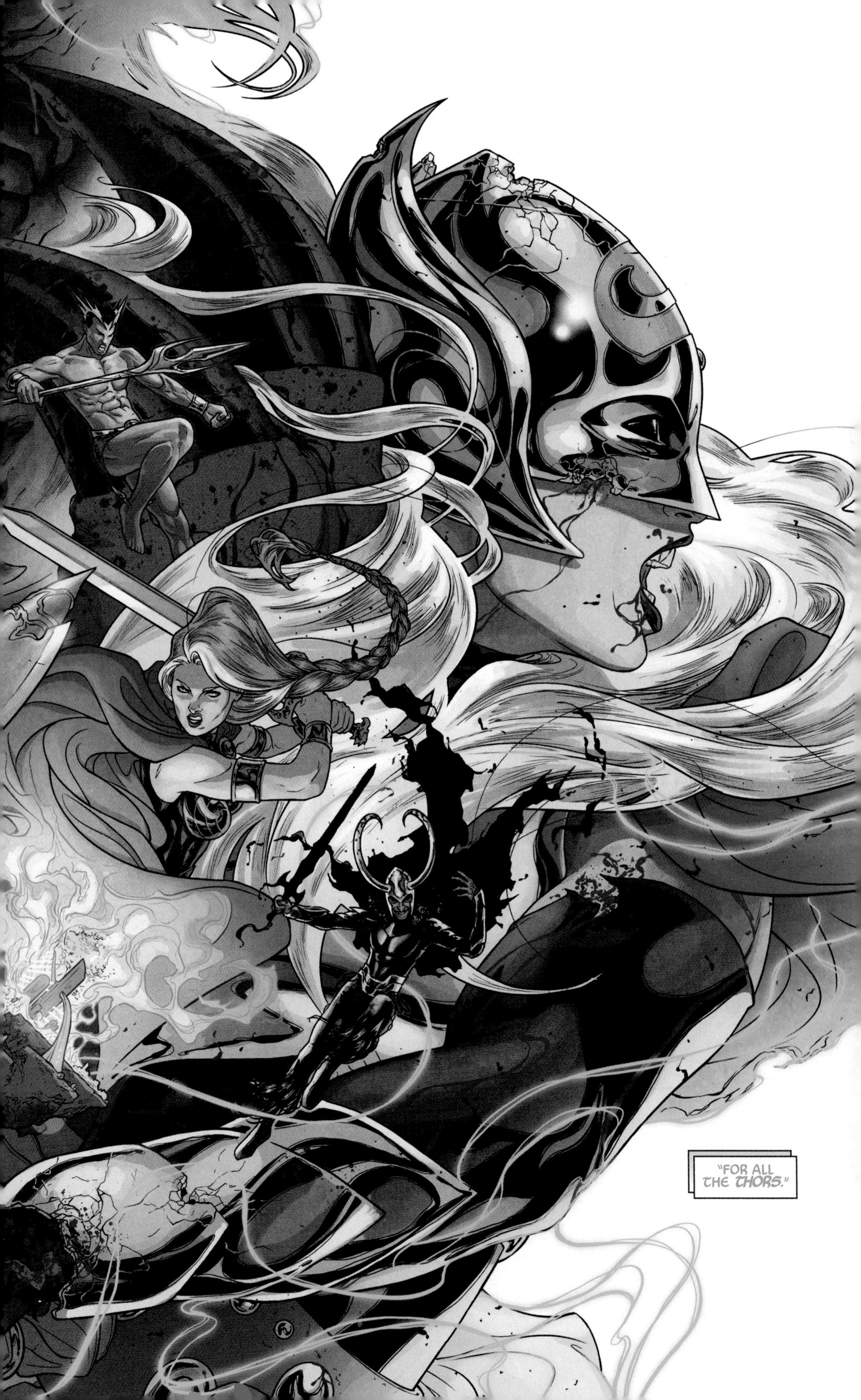
"FOR ALL
THE THORS."

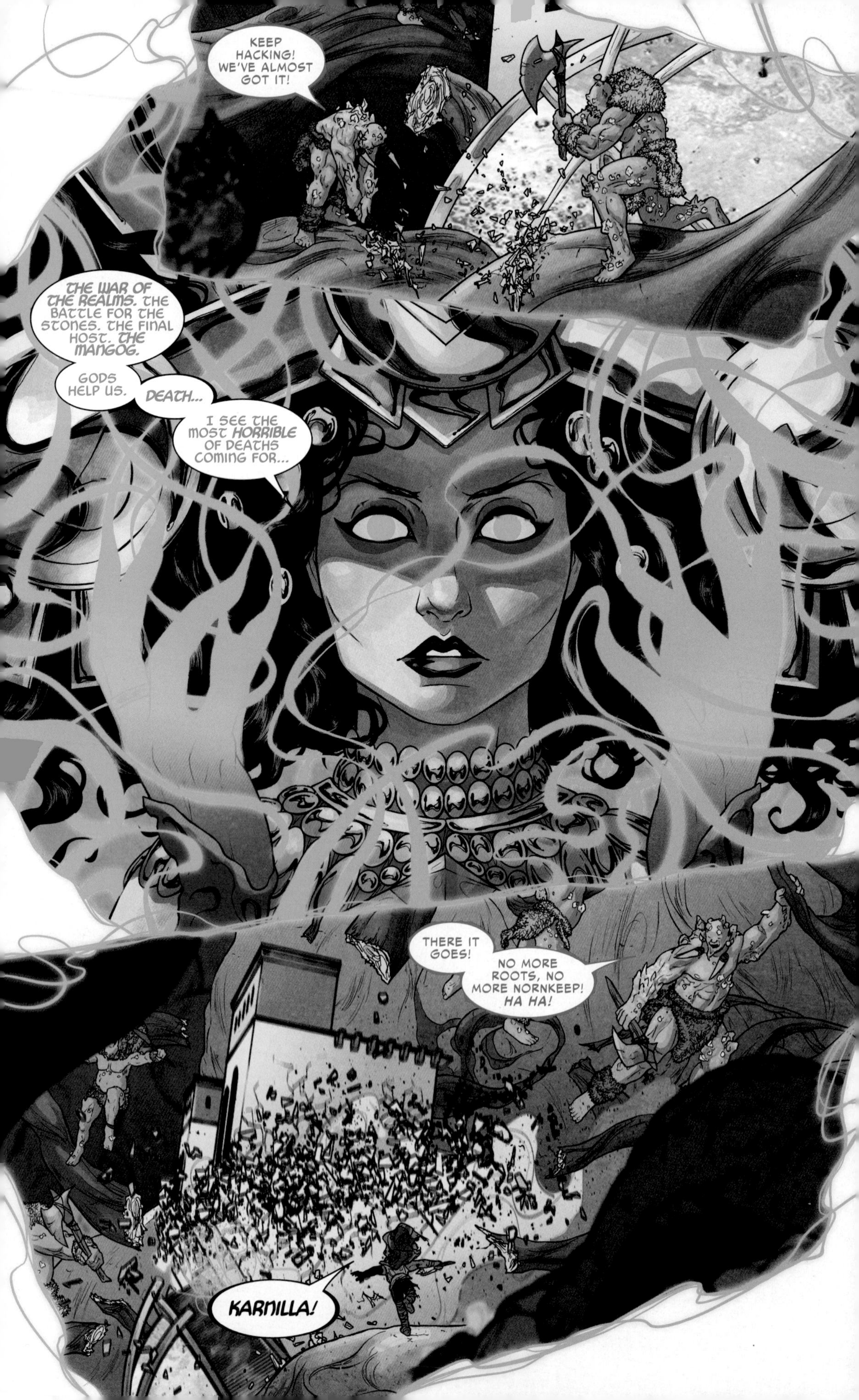
KEEP HACKING! WE'VE ALMOST GOT IT!
THE WAR OF THE REALMS. THE BATTLE FOR THE STONES. THE FINAL HOST. THE MANGOG.
GODS HELP US.
DEATH...
I SEE THE MOST HORRIBLE OF DEATHS COMING FOR...
THERE IT GOES!
NO MORE ROOTS, NO MORE NORNKEEP! HA HA!
KARNILLA!

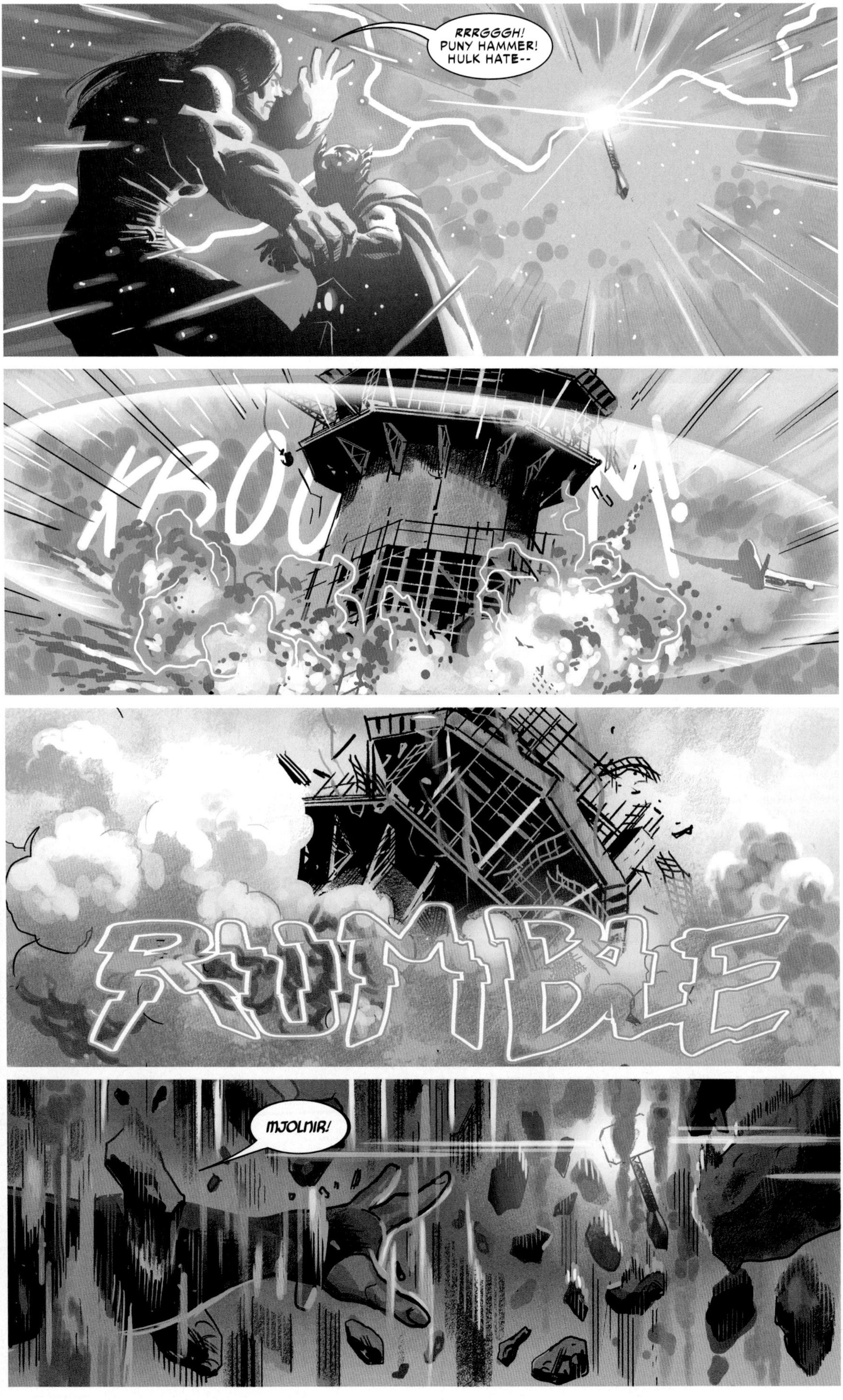
RRRGGGH! PUNY HAMMER! HULK HATE--
KRBOOM!
RUMBLE
MJOLNIR!

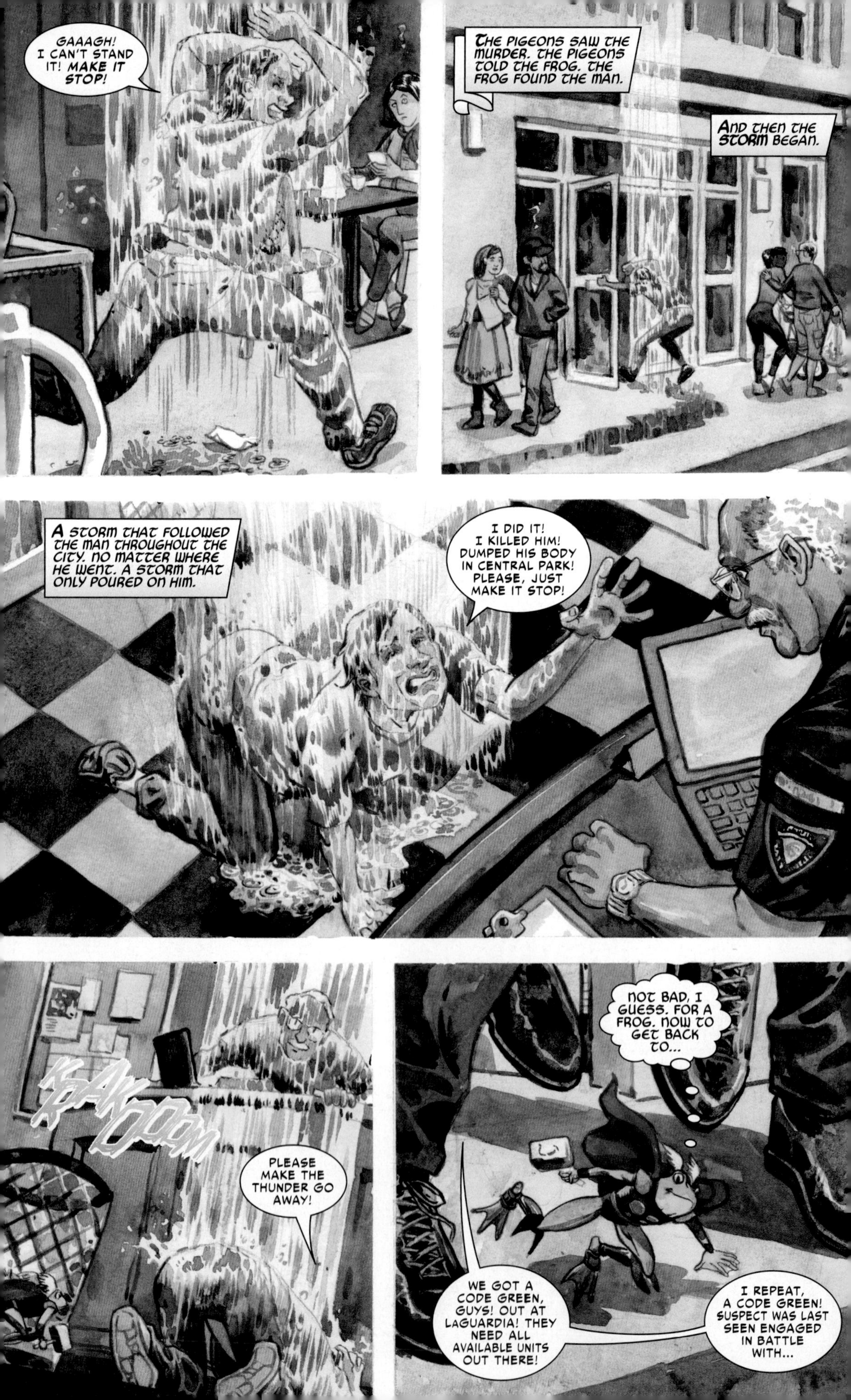
GAAAGH! I CAN'T STAND IT! MAKE IT STOP!
THE PIGEONS SAW THE MURDER. THE PIGEONS TOLD THE FROG. THE FROG FOUND THE MAN.
AND THEN THE STORM BEGAN.
A STORM THAT FOLLOWED THE MAN THROUGHOUT THE CITY. NO MATTER WHERE HE WENT. A STORM THAT ONLY POURED ON HIM.
I DID IT! I KILLED HIM! DUMPED HIS BODY IN CENTRAL PARK! PLEASE, JUST MAKE IT STOP!
KRAKOOOM
PLEASE MAKE THE THUNDER GO AWAY!
NOT BAD, I GUESS. FOR A FROG. NOW TO GET BACK TO...
WE GOT A CODE GREEN, GUYS! OUT AT LAGUARDIA! THEY NEED ALL AVAILABLE UNITS OUT THERE!
I REPEAT, A CODE GREEN! SUSPECT WAS LAST SEEN ENGAGED IN BATTLE WITH...

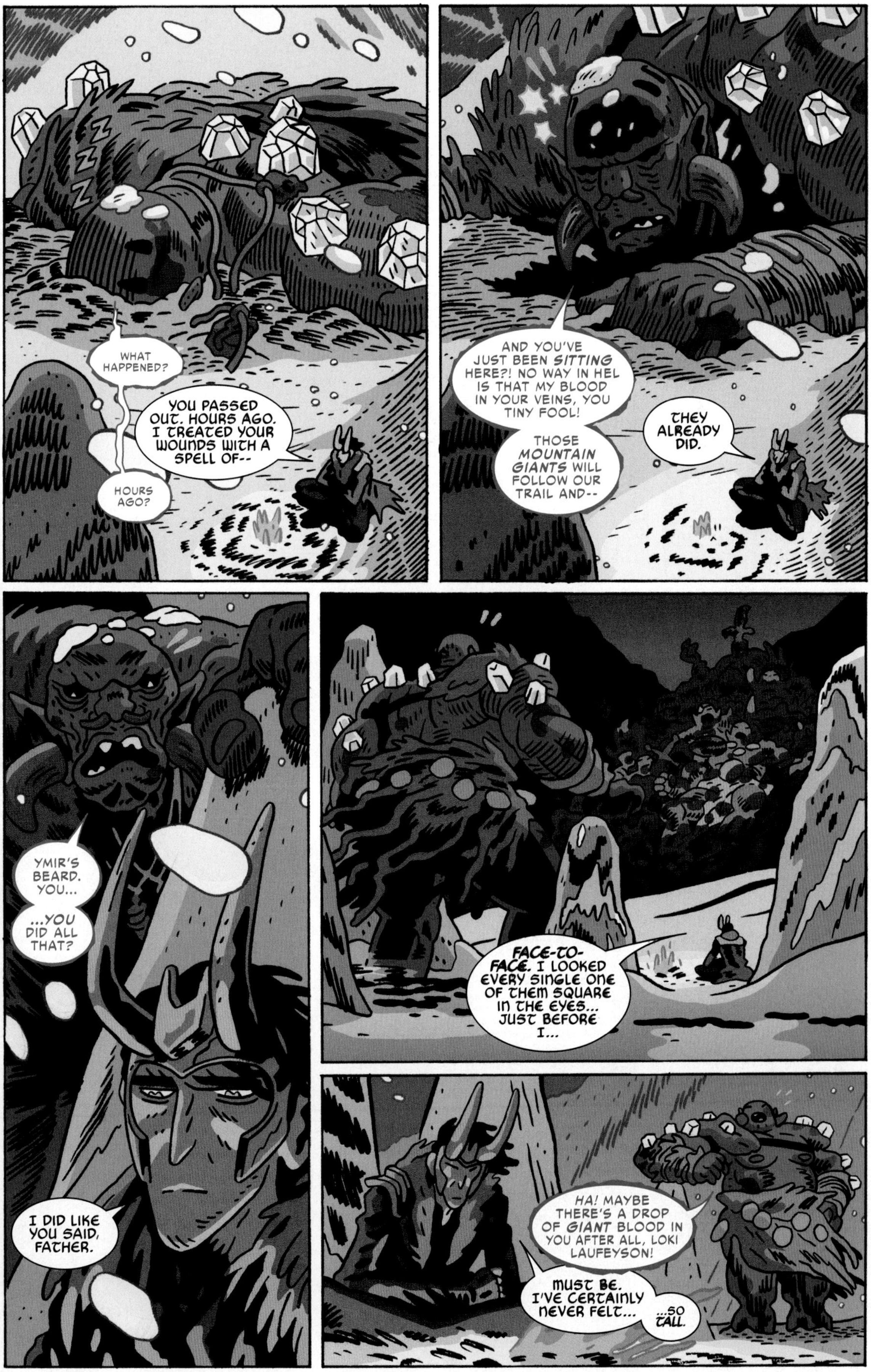

WHAT HAPPENED?
YOU PASSED OUT. HOURS AGO. I TREATED YOUR WOUNDS WITH A SPELL OF--
HOURS AGO?
AND YOU'VE JUST BEEN SITTING HERE?! NO WAY IN HEL IS THAT MY BLOOD IN YOUR VEINS, YOU TINY FOOL!
THOSE MOUNTAIN GIANTS WILL FOLLOW OUR TRAIL AND--
THEY ALREADY DID.
YMIR'S BEARD. YOU...
...YOU DID ALL THAT?
I DID LIKE YOU SAID, FATHER.
FACE-TO-FACE. I LOOKED EVERY SINGLE ONE OF THEM SQUARE IN THE EYES... JUST BEFORE I...
HA! MAYBE THERE'S A DROP OF GIANT BLOOD IN YOU AFTER ALL, LOKI LAUFEYSON!
MUST BE. I'VE CERTAINLY NEVER FELT...
...SO TALL.

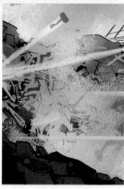

RRGGGH! MJOLNIR! I'M DOWN HERE! I'M...

NO! I'M STARTING TO *CHANGE*. AS JANE, I'LL INSTANTLY BE CRUSHED TO DEATH.

MJOLNIR! HAVE TO TOUCH MJOLNIR OR I'LL...

MJOLNIR?

WOULD YOU SETTLE FOR A *SLIVER* OF IT?

MUST BE... PASSING OUT. BECAUSE I SWEAR THAT *FROG*...

...FROG LOOKS JUST LIKE...

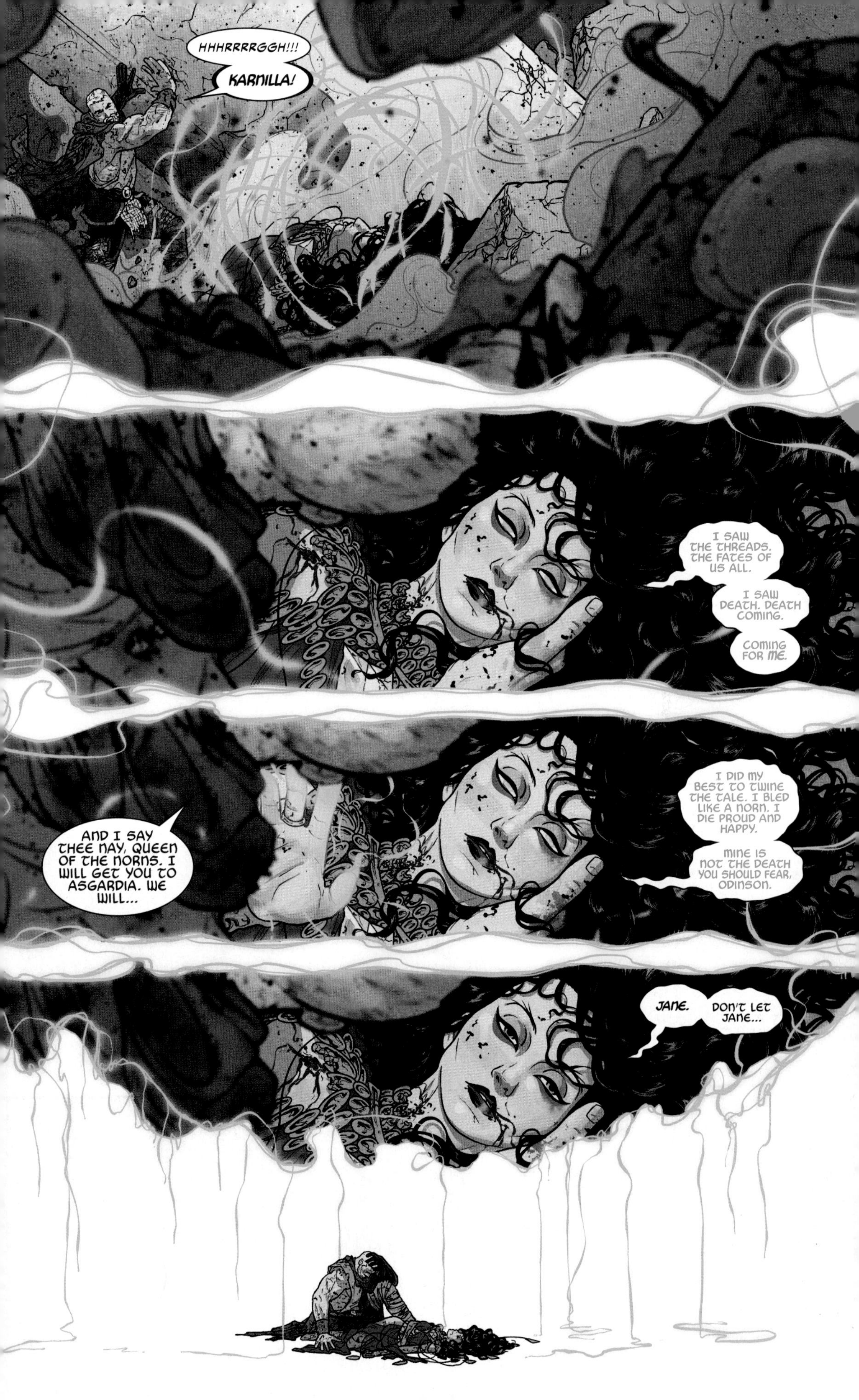
HHHRRRRGGH!!!
KARNILLA!
I SAW THE THREADS. THE FATES OF US ALL.
I SAW DEATH. DEATH COMING.
COMING FOR ME.
AND I SAY THEE NAY, QUEEN OF THE NORNS. I WILL GET YOU TO ASGARDIA. WE WILL...
I DID MY BEST TO TWINE THE TALE. I BLED LIKE A NORN. I DIE PROUD AND HAPPY.
MINE IS NOT THE DEATH YOU SHOULD FEAR, ODINSON.
JANE.
DON'T LET JANE...

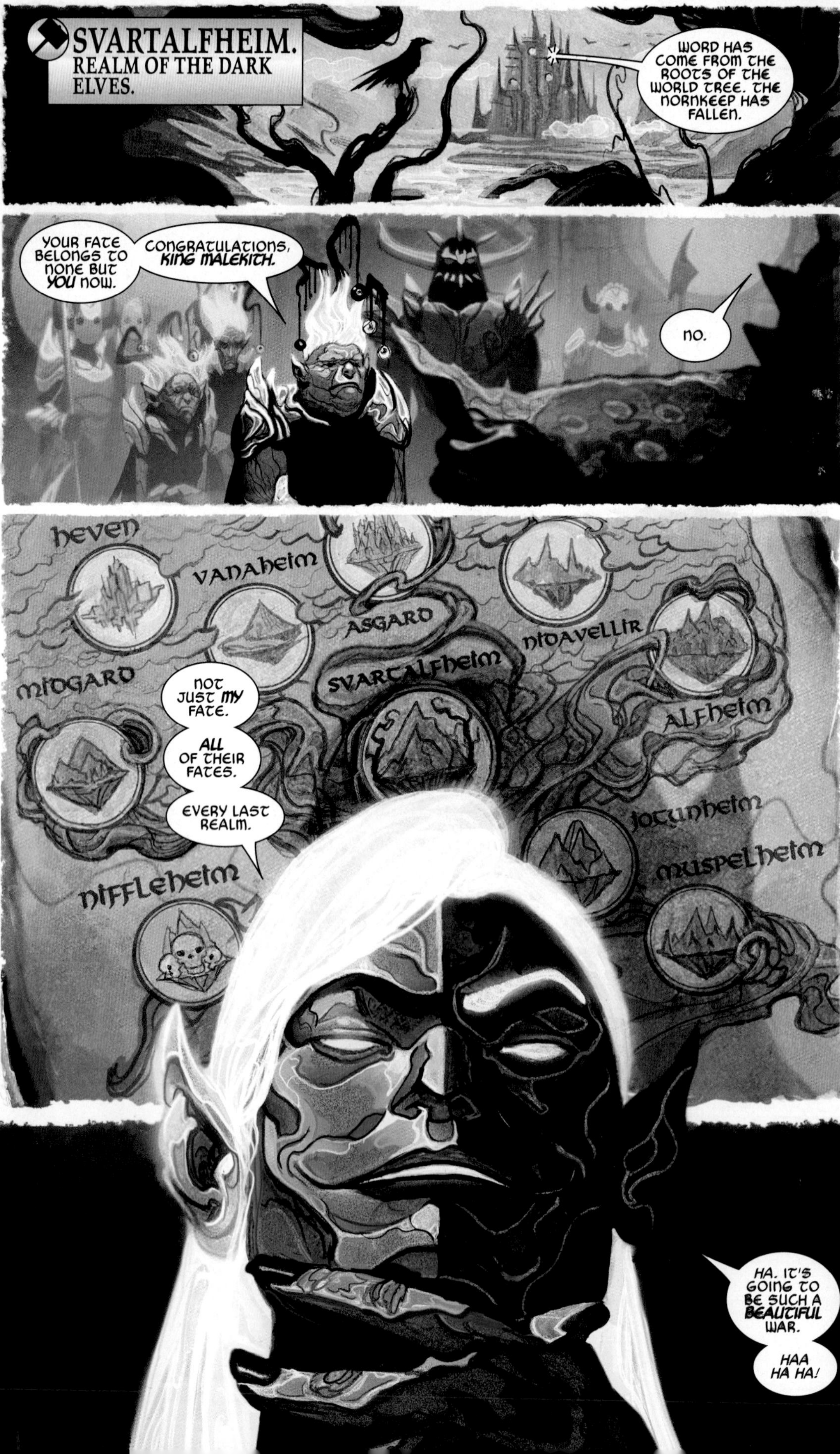
SVARTALFHEIM. REALM OF THE DARK ELVES.
WORD HAS COME FROM THE ROOTS OF THE WORLD TREE. THE NORNKEEP HAS FALLEN.
YOUR FATE BELONGS TO NONE BUT YOU NOW.
CONGRATULATIONS, KING MALEKITH.
NO.
HEVEN
VANAHEIM
ASGARD
NIDAVELLIR
MIDGARD
SVARTALFHEIM
ALFHEIM
JOTUNHEIM
MUSPELHEIM
NIFFLEHEIM
NOT JUST MY FATE.
ALL OF THEIR FATES.
EVERY LAST REALM.
HA. IT'S GOING TO BE SUCH A BEAUTIFUL WAR.
HAA HA HA!

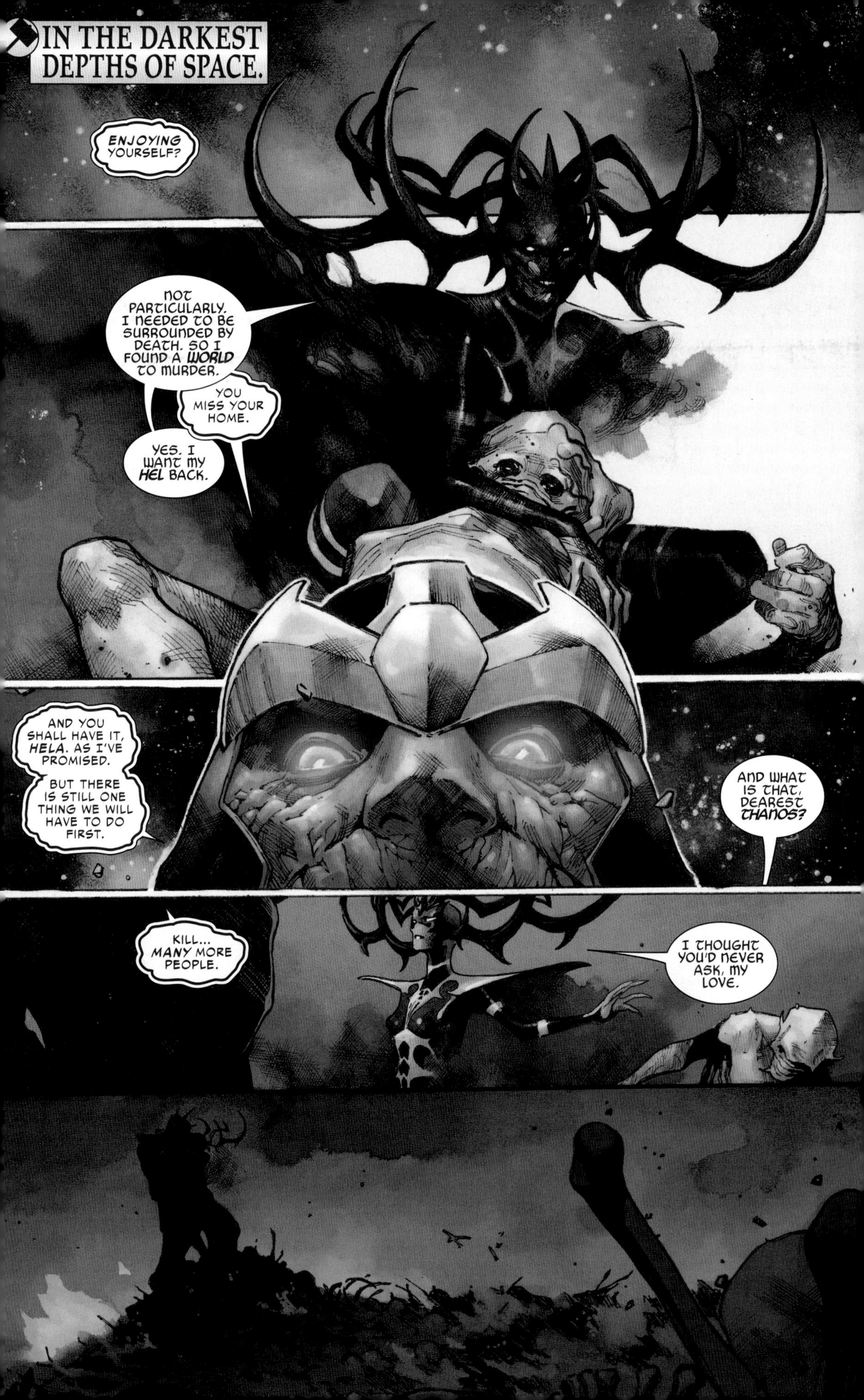

IN THE DARKEST DEPTHS OF SPACE.
ENJOYING YOURSELF?
NOT PARTICULARLY. I NEEDED TO BE SURROUNDED BY DEATH. SO I FOUND A WORLD TO MURDER.
YOU MISS YOUR HOME.
YES. I WANT MY HEL BACK.
AND YOU SHALL HAVE IT, HELA. AS I'VE PROMISED.
BUT THERE IS STILL ONE THING WE WILL HAVE TO DO FIRST.
AND WHAT IS THAT, DEAREST THANOS?
KILL... MANY MORE PEOPLE.
I THOUGHT YOU'D NEVER ASK, MY LOVE.

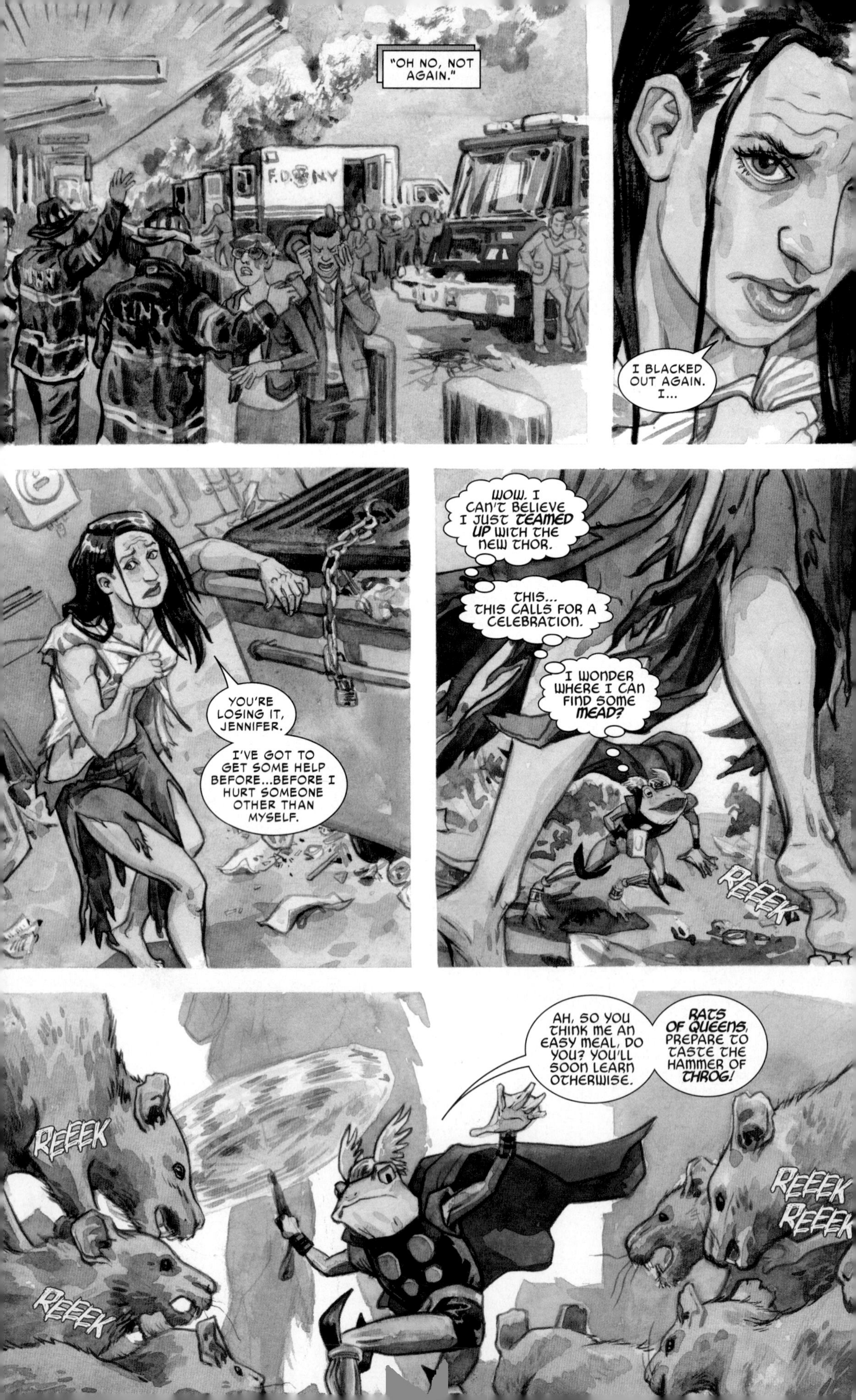
"OH NO, NOT AGAIN."
F.D.NY
I BLACKED OUT AGAIN. I...
YOU'RE LOSING IT, JENNIFER.
I'VE GOT TO GET SOME HELP BEFORE...BEFORE I HURT SOMEONE OTHER THAN MYSELF.
WOW. I CAN'T BELIEVE I JUST TEAMED UP WITH THE NEW THOR.
THIS... THIS CALLS FOR A CELEBRATION.
I WONDER WHERE I CAN FIND SOME MEAD?
REEEK
AH, SO YOU THINK ME AN EASY MEAL, DO YOU? YOU'LL SOON LEARN OTHERWISE.
RATS OF QUEENS, PREPARE TO TASTE THE HAMMER OF THROG!
REEEK
REEEK
REEEK
REEEK

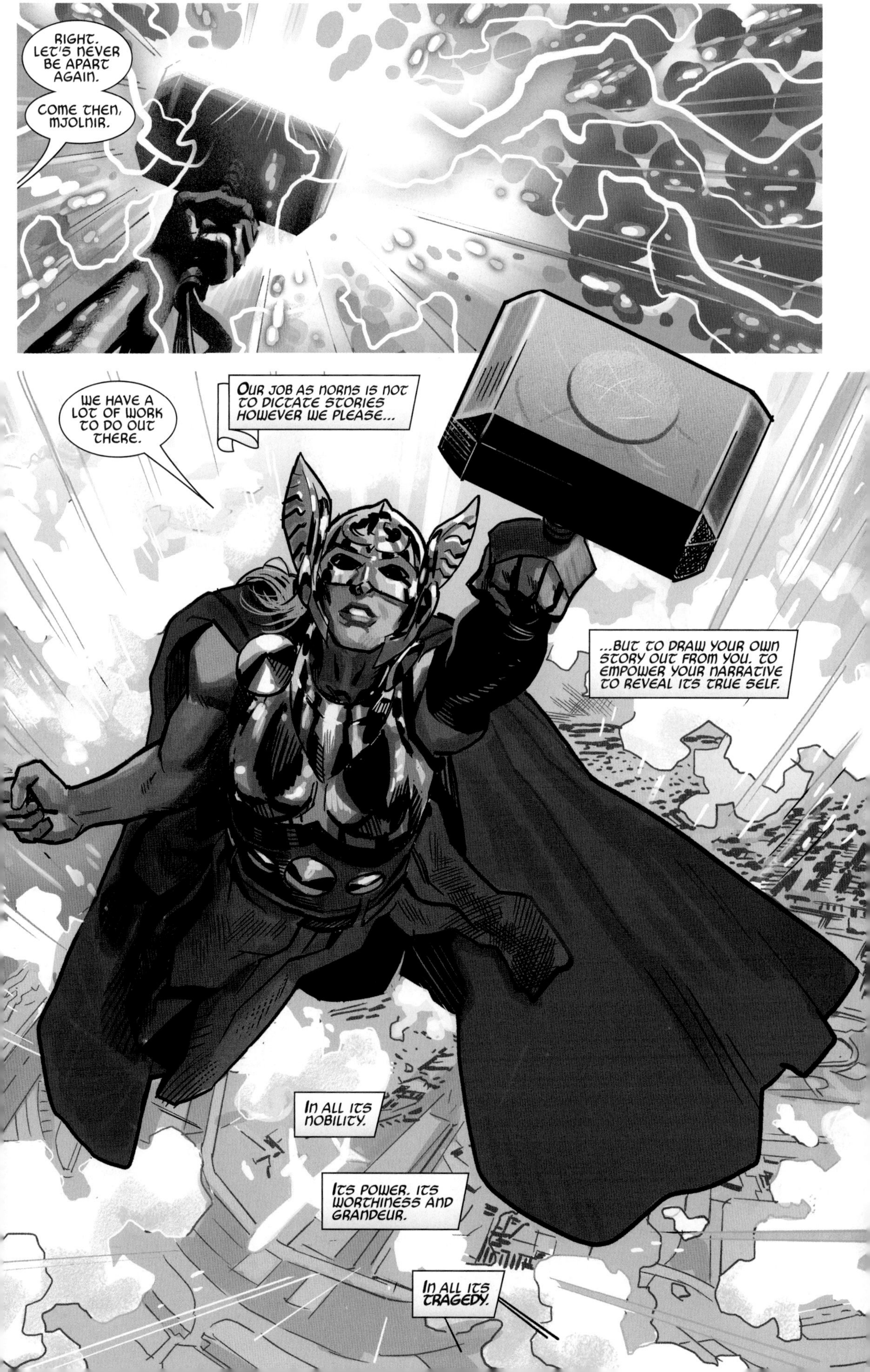
RIGHT. LET'S NEVER BE APART AGAIN.
COME THEN, MJOLNIR.
WE HAVE A LOT OF WORK TO DO OUT THERE.
OUR JOB AS NORNS IS NOT TO DICTATE STORIES HOWEVER WE PLEASE...
...BUT TO DRAW YOUR OWN STORY OUT FROM YOU. TO EMPOWER YOUR NARRATIVE TO REVEAL ITS TRUE SELF.
IN ALL ITS NOBILITY.
ITS POWER. ITS WORTHINESS AND GRANDEUR.
IN ALL ITS TRAGEDY.

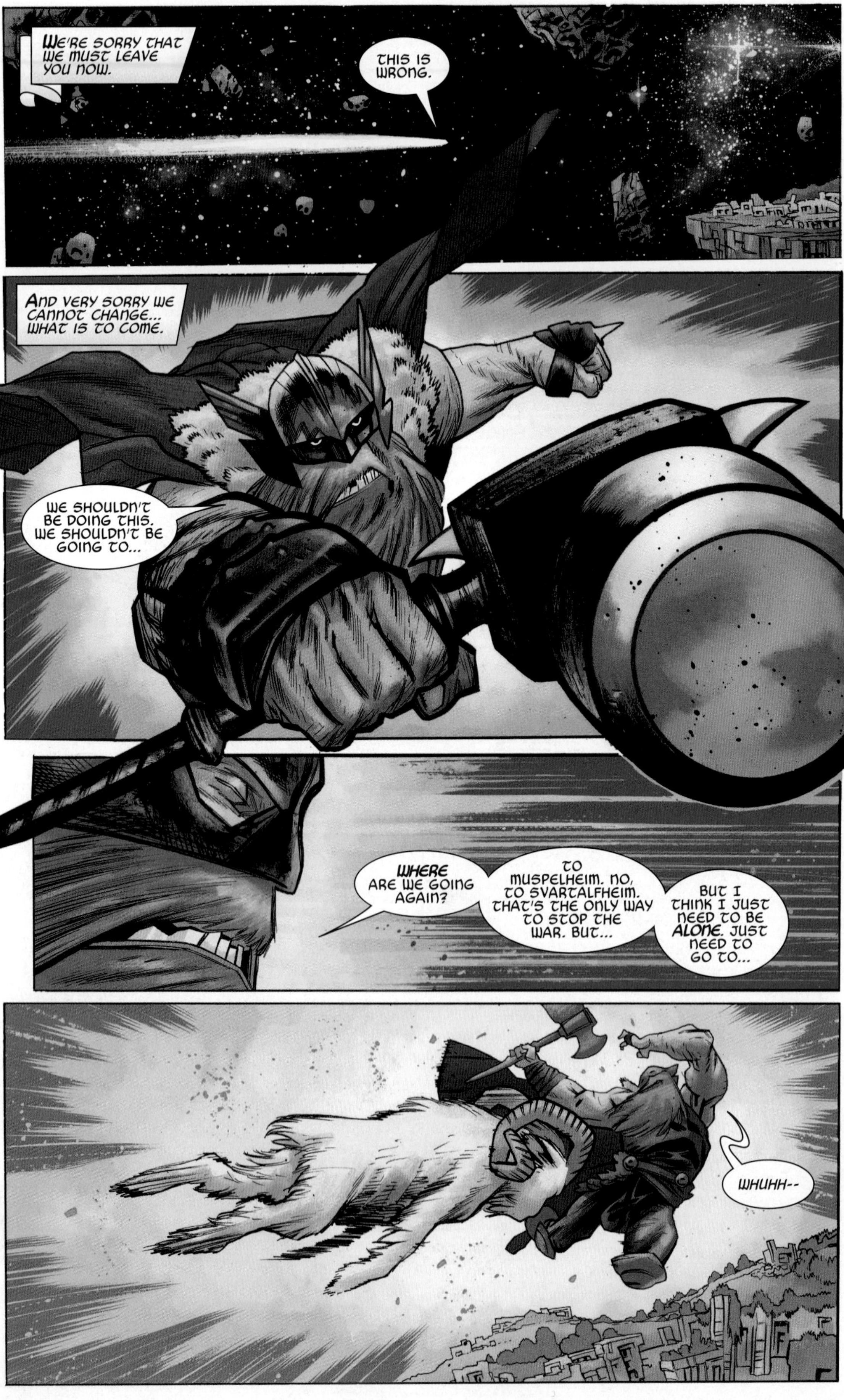
WE'RE SORRY THAT WE MUST LEAVE YOU NOW.
THIS IS WRONG.
AND VERY SORRY WE CANNOT CHANGE... WHAT IS TO COME.
WE SHOULDN'T BE DOING THIS. WE SHOULDN'T BE GOING TO...
WHERE ARE WE GOING AGAIN?
TO MUSPELHEIM. NO, TO SVARTALFHEIM. THAT'S THE ONLY WAY TO STOP THE WAR. BUT...
BUT I THINK I JUST NEED TO BE ALONE. JUST NEED TO GO TO...
WHUHH--

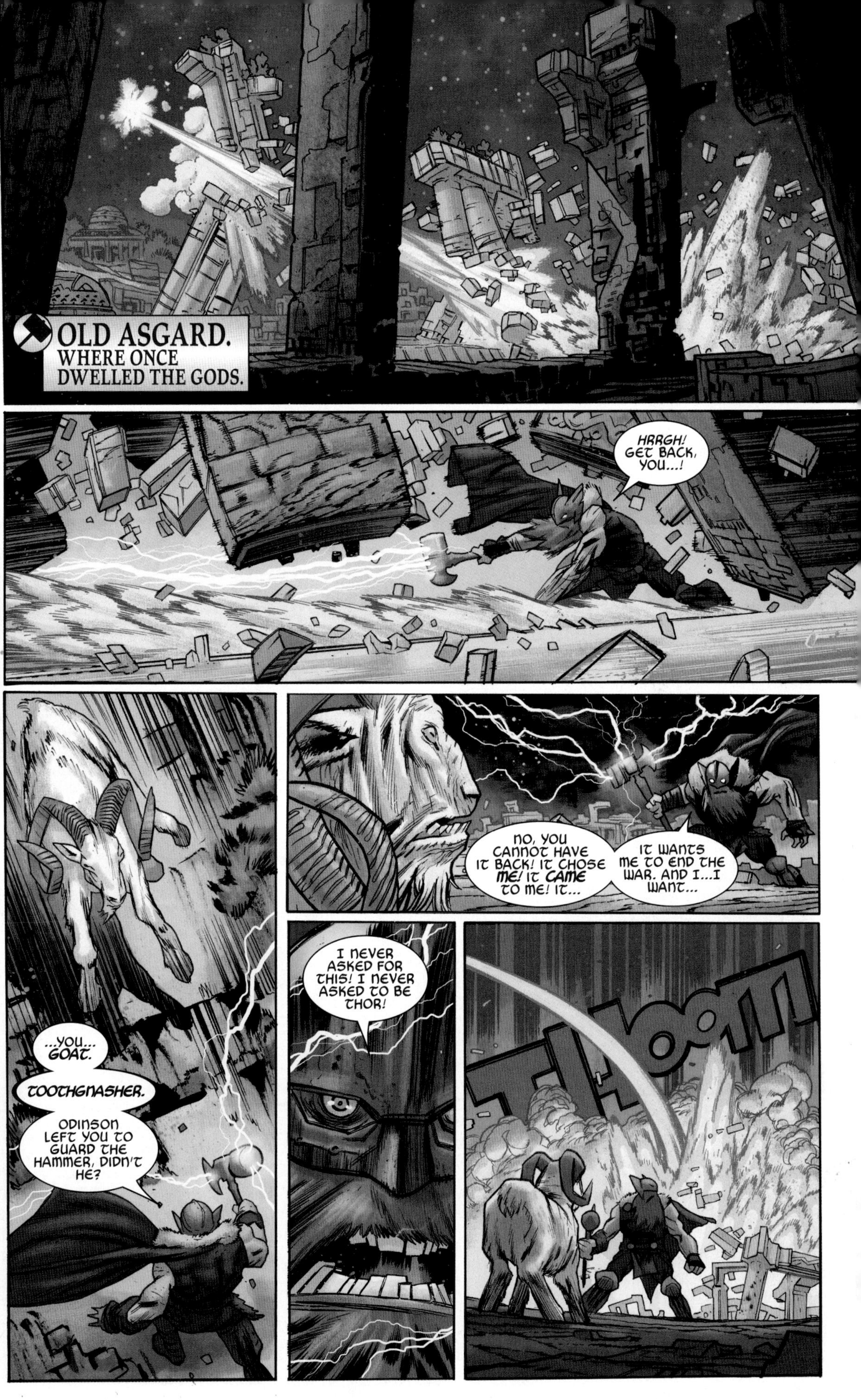

OLD ASGARD. WHERE ONCE DWELLED THE GODS.
HRRGH! GET BACK, YOU...!
NO, YOU CANNOT HAVE IT BACK! IT CHOSE ME! IT CAME TO ME! IT...
IT WANTS ME TO END THE WAR. AND I...I WANT...
...YOU... GOAT.
TOOTHGNASHER.
ODINSON LEFT YOU TO GUARD THE HAMMER, DIDN'T HE?
I NEVER ASKED FOR THIS! I NEVER ASKED TO BE THOR!
THOOM!

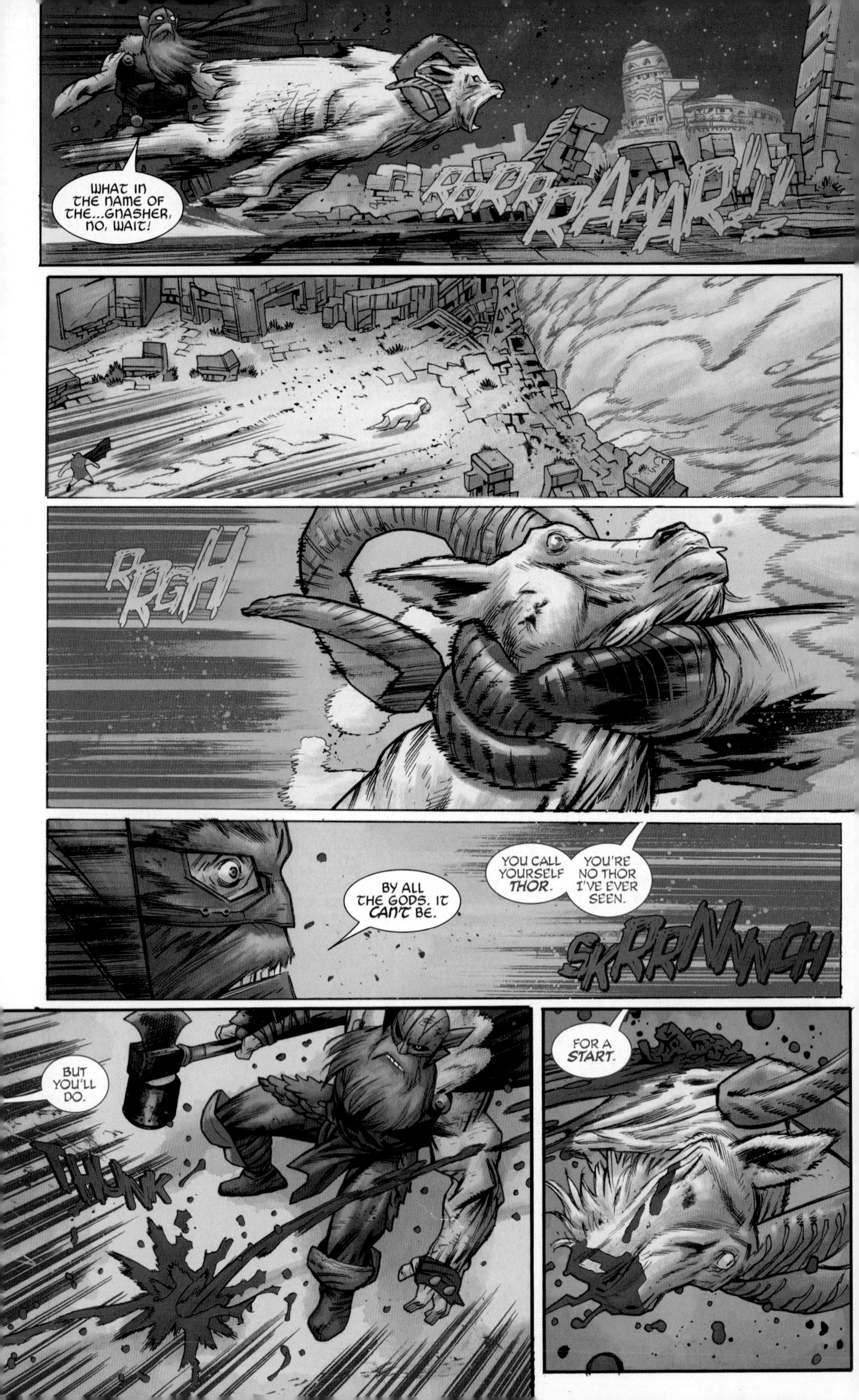
WHAT IN THE NAME OF THE...GNASHER, NO, WAIT!
RRRRRRAAAR!!!
RRGH
BY ALL THE GODS. IT CAN'T BE.
YOU CALL YOURSELF THOR.
YOU'RE NO THOR I'VE EVER SEEN.
SKRRNNNCH
BUT YOU'LL DO.
THUNK
FOR A START.

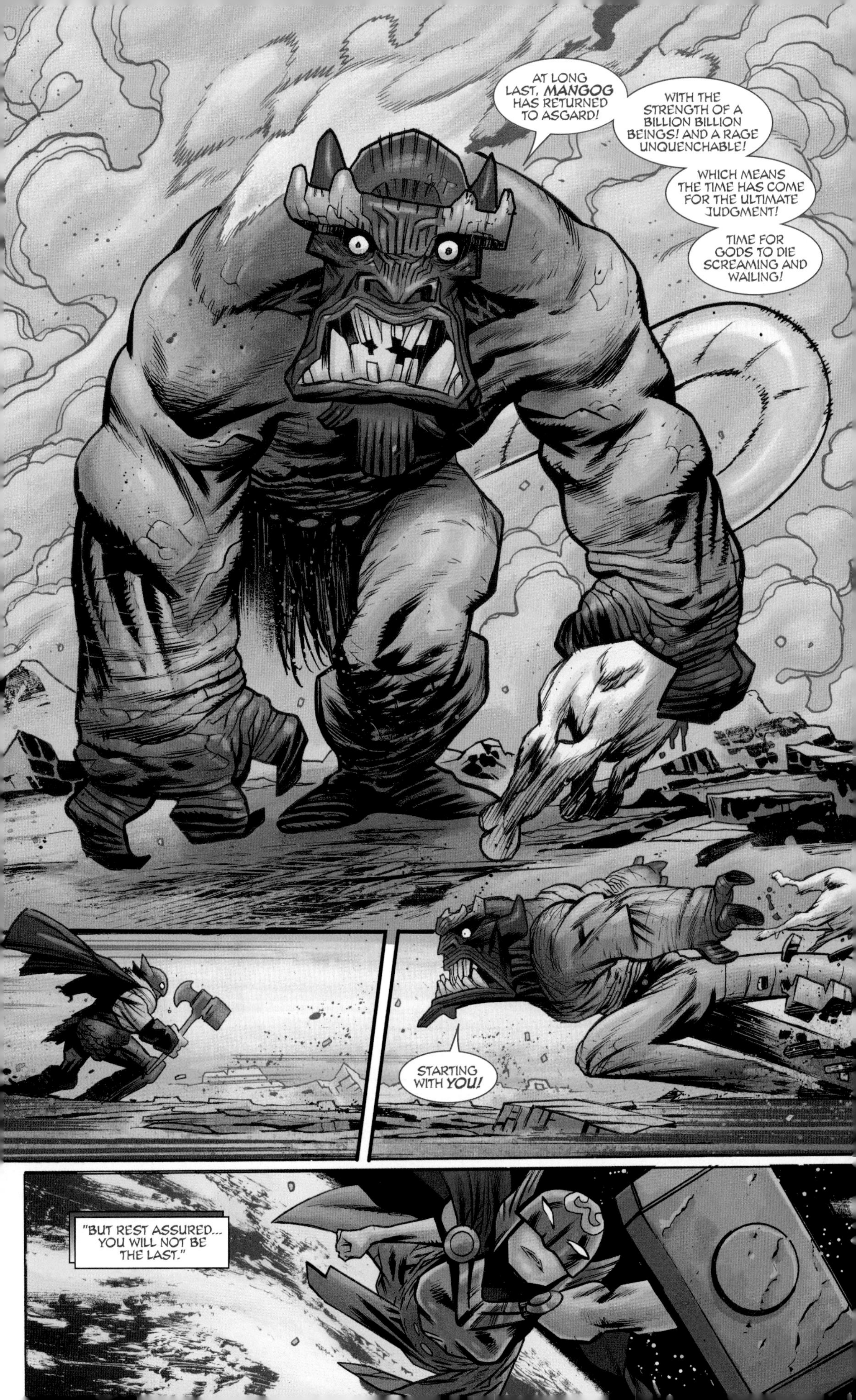
AT LONG LAST, MANGOG HAS RETURNED TO ASGARD!
WITH THE STRENGTH OF A BILLION BILLION BEINGS! AND A RAGE UNQUENCHABLE!
WHICH MEANS THE TIME HAS COME FOR THE ULTIMATE JUDGMENT!
TIME FOR GODS TO DIE SCREAMING AND WAILING!
STARTING WITH YOU!
"BUT REST ASSURED... YOU WILL NOT BE THE LAST."

# 701

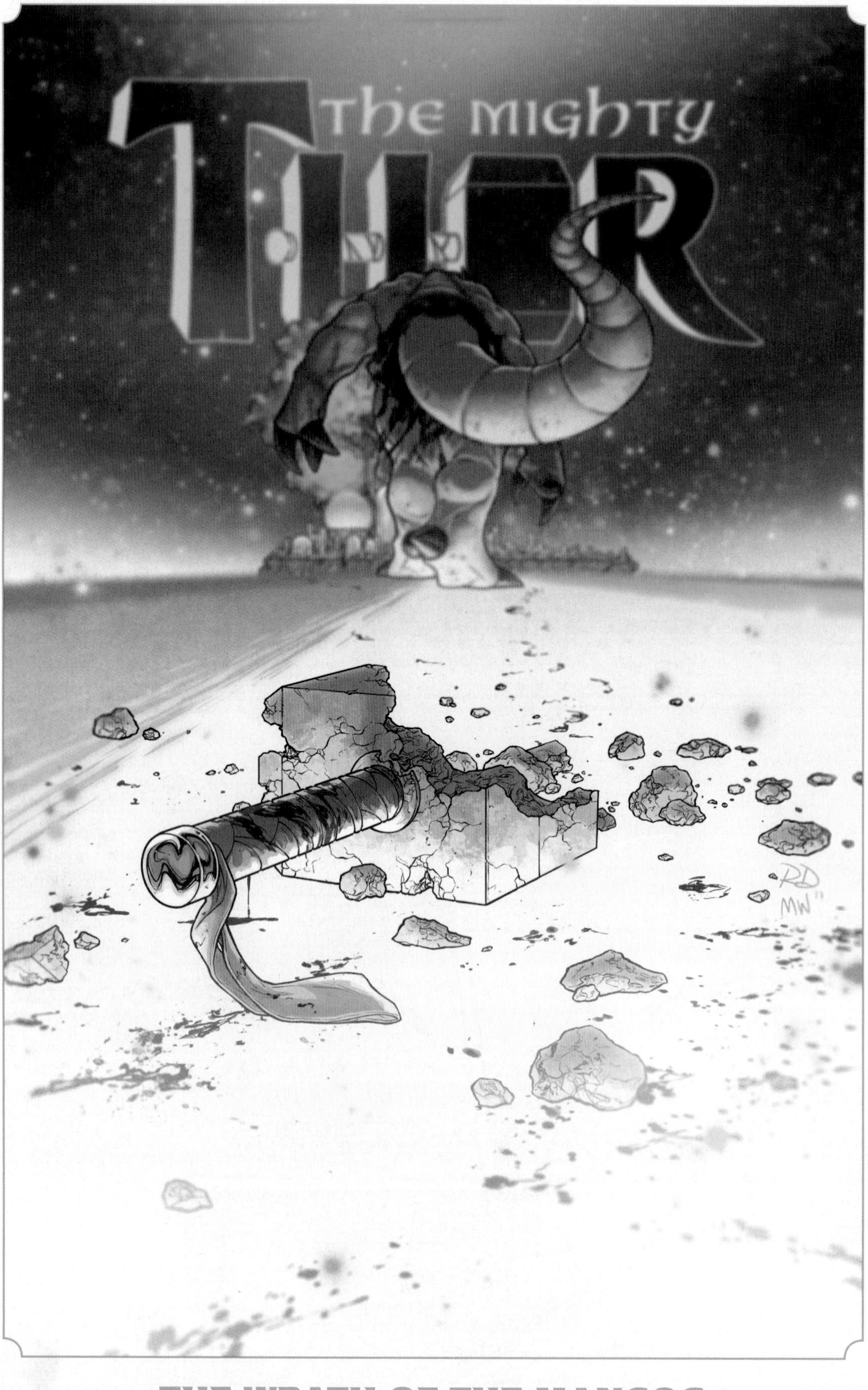
THE MIGHTY
THOR
RD
MW

## THE WRATH OF THE MANGOG

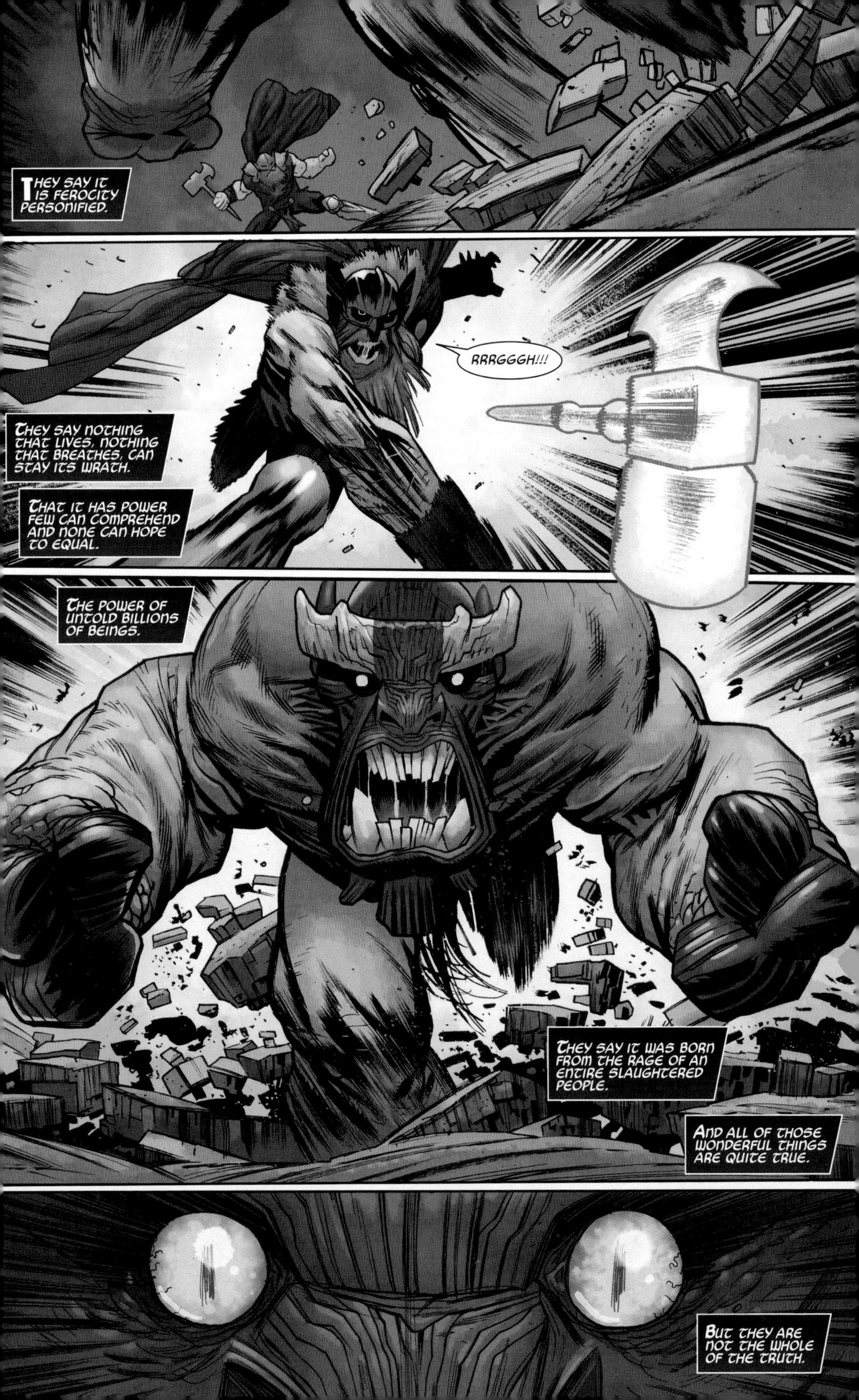
THEY SAY IT IS FEROCITY PERSONIFIED.
THEY SAY NOTHING THAT LIVES, NOTHING THAT BREATHES, CAN STAY ITS WRATH.
THAT IT HAS POWER FEW CAN COMPREHEND AND NONE CAN HOPE TO EQUAL.
RRRGGGH!!!
THE POWER OF UNTOLD BILLIONS OF BEINGS.
THEY SAY IT WAS BORN FROM THE RAGE OF AN ENTIRE SLAUGHTERED PEOPLE.
AND ALL OF THOSE WONDERFUL THINGS ARE QUITE TRUE.
BUT THEY ARE NOT THE WHOLE OF THE TRUTH.

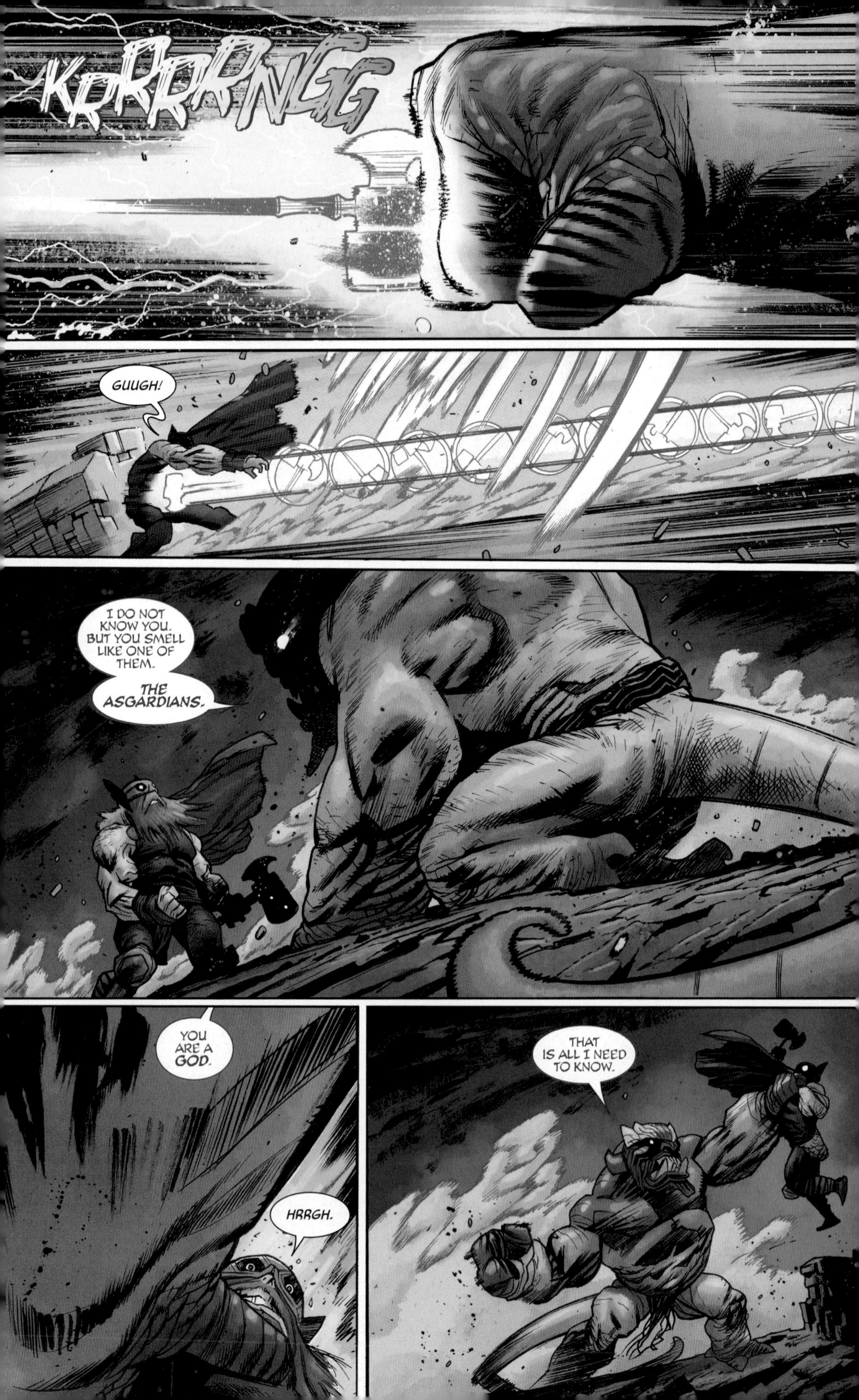

KRRRRNGG
GUUGH!
I DO NOT KNOW YOU. BUT YOU SMELL LIKE ONE OF THEM.
THE ASGARDIANS.
YOU ARE A GOD.
HRRGH.
THAT IS ALL I NEED TO KNOW.

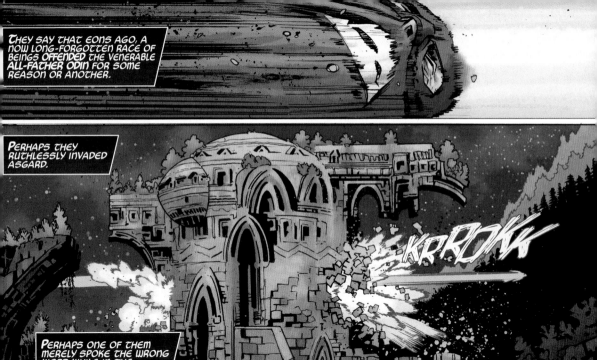

THEY SAY THAT EONS AGO, A NOW LONG-FORGOTTEN RACE OF BEINGS OFFENDED THE VENERABLE ALL-FATHER ODIN FOR SOME REASON OR ANOTHER.

PERHAPS THEY RUTHLESSLY INVADED ASGARD.

KRROKK

PERHAPS ONE OF THEM MERELY SPOKE THE WRONG WORD WHILE IN THE ALL-FATHER'S PRESENCE.

EITHER WAY, WE'LL NEVER KNOW FOR CERTAIN...

...SINCE ODIN'S RESPONSE WAS TO SLAUGHTER THEM ALL.

AN ENTIRE RACE WIPED OUT BY ONE IRATE DEITY.

BILLIONS OF BEINGS.

I AM NOT JUST... A GOD.

BUT SO GREAT WAS THEIR COLLECTIVE RAGE, THEIR UNBRIDLED HATRED, THAT IT DID NOT DISSIPATE WHEN THEY DIED.

I AM THE WAR THOR.

IT BECAME... SOMETHING ELSE.

THE GOD OF THE BLOODSTORM!

HAVE AT THEE, YOU BASTARD!

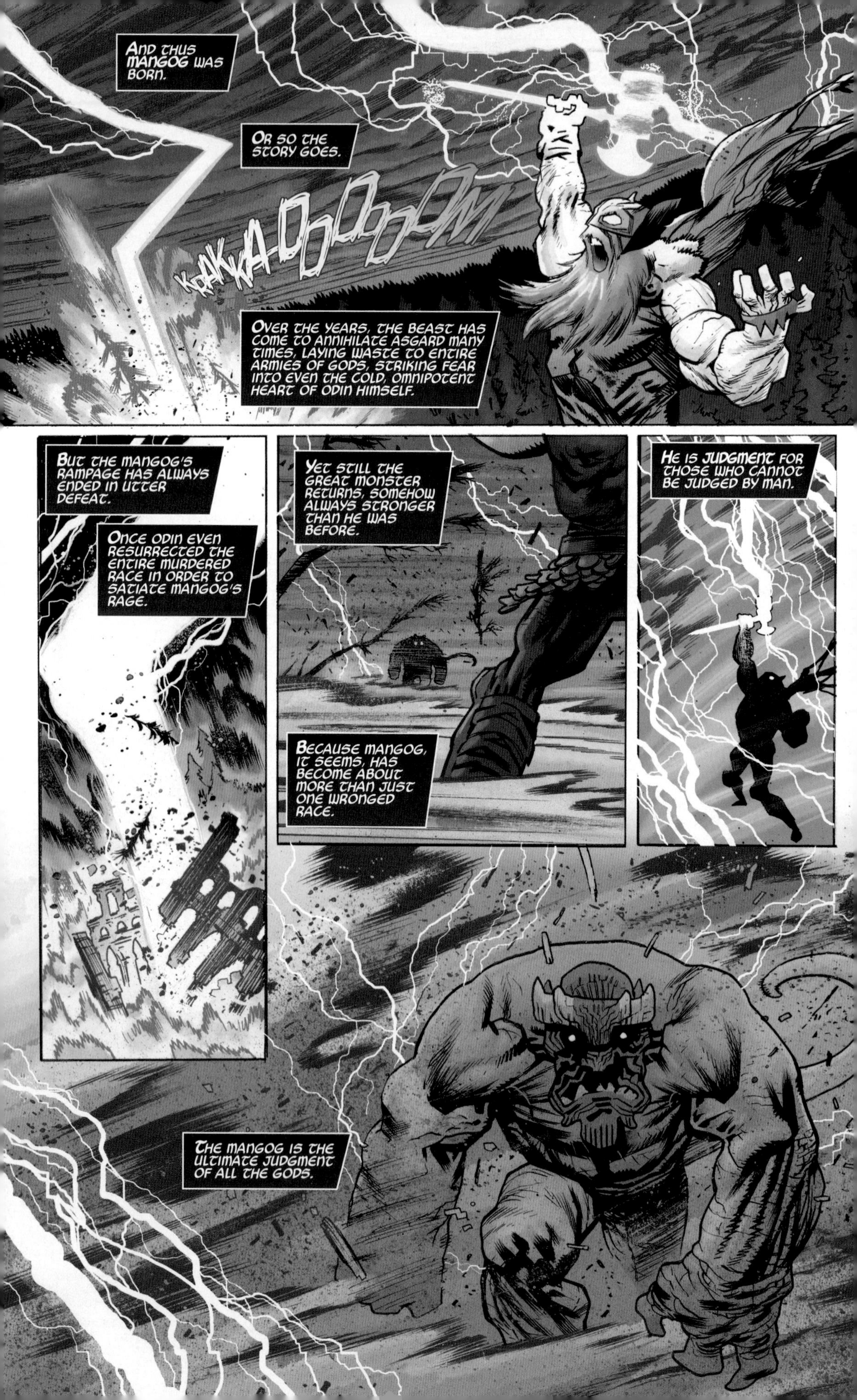

And thus Mangog was born.
Or so the story goes.
KRAKKA-DOOOOOOM
Over the years, the beast has come to annihilate Asgard many times, laying waste to entire armies of gods, striking fear into even the cold, omnipotent heart of Odin himself.
But the Mangog's rampage has always ended in utter defeat.
Once Odin even resurrected the entire murdered race in order to satiate Mangog's rage.
Yet still the great monster returns, somehow always stronger than he was before.
Because Mangog, it seems, has become about more than just one wronged race.
He is judgment for those who cannot be judged by man.
The Mangog is the ultimate judgment of all the gods.

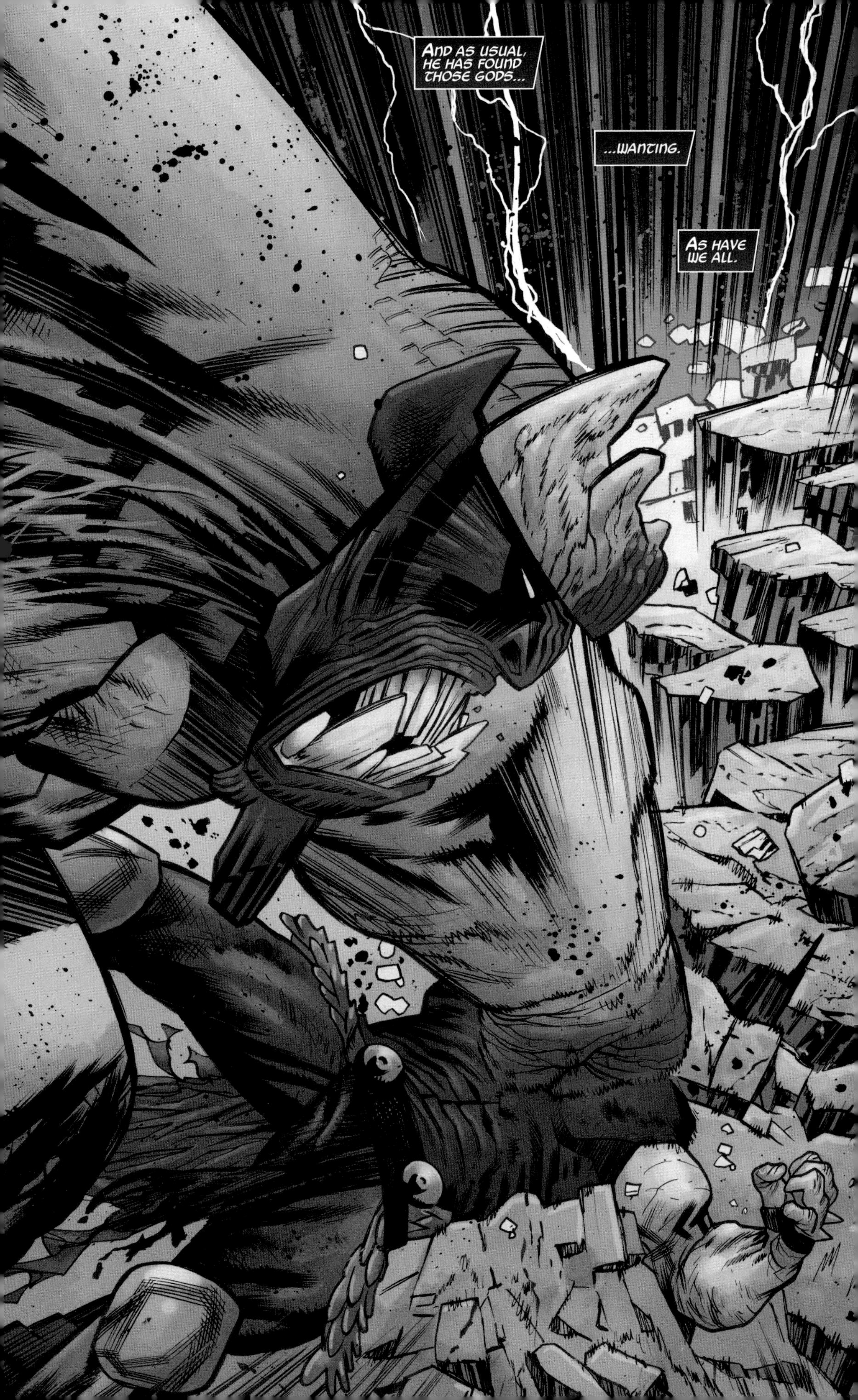
AND AS USUAL, HE HAS FOUND THOSE GODS...
...WANTING.
AS HAVE WE ALL.

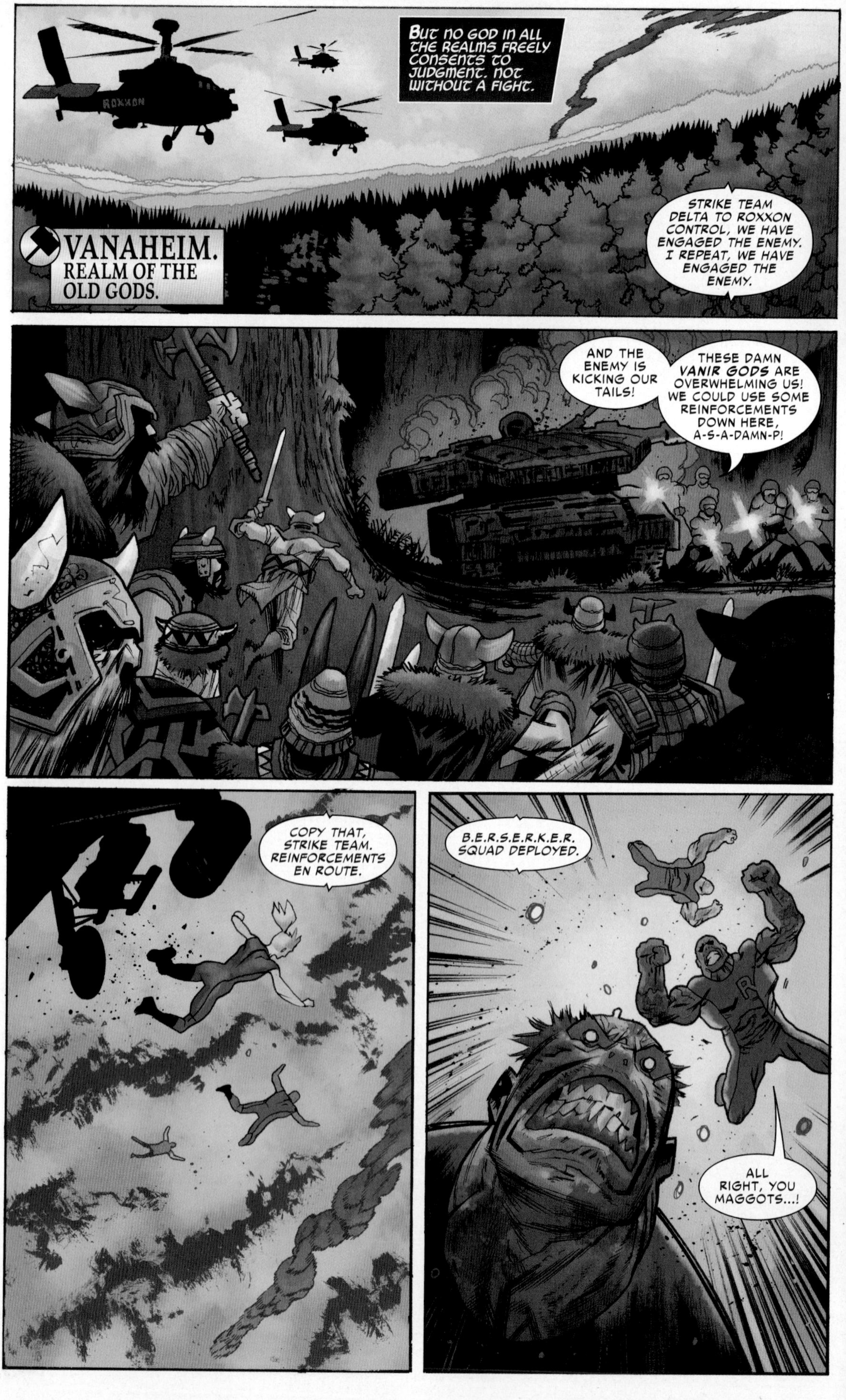
But no god in all the realms freely consents to judgment. Not without a fight.
ROXXON
VANAHEIM. REALM OF THE OLD GODS.
STRIKE TEAM DELTA TO ROXXON CONTROL, WE HAVE ENGAGED THE ENEMY. I REPEAT, WE HAVE ENGAGED THE ENEMY.
AND THE ENEMY IS KICKING OUR TAILS!
THESE DAMN VANIR GODS ARE OVERWHELMING US! WE COULD USE SOME REINFORCEMENTS DOWN HERE, A-S-A-DAMN-P!
COPY THAT, STRIKE TEAM. REINFORCEMENTS EN ROUTE.
B.E.R.S.E.R.K.E.R. SQUAD DEPLOYED.
ALL RIGHT, YOU MAGGOTS...!

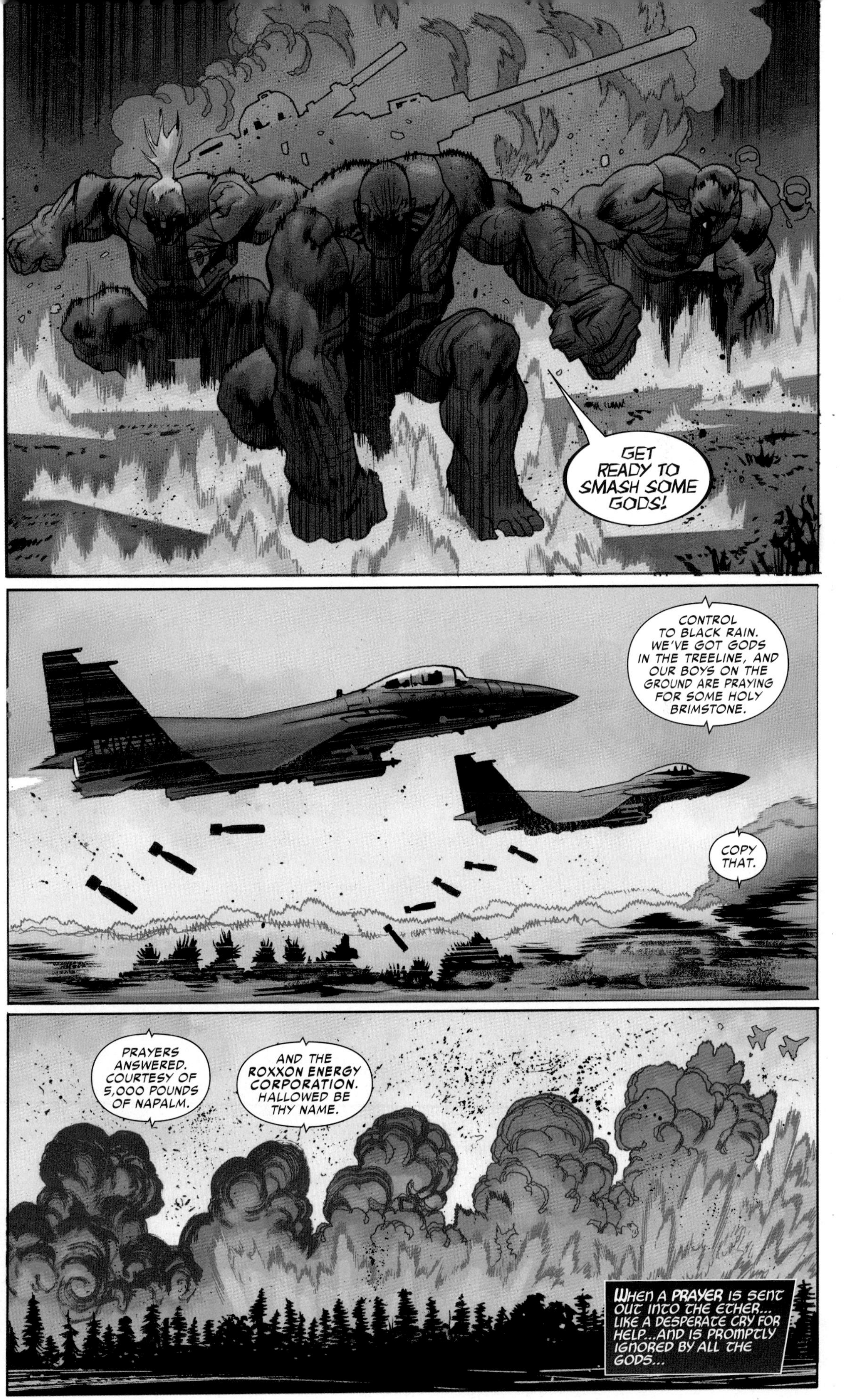
GET READY TO SMASH SOME GODS!
CONTROL TO BLACK RAIN. WE'VE GOT GODS IN THE TREELINE, AND OUR BOYS ON THE GROUND ARE PRAYING FOR SOME HOLY BRIMSTONE.
COPY THAT.
PRAYERS ANSWERED. COURTESY OF 5,000 POUNDS OF NAPALM.
AND THE ROXXON ENERGY CORPORATION. HALLOWED BE THY NAME.
WHEN A PRAYER IS SENT OUT INTO THE ETHER... LIKE A DESPERATE CRY FOR HELP...AND IS PROMPTLY IGNORED BY ALL THE GODS...

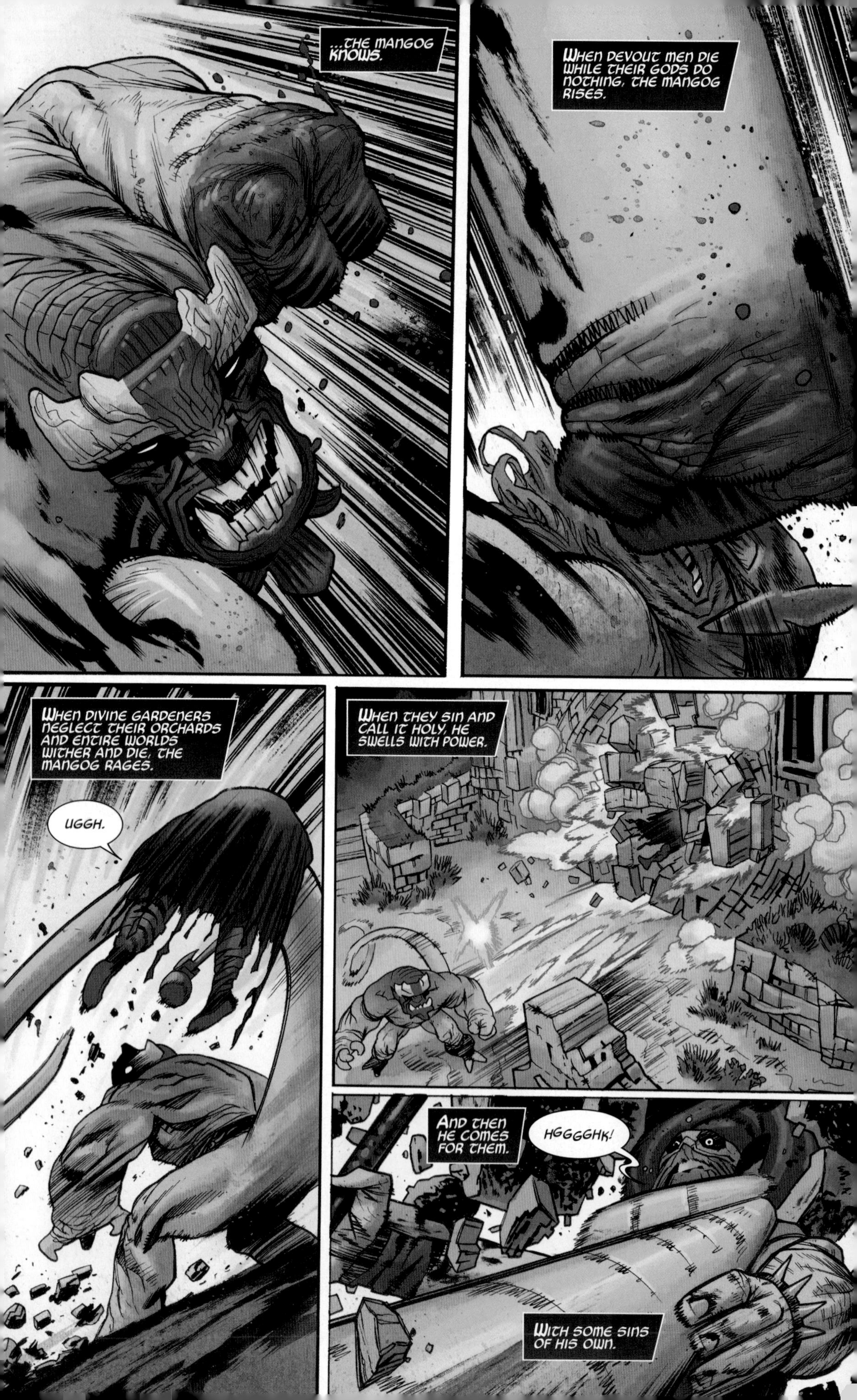
...THE MANGOG KNOWS.
WHEN DEVOUT MEN DIE WHILE THEIR GODS DO NOTHING, THE MANGOG RISES.
WHEN DIVINE GARDENERS NEGLECT THEIR ORCHARDS AND ENTIRE WORLDS WITHER AND DIE, THE MANGOG RAGES.
UGGH.
WHEN THEY SIN AND CALL IT HOLY, HE SWELLS WITH POWER.
AND THEN HE COMES FOR THEM.
HGGGGHK!
WITH SOME SINS OF HIS OWN.

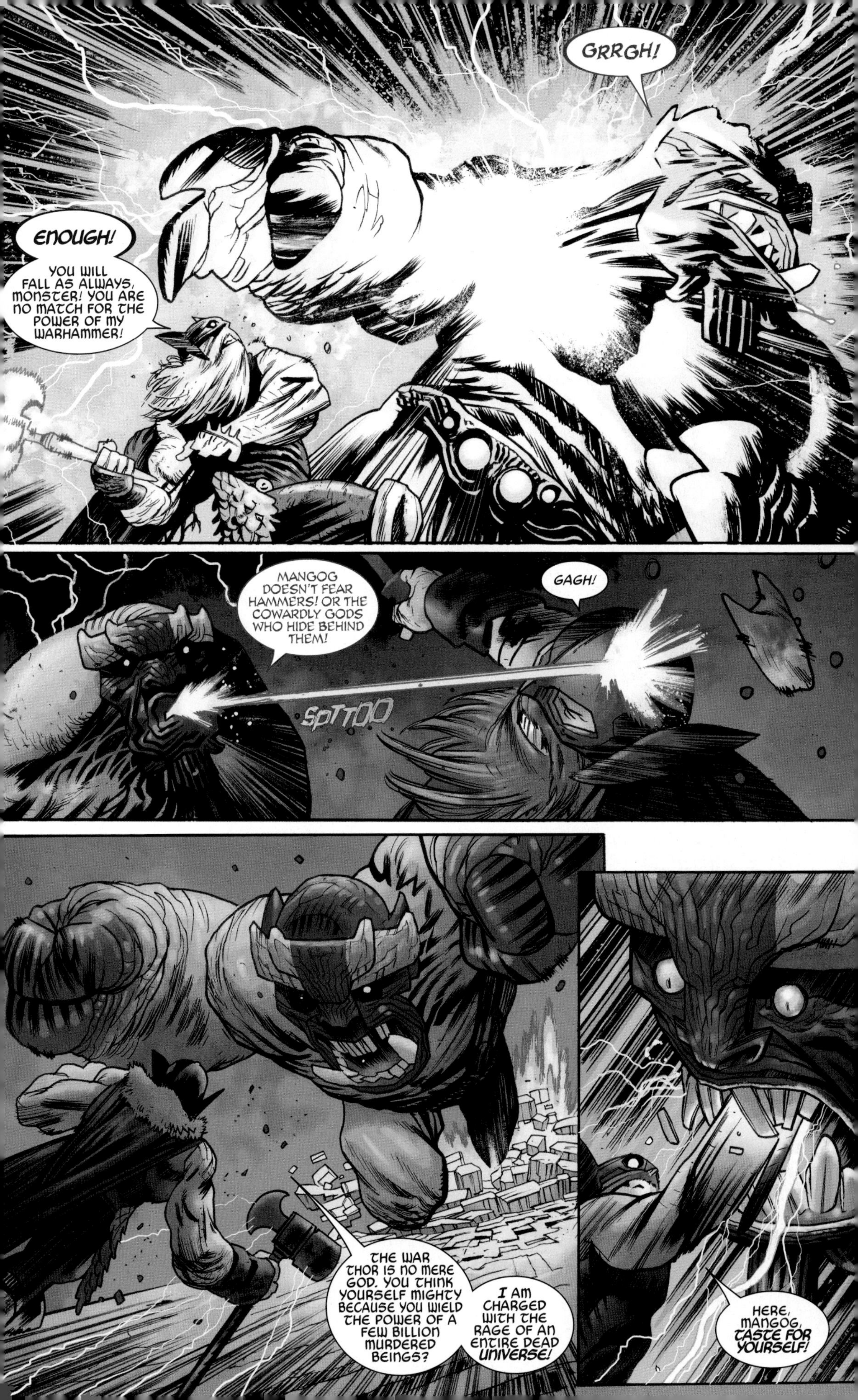
GRRGH!
ENOUGH!
YOU WILL FALL AS ALWAYS, MONSTER! YOU ARE NO MATCH FOR THE POWER OF MY WARHAMMER!
MANGOG DOESN'T FEAR HAMMERS! OR THE COWARDLY GODS WHO HIDE BEHIND THEM!
GAGH!
SPTTOO
THE WAR THOR IS NO MERE GOD. YOU THINK YOURSELF MIGHTY BECAUSE YOU WIELD THE POWER OF A FEW BILLION MURDERED BEINGS?
I AM CHARGED WITH THE RAGE OF AN ENTIRE DEAD UNIVERSE!
HERE, MANGOG, TASTE FOR YOURSELF!

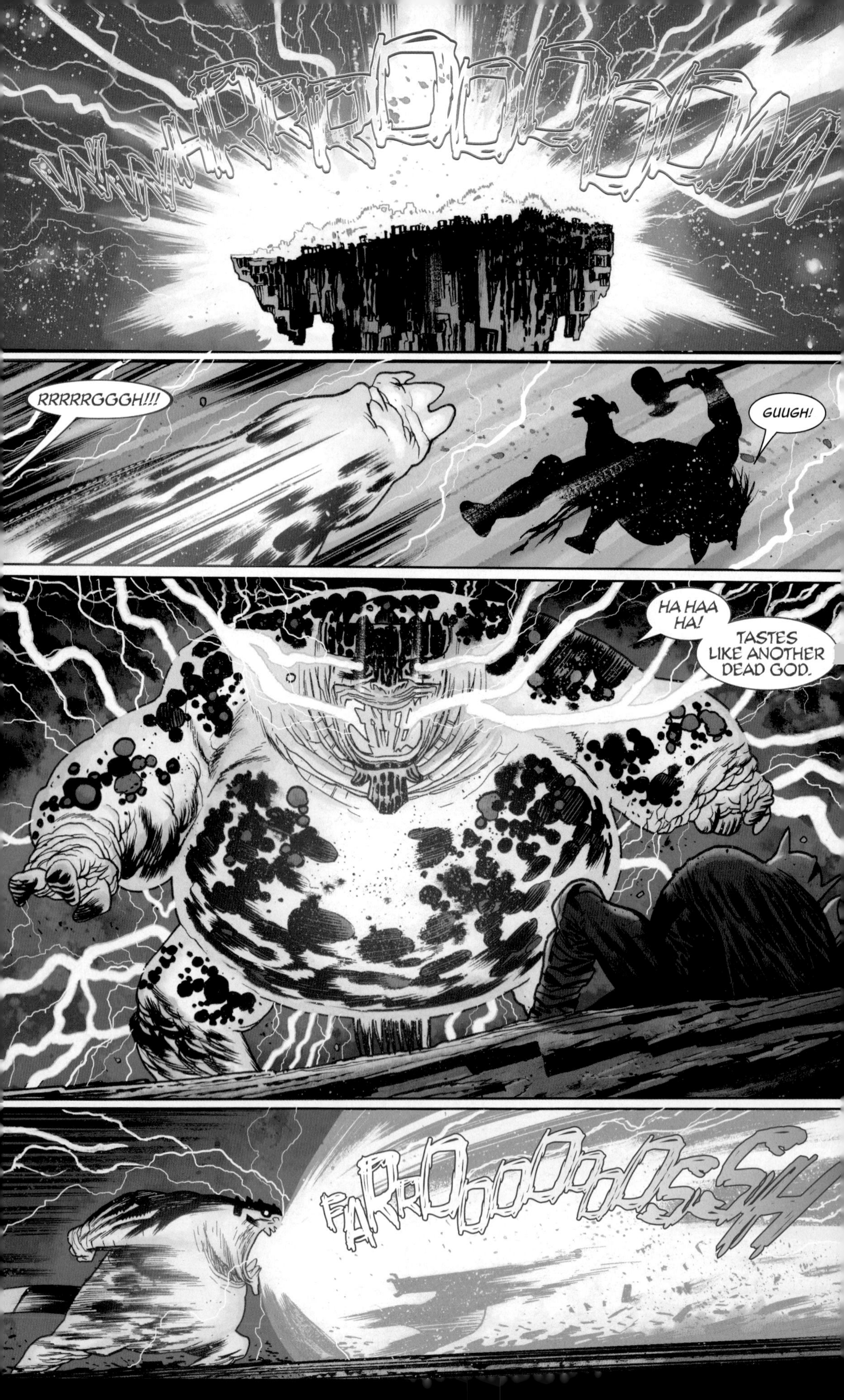
WHHHRRROOOOOOOOM
RRRRRGGGH!!!
GUUGH!
HA HAA HA!
TASTES LIKE ANOTHER DEAD GOD.
FARRROOOOOOOOSSSH

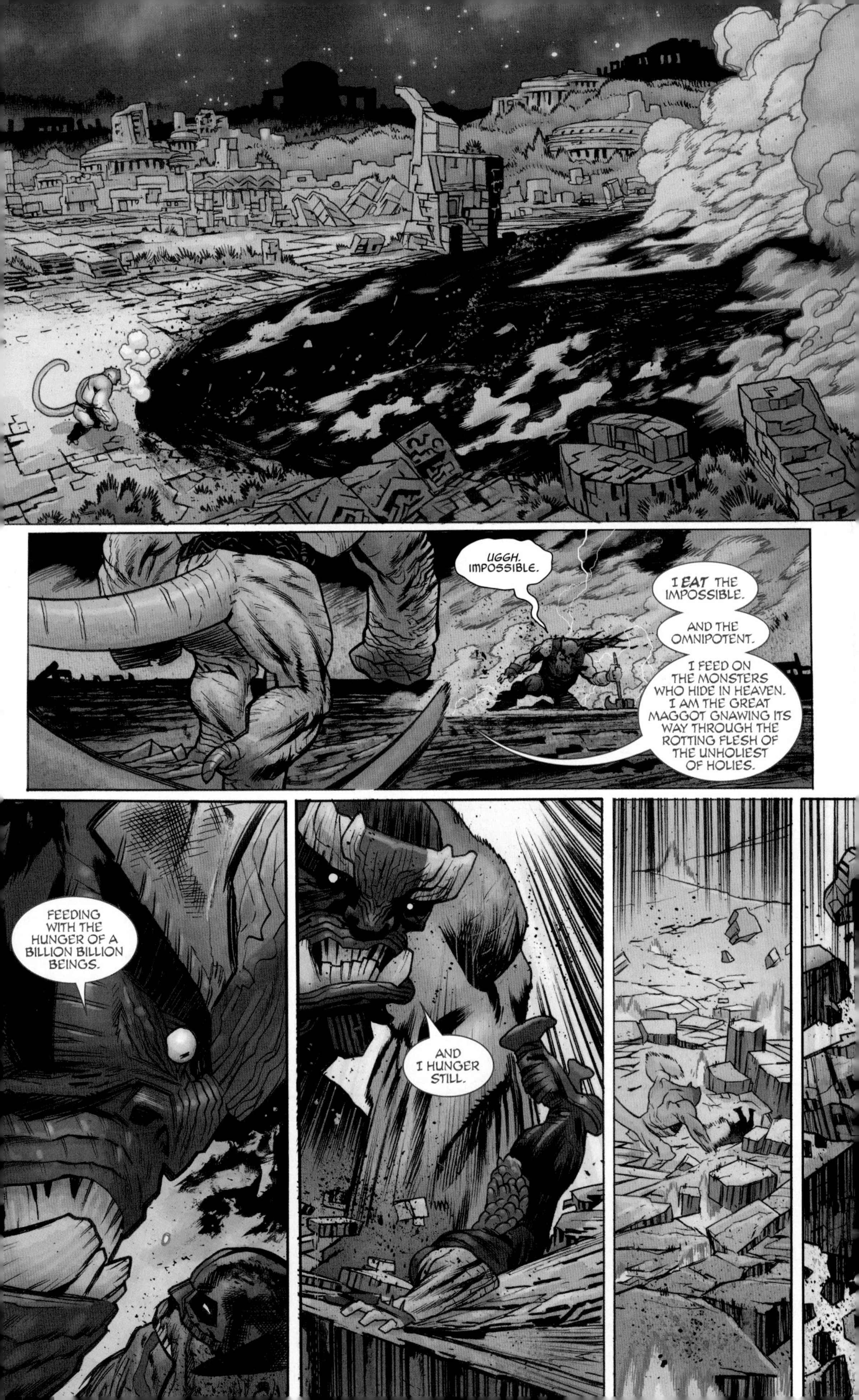
UGGH. IMPOSSIBLE.
I EAT THE IMPOSSIBLE.
AND THE OMNIPOTENT.
I FEED ON THE MONSTERS WHO HIDE IN HEAVEN. I AM THE GREAT MAGGOT GNAWING ITS WAY THROUGH THE ROTTING FLESH OF THE UNHOLIEST OF HOLIES.
FEEDING WITH THE HUNGER OF A BILLION BILLION BEINGS.
AND I HUNGER STILL.

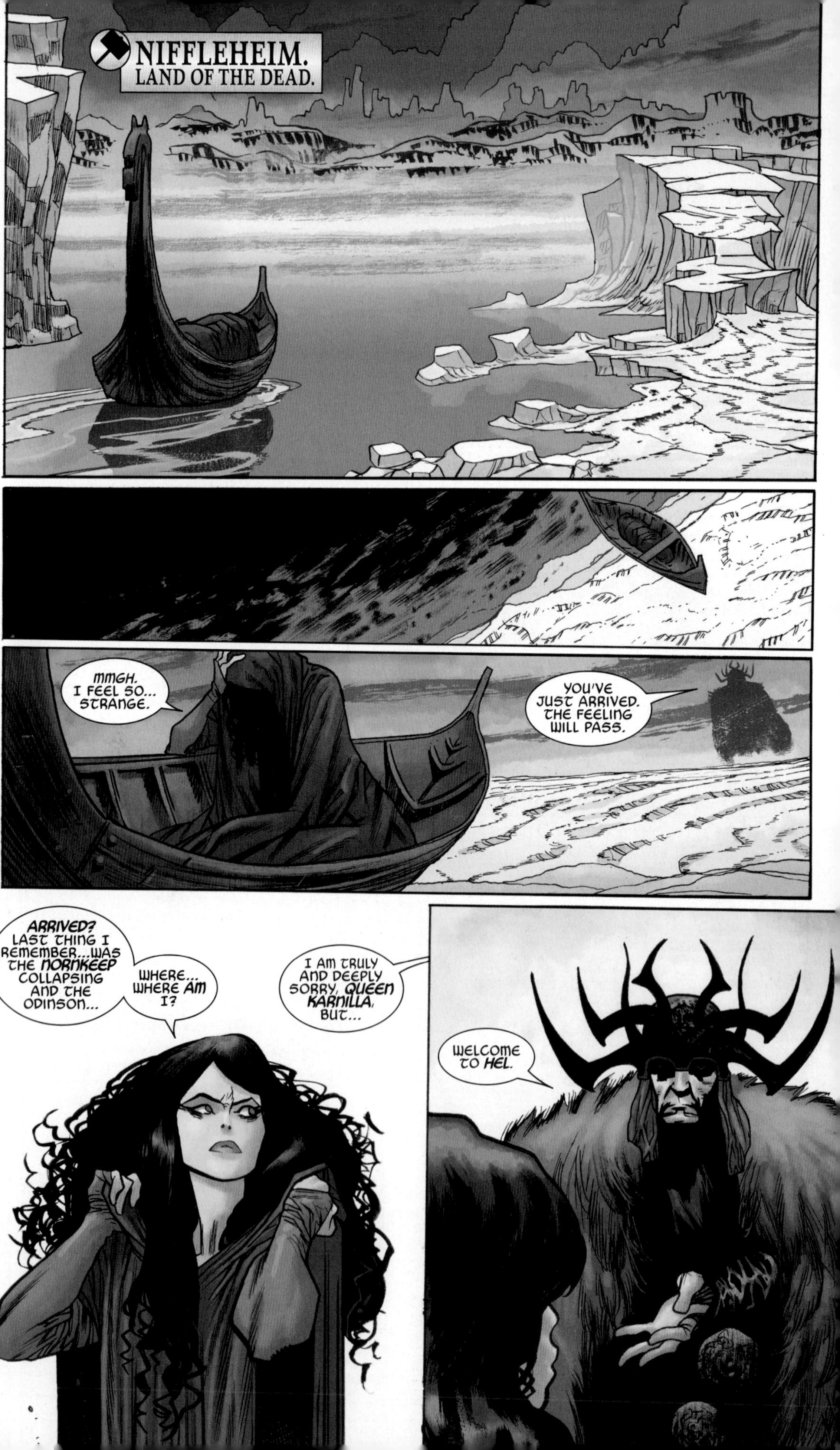
NIFFLEHEIM.
LAND OF THE DEAD.
MMGH. I FEEL SO... STRANGE.
YOU'VE JUST ARRIVED. THE FEELING WILL PASS.
ARRIVED? LAST THING I REMEMBER...WAS THE NORNKEEP COLLAPSING AND THE ODINSON...
WHERE... WHERE AM I?
I AM TRULY AND DEEPLY SORRY, QUEEN KARNILLA, BUT...
WELCOME TO HEL.

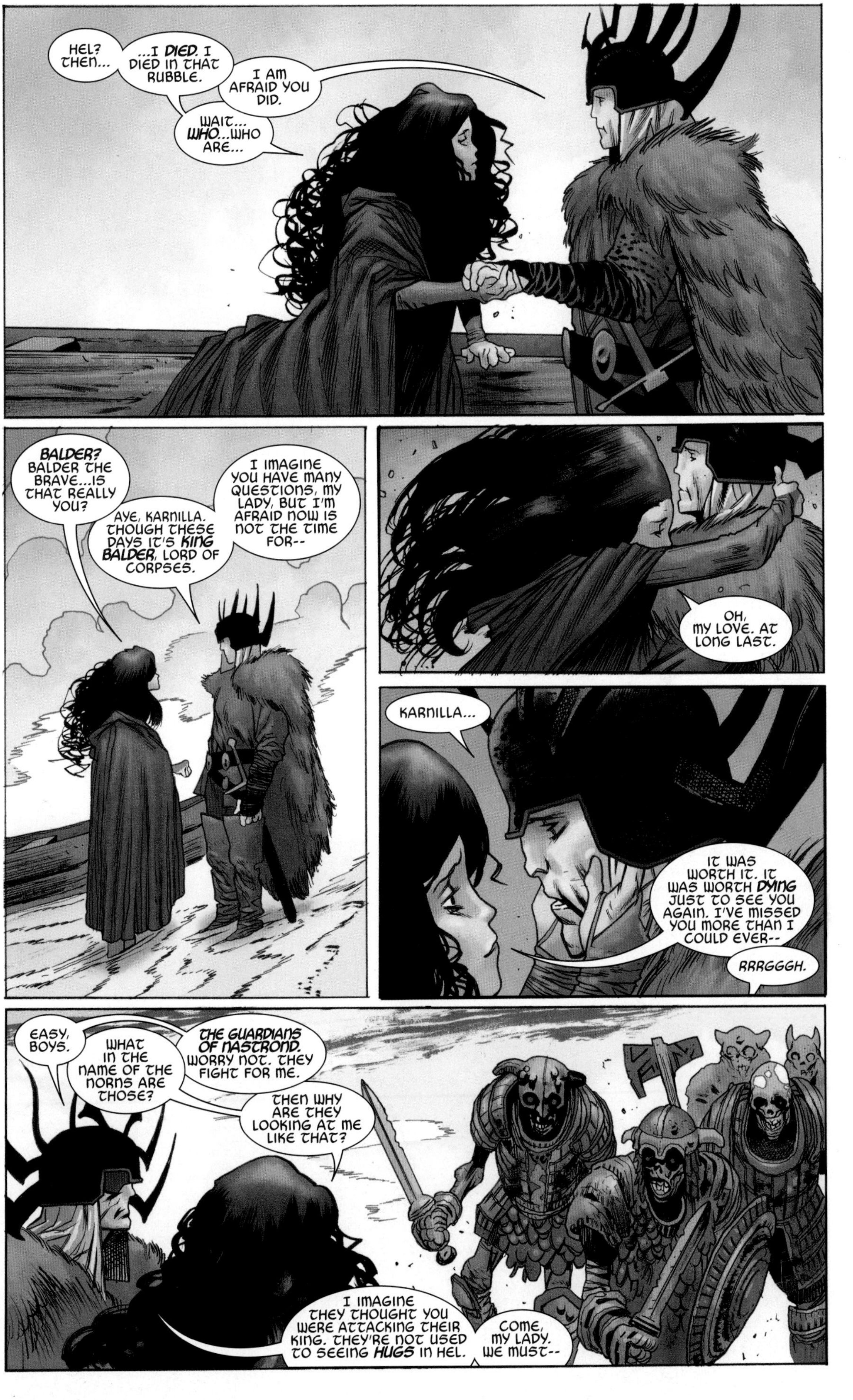
HEL? THEN...
...I DIED. I DIED IN THAT RUBBLE.
I AM AFRAID YOU DID.
WAIT... WHO...WHO ARE...
BALDER? BALDER THE BRAVE...IS THAT REALLY YOU?
AYE, KARNILLA. THOUGH THESE DAYS IT'S KING BALDER, LORD OF CORPSES.
I IMAGINE YOU HAVE MANY QUESTIONS, MY LADY, BUT I'M AFRAID NOW IS NOT THE TIME FOR--
OH, MY LOVE. AT LONG LAST.
KARNILLA...
IT WAS WORTH IT. IT WAS WORTH DYING JUST TO SEE YOU AGAIN. I'VE MISSED YOU MORE THAN I COULD EVER--
RRRGGGH.
EASY, BOYS.
WHAT IN THE NAME OF THE NORNS ARE THOSE?
THE GUARDIANS OF NASTROND. WORRY NOT. THEY FIGHT FOR ME.
THEN WHY ARE THEY LOOKING AT ME LIKE THAT?
I IMAGINE THEY THOUGHT YOU WERE ATTACKING THEIR KING. THEY'RE NOT USED TO SEEING HUGS IN HEL.
COME, MY LADY. WE MUST--

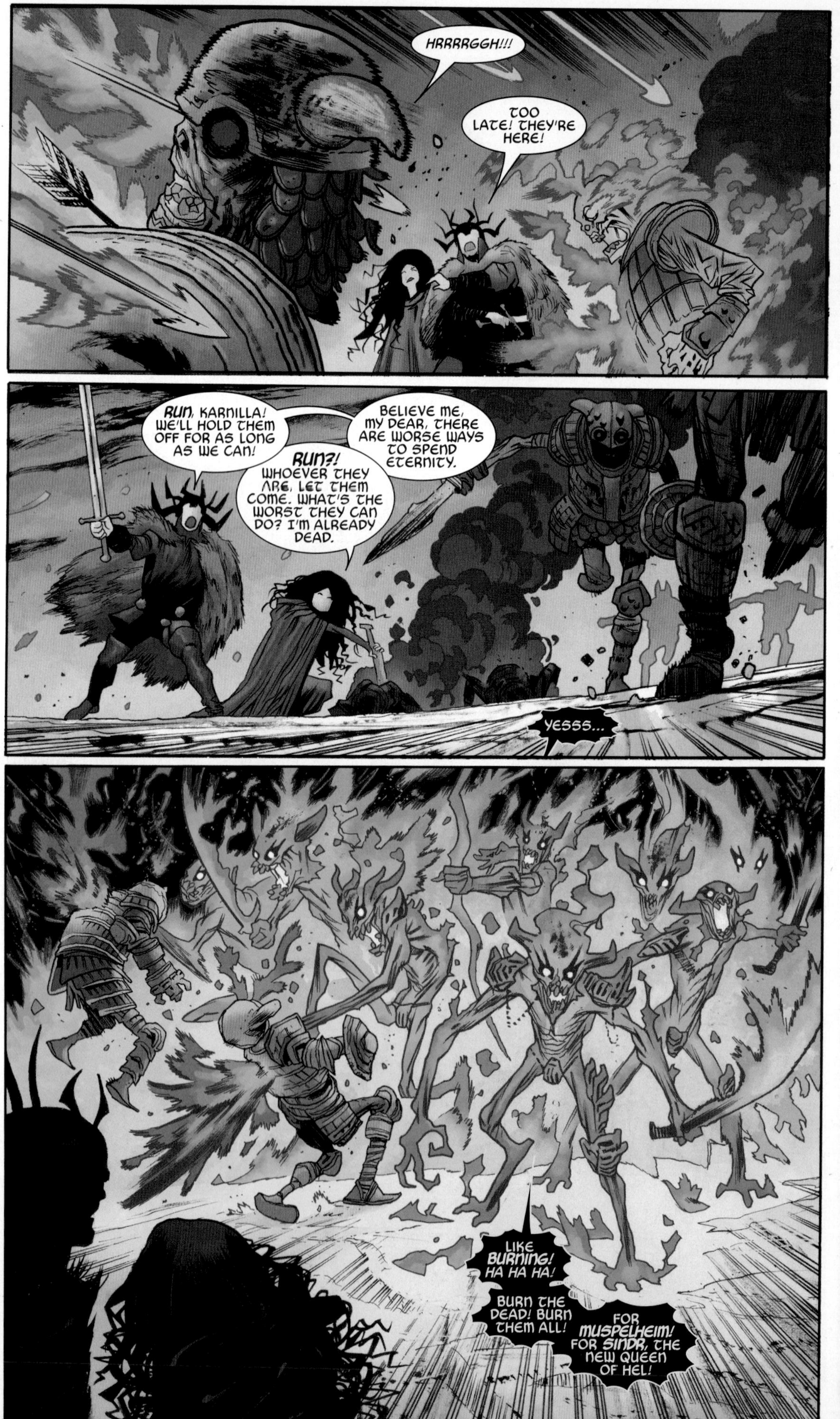
HRRRRGGH!!!
TOO LATE! THEY'RE HERE!
RUN, KARNILLA! WE'LL HOLD THEM OFF FOR AS LONG AS WE CAN!
RUN?! WHOEVER THEY ARE, LET THEM COME. WHAT'S THE WORST THEY CAN DO? I'M ALREADY DEAD.
BELIEVE ME, MY DEAR, THERE ARE WORSE WAYS TO SPEND ETERNITY.
YESSS...
LIKE BURNING! HA HA HA!
BURN THE DEAD! BURN THEM ALL!
FOR MUSPELHEIM! FOR SINDR, THE NEW QUEEN OF HEL!

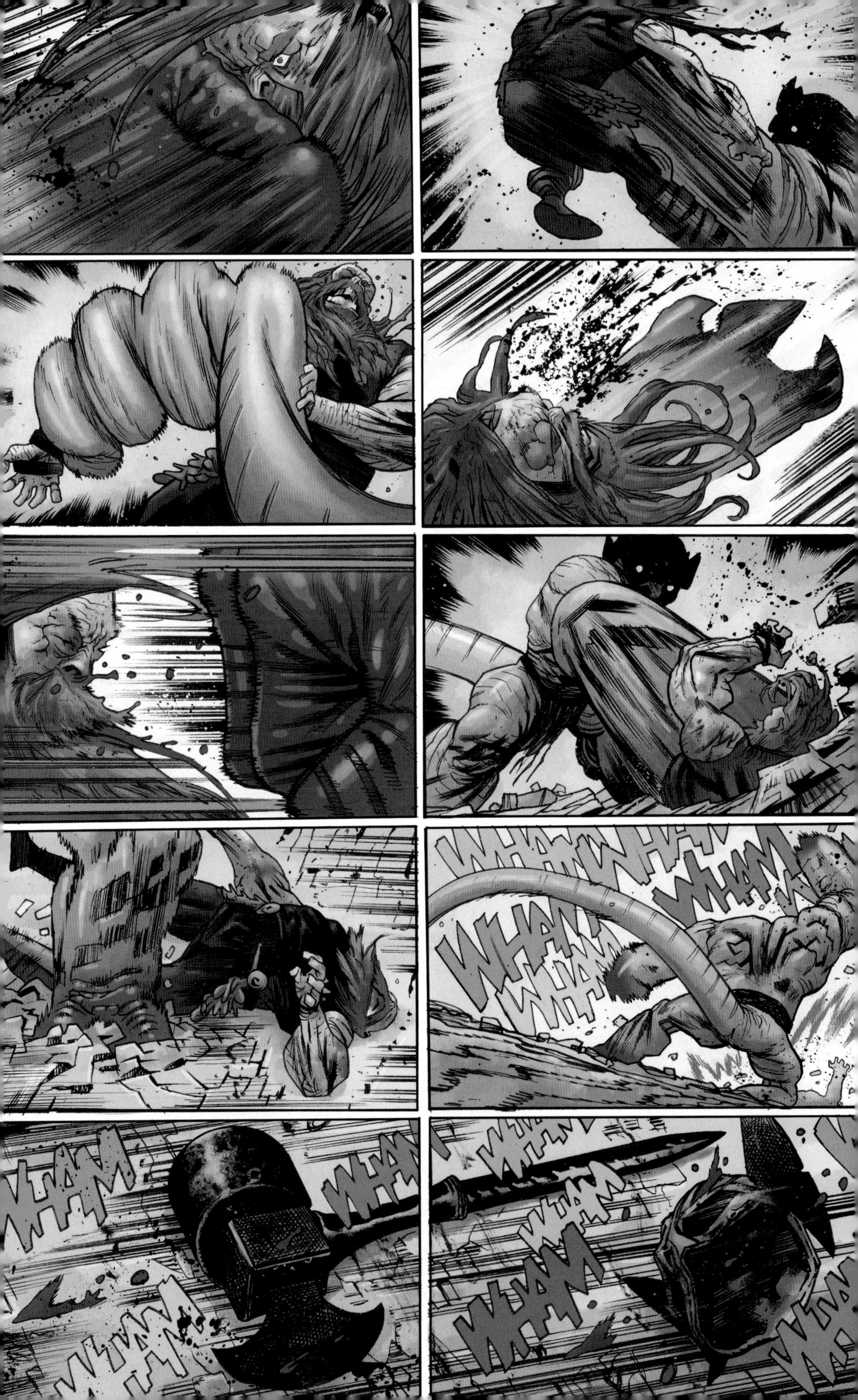
WHAM
WHAM
WHAM
WHAM
WHAM
WHAM
WHAM
WHAM
WHAM

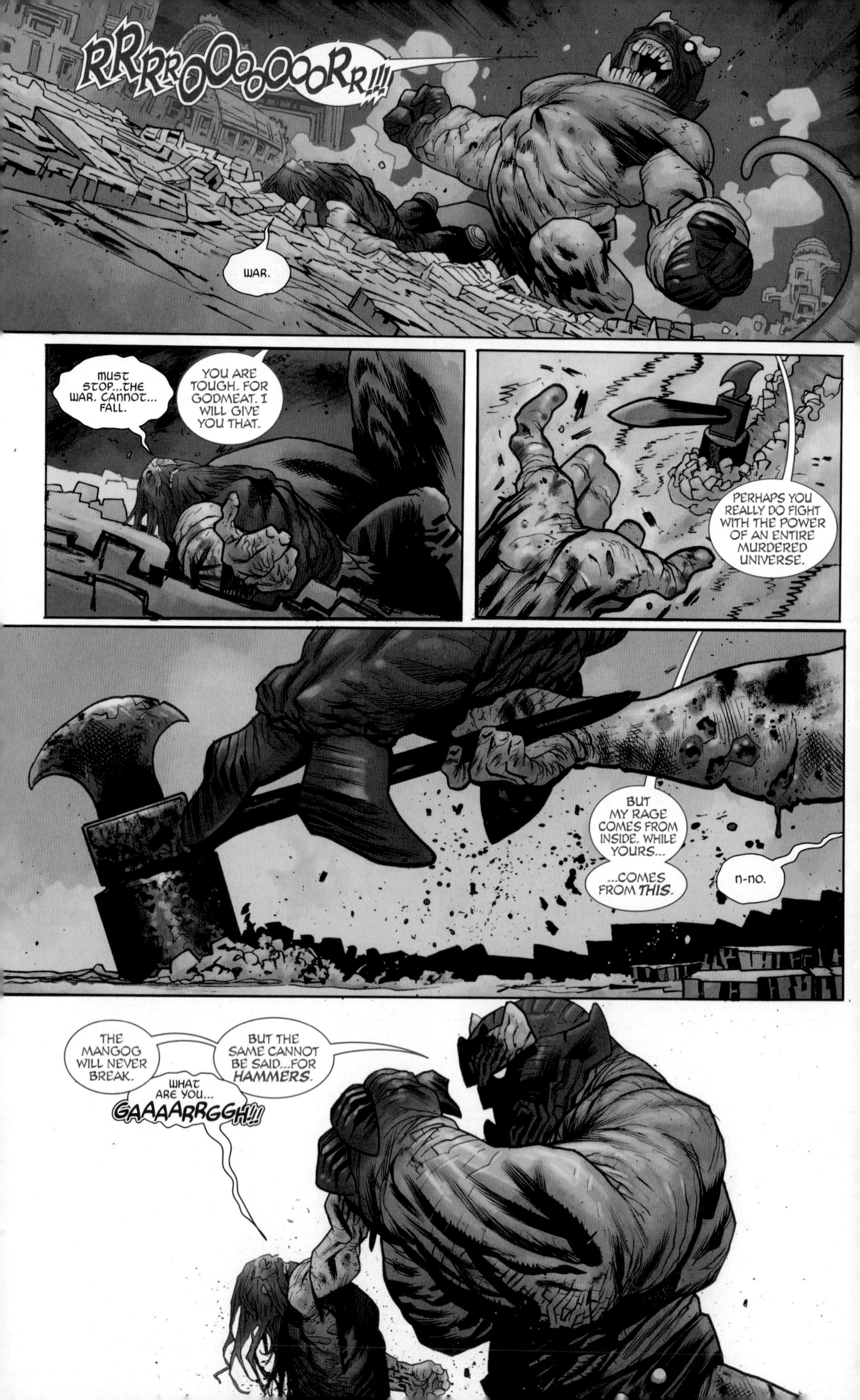
RRRROOOOOOOORRR!!!
WAR.
MUST STOP...THE WAR. CANNOT... FALL.
YOU ARE TOUGH. FOR GODMEAT. I WILL GIVE YOU THAT.
PERHAPS YOU REALLY DO FIGHT WITH THE POWER OF AN ENTIRE MURDERED UNIVERSE.
BUT MY RAGE COMES FROM INSIDE. WHILE YOURS...
...COMES FROM THIS.
n-no.
THE MANGOG WILL NEVER BREAK.
BUT THE SAME CANNOT BE SAID...FOR HAMMERS.
WHAT ARE YOU... GAAAARRGGH!!!

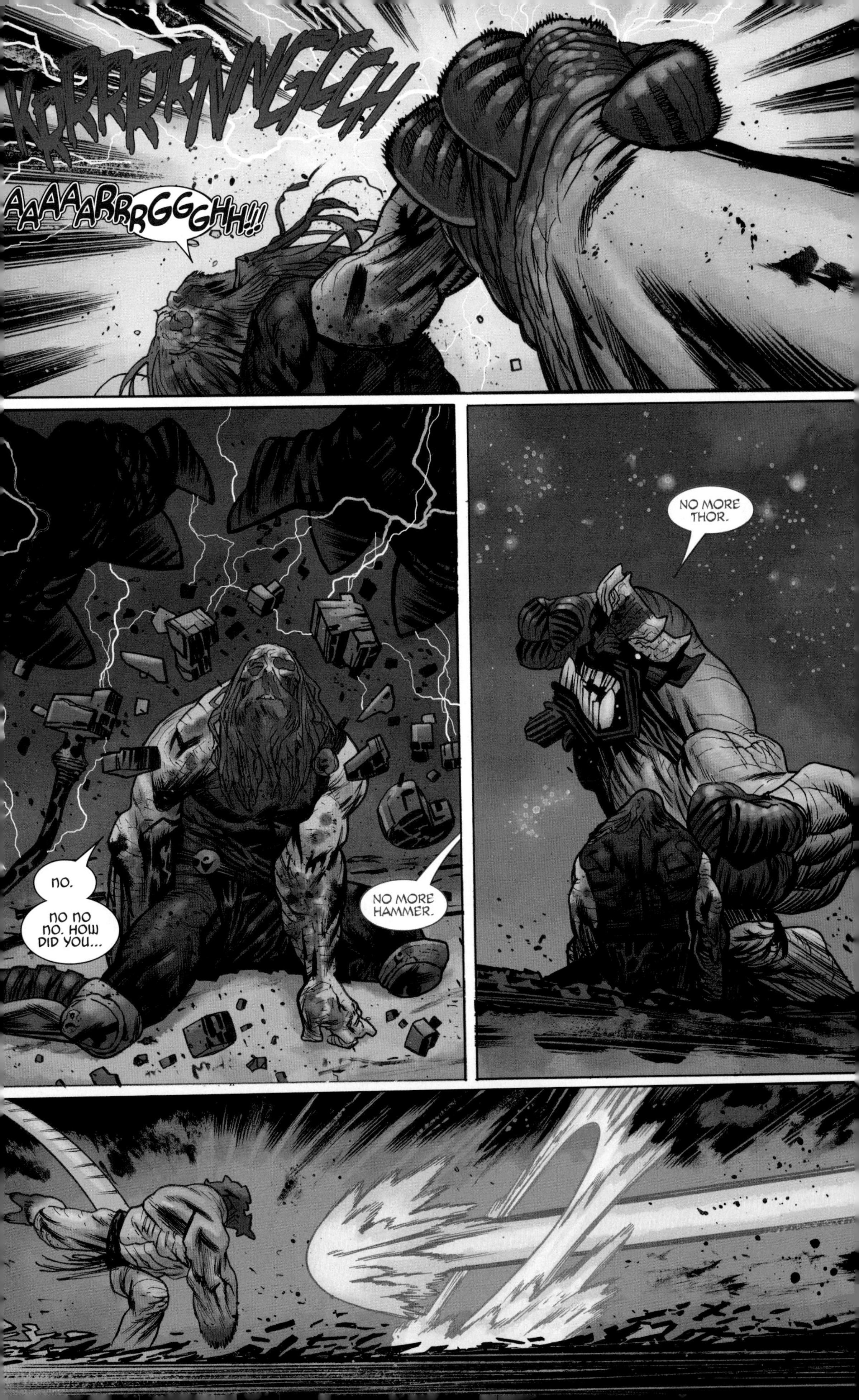

KRRRRNNGGCH
AAAAARRRRGGGHH!!!
no.
no no no. HOW DID YOU...
NO MORE HAMMER.
NO MORE THOR.

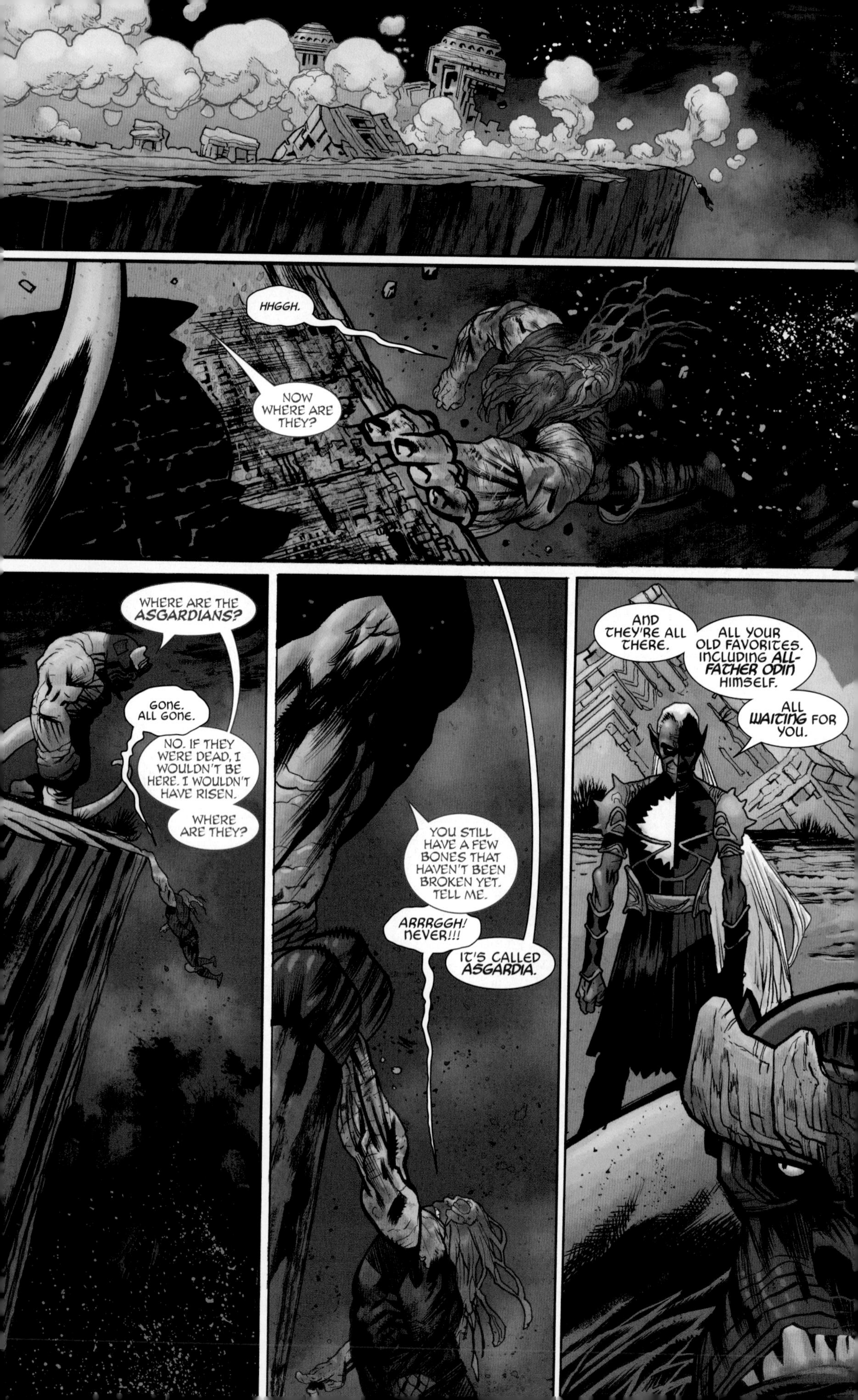
HHGGH.
NOW WHERE ARE THEY?
WHERE ARE THE ASGARDIANS?
GONE. ALL GONE.
NO. IF THEY WERE DEAD, I WOULDN'T BE HERE. I WOULDN'T HAVE RISEN.
WHERE ARE THEY?
YOU STILL HAVE A FEW BONES THAT HAVEN'T BEEN BROKEN YET. TELL ME.
ARRRGGH! NEVER!!!
IT'S CALLED ASGARDIA.
AND THEY'RE ALL THERE.
ALL YOUR OLD FAVORITES. INCLUDING ALL-FATHER ODIN HIMSELF.
ALL WAITING FOR YOU.

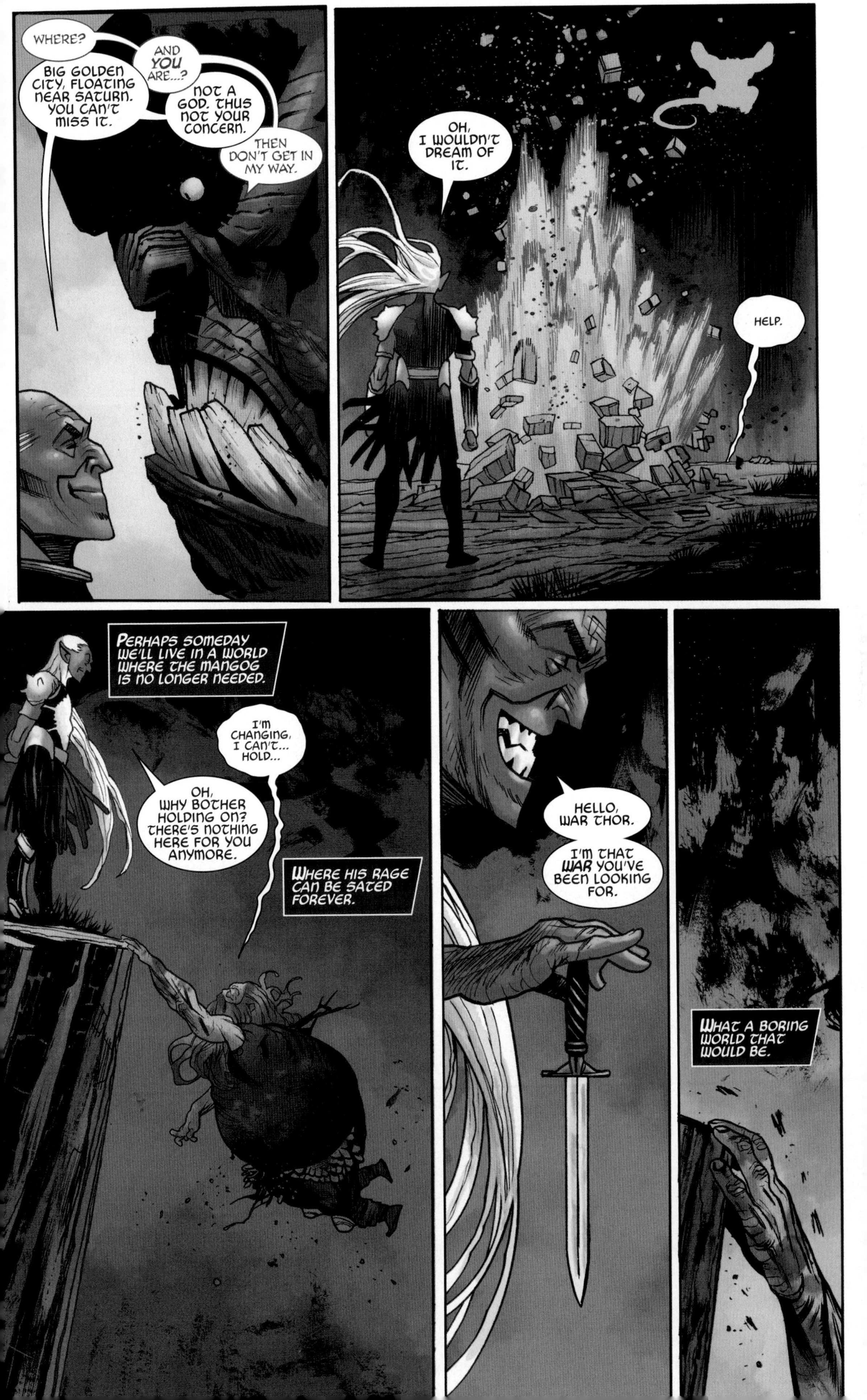
WHERE?
AND YOU ARE...?
BIG GOLDEN CITY, FLOATING NEAR SATURN. YOU CAN'T MISS IT.
NOT A GOD. THUS NOT YOUR CONCERN.
THEN DON'T GET IN MY WAY.
OH, I WOULDN'T DREAM OF IT.
HELP.
PERHAPS SOMEDAY WE'LL LIVE IN A WORLD WHERE THE MANGOG IS NO LONGER NEEDED.
I'M CHANGING, I CAN'T... HOLD...
OH, WHY BOTHER HOLDING ON? THERE'S NOTHING HERE FOR YOU ANYMORE.
WHERE HIS RAGE CAN BE SATED FOREVER.
HELLO, WAR THOR.
I'M THAT WAR YOU'VE BEEN LOOKING FOR.
WHAT A BORING WORLD THAT WOULD BE.

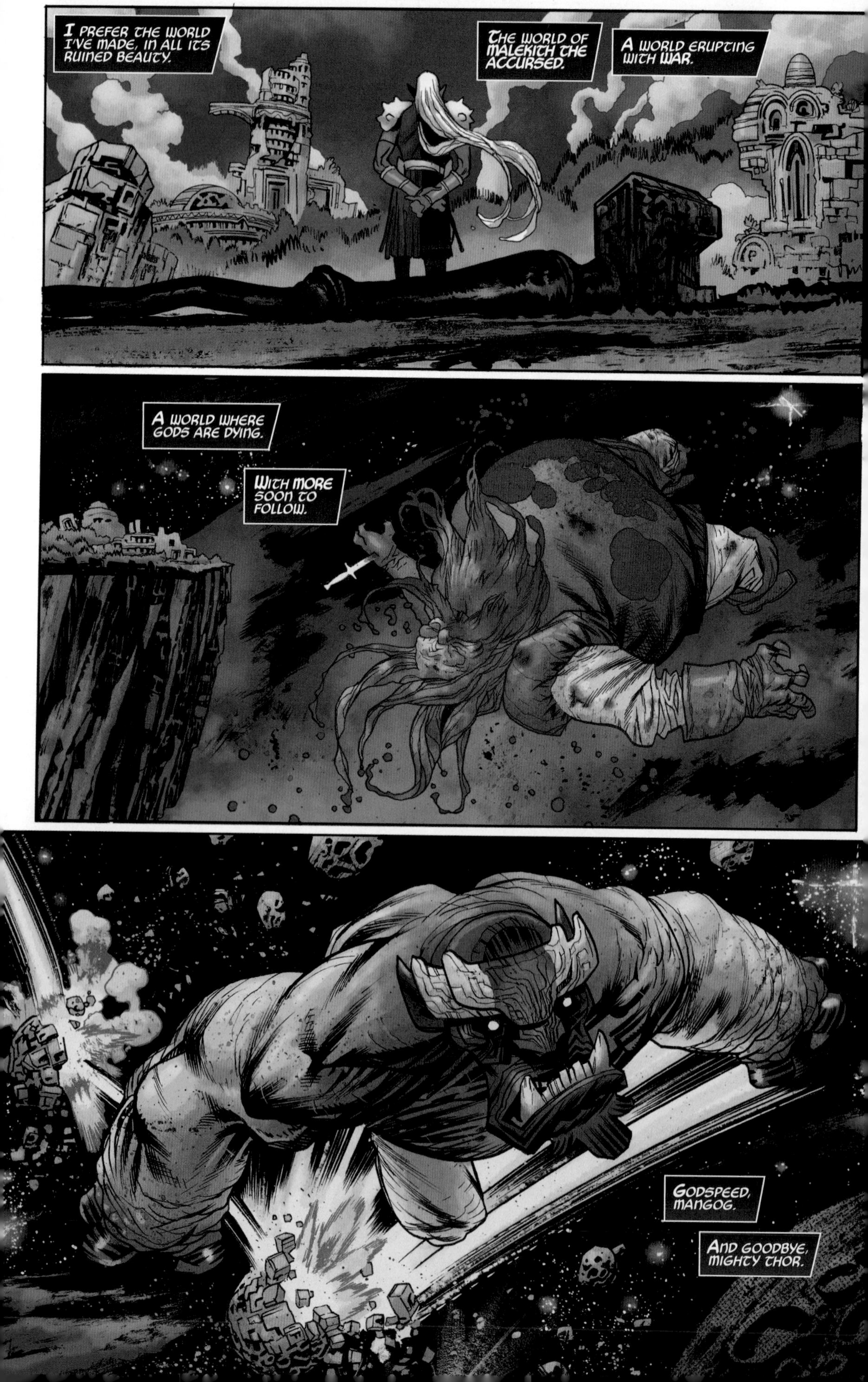
I PREFER THE WORLD I'VE MADE, IN ALL ITS RUINED BEAUTY.
THE WORLD OF MALEKITH THE ACCURSED.
A WORLD ERUPTING WITH WAR.
A WORLD WHERE GODS ARE DYING.
WITH MORE SOON TO FOLLOW.
GODSPEED, MANGOG.
AND GOODBYE, MIGHTY THOR.

# 702

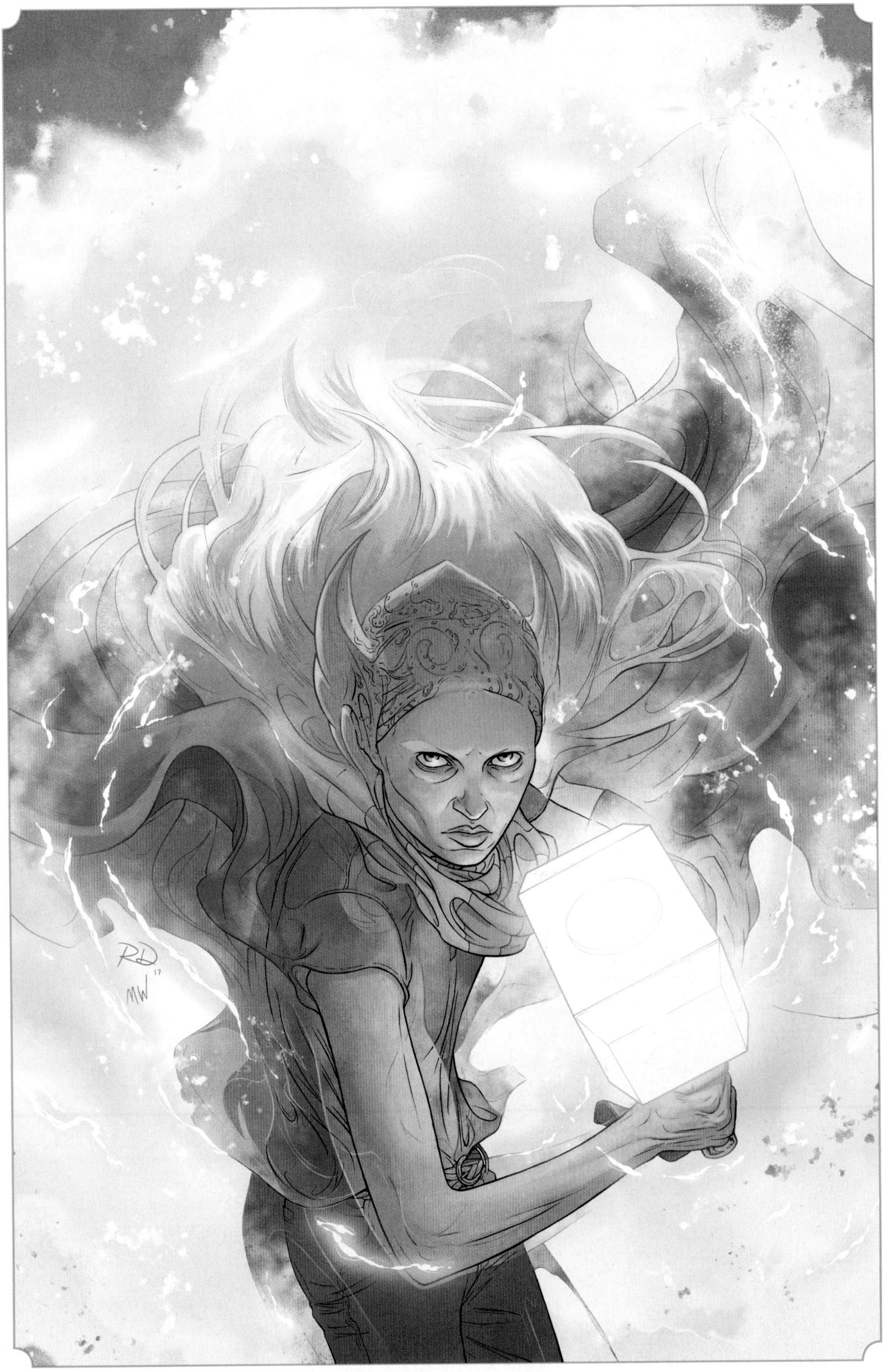

# THE LAST DAYS OF THE GODDESS OF THUNDER

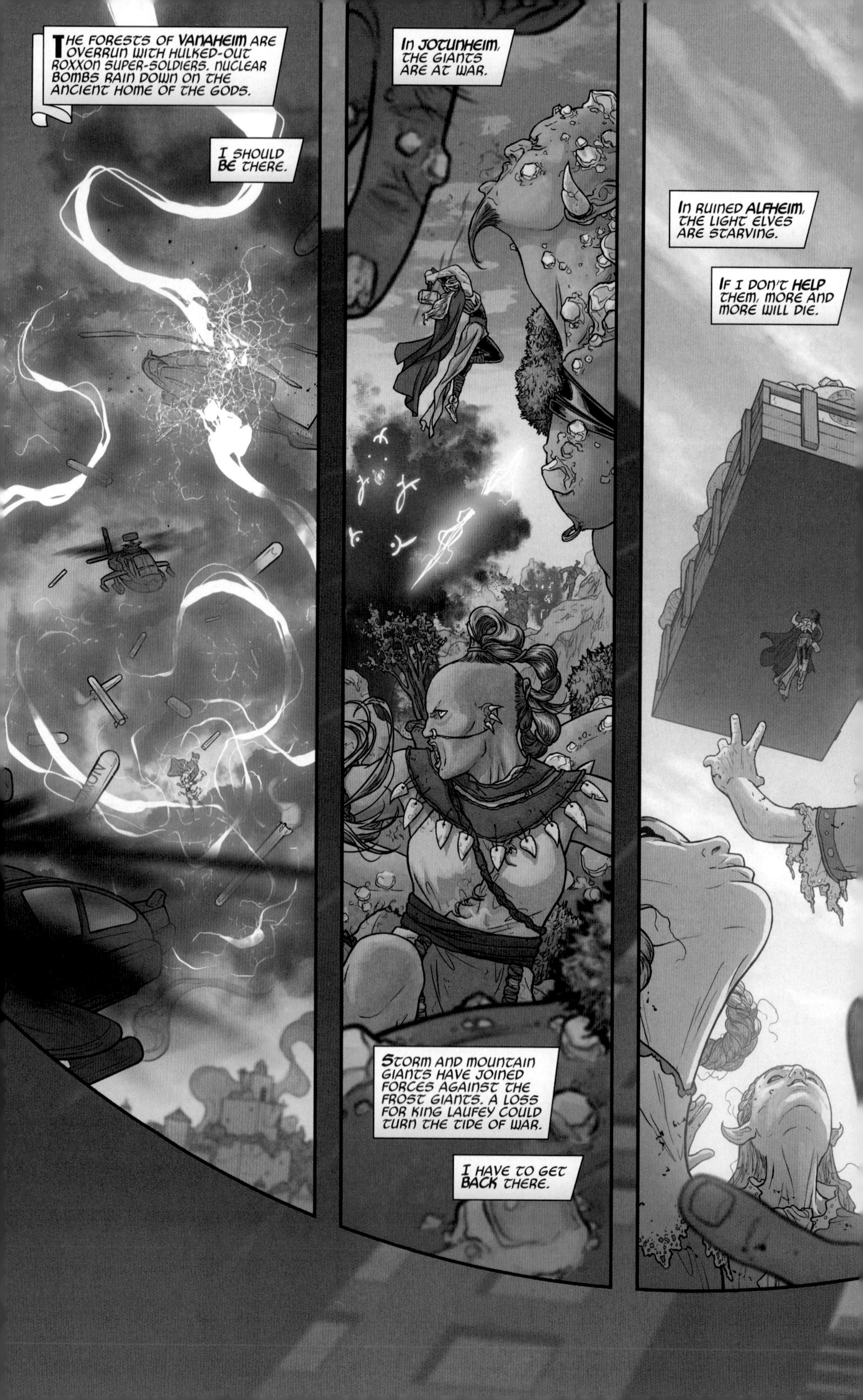
THE FORESTS OF VANAHEIM ARE OVERRUN WITH HULKED-OUT ROXXON SUPER-SOLDIERS. NUCLEAR BOMBS RAIN DOWN ON THE ANCIENT HOME OF THE GODS.
I SHOULD BE THERE.
IN JOTUNHEIM, THE GIANTS ARE AT WAR.
STORM AND MOUNTAIN GIANTS HAVE JOINED FORCES AGAINST THE FROST GIANTS. A LOSS FOR KING LAUFEY COULD TURN THE TIDE OF WAR.
I HAVE TO GET BACK THERE.
IN RUINED ALFHEIM, THE LIGHT ELVES ARE STARVING.
IF I DON'T HELP THEM, MORE AND MORE WILL DIE.

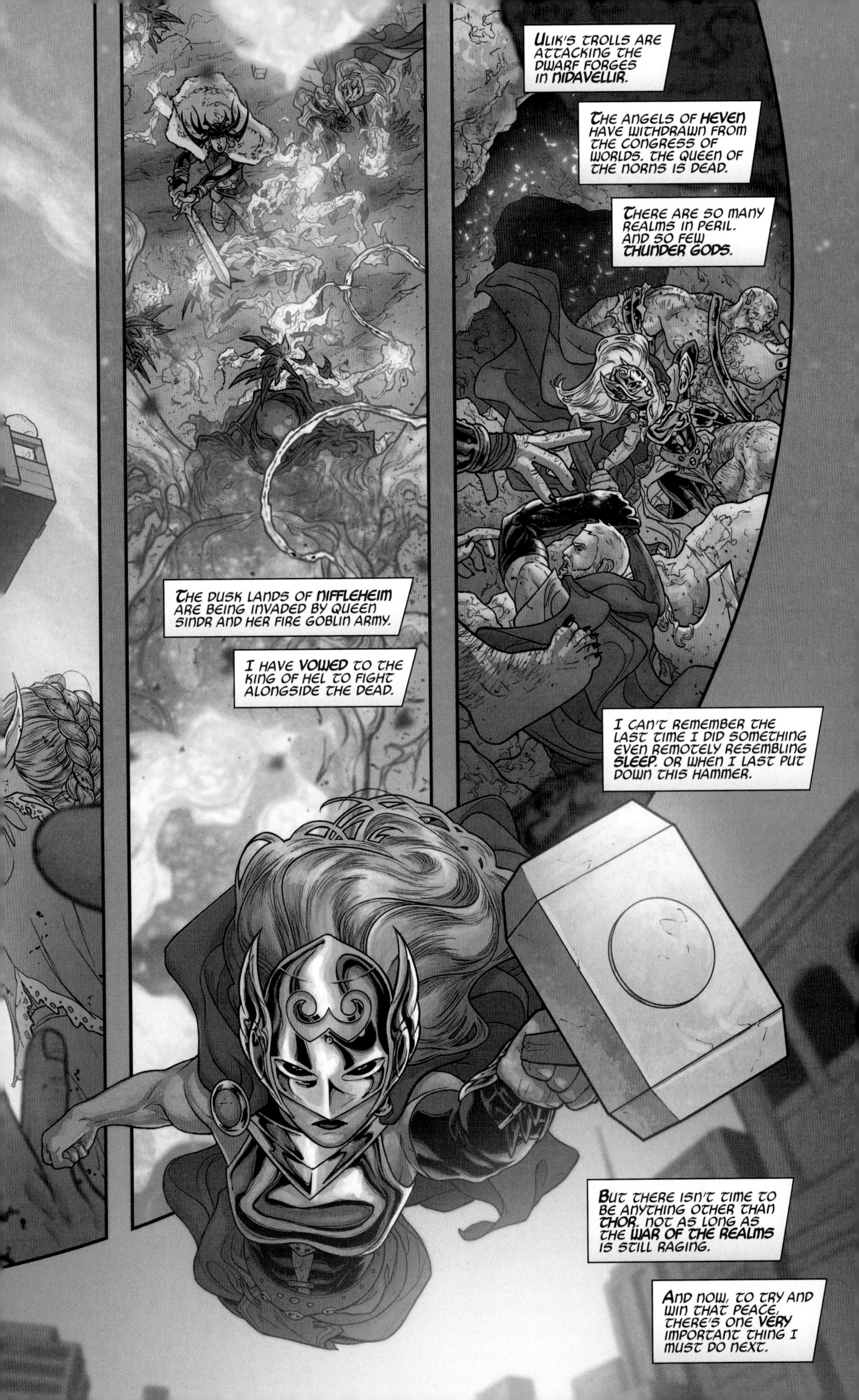

ULIK'S TROLLS ARE ATTACKING THE DWARF FORGES IN NIDAVELLIR.
THE ANGELS OF HEVEN HAVE WITHDRAWN FROM THE CONGRESS OF WORLDS. THE QUEEN OF THE NORNS IS DEAD.
THERE ARE SO MANY REALMS IN PERIL. AND SO FEW THUNDER GODS.
THE DUSK LANDS OF NIFFLEHEIM ARE BEING INVADED BY QUEEN SINDR AND HER FIRE GOBLIN ARMY.
I HAVE VOWED TO THE KING OF HEL TO FIGHT ALONGSIDE THE DEAD.
I CAN'T REMEMBER THE LAST TIME I DID SOMETHING EVEN REMOTELY RESEMBLING SLEEP. OR WHEN I LAST PUT DOWN THIS HAMMER.
BUT THERE ISN'T TIME TO BE ANYTHING OTHER THAN THOR. NOT AS LONG AS THE WAR OF THE REALMS IS STILL RAGING.
AND NOW, TO TRY AND WIN THAT PEACE, THERE'S ONE VERY IMPORTANT THING I MUST DO NEXT.

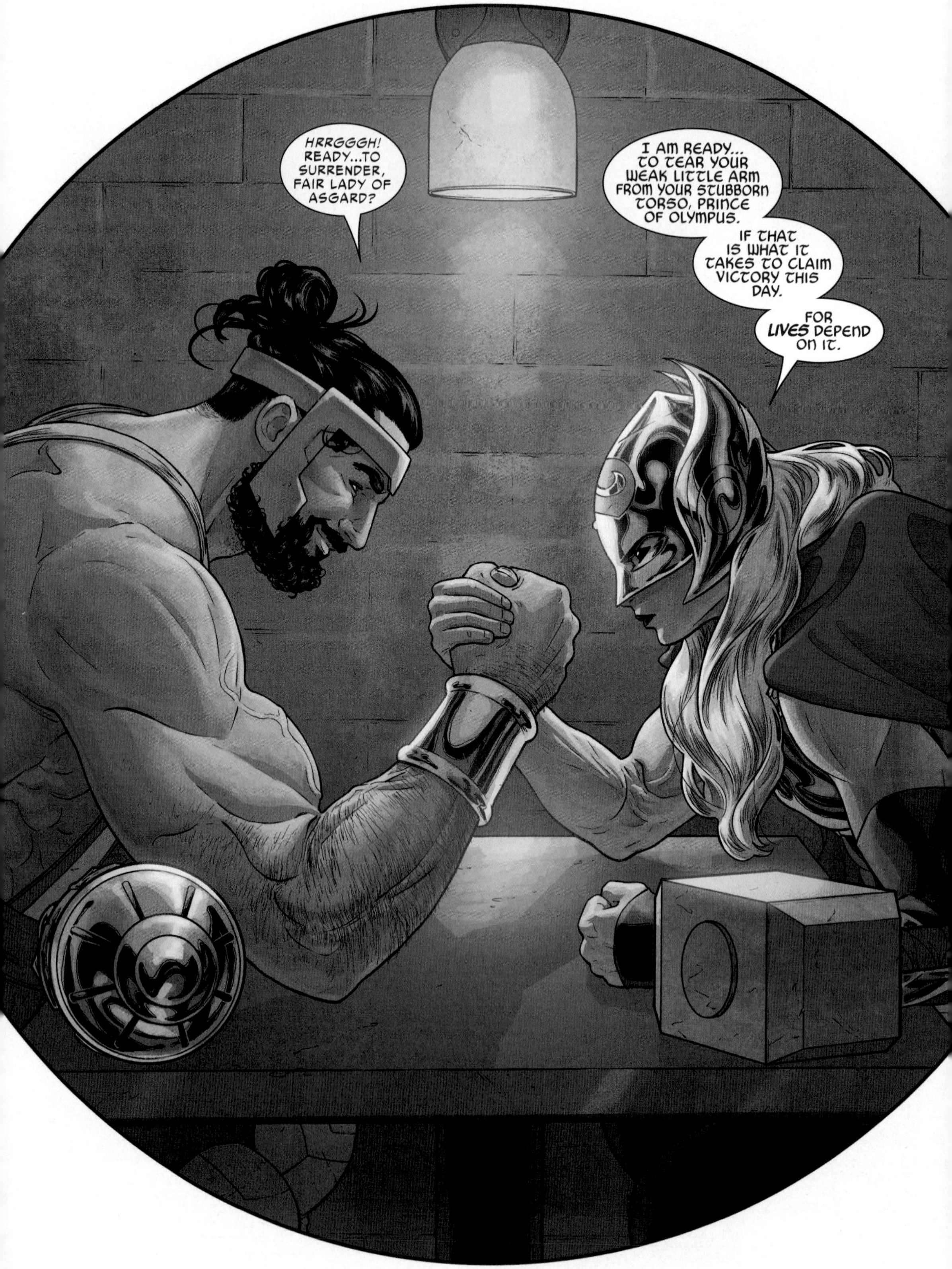
HRRGGGH! READY...TO SURRENDER, FAIR LADY OF ASGARD?
I AM READY... TO TEAR YOUR WEAK LITTLE ARM FROM YOUR STUBBORN TORSO, PRINCE OF OLYMPUS.
IF THAT IS WHAT IT TAKES TO CLAIM VICTORY THIS DAY.
FOR *LIVES* DEPEND ON IT.

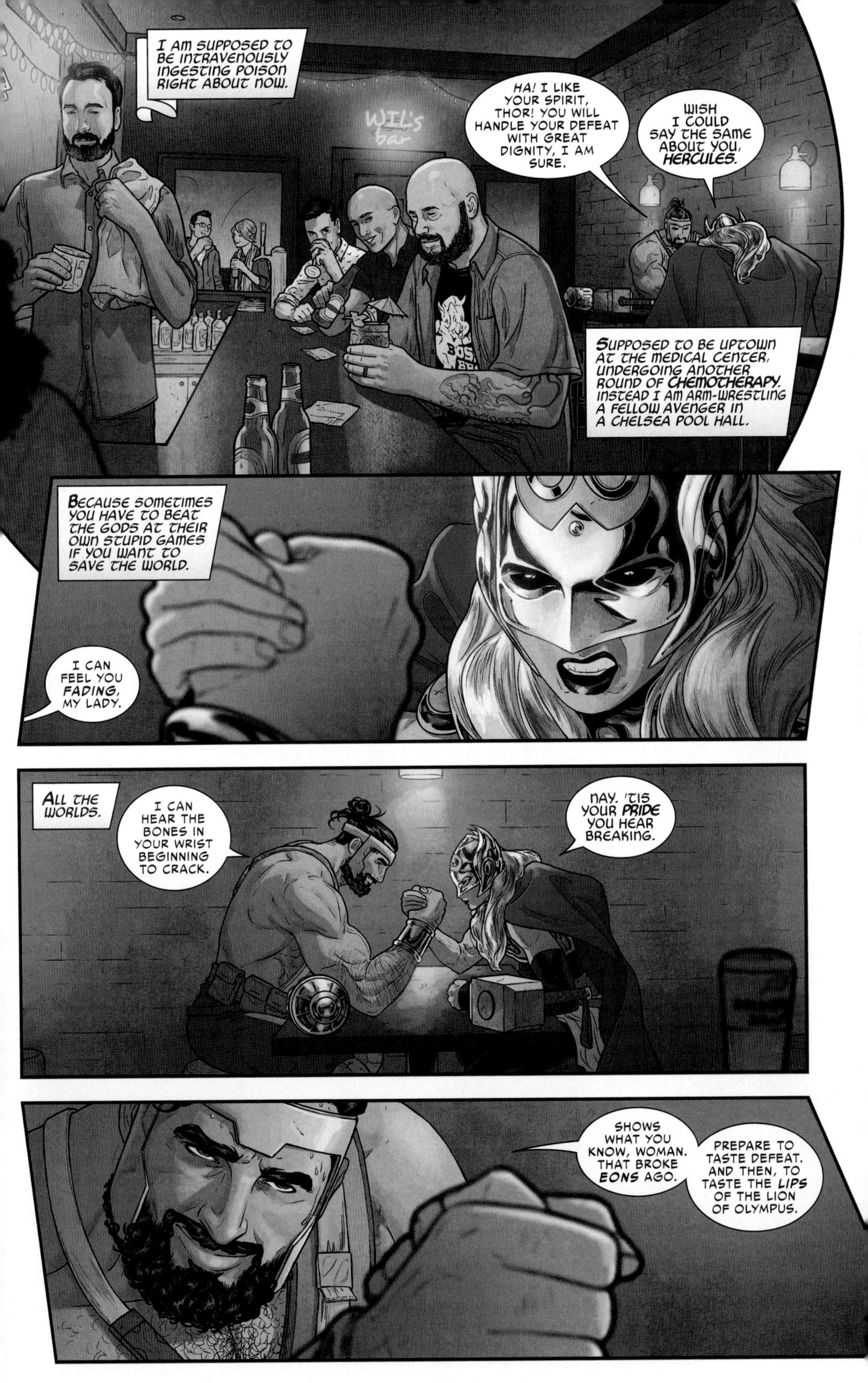
I AM SUPPOSED TO BE INTRAVENOUSLY INGESTING POISON RIGHT ABOUT NOW.
HA! I LIKE YOUR SPIRIT, THOR! YOU WILL HANDLE YOUR DEFEAT WITH GREAT DIGNITY, I AM SURE.
WISH I COULD SAY THE SAME ABOUT YOU, HERCULES.
WIL's bar
SUPPOSED TO BE UPTOWN AT THE MEDICAL CENTER, UNDERGOING ANOTHER ROUND OF CHEMOTHERAPY. INSTEAD I AM ARM-WRESTLING A FELLOW AVENGER IN A CHELSEA POOL HALL.
BECAUSE SOMETIMES YOU HAVE TO BEAT THE GODS AT THEIR OWN STUPID GAMES IF YOU WANT TO SAVE THE WORLD.
I CAN FEEL YOU FADING, MY LADY.
ALL THE WORLDS.
I CAN HEAR THE BONES IN YOUR WRIST BEGINNING TO CRACK.
NAY. 'TIS YOUR PRIDE YOU HEAR BREAKING.
SHOWS WHAT YOU KNOW, WOMAN. THAT BROKE EONS AGO.
PREPARE TO TASTE DEFEAT. AND THEN, TO TASTE THE LIPS OF THE LION OF OLYMPUS.

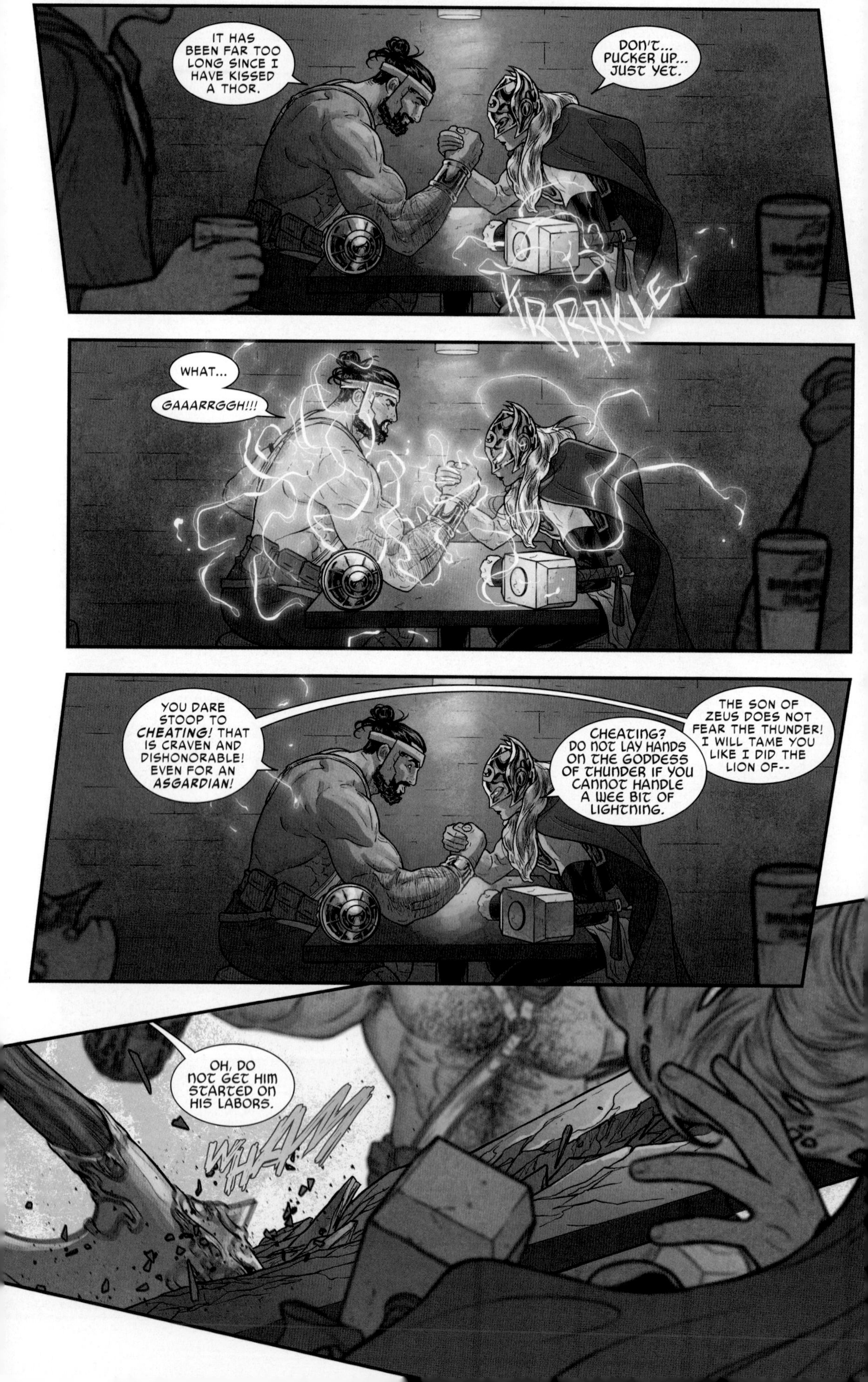
IT HAS BEEN FAR TOO LONG SINCE I HAVE KISSED A THOR.
DON'T... PUCKER UP... JUST YET.
KRRRKLE
WHAT...
GAAARRGGH!!!
YOU DARE STOOP TO CHEATING! THAT IS CRAVEN AND DISHONORABLE! EVEN FOR AN ASGARDIAN!
CHEATING? DO NOT LAY HANDS ON THE GODDESS OF THUNDER IF YOU CANNOT HANDLE A WEE BIT OF LIGHTNING.
THE SON OF ZEUS DOES NOT FEAR THE THUNDER! I WILL TAME YOU LIKE I DID THE LION OF--
OH, DO NOT GET HIM STARTED ON HIS LABORS.
WHAM

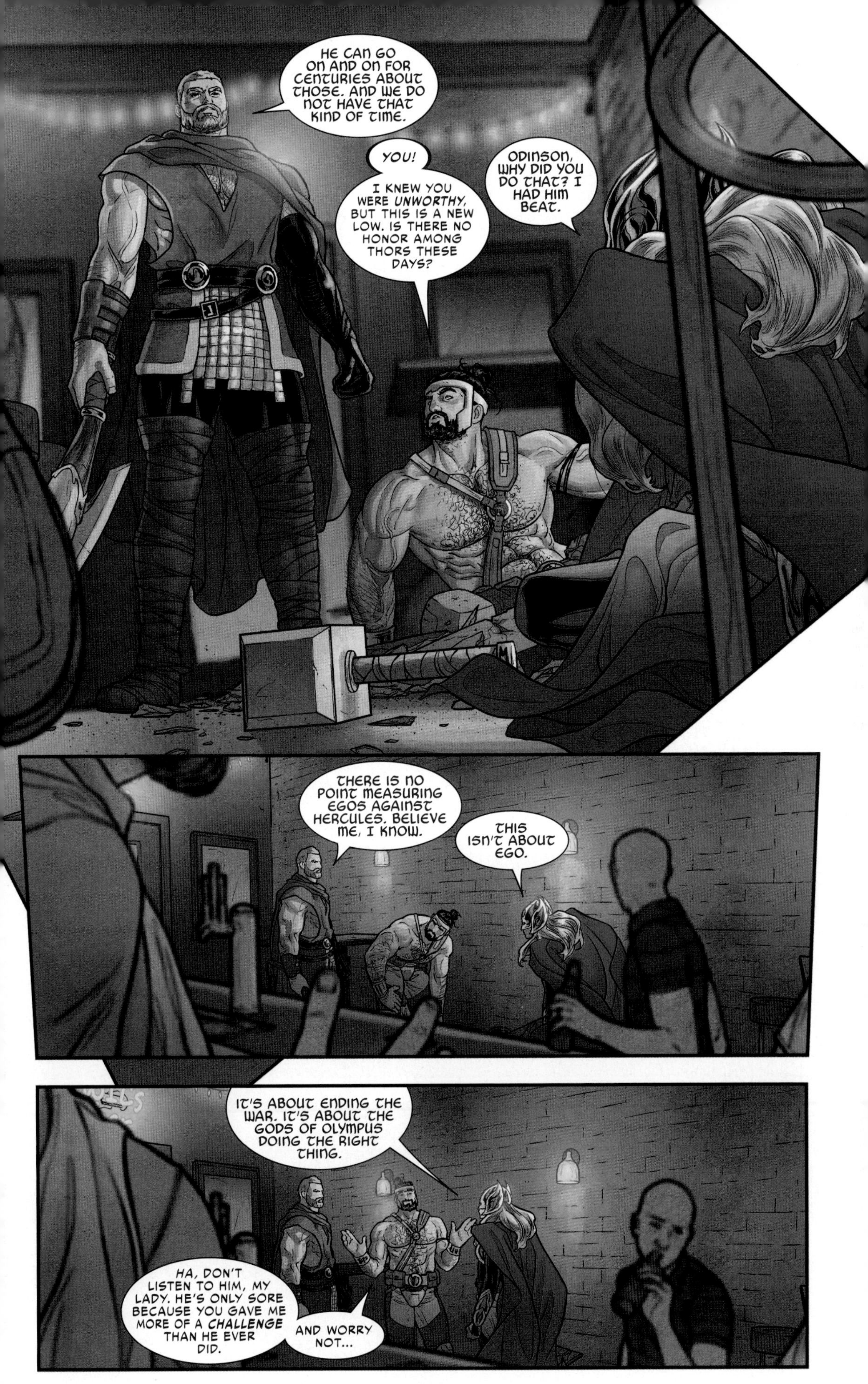
HE CAN GO ON AND ON FOR CENTURIES ABOUT THOSE. AND WE DO NOT HAVE THAT KIND OF TIME.
YOU!
I KNEW YOU WERE *UNWORTHY*, BUT THIS IS A NEW LOW. IS THERE NO HONOR AMONG THORS THESE DAYS?
ODINSON, WHY DID YOU DO THAT? I HAD HIM BEAT.
THERE IS NO POINT MEASURING EGOS AGAINST HERCULES. BELIEVE ME, I KNOW.
THIS ISN'T ABOUT EGO.
IT'S ABOUT ENDING THE WAR. IT'S ABOUT THE GODS OF OLYMPUS DOING THE RIGHT THING.
*HA*, DON'T LISTEN TO HIM, MY LADY. HE'S ONLY SORE BECAUSE YOU GAVE ME MORE OF A *CHALLENGE* THAN HE EVER DID.
AND WORRY NOT...

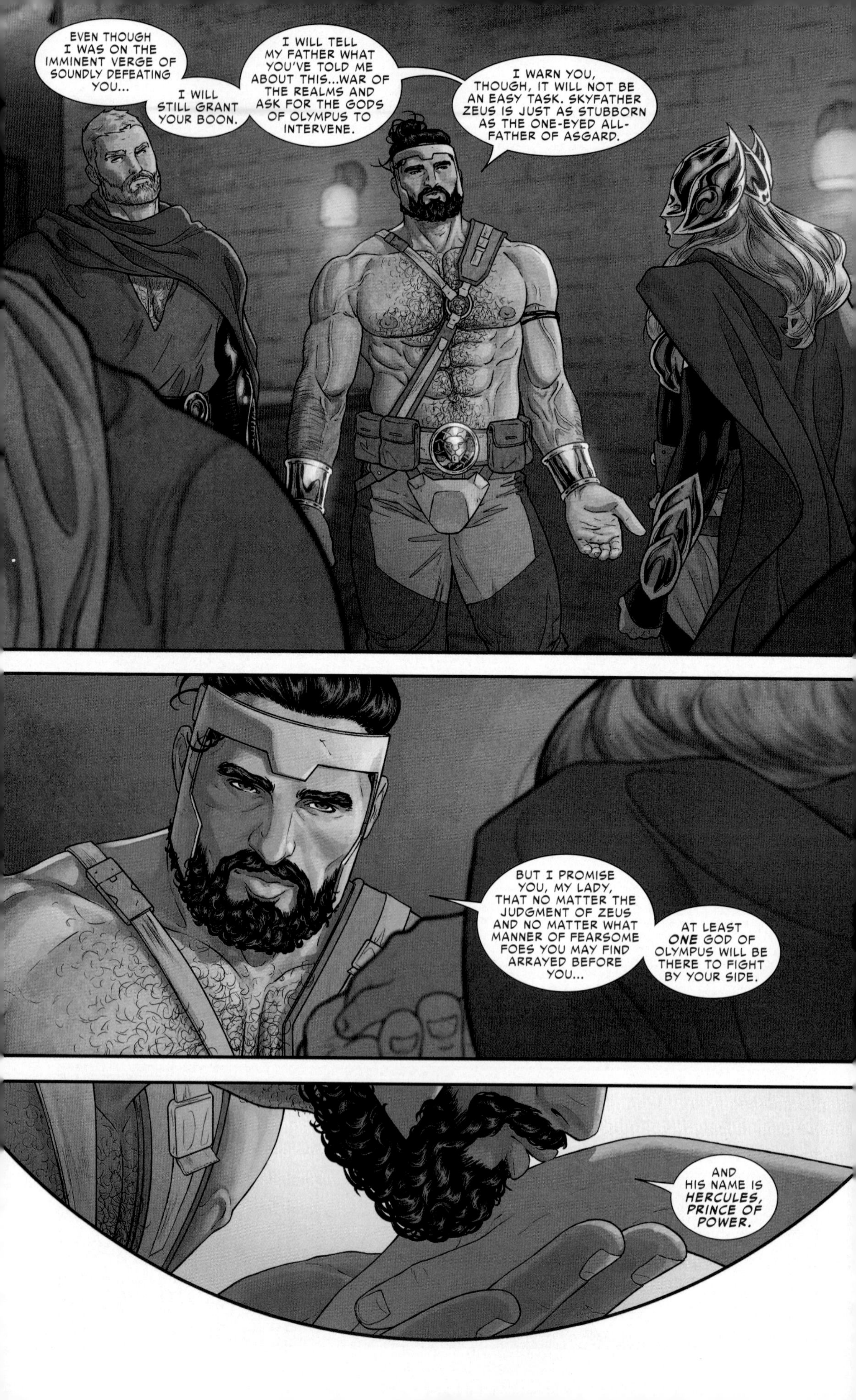
EVEN THOUGH I WAS ON THE IMMINENT VERGE OF SOUNDLY DEFEATING YOU...
I WILL STILL GRANT YOUR BOON.
I WILL TELL MY FATHER WHAT YOU'VE TOLD ME ABOUT THIS...WAR OF THE REALMS AND ASK FOR THE GODS OF OLYMPUS TO INTERVENE.
I WARN YOU, THOUGH, IT WILL NOT BE AN EASY TASK. SKYFATHER ZEUS IS JUST AS STUBBORN AS THE ONE-EYED ALL-FATHER OF ASGARD.
BUT I PROMISE YOU, MY LADY, THAT NO MATTER THE JUDGMENT OF ZEUS AND NO MATTER WHAT MANNER OF FEARSOME FOES YOU MAY FIND ARRAYED BEFORE YOU...
AT LEAST *ONE* GOD OF OLYMPUS WILL BE THERE TO FIGHT BY YOUR SIDE.
AND HIS NAME IS *HERCULES, PRINCE OF POWER.*

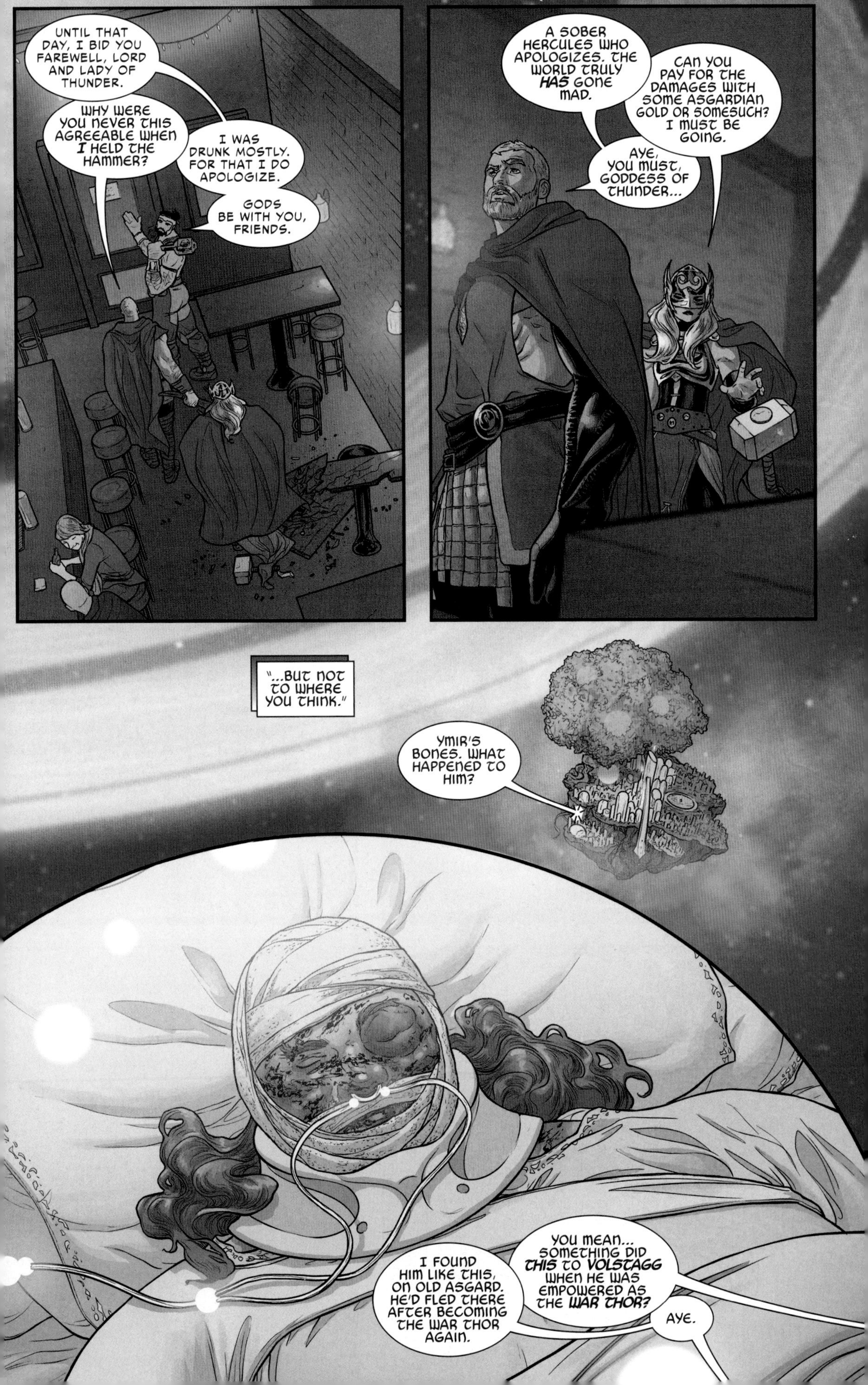
UNTIL THAT DAY, I BID YOU FAREWELL, LORD AND LADY OF THUNDER.
WHY WERE YOU NEVER THIS AGREEABLE WHEN I HELD THE HAMMER?
I WAS DRUNK MOSTLY. FOR THAT I DO APOLOGIZE.
GODS BE WITH YOU, FRIENDS.
A SOBER HERCULES WHO APOLOGIZES. THE WORLD TRULY HAS GONE MAD.
CAN YOU PAY FOR THE DAMAGES WITH SOME ASGARDIAN GOLD OR SOMESUCH? I MUST BE GOING.
AYE, YOU MUST, GODDESS OF THUNDER...
"...BUT NOT TO WHERE YOU THINK."
YMIR'S BONES. WHAT HAPPENED TO HIM?
I FOUND HIM LIKE THIS, ON OLD ASGARD. HE'D FLED THERE AFTER BECOMING THE WAR THOR AGAIN.
YOU MEAN... SOMETHING DID THIS TO VOLSTAGG WHEN HE WAS EMPOWERED AS THE WAR THOR?
AYE.

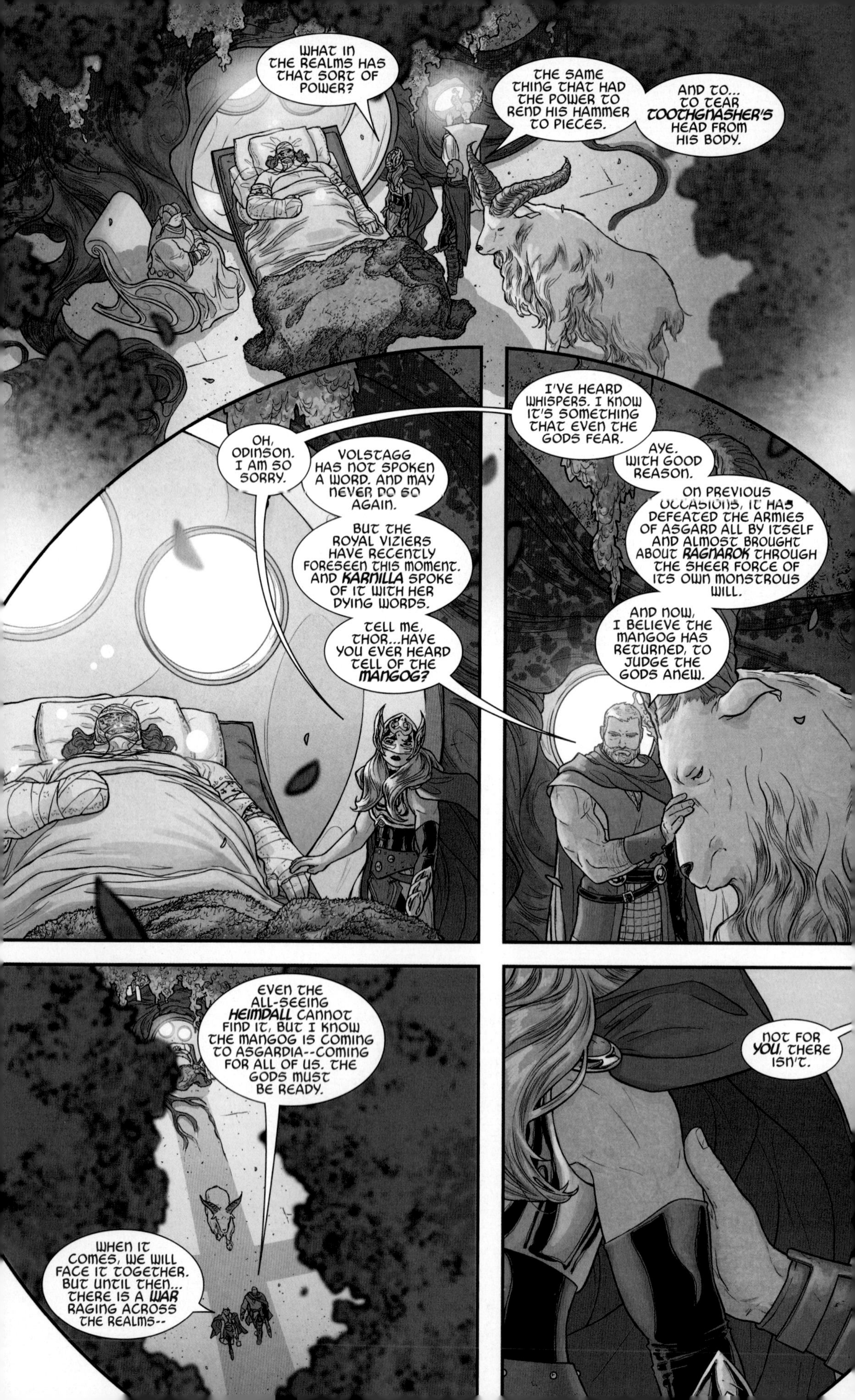
WHAT IN THE REALMS HAS THAT SORT OF POWER?
THE SAME THING THAT HAD THE POWER TO REND HIS HAMMER TO PIECES.
AND TO... TO TEAR TOOTHGNASHER'S HEAD FROM HIS BODY.
OH, ODINSON. I AM SO SORRY.
VOLSTAGG HAS NOT SPOKEN A WORD. AND MAY NEVER DO SO AGAIN.
BUT THE ROYAL VIZIERS HAVE RECENTLY FORESEEN THIS MOMENT. AND KARNILLA SPOKE OF IT WITH HER DYING WORDS.
TELL ME, THOR...HAVE YOU EVER HEARD TELL OF THE MANGOG?
I'VE HEARD WHISPERS. I KNOW IT'S SOMETHING THAT EVEN THE GODS FEAR.
AYE. WITH GOOD REASON.
ON PREVIOUS OCCASIONS, IT HAS DEFEATED THE ARMIES OF ASGARD ALL BY ITSELF AND ALMOST BROUGHT ABOUT RAGNAROK THROUGH THE SHEER FORCE OF ITS OWN MONSTROUS WILL.
AND NOW, I BELIEVE THE MANGOG HAS RETURNED, TO JUDGE THE GODS ANEW.
EVEN THE ALL-SEEING HEIMDALL CANNOT FIND IT, BUT I KNOW THE MANGOG IS COMING TO ASGARDIA--COMING FOR ALL OF US. THE GODS MUST BE READY.
WHEN IT COMES, WE WILL FACE IT TOGETHER. BUT UNTIL THEN... THERE IS A WAR RAGING ACROSS THE REALMS--
NOT FOR YOU, THERE ISN'T.

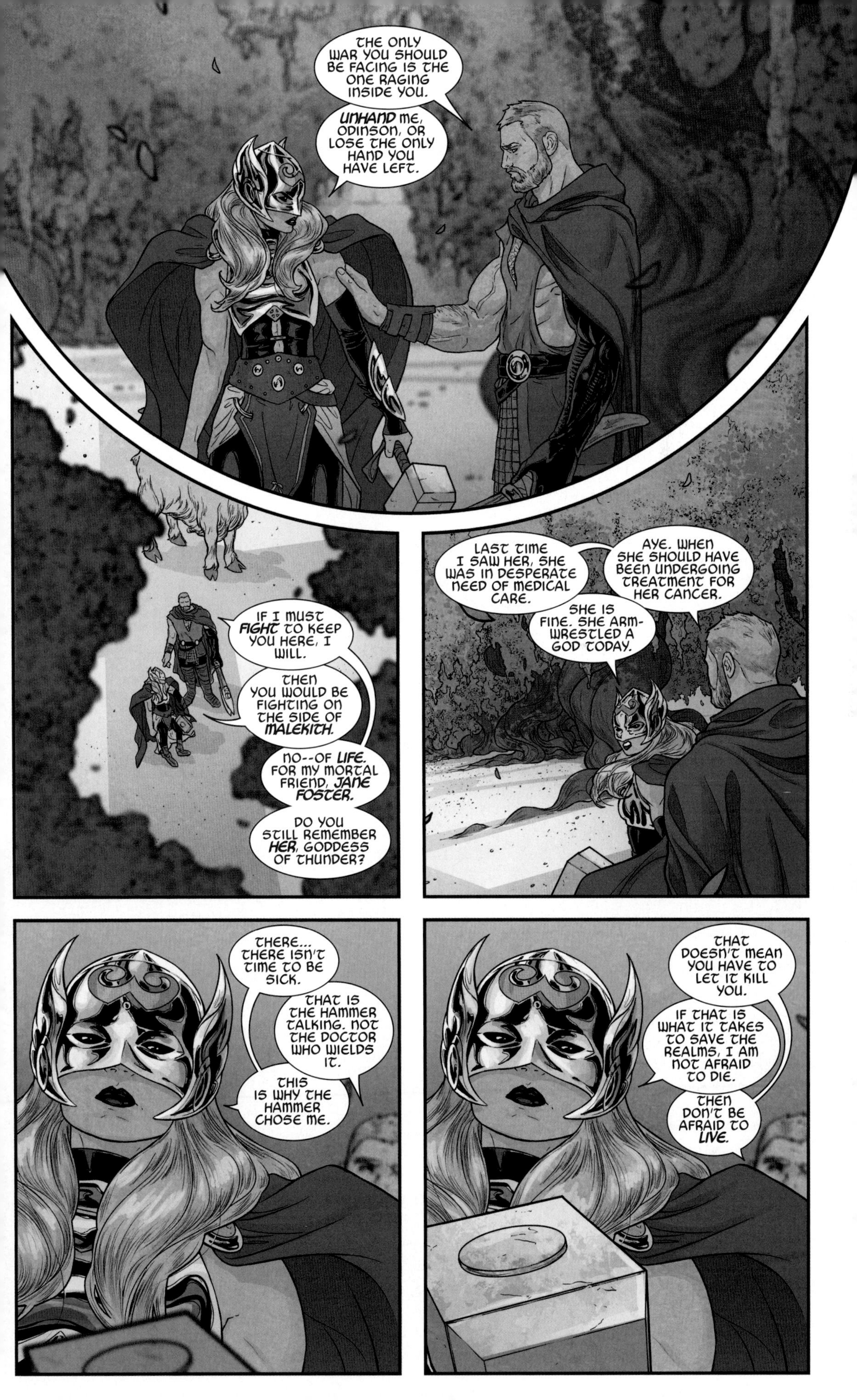
THE ONLY WAR YOU SHOULD BE FACING IS THE ONE RAGING INSIDE YOU.
UNHAND ME, ODINSON, OR LOSE THE ONLY HAND YOU HAVE LEFT.
IF I MUST FIGHT TO KEEP YOU HERE, I WILL.
THEN YOU WOULD BE FIGHTING ON THE SIDE OF MALEKITH.
NO--OF LIFE. FOR MY MORTAL FRIEND, JANE FOSTER.
DO YOU STILL REMEMBER HER, GODDESS OF THUNDER?
LAST TIME I SAW HER, SHE WAS IN DESPERATE NEED OF MEDICAL CARE.
SHE IS FINE. SHE ARM-WRESTLED A GOD TODAY.
AYE. WHEN SHE SHOULD HAVE BEEN UNDERGOING TREATMENT FOR HER CANCER.
THERE... THERE ISN'T TIME TO BE SICK.
THAT IS THE HAMMER TALKING. NOT THE DOCTOR WHO WIELDS IT.
THIS IS WHY THE HAMMER CHOSE ME.
THAT DOESN'T MEAN YOU HAVE TO LET IT KILL YOU.
IF THAT IS WHAT IT TAKES TO SAVE THE REALMS, I AM NOT AFRAID TO DIE.
THEN DON'T BE AFRAID TO LIVE.

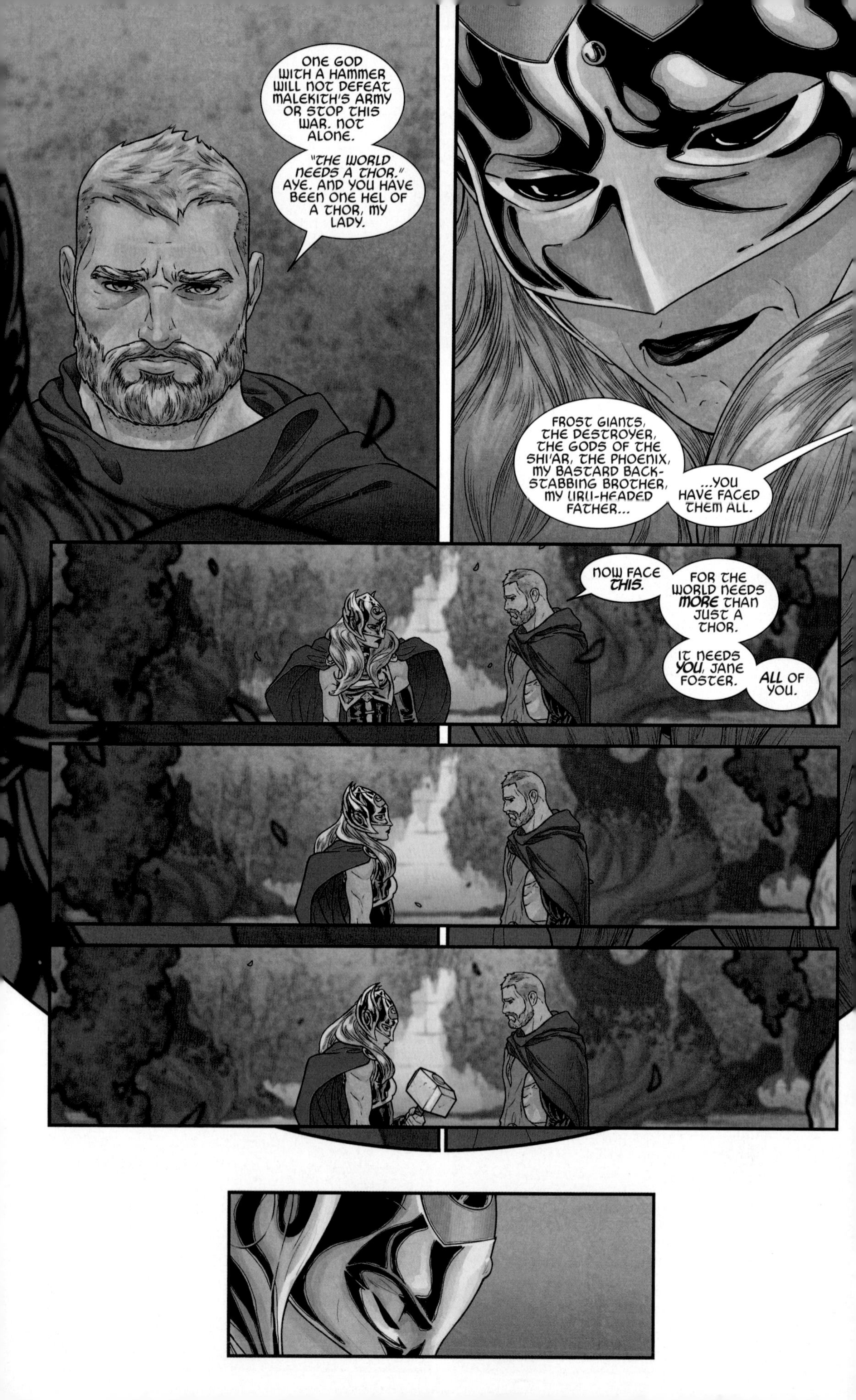
ONE GOD WITH A HAMMER WILL NOT DEFEAT MALEKITH'S ARMY OR STOP THIS WAR. NOT ALONE.
"THE WORLD NEEDS A THOR." AYE. AND YOU HAVE BEEN ONE HEL OF A THOR, MY LADY.
FROST GIANTS, THE DESTROYER, THE GODS OF THE SHI'AR, THE PHOENIX, MY BASTARD BACK-STABBING BROTHER, MY URU-HEADED FATHER...
...YOU HAVE FACED THEM ALL.
NOW FACE THIS.
FOR THE WORLD NEEDS MORE THAN JUST A THOR.
IT NEEDS YOU, JANE FOSTER.
ALL OF YOU.

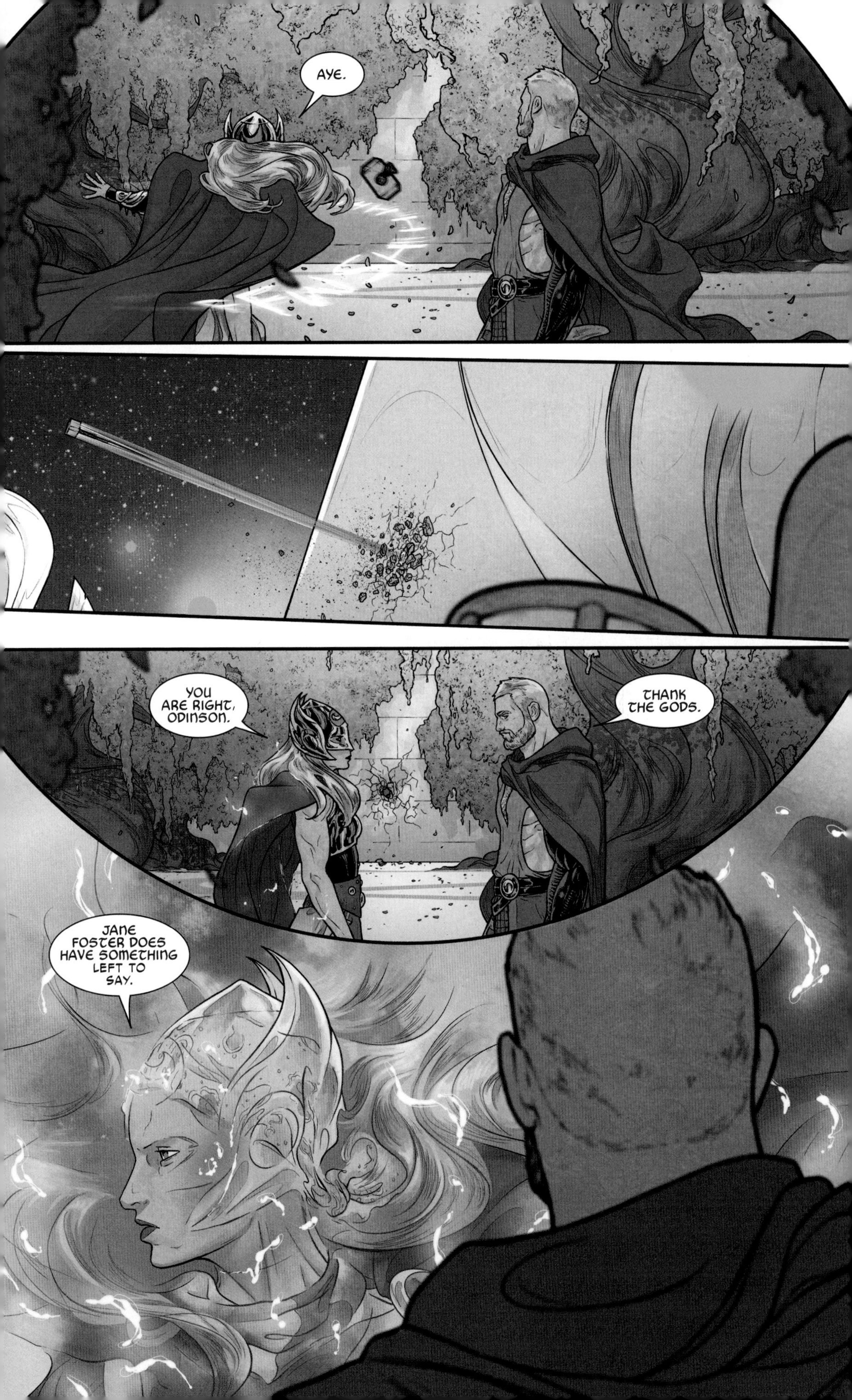
AYE.
YOU ARE RIGHT, ODINSON.
THANK THE GODS.
JANE FOSTER DOES HAVE SOMETHING LEFT TO SAY.

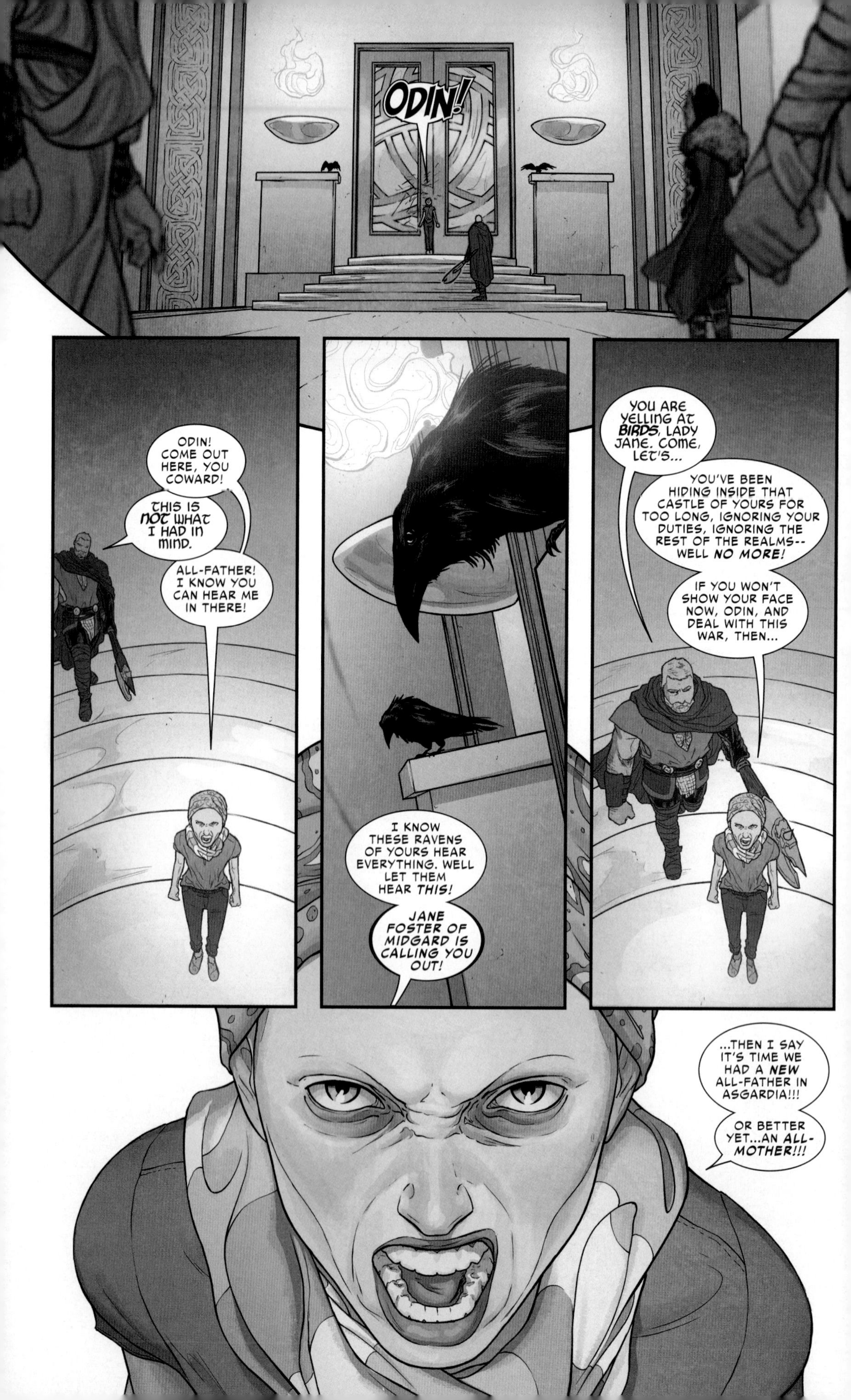

ODIN!
ODIN! COME OUT HERE, YOU COWARD!
THIS IS NOT WHAT I HAD IN MIND.
ALL-FATHER! I KNOW YOU CAN HEAR ME IN THERE!
I KNOW THESE RAVENS OF YOURS HEAR EVERYTHING. WELL LET THEM HEAR THIS!
JANE FOSTER OF MIDGARD IS CALLING YOU OUT!
YOU ARE YELLING AT BIRDS, LADY JANE. COME, LET'S...
YOU'VE BEEN HIDING INSIDE THAT CASTLE OF YOURS FOR TOO LONG, IGNORING YOUR DUTIES, IGNORING THE REST OF THE REALMS-- WELL NO MORE!
IF YOU WON'T SHOW YOUR FACE NOW, ODIN, AND DEAL WITH THIS WAR, THEN...
...THEN I SAY IT'S TIME WE HAD A NEW ALL-FATHER IN ASGARDIA!!!
OR BETTER YET...AN ALL-MOTHER!!!

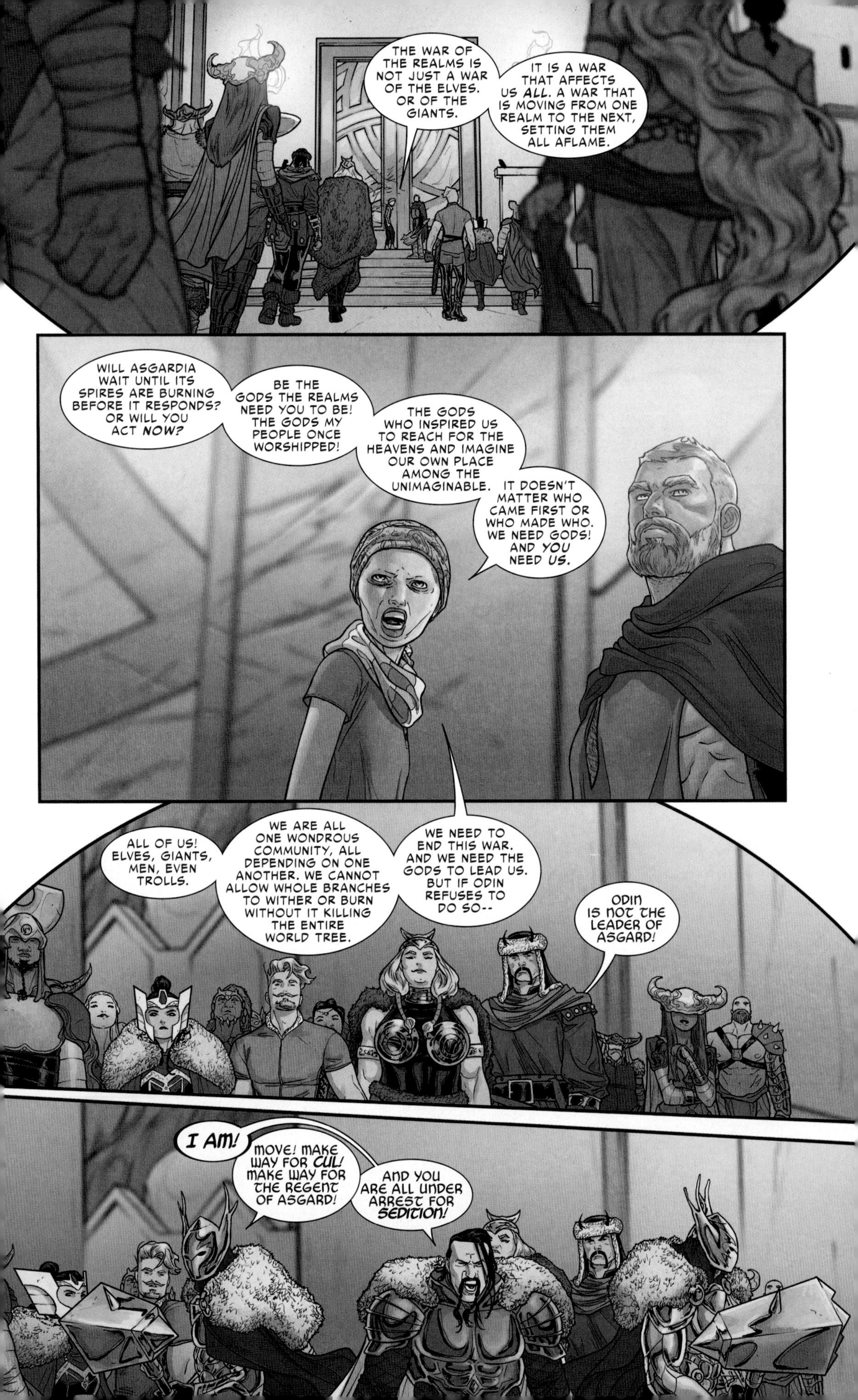
THE WAR OF THE REALMS IS NOT JUST A WAR OF THE ELVES. OR OF THE GIANTS.
IT IS A WAR THAT AFFECTS US ALL. A WAR THAT IS MOVING FROM ONE REALM TO THE NEXT, SETTING THEM ALL AFLAME.
WILL ASGARDIA WAIT UNTIL ITS SPIRES ARE BURNING BEFORE IT RESPONDS? OR WILL YOU ACT NOW?
BE THE GODS THE REALMS NEED YOU TO BE! THE GODS MY PEOPLE ONCE WORSHIPPED!
THE GODS WHO INSPIRED US TO REACH FOR THE HEAVENS AND IMAGINE OUR OWN PLACE AMONG THE UNIMAGINABLE.
IT DOESN'T MATTER WHO CAME FIRST OR WHO MADE WHO. WE NEED GODS! AND YOU NEED US.
ALL OF US! ELVES, GIANTS, MEN, EVEN TROLLS.
WE ARE ALL ONE WONDROUS COMMUNITY, ALL DEPENDING ON ONE ANOTHER. WE CANNOT ALLOW WHOLE BRANCHES TO WITHER OR BURN WITHOUT IT KILLING THE ENTIRE WORLD TREE.
WE NEED TO END THIS WAR. AND WE NEED THE GODS TO LEAD US. BUT IF ODIN REFUSES TO DO SO--
ODIN IS NOT THE LEADER OF ASGARD!
I AM!
MOVE! MAKE WAY FOR CUL! MAKE WAY FOR THE REGENT OF ASGARD!
AND YOU ARE ALL UNDER ARREST FOR SEDITION!

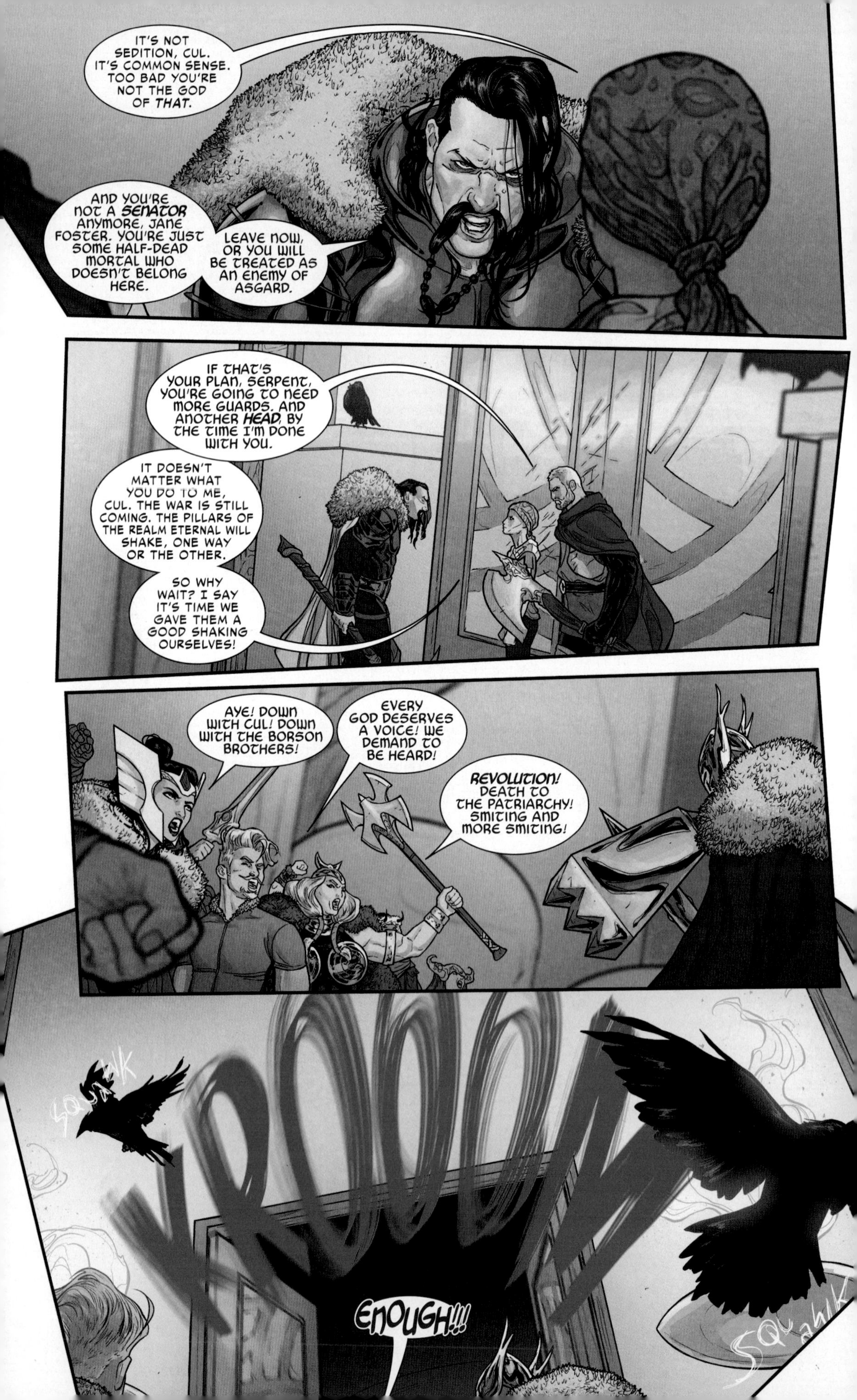

IT'S NOT SEDITION, CUL. IT'S COMMON SENSE. TOO BAD YOU'RE NOT THE GOD OF THAT.
AND YOU'RE NOT A SENATOR ANYMORE, JANE FOSTER. YOU'RE JUST SOME HALF-DEAD MORTAL WHO DOESN'T BELONG HERE.
LEAVE NOW, OR YOU WILL BE TREATED AS AN ENEMY OF ASGARD.
IF THAT'S YOUR PLAN, SERPENT, YOU'RE GOING TO NEED MORE GUARDS. AND ANOTHER HEAD, BY THE TIME I'M DONE WITH YOU.
IT DOESN'T MATTER WHAT YOU DO TO ME, CUL. THE WAR IS STILL COMING. THE PILLARS OF THE REALM ETERNAL WILL SHAKE, ONE WAY OR THE OTHER.
SO WHY WAIT? I SAY IT'S TIME WE GAVE THEM A GOOD SHAKING OURSELVES!
AYE! DOWN WITH CUL! DOWN WITH THE BORSON BROTHERS!
EVERY GOD DESERVES A VOICE! WE DEMAND TO BE HEARD!
REVOLUTION! DEATH TO THE PATRIARCHY! SMITING AND MORE SMITING!
SQUAWK
SQUAWK
ENOUGH!!!

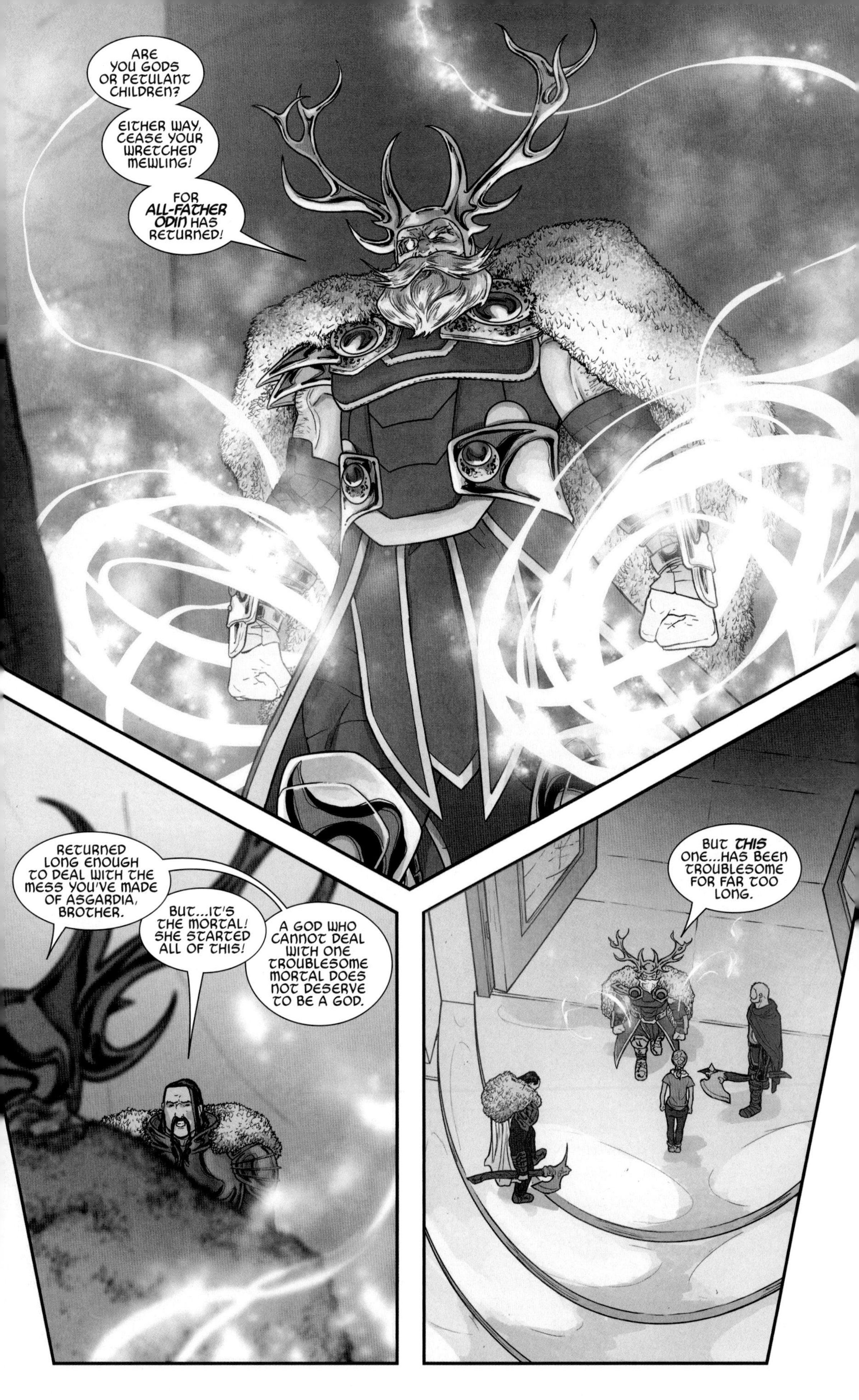
ARE YOU GODS OR PETULANT CHILDREN?
EITHER WAY, CEASE YOUR WRETCHED MEWLING!
FOR ALL-FATHER ODIN HAS RETURNED!
RETURNED LONG ENOUGH TO DEAL WITH THE MESS YOU'VE MADE OF ASGARDIA, BROTHER.
BUT...IT'S THE MORTAL! SHE STARTED ALL OF THIS!
A GOD WHO CANNOT DEAL WITH ONE TROUBLESOME MORTAL DOES NOT DESERVE TO BE A GOD.
BUT THIS ONE...HAS BEEN TROUBLESOME FOR FAR TOO LONG.

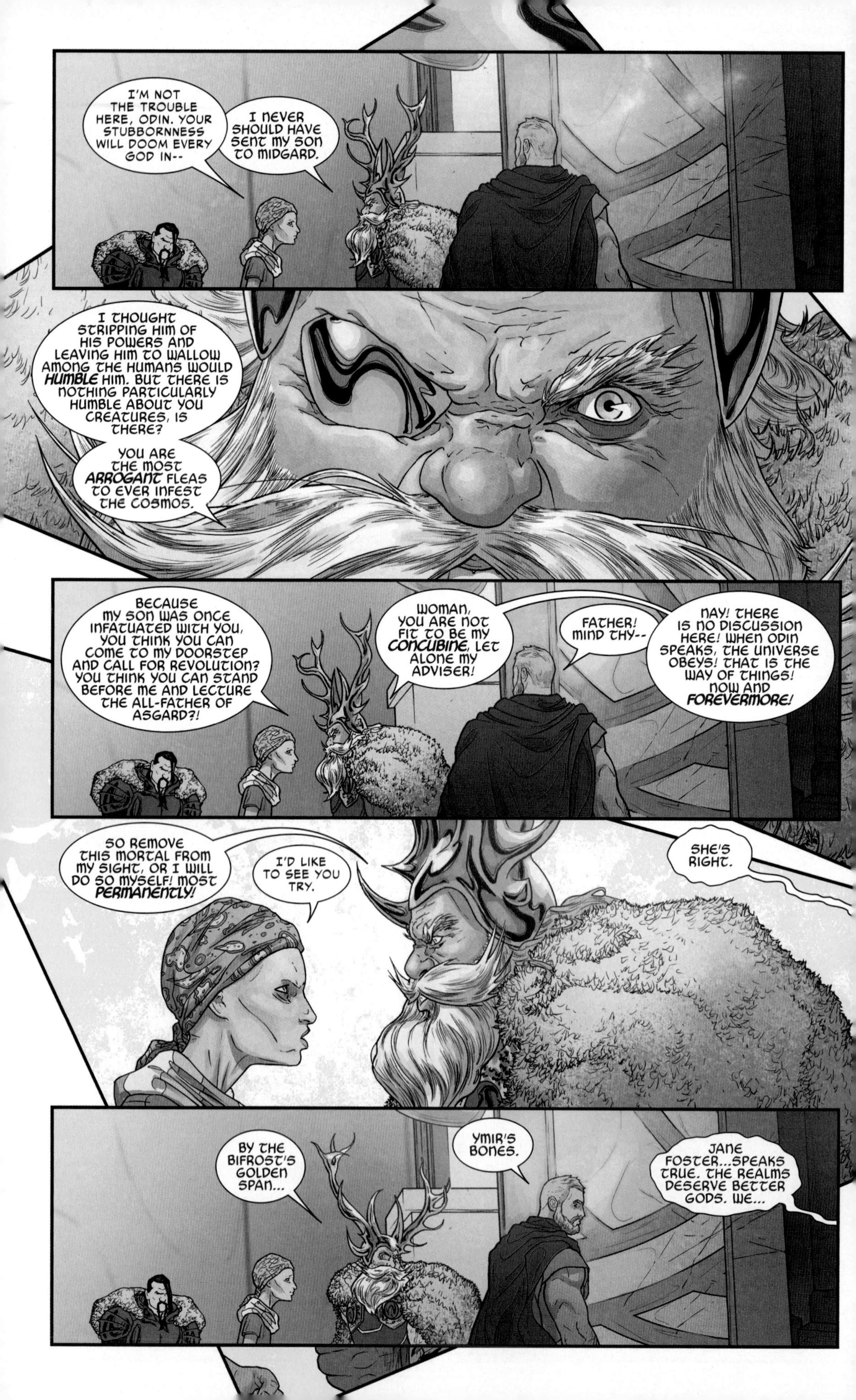
I'M NOT THE TROUBLE HERE, ODIN. YOUR STUBBORNNESS WILL DOOM EVERY GOD IN--
I NEVER SHOULD HAVE SENT MY SON TO MIDGARD.
I THOUGHT STRIPPING HIM OF HIS POWERS AND LEAVING HIM TO WALLOW AMONG THE HUMANS WOULD HUMBLE HIM. BUT THERE IS NOTHING PARTICULARLY HUMBLE ABOUT YOU CREATURES, IS THERE?
YOU ARE THE MOST ARROGANT FLEAS TO EVER INFEST THE COSMOS.
BECAUSE MY SON WAS ONCE INFATUATED WITH YOU, YOU THINK YOU CAN COME TO MY DOORSTEP AND CALL FOR REVOLUTION? YOU THINK YOU CAN STAND BEFORE ME AND LECTURE THE ALL-FATHER OF ASGARD?!
WOMAN, YOU ARE NOT FIT TO BE MY CONCUBINE, LET ALONE MY ADVISER!
FATHER! MIND THY--
NAY! THERE IS NO DISCUSSION HERE! WHEN ODIN SPEAKS, THE UNIVERSE OBEYS! THAT IS THE WAY OF THINGS! NOW AND FOREVERMORE!
SO REMOVE THIS MORTAL FROM MY SIGHT, OR I WILL DO SO MYSELF! MOST PERMANENTLY!
I'D LIKE TO SEE YOU TRY.
SHE'S RIGHT.
BY THE BIFROST'S GOLDEN SPAN...
YMIR'S BONES.
JANE FOSTER...SPEAKS TRUE. THE REALMS DESERVE BETTER GODS. WE...

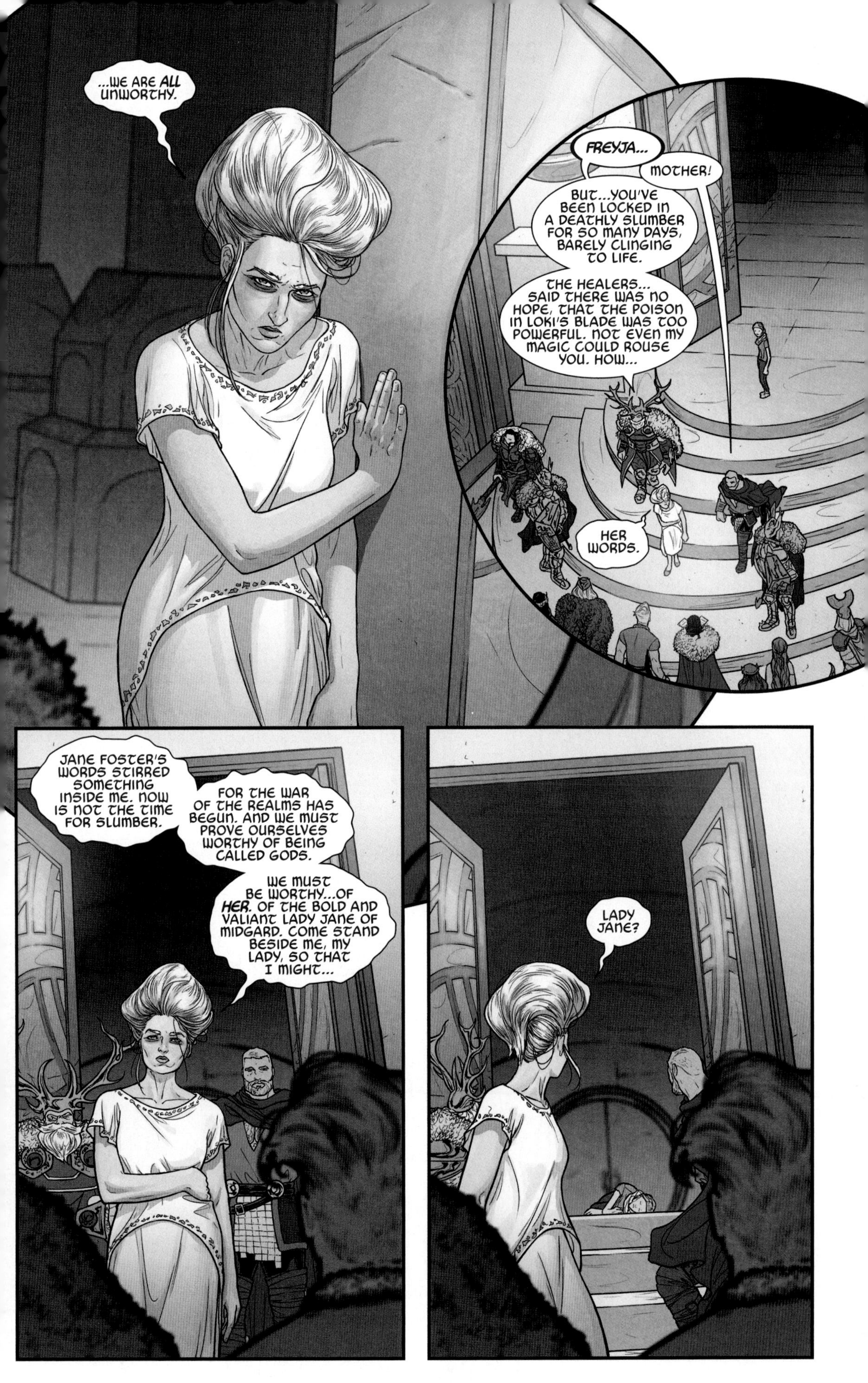

...WE ARE ALL UNWORTHY.
FREYJA...
MOTHER!
BUT...YOU'VE BEEN LOCKED IN A DEATHLY SLUMBER FOR SO MANY DAYS, BARELY CLINGING TO LIFE.
THE HEALERS... SAID THERE WAS NO HOPE, THAT THE POISON IN LOKI'S BLADE WAS TOO POWERFUL. NOT EVEN MY MAGIC COULD ROUSE YOU. HOW...
HER WORDS.
JANE FOSTER'S WORDS STIRRED SOMETHING INSIDE ME. NOW IS NOT THE TIME FOR SLUMBER.
FOR THE WAR OF THE REALMS HAS BEGUN. AND WE MUST PROVE OURSELVES WORTHY OF BEING CALLED GODS.
WE MUST BE WORTHY...OF HER. OF THE BOLD AND VALIANT LADY JANE OF MIDGARD. COME STAND BESIDE ME, MY LADY, SO THAT I MIGHT...
LADY JANE?

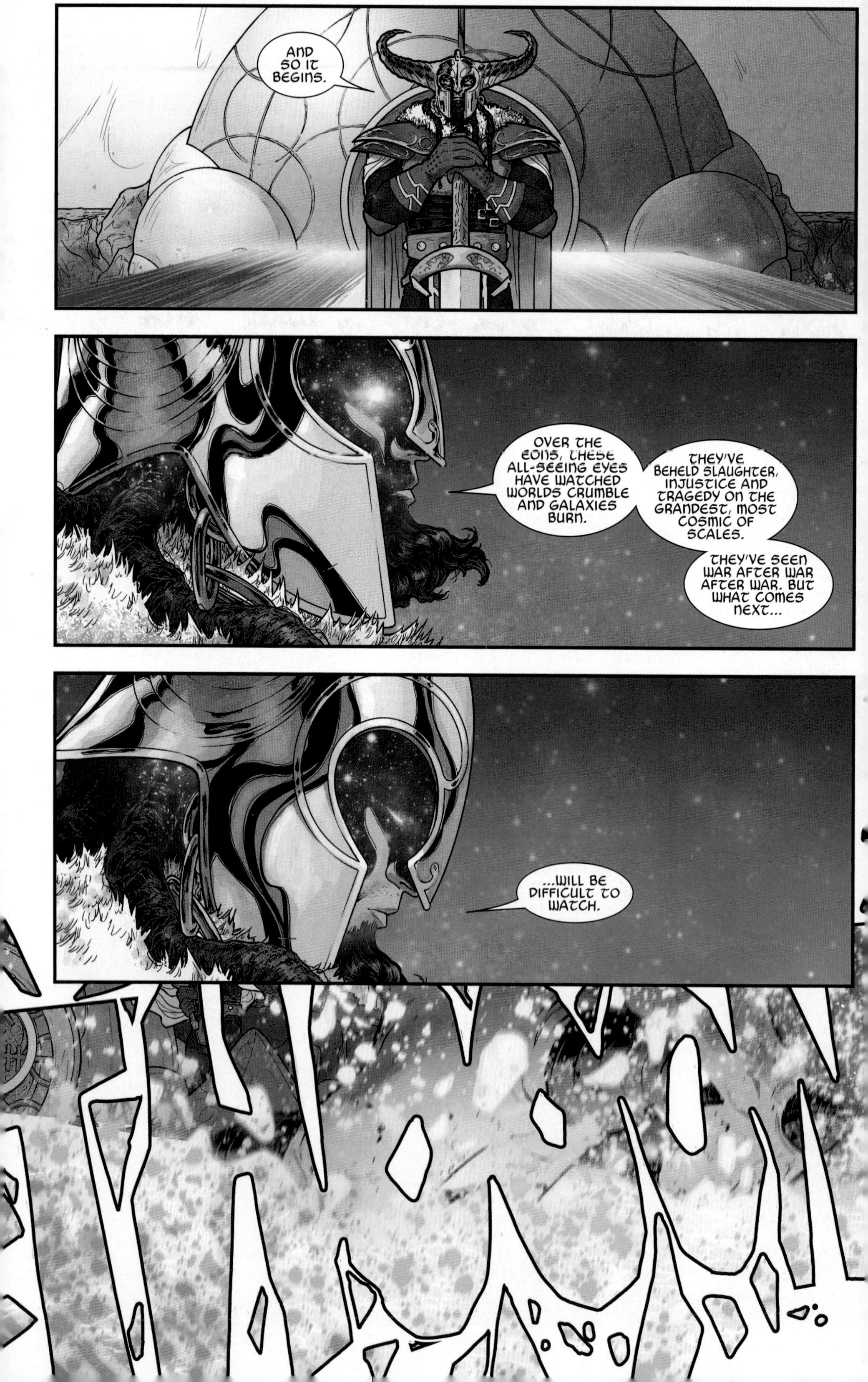
AND SO IT BEGINS.
OVER THE EONS, THESE ALL-SEEING EYES HAVE WATCHED WORLDS CRUMBLE AND GALAXIES BURN.
THEY'VE BEHELD SLAUGHTER, INJUSTICE AND TRAGEDY ON THE GRANDEST, MOST COSMIC OF SCALES.
THEY'VE SEEN WAR AFTER WAR AFTER WAR. BUT WHAT COMES NEXT...
...WILL BE DIFFICULT TO WATCH.

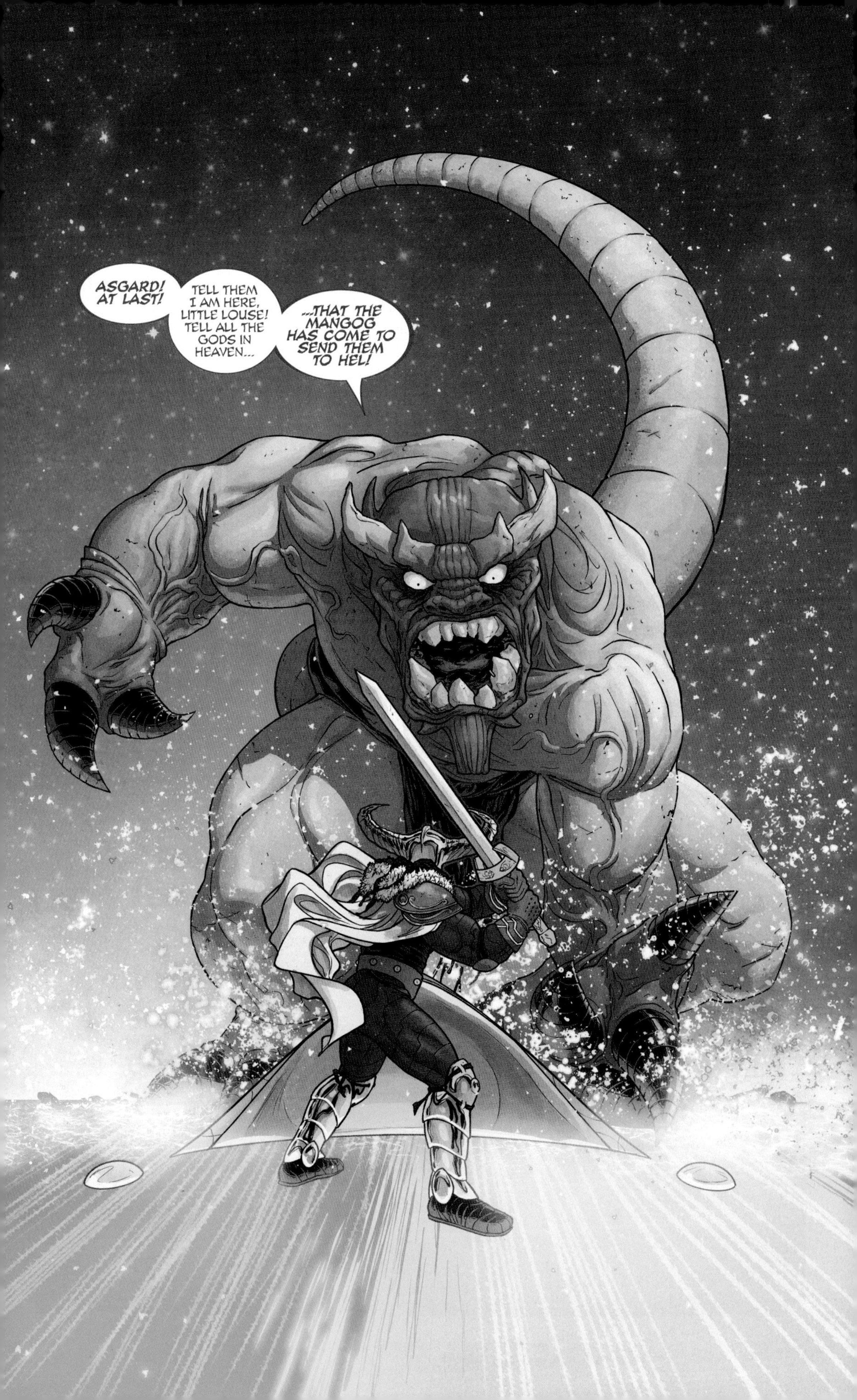
ASGARD! AT LAST!
TELL THEM I AM HERE, LITTLE LOUSE! TELL ALL THE GODS IN HEAVEN...
...THAT THE MANGOG HAS COME TO SEND THEM TO HEL!

# 703

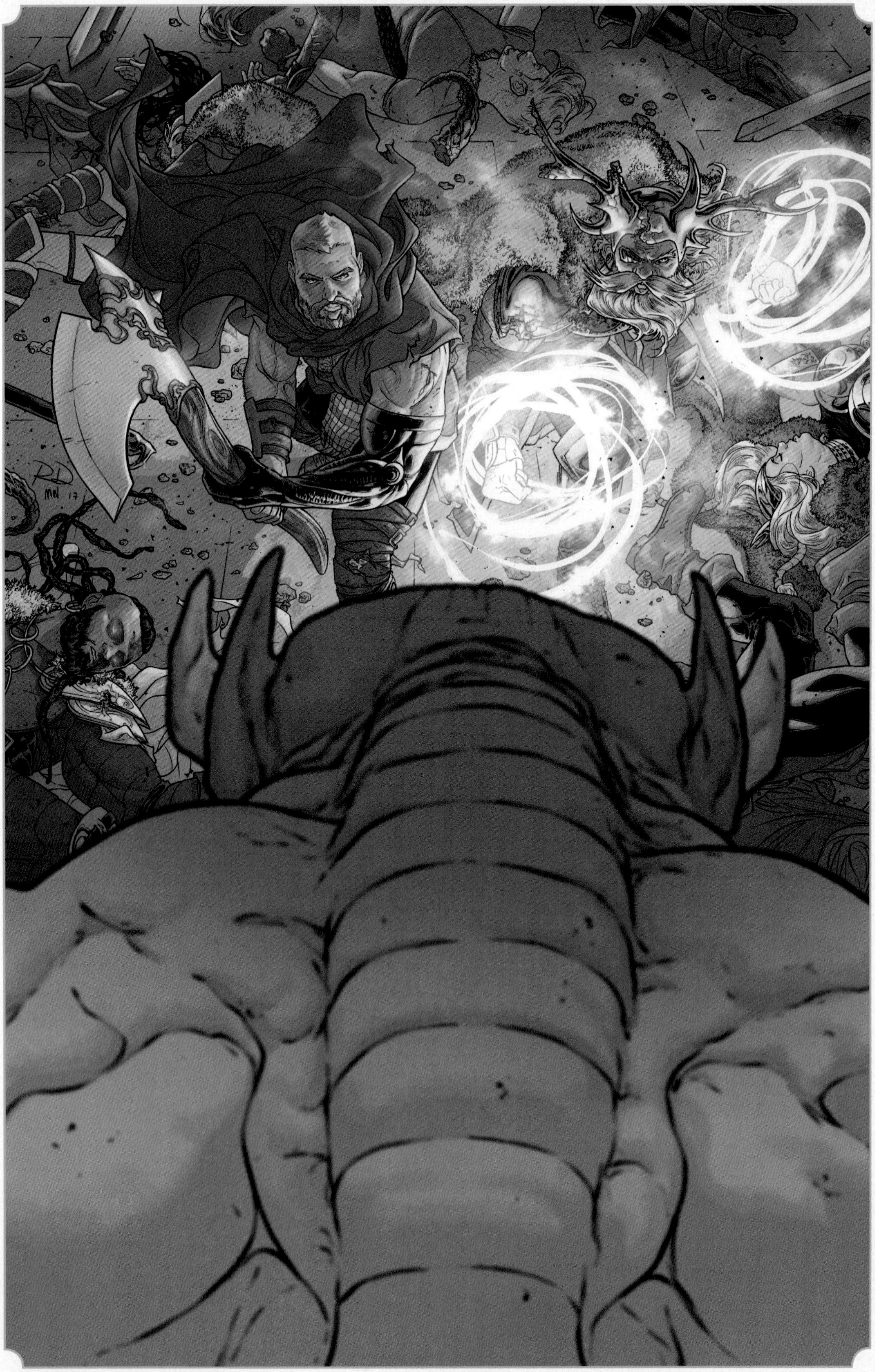

THE FALL OF ASGARD

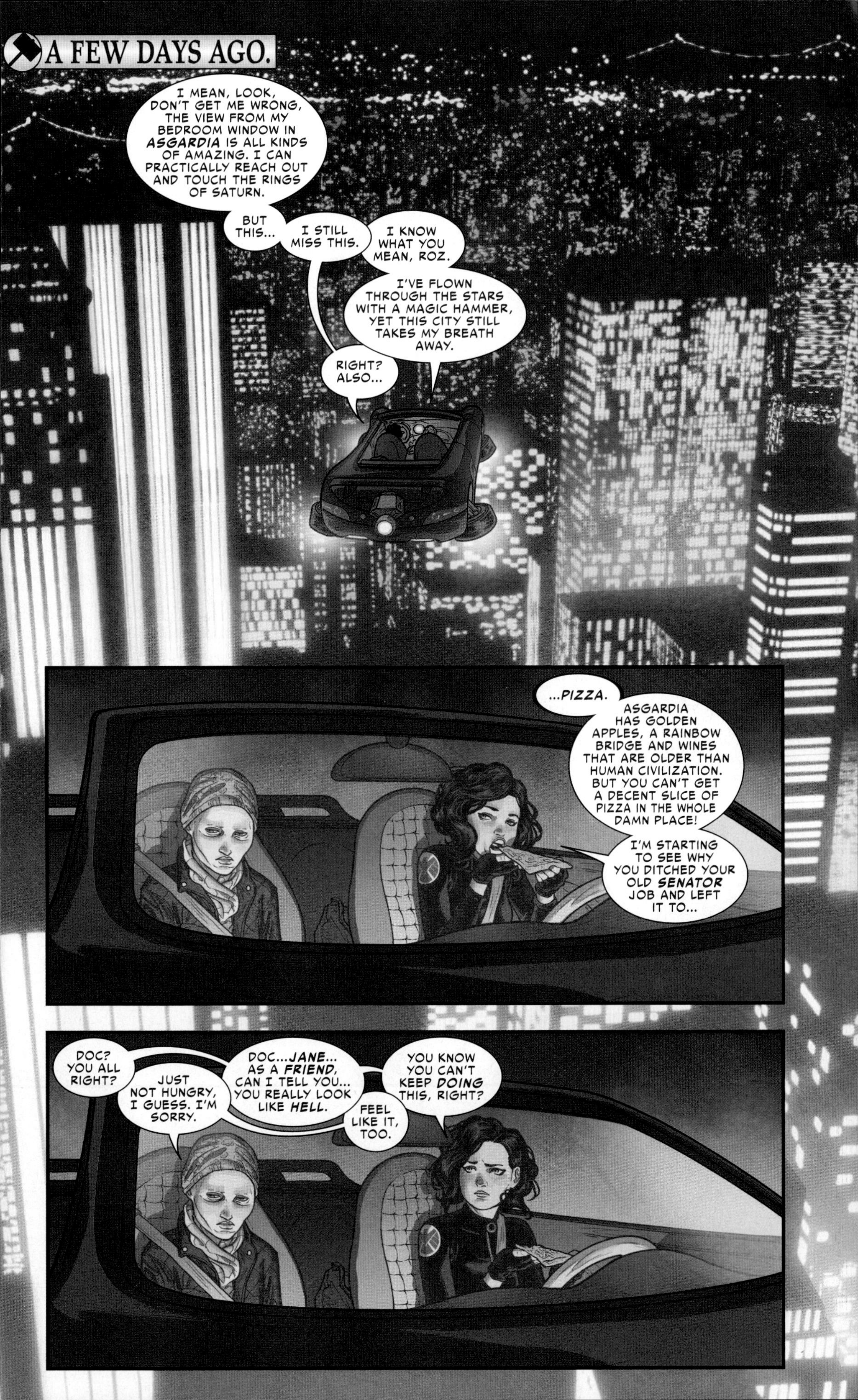
A FEW DAYS AGO.
I MEAN, LOOK, DON'T GET ME WRONG, THE VIEW FROM MY BEDROOM WINDOW IN ASGARDIA IS ALL KINDS OF AMAZING. I CAN PRACTICALLY REACH OUT AND TOUCH THE RINGS OF SATURN.
BUT THIS...
I STILL MISS THIS.
I KNOW WHAT YOU MEAN, ROZ.
I'VE FLOWN THROUGH THE STARS WITH A MAGIC HAMMER, YET THIS CITY STILL TAKES MY BREATH AWAY.
RIGHT? ALSO...
...PIZZA.
ASGARDIA HAS GOLDEN APPLES, A RAINBOW BRIDGE AND WINES THAT ARE OLDER THAN HUMAN CIVILIZATION. BUT YOU CAN'T GET A DECENT SLICE OF PIZZA IN THE WHOLE DAMN PLACE!
I'M STARTING TO SEE WHY YOU DITCHED YOUR OLD SENATOR JOB AND LEFT IT TO...
DOC? YOU ALL RIGHT?
JUST NOT HUNGRY, I GUESS. I'M SORRY.
DOC...JANE... AS A FRIEND, CAN I TELL YOU... YOU REALLY LOOK LIKE HELL.
FEEL LIKE IT, TOO.
YOU KNOW YOU CAN'T KEEP DOING THIS, RIGHT?

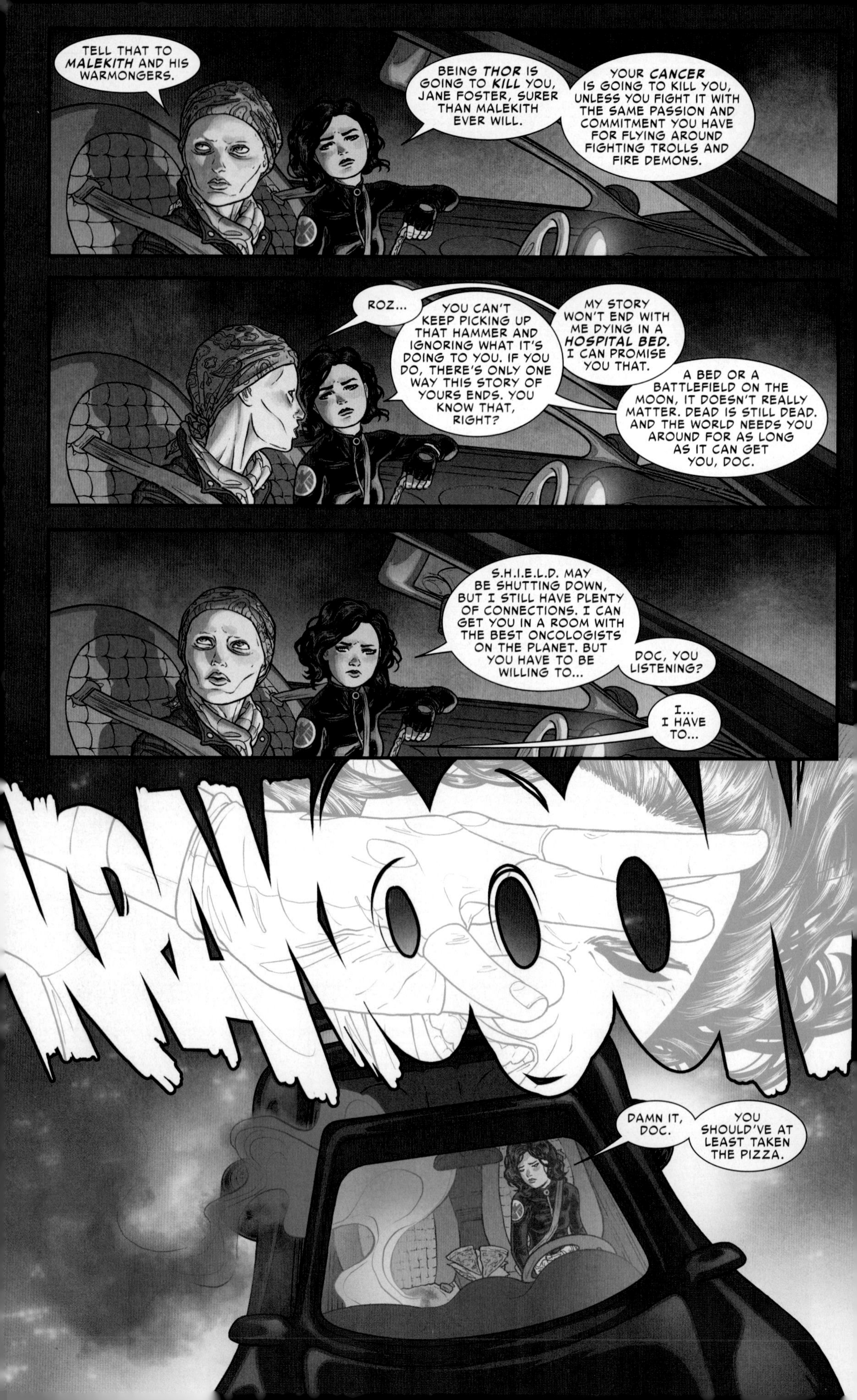
TELL THAT TO MALEKITH AND HIS WARMONGERS.
BEING THOR IS GOING TO KILL YOU, JANE FOSTER, SURER THAN MALEKITH EVER WILL.
YOUR CANCER IS GOING TO KILL YOU, UNLESS YOU FIGHT IT WITH THE SAME PASSION AND COMMITMENT YOU HAVE FOR FLYING AROUND FIGHTING TROLLS AND FIRE DEMONS.
ROZ...
YOU CAN'T KEEP PICKING UP THAT HAMMER AND IGNORING WHAT IT'S DOING TO YOU. IF YOU DO, THERE'S ONLY ONE WAY THIS STORY OF YOURS ENDS. YOU KNOW THAT, RIGHT?
MY STORY WON'T END WITH ME DYING IN A HOSPITAL BED. I CAN PROMISE YOU THAT.
A BED OR A BATTLEFIELD ON THE MOON, IT DOESN'T REALLY MATTER. DEAD IS STILL DEAD. AND THE WORLD NEEDS YOU AROUND FOR AS LONG AS IT CAN GET YOU, DOC.
S.H.I.E.L.D. MAY BE SHUTTING DOWN, BUT I STILL HAVE PLENTY OF CONNECTIONS. I CAN GET YOU IN A ROOM WITH THE BEST ONCOLOGISTS ON THE PLANET. BUT YOU HAVE TO BE WILLING TO...
DOC, YOU LISTENING?
I... I HAVE TO...
DAMN IT, DOC.
YOU SHOULD'VE AT LEAST TAKEN THE PIZZA.

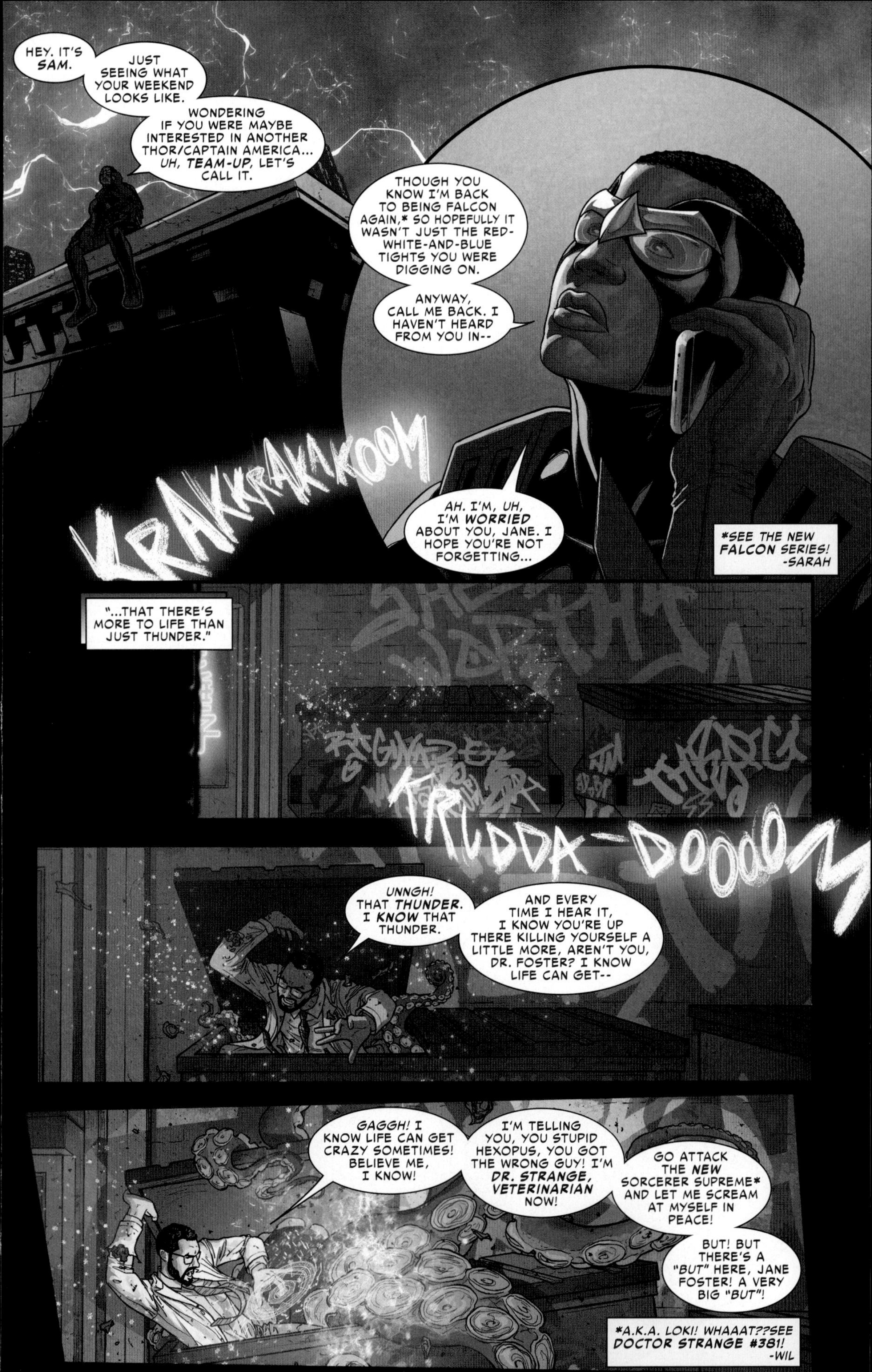

HEY. IT'S SAM.
JUST SEEING WHAT YOUR WEEKEND LOOKS LIKE.
WONDERING IF YOU WERE MAYBE INTERESTED IN ANOTHER THOR/CAPTAIN AMERICA... UH, TEAM-UP, LET'S CALL IT.
THOUGH YOU KNOW I'M BACK TO BEING FALCON AGAIN,* SO HOPEFULLY IT WASN'T JUST THE RED-WHITE-AND-BLUE TIGHTS YOU WERE DIGGING ON.
ANYWAY, CALL ME BACK. I HAVEN'T HEARD FROM YOU IN--
KRAKKRAKAKOOM
AH. I'M, UH, I'M WORRIED ABOUT YOU, JANE. I HOPE YOU'RE NOT FORGETTING...
*SEE THE NEW FALCON SERIES! -SARAH
"...THAT THERE'S MORE TO LIFE THAN JUST THUNDER."
KRUDDA-DOOOOM
UNNGH! THAT THUNDER. I KNOW THAT THUNDER.
AND EVERY TIME I HEAR IT, I KNOW YOU'RE UP THERE KILLING YOURSELF A LITTLE MORE, AREN'T YOU, DR. FOSTER? I KNOW LIFE CAN GET--
GAGGH! I KNOW LIFE CAN GET CRAZY SOMETIMES! BELIEVE ME, I KNOW!
I'M TELLING YOU, YOU STUPID HEXOPUS, YOU GOT THE WRONG GUY! I'M DR. STRANGE, VETERINARIAN NOW!
GO ATTACK THE NEW SORCERER SUPREME* AND LET ME SCREAM AT MYSELF IN PEACE!
BUT! BUT THERE'S A "BUT" HERE, JANE FOSTER! A VERY BIG "BUT"!
*A.K.A. LOKI! WHAAAT??SEE DOCTOR STRANGE #381! -WIL

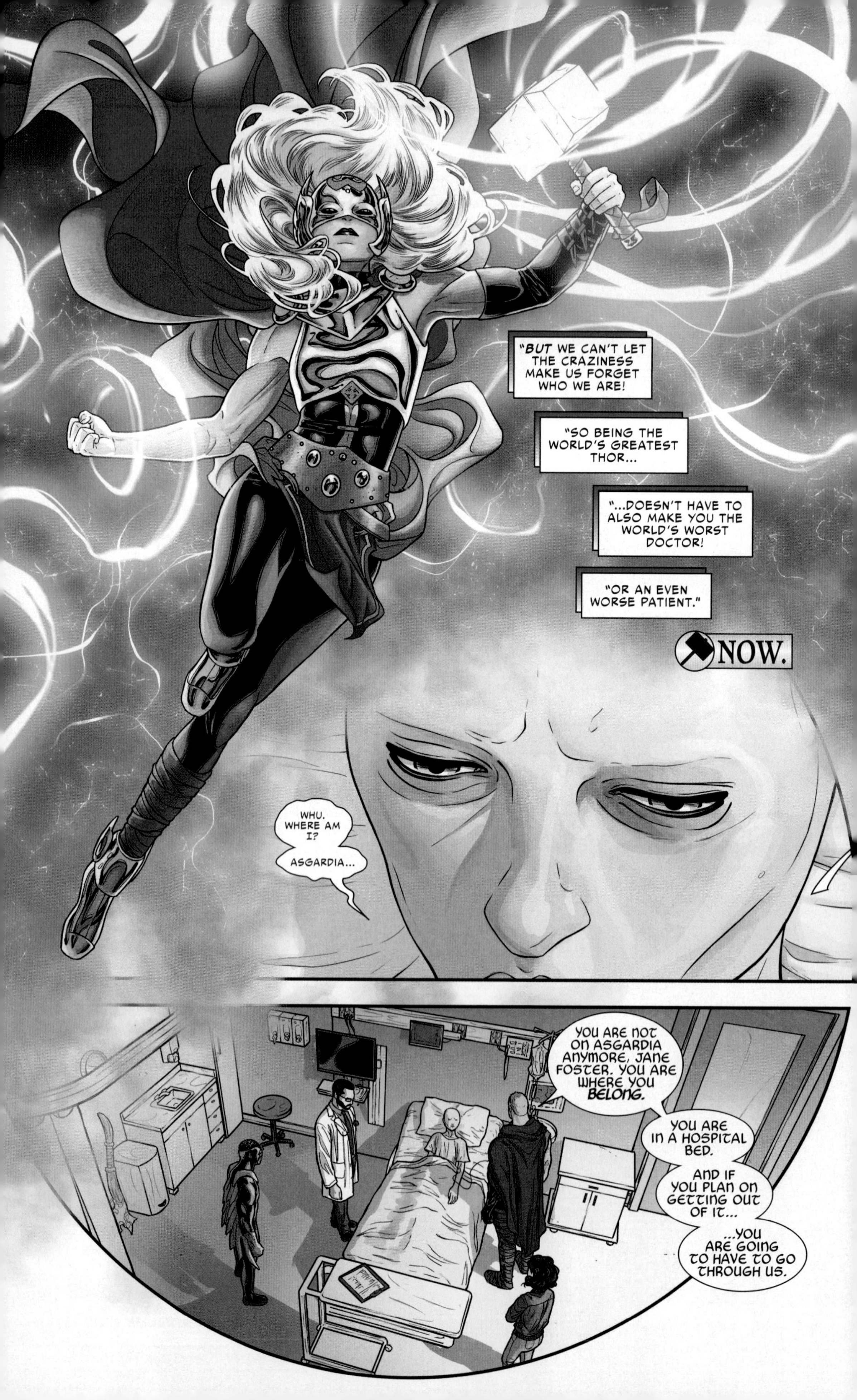
"BUT WE CAN'T LET THE CRAZINESS MAKE US FORGET WHO WE ARE!
"SO BEING THE WORLD'S GREATEST THOR...
"...DOESN'T HAVE TO ALSO MAKE YOU THE WORLD'S WORST DOCTOR!
"OR AN EVEN WORSE PATIENT."
NOW.
WHU. WHERE AM I?
ASGARDIA...
YOU ARE NOT ON ASGARDIA ANYMORE, JANE FOSTER. YOU ARE WHERE YOU BELONG.
YOU ARE IN A HOSPITAL BED.
AND IF YOU PLAN ON GETTING OUT OF IT...
...YOU ARE GOING TO HAVE TO GO THROUGH US.

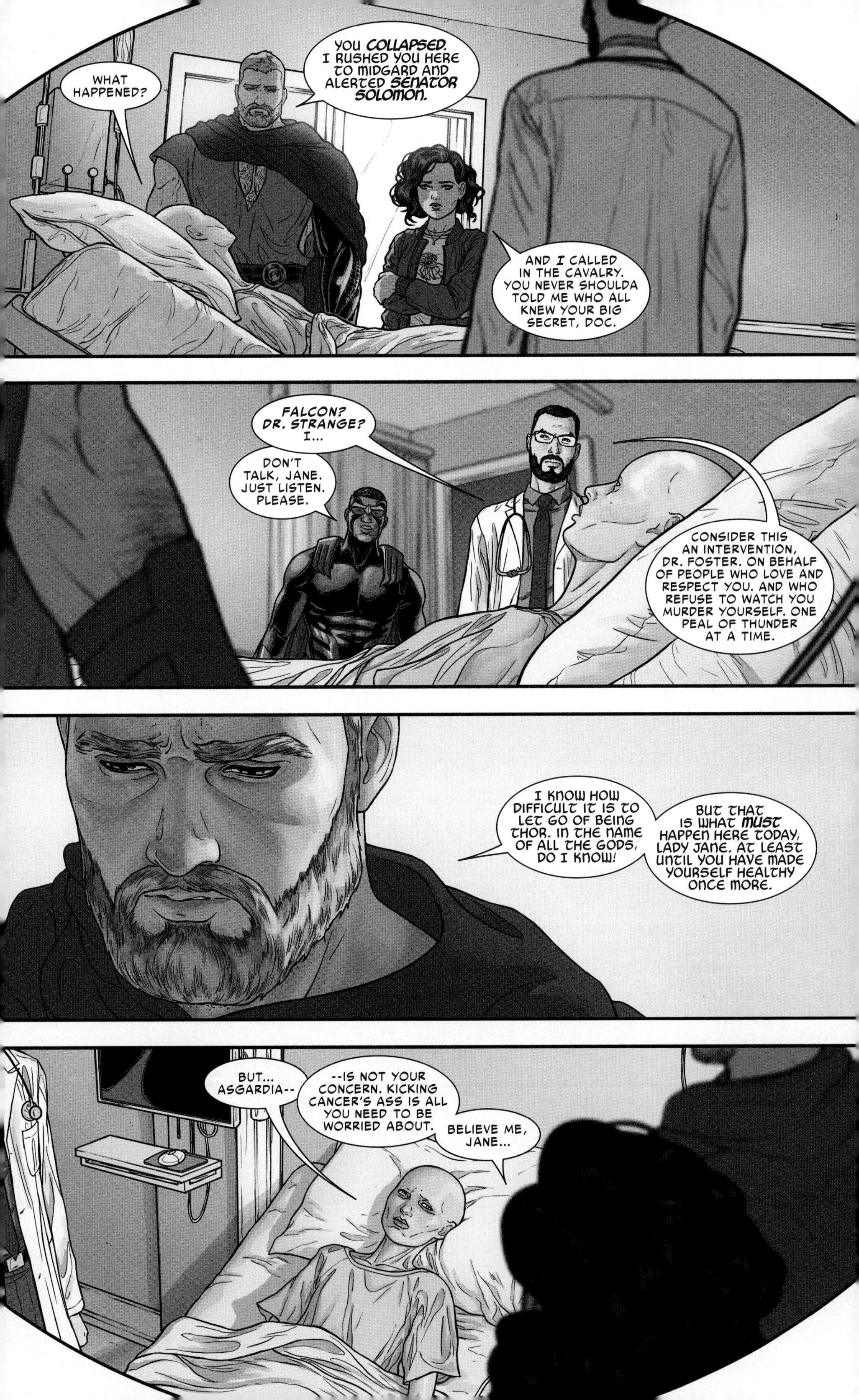
WHAT HAPPENED?
YOU COLLAPSED. I RUSHED YOU HERE TO MIDGARD AND ALERTED SENATOR SOLOMON.
AND I CALLED IN THE CAVALRY. YOU NEVER SHOULDA TOLD ME WHO ALL KNEW YOUR BIG SECRET, DOC.
FALCON? DR. STRANGE? I...
DON'T TALK, JANE. JUST LISTEN. PLEASE.
CONSIDER THIS AN INTERVENTION, DR. FOSTER. ON BEHALF OF PEOPLE WHO LOVE AND RESPECT YOU. AND WHO REFUSE TO WATCH YOU MURDER YOURSELF. ONE PEAL OF THUNDER AT A TIME.
I KNOW HOW DIFFICULT IT IS TO LET GO OF BEING THOR. IN THE NAME OF ALL THE GODS, DO I KNOW!
BUT THAT IS WHAT MUST HAPPEN HERE TODAY, LADY JANE. AT LEAST UNTIL YOU HAVE MADE YOURSELF HEALTHY ONCE MORE.
BUT... ASGARDIA--
--IS NOT YOUR CONCERN. KICKING CANCER'S ASS IS ALL YOU NEED TO BE WORRIED ABOUT.
BELIEVE ME, JANE...

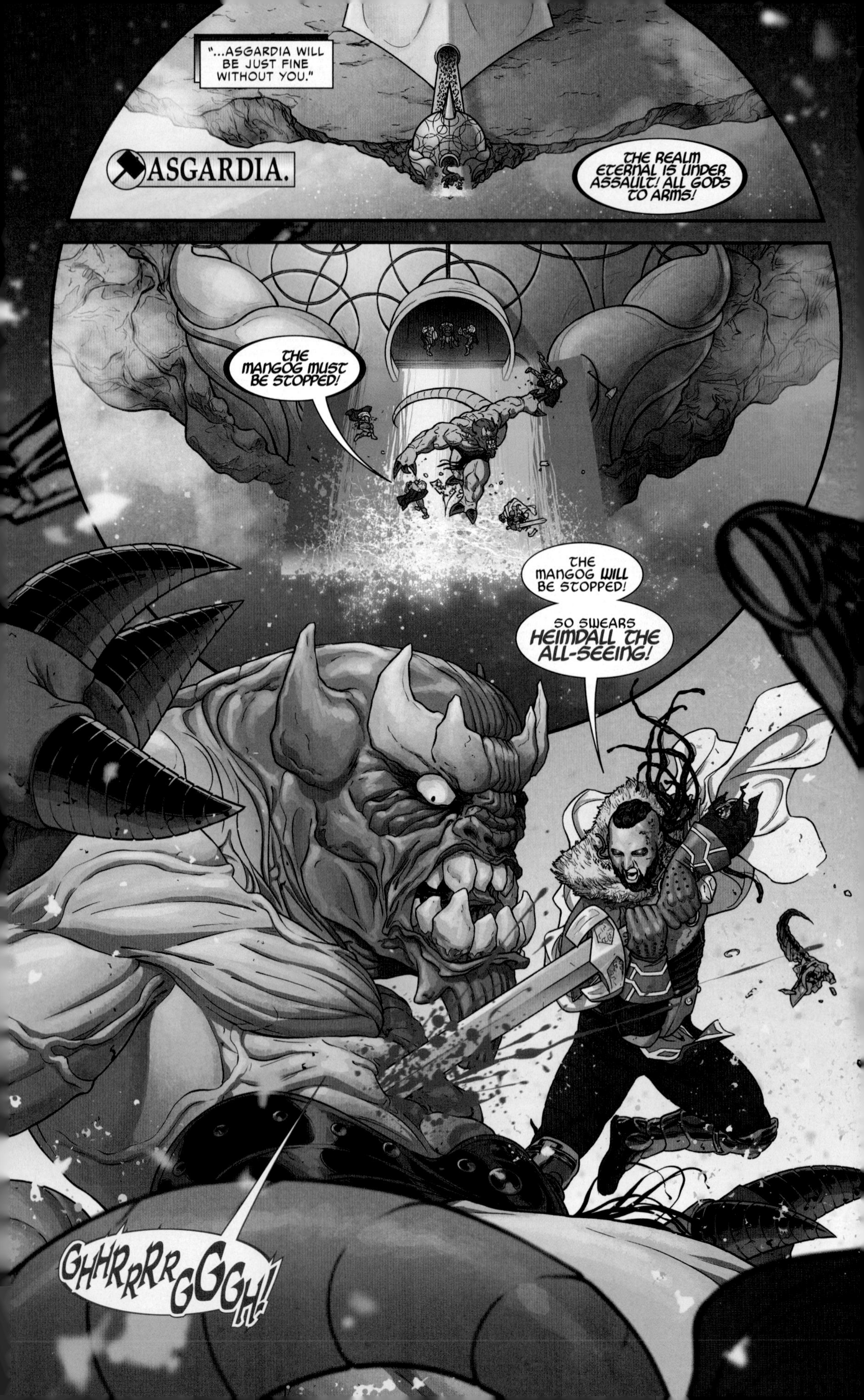
"...ASGARDIA WILL BE JUST FINE WITHOUT YOU."
ASGARDIA.
THE REALM ETERNAL IS UNDER ASSAULT! ALL GODS TO ARMS!
THE MANGOG MUST BE STOPPED!
THE MANGOG WILL BE STOPPED!
SO SWEARS HEIMDALL THE ALL-SEEING!
GHHRRRRGGGH!

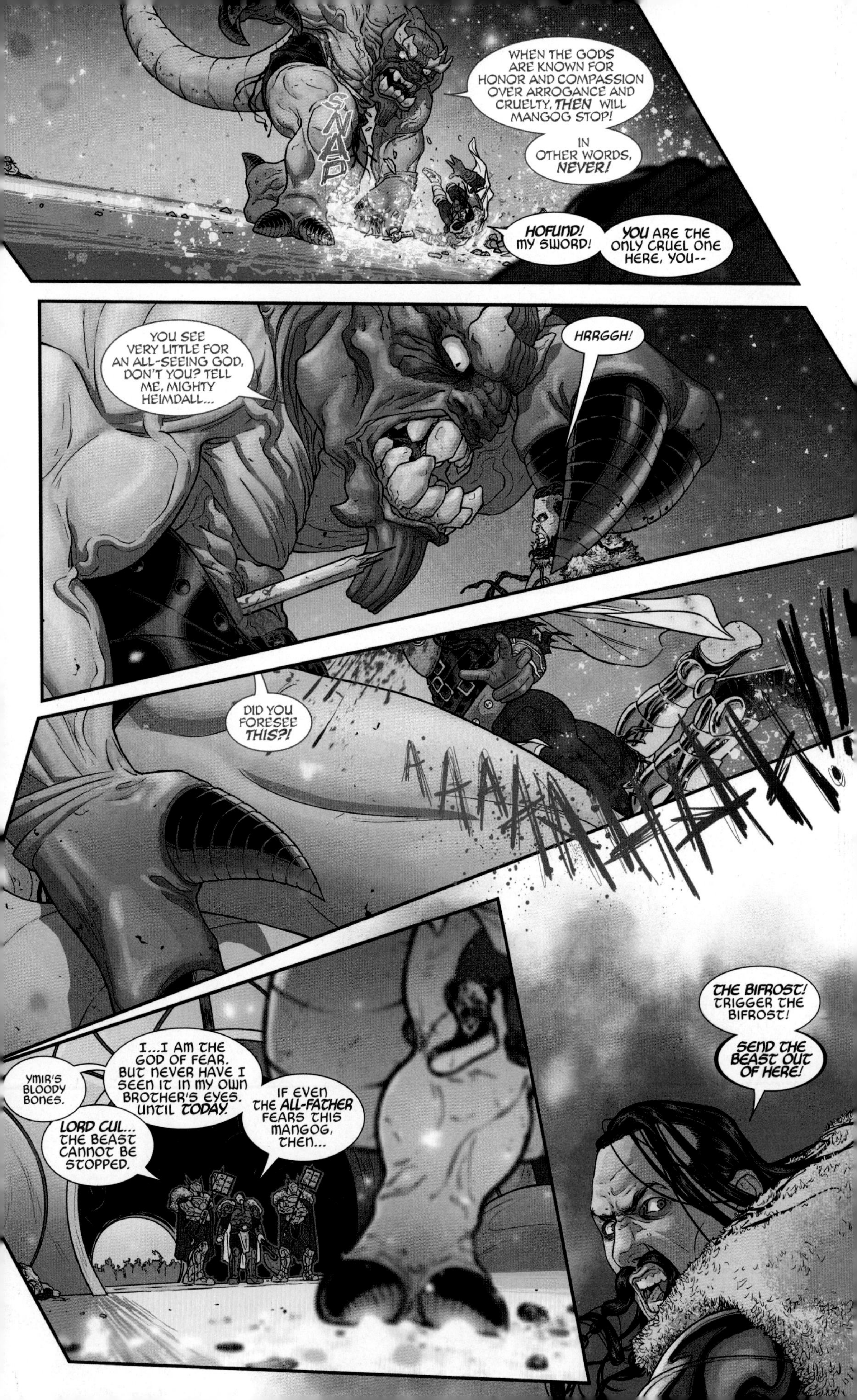
WHEN THE GODS ARE KNOWN FOR HONOR AND COMPASSION OVER ARROGANCE AND CRUELTY, THEN WILL MANGOG STOP!
IN OTHER WORDS, NEVER!
SNAP
HOFUND! MY SWORD!
YOU ARE THE ONLY CRUEL ONE HERE, YOU--
YOU SEE VERY LITTLE FOR AN ALL-SEEING GOD, DON'T YOU? TELL ME, MIGHTY HEIMDALL...
HRRGGH!
DID YOU FORESEE THIS?!
AAAAAHHHH!!
YMIR'S BLOODY BONES.
I...I AM THE GOD OF FEAR. BUT NEVER HAVE I SEEN IT IN MY OWN BROTHER'S EYES. UNTIL TODAY.
LORD CUL... THE BEAST CANNOT BE STOPPED.
IF EVEN THE ALL-FATHER FEARS THIS MANGOG, THEN...
THE BIFROST! TRIGGER THE BIFROST!
SEND THE BEAST OUT OF HERE!

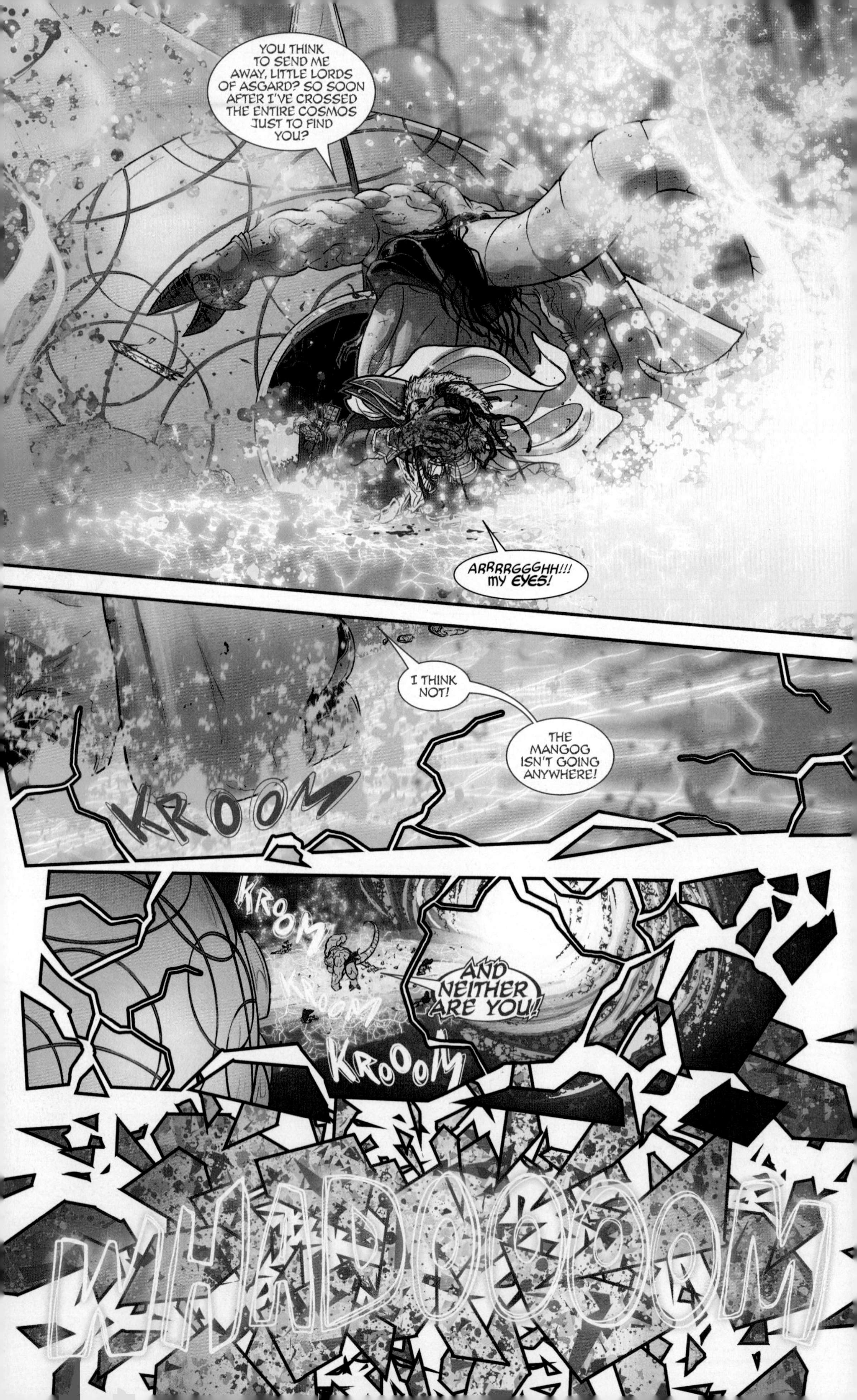
YOU THINK TO SEND ME AWAY, LITTLE LORDS OF ASGARD? SO SOON AFTER I'VE CROSSED THE ENTIRE COSMOS JUST TO FIND YOU?
ARRRRGGGHH!!! MY EYES!
I THINK NOT!
THE MANGOG ISN'T GOING ANYWHERE!
KROOM
KROOM
KROOM
AND NEITHER ARE YOU!
KROOOM
WHADOOOOM

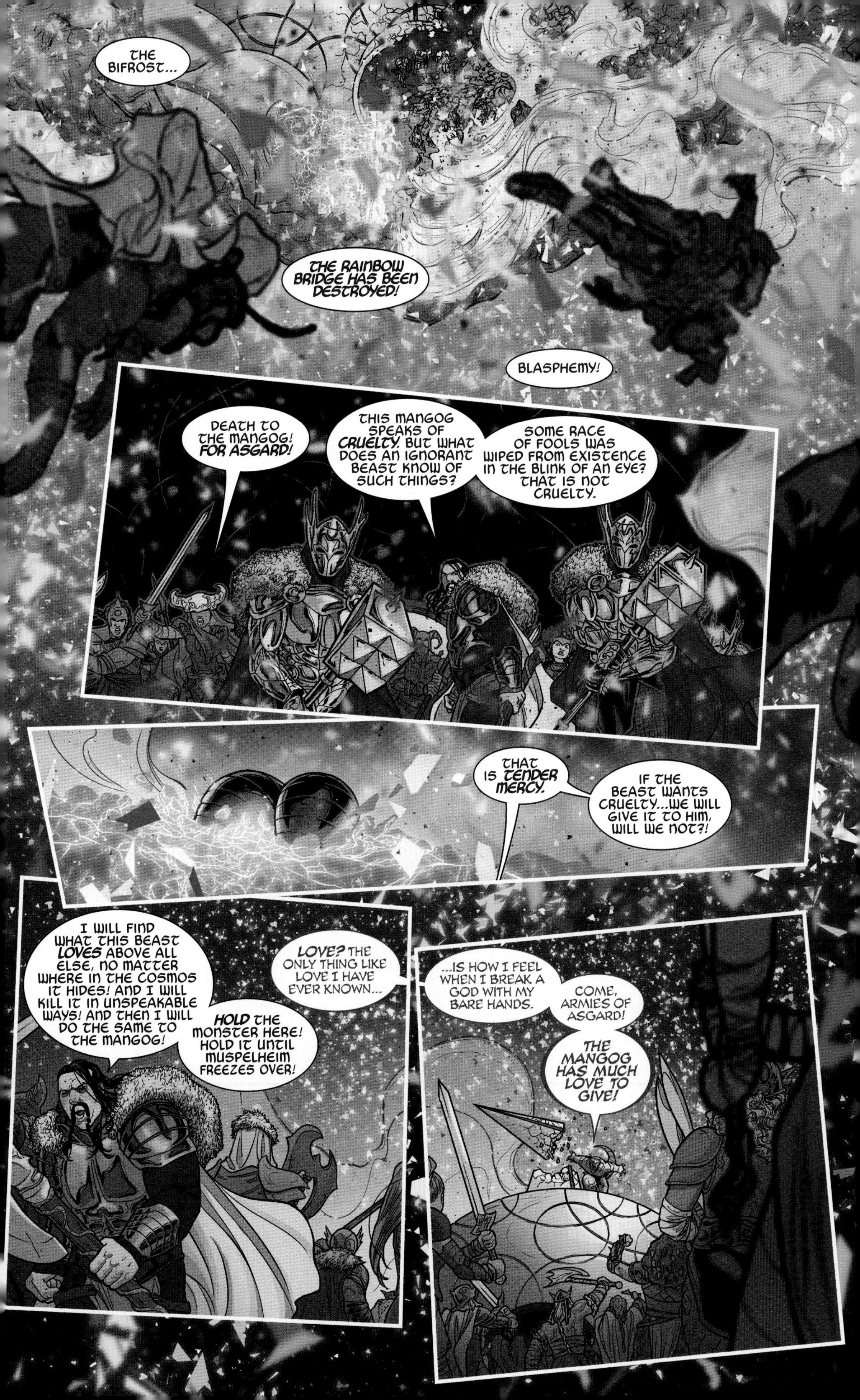
THE BIFROST...
THE RAINBOW BRIDGE HAS BEEN DESTROYED!
BLASPHEMY!
DEATH TO THE MANGOG! FOR ASGARD!
THIS MANGOG SPEAKS OF CRUELTY. BUT WHAT DOES AN IGNORANT BEAST KNOW OF SUCH THINGS?
SOME RACE OF FOOLS WAS WIPED FROM EXISTENCE IN THE BLINK OF AN EYE? THAT IS NOT CRUELTY.
THAT IS TENDER MERCY.
IF THE BEAST WANTS CRUELTY...WE WILL GIVE IT TO HIM, WILL WE NOT?!
I WILL FIND WHAT THIS BEAST LOVES ABOVE ALL ELSE, NO MATTER WHERE IN THE COSMOS IT HIDES! AND I WILL KILL IT IN UNSPEAKABLE WAYS! AND THEN I WILL DO THE SAME TO THE MANGOG!
HOLD THE MONSTER HERE! HOLD IT UNTIL MUSPELHEIM FREEZES OVER!
LOVE? THE ONLY THING LIKE LOVE I HAVE EVER KNOWN...
...IS HOW I FEEL WHEN I BREAK A GOD WITH MY BARE HANDS.
COME, ARMIES OF ASGARD!
THE MANGOG HAS MUCH LOVE TO GIVE!

THANK YOU FOR ALLOWING ME TO EXAMINE YOU LIKE THIS, DOCTOR.

LIKE I SAID, JUST DON'T GO TRYING ANY MAGICAL CURES.

I UNDERSTAND.

ARE YOU SURE YOU WOULDN'T LIKE THE REST OF US TO LEAVE THE ROOM?

NO, LET'S JUST GET THIS OVER WITH. TELL ME WHAT I ALREADY KNOW, DR. STRANGE.

WELL, I WAS NO ONCOLOGIST IN MY PREVIOUS DAY JOB, BUT I KNOW BETTER THAN ANYONE THE EFFECT *MYSTICAL FORCES* CAN HAVE ON THE BODY.

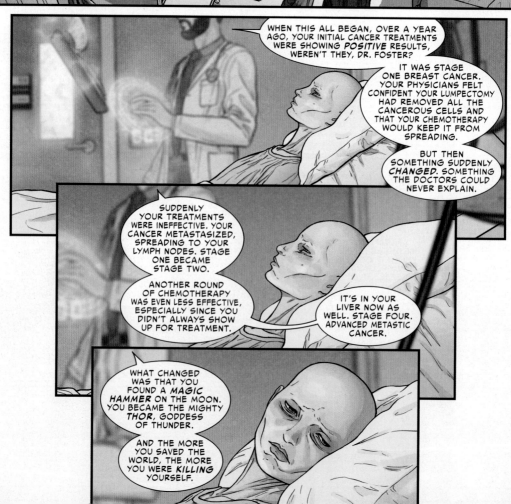

WHEN THIS ALL BEGAN, OVER A YEAR AGO, YOUR INITIAL CANCER TREATMENTS WERE SHOWING *POSITIVE* RESULTS, WEREN'T THEY, DR. FOSTER?

IT WAS STAGE ONE BREAST CANCER. YOUR PHYSICIANS FELT CONFIDENT YOUR LUMPECTOMY HAD REMOVED ALL THE CANCEROUS CELLS AND THAT YOUR CHEMOTHERAPY WOULD KEEP IT FROM SPREADING.

BUT THEN SOMETHING SUDDENLY *CHANGED.* SOMETHING THE DOCTORS COULD NEVER EXPLAIN.

SUDDENLY YOUR TREATMENTS WERE INEFFECTIVE. YOUR CANCER METASTASIZED, SPREADING TO YOUR LYMPH NODES. STAGE ONE BECAME STAGE TWO.

ANOTHER ROUND OF CHEMOTHERAPY WAS EVEN LESS EFFECTIVE, ESPECIALLY SINCE YOU DIDN'T ALWAYS SHOW UP FOR TREATMENT.

IT'S IN YOUR LIVER NOW AS WELL. STAGE FOUR. ADVANCED METASTIC CANCER.

WHAT CHANGED WAS THAT YOU FOUND A *MAGIC HAMMER* ON THE MOON. YOU BECAME THE MIGHTY *THOR,* GODDESS OF THUNDER.

AND THE MORE YOU SAVED THE WORLD, THE MORE YOU WERE *KILLING* YOURSELF.

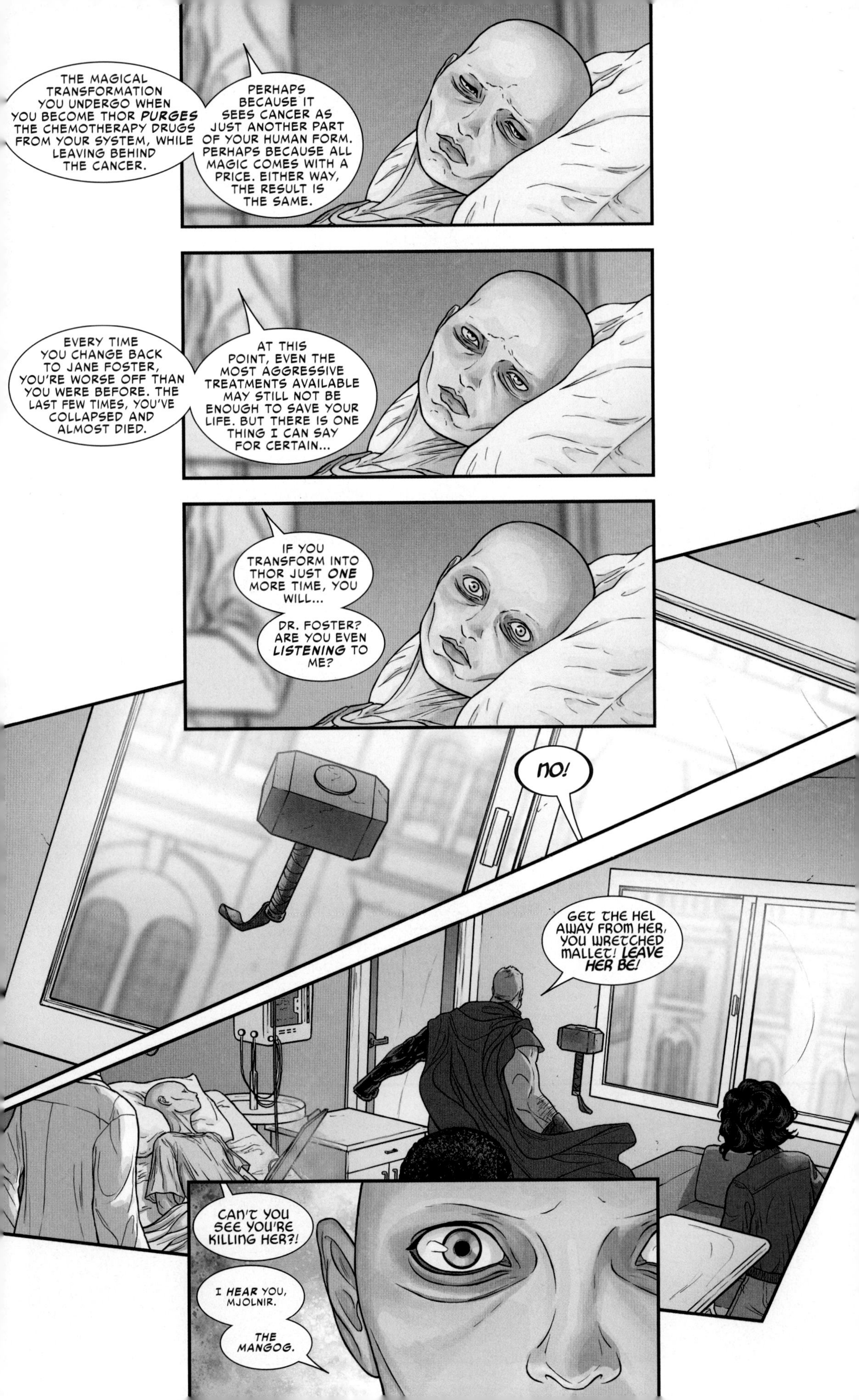
THE MAGICAL TRANSFORMATION YOU UNDERGO WHEN YOU BECOME THOR *PURGES* THE CHEMOTHERAPY DRUGS FROM YOUR SYSTEM, WHILE LEAVING BEHIND THE CANCER.
PERHAPS BECAUSE IT SEES CANCER AS JUST ANOTHER PART OF YOUR HUMAN FORM. PERHAPS BECAUSE ALL MAGIC COMES WITH A PRICE. EITHER WAY, THE RESULT IS THE SAME.
EVERY TIME YOU CHANGE BACK TO JANE FOSTER, YOU'RE WORSE OFF THAN YOU WERE BEFORE. THE LAST FEW TIMES, YOU'VE COLLAPSED AND ALMOST DIED.
AT THIS POINT, EVEN THE MOST AGGRESSIVE TREATMENTS AVAILABLE MAY STILL NOT BE ENOUGH TO SAVE YOUR LIFE. BUT THERE IS ONE THING I CAN SAY FOR CERTAIN...
IF YOU TRANSFORM INTO THOR JUST *ONE* MORE TIME, YOU WILL...
DR. FOSTER? ARE YOU EVEN *LISTENING* TO ME?
NO!
GET THE HEL AWAY FROM HER, YOU WRETCHED MALLET! *LEAVE HER BE!*
CAN'T YOU SEE YOU'RE KILLING HER?!
I *HEAR* YOU, MJOLNIR.
*THE* MANGOG.

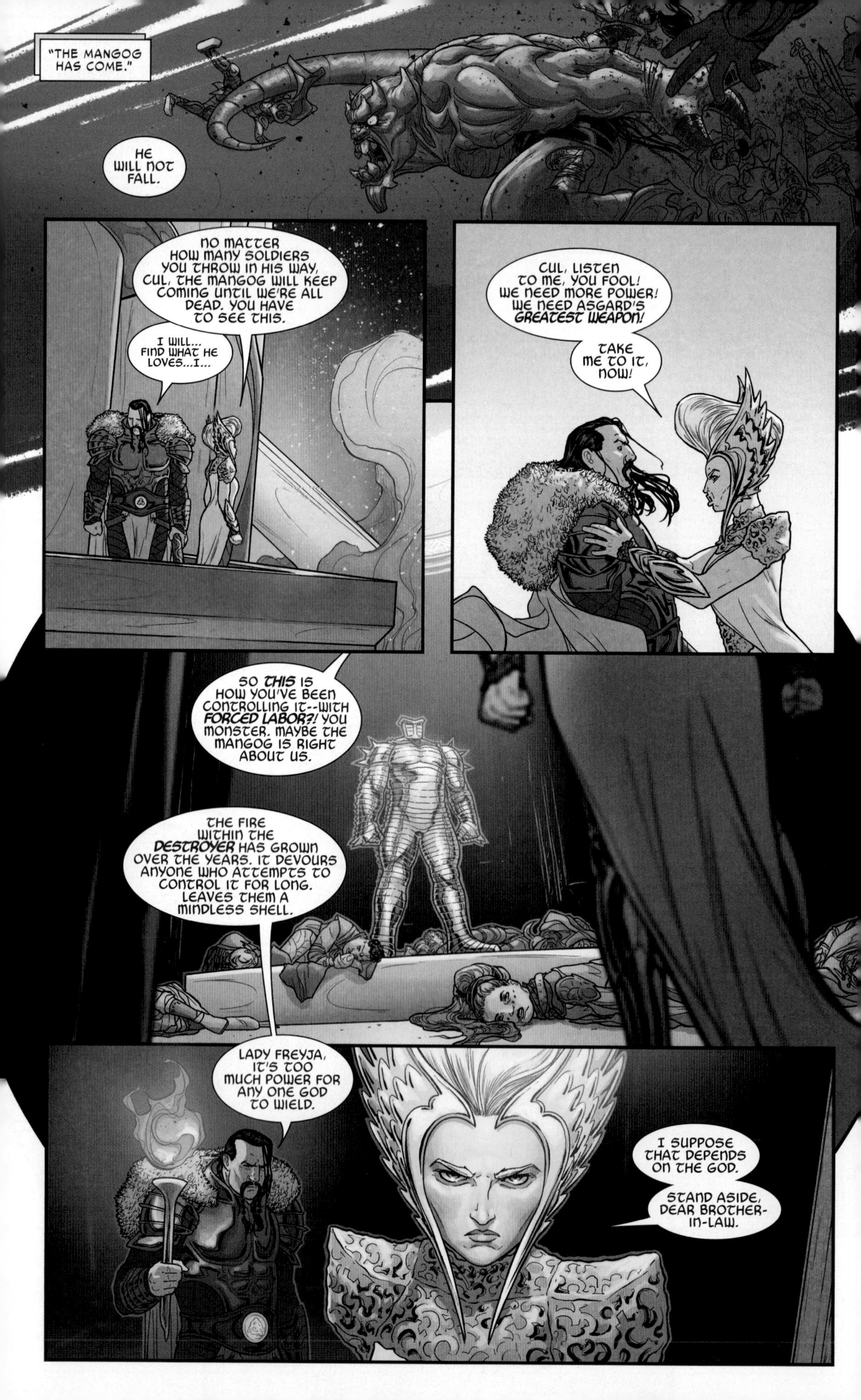

"THE MANGOG HAS COME."
HE WILL NOT FALL.
NO MATTER HOW MANY SOLDIERS YOU THROW IN HIS WAY, CUL, THE MANGOG WILL KEEP COMING UNTIL WE'RE ALL DEAD. YOU HAVE TO SEE THIS.
I WILL... FIND WHAT HE LOVES...I...
CUL, LISTEN TO ME, YOU FOOL! WE NEED MORE POWER! WE NEED ASGARD'S GREATEST WEAPON!
TAKE ME TO IT, NOW!
SO THIS IS HOW YOU'VE BEEN CONTROLLING IT--WITH FORCED LABOR?! YOU MONSTER. MAYBE THE MANGOG IS RIGHT ABOUT US.
THE FIRE WITHIN THE DESTROYER HAS GROWN OVER THE YEARS. IT DEVOURS ANYONE WHO ATTEMPTS TO CONTROL IT FOR LONG. LEAVES THEM A MINDLESS SHELL.
LADY FREYJA, IT'S TOO MUCH POWER FOR ANY ONE GOD TO WIELD.
I SUPPOSE THAT DEPENDS ON THE GOD.
STAND ASIDE, DEAR BROTHER-IN-LAW.

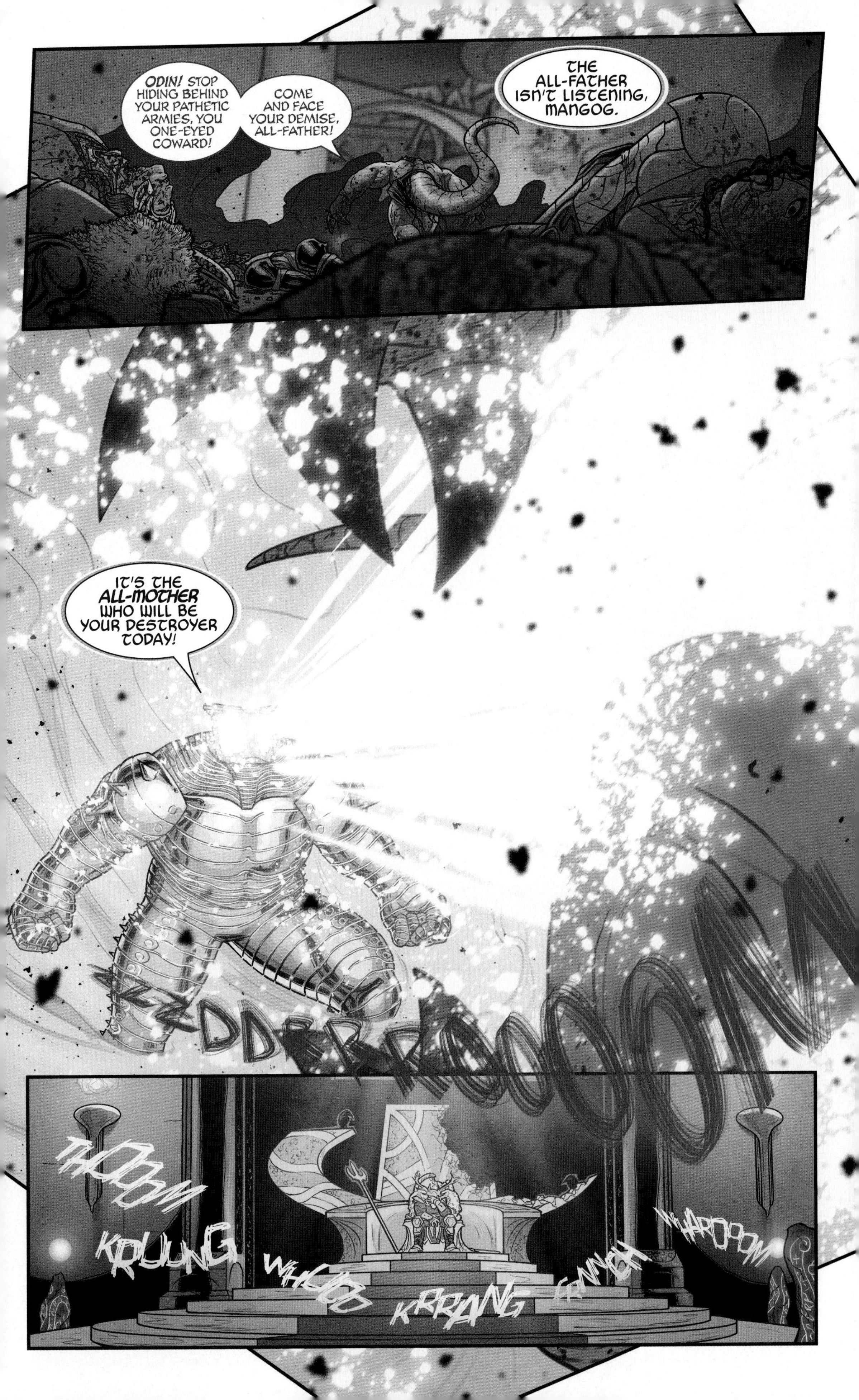
ODIN! STOP HIDING BEHIND YOUR PATHETIC ARMIES, YOU ONE-EYED COWARD!
COME AND FACE YOUR DEMISE, ALL-FATHER!
THE ALL-FATHER ISN'T LISTENING, MANGOG.
IT'S THE ALL-MOTHER WHO WILL BE YOUR DESTROYER TODAY!
KRUUNG
KRRANG

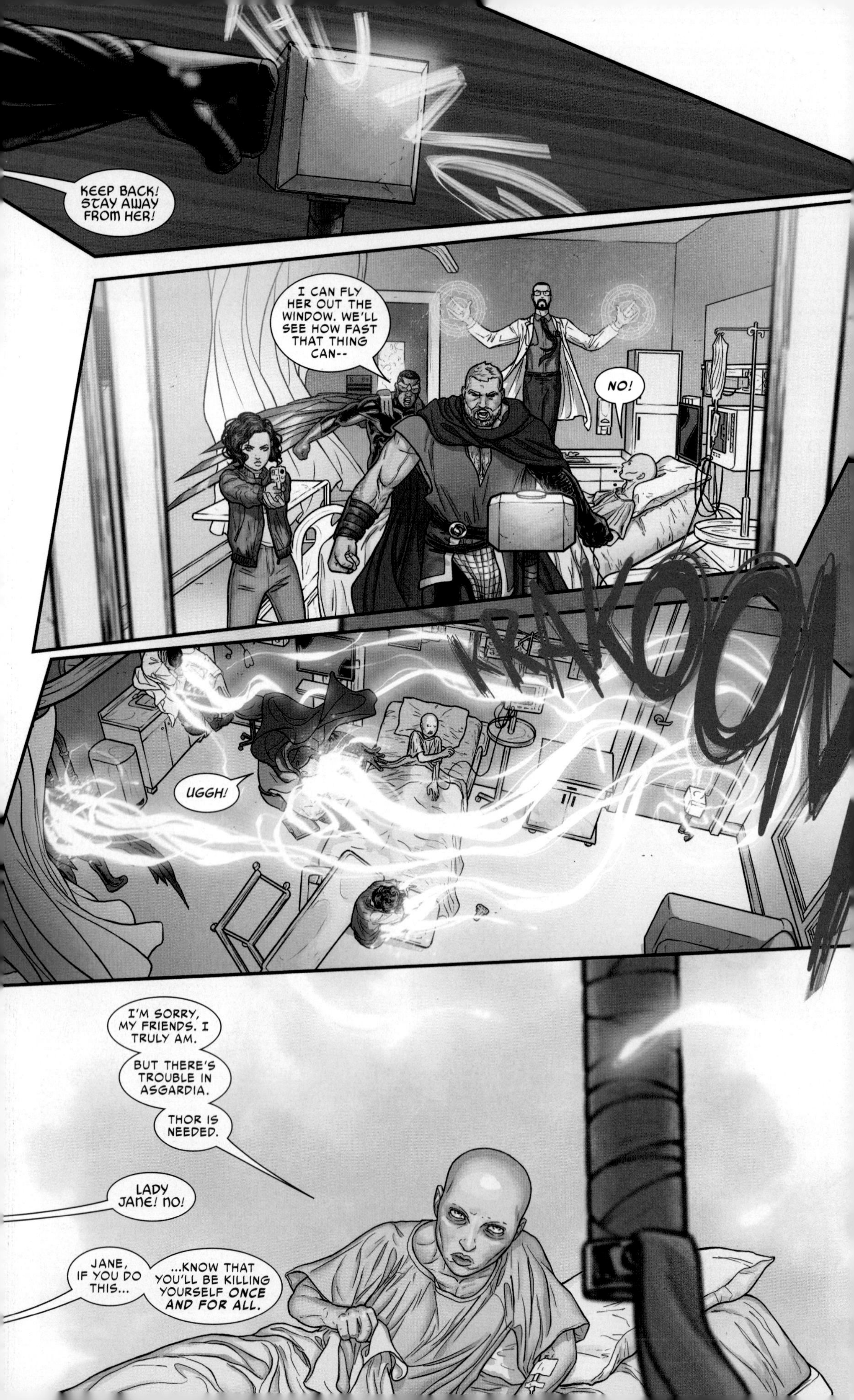
THUMM
KEEP BACK! STAY AWAY FROM HER!
I CAN FLY HER OUT THE WINDOW. WE'LL SEE HOW FAST THAT THING CAN--
NO!
KRAKOOM
UGGH!
I'M SORRY, MY FRIENDS. I TRULY AM.
BUT THERE'S TROUBLE IN ASGARDIA.
THOR IS NEEDED.
LADY JANE! NO!
JANE, IF YOU DO THIS...
...KNOW THAT YOU'LL BE KILLING YOURSELF ONCE AND FOR ALL.

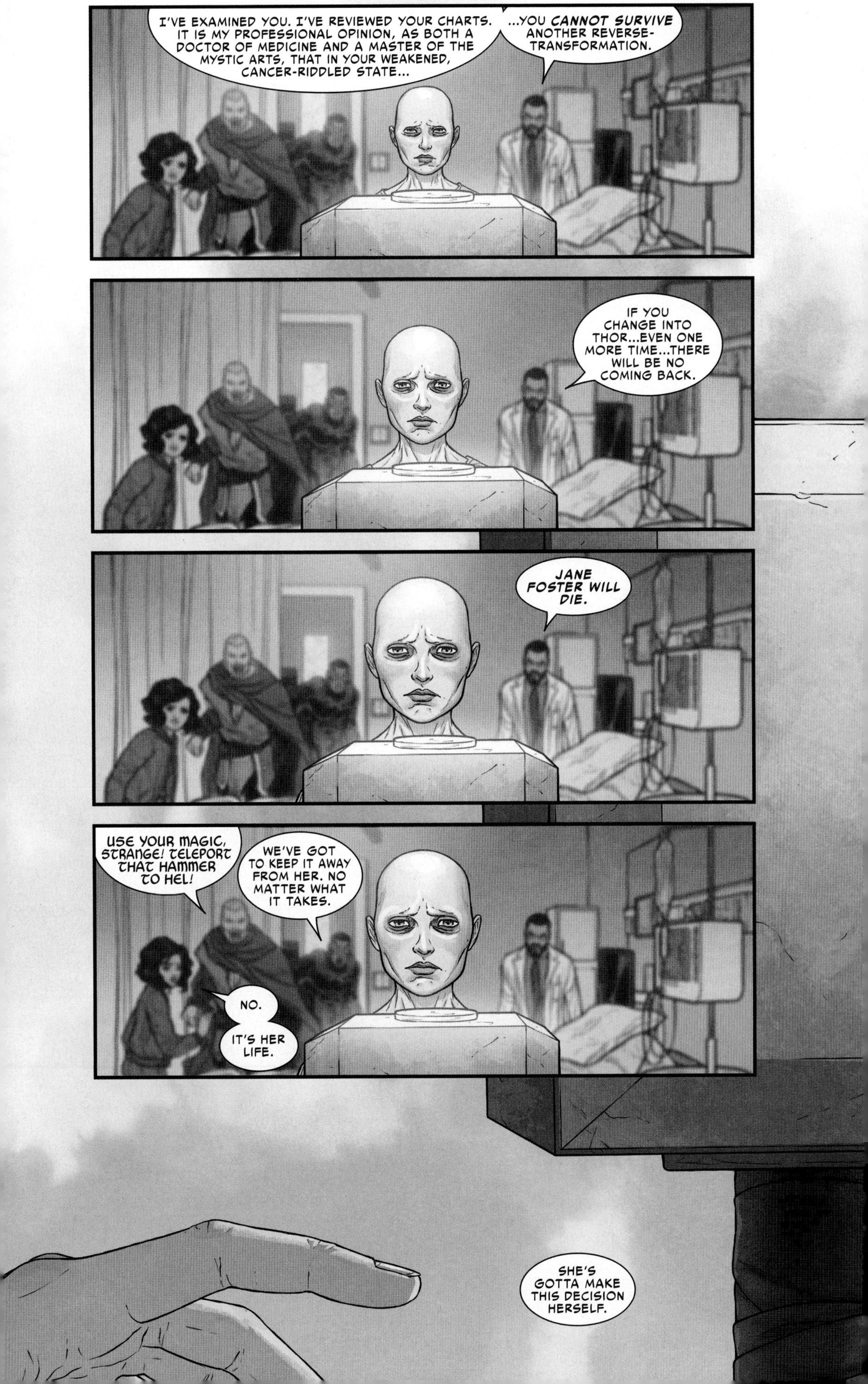
I'VE EXAMINED YOU. I'VE REVIEWED YOUR CHARTS. IT IS MY PROFESSIONAL OPINION, AS BOTH A DOCTOR OF MEDICINE AND A MASTER OF THE MYSTIC ARTS, THAT IN YOUR WEAKENED, CANCER-RIDDLED STATE...
...YOU *CANNOT SURVIVE* ANOTHER REVERSE-TRANSFORMATION.
IF YOU CHANGE INTO THOR...EVEN ONE MORE TIME...THERE WILL BE NO COMING BACK.
*JANE FOSTER WILL DIE.*
USE YOUR MAGIC, STRANGE! TELEPORT THAT HAMMER TO HEL!
WE'VE GOT TO KEEP IT AWAY FROM HER. NO MATTER WHAT IT TAKES.
NO.
IT'S HER LIFE.
SHE'S GOTTA MAKE THIS DECISION HERSELF.

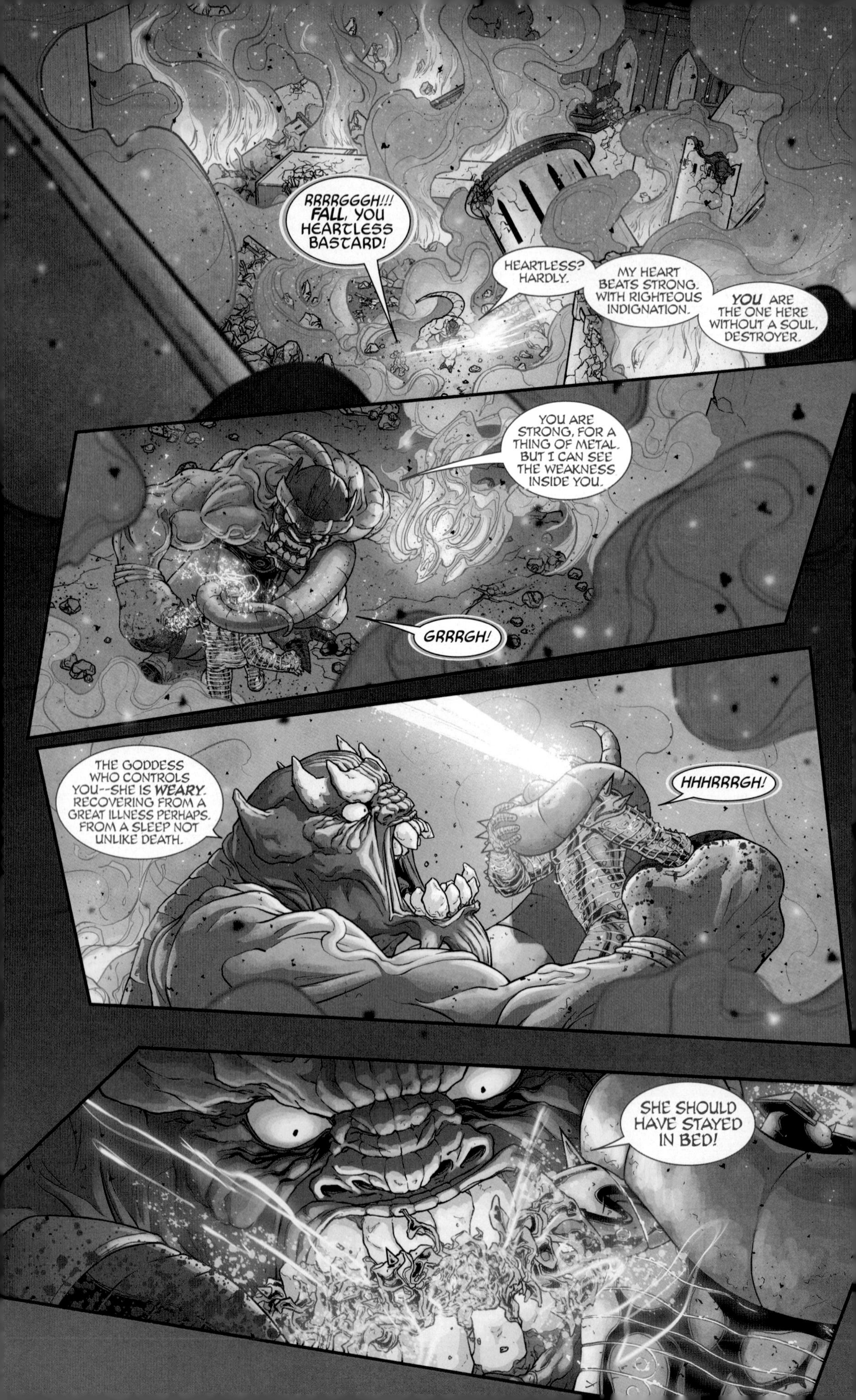
RRRRGGGH!!! FALL, YOU HEARTLESS BASTARD!
HEARTLESS? HARDLY.
MY HEART BEATS STRONG. WITH RIGHTEOUS INDIGNATION.
YOU ARE THE ONE HERE WITHOUT A SOUL, DESTROYER.
YOU ARE STRONG, FOR A THING OF METAL. BUT I CAN SEE THE WEAKNESS INSIDE YOU.
GRRRGH!
THE GODDESS WHO CONTROLS YOU--SHE IS WEARY. RECOVERING FROM A GREAT ILLNESS PERHAPS. FROM A SLEEP NOT UNLIKE DEATH.
HHHRRRGH!
SHE SHOULD HAVE STAYED IN BED!

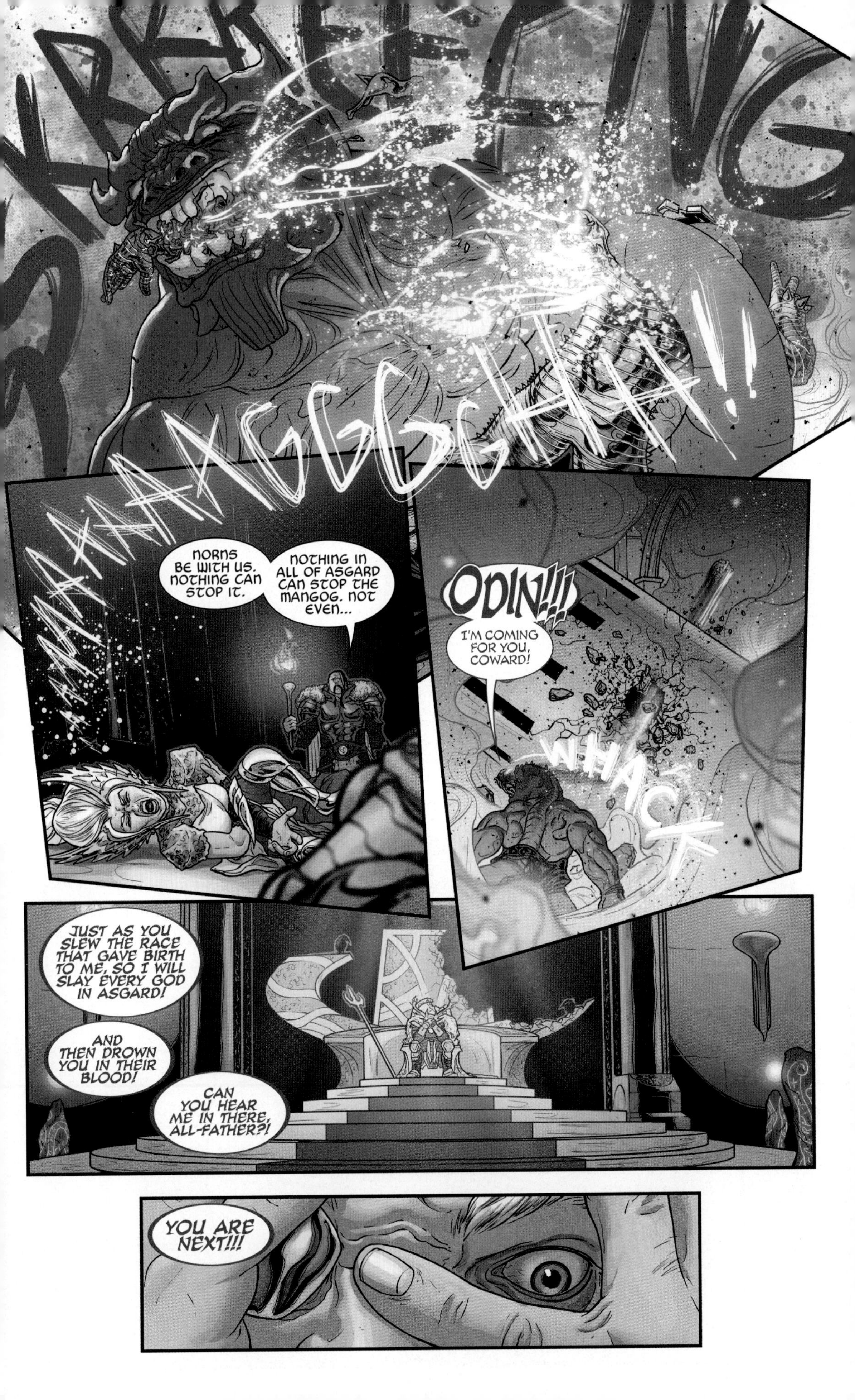
KRAKKOOOM
WHAAAAAGGGHHH!!
NORNS BE WITH US. NOTHING CAN STOP IT.
NOTHING IN ALL OF ASGARD CAN STOP THE MANGOG. NOT EVEN...
ODIN!!!!
I'M COMING FOR YOU, COWARD!
WHACK
JUST AS YOU SLEW THE RACE THAT GAVE BIRTH TO ME, SO I WILL SLAY EVERY GOD IN ASGARD!
AND THEN DROWN YOU IN THEIR BLOOD!
CAN YOU HEAR ME IN THERE, ALL-FATHER?!
YOU ARE NEXT!!!

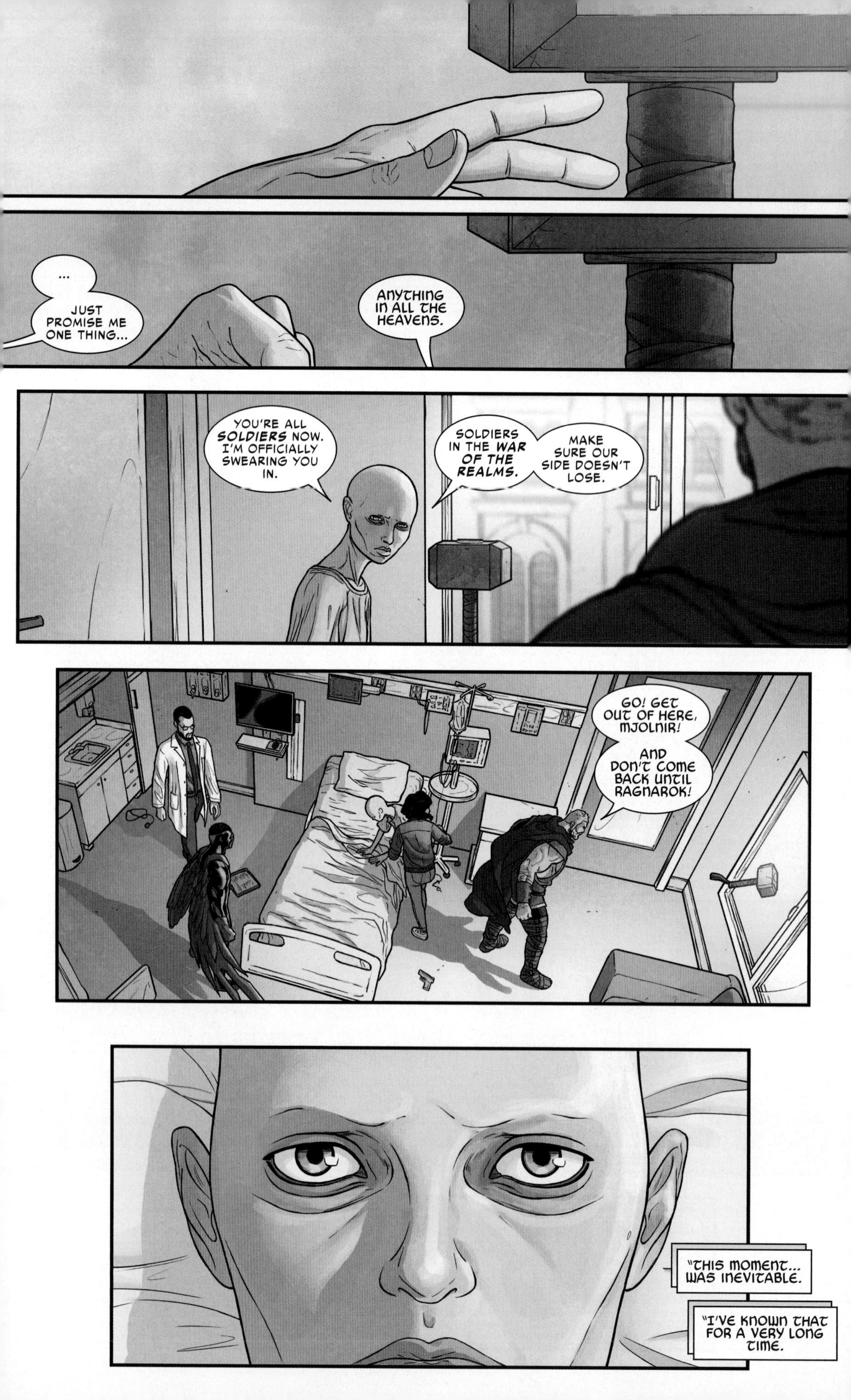
...
JUST PROMISE ME ONE THING...
ANYTHING IN ALL THE HEAVENS.
YOU'RE ALL **SOLDIERS** NOW. I'M OFFICIALLY SWEARING YOU IN.
SOLDIERS IN THE ***WAR OF THE REALMS.***
MAKE SURE OUR SIDE DOESN'T LOSE.
GO! GET OUT OF HERE, MJOLNIR!
AND DON'T COME BACK UNTIL RAGNAROK!
"THIS MOMENT... WAS INEVITABLE.
"I'VE KNOWN THAT FOR A VERY LONG TIME.

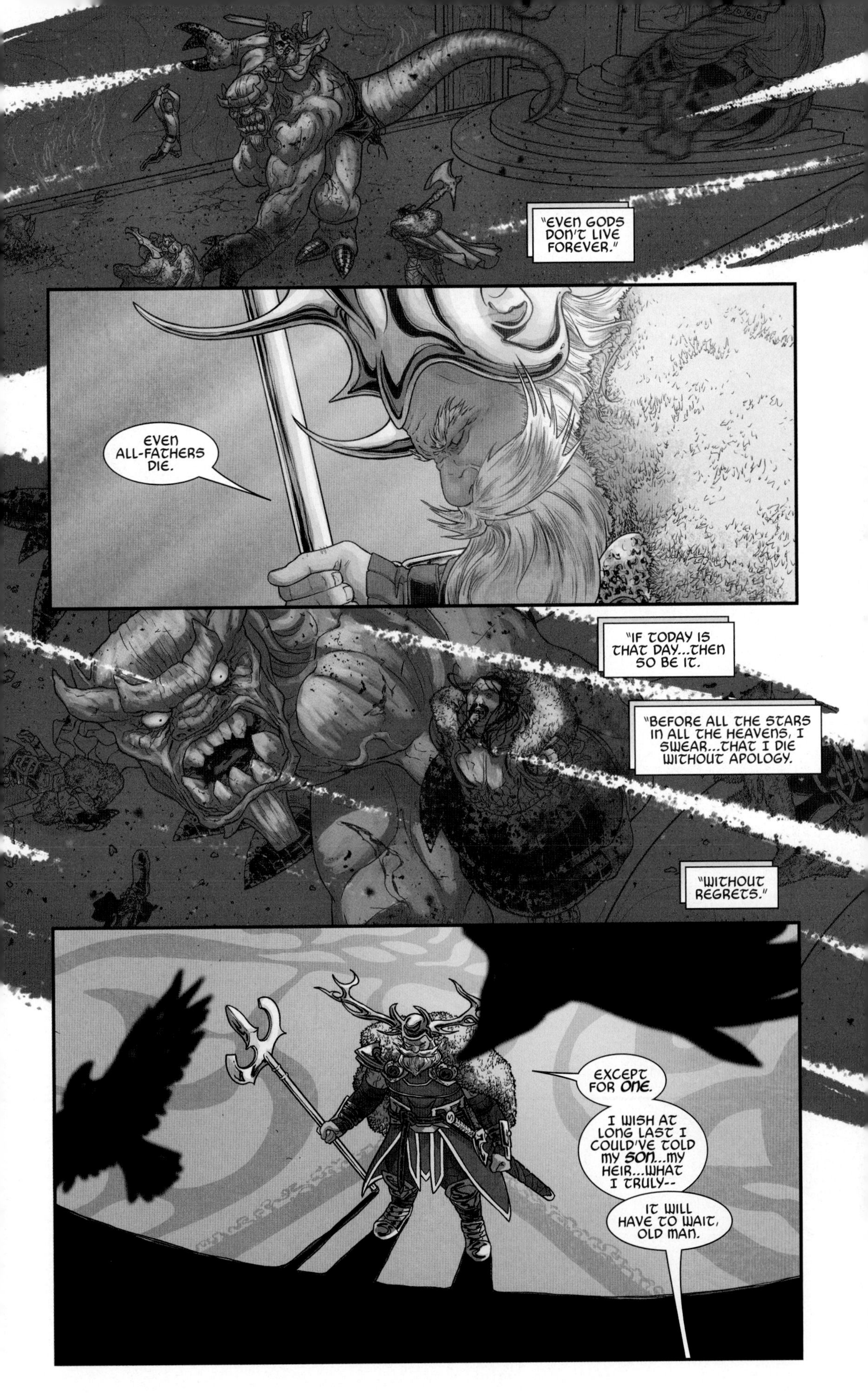
"EVEN GODS DON'T LIVE FOREVER."
EVEN ALL-FATHERS DIE.
"IF TODAY IS THAT DAY...THEN SO BE IT.
"BEFORE ALL THE STARS IN ALL THE HEAVENS, I SWEAR...THAT I DIE WITHOUT APOLOGY.
"WITHOUT REGRETS."
EXCEPT FOR ONE.
I WISH AT LONG LAST I COULD'VE TOLD MY SON...MY HEIR...WHAT I TRULY--
IT WILL HAVE TO WAIT, OLD MAN.

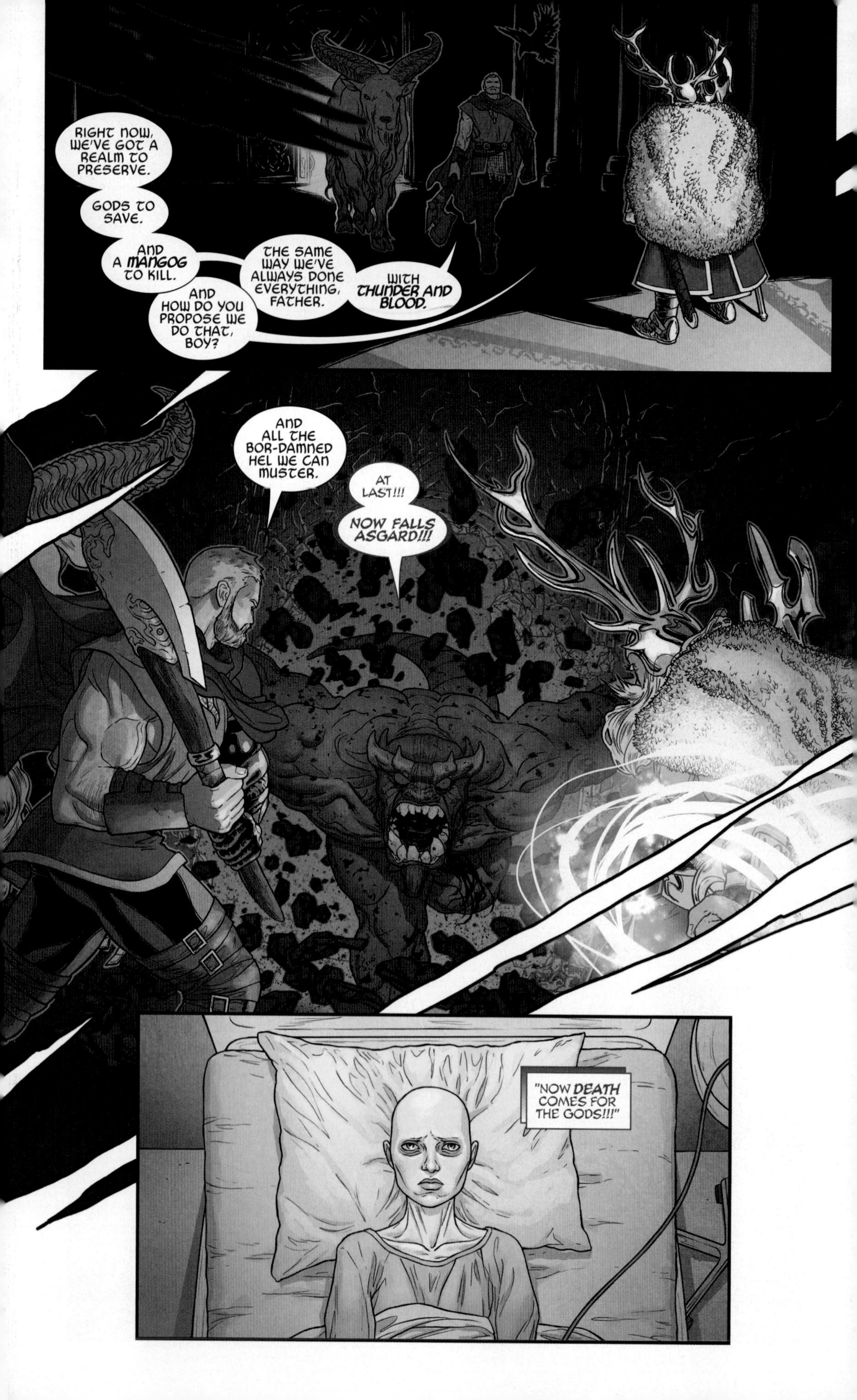
RIGHT NOW, WE'VE GOT A REALM TO PRESERVE.
GODS TO SAVE.
AND A MANGOG TO KILL.
AND HOW DO YOU PROPOSE WE DO THAT, BOY?
THE SAME WAY WE'VE ALWAYS DONE EVERYTHING, FATHER.
WITH THUNDER AND BLOOD.
AND ALL THE BOR-DAMNED HEL WE CAN MUSTER.
AT LAST!!!
NOW FALLS ASGARD!!!
"NOW DEATH COMES FOR THE GODS!!!"

# 704

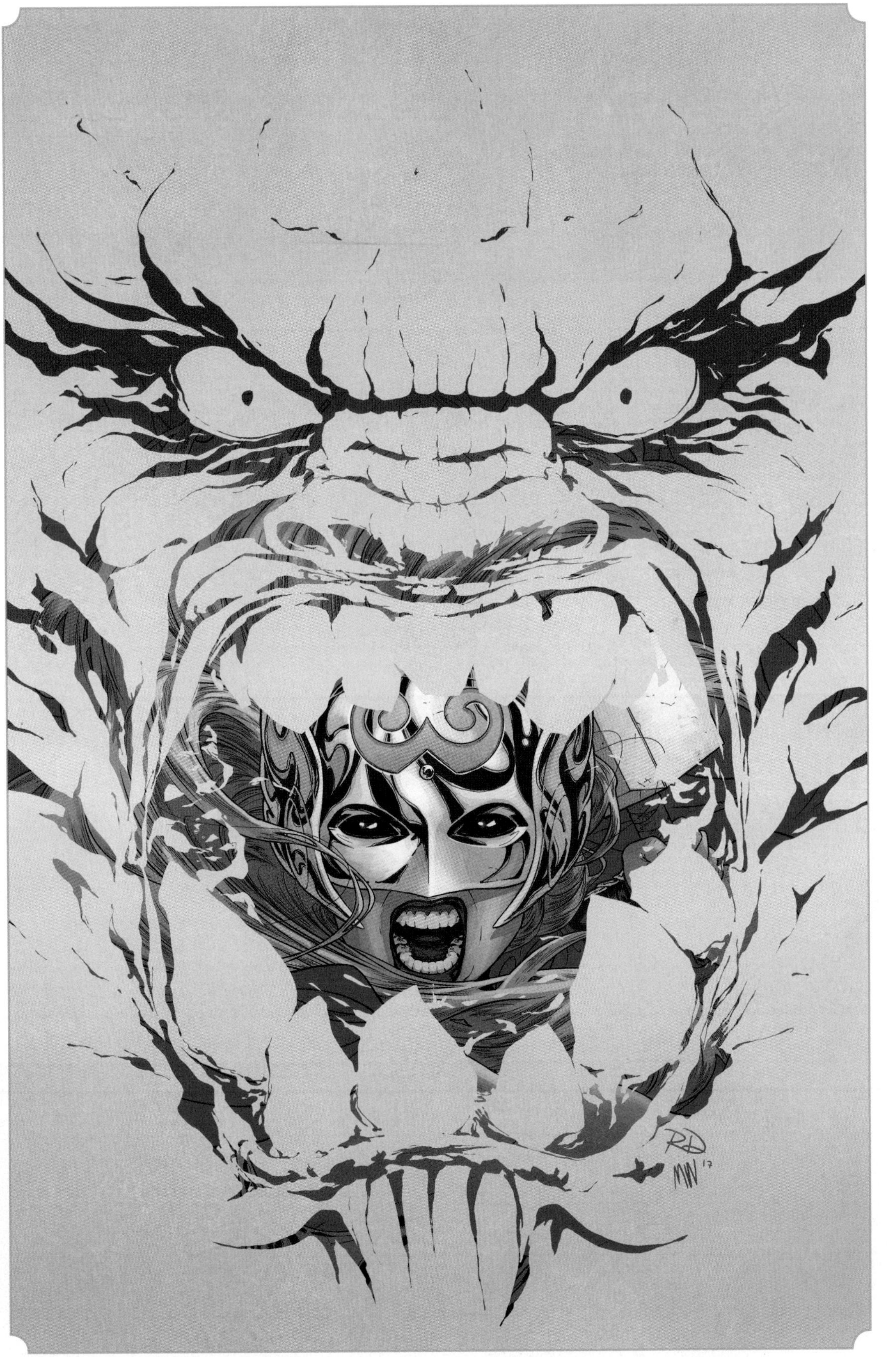

## THE GOSPEL ACCORDING TO JANE

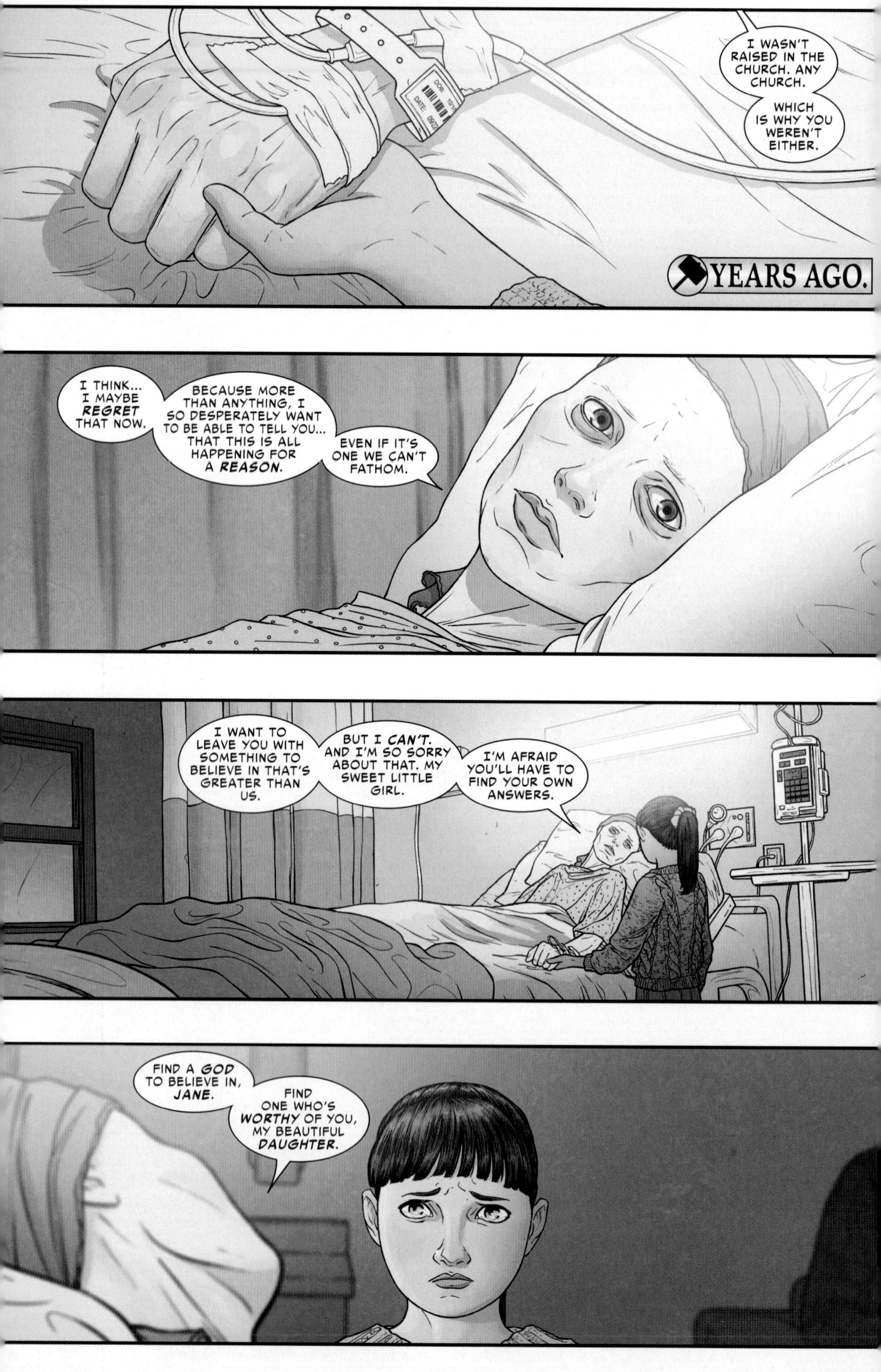
I WASN'T RAISED IN THE CHURCH. ANY CHURCH.
WHICH IS WHY YOU WEREN'T EITHER.
YEARS AGO.
I THINK... I MAYBE *REGRET* THAT NOW.
BECAUSE MORE THAN ANYTHING, I SO DESPERATELY WANT TO BE ABLE TO TELL YOU... THAT THIS IS ALL HAPPENING FOR A *REASON*.
EVEN IF IT'S ONE WE CAN'T FATHOM.
I WANT TO LEAVE YOU WITH SOMETHING TO BELIEVE IN THAT'S GREATER THAN US.
BUT I *CAN'T*. AND I'M SO SORRY ABOUT THAT. MY SWEET LITTLE GIRL.
I'M AFRAID YOU'LL HAVE TO FIND YOUR OWN ANSWERS.
FIND A *GOD* TO BELIEVE IN, *JANE*.
FIND ONE WHO'S *WORTHY* OF YOU, MY BEAUTIFUL *DAUGHTER*.

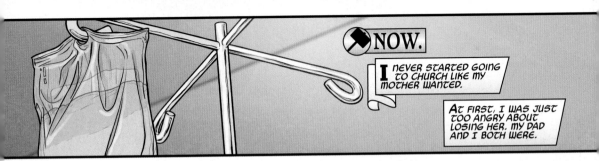

NOW.
I NEVER STARTED GOING TO CHURCH LIKE MY MOTHER WANTED.
AT FIRST, I WAS JUST TOO ANGRY ABOUT LOSING HER. MY DAD AND I BOTH WERE.
AND THE OLDER I GOT, THE MORE IT FELT FALSE TO ME, THE IDEA OF TURNING TO SOME HIGHER POWER ONLY IN THE FACE OF DEATH.
I LOVED MY MOTHER EVEN MORE FOR THAT, BECAUSE I KNEW SHE WAS DOING IT ALL FOR ME. BUT I FOUND I COULD NEVER DO WHAT SHE ASKED.
CHEMOTHERAPY DRUG
CAUTION
TRANSPORT
I COULD NEVER FIND A GOD TO BELIEVE IN.
INSTEAD THE GODS FOUND ME.
BUT THERE ARE NO GODS HERE NOW FOR ME TO LEAN ON. OR SIPHON AWAY THEIR POWER TO MAKE ME STRONGER.
AND I'VE GOT NO FAMILY LEFT, NO ONE I'M LEAVING BEHIND. THERE'S JUST ME.
AND THAT'LL HAVE TO BE ENOUGH.
MY NAME IS JANE FOSTER.
AND IF THIS IS THE STORY OF HOW I DIE... THEN KNOW THAT IT WON'T END...

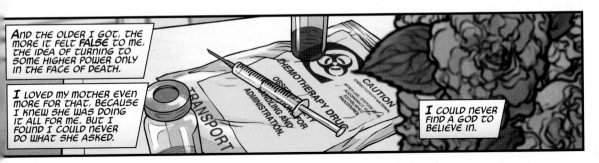

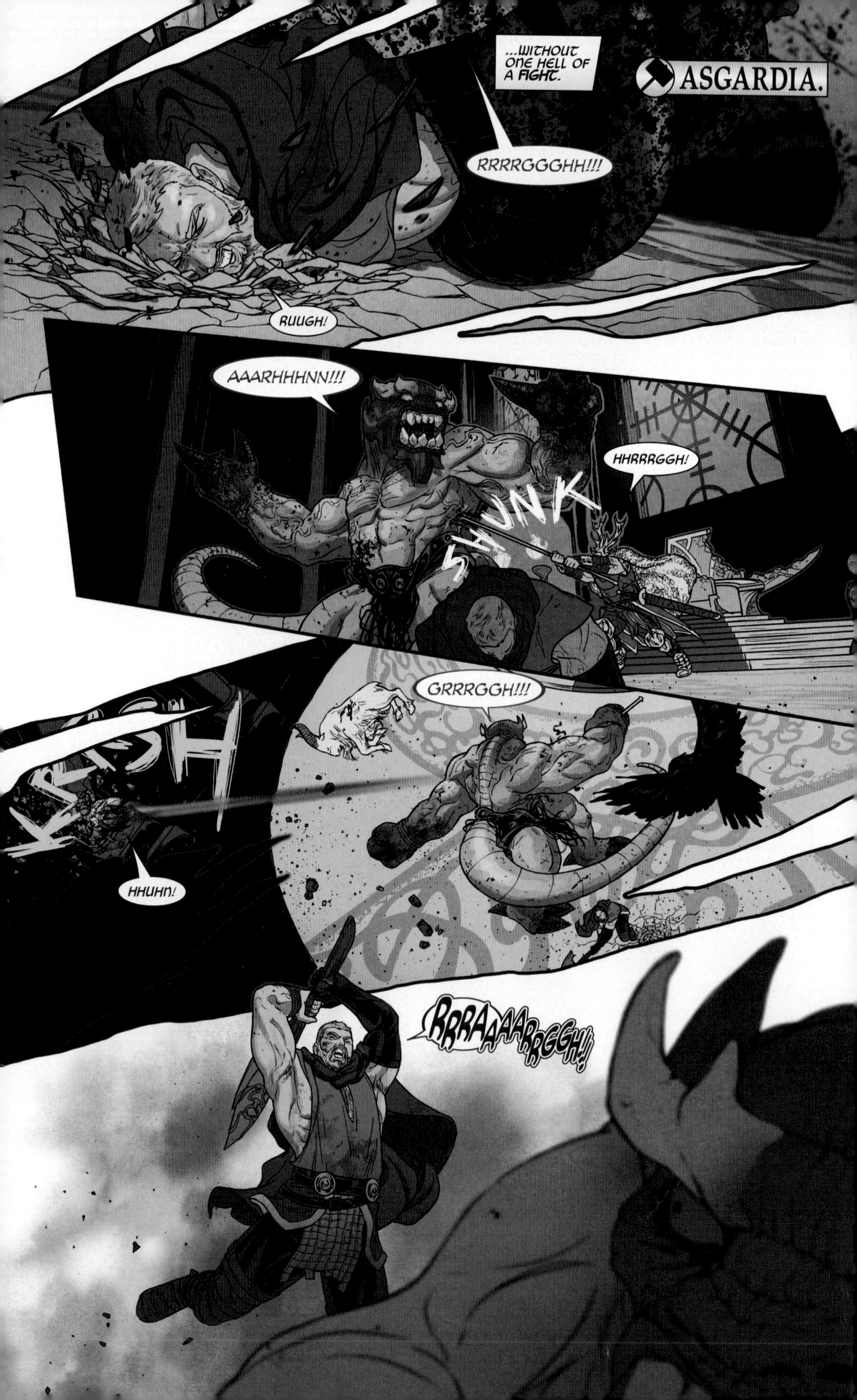
...WITHOUT ONE HELL OF A FIGHT.
ASGARDIA.
RRRRGGGHH!!!
RUUGH!
AAARHHHNN!!!
HHRRRGGH!
SHUNK
GRRRGGH!!!
KRASH
HHUHN!
RRRAAAARRGGH!!

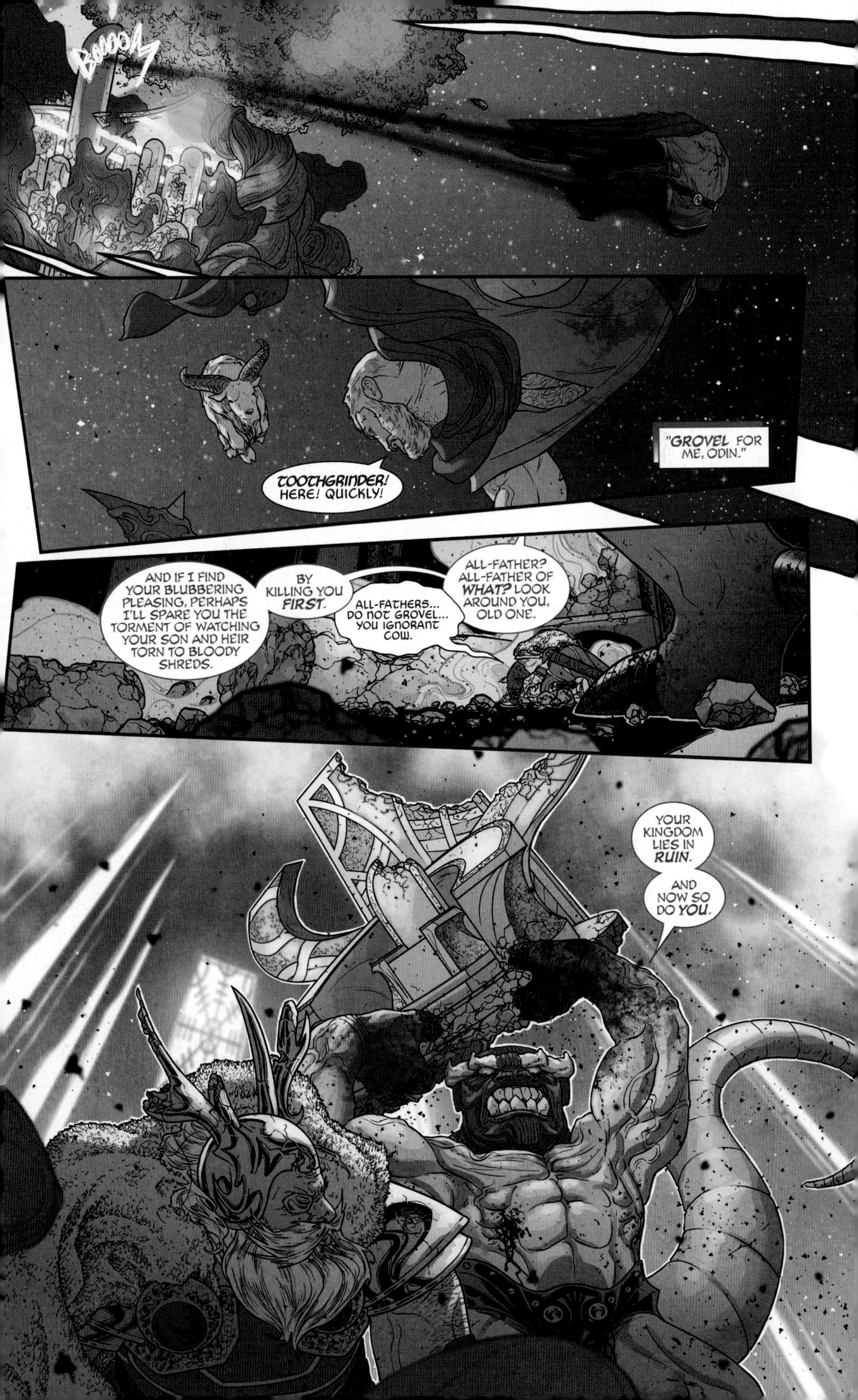
BOOOOM
TOOTHGRINDER! HERE! QUICKLY!
"GROVEL FOR ME, ODIN."
ALL-FATHER? ALL-FATHER OF WHAT? LOOK AROUND YOU, OLD ONE.
ALL-FATHERS... DO NOT GROVEL... YOU IGNORANT COW.
BY KILLING YOU FIRST.
AND IF I FIND YOUR BLUBBERING PLEASING, PERHAPS I'LL SPARE YOU THE TORMENT OF WATCHING YOUR SON AND HEIR TORN TO BLOODY SHREDS.
YOUR KINGDOM LIES IN RUIN.
AND NOW SO DO YOU.

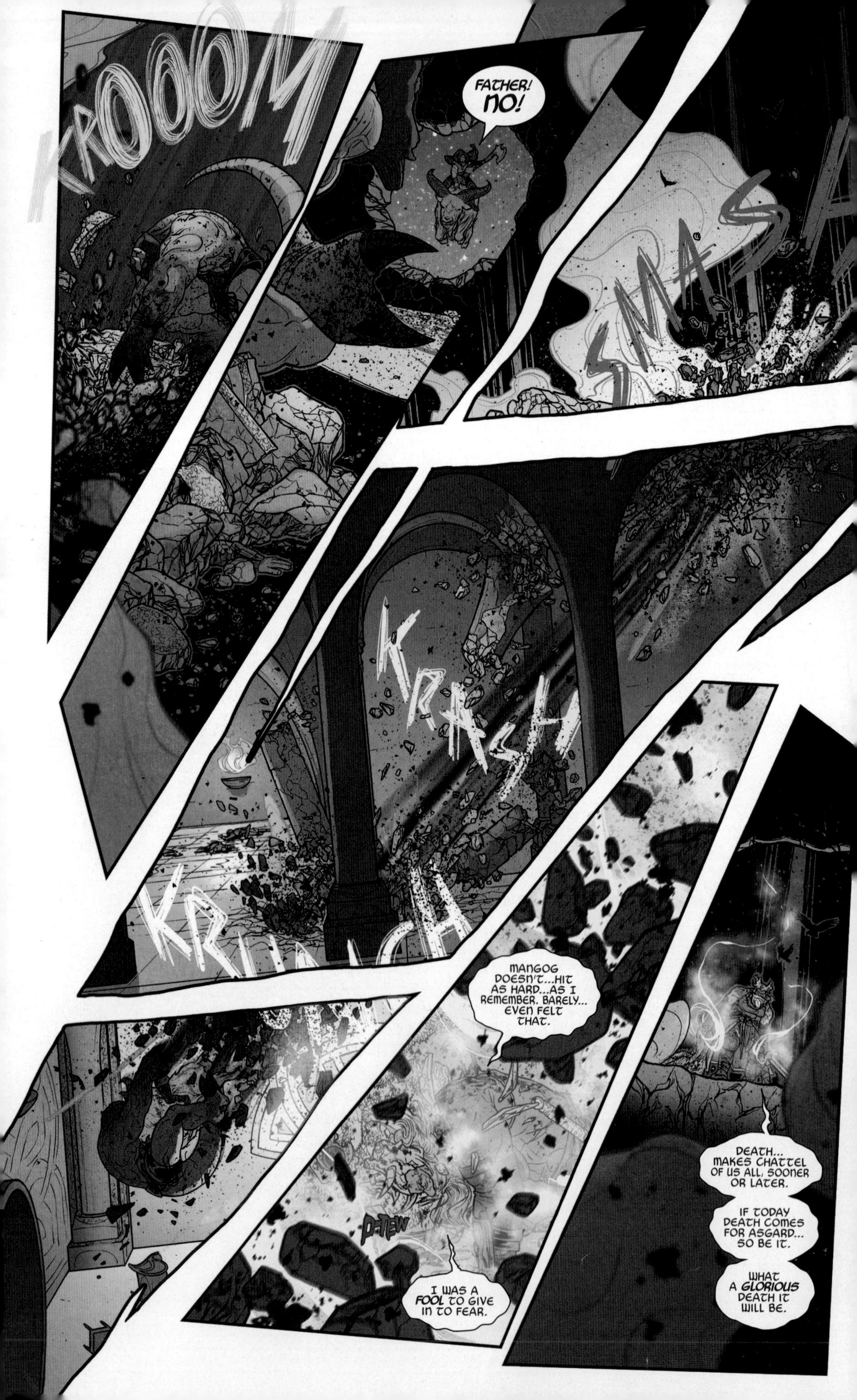
KROOOM
FATHER! NO!
SMASH
KRASH
KRUNCH
MANGOG DOESN'T...HIT AS HARD...AS I REMEMBER. BARELY... EVEN FELT THAT.
P-TEW
I WAS A FOOL TO GIVE IN TO FEAR.
DEATH... MAKES CHATTEL OF US ALL, SOONER OR LATER.
IF TODAY DEATH COMES FOR ASGARD... SO BE IT.
WHAT A GLORIOUS DEATH IT WILL BE.

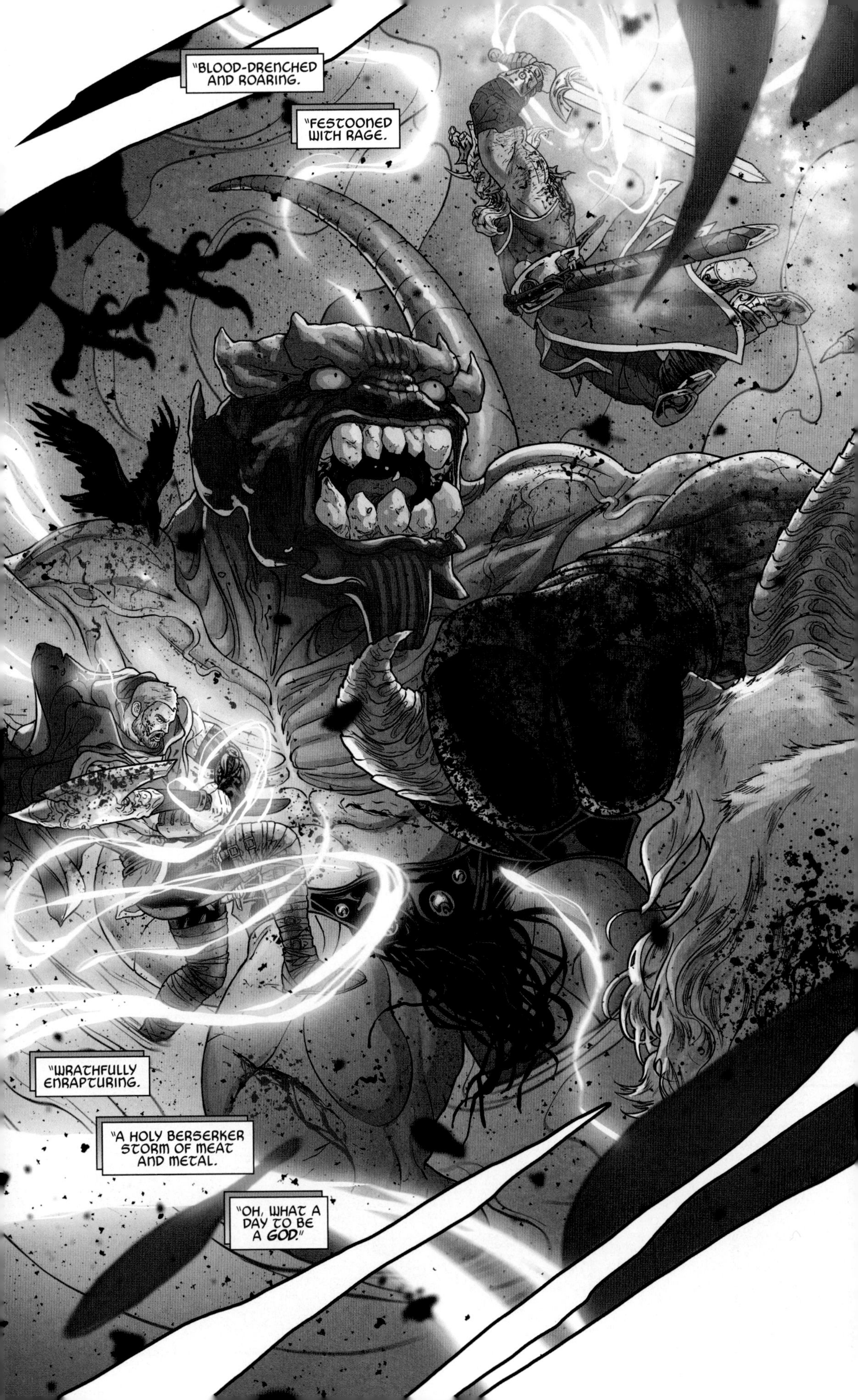
"BLOOD-DRENCHED AND ROARING.
"FESTOONED WITH RAGE.
"WRATHFULLY ENRAPTURING.
"A HOLY BERSERKER STORM OF MEAT AND METAL.
"OH, WHAT A DAY TO BE A GOD."

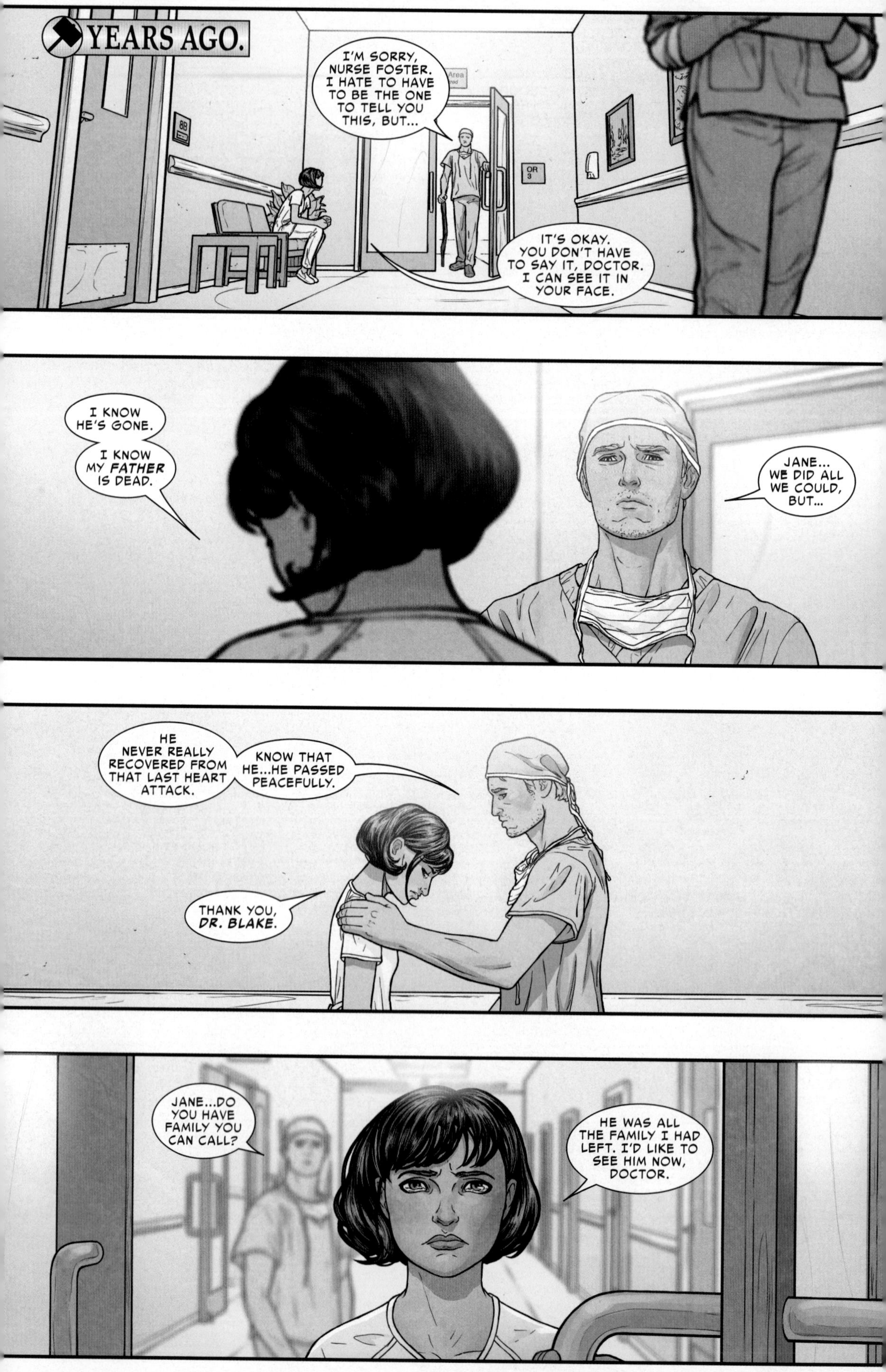
YEARS AGO.
I'M SORRY, NURSE FOSTER. I HATE TO HAVE TO BE THE ONE TO TELL YOU THIS, BUT...
IT'S OKAY. YOU DON'T HAVE TO SAY IT, DOCTOR. I CAN SEE IT IN YOUR FACE.
I KNOW HE'S GONE.
I KNOW MY *FATHER* IS DEAD.
JANE... WE DID ALL WE COULD, BUT...
HE NEVER REALLY RECOVERED FROM THAT LAST HEART ATTACK.
KNOW THAT HE...HE PASSED PEACEFULLY.
THANK YOU, *DR. BLAKE.*
JANE...DO YOU HAVE FAMILY YOU CAN CALL?
HE WAS ALL THE FAMILY I HAD LEFT. I'D LIKE TO SEE HIM NOW, DOCTOR.

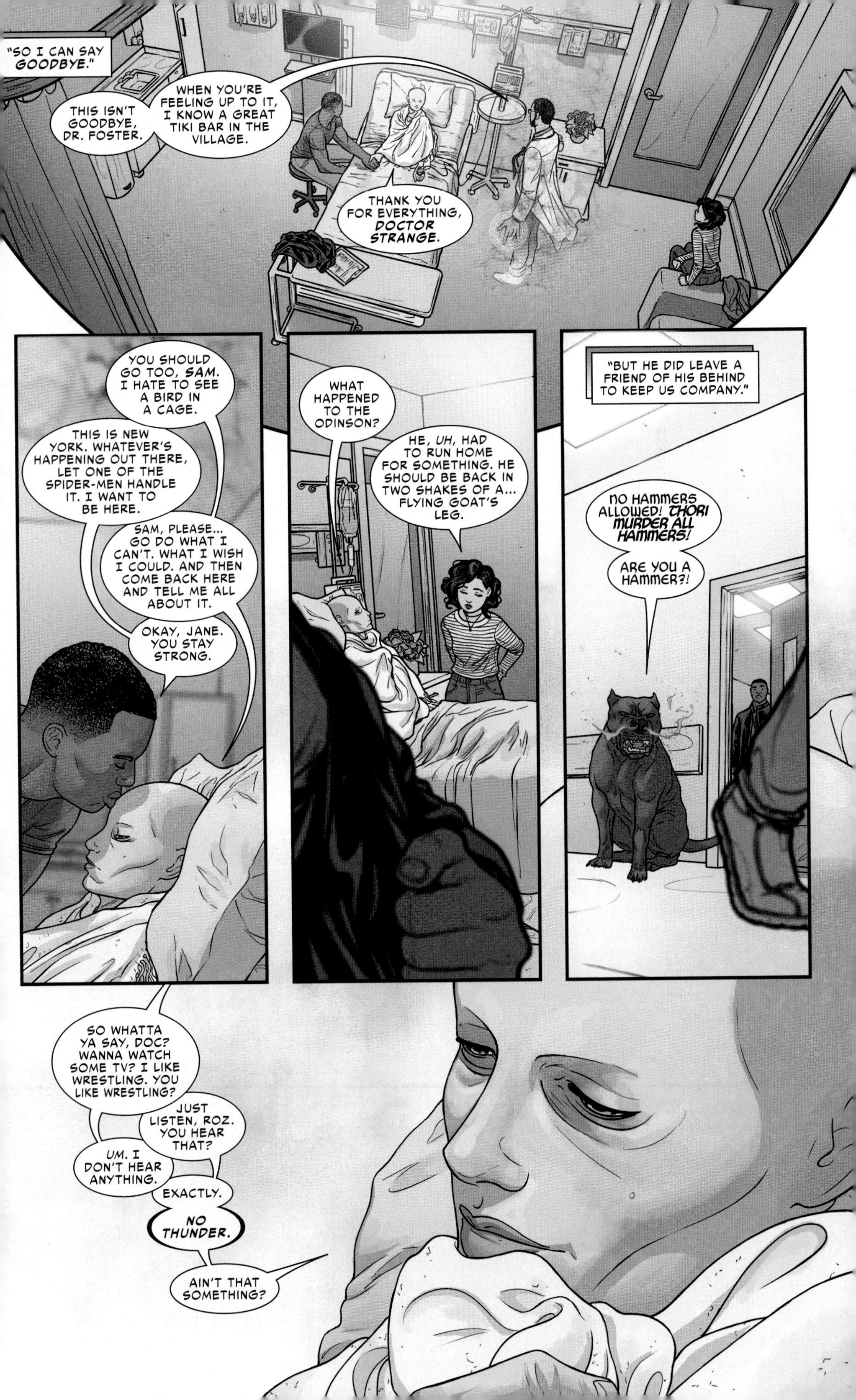
"SO I CAN SAY GOODBYE."
THIS ISN'T GOODBYE, DR. FOSTER.
WHEN YOU'RE FEELING UP TO IT, I KNOW A GREAT TIKI BAR IN THE VILLAGE.
THANK YOU FOR EVERYTHING, DOCTOR STRANGE.
YOU SHOULD GO TOO, SAM. I HATE TO SEE A BIRD IN A CAGE.
THIS IS NEW YORK. WHATEVER'S HAPPENING OUT THERE, LET ONE OF THE SPIDER-MEN HANDLE IT. I WANT TO BE HERE.
SAM, PLEASE... GO DO WHAT I CAN'T. WHAT I WISH I COULD. AND THEN COME BACK HERE AND TELL ME ALL ABOUT IT.
OKAY, JANE. YOU STAY STRONG.
WHAT HAPPENED TO THE ODINSON?
HE, UH, HAD TO RUN HOME FOR SOMETHING. HE SHOULD BE BACK IN TWO SHAKES OF A... FLYING GOAT'S LEG.
"BUT HE DID LEAVE A FRIEND OF HIS BEHIND TO KEEP US COMPANY."
NO HAMMERS ALLOWED! THORI MURDER ALL HAMMERS!
ARE YOU A HAMMER?!
SO WHATTA YA SAY, DOC? WANNA WATCH SOME TV? I LIKE WRESTLING. YOU LIKE WRESTLING?
JUST LISTEN, ROZ. YOU HEAR THAT?
UM. I DON'T HEAR ANYTHING.
EXACTLY.
NO THUNDER.
AIN'T THAT SOMETHING?

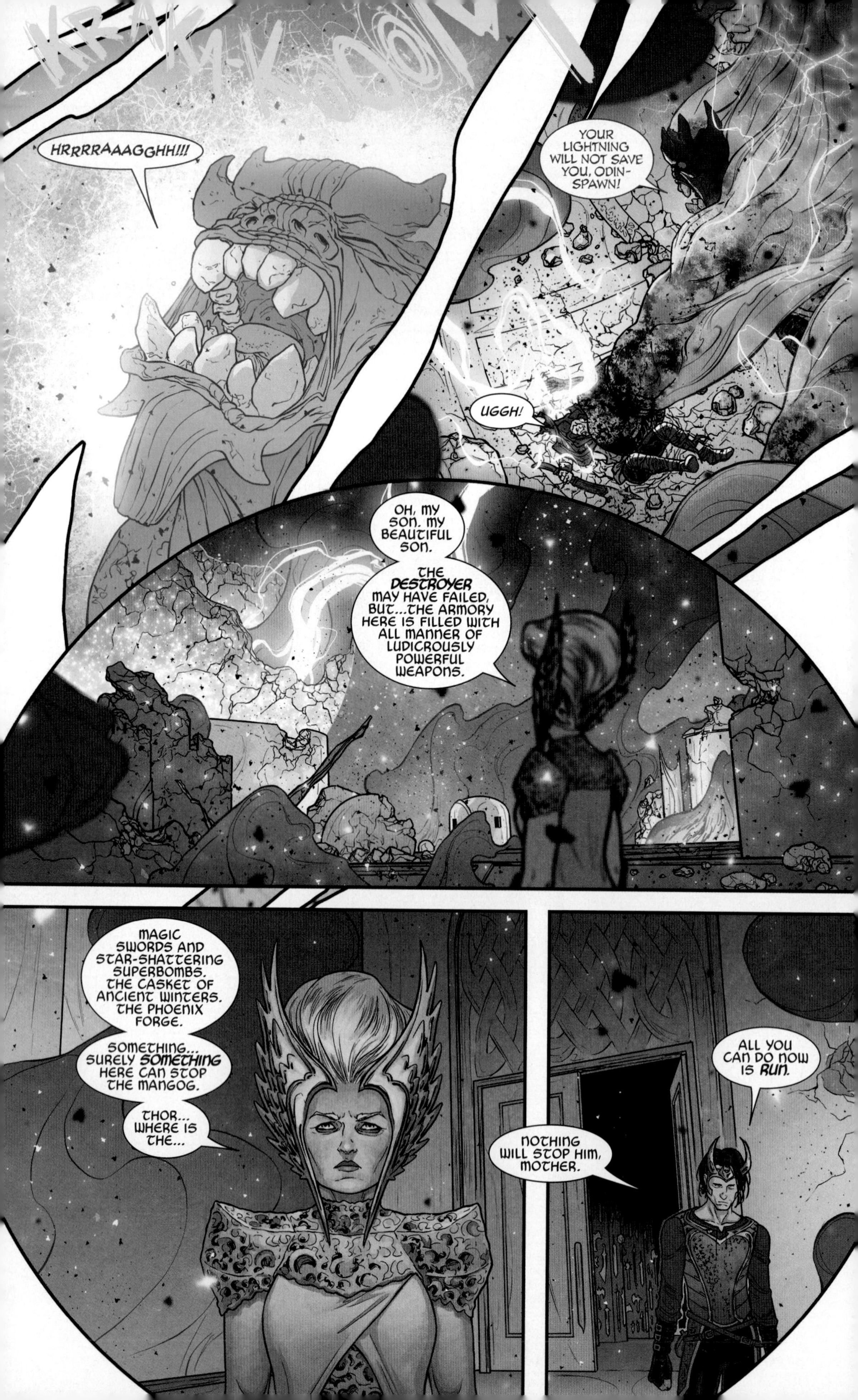
KRAKA-KOOM
HRRRRAAAGGHH!!!
YOUR LIGHTNING WILL NOT SAVE YOU, ODIN-SPAWN!
UGGH!
OH, MY SON. MY BEAUTIFUL SON.
THE DESTROYER MAY HAVE FAILED, BUT...THE ARMORY HERE IS FILLED WITH ALL MANNER OF LUDICROUSLY POWERFUL WEAPONS.
MAGIC SWORDS AND STAR-SHATTERING SUPERBOMBS. THE CASKET OF ANCIENT WINTERS. THE PHOENIX FORGE.
SOMETHING... SURELY SOMETHING HERE CAN STOP THE MANGOG.
THOR... WHERE IS THE...
NOTHING WILL STOP HIM, MOTHER.
ALL YOU CAN DO NOW IS RUN.

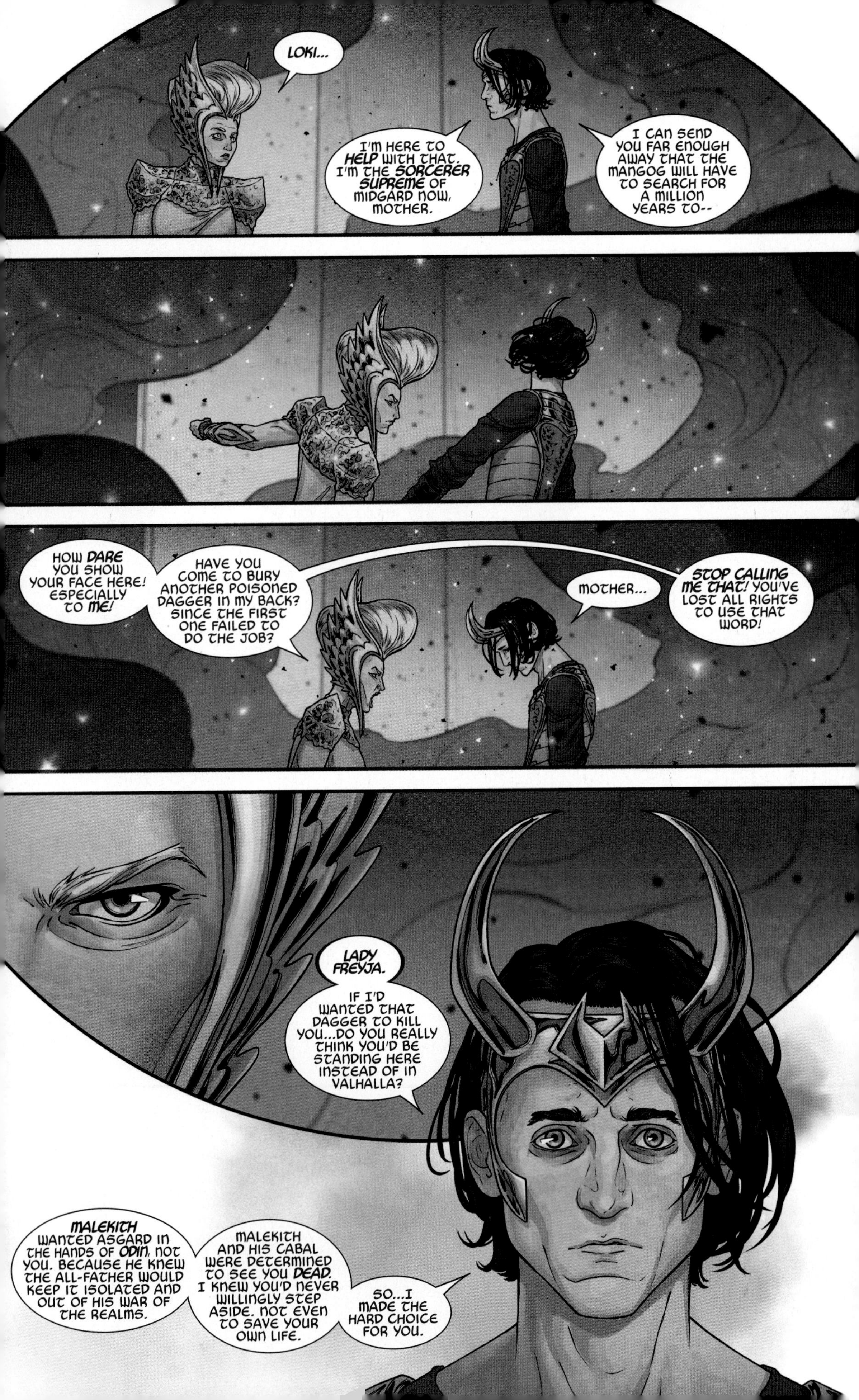
LOKI...
I'M HERE TO HELP WITH THAT. I'M THE SORCERER SUPREME OF MIDGARD NOW, MOTHER.
I CAN SEND YOU FAR ENOUGH AWAY THAT THE MANGOG WILL HAVE TO SEARCH FOR A MILLION YEARS TO--
HOW DARE YOU SHOW YOUR FACE HERE! ESPECIALLY TO ME!
HAVE YOU COME TO BURY ANOTHER POISONED DAGGER IN MY BACK? SINCE THE FIRST ONE FAILED TO DO THE JOB?
MOTHER...
STOP CALLING ME THAT! YOU'VE LOST ALL RIGHTS TO USE THAT WORD!
LADY FREYJA.
IF I'D WANTED THAT DAGGER TO KILL YOU...DO YOU REALLY THINK YOU'D BE STANDING HERE INSTEAD OF IN VALHALLA?
MALEKITH WANTED ASGARD IN THE HANDS OF ODIN, NOT YOU. BECAUSE HE KNEW THE ALL-FATHER WOULD KEEP IT ISOLATED AND OUT OF HIS WAR OF THE REALMS.
MALEKITH AND HIS CABAL WERE DETERMINED TO SEE YOU DEAD. I KNEW YOU'D NEVER WILLINGLY STEP ASIDE. NOT EVEN TO SAVE YOUR OWN LIFE.
SO...I MADE THE HARD CHOICE FOR YOU.

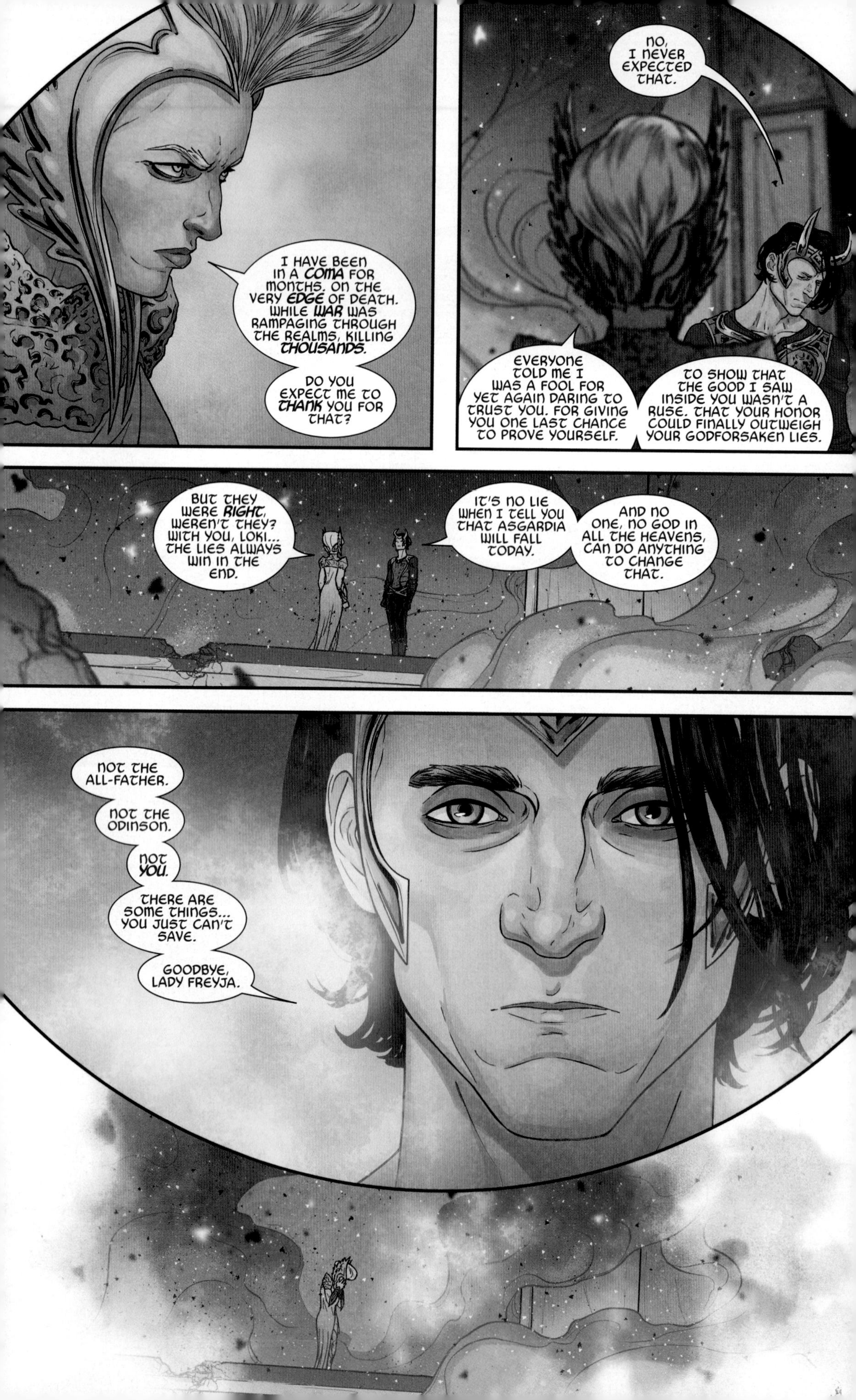
I HAVE BEEN IN A COMA FOR MONTHS. ON THE VERY EDGE OF DEATH. WHILE WAR WAS RAMPAGING THROUGH THE REALMS, KILLING THOUSANDS.
DO YOU EXPECT ME TO THANK YOU FOR THAT?
NO, I NEVER EXPECTED THAT.
EVERYONE TOLD ME I WAS A FOOL FOR YET AGAIN DARING TO TRUST YOU. FOR GIVING YOU ONE LAST CHANCE TO PROVE YOURSELF.
TO SHOW THAT THE GOOD I SAW INSIDE YOU WASN'T A RUSE. THAT YOUR HONOR COULD FINALLY OUTWEIGH YOUR GODFORSAKEN LIES.
BUT THEY WERE RIGHT, WEREN'T THEY? WITH YOU, LOKI... THE LIES ALWAYS WIN IN THE END.
IT'S NO LIE WHEN I TELL YOU THAT ASGARDIA WILL FALL TODAY.
AND NO ONE, NO GOD IN ALL THE HEAVENS, CAN DO ANYTHING TO CHANGE THAT.
NOT THE ALL-FATHER.
NOT THE ODINSON.
NOT YOU.
THERE ARE SOME THINGS... YOU JUST CAN'T SAVE.
GOODBYE, LADY FREYJA.

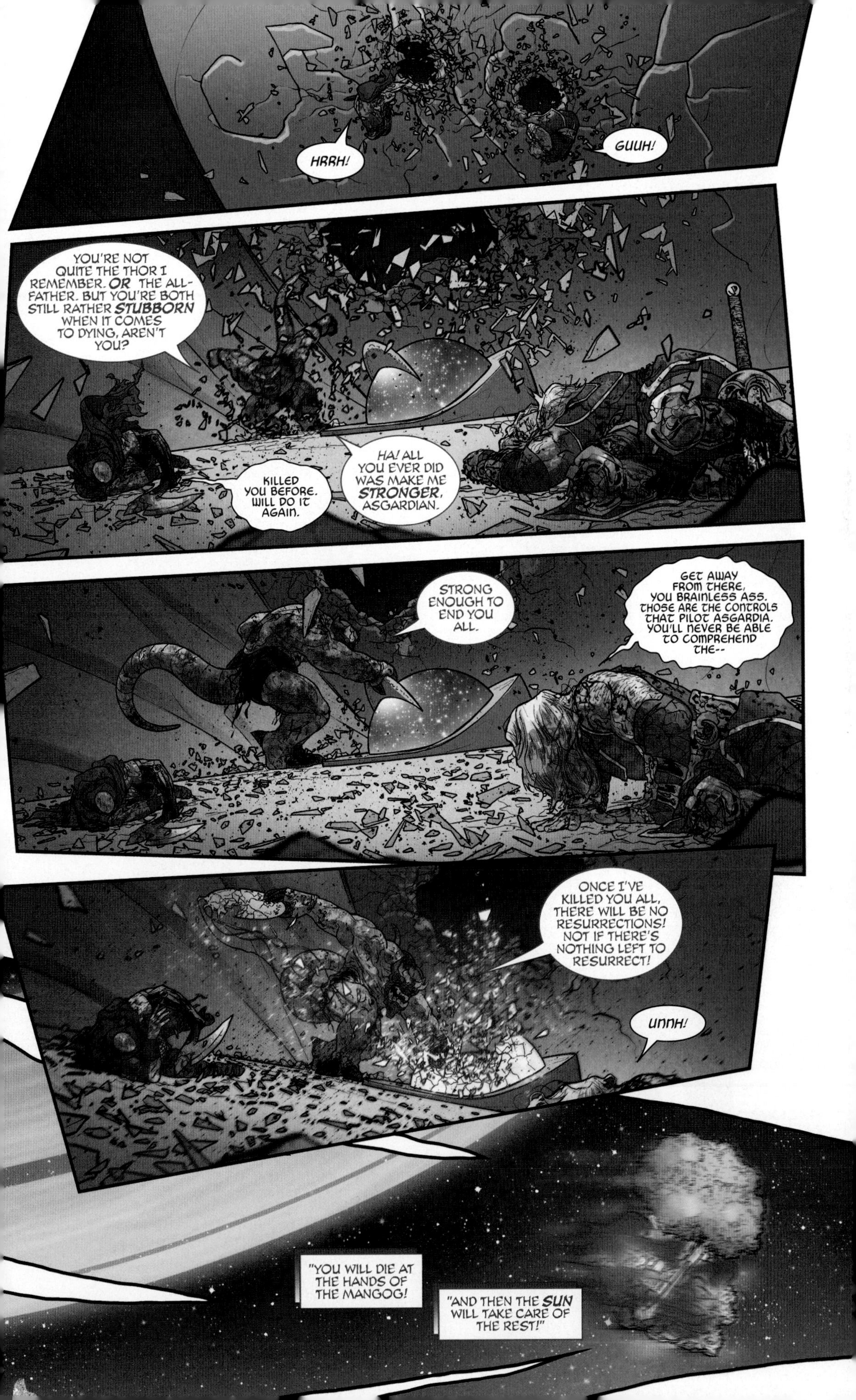
HRRH!
GUUH!
YOU'RE NOT QUITE THE THOR I REMEMBER. OR THE ALL-FATHER. BUT YOU'RE BOTH STILL RATHER STUBBORN WHEN IT COMES TO DYING, AREN'T YOU?
KILLED YOU BEFORE. WILL DO IT AGAIN.
HA! ALL YOU EVER DID WAS MAKE ME STRONGER, ASGARDIAN.
STRONG ENOUGH TO END YOU ALL.
GET AWAY FROM THERE, YOU BRAINLESS ASS. THOSE ARE THE CONTROLS THAT PILOT ASGARDIA. YOU'LL NEVER BE ABLE TO COMPREHEND THE--
ONCE I'VE KILLED YOU ALL, THERE WILL BE NO RESURRECTIONS! NOT IF THERE'S NOTHING LEFT TO RESURRECT!
UNNH!
"YOU WILL DIE AT THE HANDS OF THE MANGOG!
"AND THEN THE SUN WILL TAKE CARE OF THE REST!"

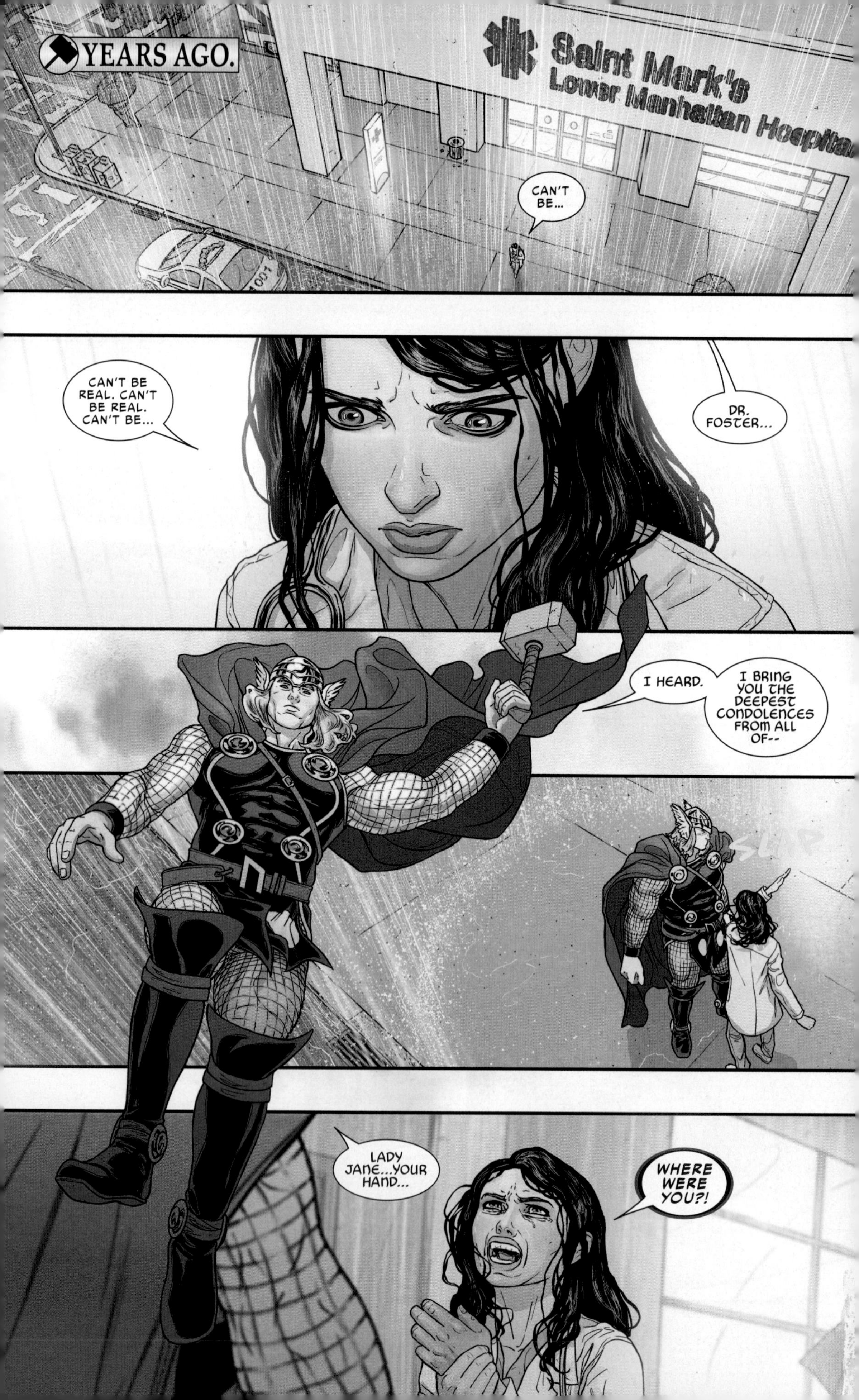
YEARS AGO.
Saint Mark's
Lower Manhattan Hospital
CAN'T BE...
CAN'T BE REAL. CAN'T BE REAL. CAN'T BE...
DR. FOSTER...
I HEARD.
I BRING YOU THE DEEPEST CONDOLENCES FROM ALL OF--
SLAP
LADY JANE...YOUR HAND...
WHERE WERE YOU?!

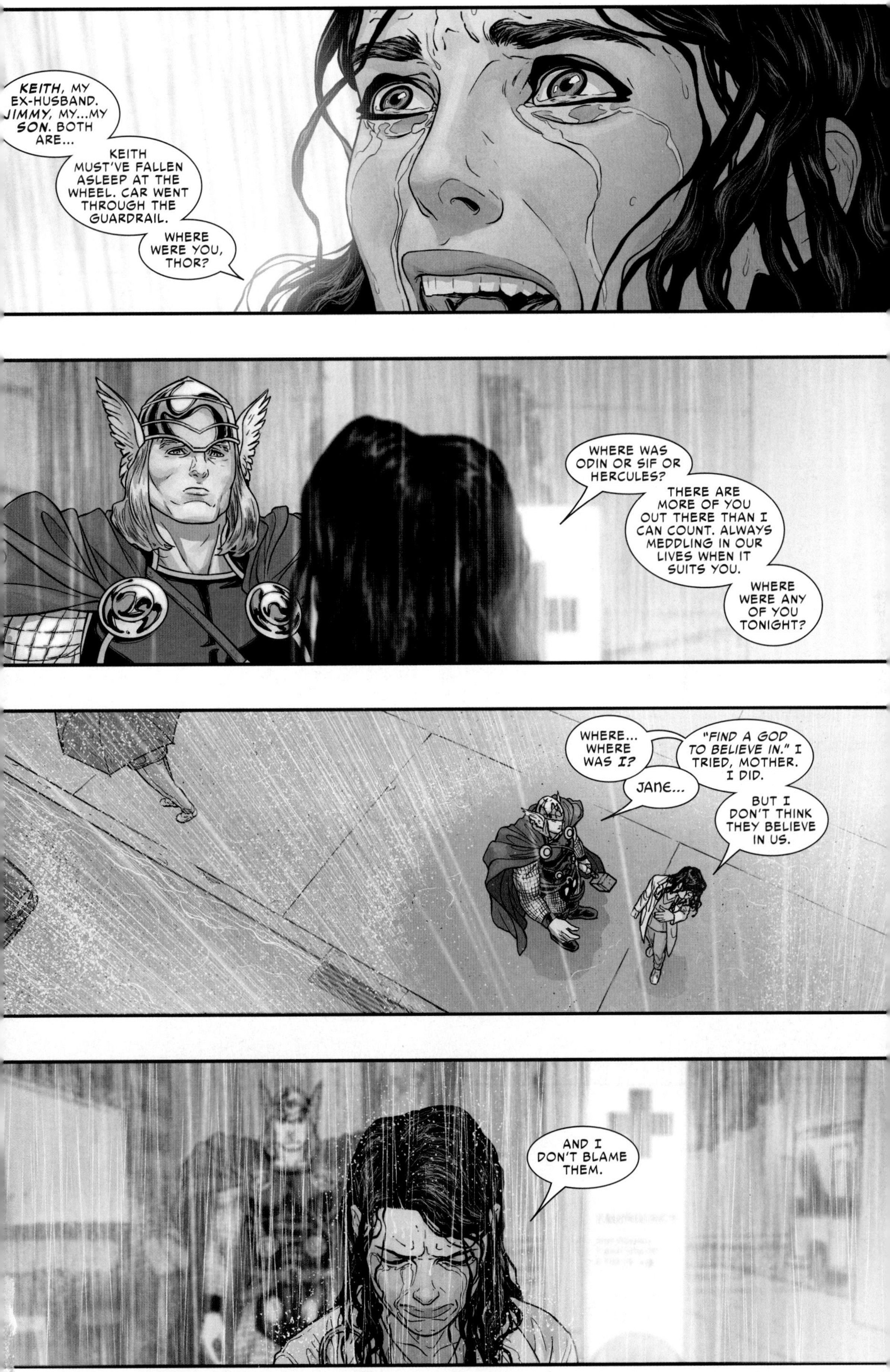
KEITH, MY EX-HUSBAND. JIMMY, MY...MY SON. BOTH ARE...
KEITH MUST'VE FALLEN ASLEEP AT THE WHEEL. CAR WENT THROUGH THE GUARDRAIL.
WHERE WERE YOU, THOR?
WHERE WAS ODIN OR SIF OR HERCULES?
THERE ARE MORE OF YOU OUT THERE THAN I CAN COUNT. ALWAYS MEDDLING IN OUR LIVES WHEN IT SUITS YOU.
WHERE WERE ANY OF YOU TONIGHT?
WHERE... WHERE WAS I?
JANE...
"FIND A GOD TO BELIEVE IN." I TRIED, MOTHER. I DID.
BUT I DON'T THINK THEY BELIEVE IN US.
AND I DON'T BLAME THEM.

HEY, BONNIE.

DR. FOSTER. HAVEN'T SEEN YOU IN A WHILE.

IN THIS WARD, I GET WORRIED WHEN I DON'T SEE FOLKS FOR A WHILE.

I'M STILL KICKING. HOW ABOUT YOU?

EH, THE NURSES TELL ME I'M STILL ALIVE. BUT SOME DAYS I AIN'T SO SURE.

I TOLD YOU, BONNIE, YOU GOTTA BE AROUND TO KEEP THAT *FLOWER* ALIVE, AFTER ALL THE TROUBLE I WENT THROUGH.

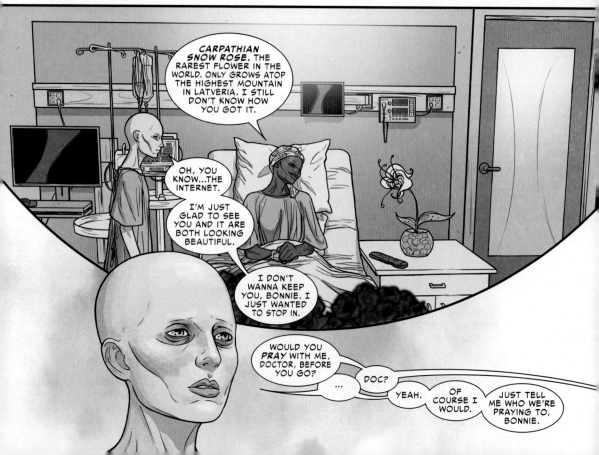

*CARPATHIAN SNOW ROSE.* THE RAREST FLOWER IN THE WORLD. ONLY GROWS ATOP THE HIGHEST MOUNTAIN IN LATVERIA. I STILL DON'T KNOW HOW YOU GOT IT.

OH, YOU KNOW...THE INTERNET.

I'M JUST GLAD TO SEE YOU AND IT ARE BOTH LOOKING BEAUTIFUL.

I DON'T WANNA KEEP YOU, BONNIE. I JUST WANTED TO STOP IN.

WOULD YOU *PRAY* WITH ME, DOCTOR, BEFORE YOU GO?

...

DOC?

YEAH.

OF COURSE I WOULD.

JUST TELL ME WHO WE'RE PRAYING TO, BONNIE.

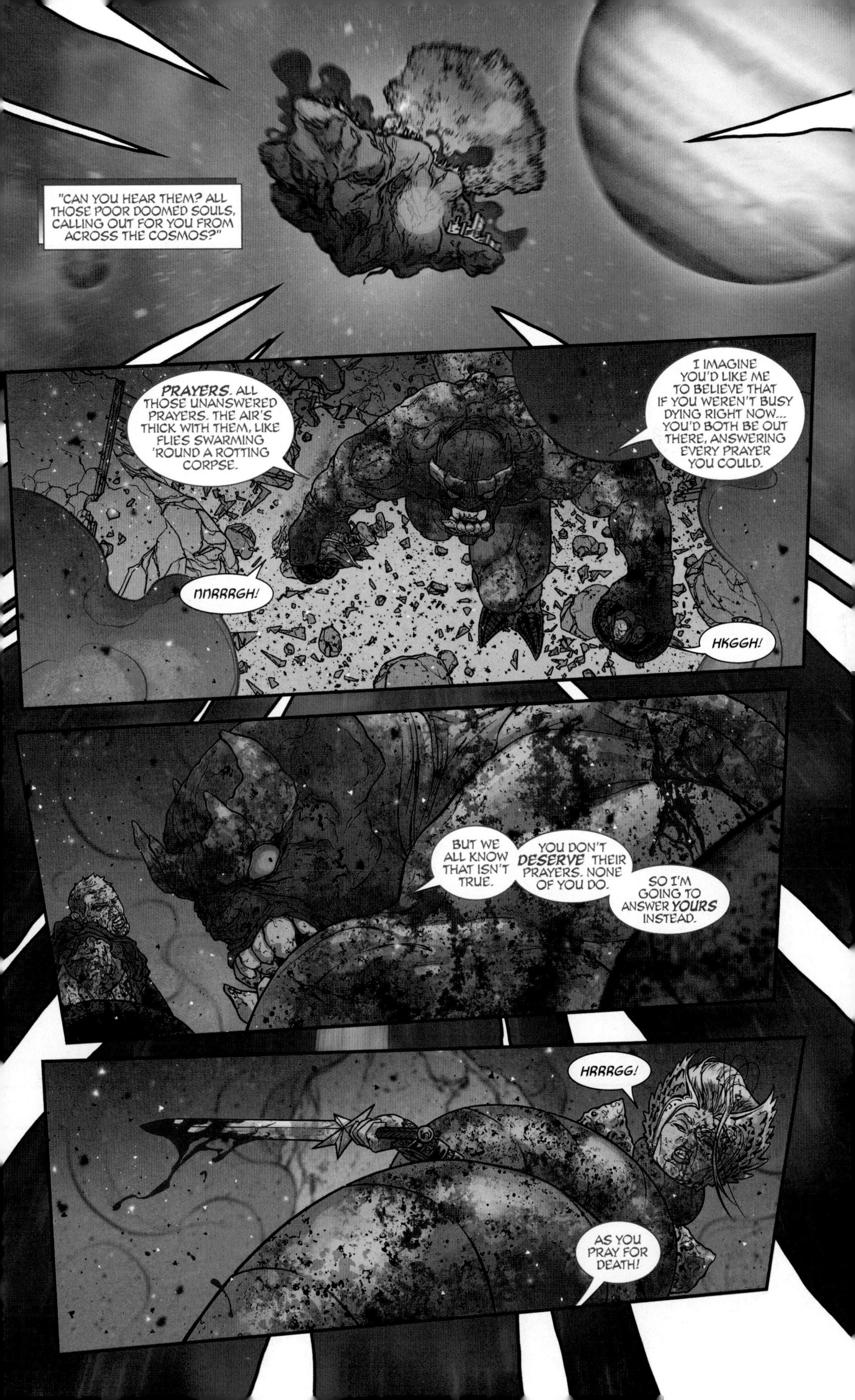
"CAN YOU HEAR THEM? ALL THOSE POOR DOOMED SOULS, CALLING OUT FOR YOU FROM ACROSS THE COSMOS?"
PRAYERS. ALL THOSE UNANSWERED PRAYERS. THE AIR'S THICK WITH THEM, LIKE FLIES SWARMING 'ROUND A ROTTING CORPSE.
I IMAGINE YOU'D LIKE ME TO BELIEVE THAT IF YOU WEREN'T BUSY DYING RIGHT NOW... YOU'D BOTH BE OUT THERE, ANSWERING EVERY PRAYER YOU COULD.
NNRRRGH!
HKGGH!
BUT WE ALL KNOW THAT ISN'T TRUE.
YOU DON'T DESERVE THEIR PRAYERS. NONE OF YOU DO.
SO I'M GOING TO ANSWER YOURS INSTEAD.
HRRRGG!
AS YOU PRAY FOR DEATH!

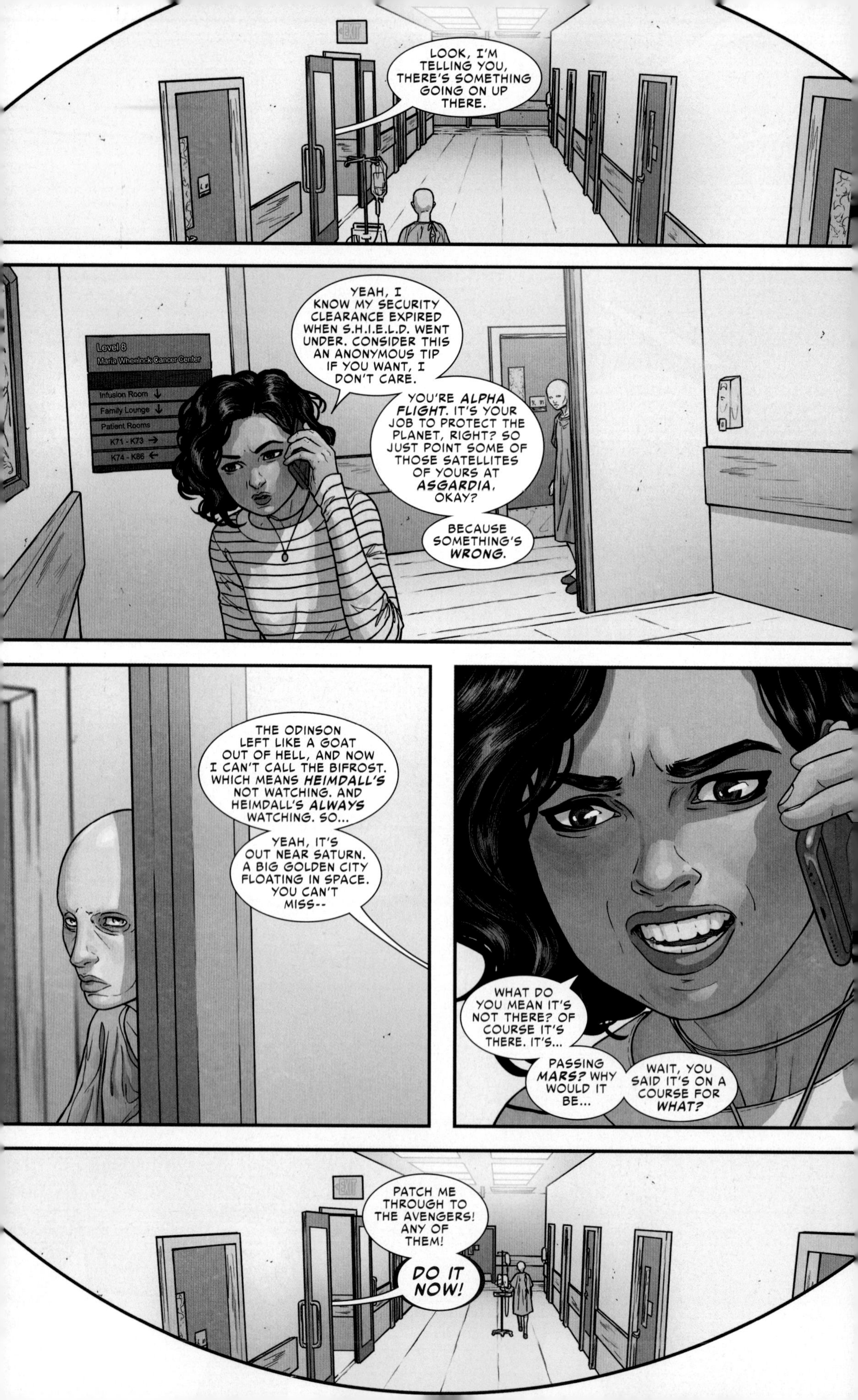
EXIT
LOOK, I'M TELLING YOU, THERE'S SOMETHING GOING ON UP THERE.
Level 8
Maria Wheelock Cancer Center
Infusion Room
Family Lounge
Patient Rooms
K71 - K73
K74 - K86
YEAH, I KNOW MY SECURITY CLEARANCE EXPIRED WHEN S.H.I.E.L.D. WENT UNDER. CONSIDER THIS AN ANONYMOUS TIP IF YOU WANT, I DON'T CARE.
YOU'RE ALPHA FLIGHT. IT'S YOUR JOB TO PROTECT THE PLANET, RIGHT? SO JUST POINT SOME OF THOSE SATELLITES OF YOURS AT ASGARDIA, OKAY?
BECAUSE SOMETHING'S WRONG.
THE ODINSON LEFT LIKE A GOAT OUT OF HELL, AND NOW I CAN'T CALL THE BIFROST. WHICH MEANS HEIMDALL'S NOT WATCHING. AND HEIMDALL'S ALWAYS WATCHING. SO...
YEAH, IT'S OUT NEAR SATURN. A BIG GOLDEN CITY FLOATING IN SPACE. YOU CAN'T MISS--
WHAT DO YOU MEAN IT'S NOT THERE? OF COURSE IT'S THERE. IT'S...
PASSING MARS? WHY WOULD IT BE...
WAIT, YOU SAID IT'S ON A COURSE FOR WHAT?
EXIT
PATCH ME THROUGH TO THE AVENGERS! ANY OF THEM!
DO IT NOW!

RAWF HAMMER!

RAWF RAWF MURDER!

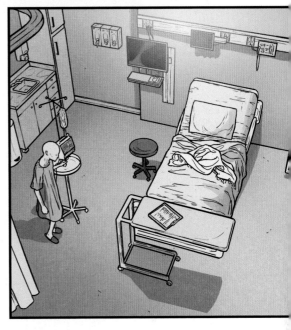

I WOULD'VE *BEATEN* YOU, YOU LITTLE CANCEROUS SONS OF BITCHES.

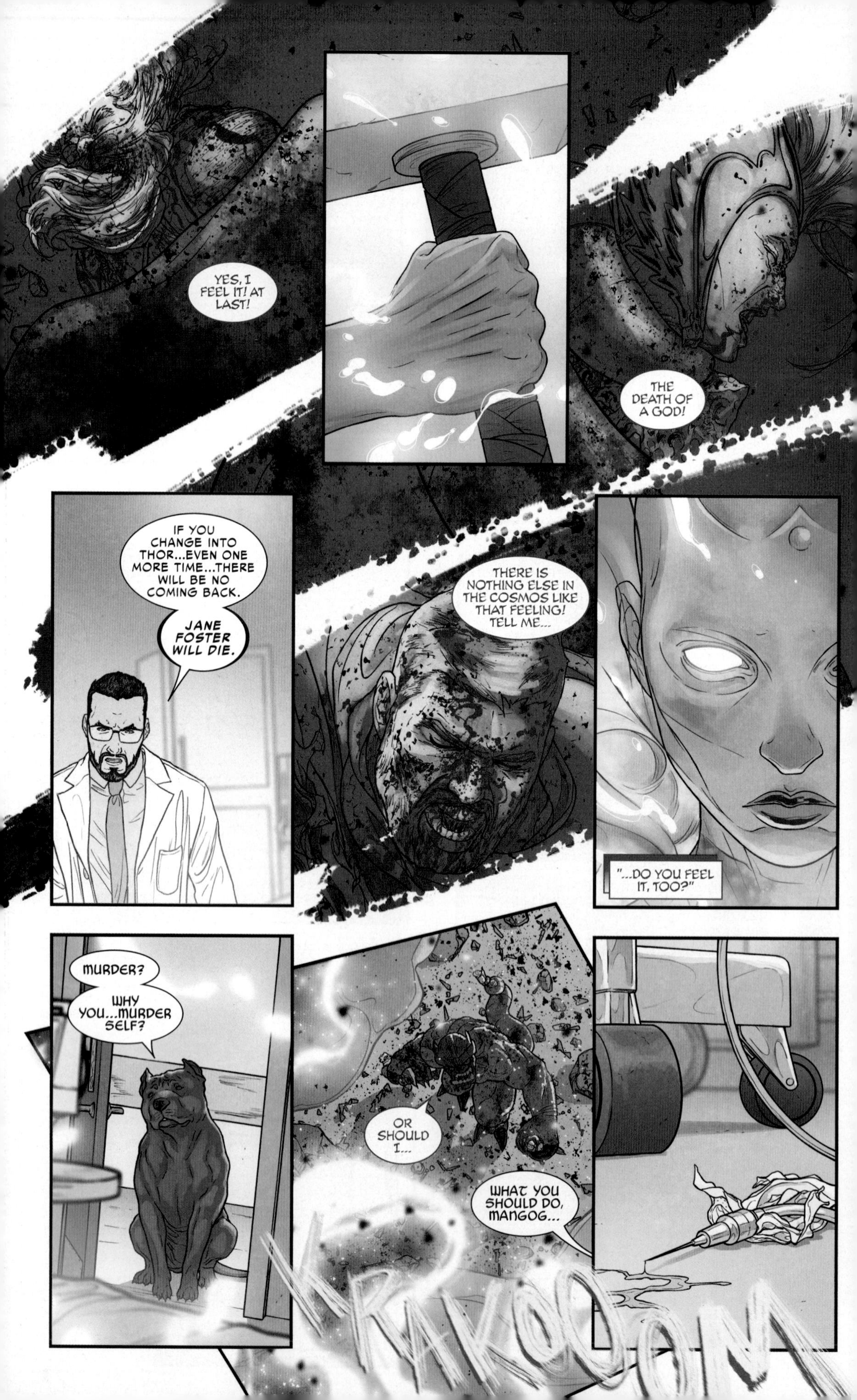
YES, I FEEL IT! AT LAST!
THE DEATH OF A GOD!
IF YOU CHANGE INTO THOR...EVEN ONE MORE TIME...THERE WILL BE NO COMING BACK.
JANE FOSTER WILL DIE.
THERE IS NOTHING ELSE IN THE COSMOS LIKE THAT FEELING! TELL ME...
"...DO YOU FEEL IT, TOO?"
MURDER?
WHY YOU...MURDER SELF?
OR SHOULD I...
WHAT YOU SHOULD DO, MANGOG...
KRAKOOOM

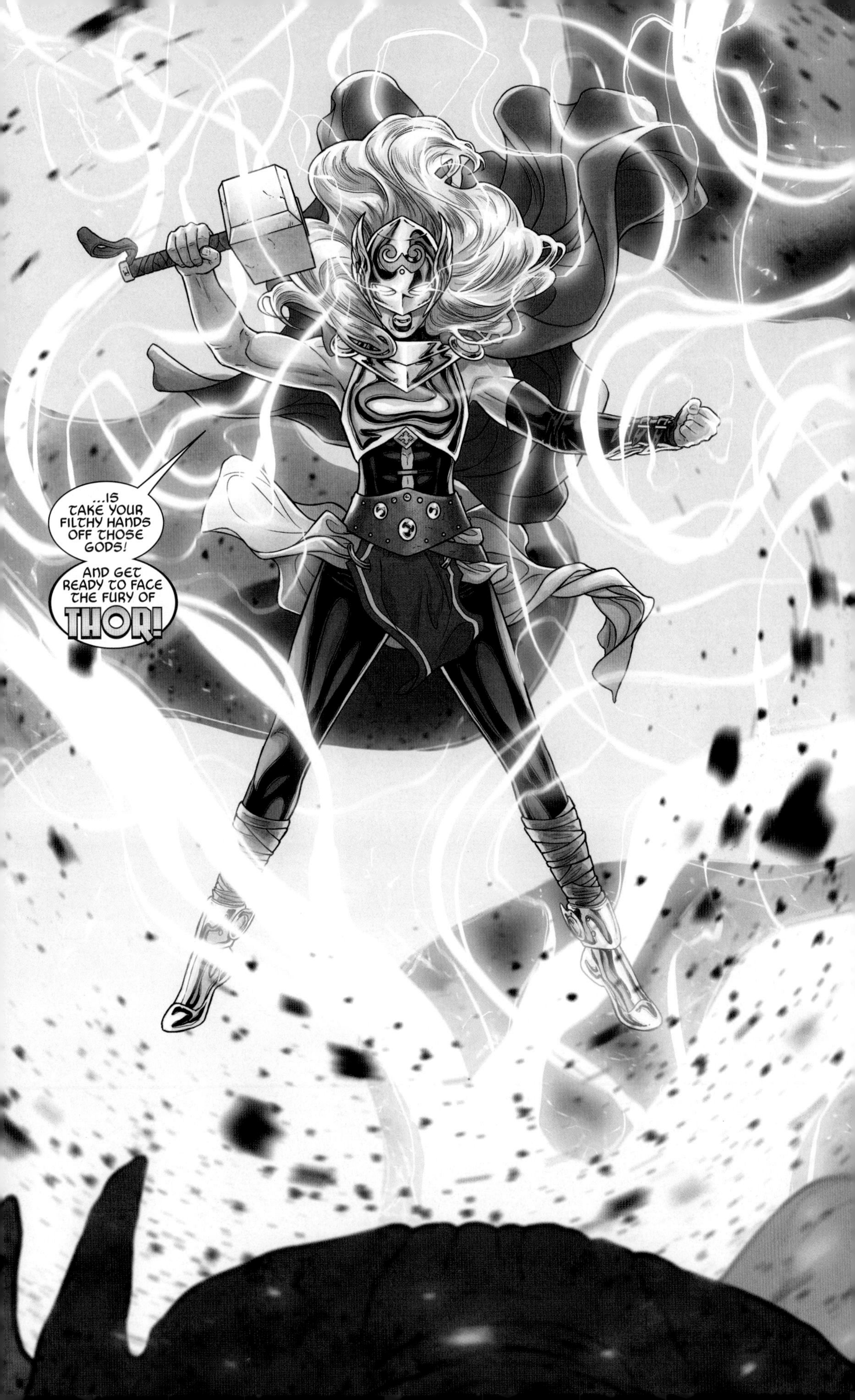
...IS TAKE YOUR FILTHY HANDS OFF THOSE GODS!
AND GET READY TO FACE THE FURY OF THOR!

# 705

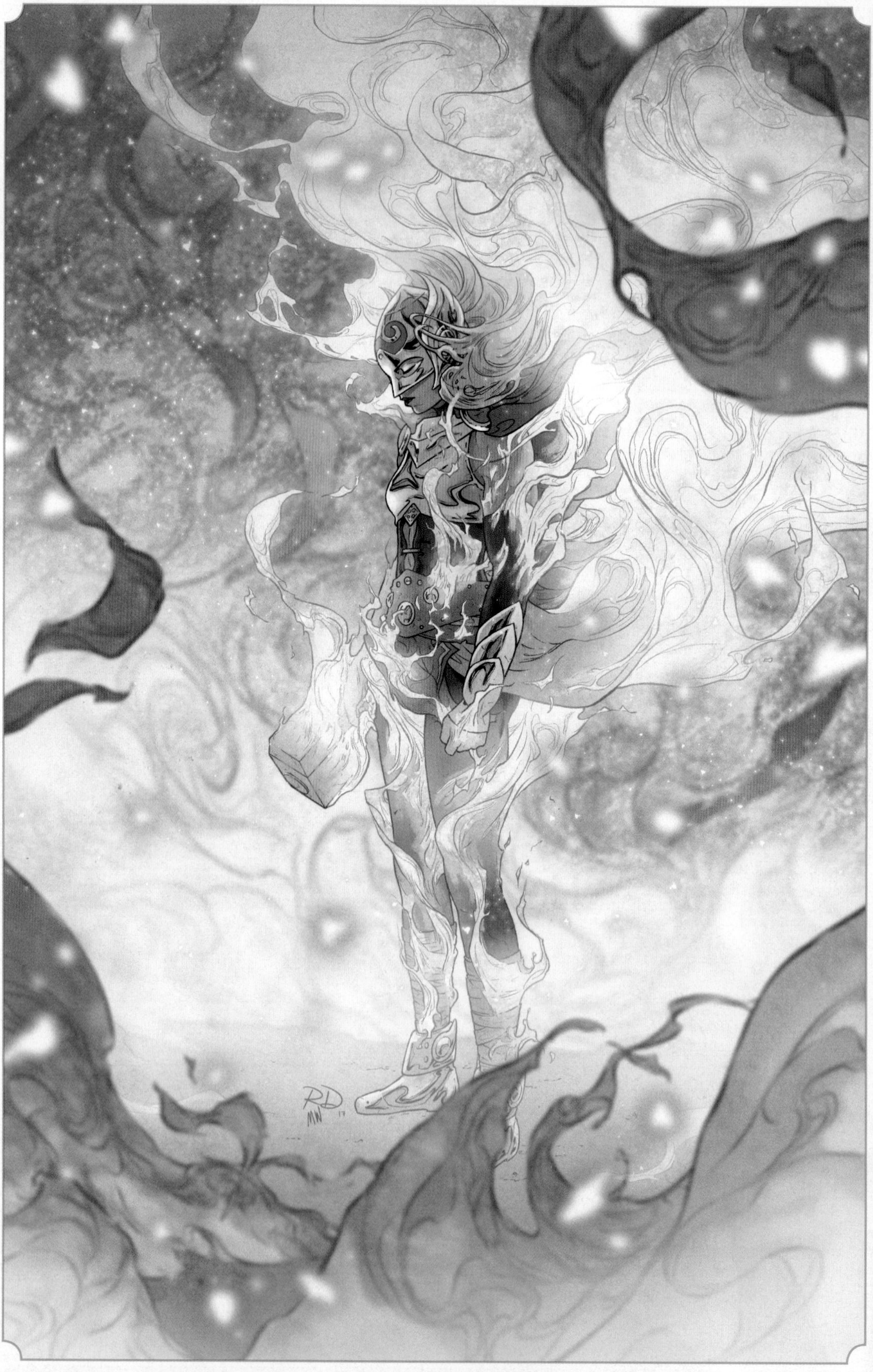

SUNDOWN

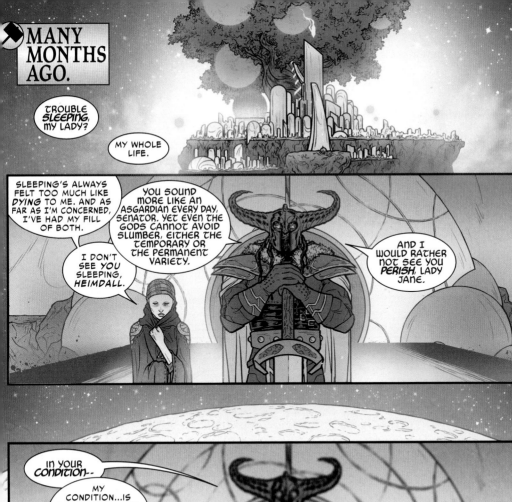

TROUBLE *SLEEPING*, MY LADY?

MY WHOLE LIFE.

SLEEPING'S ALWAYS FELT TOO MUCH LIKE *DYING* TO ME. AND AS FAR AS I'M CONCERNED, I'VE HAD MY FILL OF BOTH.

YOU SOUND MORE LIKE AN ASGARDIAN EVERY DAY, SENATOR. YET EVEN THE GODS CANNOT AVOID SLUMBER, EITHER THE TEMPORARY OR THE PERMANENT VARIETY.

I DON'T SEE *YOU* SLEEPING, *HEIMDALL.*

AND I WOULD RATHER NOT SEE YOU *PERISH*, LADY JANE.

IN YOUR *CONDITION--*

MY CONDITION...IS A *RESTLESS* ONE. AND I IMAGINE WE BOTH KNOW WHY.

I HAVE A *VOICE* IN MY HEAD, HEIMDALL. AND I WON'T INSULT YOU BY LYING ABOUT WHAT IT WANTS ME TO DO.

JUST SEND ME THERE. BEFORE I COME TO MY SENSES.

YOU ARE A SENATOR IN THE *CONGRESS OF WORLDS*, JANE FOSTER. THE *BIFROST* IS YOURS TO COMMAND.

MAY THE GODS BE WITH YOU.

THOUGH PERHAPS YOU WOULD'VE BEEN FAR BETTER OFF...

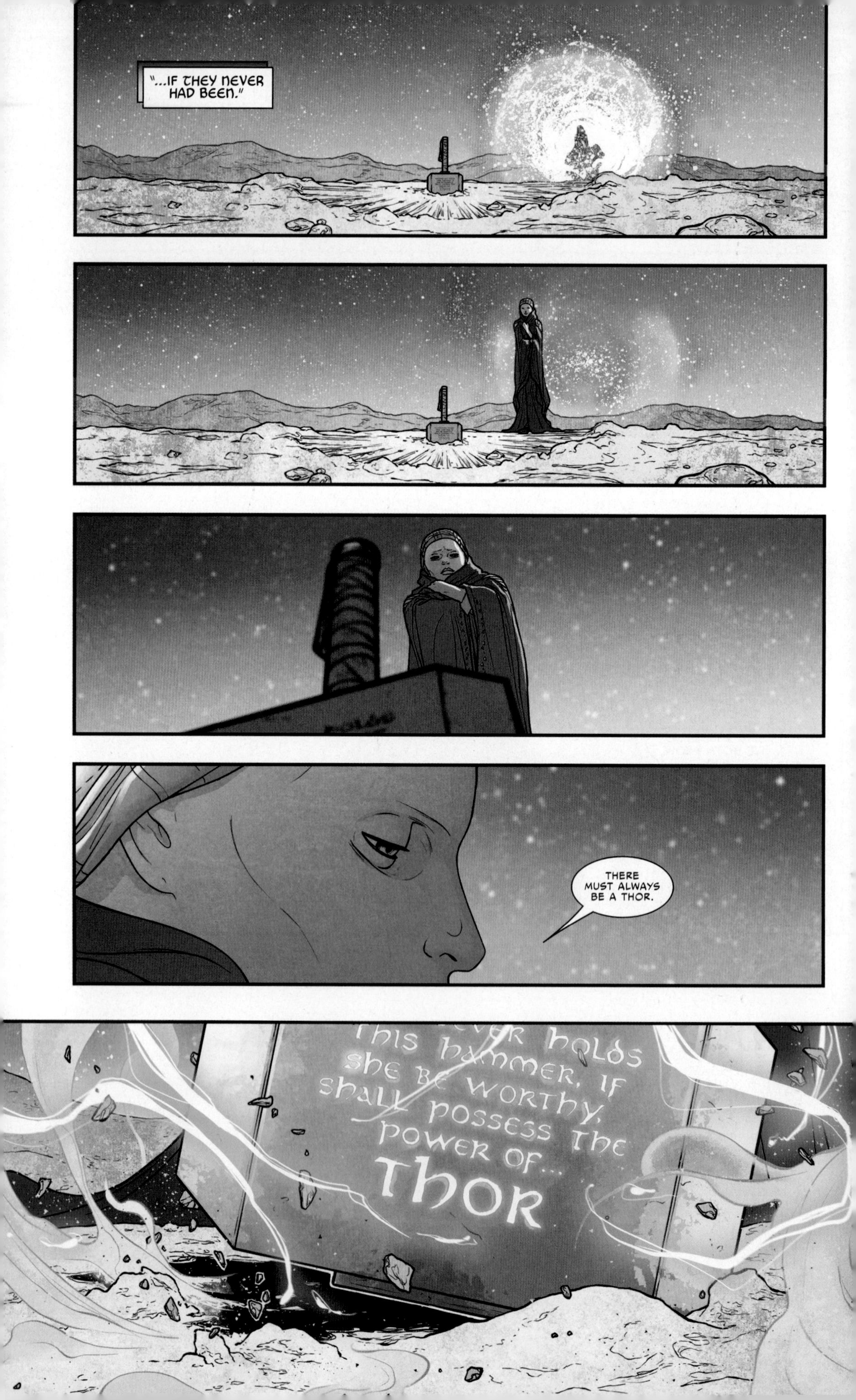
"...IF THEY NEVER HAD BEEN."
THERE MUST ALWAYS BE A THOR.
this hammer, if
she be worthy,
shall possess the
power of...
THOR

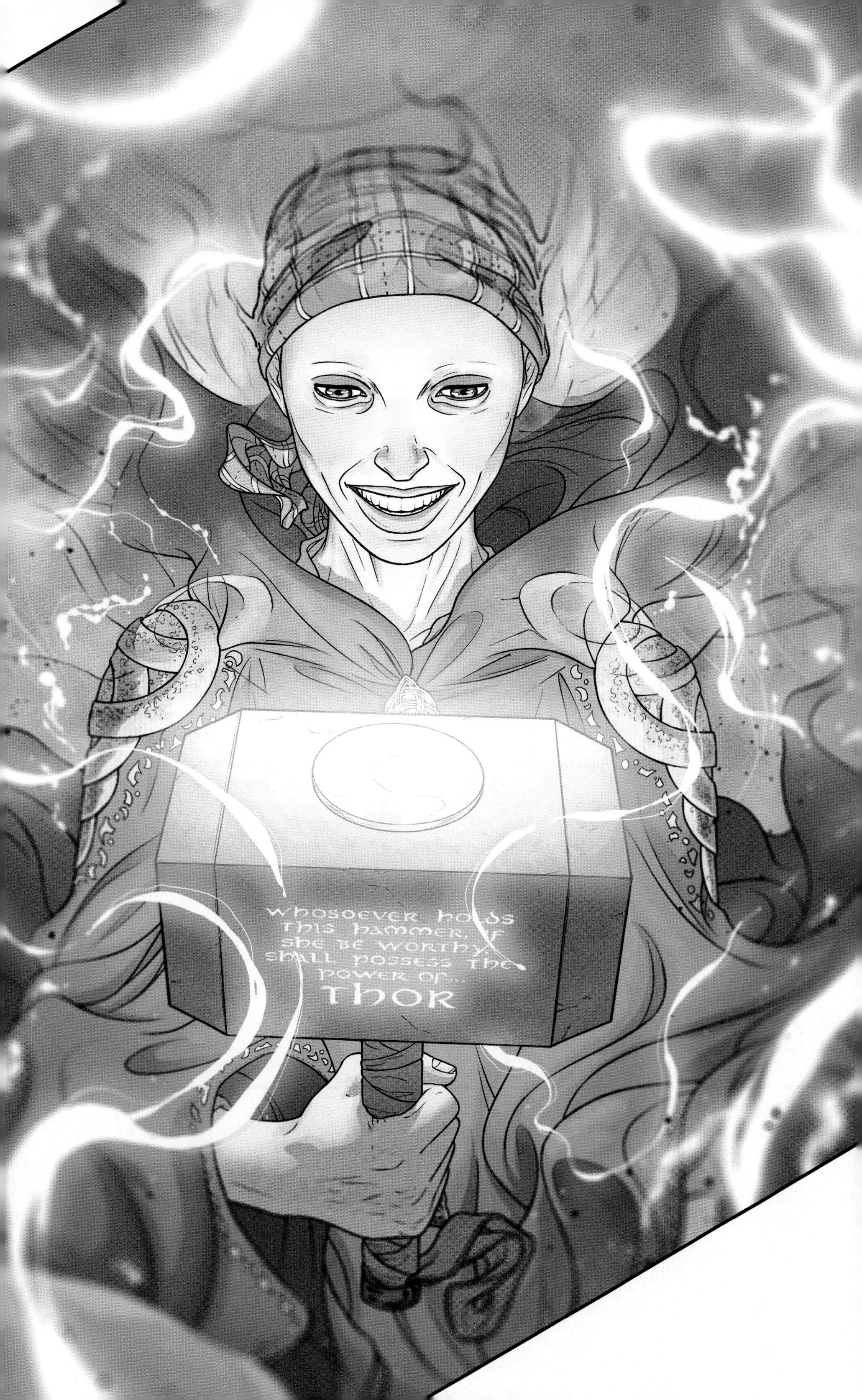
WHOSOEVER HOLDS THIS HAMMER, IF SHE BE WORTHY, SHALL POSSESS THE POWER OF...
THOR

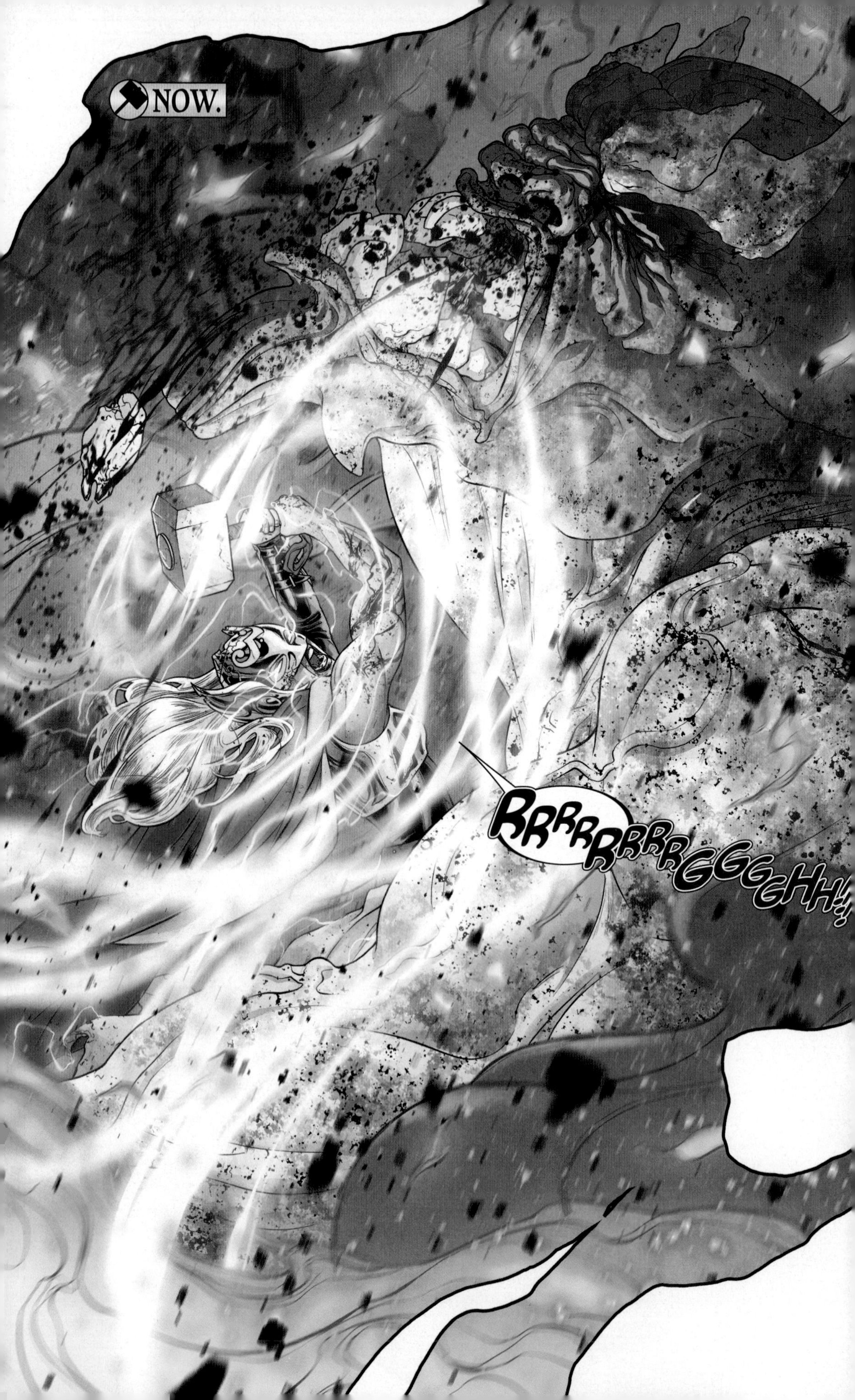
NOW.
RRRRRRRRRGGGGHH!!

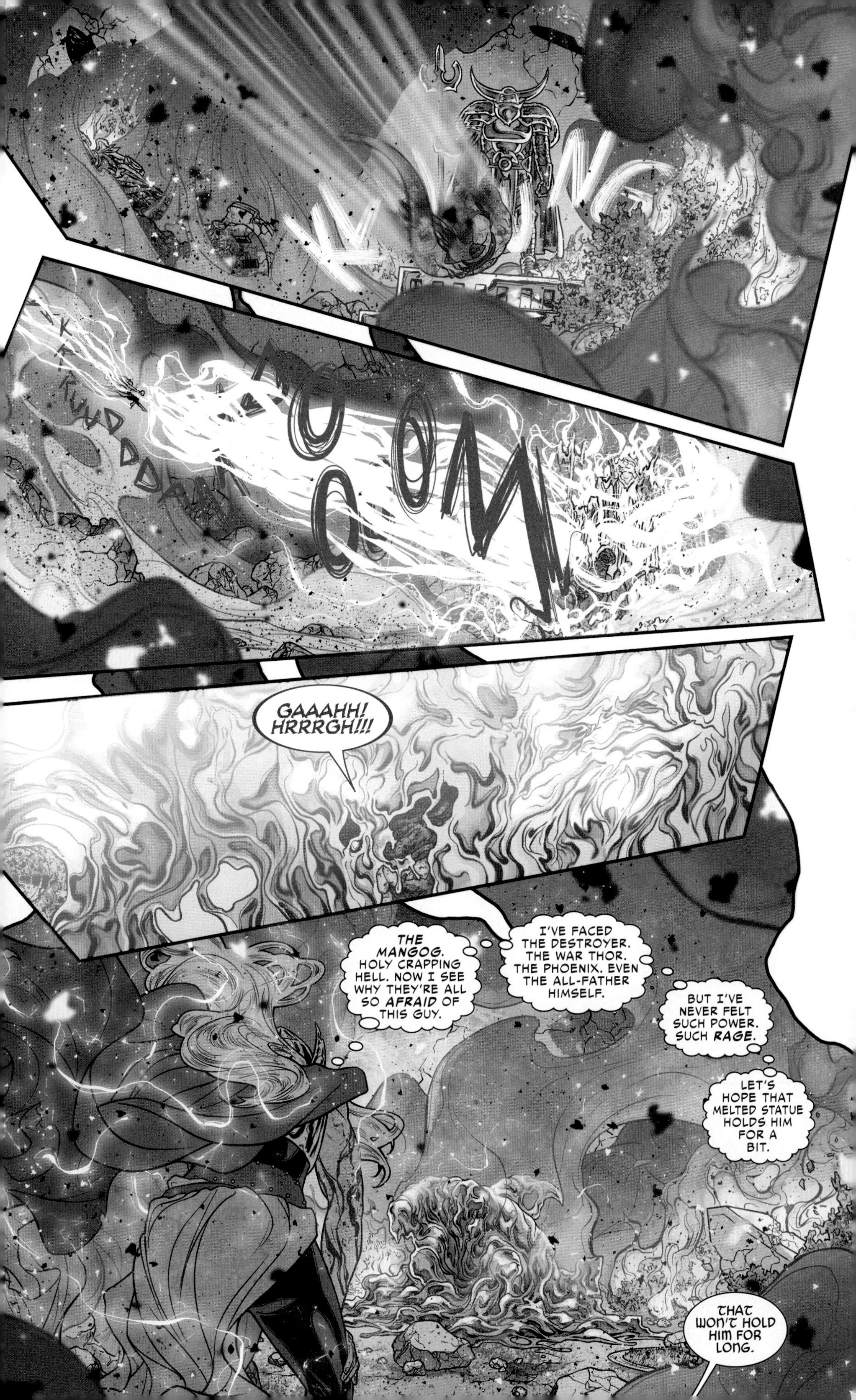
KKUNG
KRUDDDDAM
KRAKOOOM
GAAAHH! HRRRGH!!!
THE MANGOG. HOLY CRAPPING HELL. NOW I SEE WHY THEY'RE ALL SO AFRAID OF THIS GUY.
I'VE FACED THE DESTROYER. THE WAR THOR. THE PHOENIX. EVEN THE ALL-FATHER HIMSELF.
BUT I'VE NEVER FELT SUCH POWER. SUCH RAGE.
LET'S HOPE THAT MELTED STATUE HOLDS HIM FOR A BIT.
THAT WON'T HOLD HIM FOR LONG.

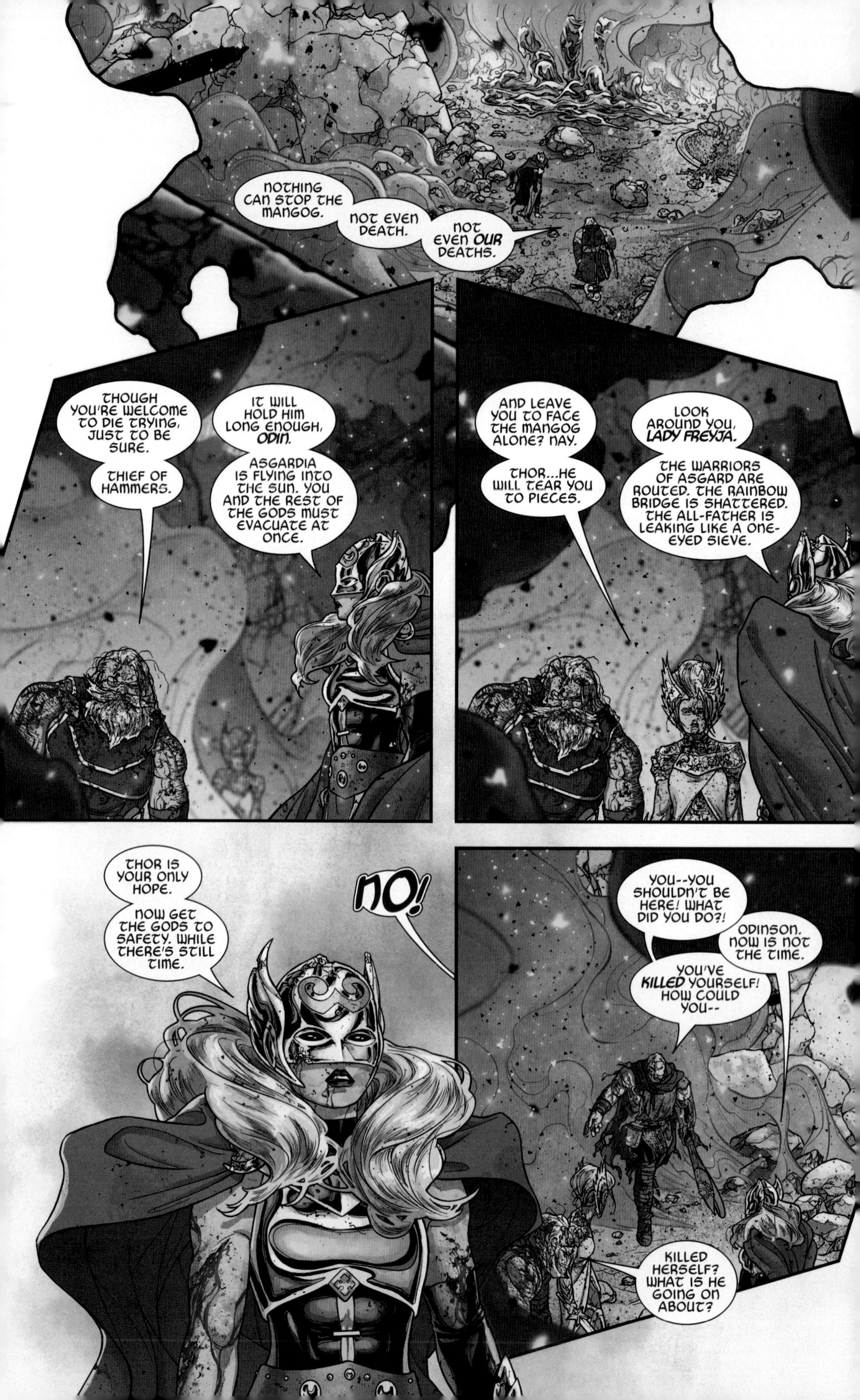
NOTHING CAN STOP THE MANGOG.
NOT EVEN DEATH.
NOT EVEN OUR DEATHS.
IT WILL HOLD HIM LONG ENOUGH, ODIN.
ASGARDIA IS FLYING INTO THE SUN. YOU AND THE REST OF THE GODS MUST EVACUATE AT ONCE.
THOUGH YOU'RE WELCOME TO DIE TRYING, JUST TO BE SURE.
THIEF OF HAMMERS.
LOOK AROUND YOU, LADY FREYJA.
THE WARRIORS OF ASGARD ARE ROUTED. THE RAINBOW BRIDGE IS SHATTERED. THE ALL-FATHER IS LEAKING LIKE A ONE-EYED SIEVE.
AND LEAVE YOU TO FACE THE MANGOG ALONE? NAY.
THOR...HE WILL TEAR YOU TO PIECES.
THOR IS YOUR ONLY HOPE.
NOW GET THE GODS TO SAFETY. WHILE THERE'S STILL TIME.
NO!
YOU--YOU SHOULDN'T BE HERE! WHAT DID YOU DO?!
ODINSON. NOW IS NOT THE TIME.
YOU'VE KILLED YOURSELF! HOW COULD YOU--
KILLED HERSELF? WHAT IS HE GOING ON ABOUT?

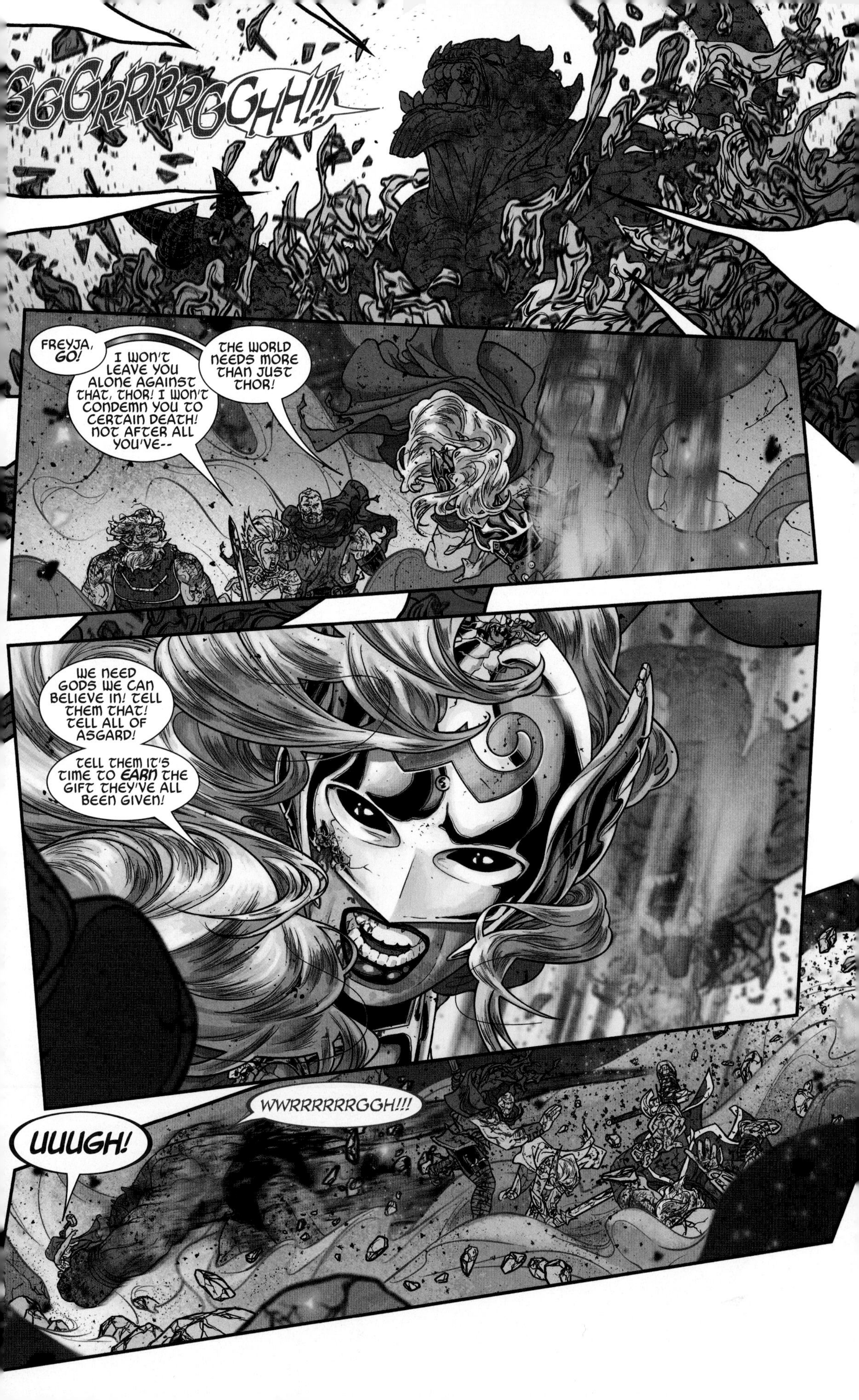

SGGRRRRRGGHH!!!
FREYJA, GO!
I WON'T LEAVE YOU ALONE AGAINST THAT, THOR! I WON'T CONDEMN YOU TO CERTAIN DEATH! NOT AFTER ALL YOU'VE--
THE WORLD NEEDS MORE THAN JUST THOR!
WE NEED GODS WE CAN BELIEVE IN! TELL THEM THAT! TELL ALL OF ASGARD!
TELL THEM IT'S TIME TO EARN THE GIFT THEY'VE ALL BEEN GIVEN!
WWRRRRRRGGH!!!
UUUGH!

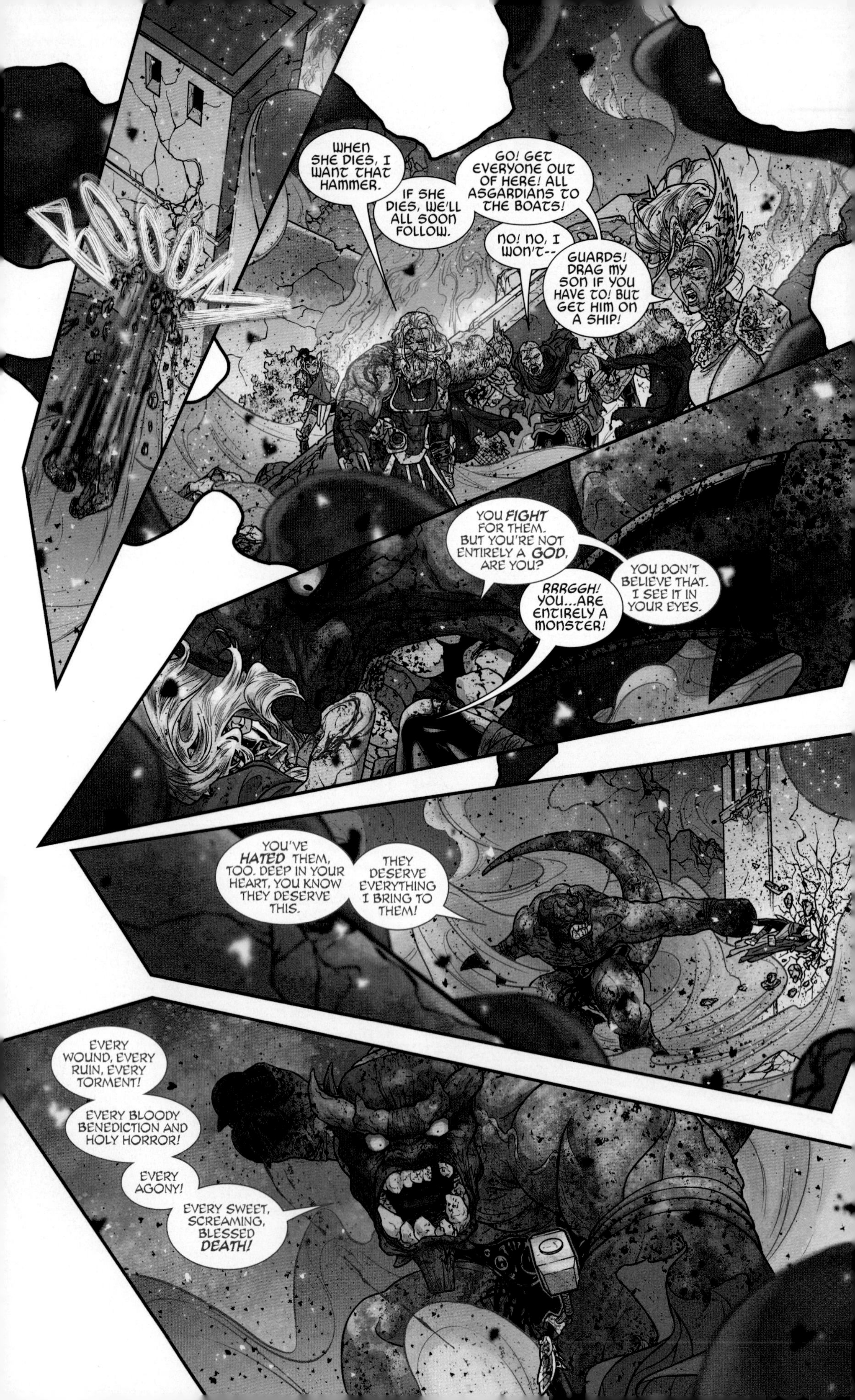
BOOOOM
WHEN SHE DIES, I WANT THAT HAMMER.
IF SHE DIES, WE'LL ALL SOON FOLLOW.
GO! GET EVERYONE OUT OF HERE! ALL ASGARDIANS TO THE BOATS!
NO! NO, I WON'T--
GUARDS! DRAG MY SON IF YOU HAVE TO! BUT GET HIM ON A SHIP!
YOU FIGHT FOR THEM. BUT YOU'RE NOT ENTIRELY A GOD, ARE YOU?
RRRGGH! YOU...ARE ENTIRELY A MONSTER!
YOU DON'T BELIEVE THAT. I SEE IT IN YOUR EYES.
YOU'VE HATED THEM, TOO. DEEP IN YOUR HEART, YOU KNOW THEY DESERVE THIS.
THEY DESERVE EVERYTHING I BRING TO THEM!
EVERY WOUND, EVERY RUIN, EVERY TORMENT!
EVERY BLOODY BENEDICTION AND HOLY HORROR!
EVERY AGONY!
EVERY SWEET, SCREAMING, BLESSED DEATH!

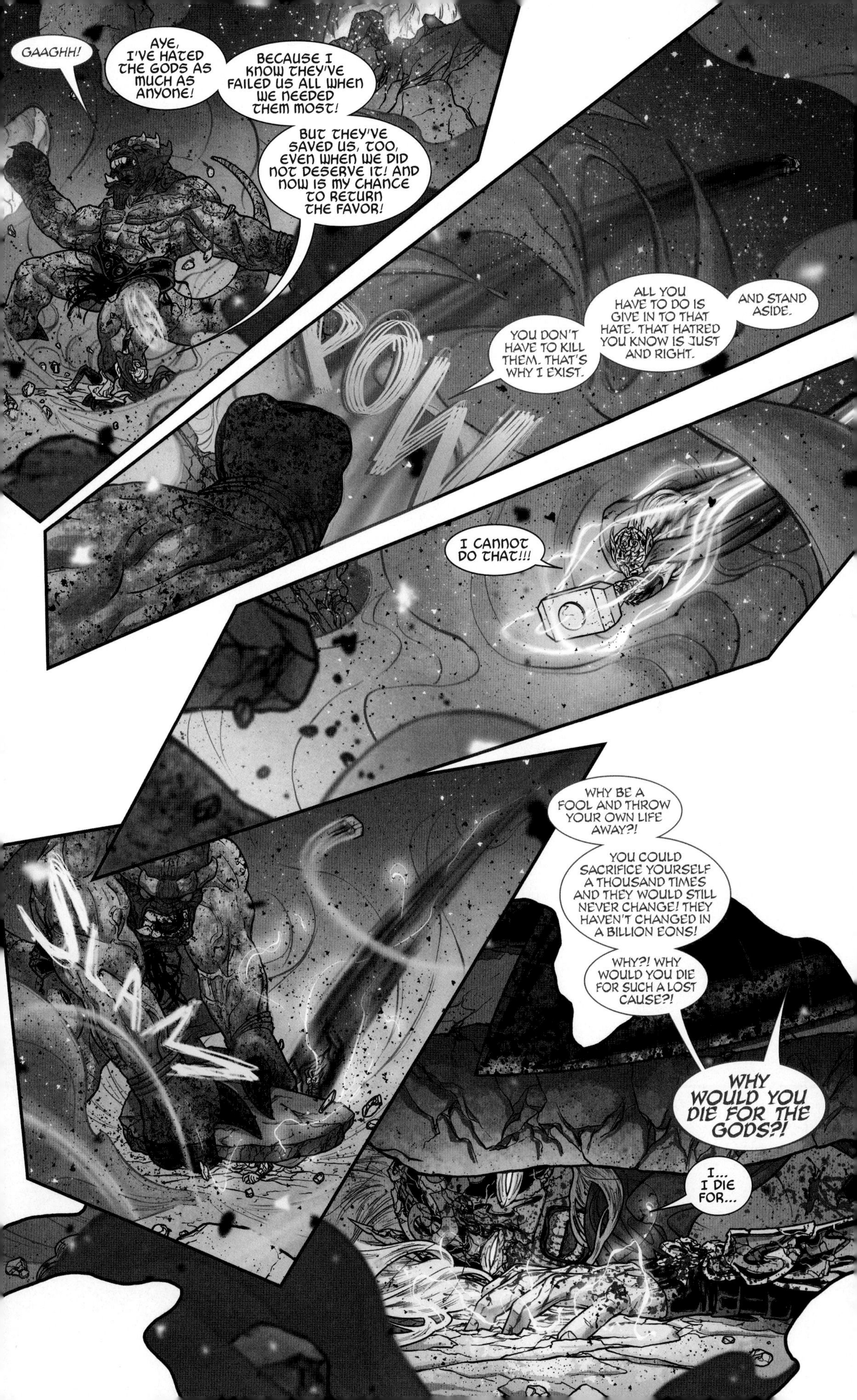

GAAGHH!
AYE, I'VE HATED THE GODS AS MUCH AS ANYONE!
BECAUSE I KNOW THEY'VE FAILED US ALL WHEN WE NEEDED THEM MOST!
BUT THEY'VE SAVED US, TOO, EVEN WHEN WE DID NOT DESERVE IT! AND NOW IS MY CHANCE TO RETURN THE FAVOR!
POW
YOU DON'T HAVE TO KILL THEM. THAT'S WHY I EXIST.
ALL YOU HAVE TO DO IS GIVE IN TO THAT HATE. THAT HATRED YOU KNOW IS JUST AND RIGHT.
AND STAND ASIDE.
I CANNOT DO THAT!!!
SLAM
WHY BE A FOOL AND THROW YOUR OWN LIFE AWAY?!
YOU COULD SACRIFICE YOURSELF A THOUSAND TIMES AND THEY WOULD STILL NEVER CHANGE! THEY HAVEN'T CHANGED IN A BILLION EONS!
WHY?! WHY WOULD YOU DIE FOR SUCH A LOST CAUSE?!
WHY WOULD YOU DIE FOR THE GODS?!
I... I DIE FOR...

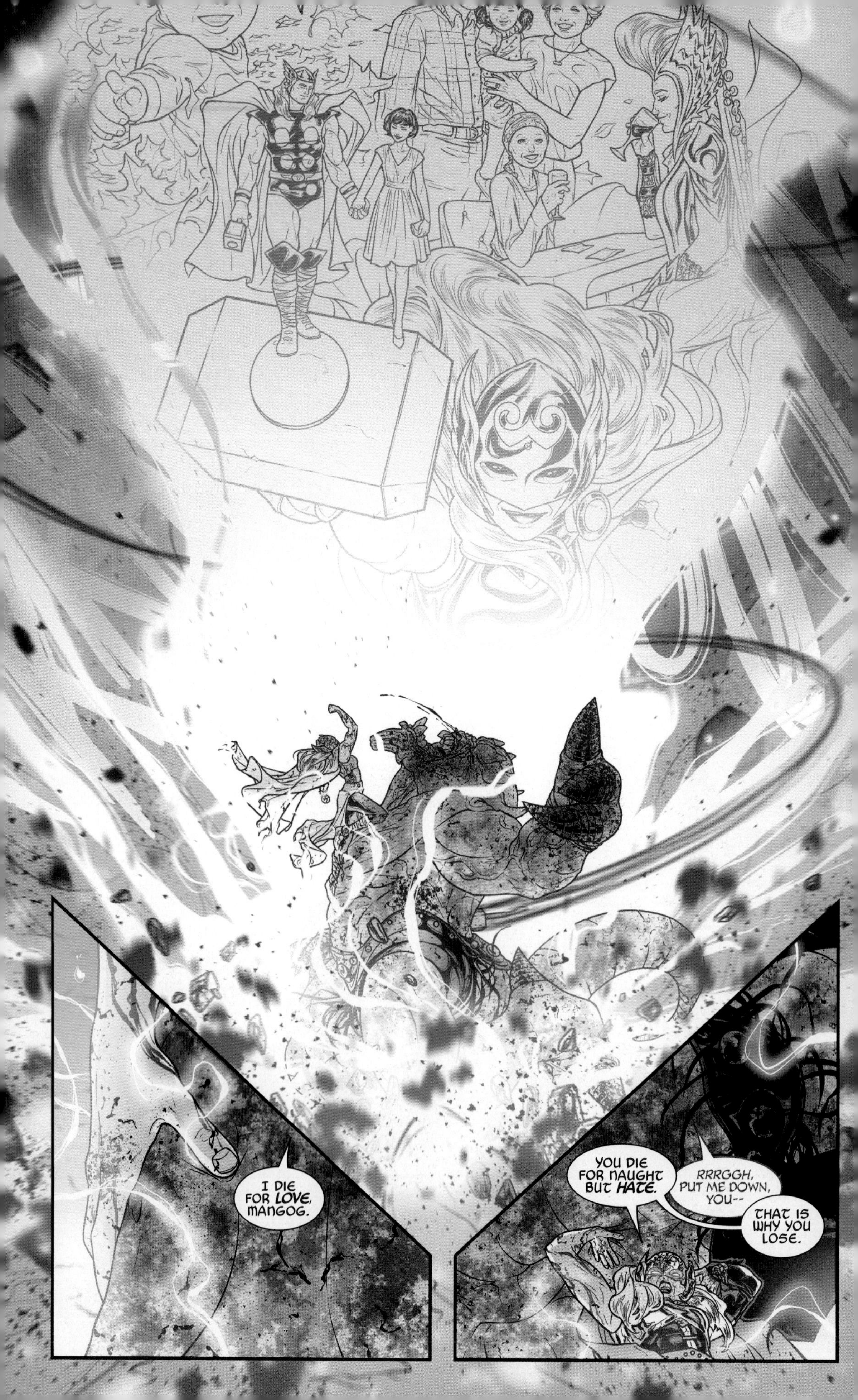
I DIE FOR LOVE, MANGOG.
YOU DIE FOR NAUGHT BUT HATE.
RRRGGH, PUT ME DOWN, YOU--
THAT IS WHY YOU LOSE.

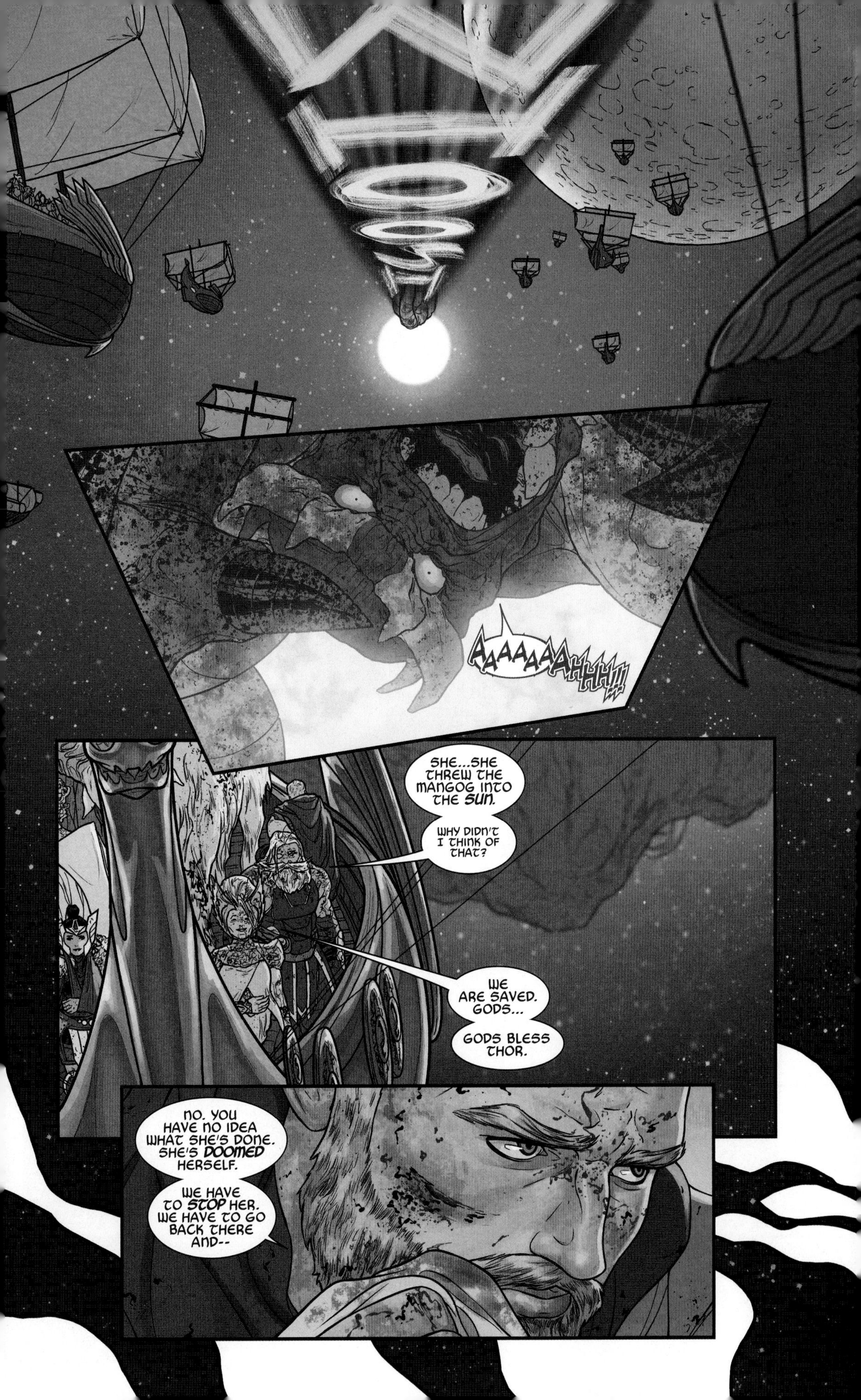
AAAAAAAHHHH!!!
SHE...SHE THREW THE MANGOG INTO THE SUN.
WHY DIDN'T I THINK OF THAT?
WE ARE SAVED. GODS...
GODS BLESS THOR.
NO. YOU HAVE NO IDEA WHAT SHE'S DONE. SHE'S DOOMED HERSELF.
WE HAVE TO STOP HER. WE HAVE TO GO BACK THERE AND--

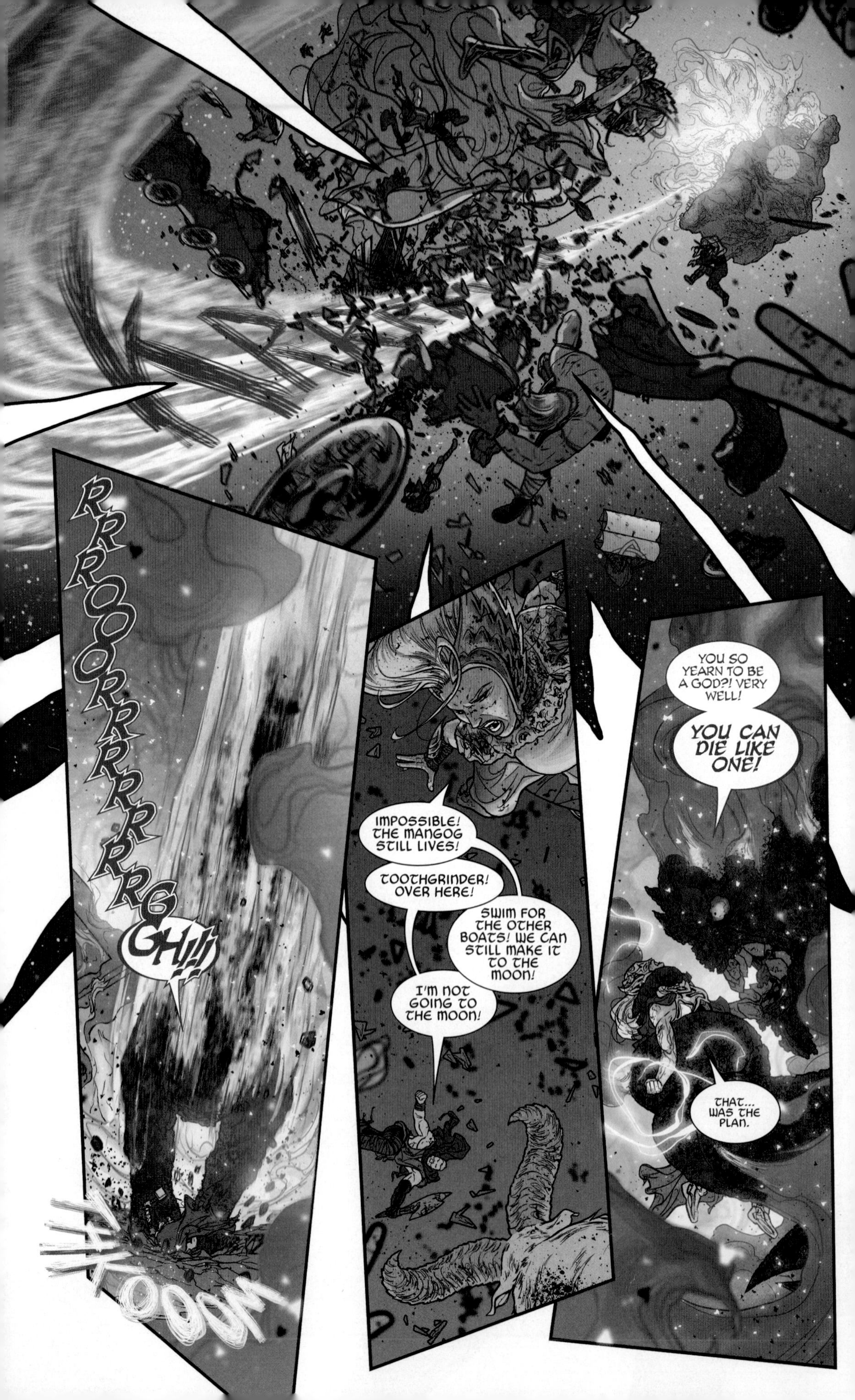

RRROOORRRRRRRRRGGH!!!
THKOOOM
IMPOSSIBLE! THE MANGOG STILL LIVES!
TOOTHGRINDER! OVER HERE!
SWIM FOR THE OTHER BOATS! WE CAN STILL MAKE IT TO THE MOON!
I'M NOT GOING TO THE MOON!
YOU SO YEARN TO BE A GOD?! VERY WELL!
YOU CAN DIE LIKE ONE!
THAT... WAS THE PLAN.

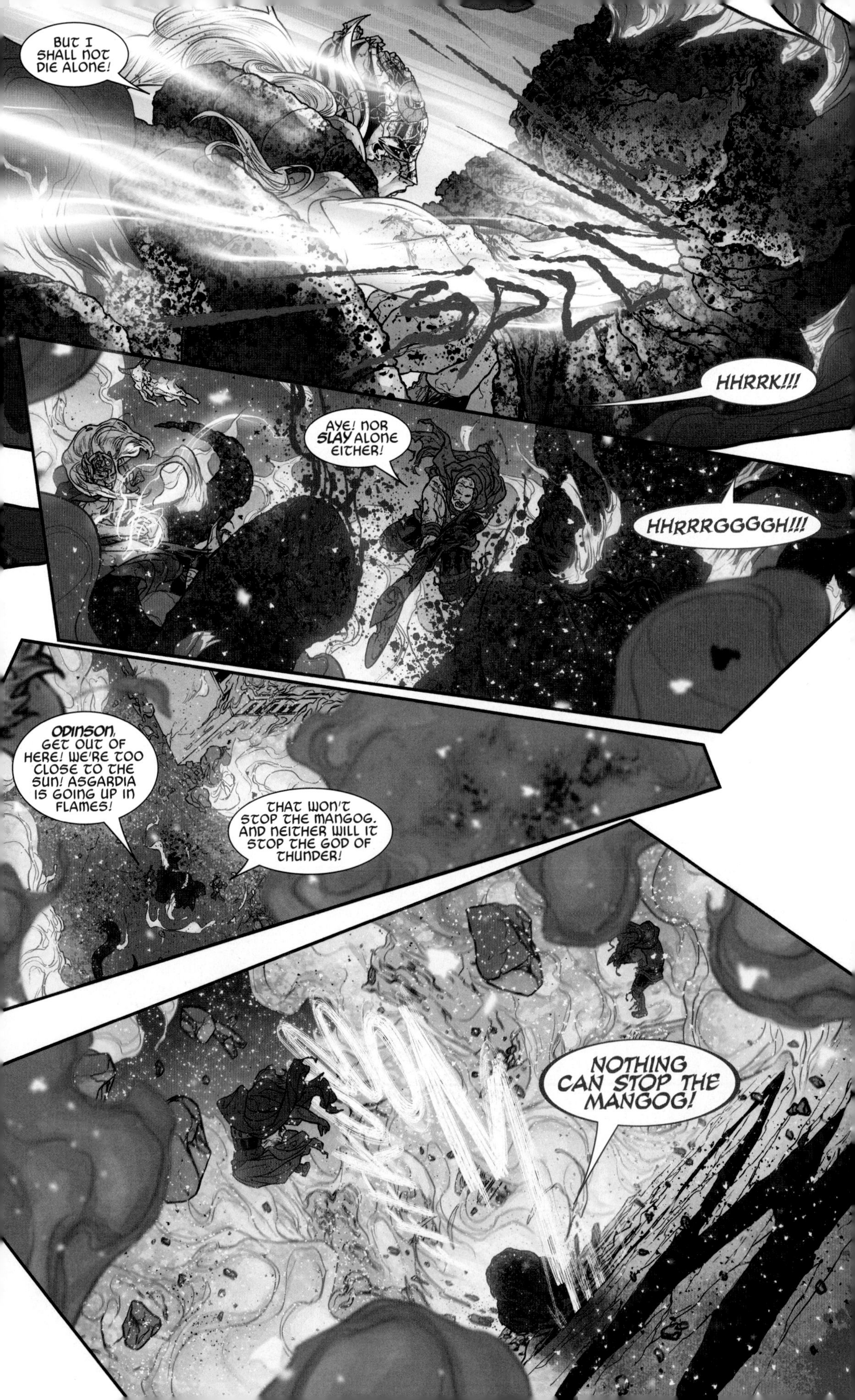
BUT I SHALL NOT DIE ALONE!
HHRRK!!!
AYE! NOR SLAY ALONE EITHER!
HHRRRGGGGH!!!
ODINSON, GET OUT OF HERE! WE'RE TOO CLOSE TO THE SUN! ASGARDIA IS GOING UP IN FLAMES!
THAT WON'T STOP THE MANGOG. AND NEITHER WILL IT STOP THE GOD OF THUNDER!
NOTHING CAN STOP THE MANGOG!

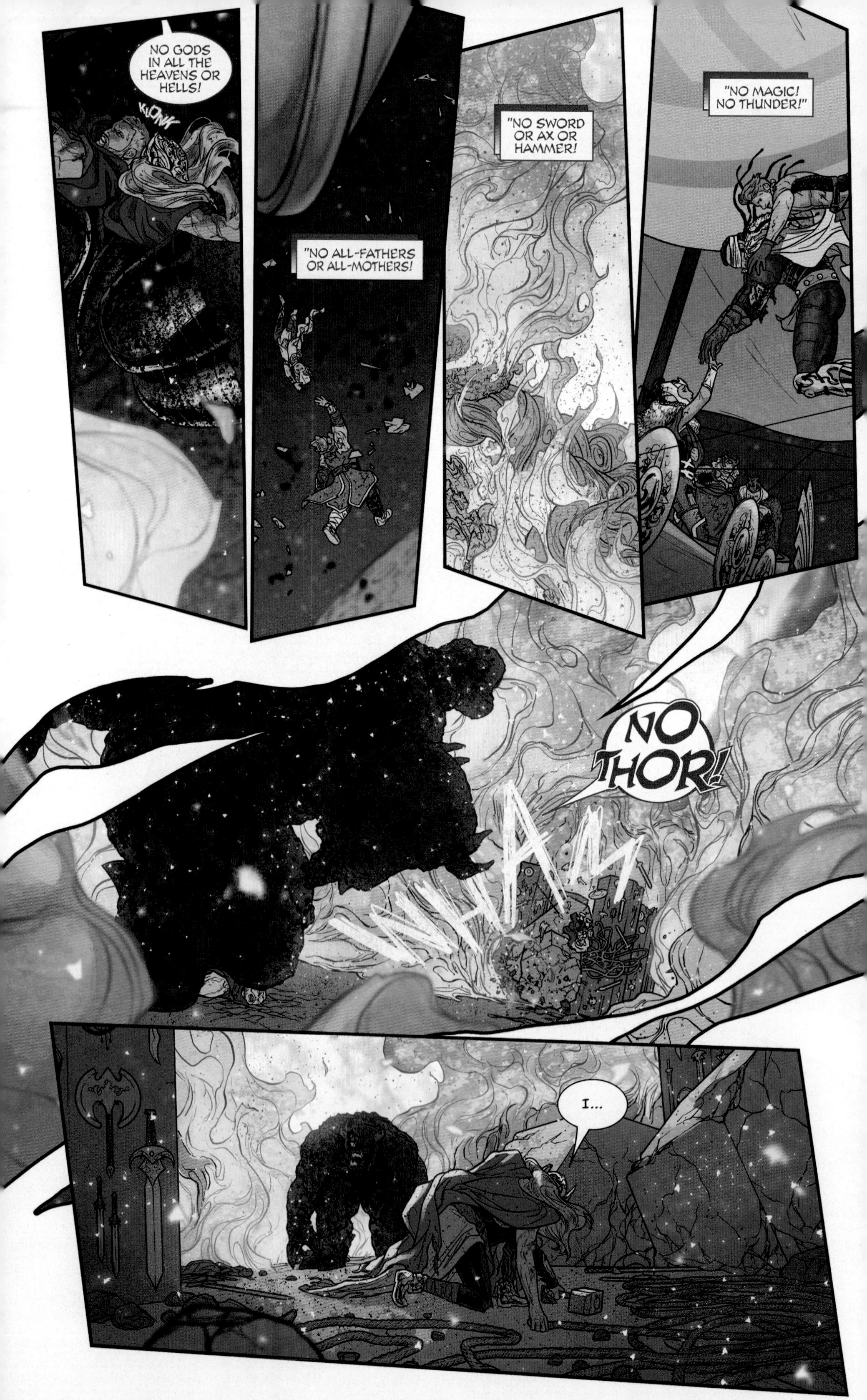
NO GODS IN ALL THE HEAVENS OR HELLS!
KLONK
"NO ALL-FATHERS OR ALL-MOTHERS!
"NO SWORD OR AX OR HAMMER!
"NO MAGIC! NO THUNDER!"
NO THOR!
WHAM
I...

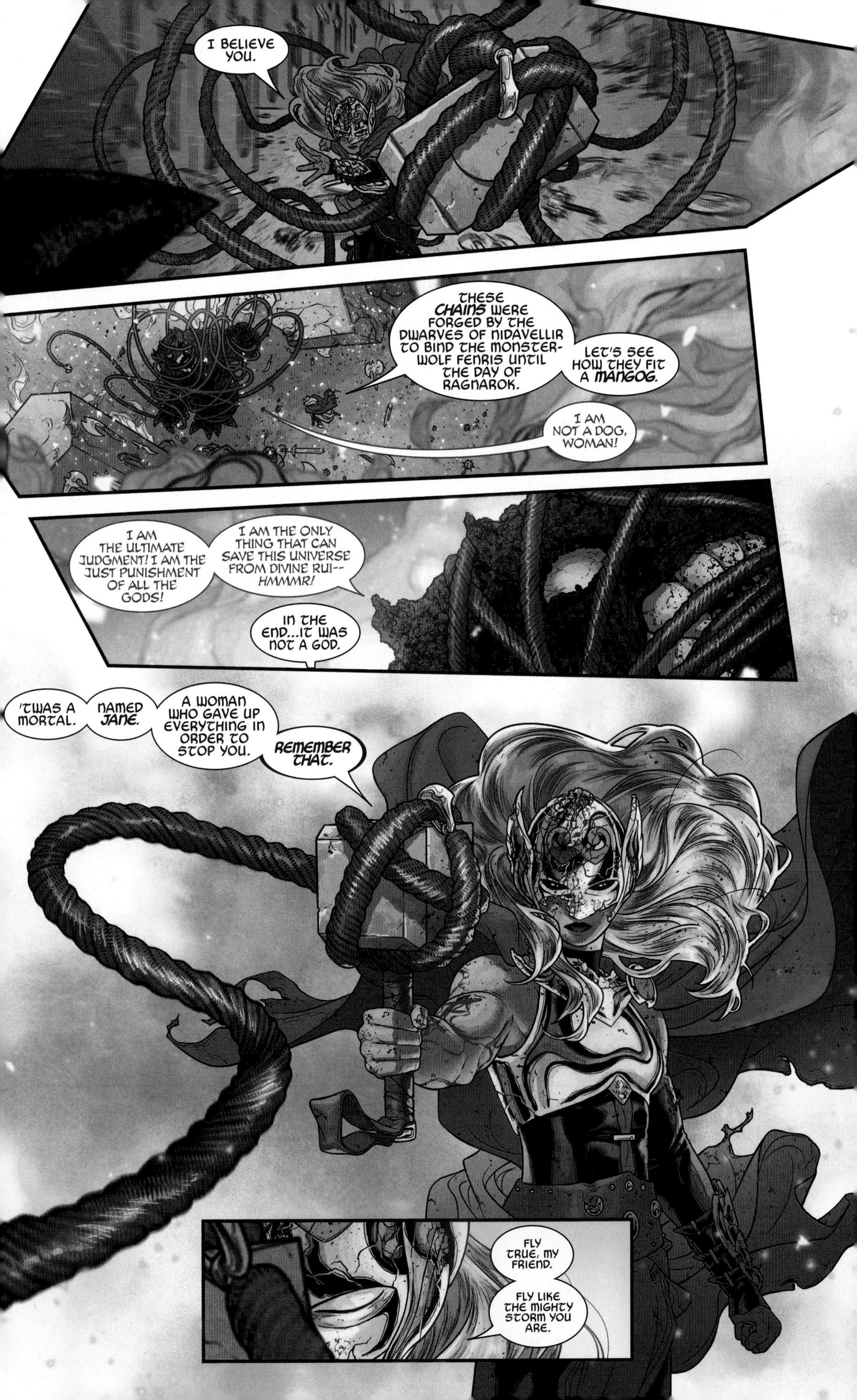
I BELIEVE YOU.
THESE CHAINS WERE FORGED BY THE DWARVES OF NIDAVELLIR TO BIND THE MONSTER-WOLF FENRIS UNTIL THE DAY OF RAGNAROK.
LET'S SEE HOW THEY FIT A MANGOG.
I AM NOT A DOG, WOMAN!
I AM THE ULTIMATE JUDGMENT! I AM THE JUST PUNISHMENT OF ALL THE GODS!
I AM THE ONLY THING THAT CAN SAVE THIS UNIVERSE FROM DIVINE RUI-- HMMMR!
IN THE END...IT WAS NOT A GOD.
'TWAS A MORTAL.
NAMED JANE.
A WOMAN WHO GAVE UP EVERYTHING IN ORDER TO STOP YOU.
REMEMBER THAT.
FLY TRUE, MY FRIEND.
FLY LIKE THE MIGHTY STORM YOU ARE.

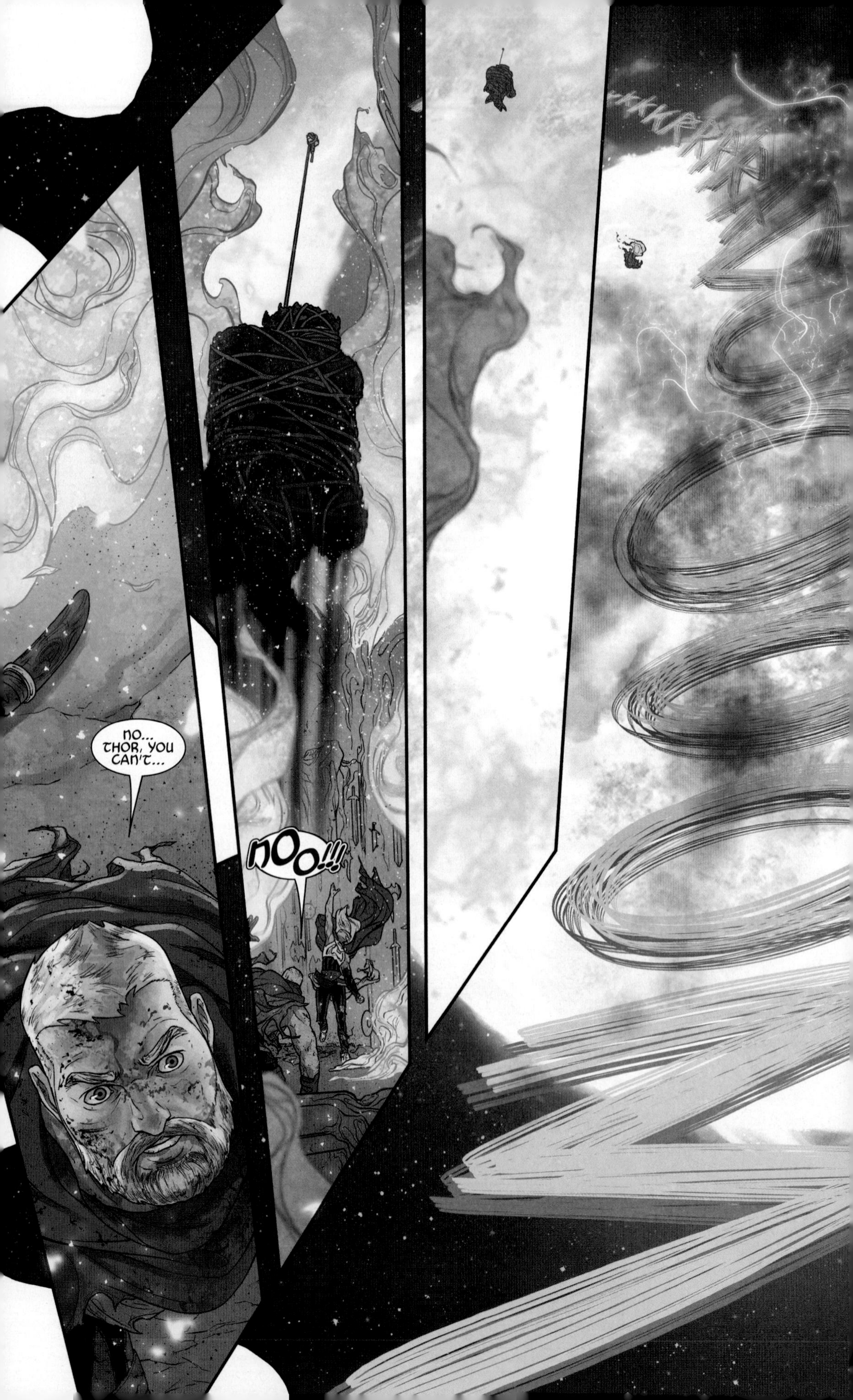
NO... THOR, YOU CAN'T...
NOO!!!

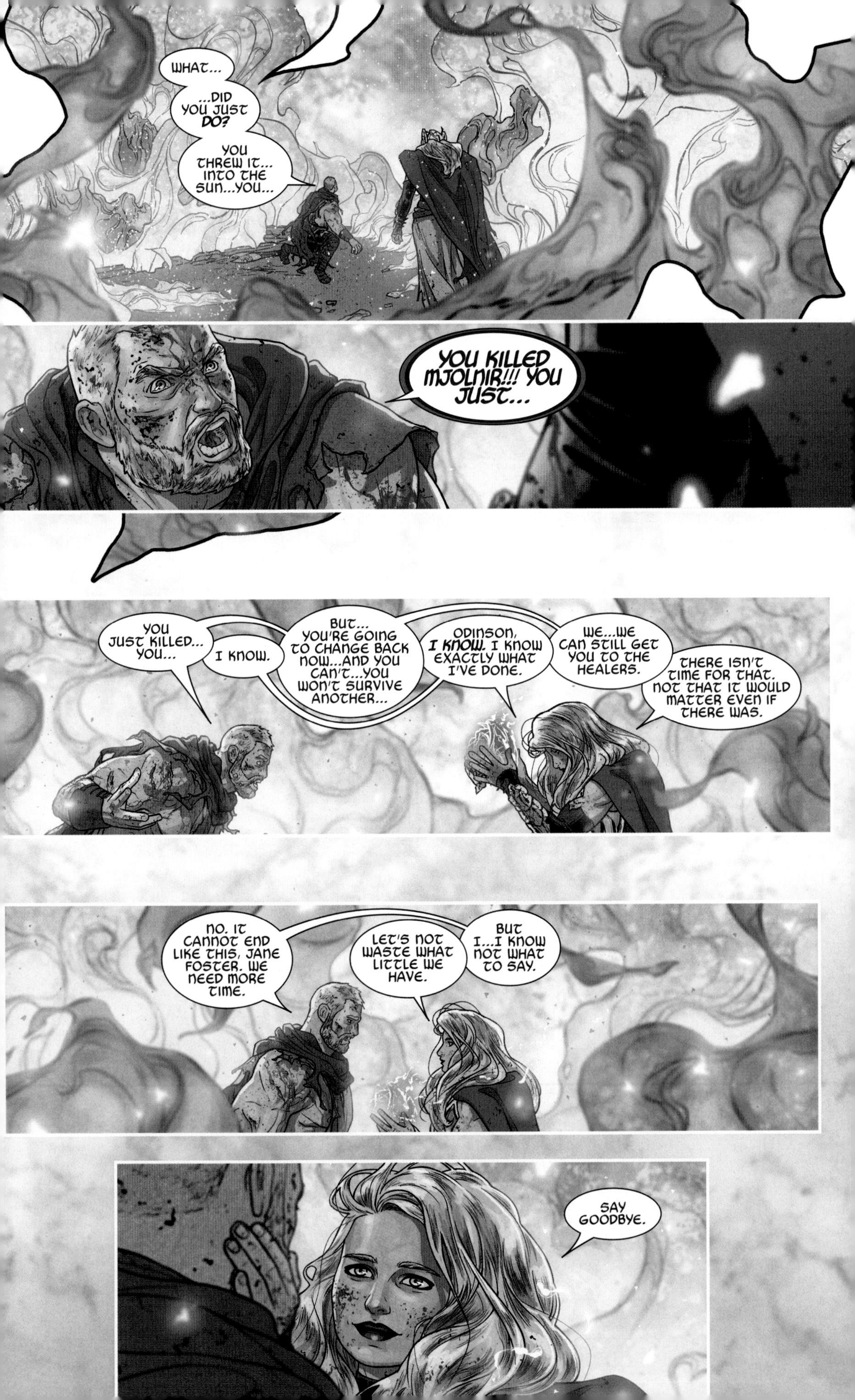
WHAT...
...DID YOU JUST DO?
YOU THREW IT... INTO THE SUN...YOU...
YOU KILLED MJOLNIR!!! YOU JUST...
YOU JUST KILLED... YOU...
I KNOW.
BUT... YOU'RE GOING TO CHANGE BACK NOW...AND YOU CAN'T...YOU WON'T SURVIVE ANOTHER...
ODINSON, I KNOW. I KNOW EXACTLY WHAT I'VE DONE.
WE...WE CAN STILL GET YOU TO THE HEALERS.
THERE ISN'T TIME FOR THAT. NOT THAT IT WOULD MATTER EVEN IF THERE WAS.
NO. IT CANNOT END LIKE THIS, JANE FOSTER. WE NEED MORE TIME.
LET'S NOT WASTE WHAT LITTLE WE HAVE.
BUT I...I KNOW NOT WHAT TO SAY.
SAY GOODBYE.

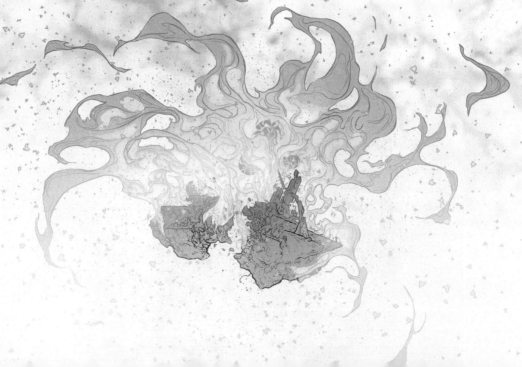

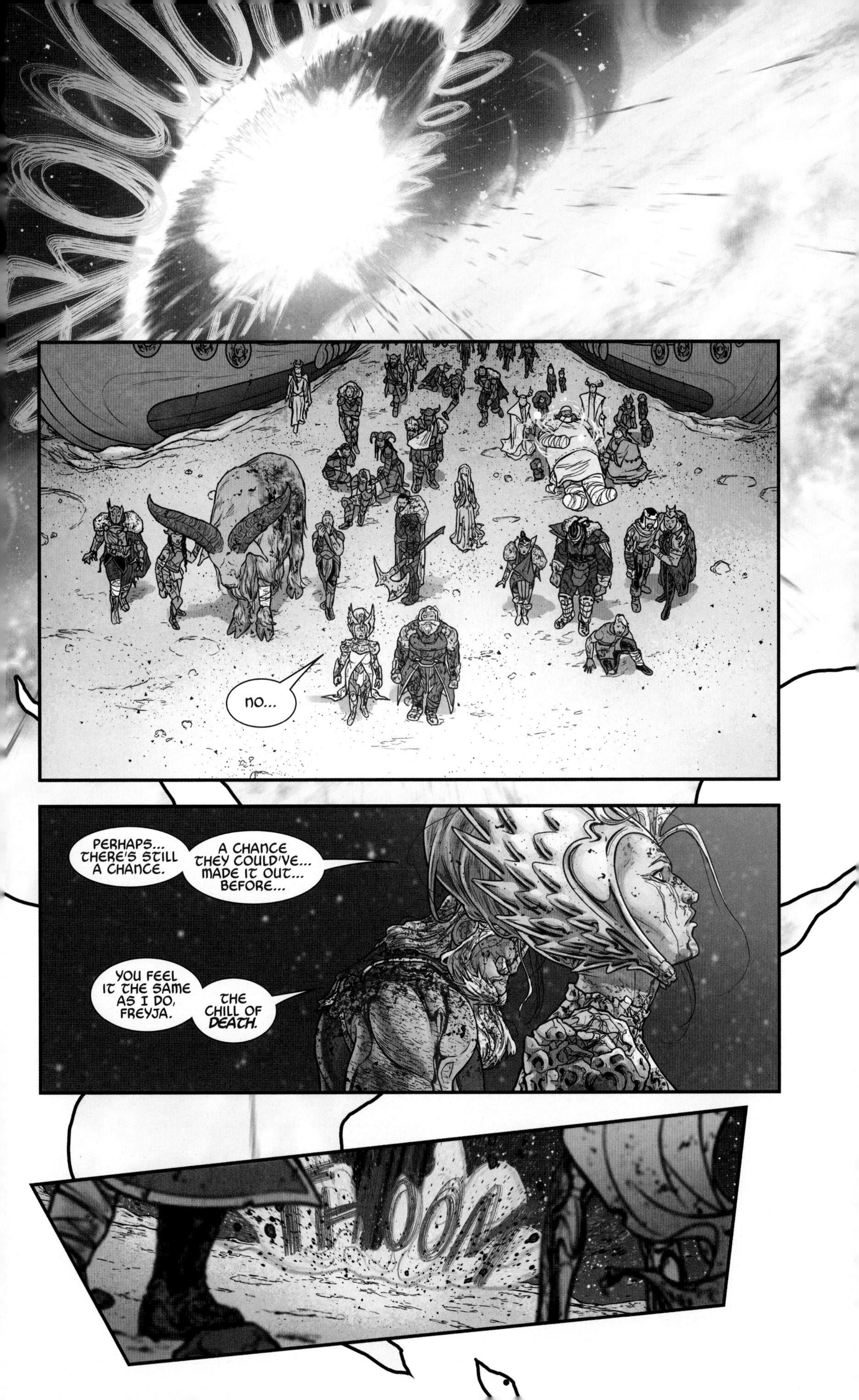
no...
PERHAPS... THERE'S STILL A CHANCE.
A CHANCE THEY COULD'VE... MADE IT OUT... BEFORE...
YOU FEEL IT THE SAME AS I DO, FREYJA.
THE CHILL OF DEATH.
THOOM

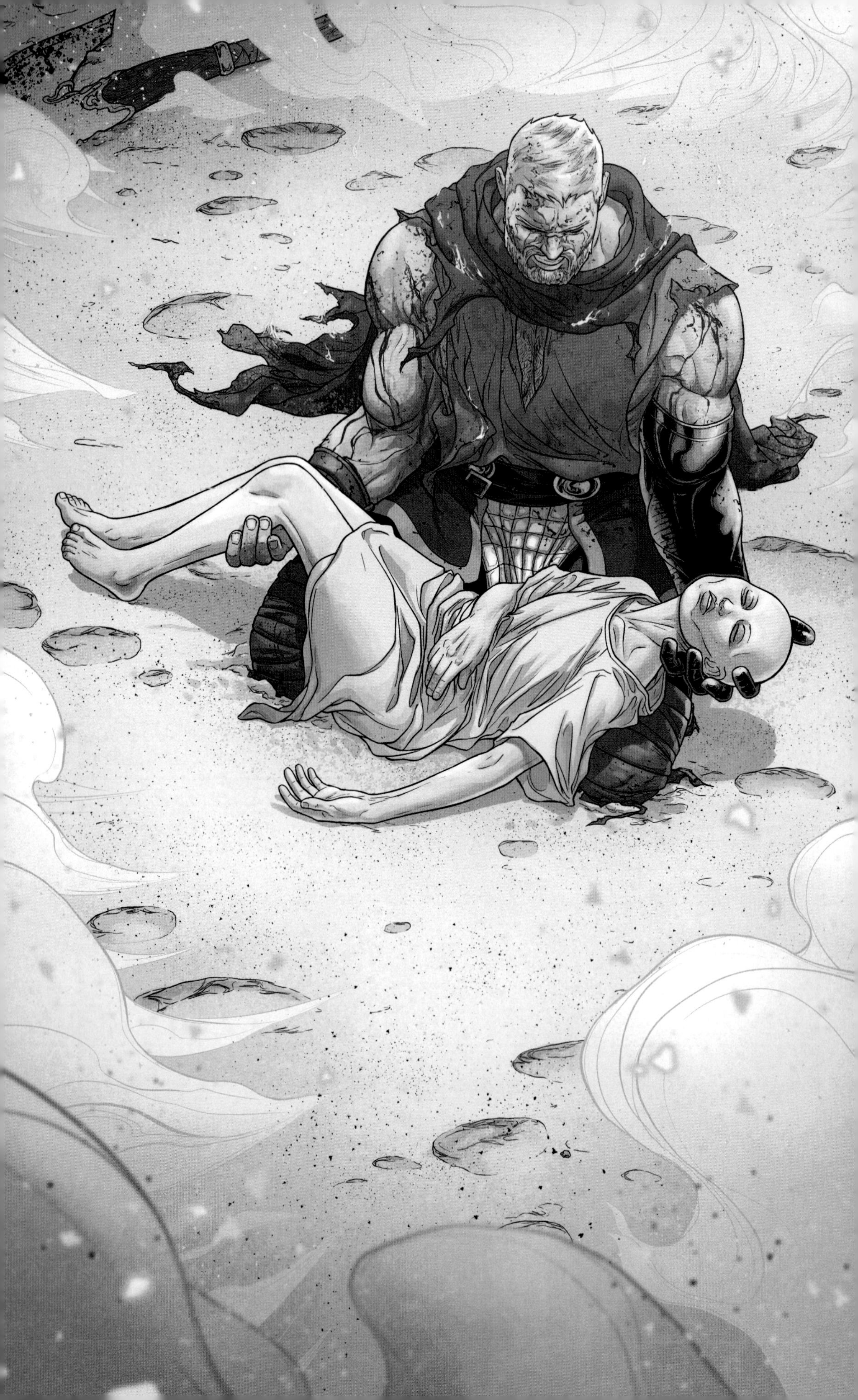

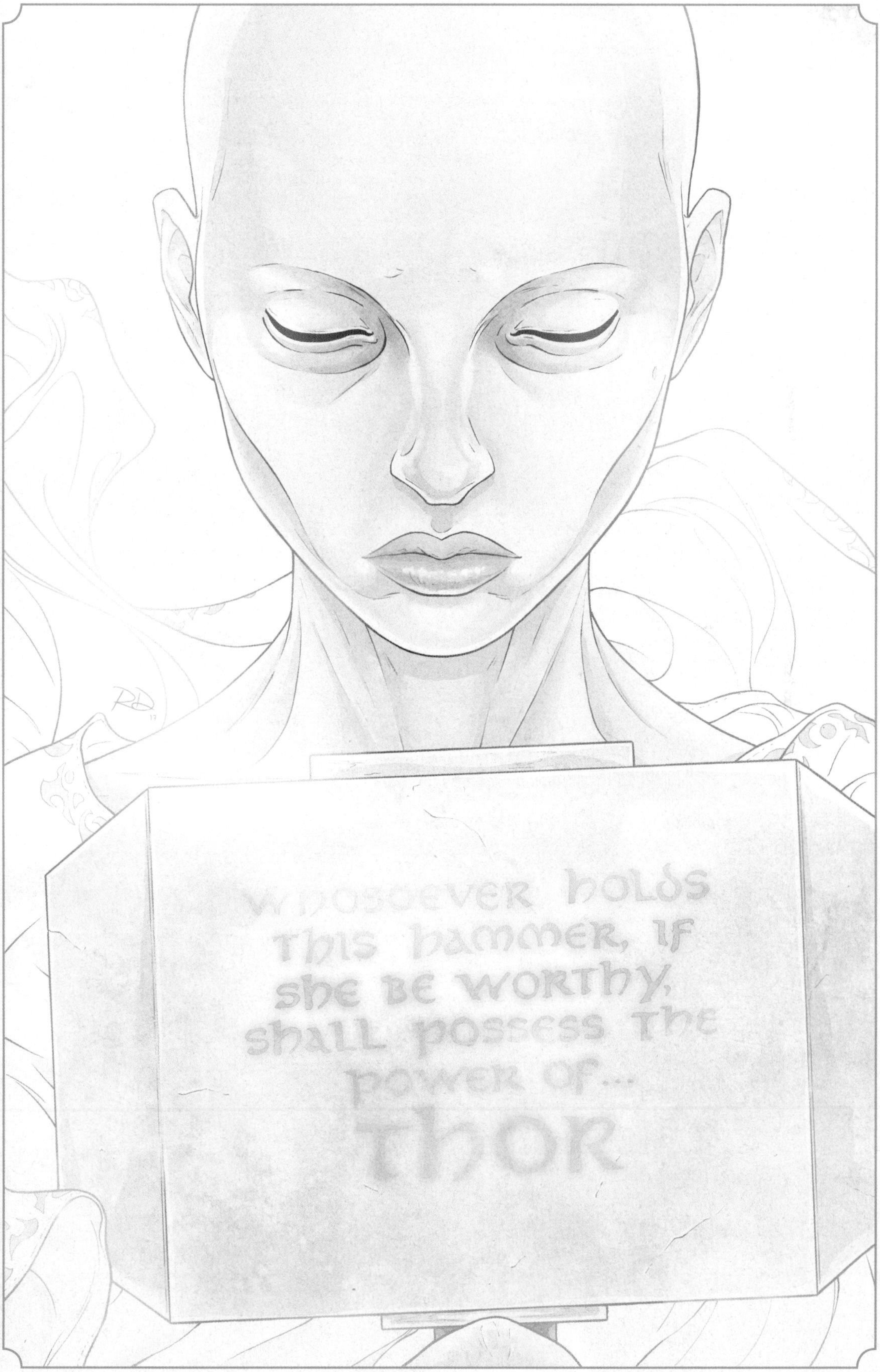
WHOSOEVER HOLDS THIS HAMMER, IF SHE BE WORTHY, SHALL POSSESS THE POWER OF...
THOR

AT THE GATES OF VALHALLA

NO! THIS CAN'T BE HOW IT ENDS! HEALERS!
WHERE ARE THE BOR-DAMNED HEALERS?!
JANE FOSTER.
JANE FOSTER OF MIDGARD WAS THE NEW THOR. I...HAD NO IDEA.
A MORTAL. A DISEASED ONE AT THAT--
--A SICKLY MORTAL JUST SAVED THE GODS OF ASGARD.
HRRPH.
RGGHH!
RRRRGGGGH!!!
HELP HER! SOMEONE SAVE HER!
HEIMDALL, IS SHE TRULY...
EVEN BLINDED, I CAN SEE THE TRUTH, SIF. I AM AFRAID IT IS TOO LATE, DEAR SISTER.

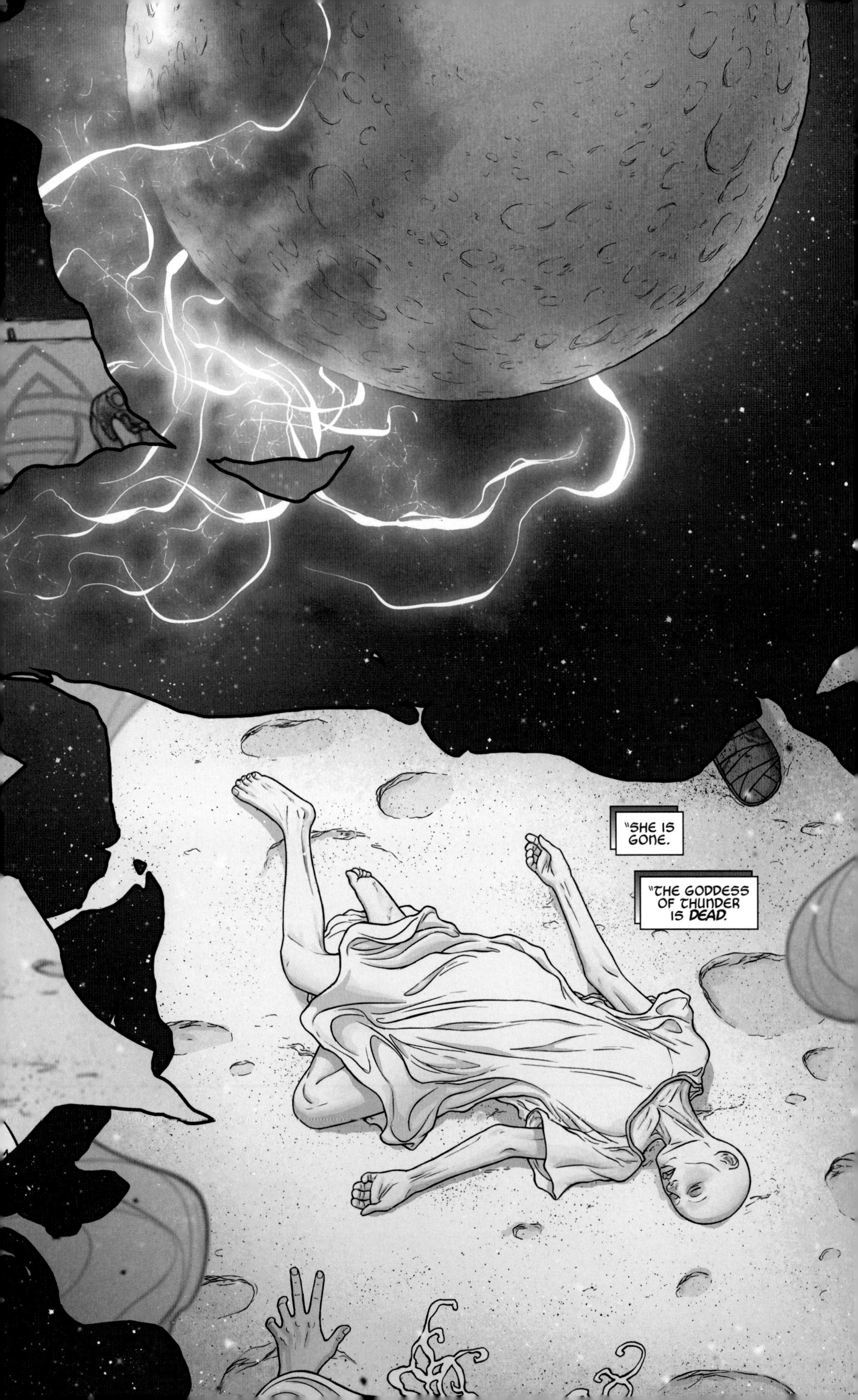
"SHE IS GONE.
"THE GODDESS OF THUNDER IS DEAD.

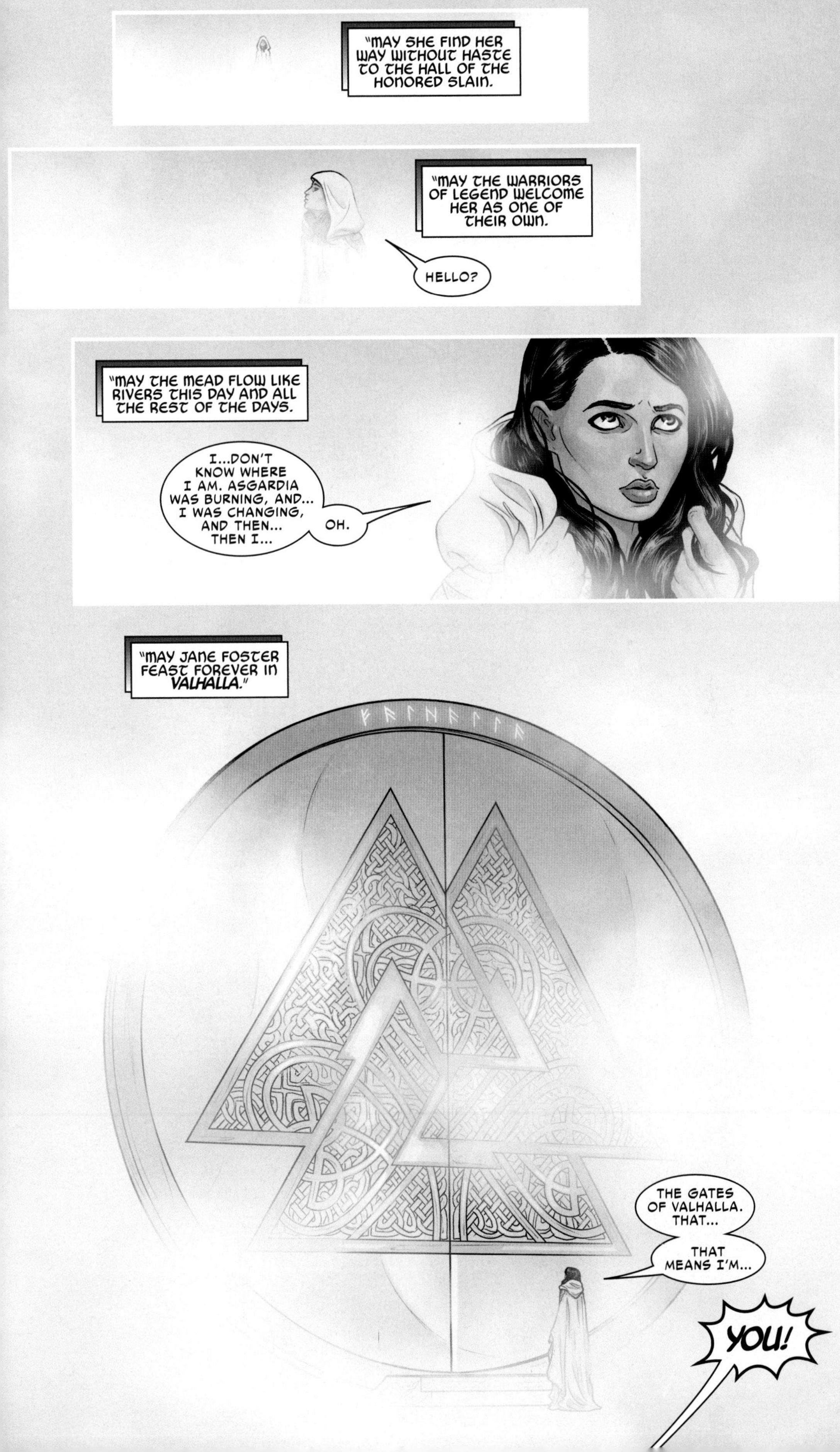
"MAY SHE FIND HER WAY WITHOUT HASTE TO THE HALL OF THE HONORED SLAIN.
"MAY THE WARRIORS OF LEGEND WELCOME HER AS ONE OF THEIR OWN.
HELLO?
"MAY THE MEAD FLOW LIKE RIVERS THIS DAY AND ALL THE REST OF THE DAYS.
I...DON'T KNOW WHERE I AM. ASGARDIA WAS BURNING, AND... I WAS CHANGING, AND THEN... THEN I...
OH.
"MAY JANE FOSTER FEAST FOREVER IN *VALHALLA*."
THE GATES OF VALHALLA. THAT...
THAT MEANS I'M...
*YOU!*

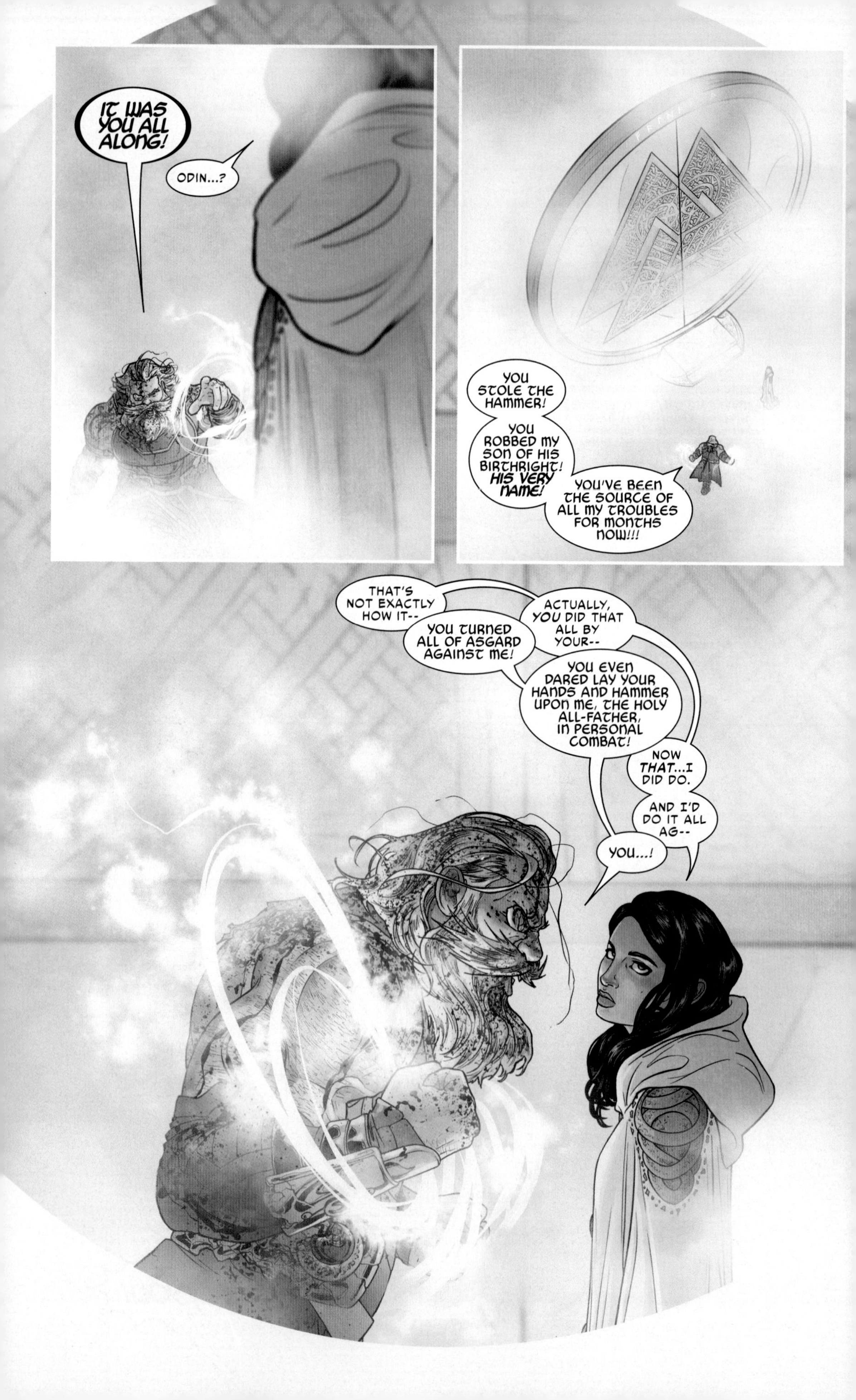
IT WAS YOU ALL ALONG!
ODIN...?
YOU STOLE THE HAMMER!
YOU ROBBED MY SON OF HIS BIRTHRIGHT! HIS VERY NAME!
YOU'VE BEEN THE SOURCE OF ALL MY TROUBLES FOR MONTHS NOW!!!
THAT'S NOT EXACTLY HOW IT--
YOU TURNED ALL OF ASGARD AGAINST ME!
ACTUALLY, YOU DID THAT ALL BY YOUR--
YOU EVEN DARED LAY YOUR HANDS AND HAMMER UPON ME, THE HOLY ALL-FATHER, IN PERSONAL COMBAT!
NOW THAT...I DID DO.
AND I'D DO IT ALL AG--
YOU...!

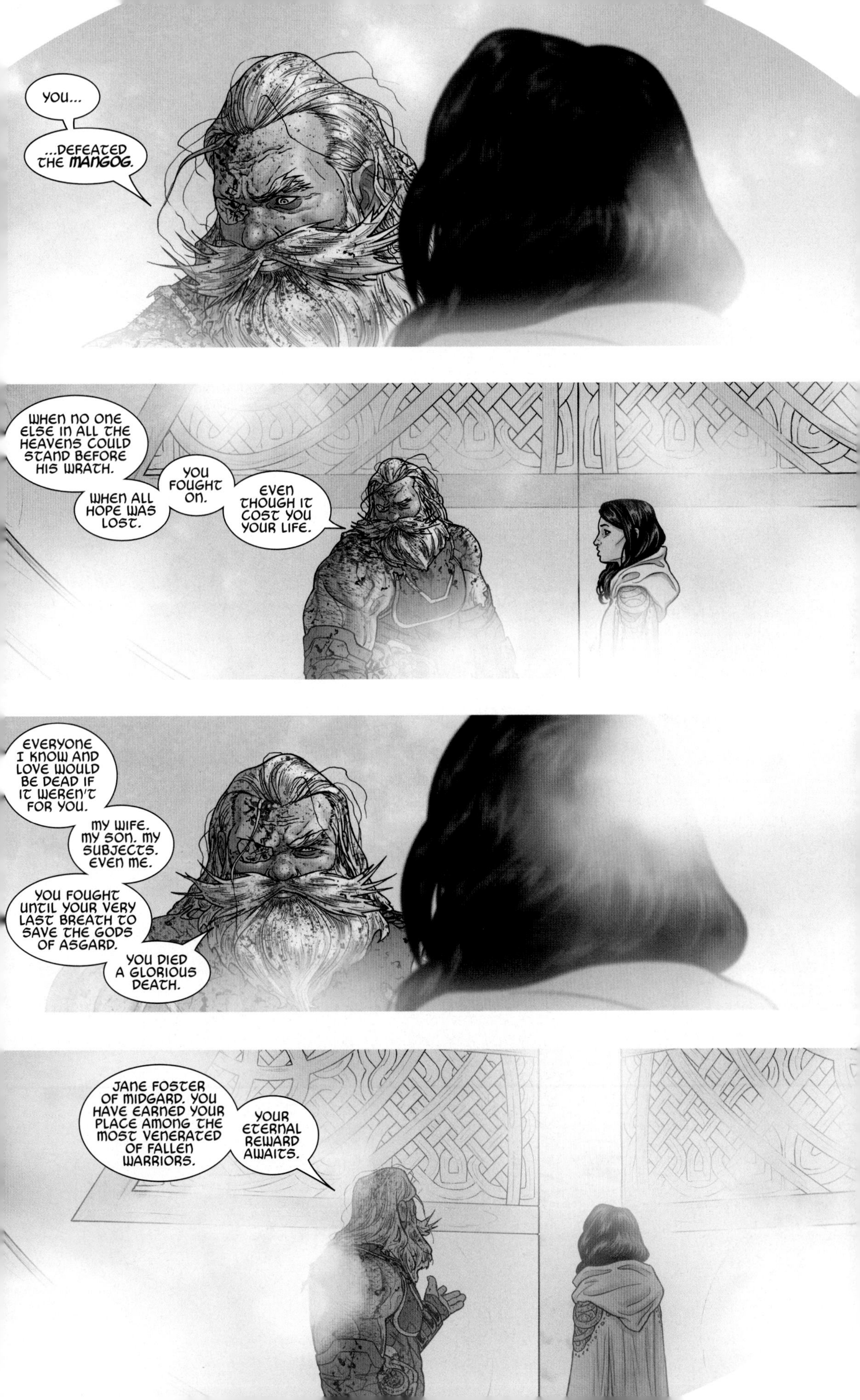
YOU...
...DEFEATED THE MANGOG.
WHEN NO ONE ELSE IN ALL THE HEAVENS COULD STAND BEFORE HIS WRATH.
WHEN ALL HOPE WAS LOST.
YOU FOUGHT ON.
EVEN THOUGH IT COST YOU YOUR LIFE.
EVERYONE I KNOW AND LOVE WOULD BE DEAD IF IT WEREN'T FOR YOU.
MY WIFE. MY SON. MY SUBJECTS. EVEN ME.
YOU FOUGHT UNTIL YOUR VERY LAST BREATH TO SAVE THE GODS OF ASGARD.
YOU DIED A GLORIOUS DEATH.
JANE FOSTER OF MIDGARD. YOU HAVE EARNED YOUR PLACE AMONG THE MOST VENERATED OF FALLEN WARRIORS.
YOUR ETERNAL REWARD AWAITS.

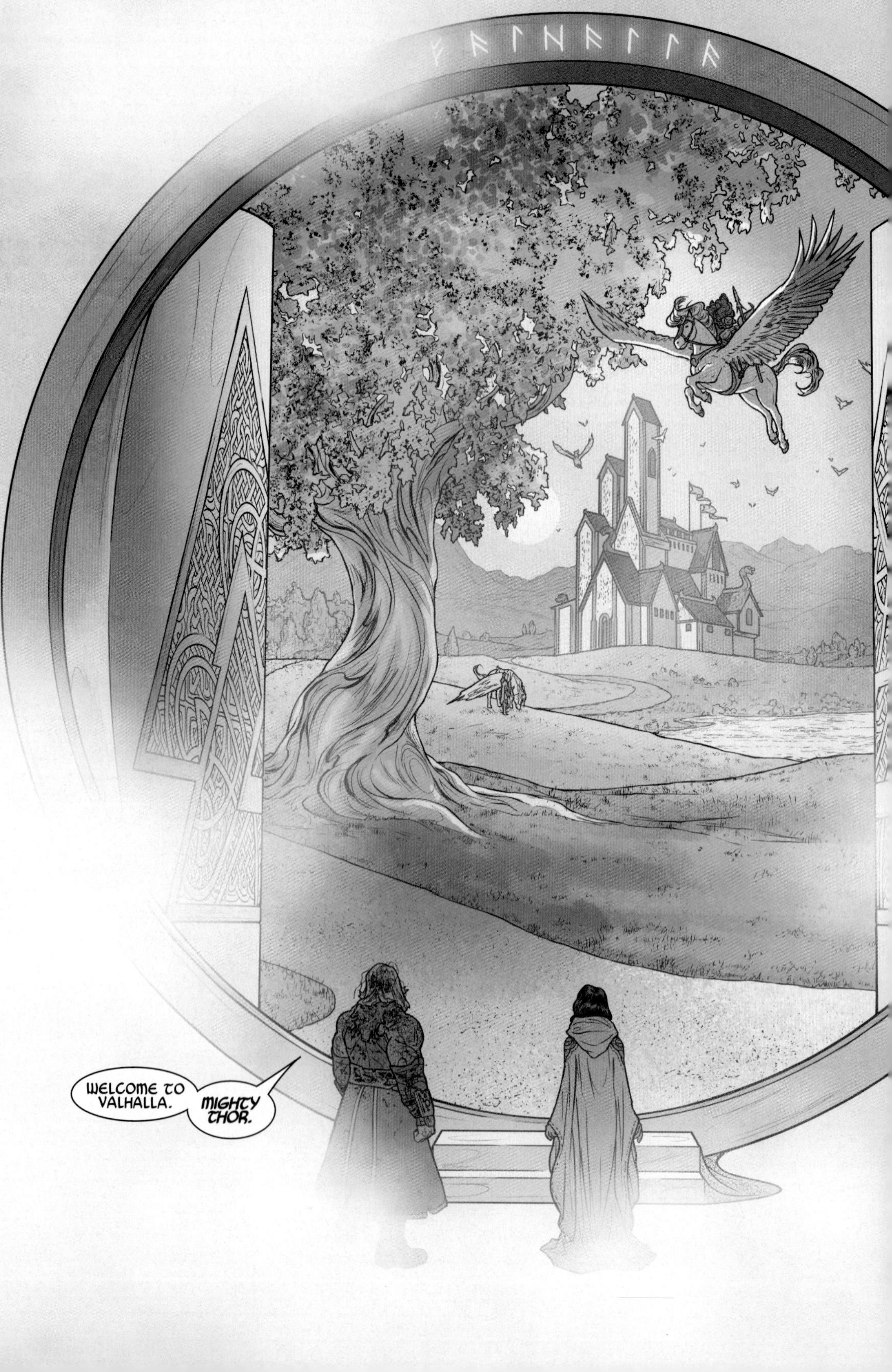

WELCOME TO VALHALLA.
MIGHTY THOR.

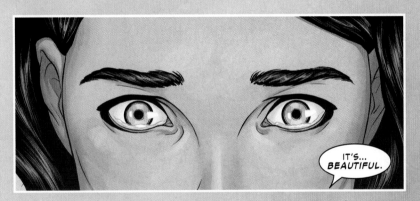

IT'S... BEAUTIFUL.

WHY DO YOU HESITATE? A GREAT FEAST IS ABOUT TO BEGIN, IN YOUR HONOR.

BE NOT AFRAID. YOU HAVE NOTHING MORE TO FEAR FROM ME OR ANYONE ELSE EVER AGAIN.

ALL WHO FALL VALIANTLY IN BATTLE ARE CHILDREN OF ODIN. SO TELL ME...

WHAT TROUBLES THEE, DAUGHTER JANE?

I... I WASN'T READY.

I WASN'T READY TO DIE.

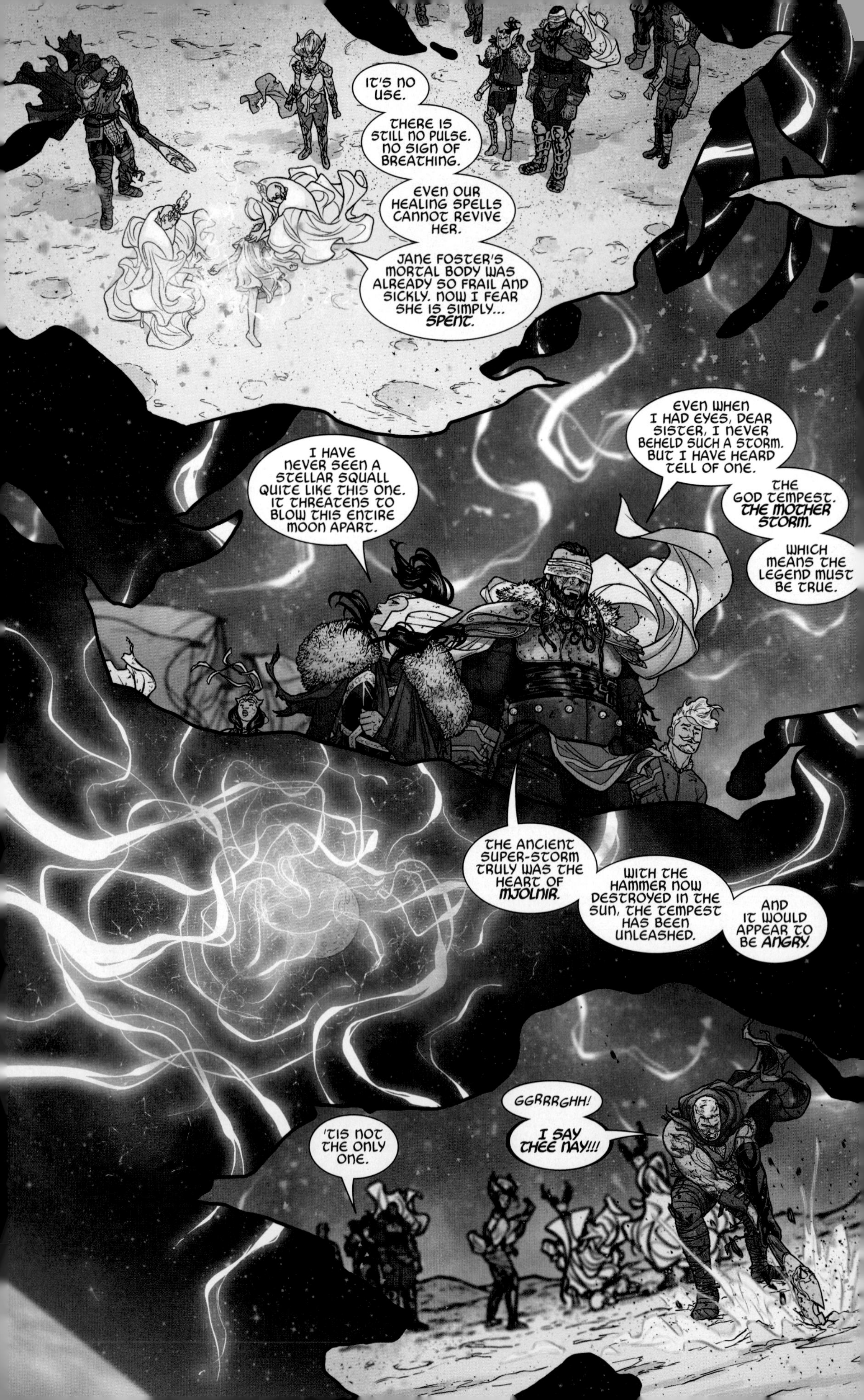
IT'S NO USE.
THERE IS STILL NO PULSE. NO SIGN OF BREATHING.
EVEN OUR HEALING SPELLS CANNOT REVIVE HER.
JANE FOSTER'S MORTAL BODY WAS ALREADY SO FRAIL AND SICKLY. NOW I FEAR SHE IS SIMPLY... SPENT.
I HAVE NEVER SEEN A STELLAR SQUALL QUITE LIKE THIS ONE. IT THREATENS TO BLOW THIS ENTIRE MOON APART.
EVEN WHEN I HAD EYES, DEAR SISTER, I NEVER BEHELD SUCH A STORM. BUT I HAVE HEARD TELL OF ONE.
THE GOD TEMPEST. THE MOTHER STORM.
WHICH MEANS THE LEGEND MUST BE TRUE.
THE ANCIENT SUPER-STORM TRULY WAS THE HEART OF MJOLNIR.
WITH THE HAMMER NOW DESTROYED IN THE SUN, THE TEMPEST HAS BEEN UNLEASHED.
AND IT WOULD APPEAR TO BE ANGRY.
'TIS NOT THE ONLY ONE.
GGRRRGHH!
I SAY THEE NAY!!!

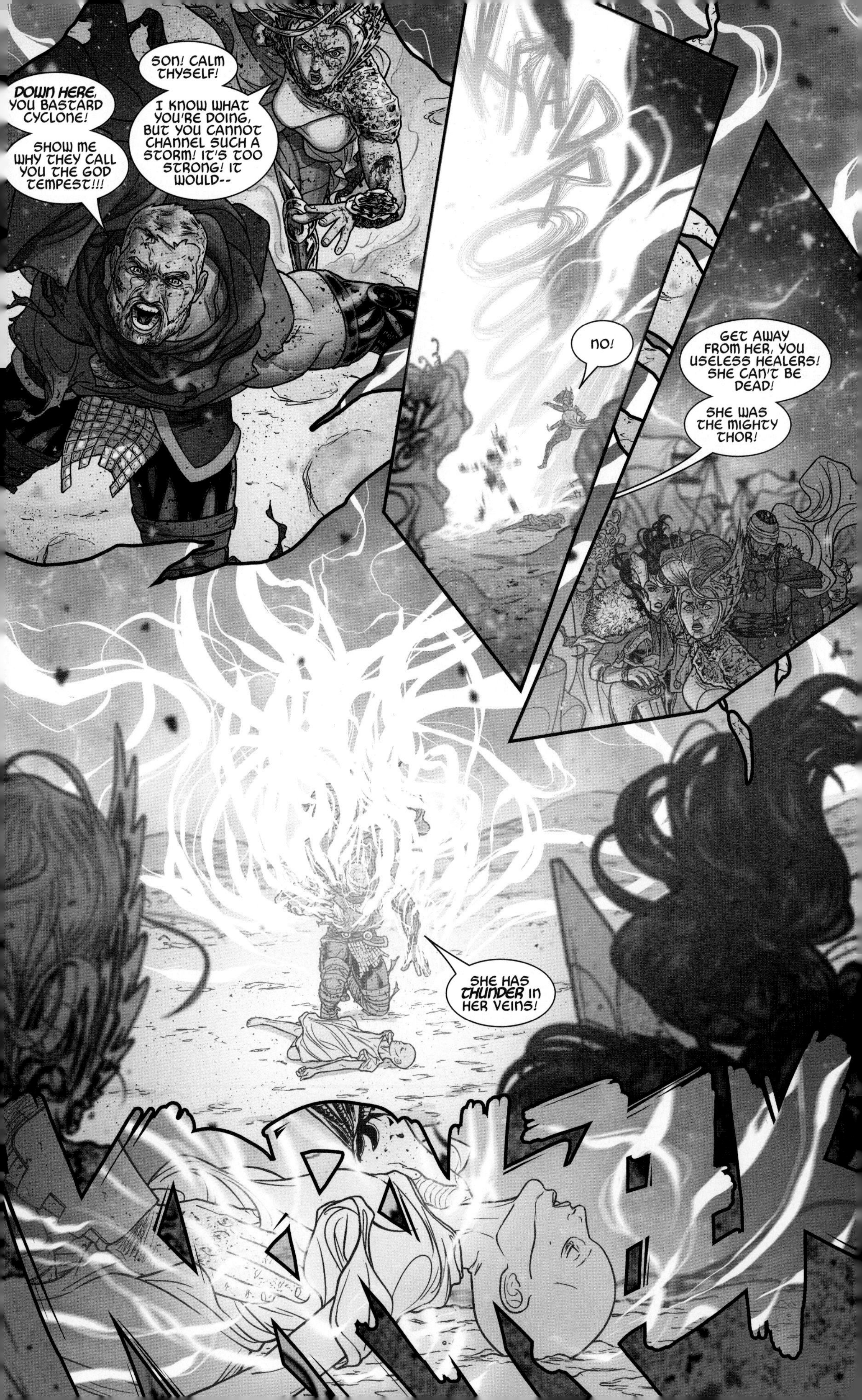
DOWN HERE, YOU BASTARD CYCLONE!
SHOW ME WHY THEY CALL YOU THE GOD TEMPEST!!!
SON! CALM THYSELF!
I KNOW WHAT YOU'RE DOING, BUT YOU CANNOT CHANNEL SUCH A STORM! IT'S TOO STRONG! IT WOULD--
NO!
GET AWAY FROM HER, YOU USELESS HEALERS! SHE CAN'T BE DEAD!
SHE WAS THE MIGHTY THOR!
SHE HAS THUNDER IN HER VEINS!

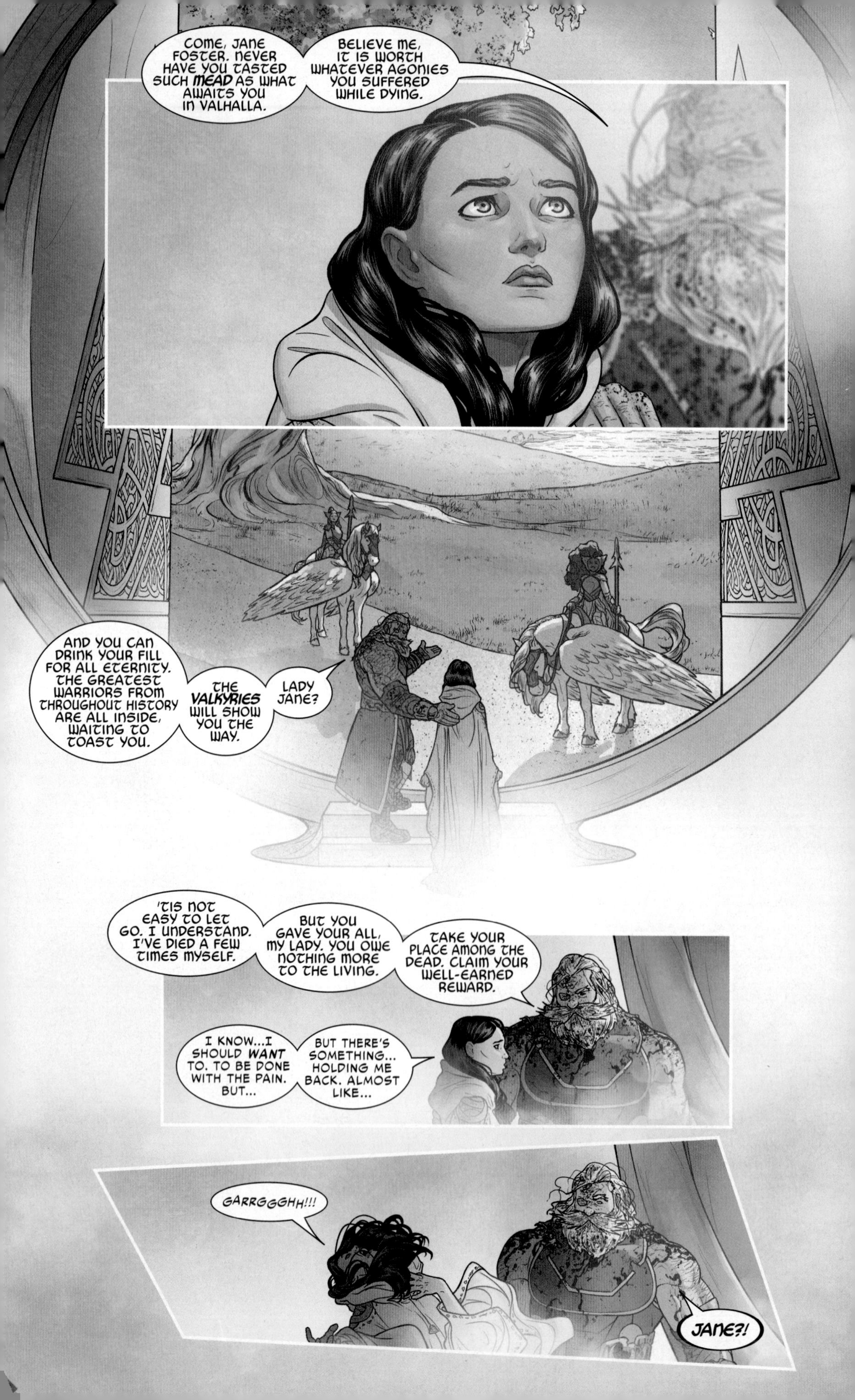
COME, JANE FOSTER. NEVER HAVE YOU TASTED SUCH MEAD AS WHAT AWAITS YOU IN VALHALLA.
BELIEVE ME, IT IS WORTH WHATEVER AGONIES YOU SUFFERED WHILE DYING.
AND YOU CAN DRINK YOUR FILL FOR ALL ETERNITY. THE GREATEST WARRIORS FROM THROUGHOUT HISTORY ARE ALL INSIDE, WAITING TO TOAST YOU.
THE VALKYRIES WILL SHOW YOU THE WAY.
LADY JANE?
'TIS NOT EASY TO LET GO. I UNDERSTAND. I'VE DIED A FEW TIMES MYSELF.
BUT YOU GAVE YOUR ALL, MY LADY. YOU OWE NOTHING MORE TO THE LIVING.
TAKE YOUR PLACE AMONG THE DEAD. CLAIM YOUR WELL-EARNED REWARD.
I KNOW...I SHOULD WANT TO. TO BE DONE WITH THE PAIN. BUT...
BUT THERE'S SOMETHING... HOLDING ME BACK. ALMOST LIKE...
GARRGGGHH!!!
JANE?!

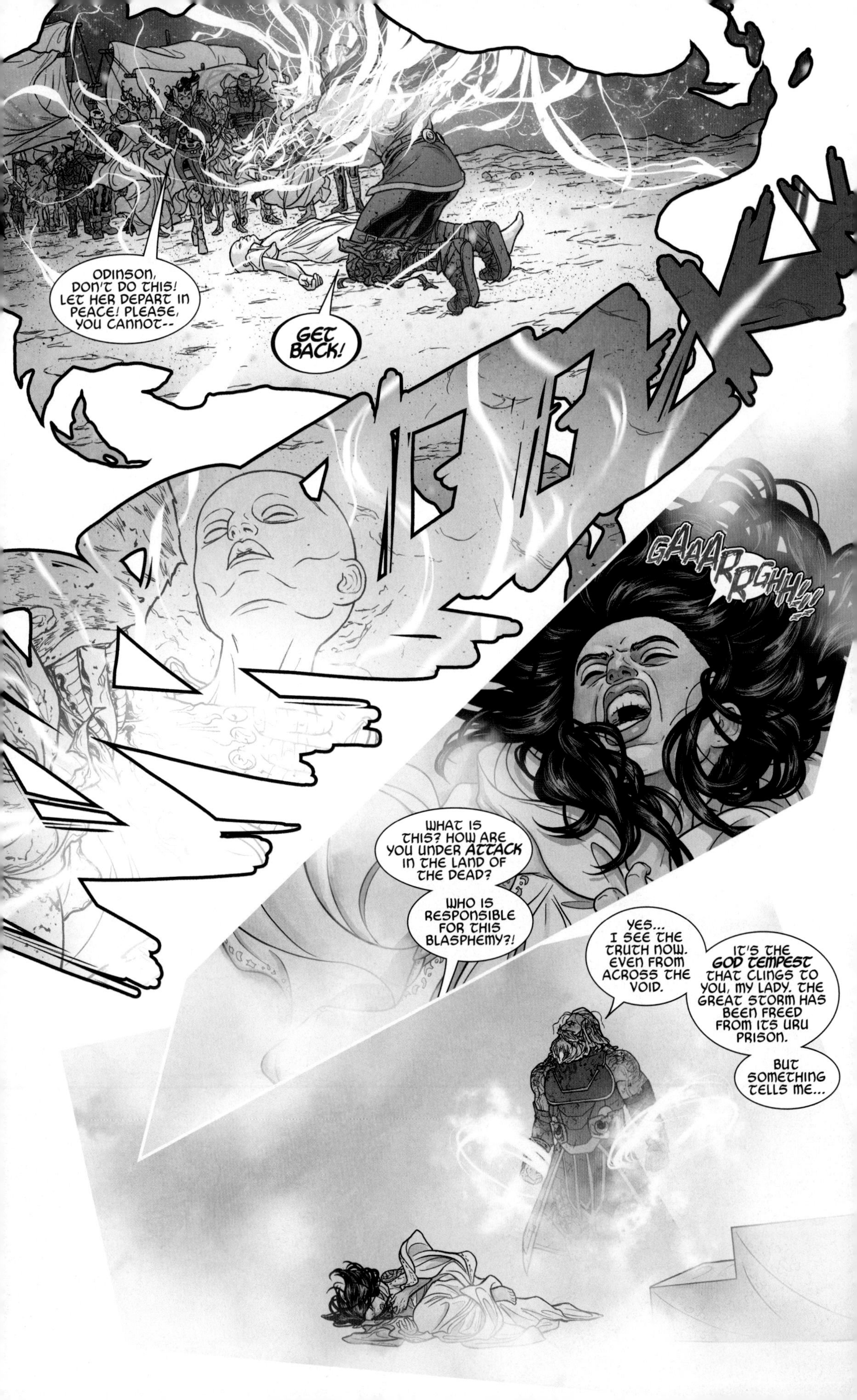
ODINSON, DON'T DO THIS! LET HER DEPART IN PEACE! PLEASE, YOU CANNOT--
GET BACK!
GAAAARRGHH!!
WHAT IS THIS? HOW ARE YOU UNDER ATTACK IN THE LAND OF THE DEAD?
WHO IS RESPONSIBLE FOR THIS BLASPHEMY?!
YES... I SEE THE TRUTH NOW. EVEN FROM ACROSS THE VOID.
IT'S THE GOD TEMPEST THAT CLINGS TO YOU, MY LADY. THE GREAT STORM HAS BEEN FREED FROM ITS URU PRISON.
BUT SOMETHING TELLS ME...

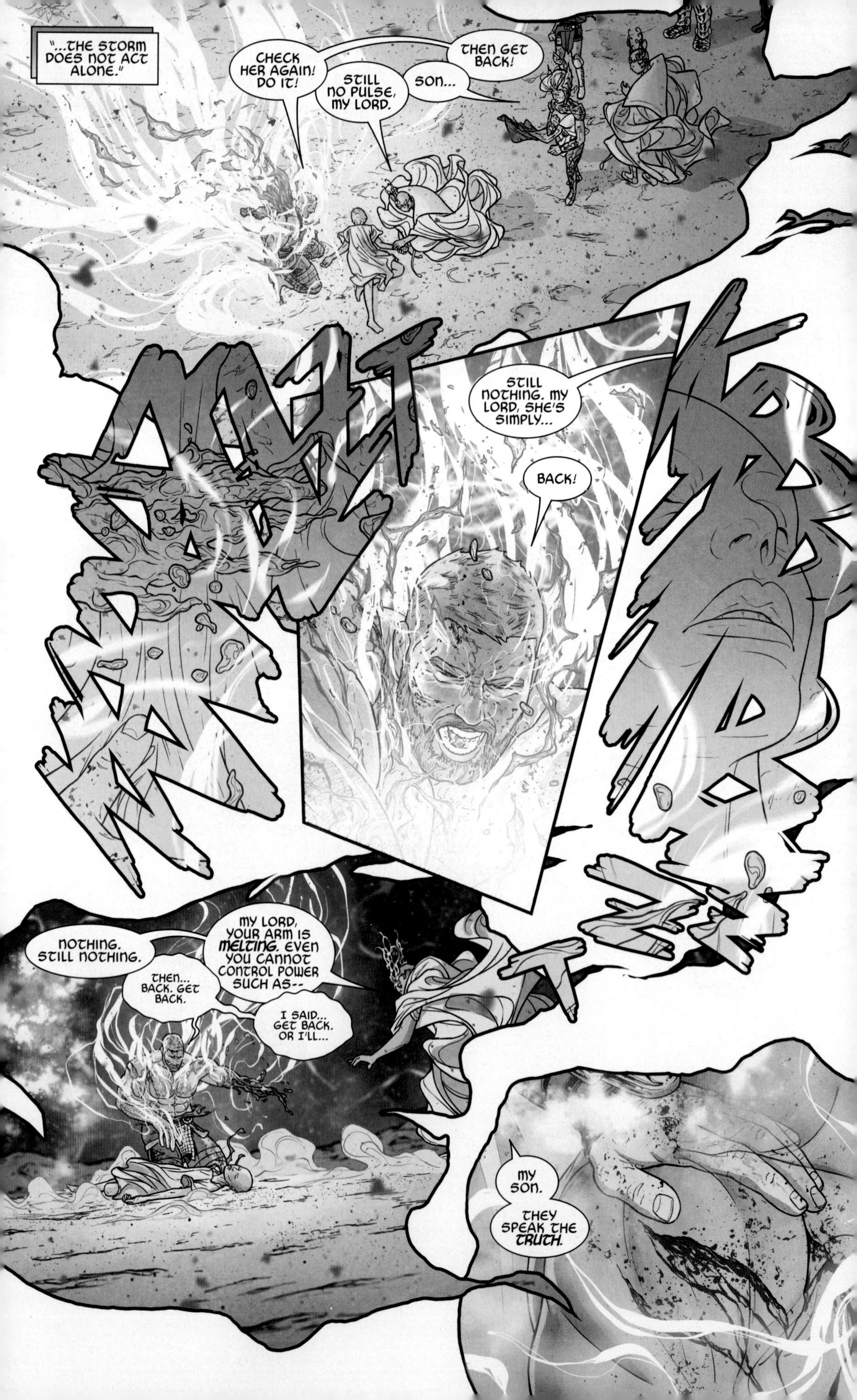
"...THE STORM DOES NOT ACT ALONE."
CHECK HER AGAIN! DO IT!
STILL NO PULSE, MY LORD.
SON...
THEN GET BACK!
STILL NOTHING. MY LORD, SHE'S SIMPLY...
BACK!
NOTHING. STILL NOTHING.
MY LORD, YOUR ARM IS *MELTING*. EVEN YOU CANNOT CONTROL POWER SUCH AS--
THEN... BACK. GET BACK.
I SAID... GET BACK. OR I'LL...
MY SON.
THEY SPEAK THE *TRUTH*.

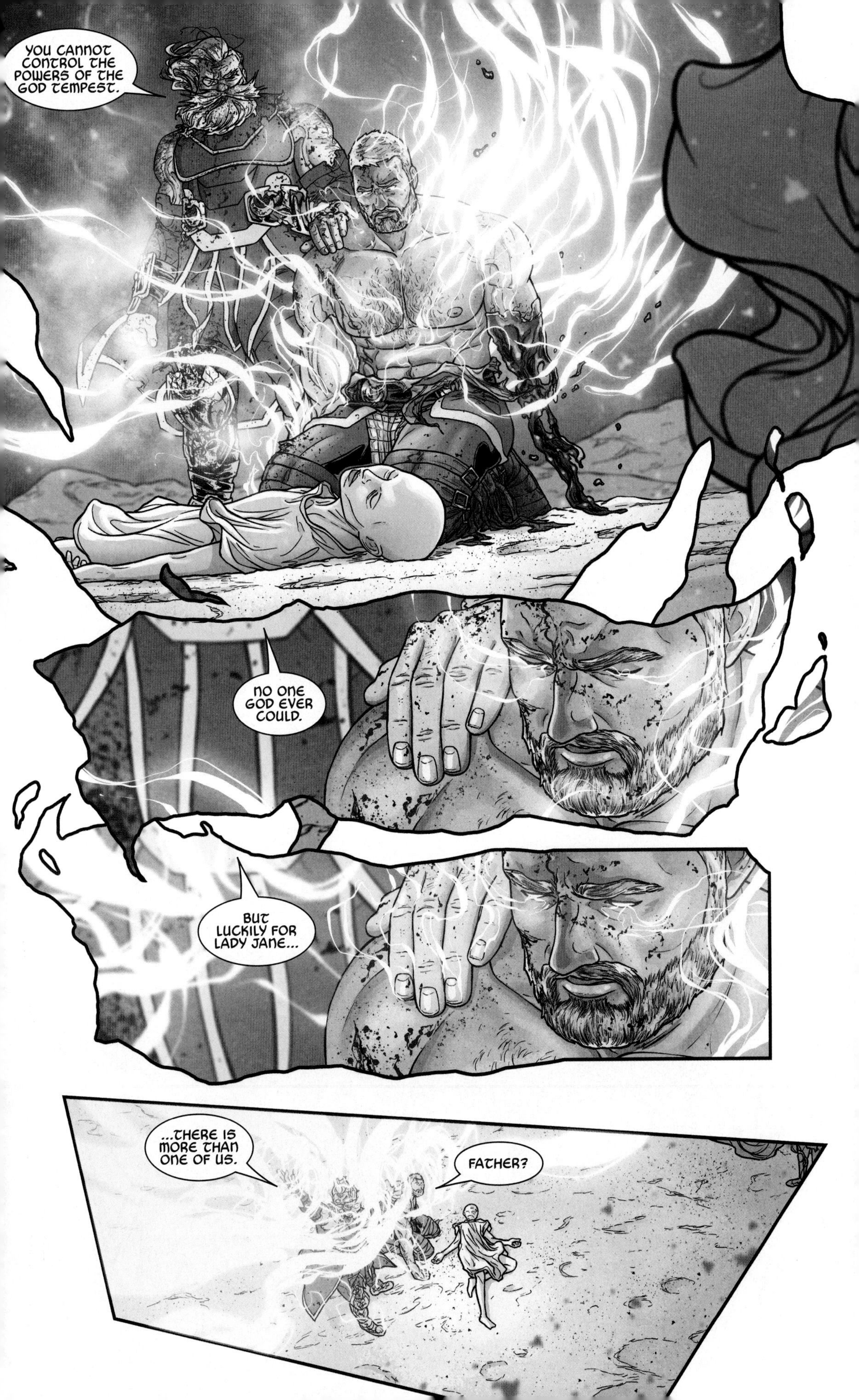
YOU CANNOT CONTROL THE POWERS OF THE GOD TEMPEST.
NO ONE GOD EVER COULD.
BUT LUCKILY FOR LADY JANE...
...THERE IS MORE THAN ONE OF US.
FATHER?

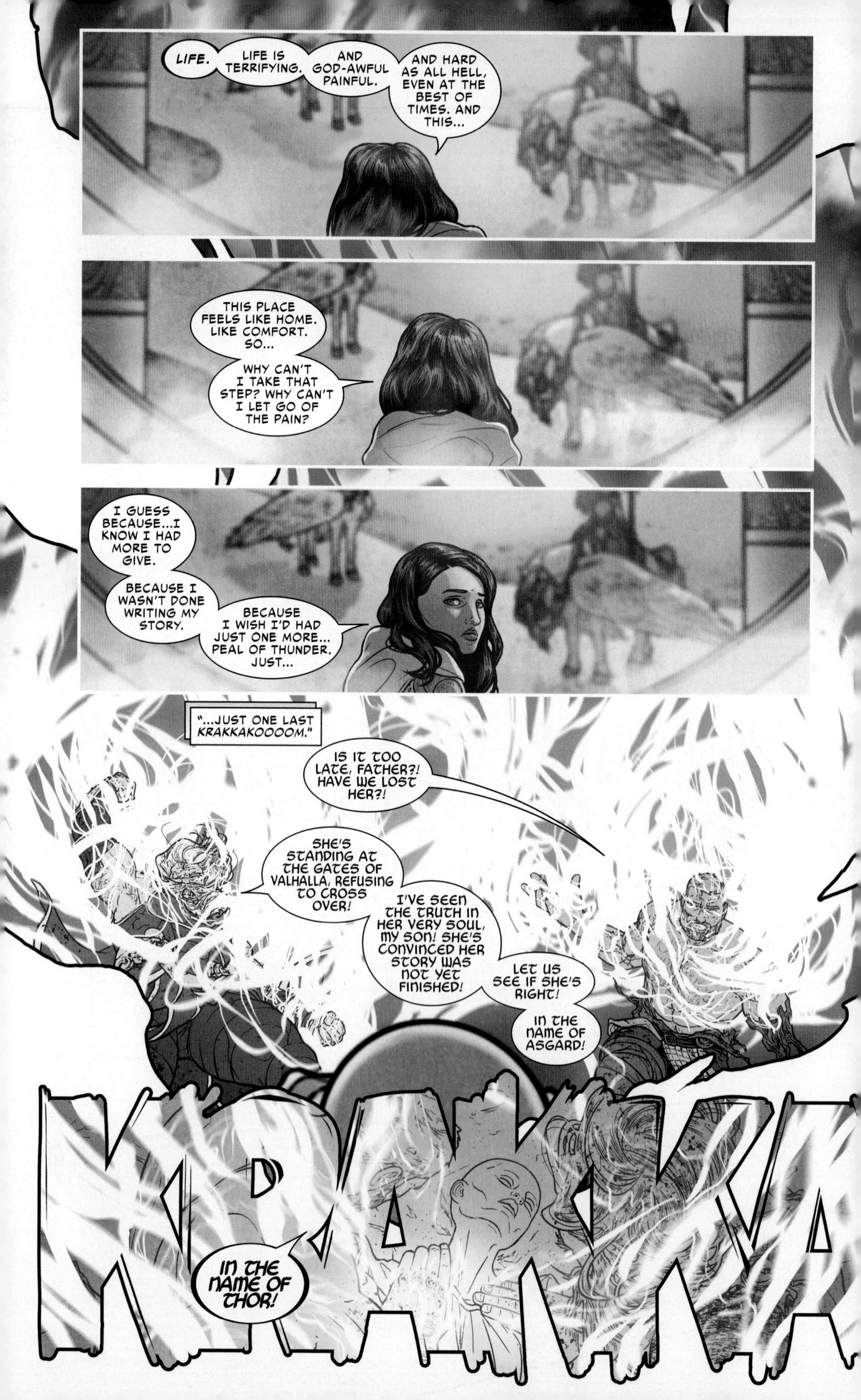
LIFE.
LIFE IS TERRIFYING.
AND GOD-AWFUL PAINFUL.
AND HARD AS ALL HELL, EVEN AT THE BEST OF TIMES. AND THIS...
THIS PLACE FEELS LIKE HOME. LIKE COMFORT. SO...
WHY CAN'T I TAKE THAT STEP? WHY CAN'T I LET GO OF THE PAIN?
I GUESS BECAUSE...I KNOW I HAD MORE TO GIVE.
BECAUSE I WASN'T DONE WRITING MY STORY.
BECAUSE I WISH I'D HAD JUST ONE MORE... PEAL OF THUNDER. JUST...
"...JUST ONE LAST KRAKKAKOOOOM."
IS IT TOO LATE, FATHER?! HAVE WE LOST HER?!
SHE'S STANDING AT THE GATES OF VALHALLA, REFUSING TO CROSS OVER!
I'VE SEEN THE TRUTH IN HER VERY SOUL, MY SON! SHE'S CONVINCED HER STORY WAS NOT YET FINISHED!
LET US SEE IF SHE'S RIGHT!
IN THE NAME OF ASGARD!
IN THE NAME OF THOR!
KRAKKA

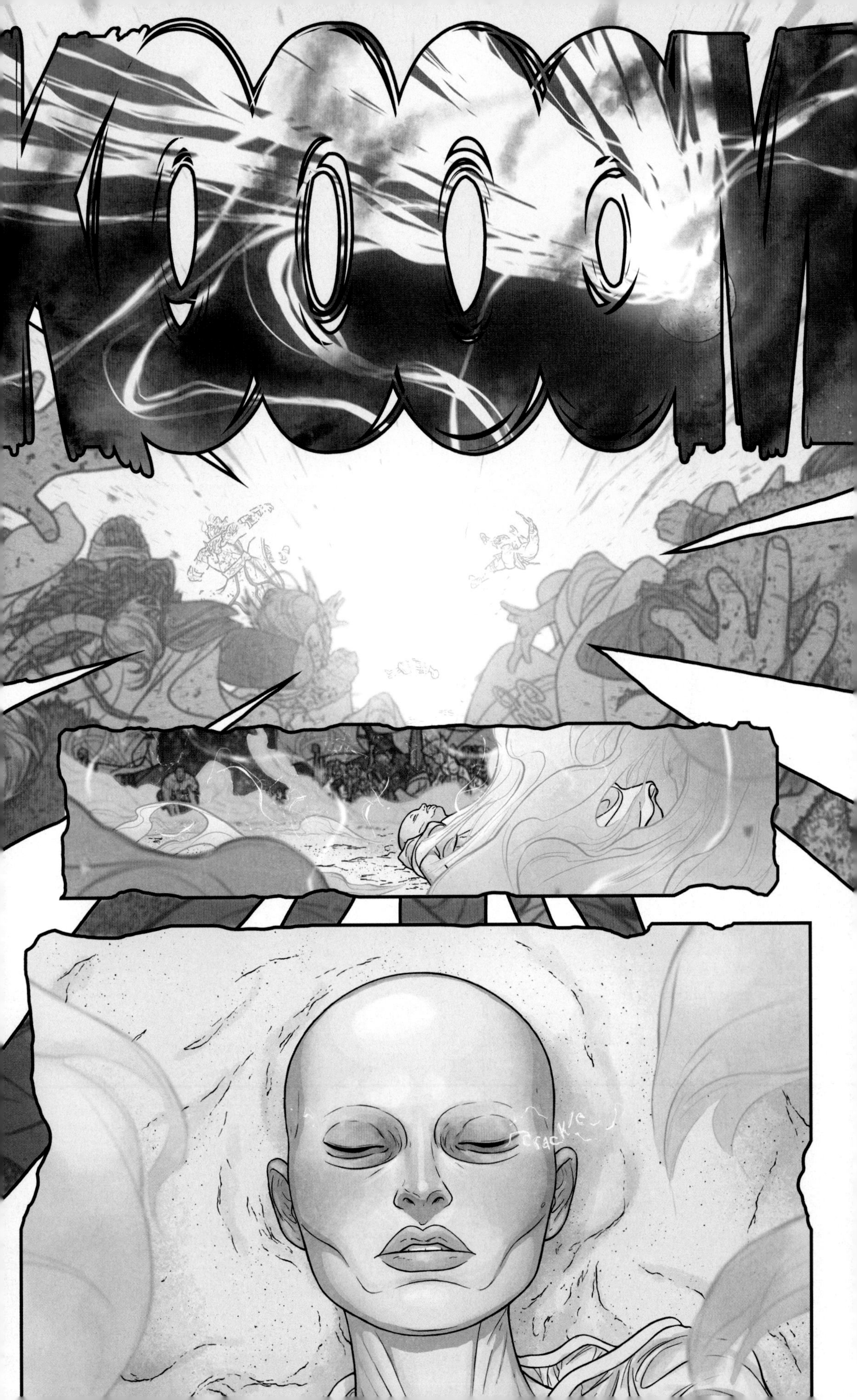
KOOOOM
crackle

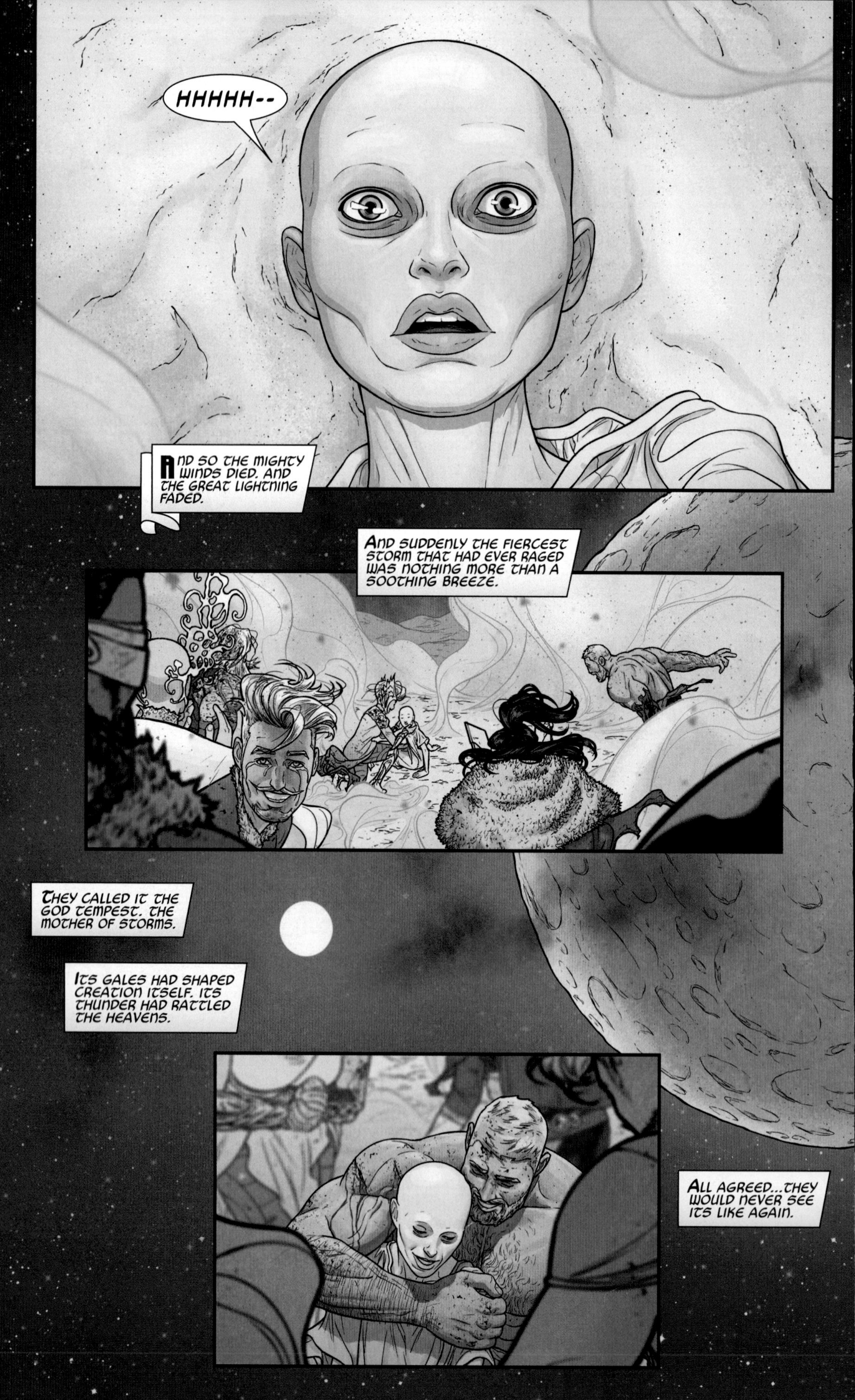
HHHHH--
AND SO THE MIGHTY WINDS DIED. AND THE GREAT LIGHTNING FADED.
AND SUDDENLY THE FIERCEST STORM THAT HAD EVER RAGED WAS NOTHING MORE THAN A SOOTHING BREEZE.
THEY CALLED IT THE GOD TEMPEST. THE MOTHER OF STORMS.
ITS GALES HAD SHAPED CREATION ITSELF. ITS THUNDER HAD RATTLED THE HEAVENS.
ALL AGREED...THEY WOULD NEVER SEE ITS LIKE AGAIN.

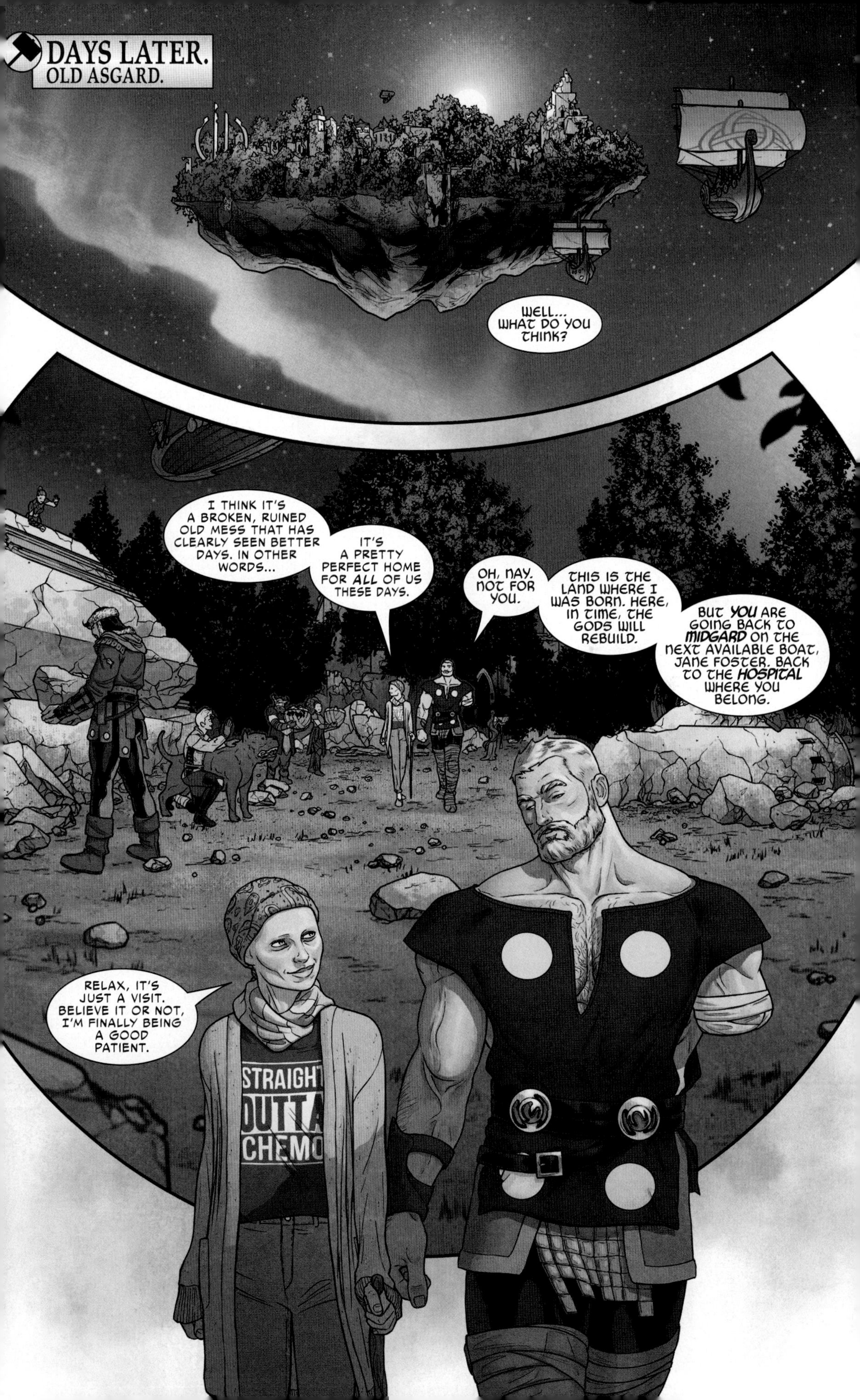
DAYS LATER.
OLD ASGARD.
WELL... WHAT DO YOU THINK?
I THINK IT'S A BROKEN, RUINED OLD MESS THAT HAS CLEARLY SEEN BETTER DAYS. IN OTHER WORDS...
IT'S A PRETTY PERFECT HOME FOR ALL OF US THESE DAYS.
OH, NAY. NOT FOR YOU.
THIS IS THE LAND WHERE I WAS BORN. HERE, IN TIME, THE GODS WILL REBUILD.
BUT YOU ARE GOING BACK TO MIDGARD ON THE NEXT AVAILABLE BOAT, JANE FOSTER. BACK TO THE HOSPITAL WHERE YOU BELONG.
RELAX, IT'S JUST A VISIT. BELIEVE IT OR NOT, I'M FINALLY BEING A GOOD PATIENT.
STRAIGHT OUTTA CHEMO

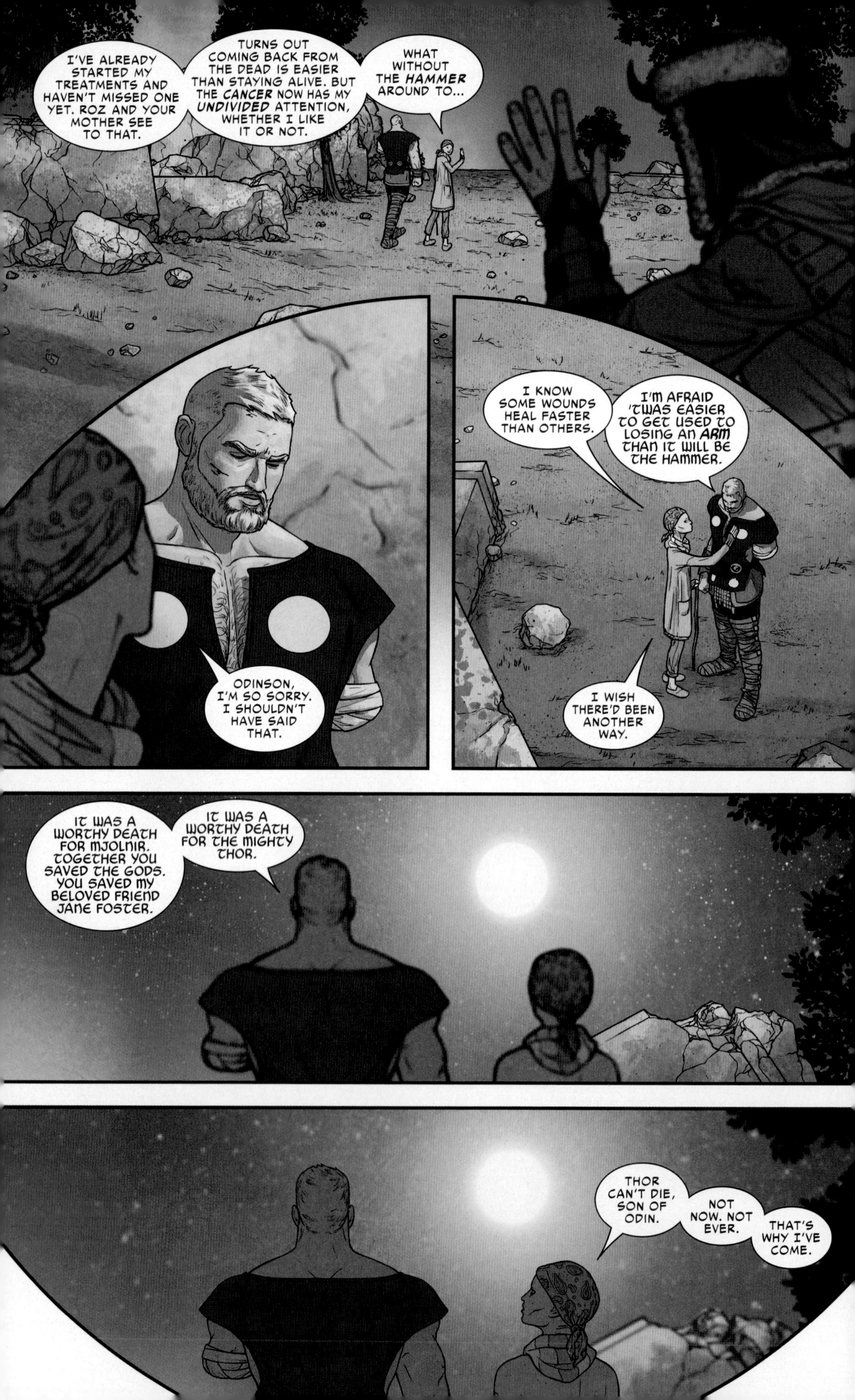

I'VE ALREADY STARTED MY TREATMENTS AND HAVEN'T MISSED ONE YET. ROZ AND YOUR MOTHER SEE TO THAT.
TURNS OUT COMING BACK FROM THE DEAD IS EASIER THAN STAYING ALIVE. BUT THE CANCER NOW HAS MY UNDIVIDED ATTENTION, WHETHER I LIKE IT OR NOT.
WHAT WITHOUT THE HAMMER AROUND TO...
ODINSON, I'M SO SORRY. I SHOULDN'T HAVE SAID THAT.
I KNOW SOME WOUNDS HEAL FASTER THAN OTHERS.
I'M AFRAID 'TWAS EASIER TO GET USED TO LOSING AN ARM THAN IT WILL BE THE HAMMER.
I WISH THERE'D BEEN ANOTHER WAY.
IT WAS A WORTHY DEATH FOR MJOLNIR. TOGETHER YOU SAVED THE GODS. YOU SAVED MY BELOVED FRIEND JANE FOSTER.
IT WAS A WORTHY DEATH FOR THE MIGHTY THOR.
THOR CAN'T DIE, SON OF ODIN.
NOT NOW. NOT EVER.
THAT'S WHY I'VE COME.

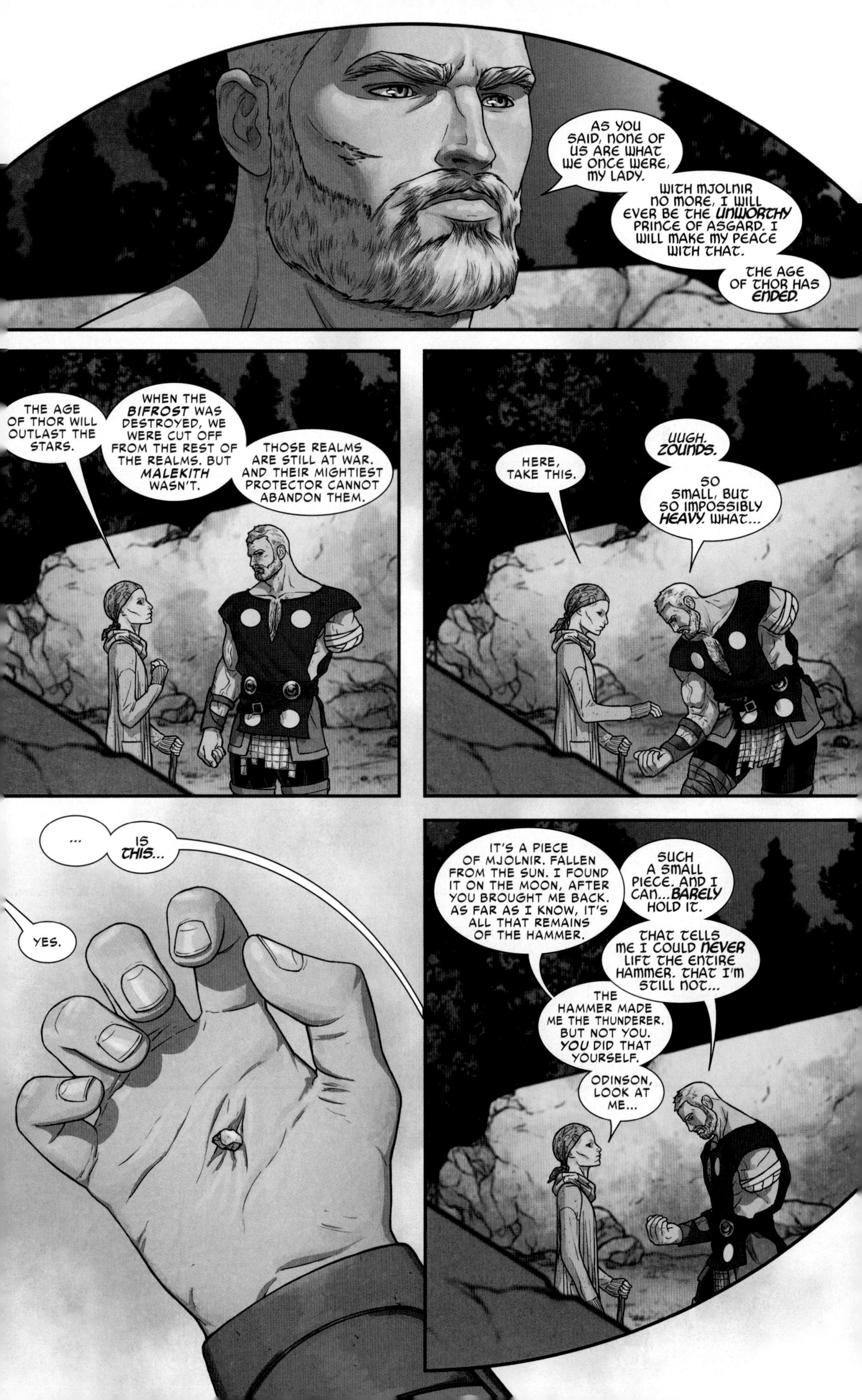

AS YOU SAID, NONE OF US ARE WHAT WE ONCE WERE, MY LADY.
WITH MJOLNIR NO MORE, I WILL EVER BE THE UNWORTHY PRINCE OF ASGARD. I WILL MAKE MY PEACE WITH THAT.
THE AGE OF THOR HAS ENDED.
THE AGE OF THOR WILL OUTLAST THE STARS.
WHEN THE BIFROST WAS DESTROYED, WE WERE CUT OFF FROM THE REST OF THE REALMS. BUT MALEKITH WASN'T.
THOSE REALMS ARE STILL AT WAR. AND THEIR MIGHTIEST PROTECTOR CANNOT ABANDON THEM.
HERE, TAKE THIS.
UUGH. ZOUNDS.
SO SMALL, BUT SO IMPOSSIBLY HEAVY. WHAT...
...
IS THIS...
YES.
IT'S A PIECE OF MJOLNIR. FALLEN FROM THE SUN. I FOUND IT ON THE MOON, AFTER YOU BROUGHT ME BACK. AS FAR AS I KNOW, IT'S ALL THAT REMAINS OF THE HAMMER.
SUCH A SMALL PIECE. AND I CAN...BARELY HOLD IT.
THAT TELLS ME I COULD NEVER LIFT THE ENTIRE HAMMER. THAT I'M STILL NOT...
THE HAMMER MADE ME THE THUNDERER. BUT NOT YOU. YOU DID THAT YOURSELF.
ODINSON, LOOK AT ME...

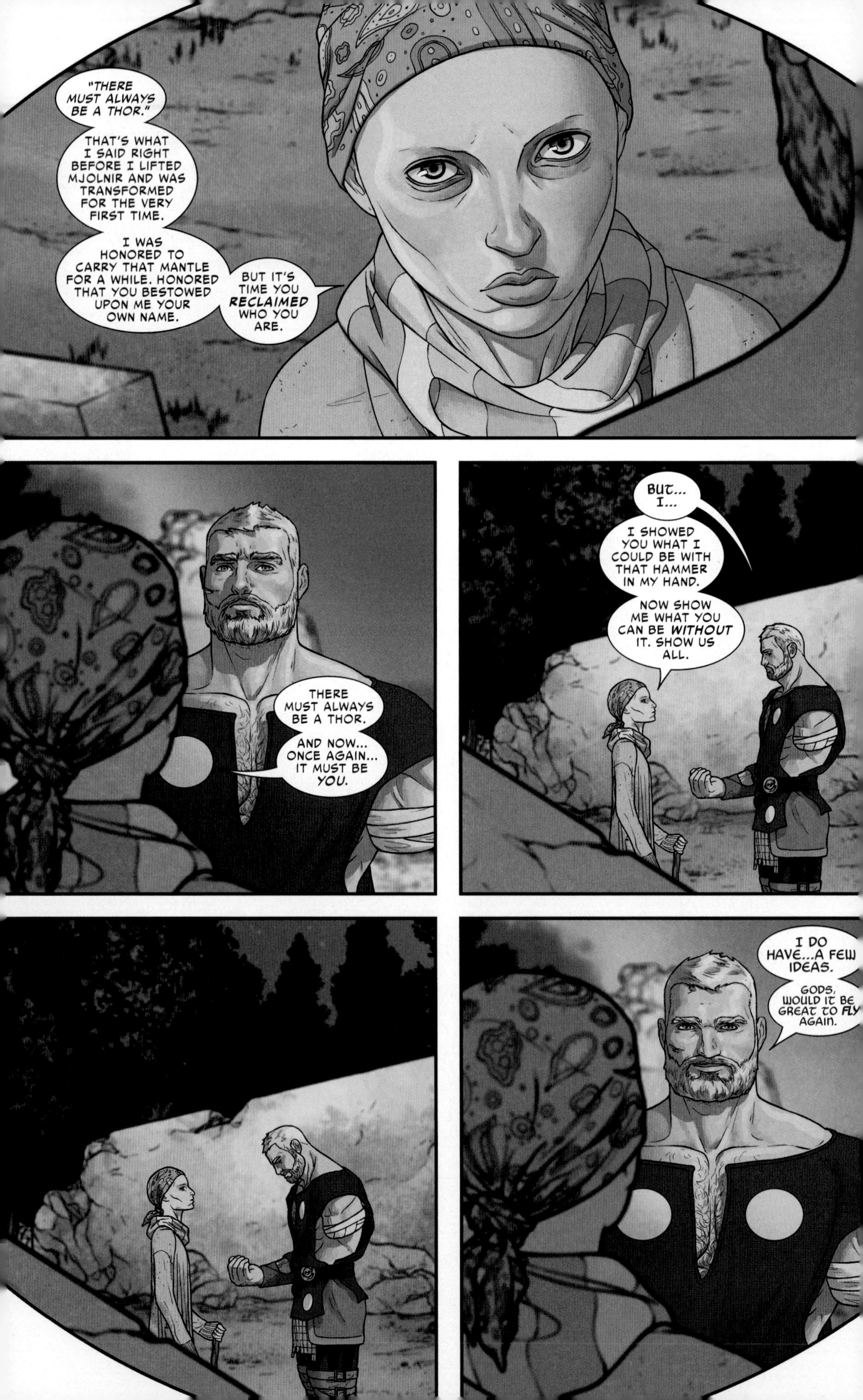
"THERE MUST ALWAYS BE A THOR."
THAT'S WHAT I SAID RIGHT BEFORE I LIFTED MJOLNIR AND WAS TRANSFORMED FOR THE VERY FIRST TIME.
I WAS HONORED TO CARRY THAT MANTLE FOR A WHILE. HONORED THAT YOU BESTOWED UPON ME YOUR OWN NAME.
BUT IT'S TIME YOU *RECLAIMED* WHO YOU ARE.
THERE MUST ALWAYS BE A THOR.
AND NOW... ONCE AGAIN... IT MUST BE *YOU*.
BUT... I...
I SHOWED YOU WHAT I COULD BE WITH THAT HAMMER IN MY HAND.
NOW SHOW ME WHAT YOU CAN BE *WITHOUT* IT. SHOW US ALL.
I DO HAVE...A FEW IDEAS.
GODS, WOULD IT BE GREAT TO *FLY* AGAIN.

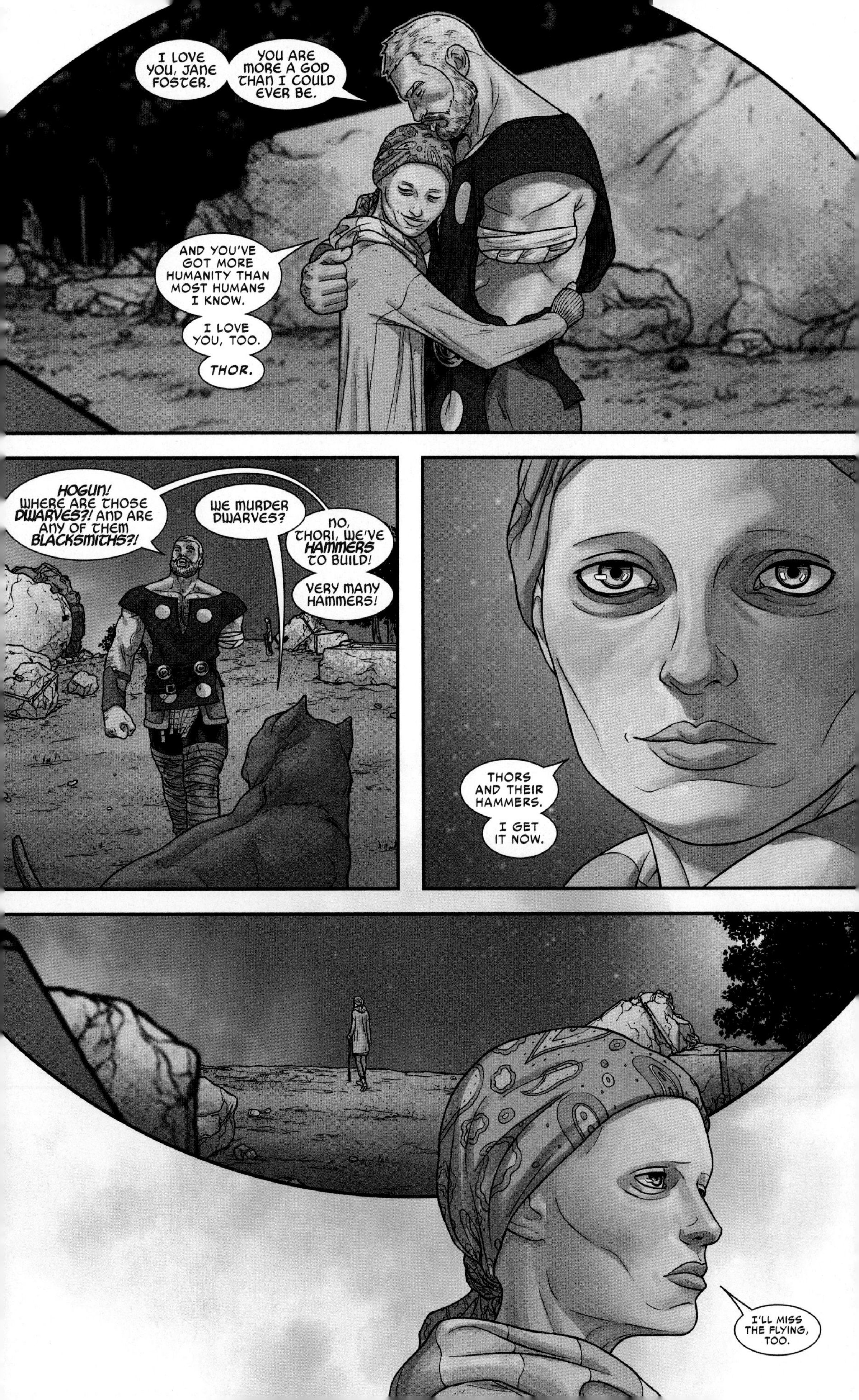
I LOVE YOU, JANE FOSTER.
YOU ARE MORE A GOD THAN I COULD EVER BE.
AND YOU'VE GOT MORE HUMANITY THAN MOST HUMANS I KNOW.
I LOVE YOU, TOO.
THOR.
HOGUN! WHERE ARE THOSE DWARVES?! AND ARE ANY OF THEM BLACKSMITHS?!
WE MURDER DWARVES?
NO, THORI, WE'VE HAMMERS TO BUILD!
VERY MANY HAMMERS!
THORS AND THEIR HAMMERS.
I GET IT NOW.
I'LL MISS THE FLYING, TOO.

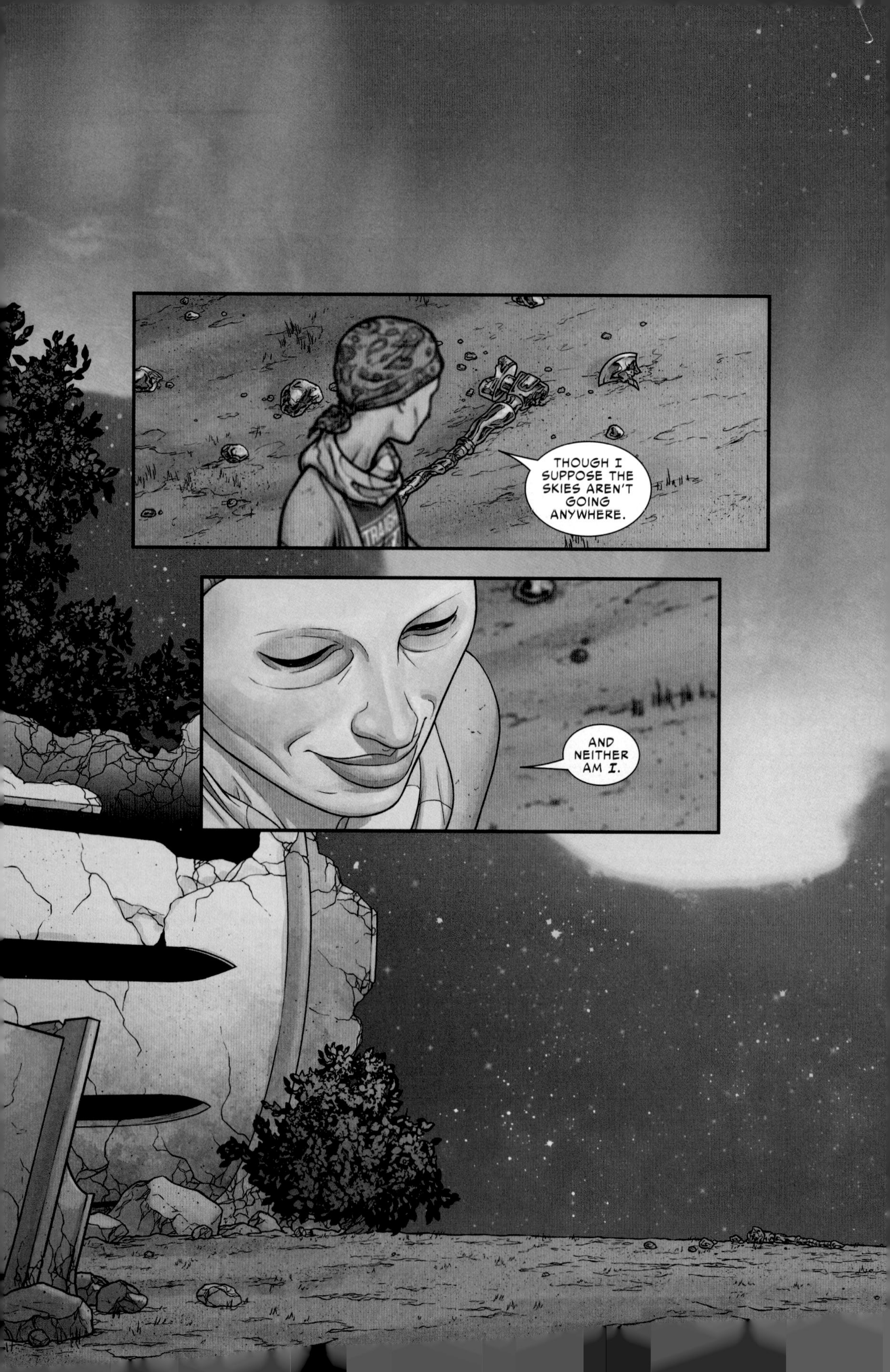
THOUGH I SUPPOSE THE SKIES AREN'T GOING ANYWHERE.
AND NEITHER AM I.

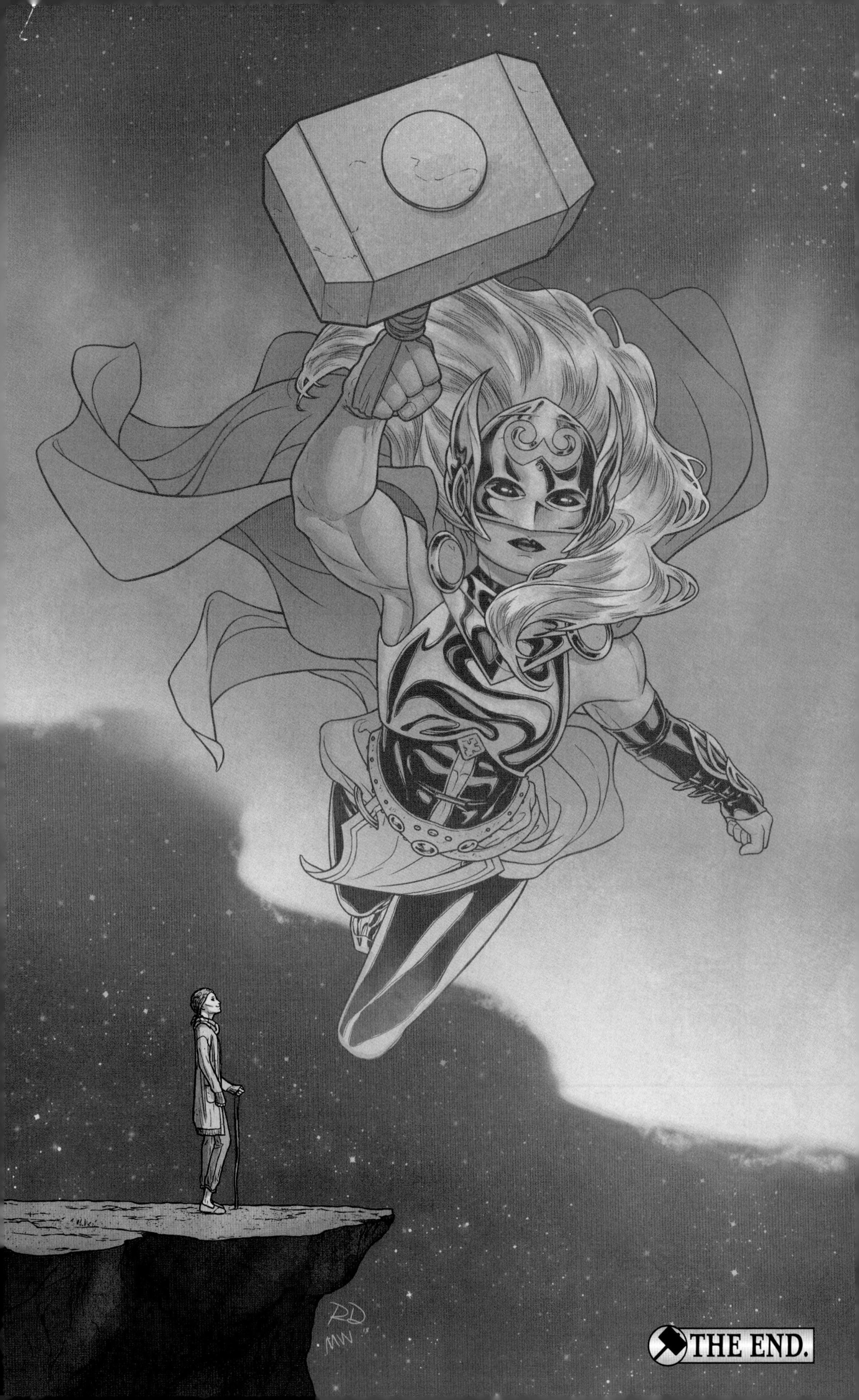
THE END.

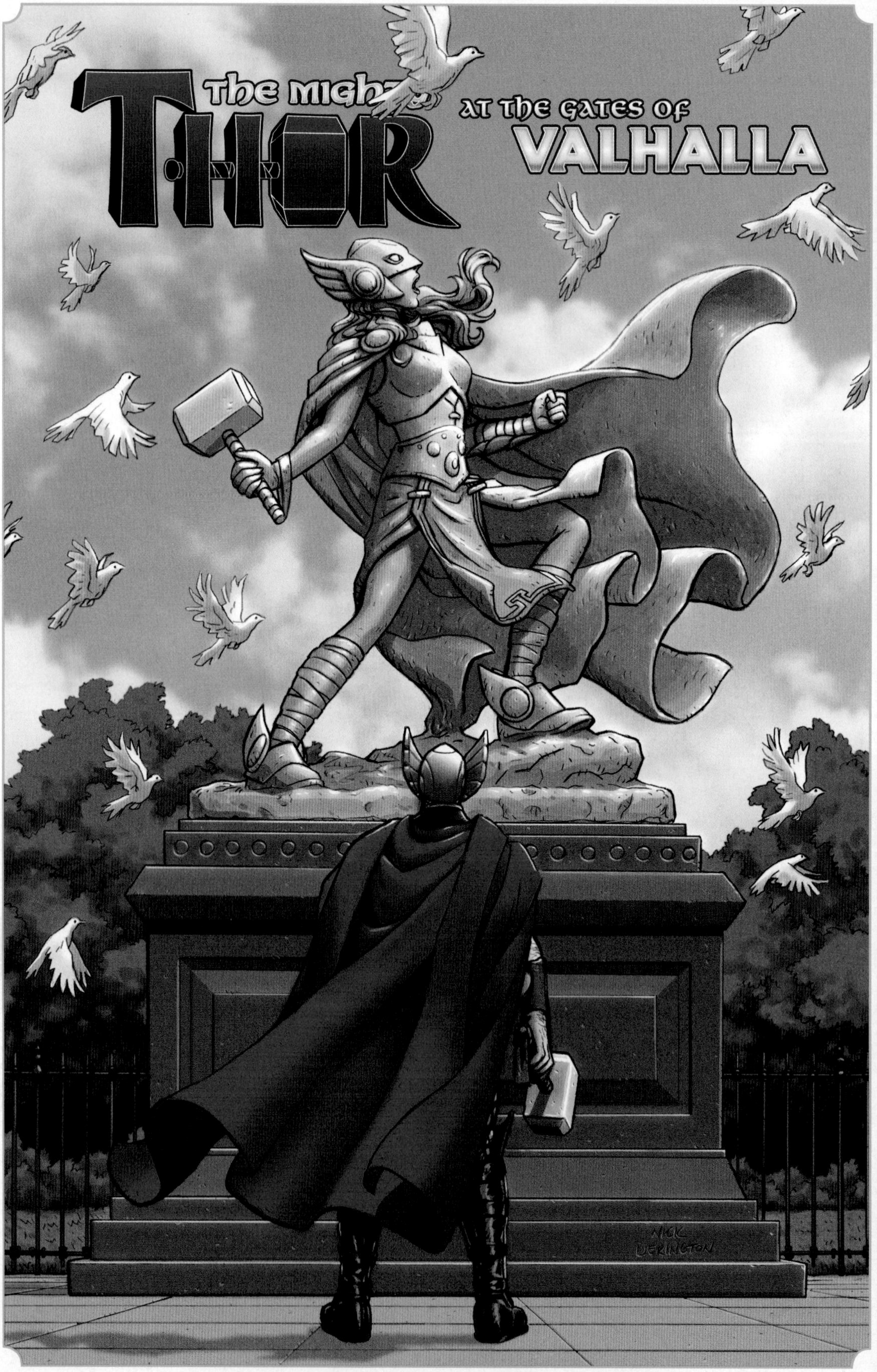
The Migh
THOR
at the Gates of
VALHALLA
NICK DERINGTON

# THE TOMORROW GIRLS
# &
# THE LORD OF THE REALMS

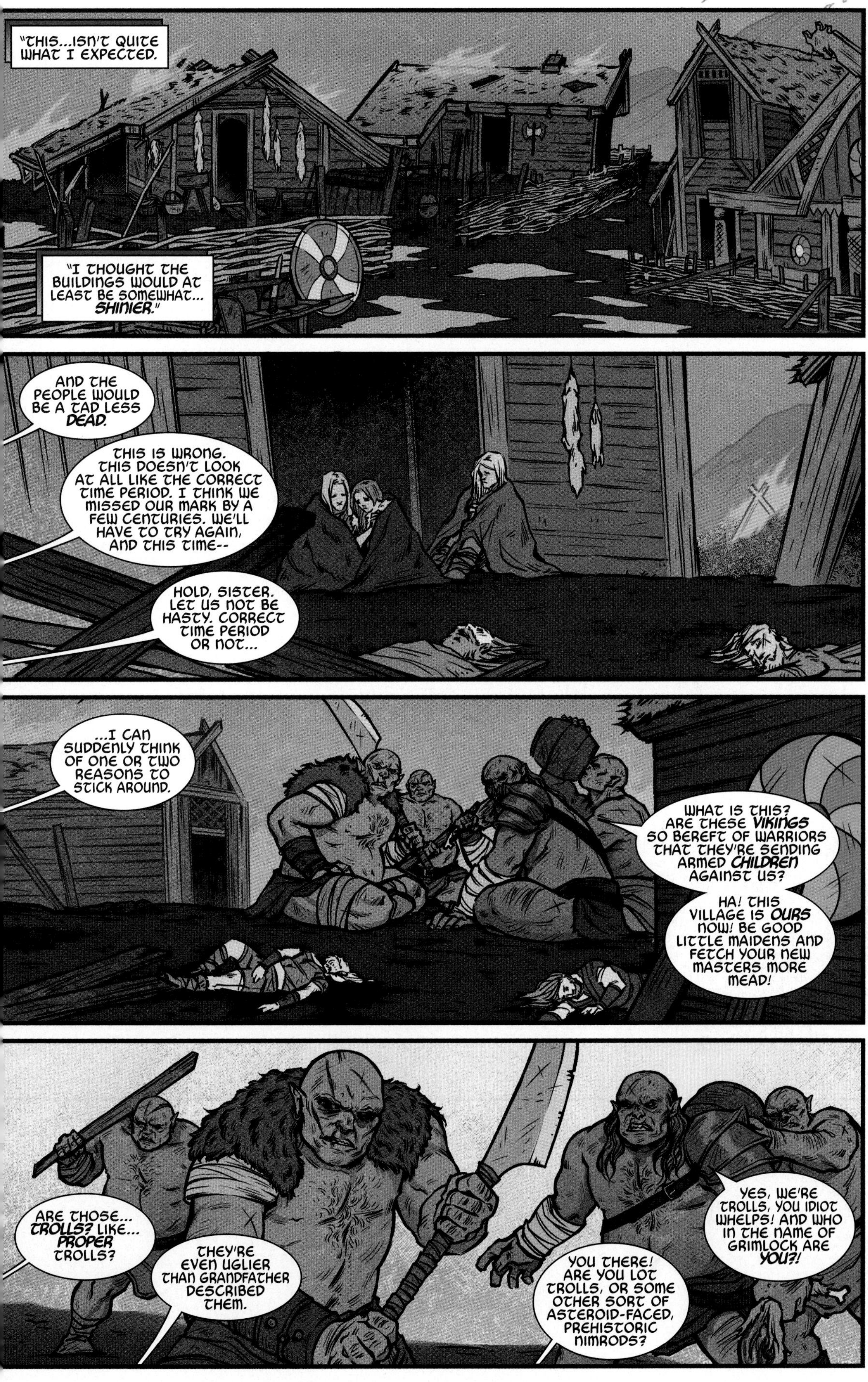
"THIS...ISN'T QUITE WHAT I EXPECTED.
"I THOUGHT THE BUILDINGS WOULD AT LEAST BE SOMEWHAT... SHINIER."
AND THE PEOPLE WOULD BE A TAD LESS DEAD.
THIS IS WRONG. THIS DOESN'T LOOK AT ALL LIKE THE CORRECT TIME PERIOD. I THINK WE MISSED OUR MARK BY A FEW CENTURIES. WE'LL HAVE TO TRY AGAIN, AND THIS TIME--
HOLD, SISTER. LET US NOT BE HASTY. CORRECT TIME PERIOD OR NOT...
...I CAN SUDDENLY THINK OF ONE OR TWO REASONS TO STICK AROUND.
WHAT IS THIS? ARE THESE VIKINGS SO BEREFT OF WARRIORS THAT THEY'RE SENDING ARMED CHILDREN AGAINST US?
HA! THIS VILLAGE IS OURS NOW! BE GOOD LITTLE MAIDENS AND FETCH YOUR NEW MASTERS MORE MEAD!
ARE THOSE... TROLLS? LIKE... PROPER TROLLS?
THEY'RE EVEN UGLIER THAN GRANDFATHER DESCRIBED THEM.
YOU THERE! ARE YOU LOT TROLLS, OR SOME OTHER SORT OF ASTEROID-FACED, PREHISTORIC NIMRODS?
YES, WE'RE TROLLS, YOU IDIOT WHELPS! AND WHO IN THE NAME OF GRIMLOCK ARE YOU?!

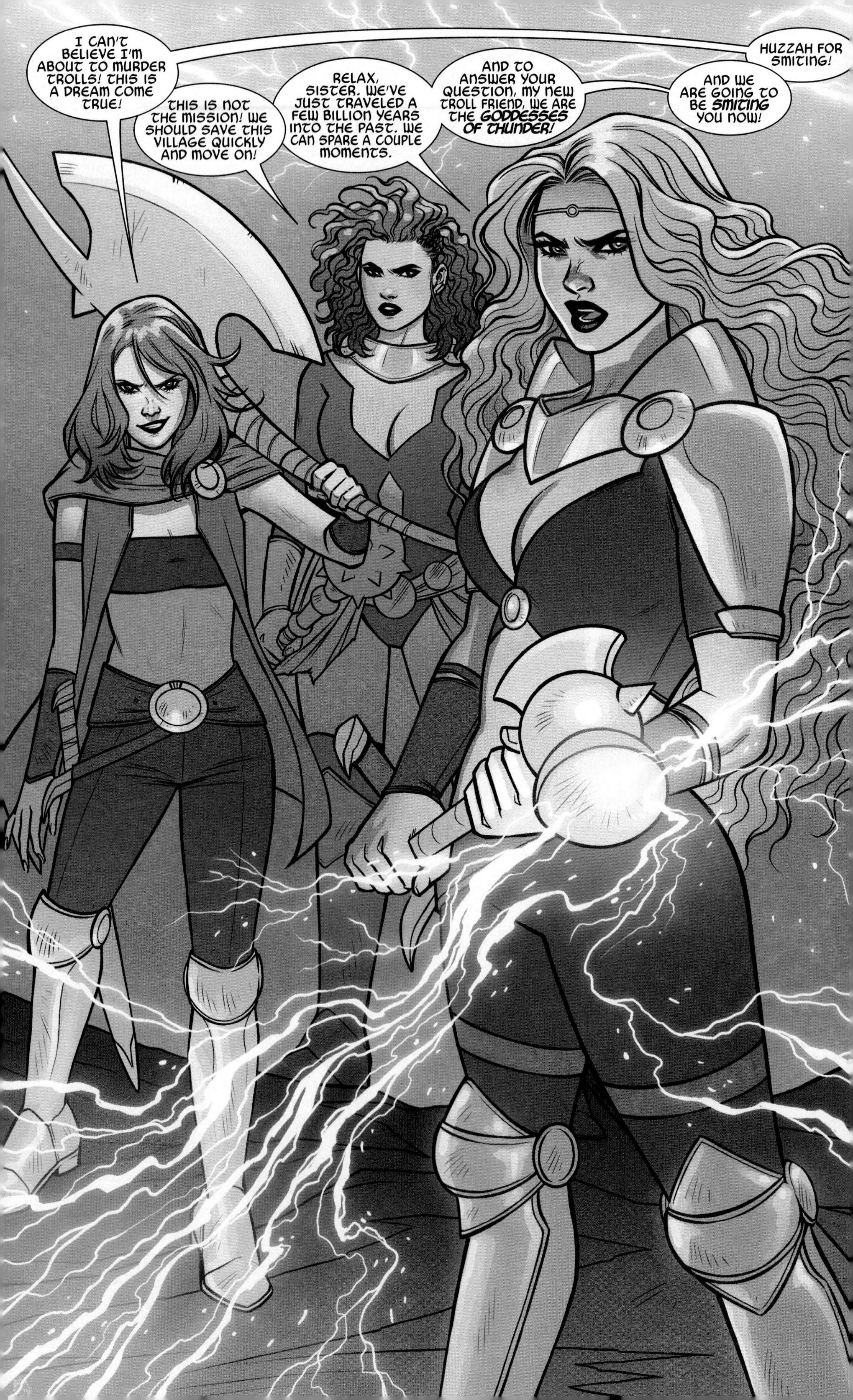

I CAN'T BELIEVE I'M ABOUT TO MURDER TROLLS! THIS IS A DREAM COME TRUE!
THIS IS NOT THE MISSION! WE SHOULD SAVE THIS VILLAGE QUICKLY AND MOVE ON!
RELAX, SISTER. WE'VE JUST TRAVELED A FEW BILLION YEARS INTO THE PAST. WE CAN SPARE A COUPLE MOMENTS.
AND TO ANSWER YOUR QUESTION, MY NEW TROLL FRIEND, WE ARE THE GODDESSES OF THUNDER!
HUZZAH FOR SMITING!
AND WE ARE GOING TO BE SMITING YOU NOW!

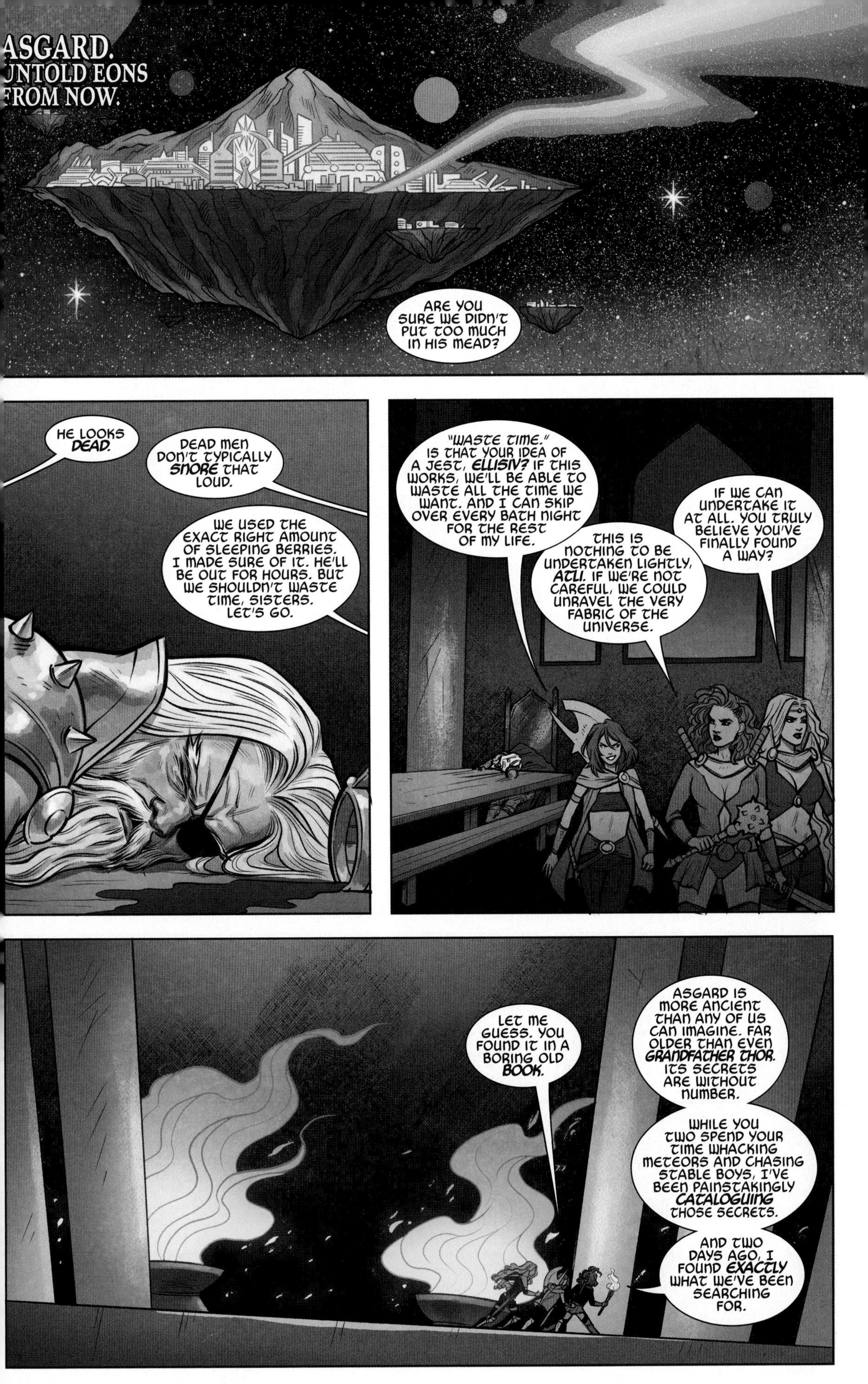
ASGARD. UNTOLD EONS FROM NOW.
ARE YOU SURE WE DIDN'T PUT TOO MUCH IN HIS MEAD?
HE LOOKS DEAD.
DEAD MEN DON'T TYPICALLY SNORE THAT LOUD.
WE USED THE EXACT RIGHT AMOUNT OF SLEEPING BERRIES. I MADE SURE OF IT. HE'LL BE OUT FOR HOURS. BUT WE SHOULDN'T WASTE TIME, SISTERS. LET'S GO.
"WASTE TIME." IS THAT YOUR IDEA OF A JEST, ELLISIV? IF THIS WORKS, WE'LL BE ABLE TO WASTE ALL THE TIME WE WANT. AND I CAN SKIP OVER EVERY BATH NIGHT FOR THE REST OF MY LIFE.
THIS IS NOTHING TO BE UNDERTAKEN LIGHTLY, ATLI. IF WE'RE NOT CAREFUL, WE COULD UNRAVEL THE VERY FABRIC OF THE UNIVERSE.
IF WE CAN UNDERTAKE IT AT ALL. YOU TRULY BELIEVE YOU'VE FINALLY FOUND A WAY?
LET ME GUESS. YOU FOUND IT IN A BORING OLD BOOK.
ASGARD IS MORE ANCIENT THAN ANY OF US CAN IMAGINE. FAR OLDER THAN EVEN GRANDFATHER THOR. ITS SECRETS ARE WITHOUT NUMBER.
WHILE YOU TWO SPEND YOUR TIME WHACKING METEORS AND CHASING STABLE BOYS, I'VE BEEN PAINSTAKINGLY CATALOGUING THOSE SECRETS.
AND TWO DAYS AGO, I FOUND EXACTLY WHAT WE'VE BEEN SEARCHING FOR.

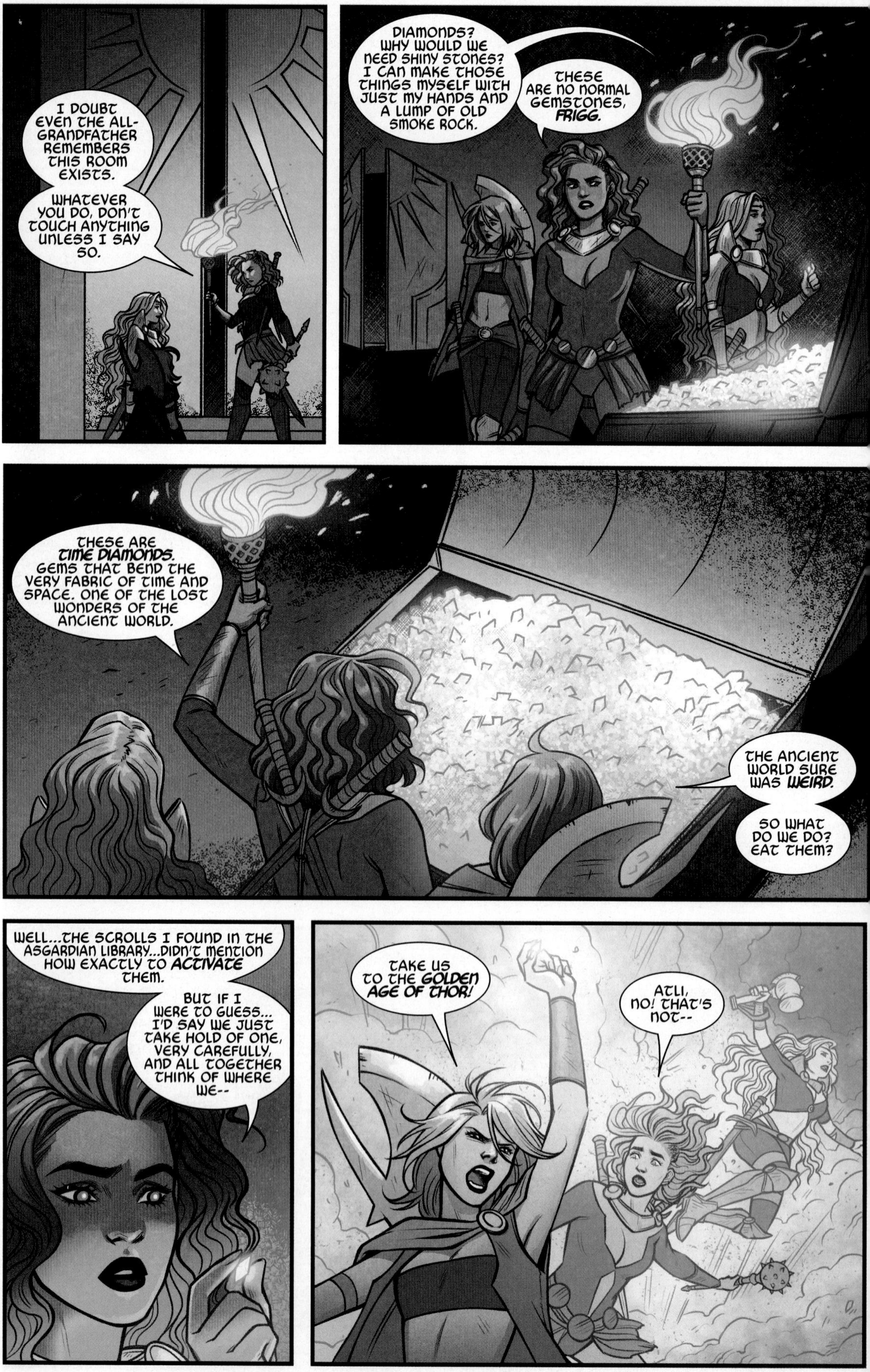

I DOUBT EVEN THE ALL-GRANDFATHER REMEMBERS THIS ROOM EXISTS.
WHATEVER YOU DO, DON'T TOUCH ANYTHING UNLESS I SAY SO.
DIAMONDS? WHY WOULD WE NEED SHINY STONES? I CAN MAKE THOSE THINGS MYSELF WITH JUST MY HANDS AND A LUMP OF OLD SMOKE ROCK.
THESE ARE NO NORMAL GEMSTONES, FRIGG.
THESE ARE TIME DIAMONDS. GEMS THAT BEND THE VERY FABRIC OF TIME AND SPACE. ONE OF THE LOST WONDERS OF THE ANCIENT WORLD.
THE ANCIENT WORLD SURE WAS WEIRD.
SO WHAT DO WE DO? EAT THEM?
WELL...THE SCROLLS I FOUND IN THE ASGARDIAN LIBRARY...DIDN'T MENTION HOW EXACTLY TO ACTIVATE THEM.
BUT IF I WERE TO GUESS... I'D SAY WE JUST TAKE HOLD OF ONE, VERY CAREFULLY, AND ALL TOGETHER THINK OF WHERE WE--
TAKE US TO THE GOLDEN AGE OF THOR!
ATLI, NO! THAT'S NOT--

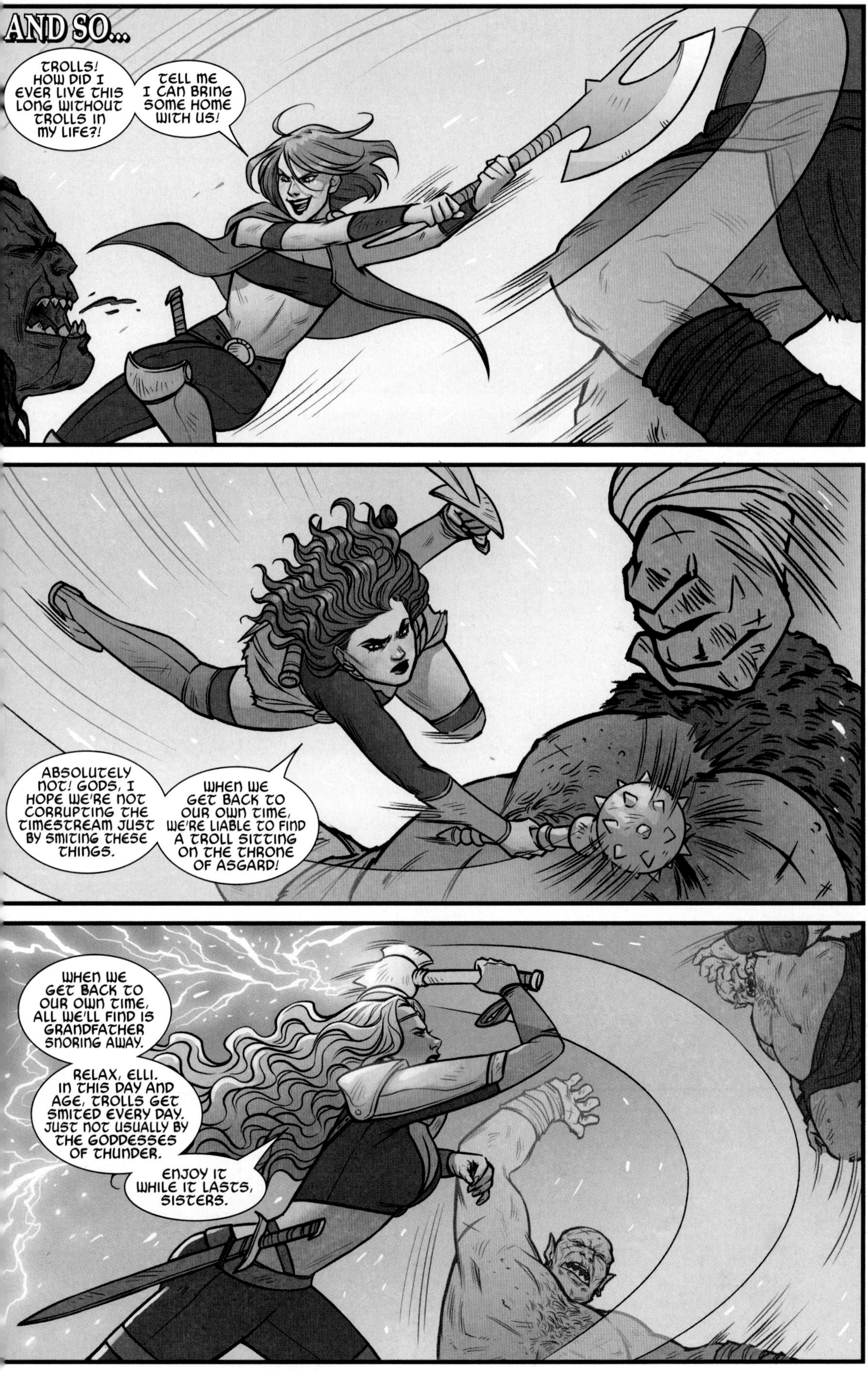
AND SO...
TROLLS! HOW DID I EVER LIVE THIS LONG WITHOUT TROLLS IN MY LIFE?!
TELL ME I CAN BRING SOME HOME WITH US!
ABSOLUTELY NOT! GODS, I HOPE WE'RE NOT CORRUPTING THE TIMESTREAM JUST BY SMITING THESE THINGS.
WHEN WE GET BACK TO OUR OWN TIME, WE'RE LIABLE TO FIND A TROLL SITTING ON THE THRONE OF ASGARD!
WHEN WE GET BACK TO OUR OWN TIME, ALL WE'LL FIND IS GRANDFATHER SNORING AWAY.
RELAX, ELLI. IN THIS DAY AND AGE, TROLLS GET SMITED EVERY DAY. JUST NOT USUALLY BY THE GODDESSES OF THUNDER.
ENJOY IT WHILE IT LASTS, SISTERS.

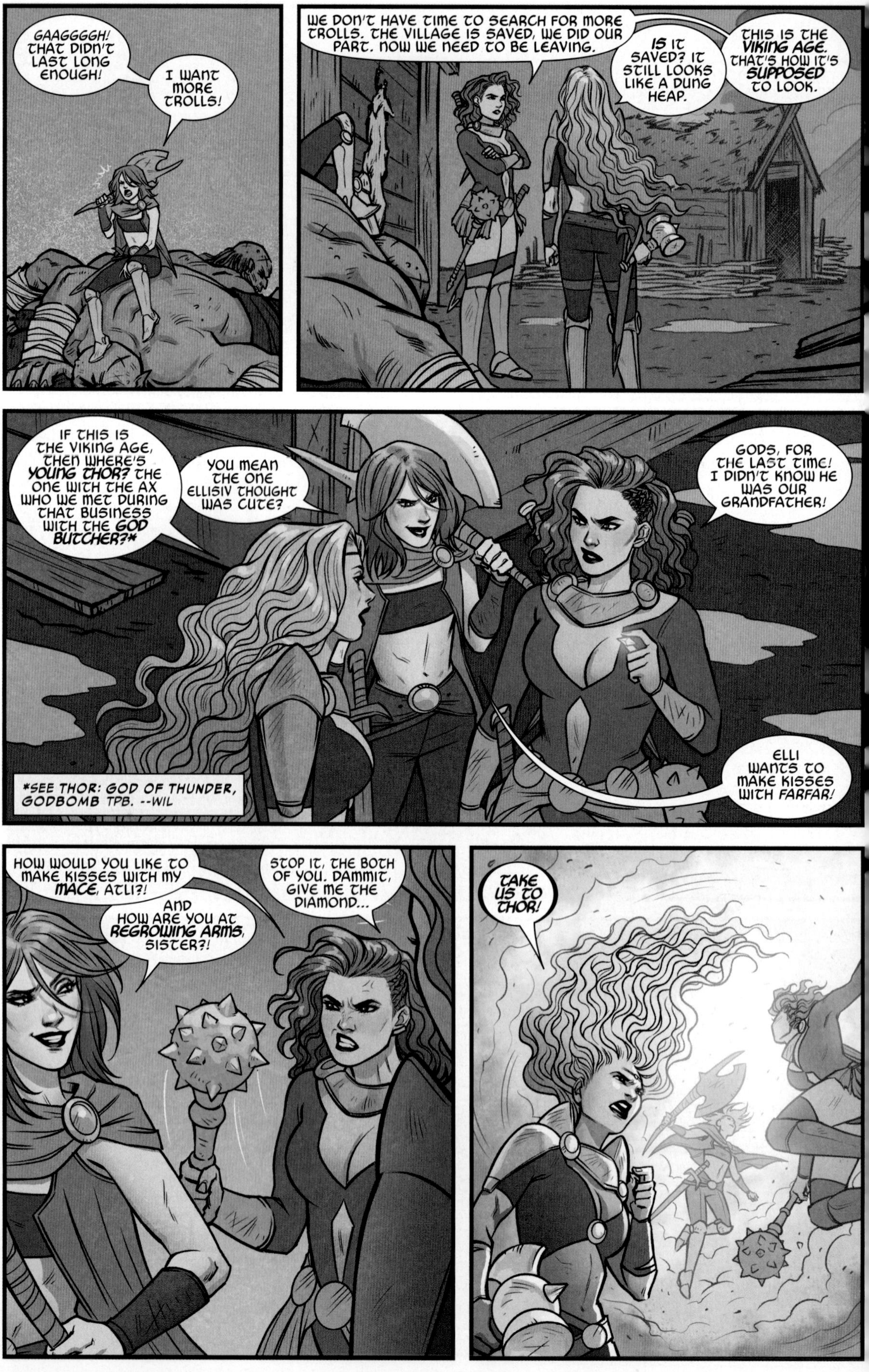
GAAGGGGH! THAT DIDN'T LAST LONG ENOUGH!
I WANT MORE TROLLS!
WE DON'T HAVE TIME TO SEARCH FOR MORE TROLLS. THE VILLAGE IS SAVED, WE DID OUR PART. NOW WE NEED TO BE LEAVING.
IS IT SAVED? IT STILL LOOKS LIKE A DUNG HEAP.
THIS IS THE VIKING AGE. THAT'S HOW IT'S SUPPOSED TO LOOK.
IF THIS IS THE VIKING AGE, THEN WHERE'S YOUNG THOR? THE ONE WITH THE AX WHO WE MET DURING THAT BUSINESS WITH THE GOD BUTCHER?*
YOU MEAN THE ONE ELLISIV THOUGHT WAS CUTE?
GODS, FOR THE LAST TIME! I DIDN'T KNOW HE WAS OUR GRANDFATHER!
*SEE THOR: GOD OF THUNDER, GODBOMB TPB. --WIL
ELLI WANTS TO MAKE KISSES WITH FARFAR!
HOW WOULD YOU LIKE TO MAKE KISSES WITH MY MACE, ATLI?!
AND HOW ARE YOU AT REGROWING ARMS, SISTER?!
STOP IT, THE BOTH OF YOU. DAMMIT, GIVE ME THE DIAMOND...
TAKE US TO THOR!

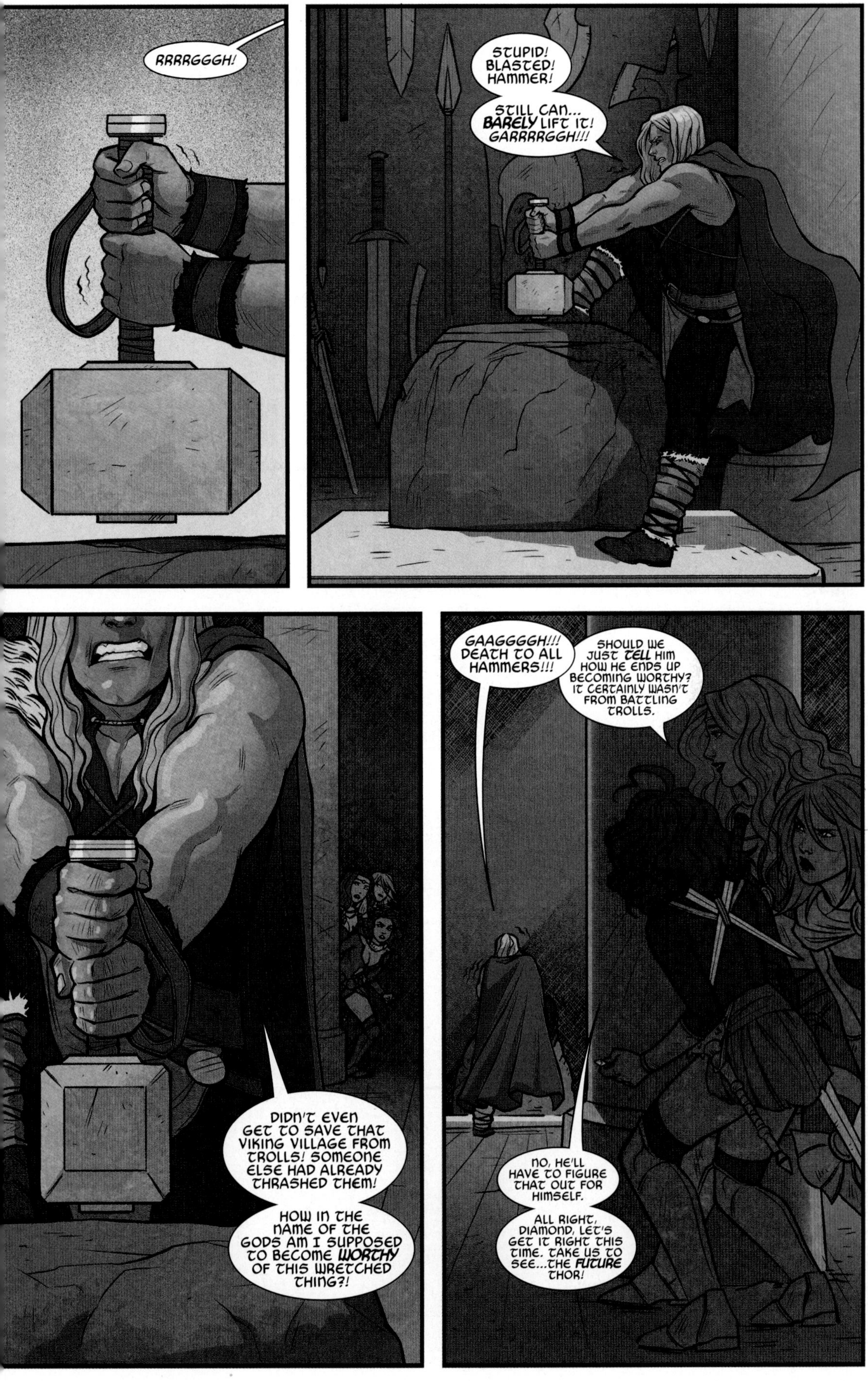
RRRRGGGH!
STUPID! BLASTED! HAMMER!
STILL CAN... BARELY LIFT IT! GARRRRGGH!!!
DIDN'T EVEN GET TO SAVE THAT VIKING VILLAGE FROM TROLLS! SOMEONE ELSE HAD ALREADY THRASHED THEM!
HOW IN THE NAME OF THE GODS AM I SUPPOSED TO BECOME WORTHY OF THIS WRETCHED THING?!
GAAGGGGH!!! DEATH TO ALL HAMMERS!!!
SHOULD WE JUST TELL HIM HOW HE ENDS UP BECOMING WORTHY? IT CERTAINLY WASN'T FROM BATTLING TROLLS.
NO, HE'LL HAVE TO FIGURE THAT OUT FOR HIMSELF.
ALL RIGHT, DIAMOND, LET'S GET IT RIGHT THIS TIME. TAKE US TO SEE...THE FUTURE THOR!

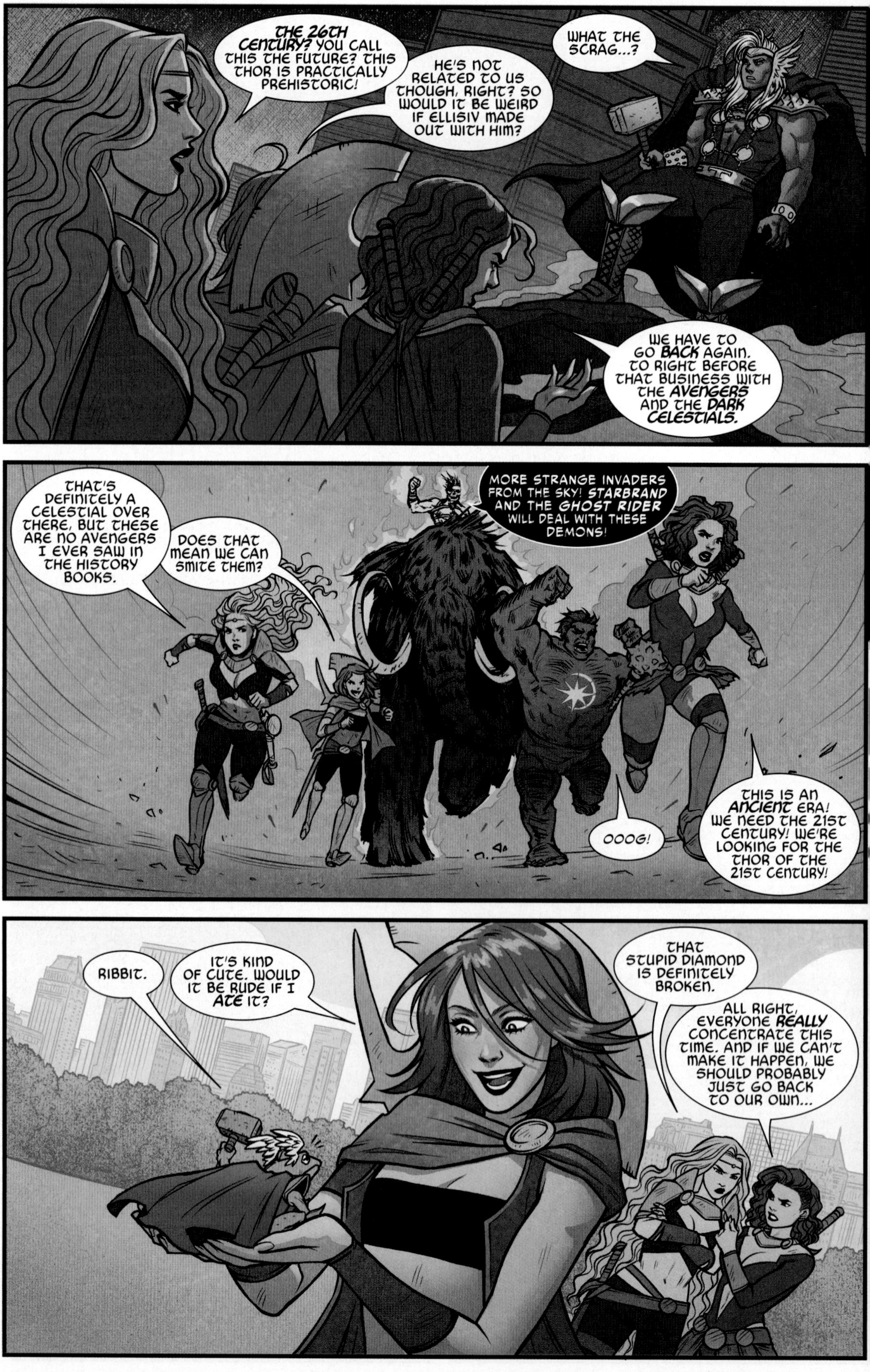
THE 26TH CENTURY? YOU CALL THIS THE FUTURE? THIS THOR IS PRACTICALLY PREHISTORIC!
HE'S NOT RELATED TO US THOUGH, RIGHT? SO WOULD IT BE WEIRD IF ELLISIV MADE OUT WITH HIM?
WHAT THE SCRAG...?
WE HAVE TO GO BACK AGAIN. TO RIGHT BEFORE THAT BUSINESS WITH THE AVENGERS AND THE DARK CELESTIALS.
THAT'S DEFINITELY A CELESTIAL OVER THERE, BUT THESE ARE NO AVENGERS I EVER SAW IN THE HISTORY BOOKS.
DOES THAT MEAN WE CAN SMITE THEM?
MORE STRANGE INVADERS FROM THE SKY! STARBRAND AND THE GHOST RIDER WILL DEAL WITH THESE DEMONS!
OOOG!
THIS IS AN ANCIENT ERA! WE NEED THE 21ST CENTURY! WE'RE LOOKING FOR THE THOR OF THE 21ST CENTURY!
RIBBIT.
IT'S KIND OF CUTE. WOULD IT BE RUDE IF I ATE IT?
THAT STUPID DIAMOND IS DEFINITELY BROKEN.
ALL RIGHT, EVERYONE REALLY CONCENTRATE THIS TIME. AND IF WE CAN'T MAKE IT HAPPEN, WE SHOULD PROBABLY JUST GO BACK TO OUR OWN...

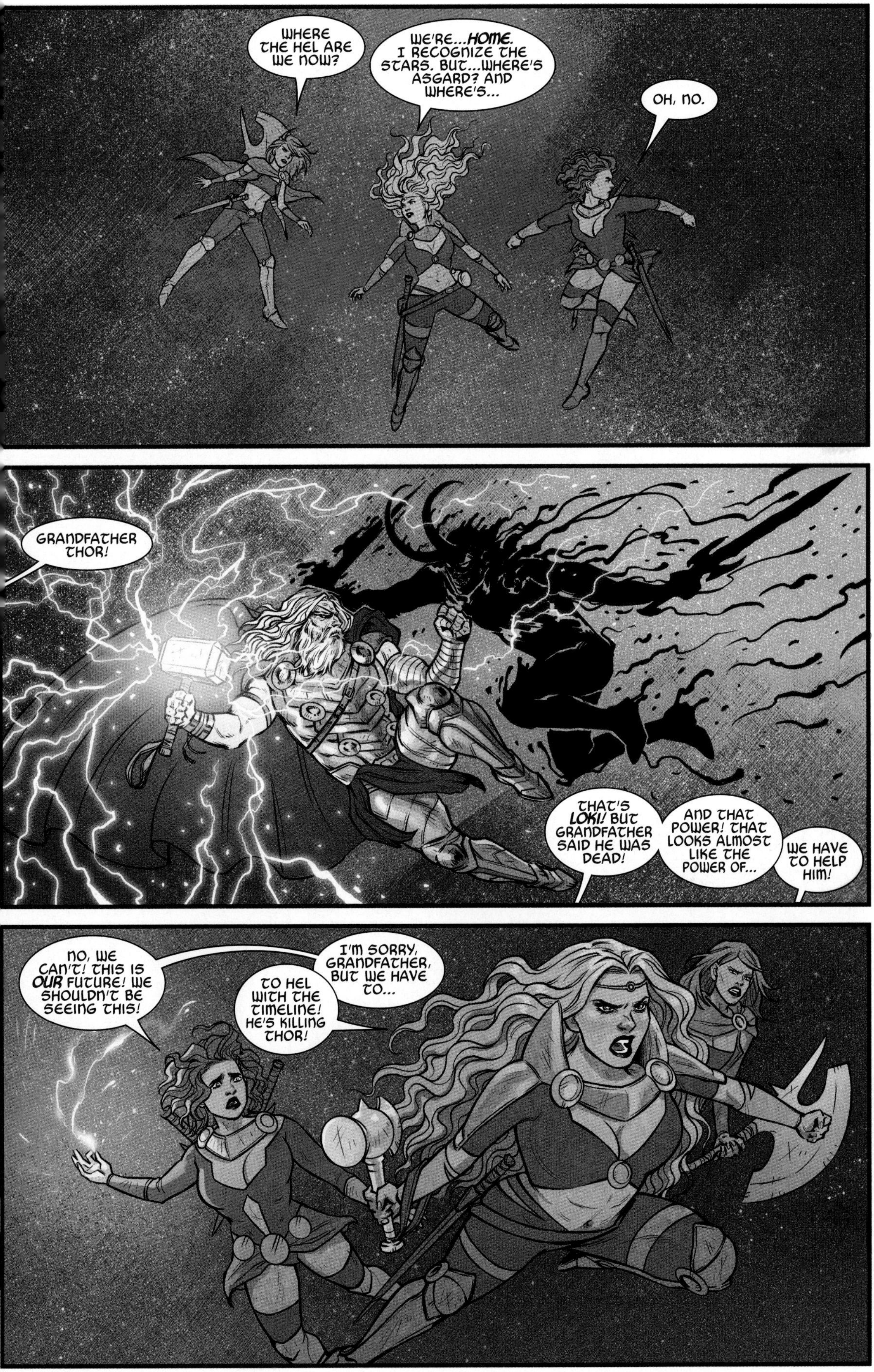
WHERE THE HEL ARE WE NOW?
WE'RE...HOME. I RECOGNIZE THE STARS. BUT...WHERE'S ASGARD? AND WHERE'S...
OH, NO.
GRANDFATHER THOR!
THAT'S LOKI! BUT GRANDFATHER SAID HE WAS DEAD!
AND THAT POWER! THAT LOOKS ALMOST LIKE THE POWER OF...
WE HAVE TO HELP HIM!
NO, WE CAN'T! THIS IS OUR FUTURE! WE SHOULDN'T BE SEEING THIS!
I'M SORRY, GRANDFATHER, BUT WE HAVE TO...
TO HEL WITH THE TIMELINE! HE'S KILLING THOR!

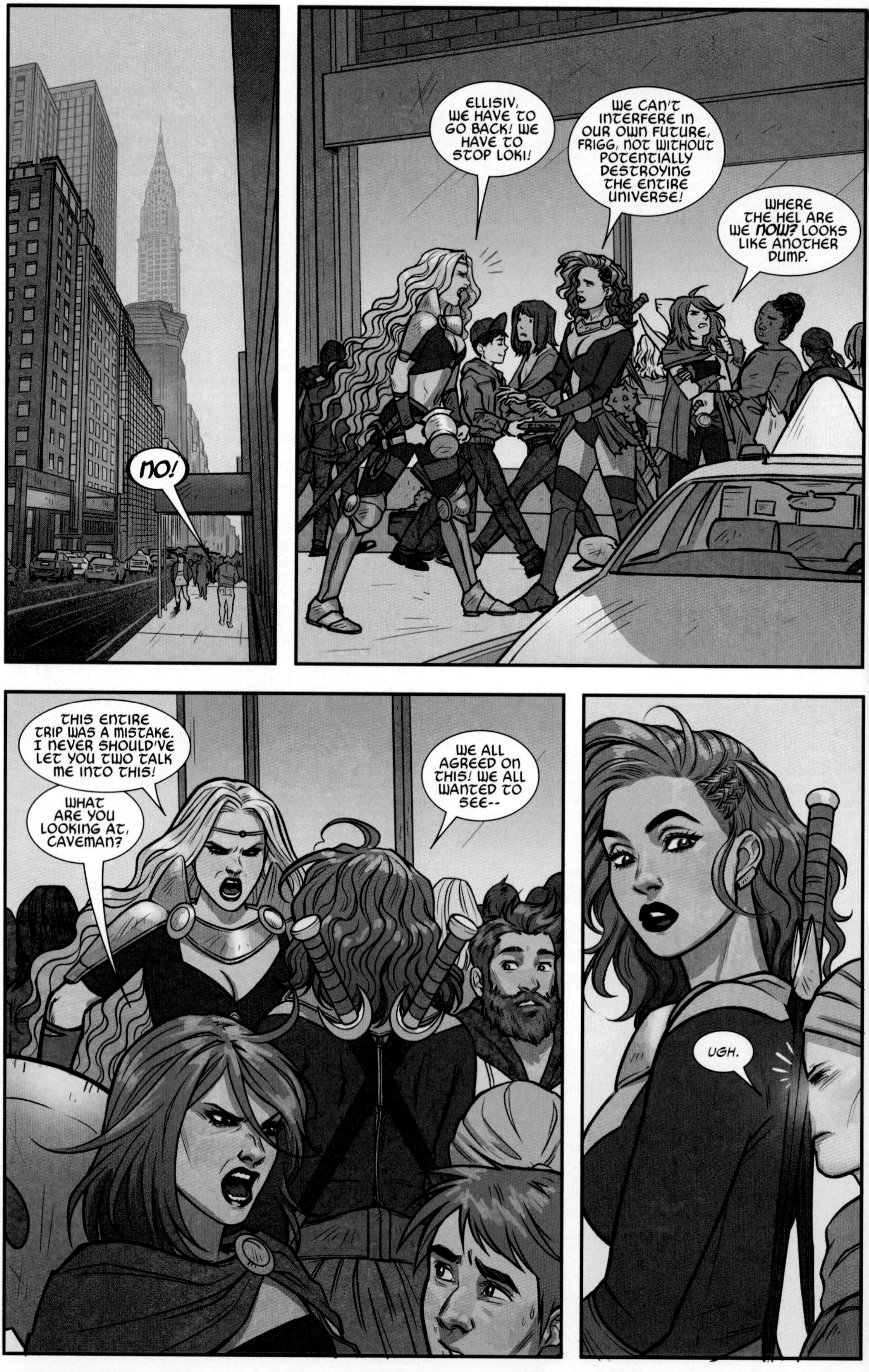

NO!
ELLISIV, WE HAVE TO GO BACK! WE HAVE TO STOP LOKI!
WE CAN'T INTERFERE IN OUR OWN FUTURE, FRIGG, NOT WITHOUT POTENTIALLY DESTROYING THE ENTIRE UNIVERSE!
WHERE THE HEL ARE WE NOW? LOOKS LIKE ANOTHER DUMP.
THIS ENTIRE TRIP WAS A MISTAKE. I NEVER SHOULD'VE LET YOU TWO TALK ME INTO THIS!
WHAT ARE YOU LOOKING AT, CAVEMAN?
WE ALL AGREED ON THIS! WE ALL WANTED TO SEE--
UGH.

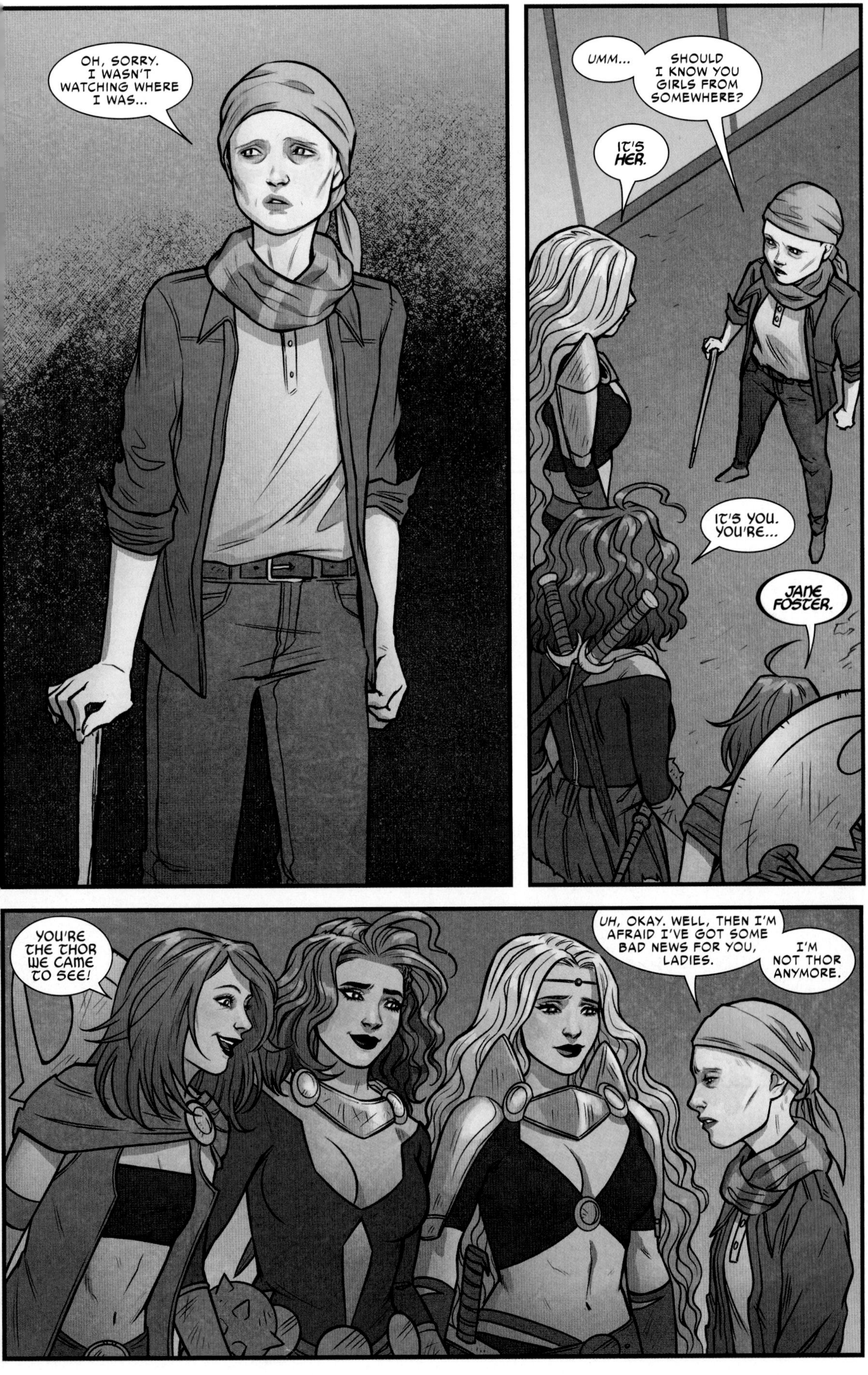
OH, SORRY. I WASN'T WATCHING WHERE I WAS...
UMM...
SHOULD I KNOW YOU GIRLS FROM SOMEWHERE?
IT'S HER.
IT'S YOU. YOU'RE...
JANE FOSTER.
YOU'RE THE THOR WE CAME TO SEE!
UH, OKAY. WELL, THEN I'M AFRAID I'VE GOT SOME BAD NEWS FOR YOU, LADIES.
I'M NOT THOR ANYMORE.

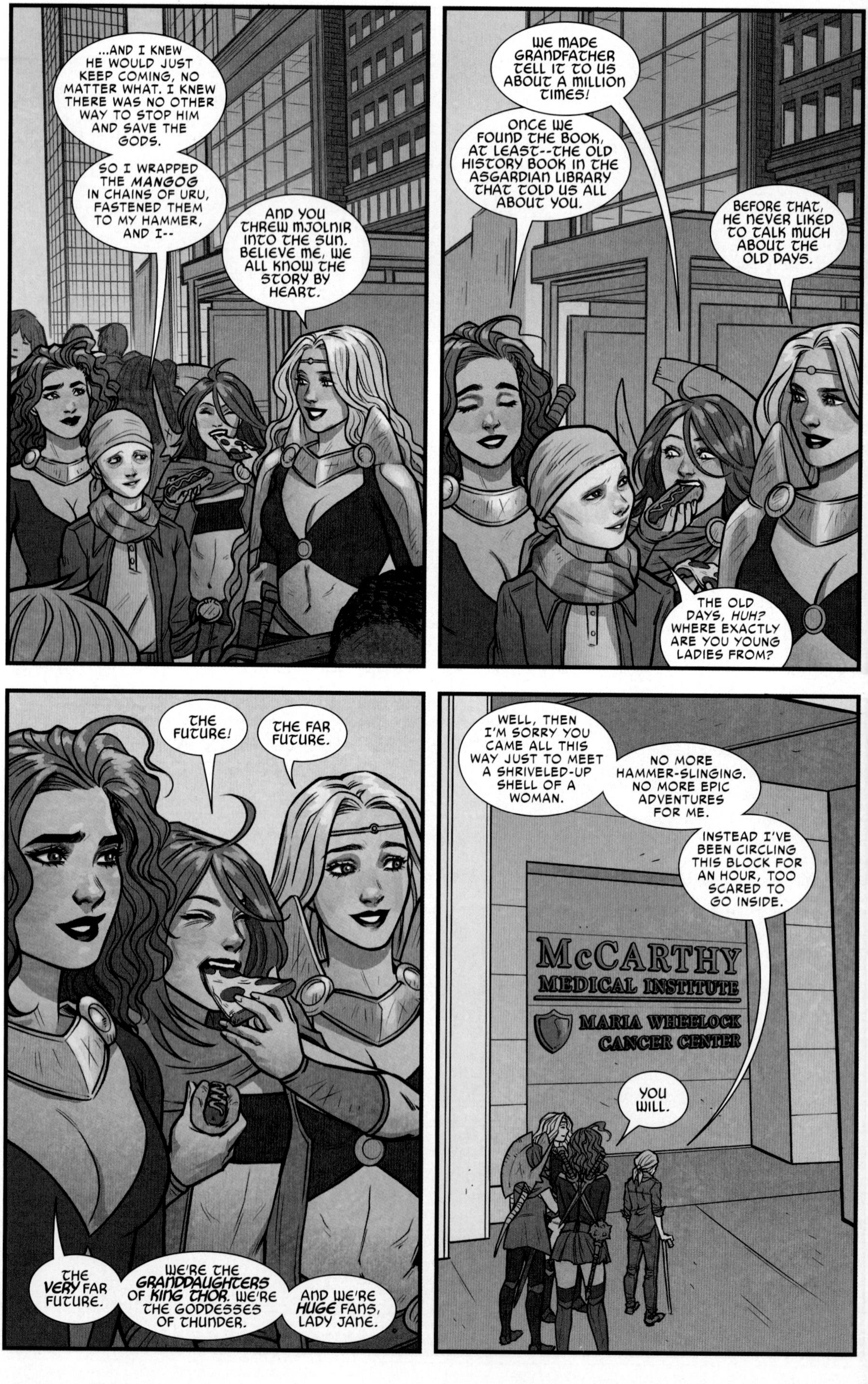
...AND I KNEW HE WOULD JUST KEEP COMING, NO MATTER WHAT. I KNEW THERE WAS NO OTHER WAY TO STOP HIM AND SAVE THE GODS.
SO I WRAPPED THE *MANGOG* IN CHAINS OF URU, FASTENED THEM TO MY HAMMER, AND I--
AND YOU THREW MJOLNIR INTO THE SUN. BELIEVE ME, WE ALL KNOW THE STORY BY HEART.
WE MADE GRANDFATHER TELL IT TO US ABOUT A MILLION TIMES!
ONCE WE FOUND THE BOOK, AT LEAST--THE OLD HISTORY BOOK IN THE ASGARDIAN LIBRARY THAT TOLD US ALL ABOUT YOU.
BEFORE THAT, HE NEVER LIKED TO TALK MUCH ABOUT THE OLD DAYS.
THE OLD DAYS, *HUH?* WHERE EXACTLY ARE YOU YOUNG LADIES FROM?
THE FUTURE!
THE FAR FUTURE.
THE *VERY* FAR FUTURE.
WE'RE THE *GRANDDAUGHTERS* OF *KING THOR*. WE'RE THE GODDESSES OF THUNDER.
AND WE'RE *HUGE* FANS, LADY JANE.
WELL, THEN I'M SORRY YOU CAME ALL THIS WAY JUST TO MEET A SHRIVELED-UP SHELL OF A WOMAN.
NO MORE HAMMER-SLINGING. NO MORE EPIC ADVENTURES FOR ME.
INSTEAD I'VE BEEN CIRCLING THIS BLOCK FOR AN HOUR, TOO SCARED TO GO INSIDE.
McCARTHY MEDICAL INSTITUTE
MARIA WHEELOCK CANCER CENTER
YOU WILL.

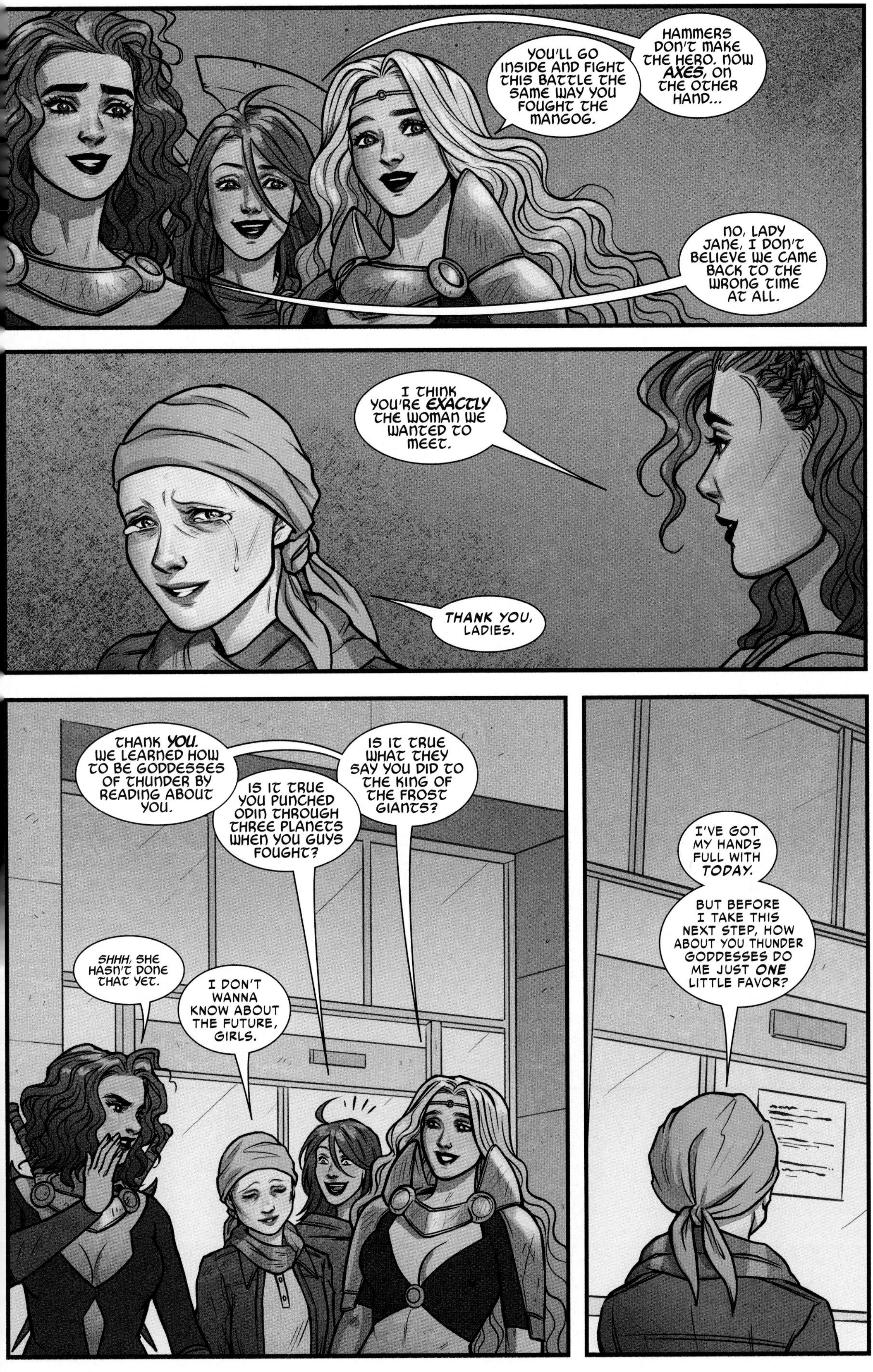
YOU'LL GO INSIDE AND FIGHT THIS BATTLE THE SAME WAY YOU FOUGHT THE MANGOG.
HAMMERS DON'T MAKE THE HERO. NOW AXES, ON THE OTHER HAND...
NO, LADY JANE, I DON'T BELIEVE WE CAME BACK TO THE WRONG TIME AT ALL.
I THINK YOU'RE EXACTLY THE WOMAN WE WANTED TO MEET.
THANK YOU, LADIES.
THANK YOU. WE LEARNED HOW TO BE GODDESSES OF THUNDER BY READING ABOUT YOU.
IS IT TRUE WHAT THEY SAY YOU DID TO THE KING OF THE FROST GIANTS?
IS IT TRUE YOU PUNCHED ODIN THROUGH THREE PLANETS WHEN YOU GUYS FOUGHT?
SHHH, SHE HASN'T DONE THAT YET.
I DON'T WANNA KNOW ABOUT THE FUTURE, GIRLS.
I'VE GOT MY HANDS FULL WITH TODAY.
BUT BEFORE I TAKE THIS NEXT STEP, HOW ABOUT YOU THUNDER GODDESSES DO ME JUST ONE LITTLE FAVOR?

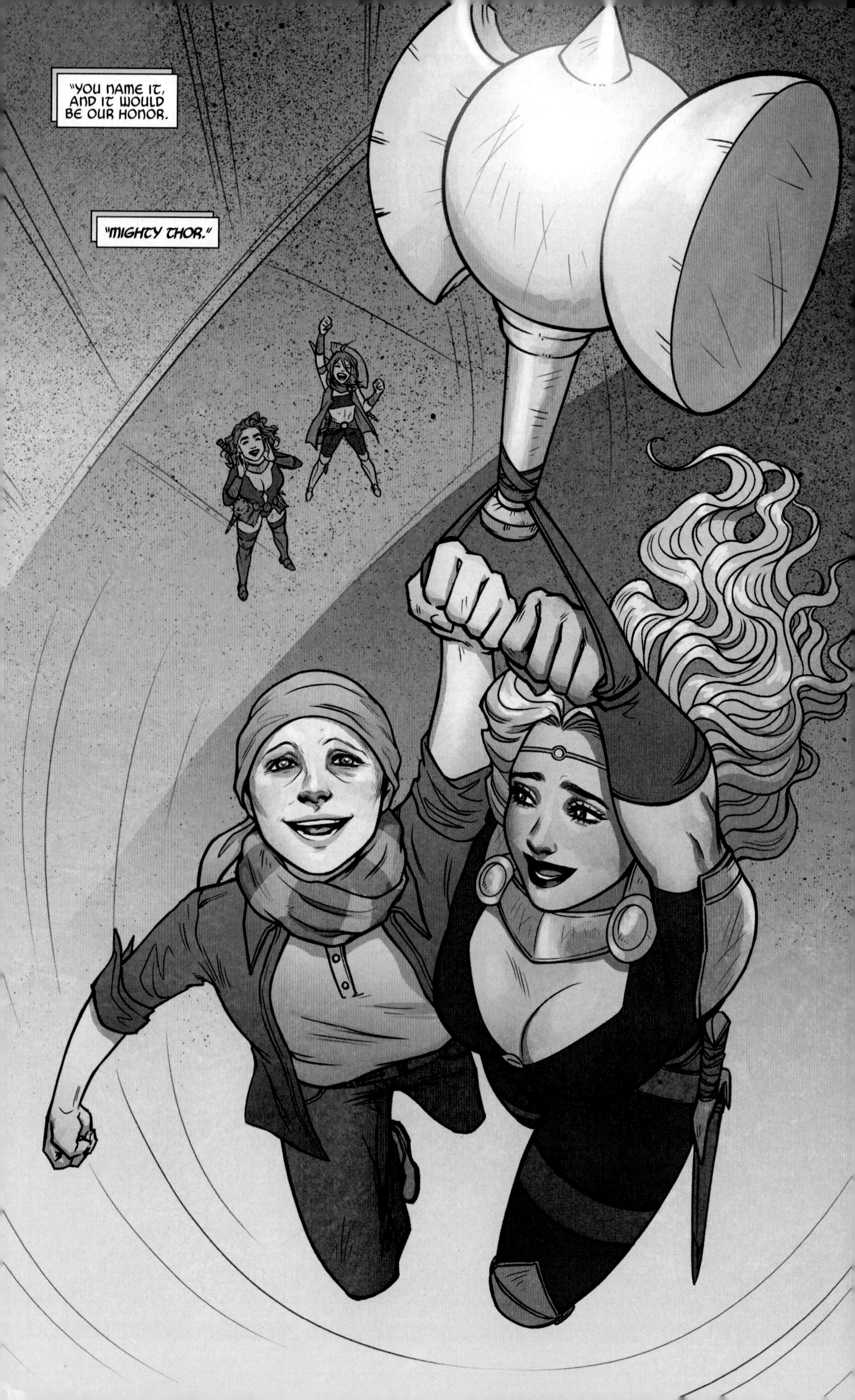
"YOU NAME IT, AND IT WOULD BE OUR HONOR.
"MIGHTY THOR."

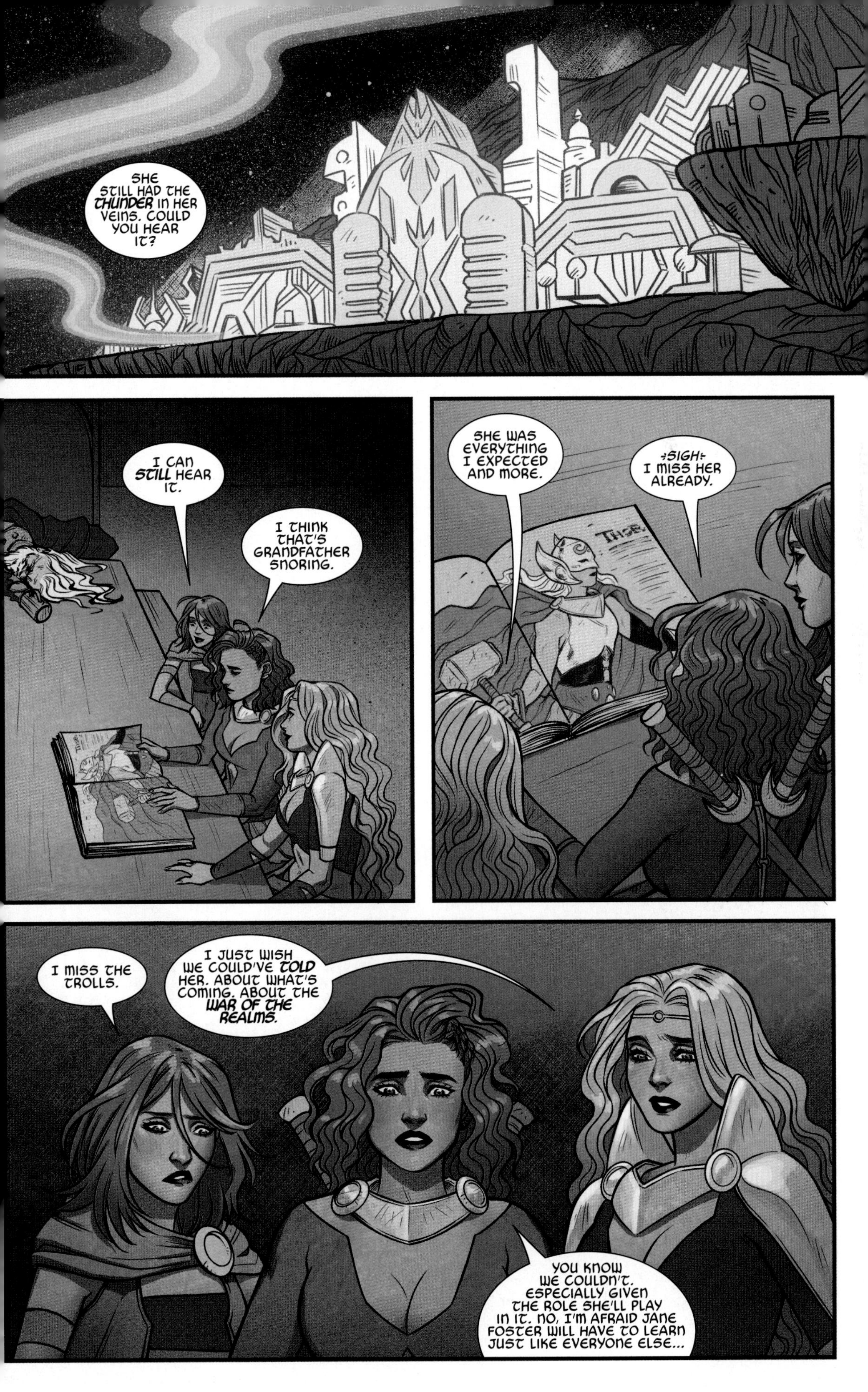
SHE STILL HAD THE THUNDER IN HER VEINS. COULD YOU HEAR IT?
I CAN STILL HEAR IT.
I THINK THAT'S GRANDFATHER SNORING.
SHE WAS EVERYTHING I EXPECTED AND MORE.
SIGH I MISS HER ALREADY.
THOR
I MISS THE TROLLS.
I JUST WISH WE COULD'VE TOLD HER. ABOUT WHAT'S COMING. ABOUT THE WAR OF THE REALMS.
YOU KNOW WE COULDN'T. ESPECIALLY GIVEN THE ROLE SHE'LL PLAY IN IT. NO, I'M AFRAID JANE FOSTER WILL HAVE TO LEARN JUST LIKE EVERYONE ELSE...

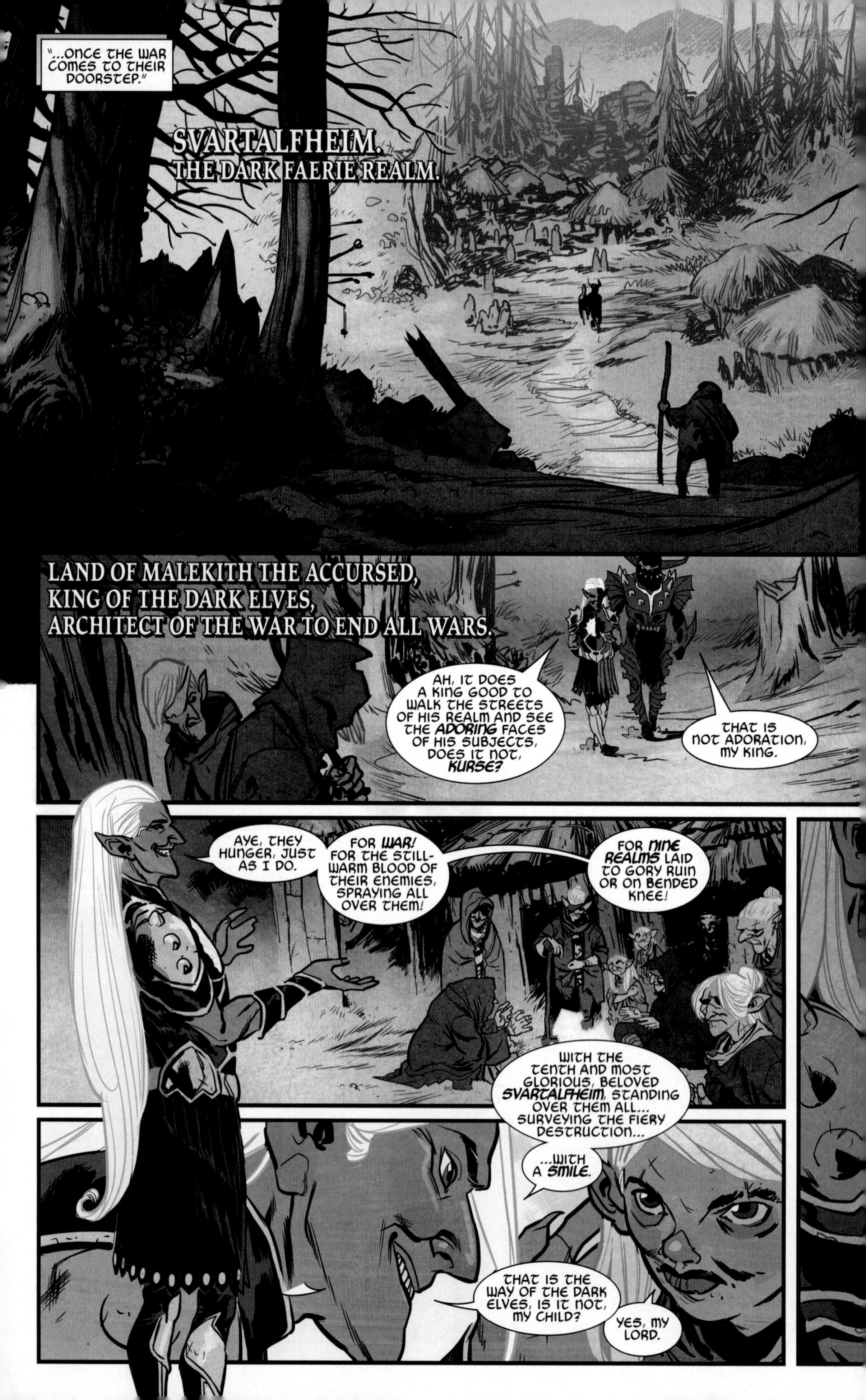
"...ONCE THE WAR COMES TO THEIR DOORSTEP."
SVARTALFHEIM. THE DARK FAERIE REALM.
LAND OF MALEKITH THE ACCURSED, KING OF THE DARK ELVES, ARCHITECT OF THE WAR TO END ALL WARS.
AH, IT DOES A KING GOOD TO WALK THE STREETS OF HIS REALM AND SEE THE ADORING FACES OF HIS SUBJECTS, DOES IT NOT, KURSE?
THAT IS NOT ADORATION, MY KING.
AYE, THEY HUNGER, JUST AS I DO.
FOR WAR! FOR THE STILL-WARM BLOOD OF THEIR ENEMIES, SPRAYING ALL OVER THEM!
FOR NINE REALMS LAID TO GORY RUIN OR ON BENDED KNEE!
WITH THE TENTH AND MOST GLORIOUS, BELOVED SVARTALFHEIM, STANDING OVER THEM ALL... SURVEYING THE FIERY DESTRUCTION...
...WITH A SMILE.
THAT IS THE WAY OF THE DARK ELVES, IS IT NOT, MY CHILD?
YES, MY LORD.

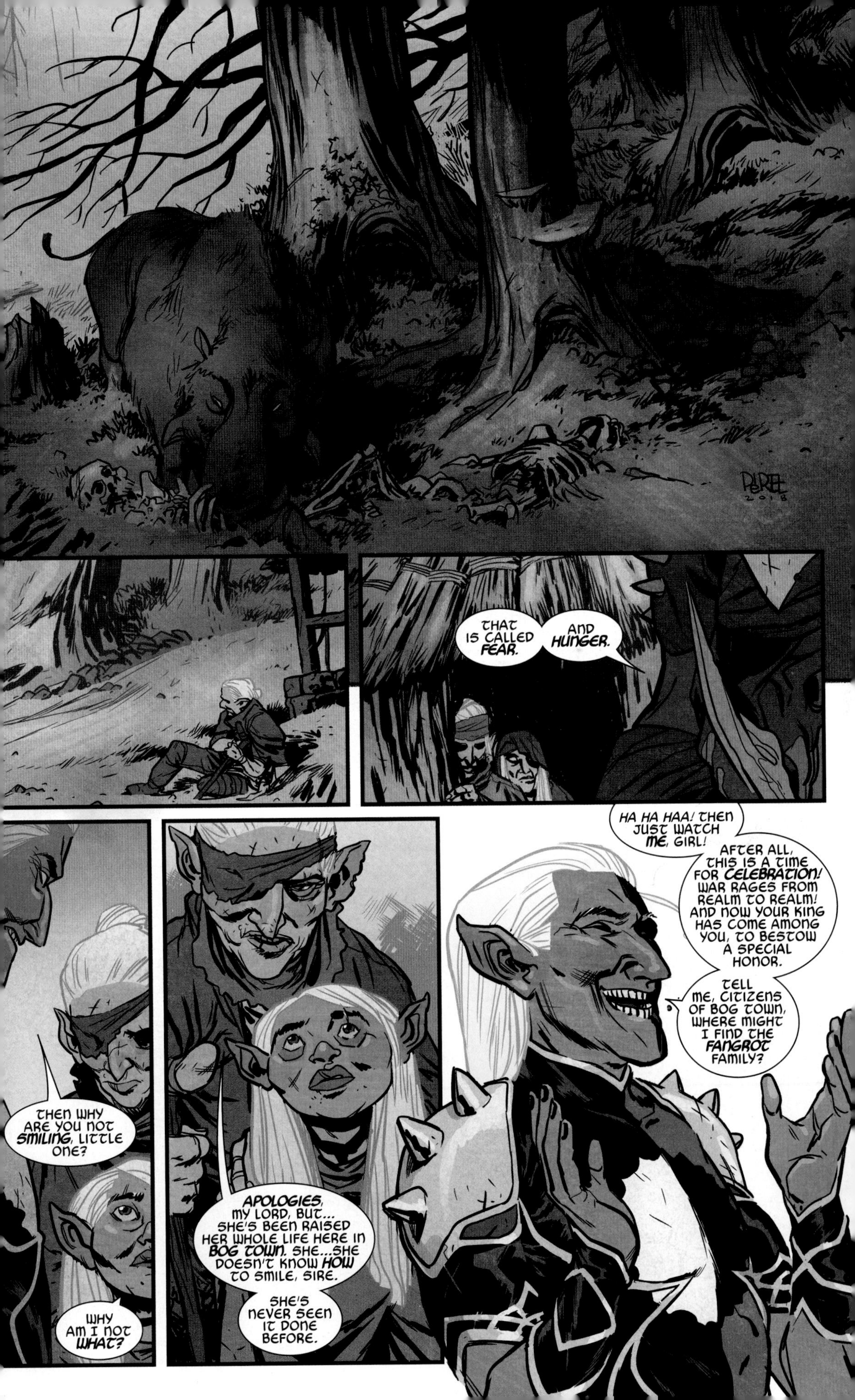

THAT IS CALLED FEAR.
AND HUNGER.
THEN WHY ARE YOU NOT SMILING, LITTLE ONE?
WHY AM I NOT WHAT?
APOLOGIES, MY LORD, BUT... SHE'S BEEN RAISED HER WHOLE LIFE HERE IN BOG TOWN. SHE...SHE DOESN'T KNOW HOW TO SMILE, SIRE.
SHE'S NEVER SEEN IT DONE BEFORE.
HA HA HAA! THEN JUST WATCH ME, GIRL!
AFTER ALL, THIS IS A TIME FOR CELEBRATION! WAR RAGES FROM REALM TO REALM! AND NOW YOUR KING HAS COME AMONG YOU, TO BESTOW A SPECIAL HONOR.
TELL ME, CITIZENS OF BOG TOWN, WHERE MIGHT I FIND THE FANGROT FAMILY?

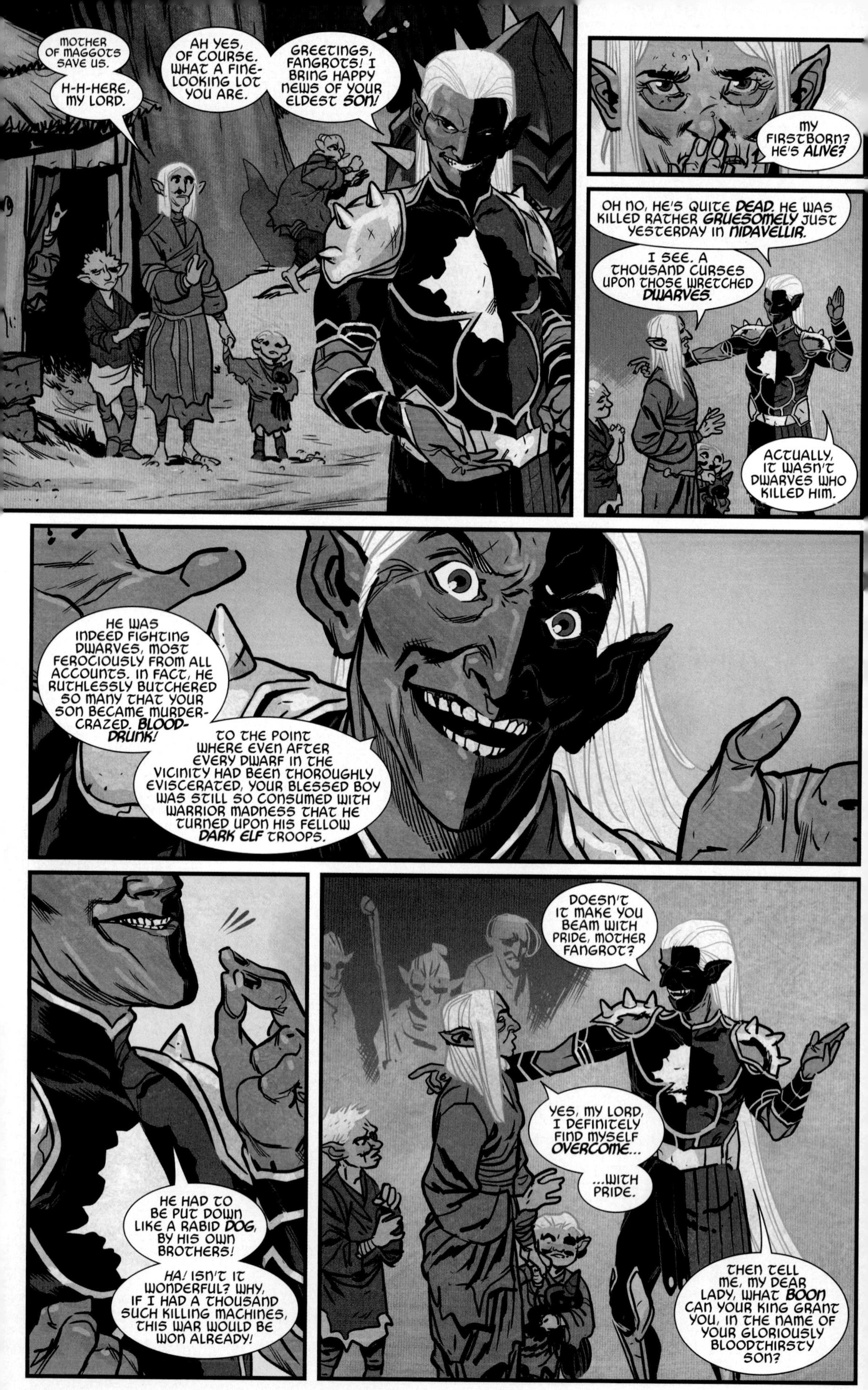
MOTHER OF MAGGOTS SAVE US.
H-H-HERE, MY LORD.
AH YES, OF COURSE. WHAT A FINE-LOOKING LOT YOU ARE.
GREETINGS, FANGROTS! I BRING HAPPY NEWS OF YOUR ELDEST SON!
MY FIRSTBORN? HE'S ALIVE?
OH NO, HE'S QUITE DEAD. HE WAS KILLED RATHER GRUESOMELY JUST YESTERDAY IN NIDAVELLIR.
I SEE. A THOUSAND CURSES UPON THOSE WRETCHED DWARVES.
ACTUALLY, IT WASN'T DWARVES WHO KILLED HIM.
HE WAS INDEED FIGHTING DWARVES, MOST FEROCIOUSLY FROM ALL ACCOUNTS. IN FACT, HE RUTHLESSLY BUTCHERED SO MANY THAT YOUR SON BECAME MURDER-CRAZED. BLOOD-DRUNK!
TO THE POINT WHERE EVEN AFTER EVERY DWARF IN THE VICINITY HAD BEEN THOROUGHLY EVISCERATED, YOUR BLESSED BOY WAS STILL SO CONSUMED WITH WARRIOR MADNESS THAT HE TURNED UPON HIS FELLOW DARK ELF TROOPS.
HE HAD TO BE PUT DOWN LIKE A RABID DOG, BY HIS OWN BROTHERS!
HA! ISN'T IT WONDERFUL? WHY, IF I HAD A THOUSAND SUCH KILLING MACHINES, THIS WAR WOULD BE WON ALREADY!
DOESN'T IT MAKE YOU BEAM WITH PRIDE, MOTHER FANGROT?
YES, MY LORD, I DEFINITELY FIND MYSELF OVERCOME...
...WITH PRIDE.
THEN TELL ME, MY DEAR LADY, WHAT BOON CAN YOUR KING GRANT YOU, IN THE NAME OF YOUR GLORIOUSLY BLOODTHIRSTY SON?

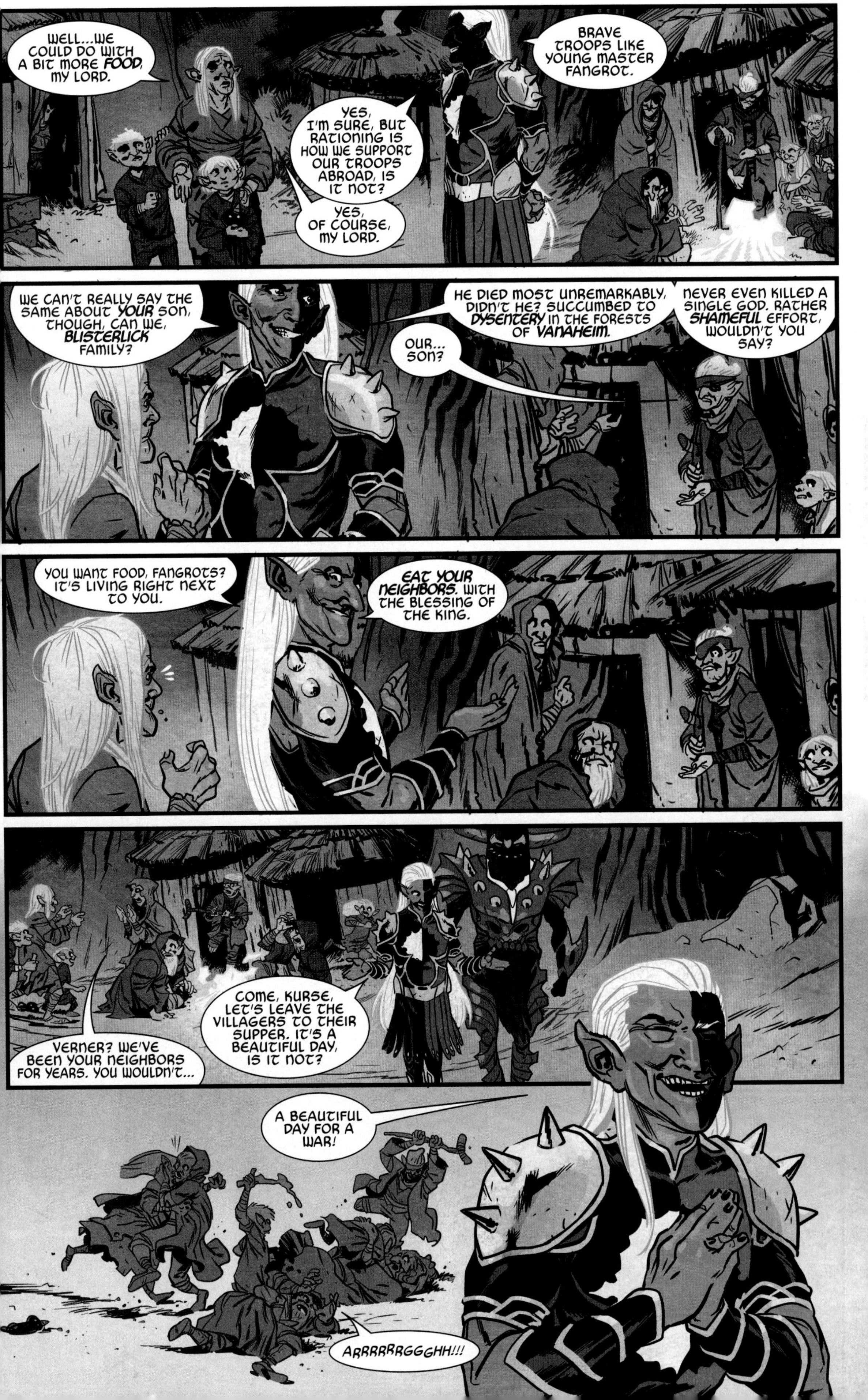
WELL...WE COULD DO WITH A BIT MORE FOOD, MY LORD.
YES, I'M SURE, BUT RATIONING IS HOW WE SUPPORT OUR TROOPS ABROAD, IS IT NOT?
YES, OF COURSE, MY LORD.
BRAVE TROOPS LIKE YOUNG MASTER FANGROT.
WE CAN'T REALLY SAY THE SAME ABOUT YOUR SON, THOUGH, CAN WE, BLISTERLICK FAMILY?
HE DIED MOST UNREMARKABLY, DIDN'T HE? SUCCUMBED TO DYSENTERY IN THE FORESTS OF VANAHEIM.
OUR... SON?
NEVER EVEN KILLED A SINGLE GOD. RATHER SHAMEFUL EFFORT, WOULDN'T YOU SAY?
YOU WANT FOOD, FANGROTS? IT'S LIVING RIGHT NEXT TO YOU.
EAT YOUR NEIGHBORS. WITH THE BLESSING OF THE KING.
VERNER? WE'VE BEEN YOUR NEIGHBORS FOR YEARS. YOU WOULDN'T...
COME, KURSE, LET'S LEAVE THE VILLAGERS TO THEIR SUPPER. IT'S A BEAUTIFUL DAY, IS IT NOT?
A BEAUTIFUL DAY FOR A WAR!
ARRRRRRGGGHH!!!

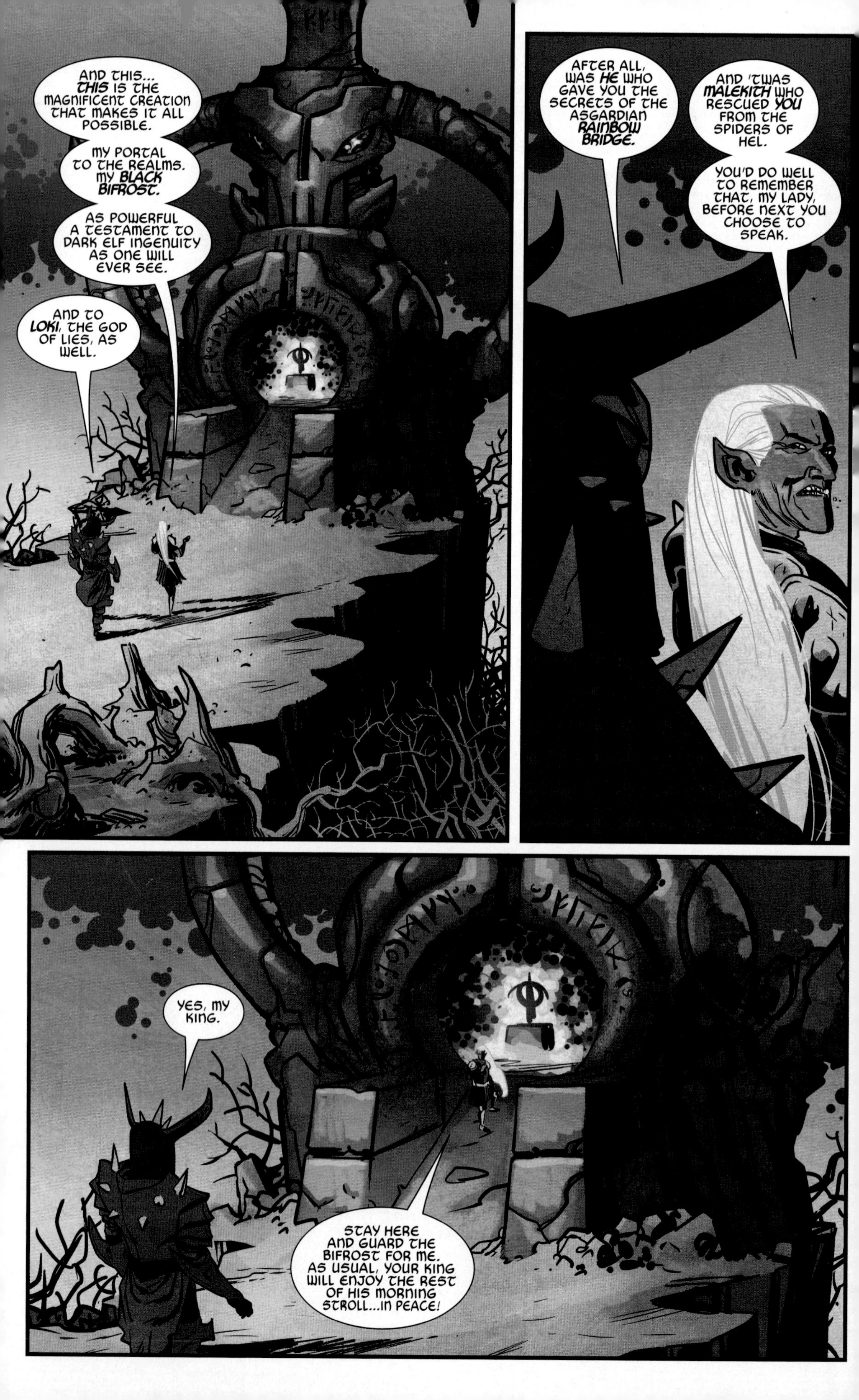
AND THIS... THIS IS THE MAGNIFICENT CREATION THAT MAKES IT ALL POSSIBLE.
MY PORTAL TO THE REALMS. MY BLACK BIFROST.
AS POWERFUL A TESTAMENT TO DARK ELF INGENUITY AS ONE WILL EVER SEE.
AND TO LOKI, THE GOD OF LIES, AS WELL.
AFTER ALL, WAS HE WHO GAVE YOU THE SECRETS OF THE ASGARDIAN RAINBOW BRIDGE.
AND 'TWAS MALEKITH WHO RESCUED YOU FROM THE SPIDERS OF HEL.
YOU'D DO WELL TO REMEMBER THAT, MY LADY, BEFORE NEXT YOU CHOOSE TO SPEAK.
YES, MY KING.
STAY HERE AND GUARD THE BIFROST FOR ME. AS USUAL, YOUR KING WILL ENJOY THE REST OF HIS MORNING STROLL...IN PEACE!

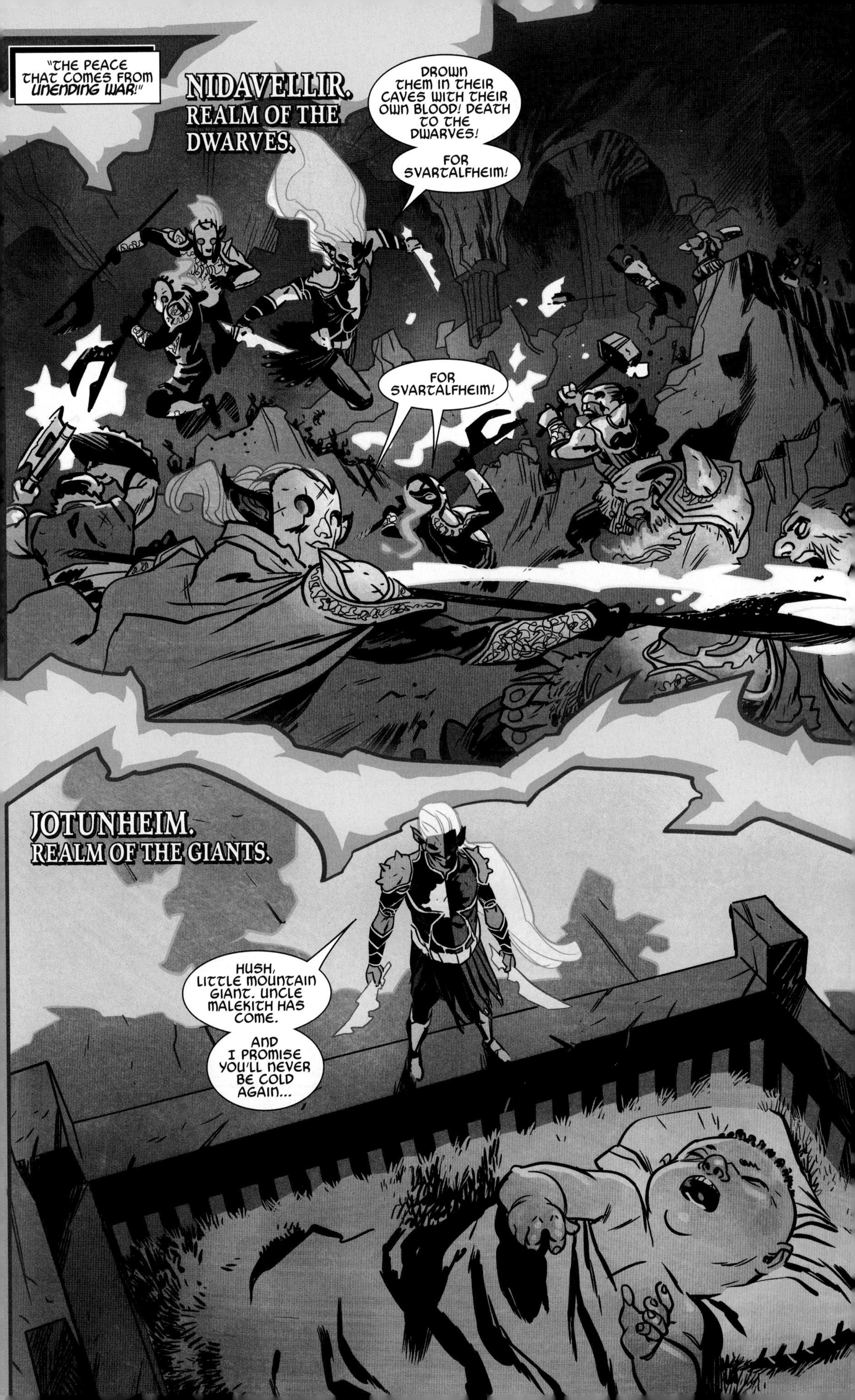
"THE PEACE THAT COMES FROM UNENDING WAR!"
NIDAVELLIR. REALM OF THE DWARVES.
DROWN THEM IN THEIR CAVES WITH THEIR OWN BLOOD! DEATH TO THE DWARVES!
FOR SVARTALFHEIM!
FOR SVARTALFHEIM!
JOTUNHEIM. REALM OF THE GIANTS.
HUSH, LITTLE MOUNTAIN GIANT. UNCLE MALEKITH HAS COME.
AND I PROMISE YOU'LL NEVER BE COLD AGAIN...

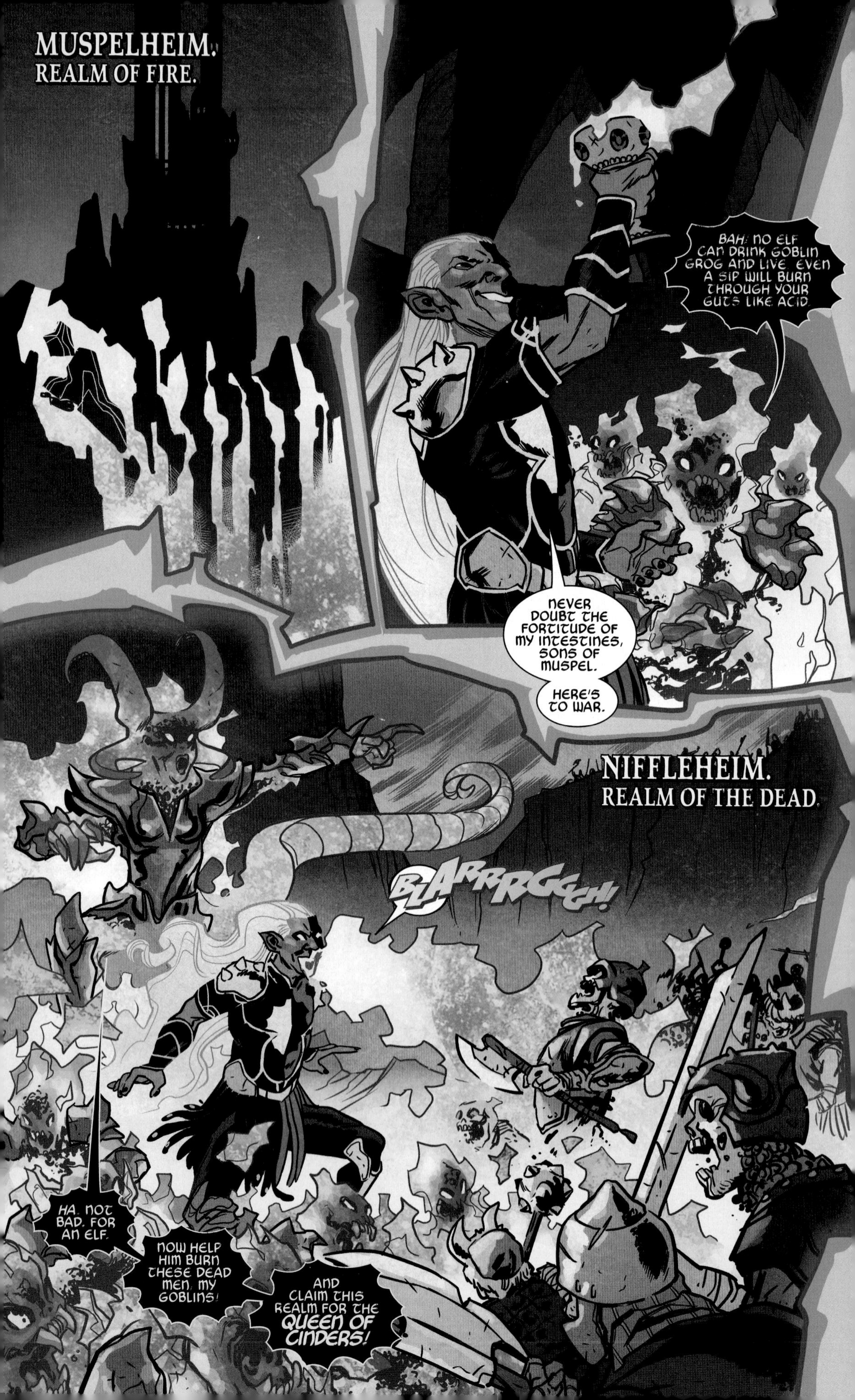
MUSPELHEIM.
REALM OF FIRE.
BAH! NO ELF CAN DRINK GOBLIN GROG AND LIVE. EVEN A SIP WILL BURN THROUGH YOUR GUTS LIKE ACID.
NEVER DOUBT THE FORTITUDE OF MY INTESTINES, SONS OF MUSPEL.
HERE'S TO WAR.
NIFFLEHEIM.
REALM OF THE DEAD.
BLARRRGGGH!
HA. NOT BAD. FOR AN ELF.
NOW HELP HIM BURN THESE DEAD MEN, MY GOBLINS!
AND CLAIM THIS REALM FOR THE QUEEN OF CINDERS!

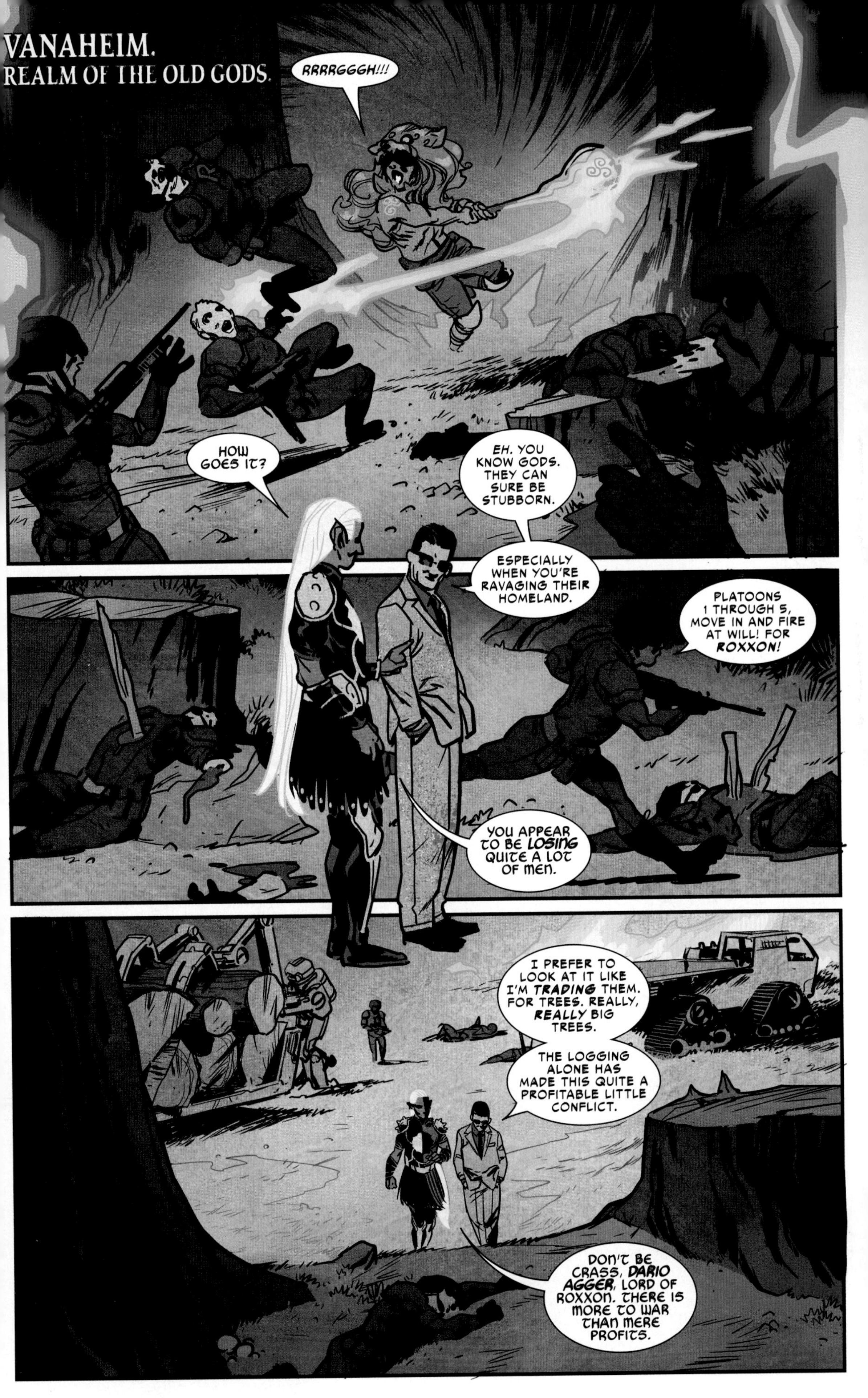
VANAHEIM.
REALM OF THE OLD GODS.
RRRRGGGH!!!
HOW GOES IT?
EH. YOU KNOW GODS. THEY CAN SURE BE STUBBORN.
ESPECIALLY WHEN YOU'RE RAVAGING THEIR HOMELAND.
PLATOONS 1 THROUGH 5, MOVE IN AND FIRE AT WILL! FOR ROXXON!
YOU APPEAR TO BE LOSING QUITE A LOT OF MEN.
I PREFER TO LOOK AT IT LIKE I'M TRADING THEM. FOR TREES. REALLY, REALLY BIG TREES.
THE LOGGING ALONE HAS MADE THIS QUITE A PROFITABLE LITTLE CONFLICT.
DON'T BE CRASS, DARIO AGGER, LORD OF ROXXON. THERE IS MORE TO WAR THAN MERE PROFITS.

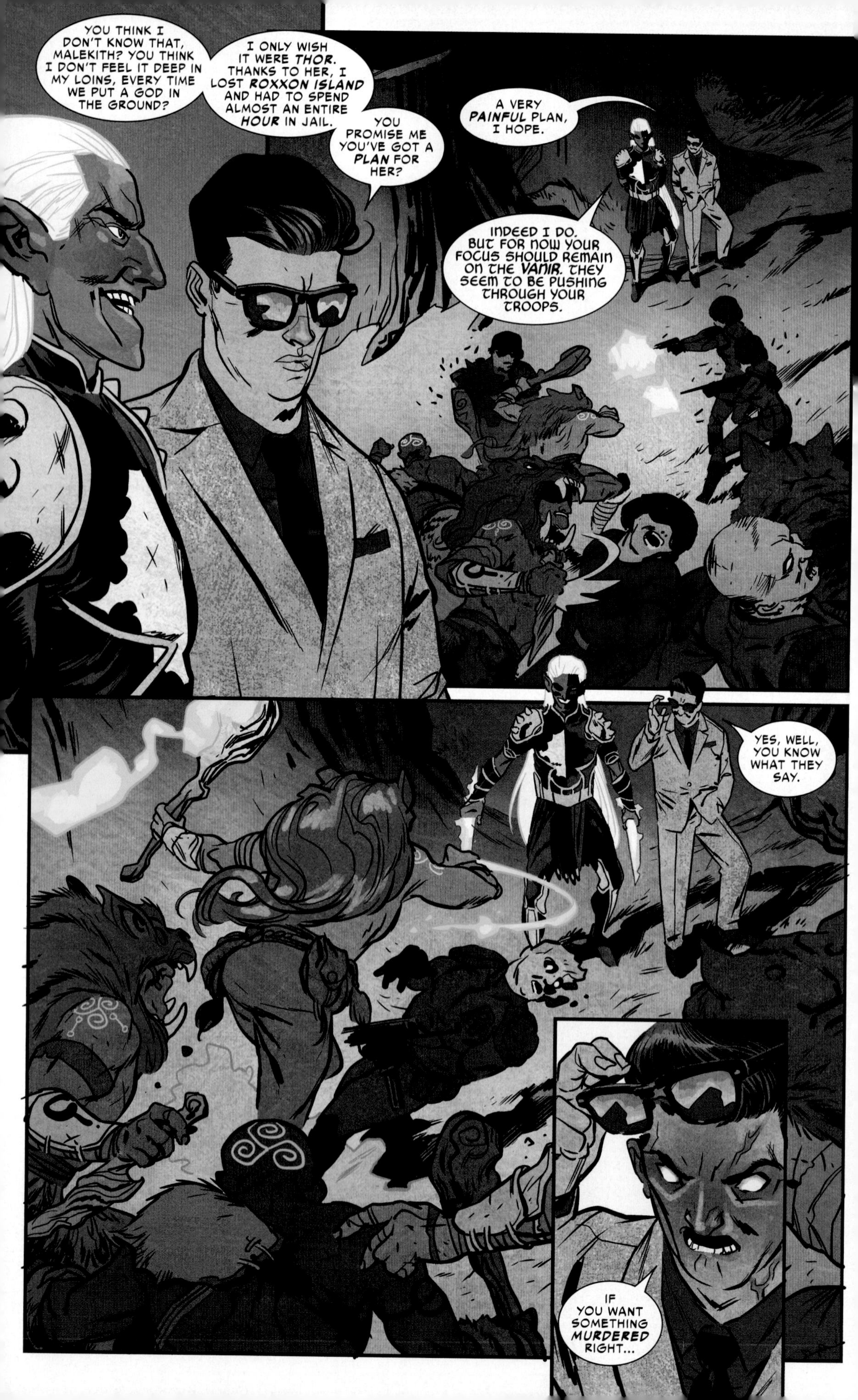
YOU THINK I DON'T KNOW THAT, MALEKITH? YOU THINK I DON'T FEEL IT DEEP IN MY LOINS, EVERY TIME WE PUT A GOD IN THE GROUND?
I ONLY WISH IT WERE THOR. THANKS TO HER, I LOST ROXXON ISLAND AND HAD TO SPEND ALMOST AN ENTIRE HOUR IN JAIL.
YOU PROMISE ME YOU'VE GOT A PLAN FOR HER?
A VERY PAINFUL PLAN, I HOPE.
INDEED I DO. BUT FOR NOW YOUR FOCUS SHOULD REMAIN ON THE VANIR. THEY SEEM TO BE PUSHING THROUGH YOUR TROOPS.
YES, WELL, YOU KNOW WHAT THEY SAY.
IF YOU WANT SOMETHING MURDERED RIGHT...

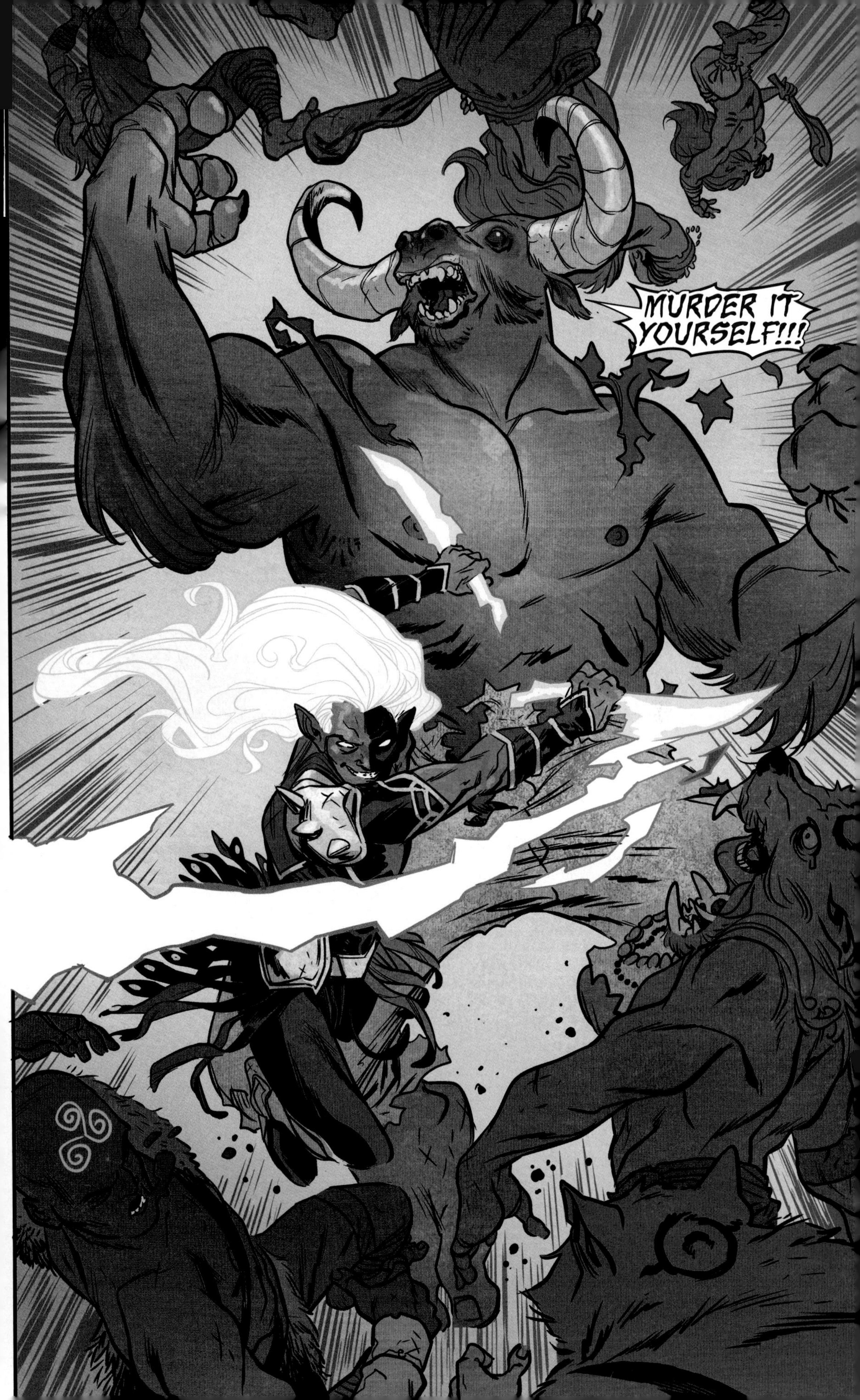
MURDER IT YOURSELF!!!

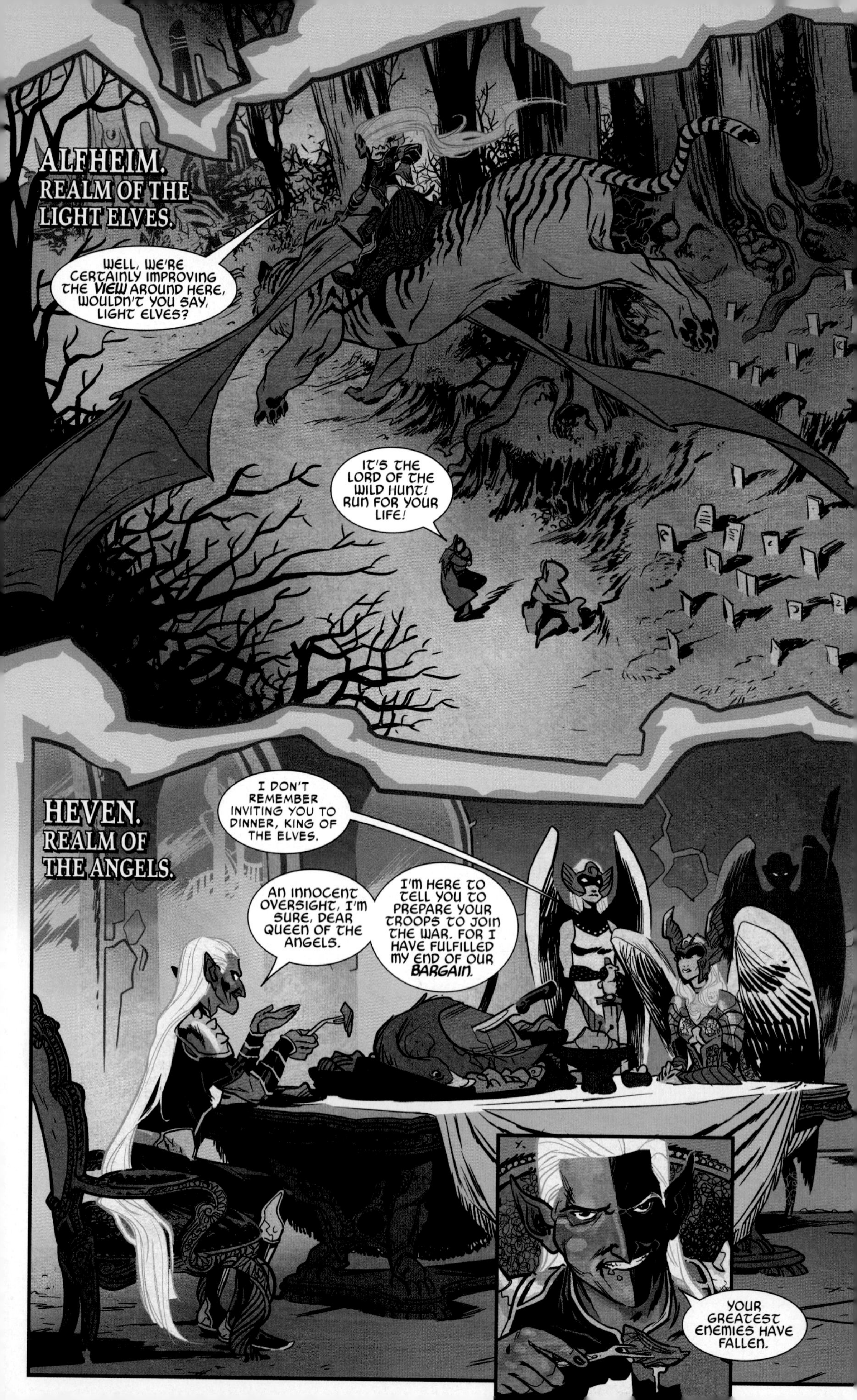
ALFHEIM. REALM OF THE LIGHT ELVES.
WELL, WE'RE CERTAINLY IMPROVING THE VIEW AROUND HERE, WOULDN'T YOU SAY, LIGHT ELVES?
IT'S THE LORD OF THE WILD HUNT! RUN FOR YOUR LIFE!
HEVEN. REALM OF THE ANGELS.
I DON'T REMEMBER INVITING YOU TO DINNER, KING OF THE ELVES.
AN INNOCENT OVERSIGHT, I'M SURE, DEAR QUEEN OF THE ANGELS.
I'M HERE TO TELL YOU TO PREPARE YOUR TROOPS TO JOIN THE WAR. FOR I HAVE FULFILLED MY END OF OUR BARGAIN.
YOUR GREATEST ENEMIES HAVE FALLEN.

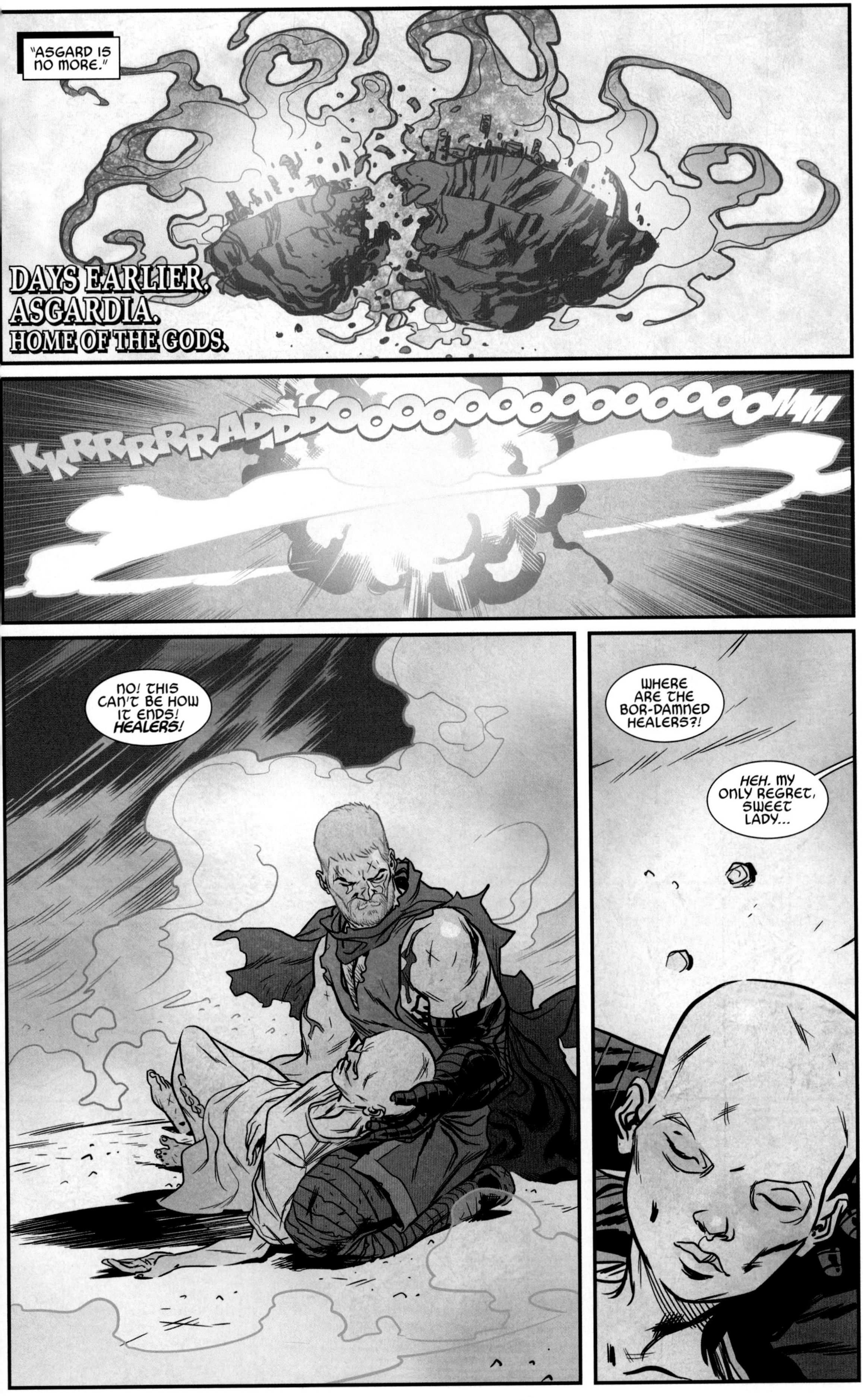
"ASGARD IS NO MORE."
DAYS EARLIER. ASGARDIA. HOME OF THE GODS.
KKRRRRRADDDOOOOOOOOOOOOOOOOOMM
NO! THIS CAN'T BE HOW IT ENDS! *HEALERS!*
WHERE ARE THE BOR-DAMNED HEALERS?!
HEH. MY ONLY REGRET, SWEET LADY...

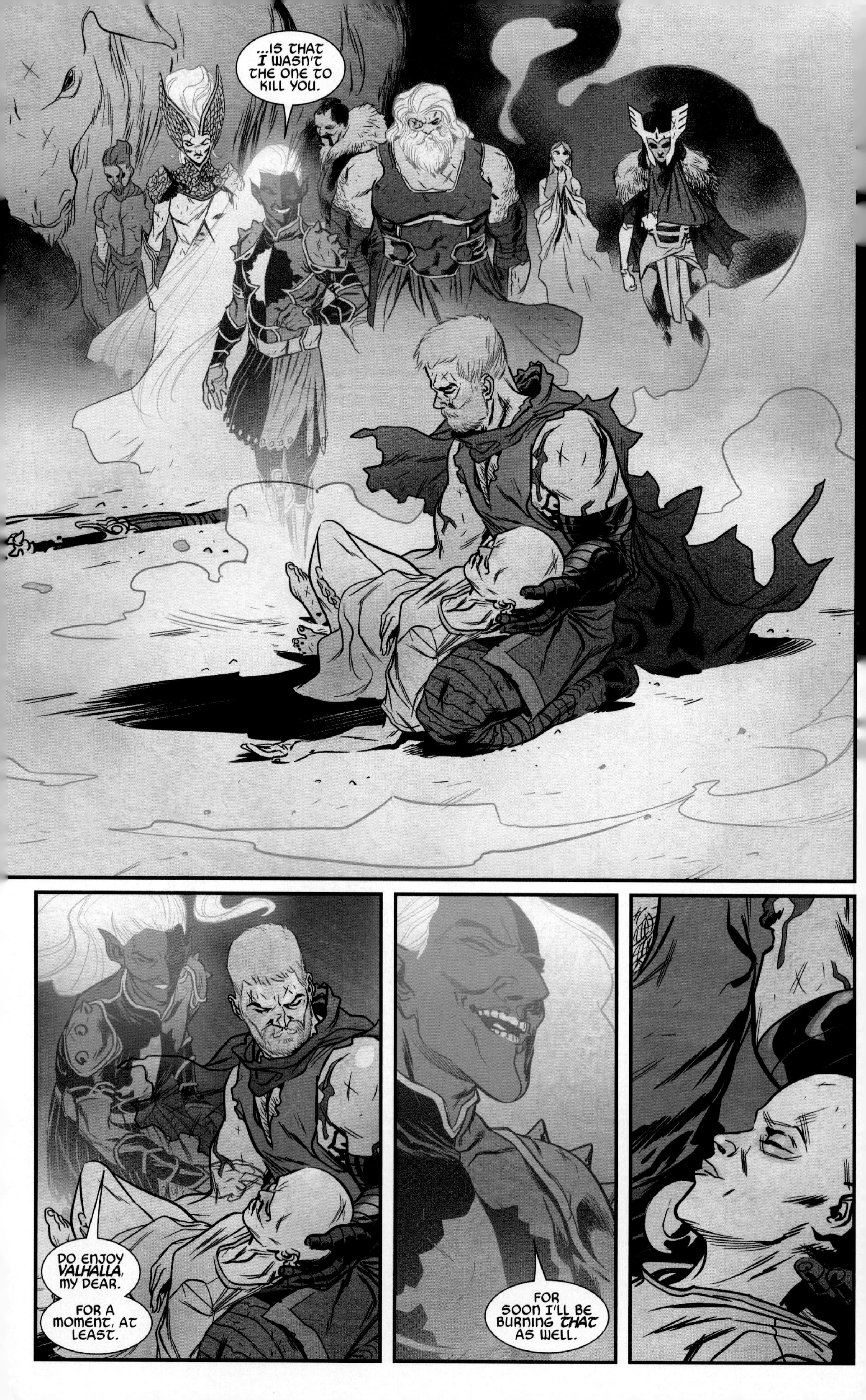
...IS THAT I WASN'T THE ONE TO KILL YOU.
DO ENJOY VALHALLA, MY DEAR.
FOR A MOMENT, AT LEAST.
FOR SOON I'LL BE BURNING THAT AS WELL.

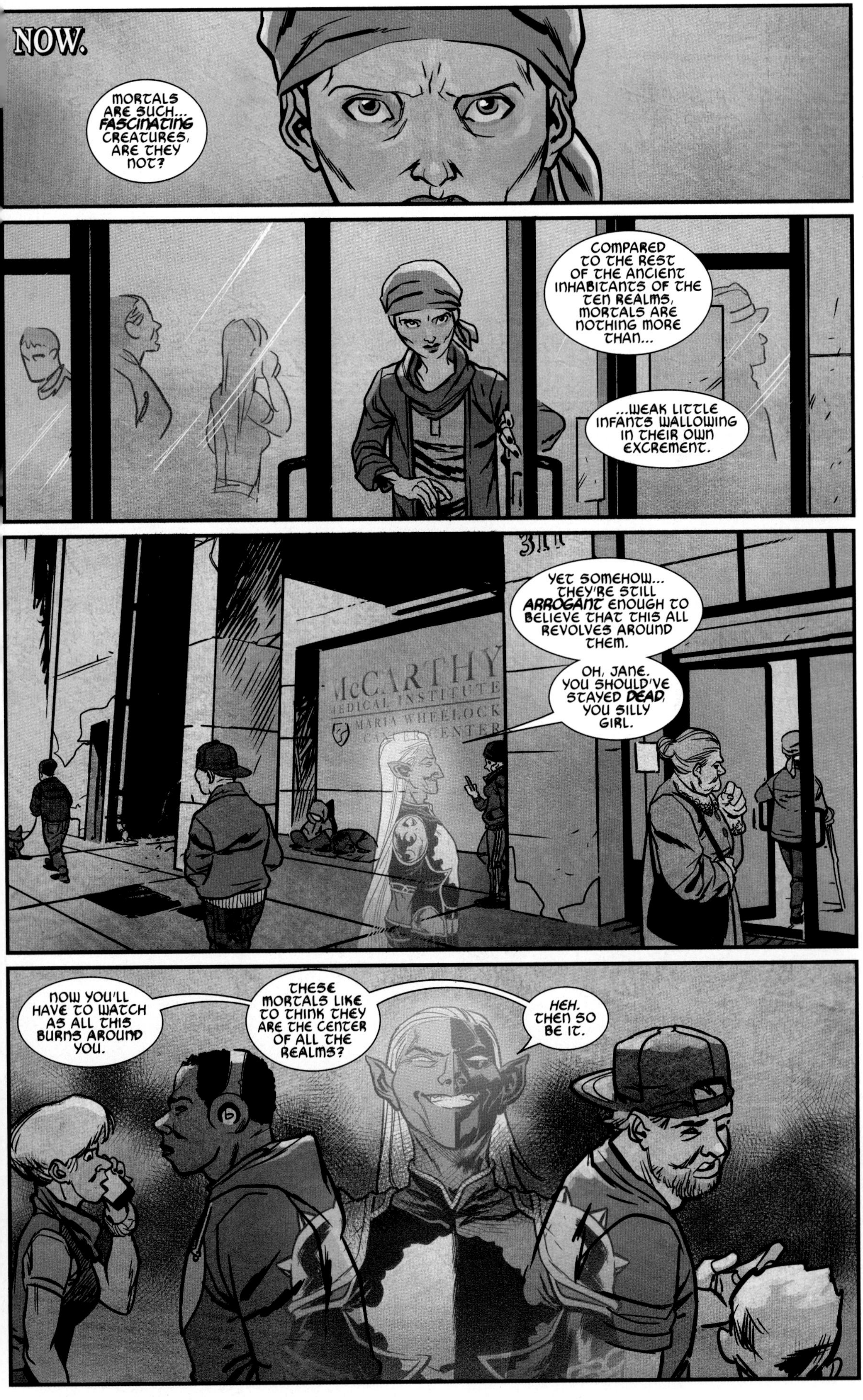
NOW.
MORTALS ARE SUCH... FASCINATING CREATURES, ARE THEY NOT?
COMPARED TO THE REST OF THE ANCIENT INHABITANTS OF THE TEN REALMS, MORTALS ARE NOTHING MORE THAN...
...WEAK LITTLE INFANTS WALLOWING IN THEIR OWN EXCREMENT.
YET SOMEHOW... THEY'RE STILL ARROGANT ENOUGH TO BELIEVE THAT THIS ALL REVOLVES AROUND THEM.
OH, JANE. YOU SHOULD'VE STAYED DEAD, YOU SILLY GIRL.
McCARTHY
MEDICAL INSTITUTE
MARIA WHEELOCK
NOW YOU'LL HAVE TO WATCH AS ALL THIS BURNS AROUND YOU.
THESE MORTALS LIKE TO THINK THEY ARE THE CENTER OF ALL THE REALMS?
HEH. THEN SO BE IT.

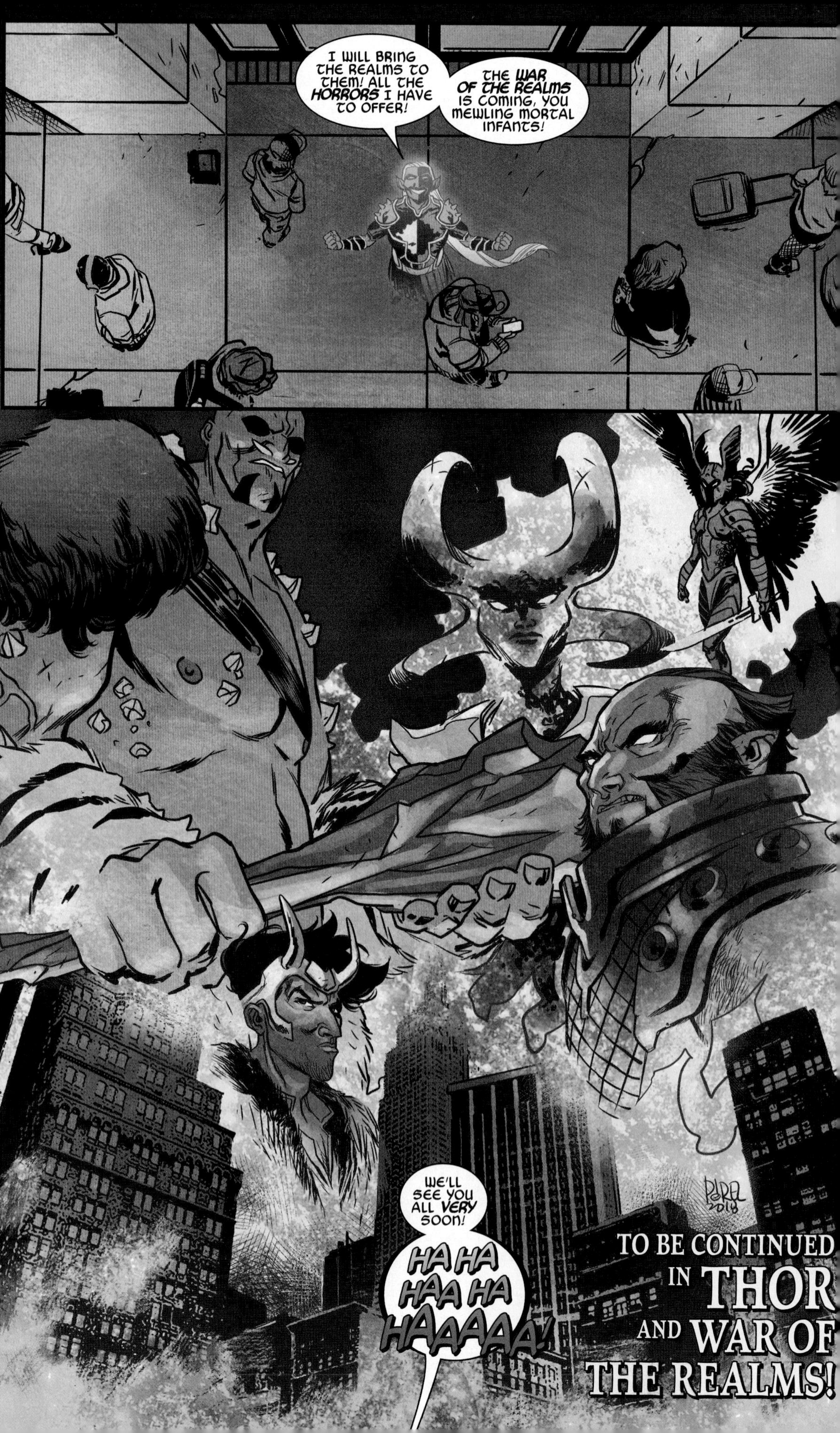
I WILL BRING THE REALMS TO THEM! ALL THE HORRORS I HAVE TO OFFER!
THE WAR OF THE REALMS IS COMING, YOU MEWLING MORTAL INFANTS!
WE'LL SEE YOU ALL VERY SOON!
HA HA HAA HA HAAAAA!
TO BE CONTINUED IN THOR AND WAR OF THE REALMS!

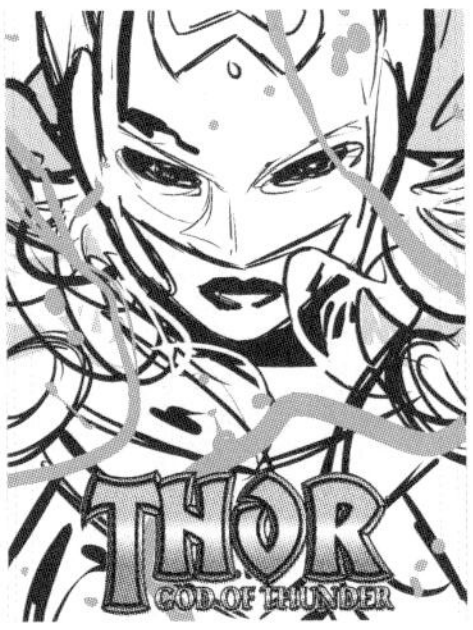
THOR
GOD OF THUNDER

This is the first drawing I did of Jane: a layout for what was originally just a variant cover. I never thought that nearly four years after drawing this, I'd be sitting here in a Jane Thor T-shirt, with a Jane Thor Funko figure on my desk, writing a letter to commemorate the last issue of Jane's long-running series.

That variant cover turned into the main cover and a new job for me. I thought the book would be a good fit (I love fantasy and mythology, billowing capes and flowing hair!), but I was still pretty nervous. I'd just started working for Marvel a few months before, I'd just gotten married – there was a lot of new going on. Plus, Jason's GOD OF THUNDER was one of my favorite comics, and following Esad's art had me intimidated. I wondered if our book would be as good, if it would sell, if anyone would care about this new Thor. And then I see Whoopi Goldberg pointing to my art on *The View.* And then Thor's identity is revealed and I start getting messages from readers saying how much Jane means to them.

I saved a screengrab of Whoopi pointing to the issue #1 cover. In the same folder, I've saved your messages. Thank you for sharing your stories about how you relate to Jane's struggle, or just for writing to say how much you like the book. I know we put you through the emotional wringer with this arc (sorry!), but I hope we did right by you with the finale. I hope we did Jane justice.

This is my last THOR issue, and I'll miss drawing Jane. But I'm thrilled that she has a complete story told by the same creative team (with some fantastic guests). I'm incredibly proud of the work everyone's done. Thank you to Jason for the brilliant ideas, amazing writing and thoughtful scripts, to Matt for the smart and unbelievably gorgeous colors, to Joe for stylishly making everything flow together, to Sarah (and past editors Jon Moisan, Charles Beacham and Chris Robinson!) for steering the ship so well, and to Wil for the guidance, thoughtfulness and opportunity.

I really lucked out, getting to work with some of the absolute best. Here's hoping that down the line, the rainbow bridge gets fixed and we all get teleported back to Asgard together.

In the meantime, I'm excited to see where Jason takes his amazing Thor saga, and I'm sure I'll be drooling over Mike del Mundo's art for it. I have more with Marvel in the pipeline, and I'll share as soon as I can.

Drawing THOR became an absolute dream project, one that will always mean the world to me. Thank you all so much for supporting Jane (and me, and the whole team)!

KRAKKAKOOOOM!
Russell

I never expected all this.

Before Jane became Thor, I'd never had fans come up to me in tears at signings, relating stories of their loved ones who'd passed or of their own battles with cancer.

Before Jane, I'd never had so many people screaming at me on Twitter, so enraged, oftentimes over a book they hadn't even read.

I'd never had a character I helped shape explode so epically, becoming toys and statues and cosplay at every con I've attended since.

Before Jane, I'd never cried while writing a script.

I've never been as emotionally invested in a super hero as I've been in her. And I've never felt such a profound emotional response from the fans as what Jane has generated.

I never imagined she'd become this important to so many people, including myself.

It all started when then-EIC Axel Alonso called and offered me the chance to relaunch THOR after my GOD OF THUNDER run. We agreed that it'd be a great opportunity to have someone else carry the mantle. Since I first took over the character, I knew at some point I wanted to do a Beta Ray Bill sorta story, where Thor's hammer would change hands. And for a while I'd had a vague idea about it being Thor's stepmom Freyja who'd eventually wield Mjolnir.

But as soon as we talked about the relaunch, I knew it had to be Jane.

I'd already shown that Jane was dealing with breast cancer. And as soon as I imagined her becoming Thor, the entire story clicked into place, right up through these last few issues, in a way that stories don't often do, not for me at least, not without a lot of pushing and pulling.

For years, I both eagerly awaited and thoroughly dreaded having to write this "Death of Thor" story. And for the last few months, I've felt the same way every single time I'd get a new email from Russell.

Not enough can be said about what Russell Dauterman and Matthew Wilson have accomplished together on this series. They have brought Jane to life and made her entire world sing and explode and burn in ways that should be remembered and studied and idolized for many eons to come. I cannot possibly thank them enough for all their amazing work, but I'll gladly spend the rest of my mortal life attempting to do so. In other words, the drinks are always on me, boys.

And those thanks and free drinks also go out to everyone else who's worked on the series, including letterer Joe Sabino and all the stellar guest artists, cover artists and assistant editors along the way. And even bigger thanks to editor Wil Moss, who has some of the best artistic tastes and creative instincts of any editor I've ever known. Another round of mead for all of you!

But most especially, thanks to you, the readers. For embracing Jane the way you have. For making her so much a part of your own lives. For making this entire run one of the most rewarding creative and emotional experiences of my entire life.

I'll never forget this Thor. And I'll never forget all of you. And I hope we'll all see each other again, in some other thunderous stories down the road.

Stay worthy.
Jason Aaron
KC, March 2018

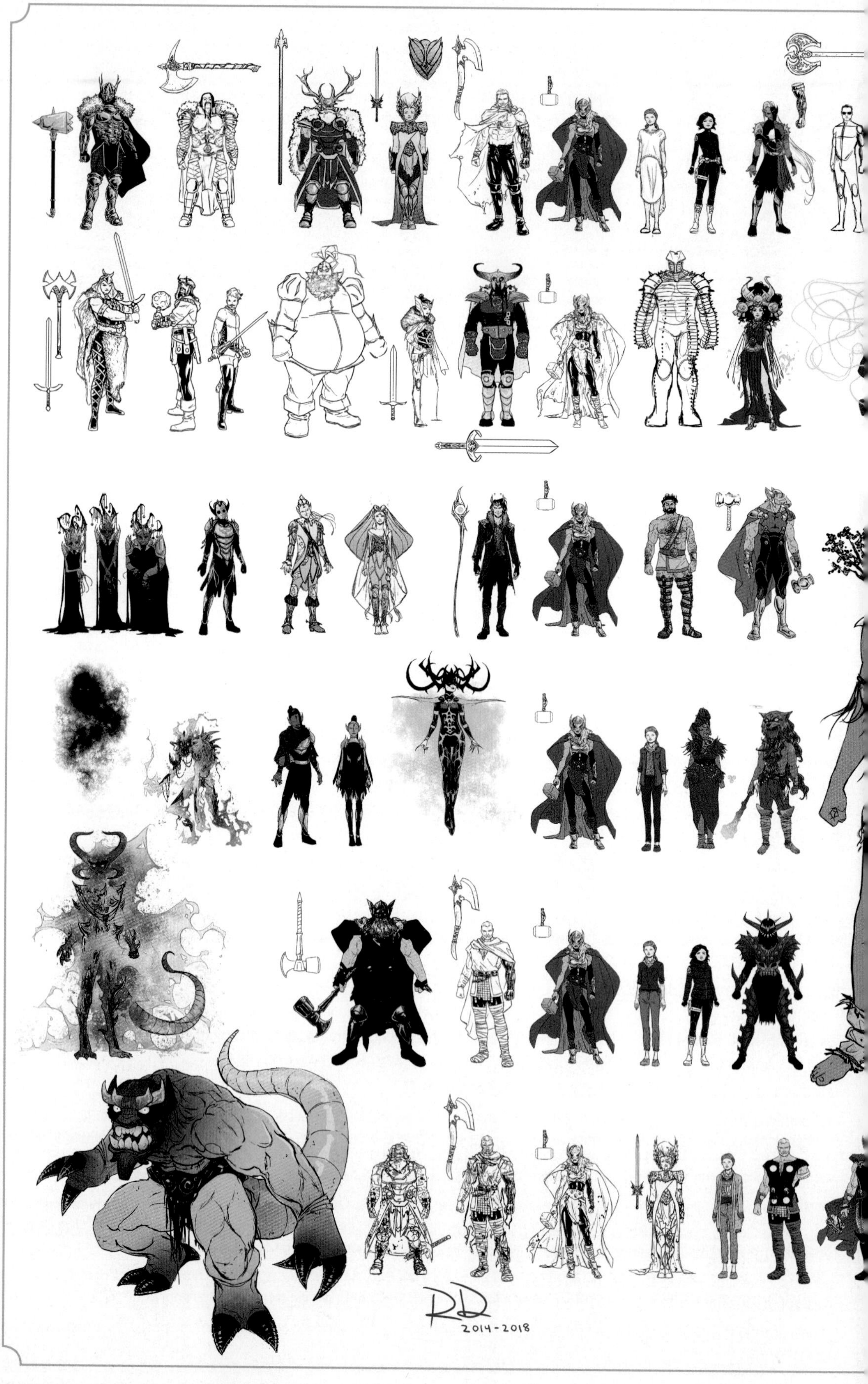
RD
2014-2018

RUSSELL DAUTERMAN CREATED A HEIGHT CHART WITH ALL OF HIS CHARACTER MODELS TO KEEP TRACK OF THEIR RELATIVE SIZES, ADDING CHARACTERS AS THE SERIES WENT ALONG. THIS IS THE RESULTING IMAGE!

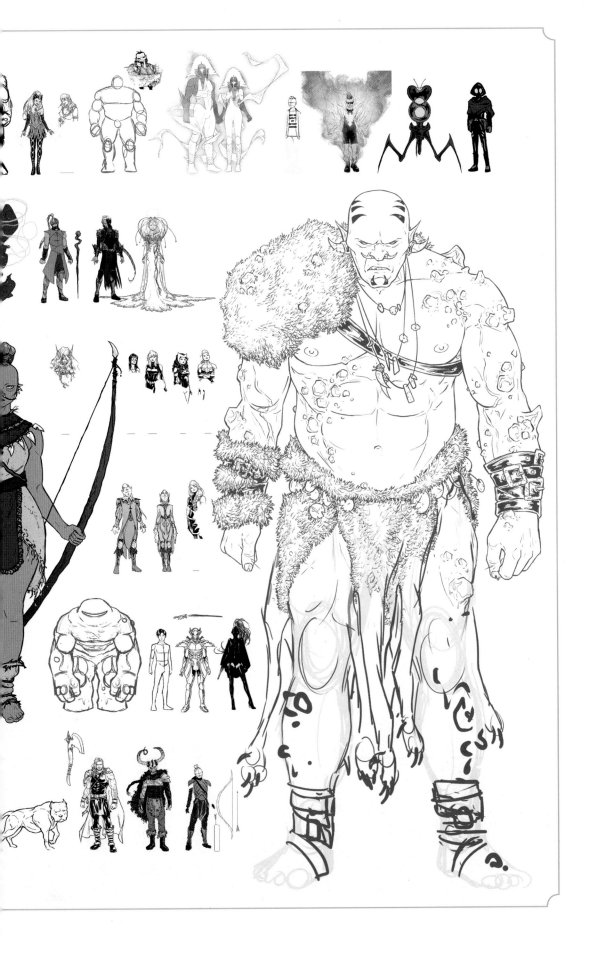

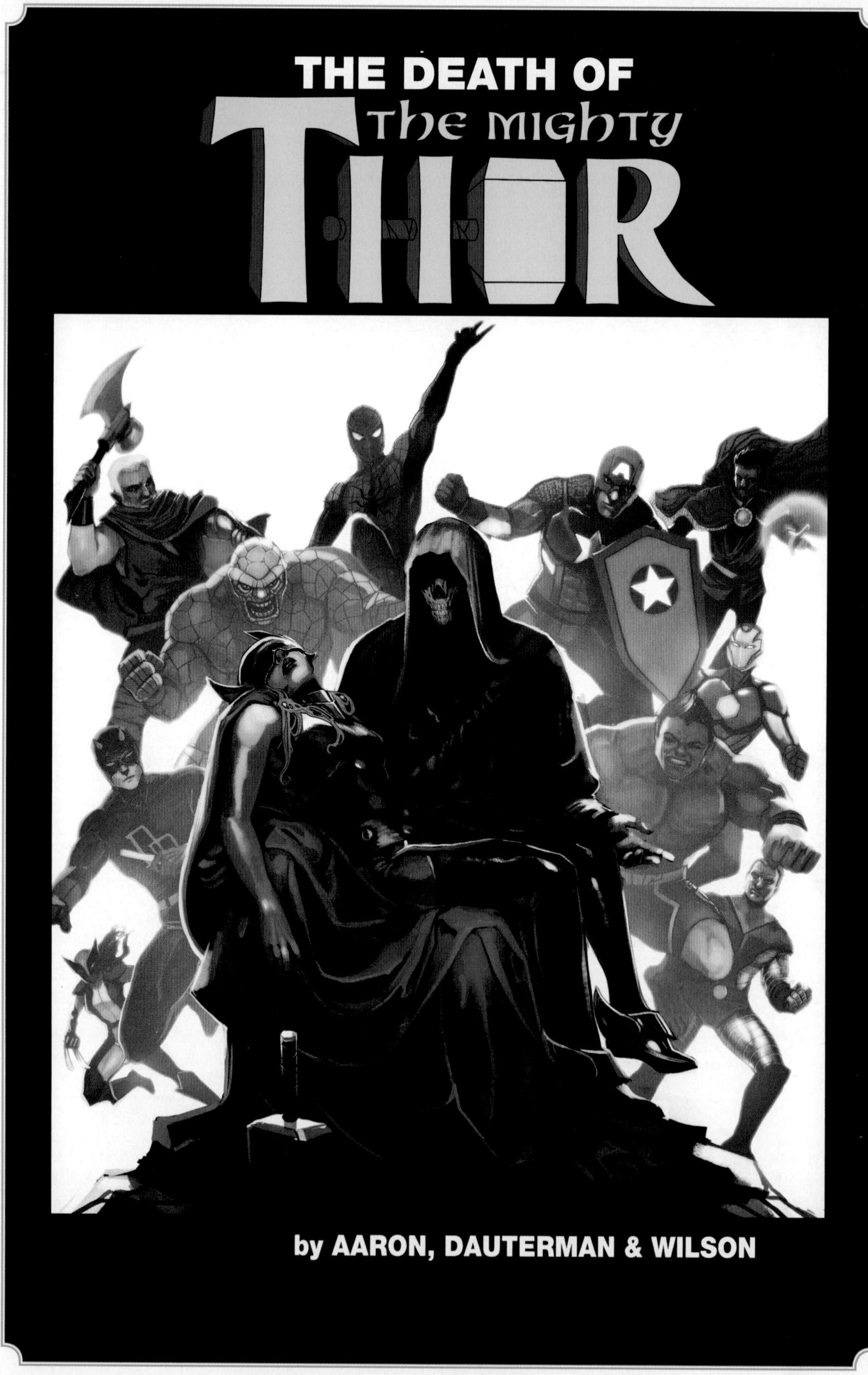
THE DEATH OF
The Mighty
THOR
by AARON, DAUTERMAN & WILSON

MIGHTY THOR #700 HOMAGE VARIANT
BY **STEPHANIE HANS**

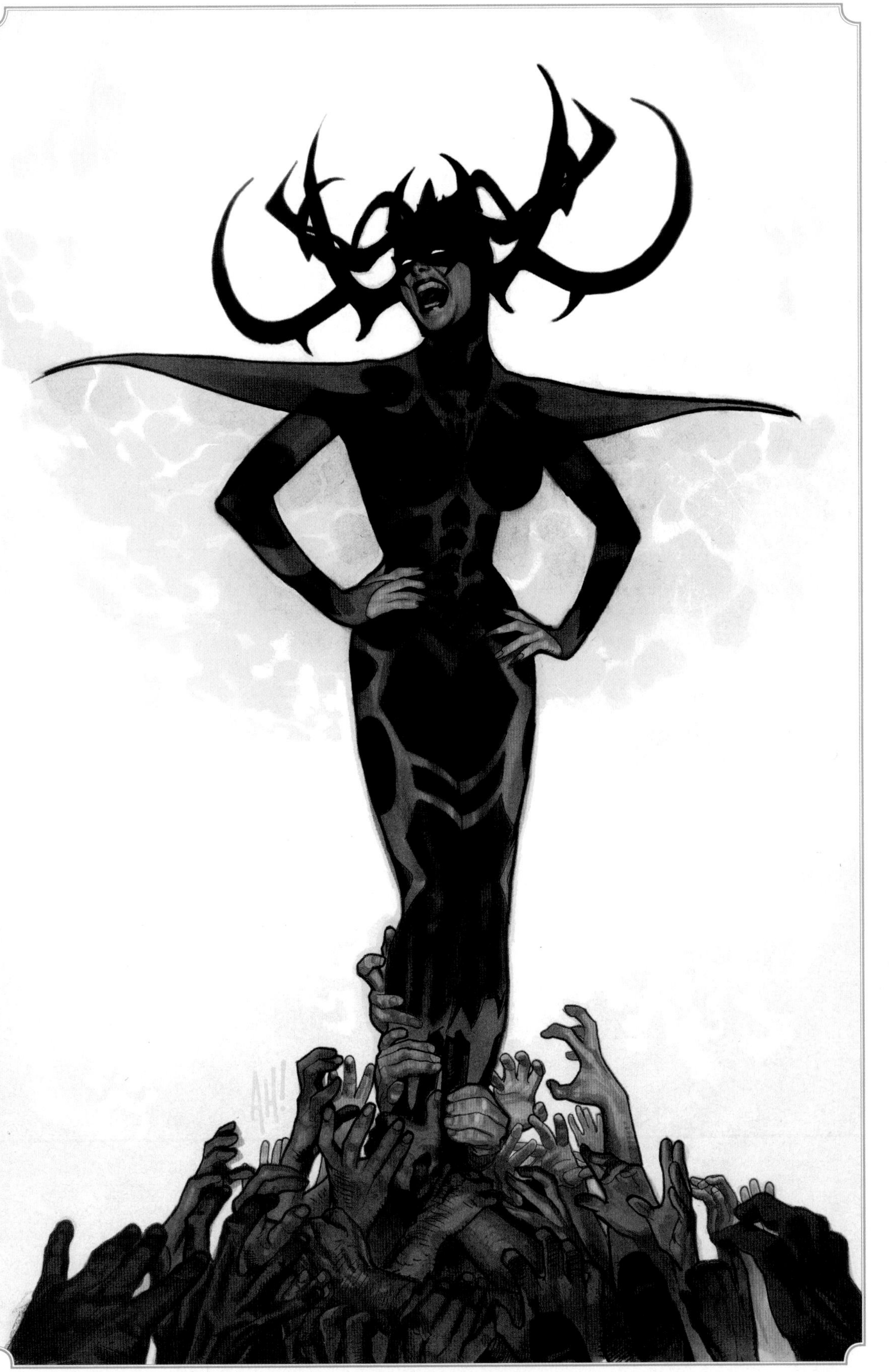

MIGHTY THOR #700 VARIANT
BY **ADAM HUGHES**

# HOW TO DRAW MJOLNIR
## IN SIX EASY STEPS!
### BY CHIP "WORTHLESS" ZDARSKY

Wow! A "sketch variant cover"! Studies show that drawing
keeps you mentally acute and generally unpopular!
Anyway, here's a fun and informative step-by-step guide!

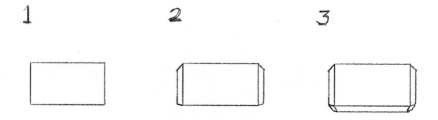

**1**

First step: make a rectangle!
Easy, right? Roughly twice as
long as it is tall!

**2**

Now, even though we didn't
draw the rectangle in
perspective, we'll do a slight
cheat here, and draw its
bevels slightly slanted
downward!

**3**

Now, copy the entire bottom
line just underneath, but
make it a little smaller for
receding perspective. Then
connect the points!

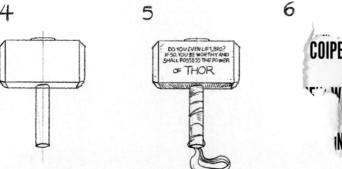

**4**

DO YOU EVEN LIFT, BRO?
IF SO, YOU BE WORTHY AND
SHALL POSSESS THE POWER
OF THOR

Place a cylinder, like a paper
towel roll, below the
hammer's head, and then
show the hints of a larger disc
above! A center guide line will
help you place these!

**5**

Add a loose strap at the base and
wrap the handle in leather! Then, add
some shading and little details for the
stone and handle! I forget the quote
that's on the hammer, but it's
something like this. Basically to lift it
you have to be worthy, like, SUPER
worthy, or it will NOT budge. Done!

**6**

COIPEL & STEV

WILS

N); A

Now, protect your comic by
picking it up and placing it in
a bag and—oh.

Uh.

MIGHTY THOR #700 HOW TO DRAW VARIANT
BY **CHIP ZDARSKY**

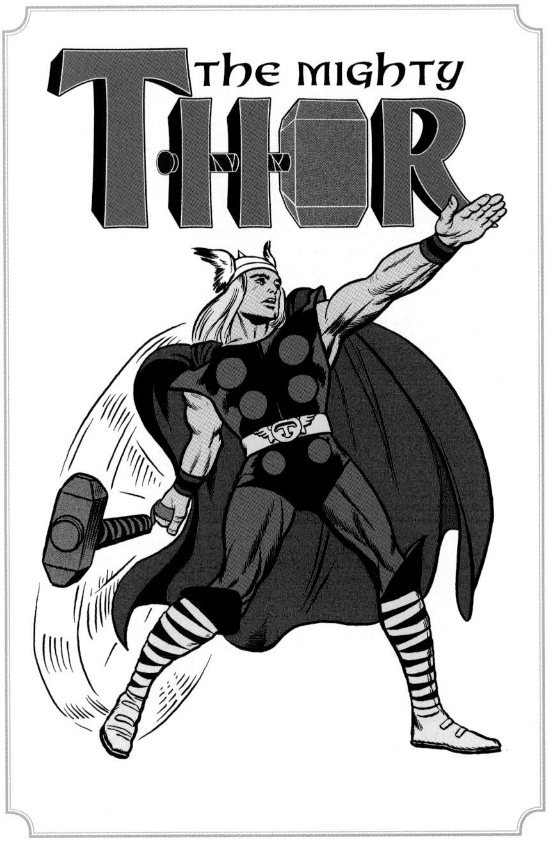
THE MIGHTY
THOR

MIGHTY THOR #700 1965 T-SHIRT VARIANT
BY **JACK KIRBY & DICK AYERS**

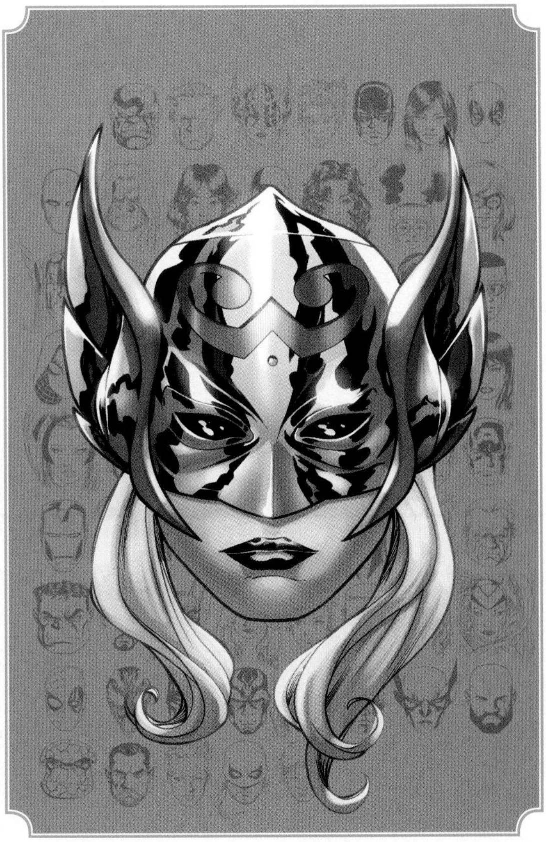

MIGHTY THOR #700 LEGACY HEADSHOT VARIANT
BY **MIKE McKONE & RACHELLE ROSENBERG**

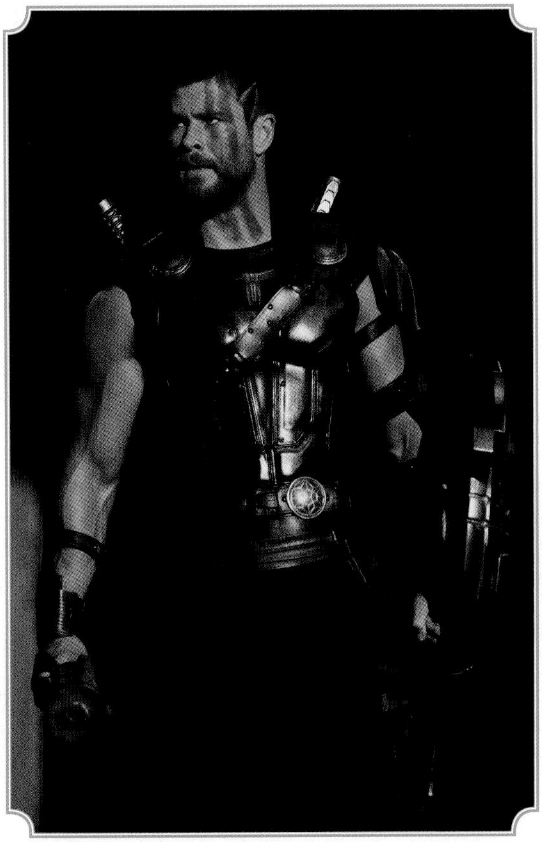

MIGHTY THOR #700 MOVIE VARIANT

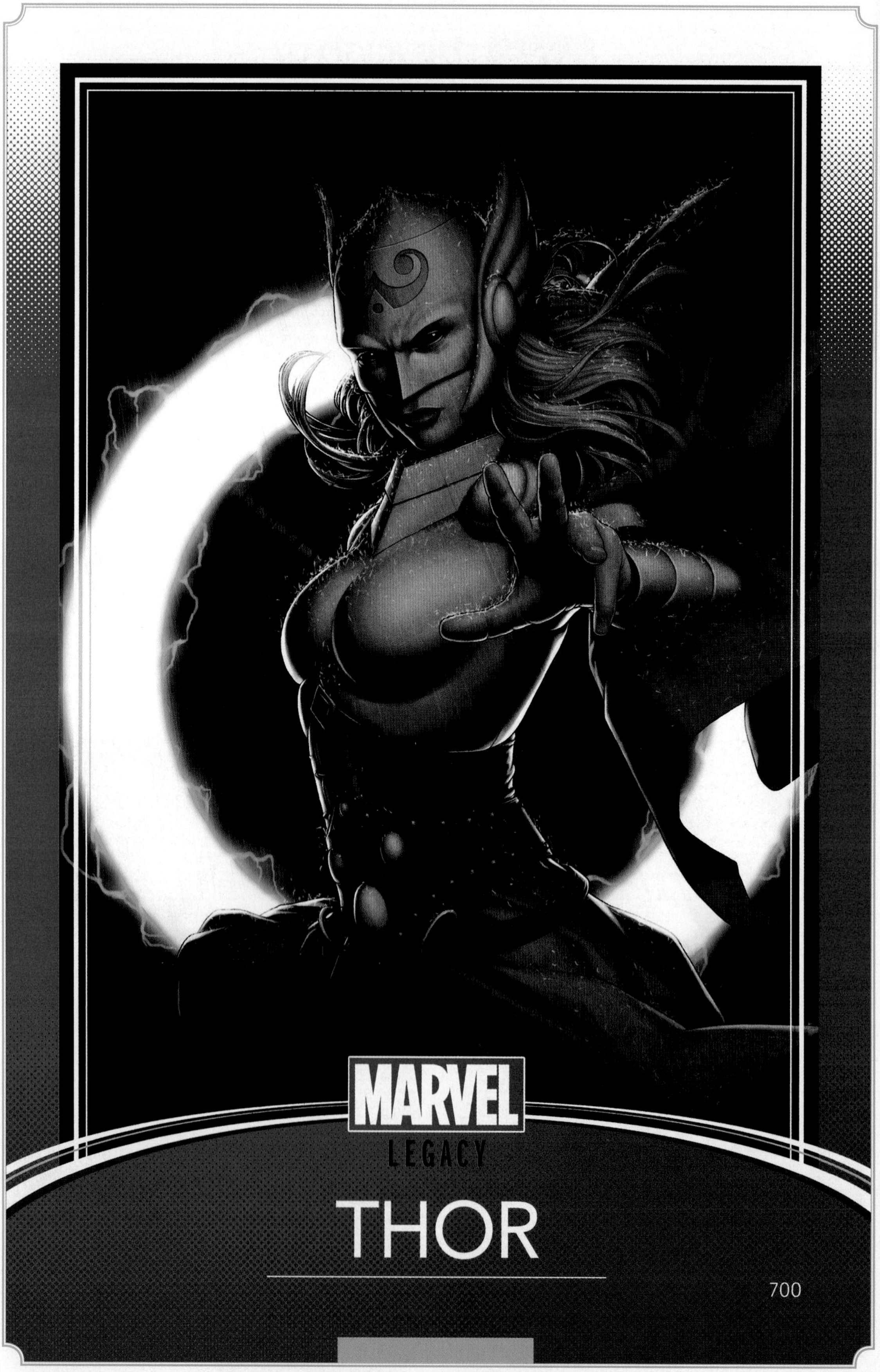
MARVEL
LEGACY
THOR
700

MIGHTY THOR #700 TRADING CARD VARIANT
BY **JOHN TYLER CHRISTOPHER**

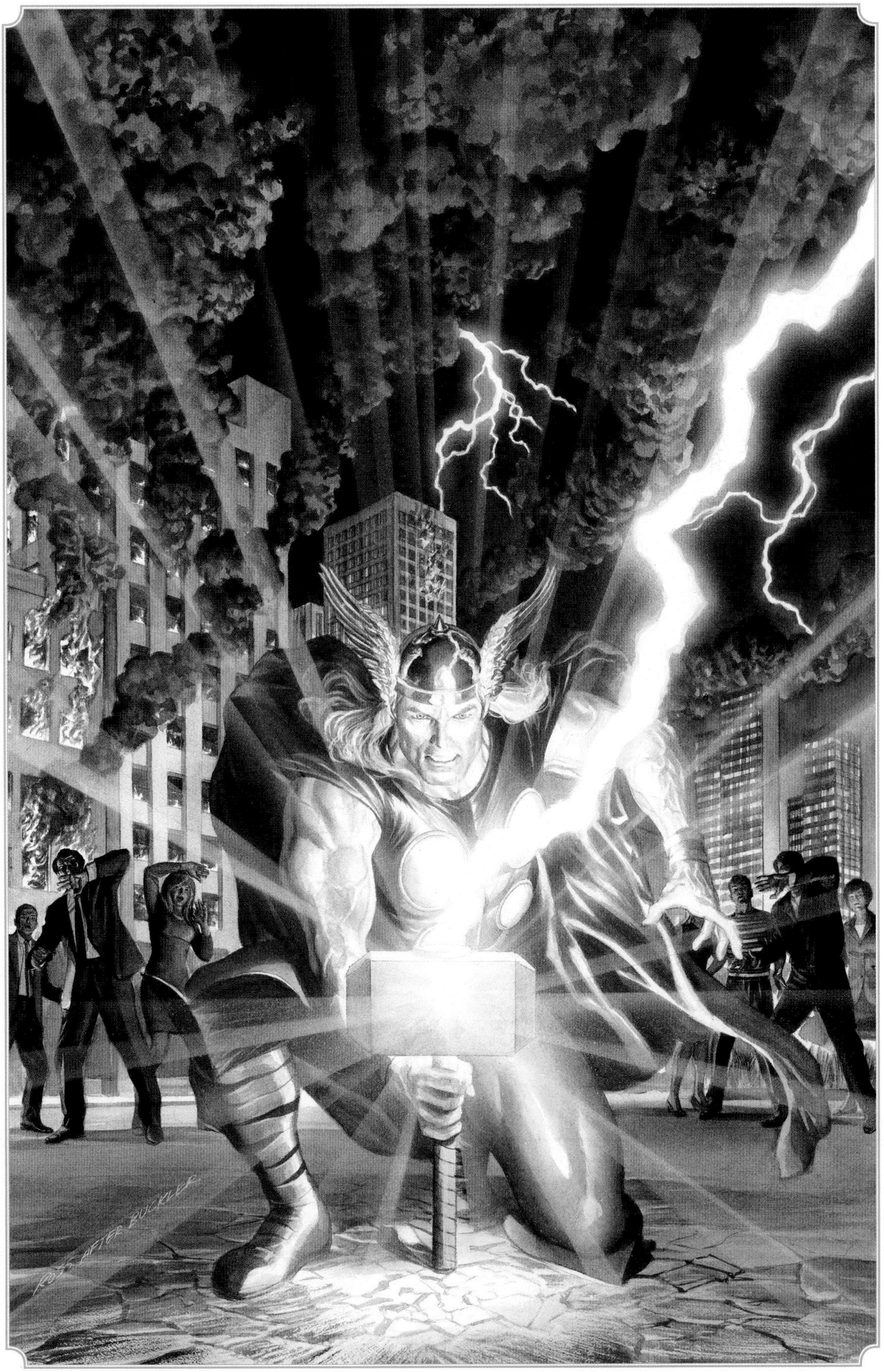

MIGHTY THOR #701 VARIANT
BY **ALEX ROSS**

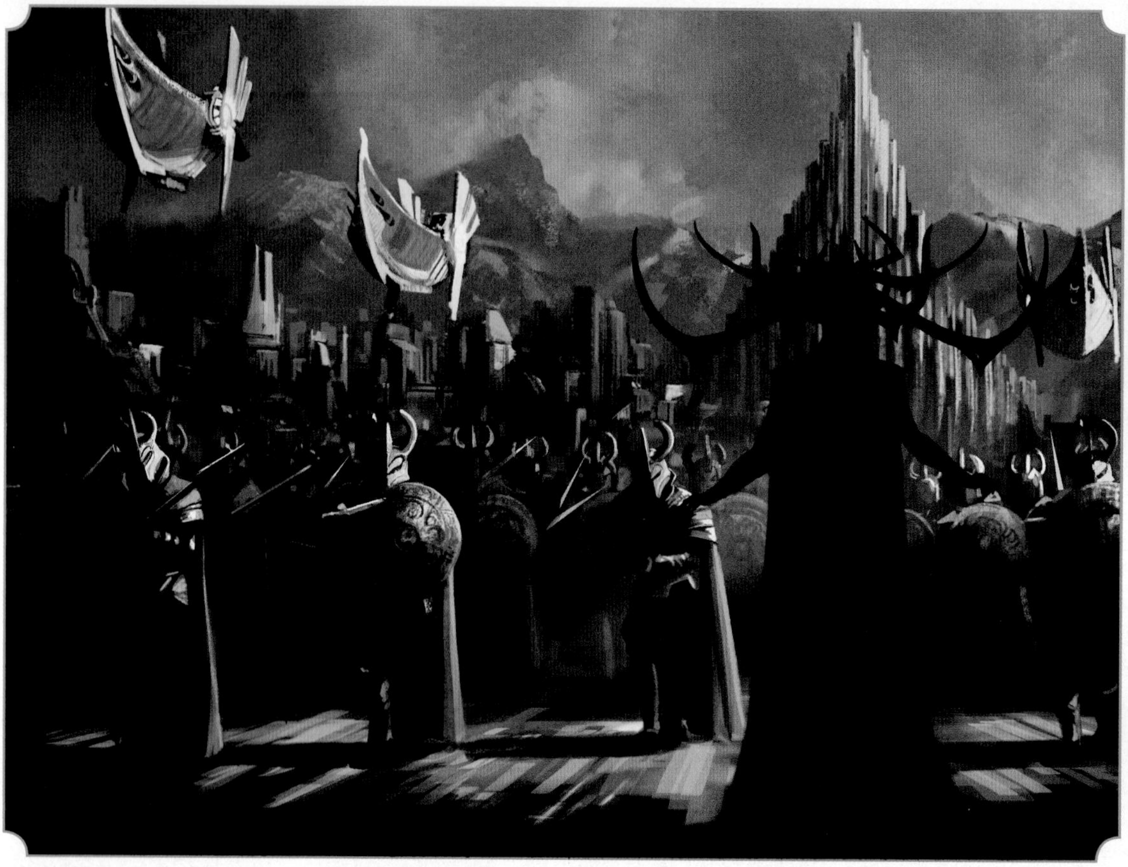

MIGHTY THOR #700 MOVIE VARIANT
BY **JACKSON SZE**

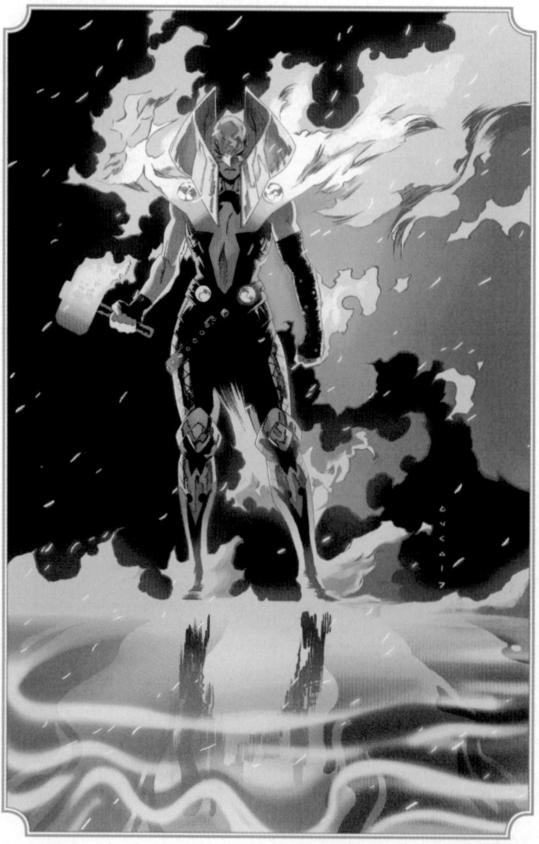

MIGHTY THOR #702 PHOENIX VARIANT
BY **KRIS ANKA**

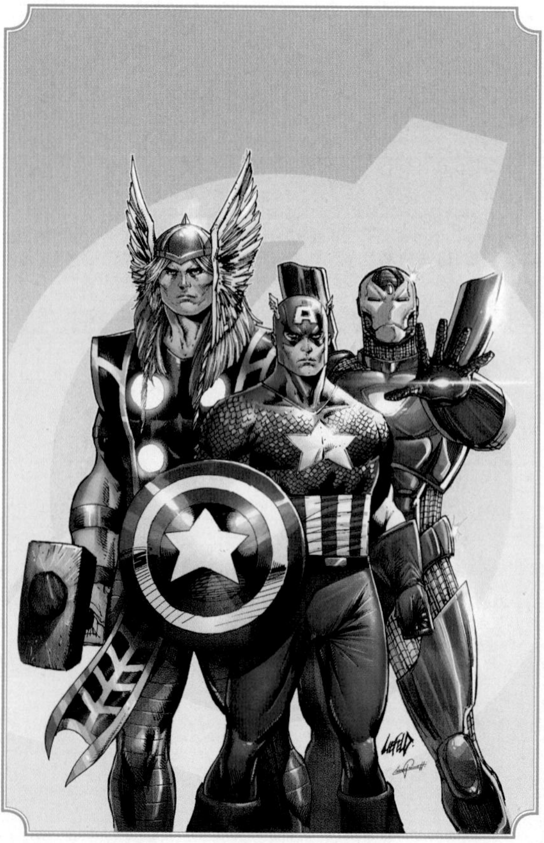

MIGHTY THOR #704 HEROES REBORN VARIANT
BY **ROB LIEFELD & LEO PACIAROTTI**

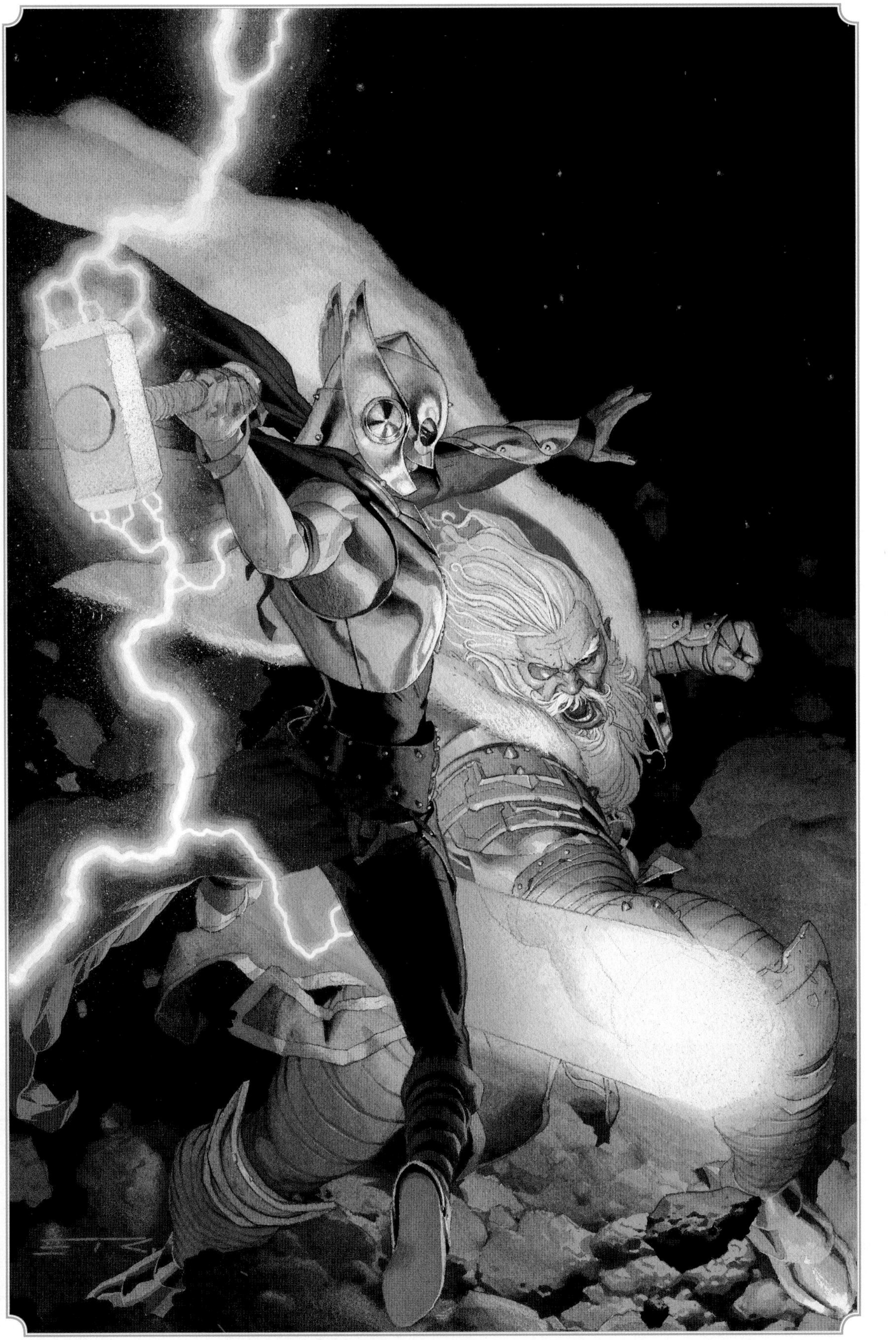

MIGHTY THOR #705 VARIANT
BY **ESAD RIBIĆ**

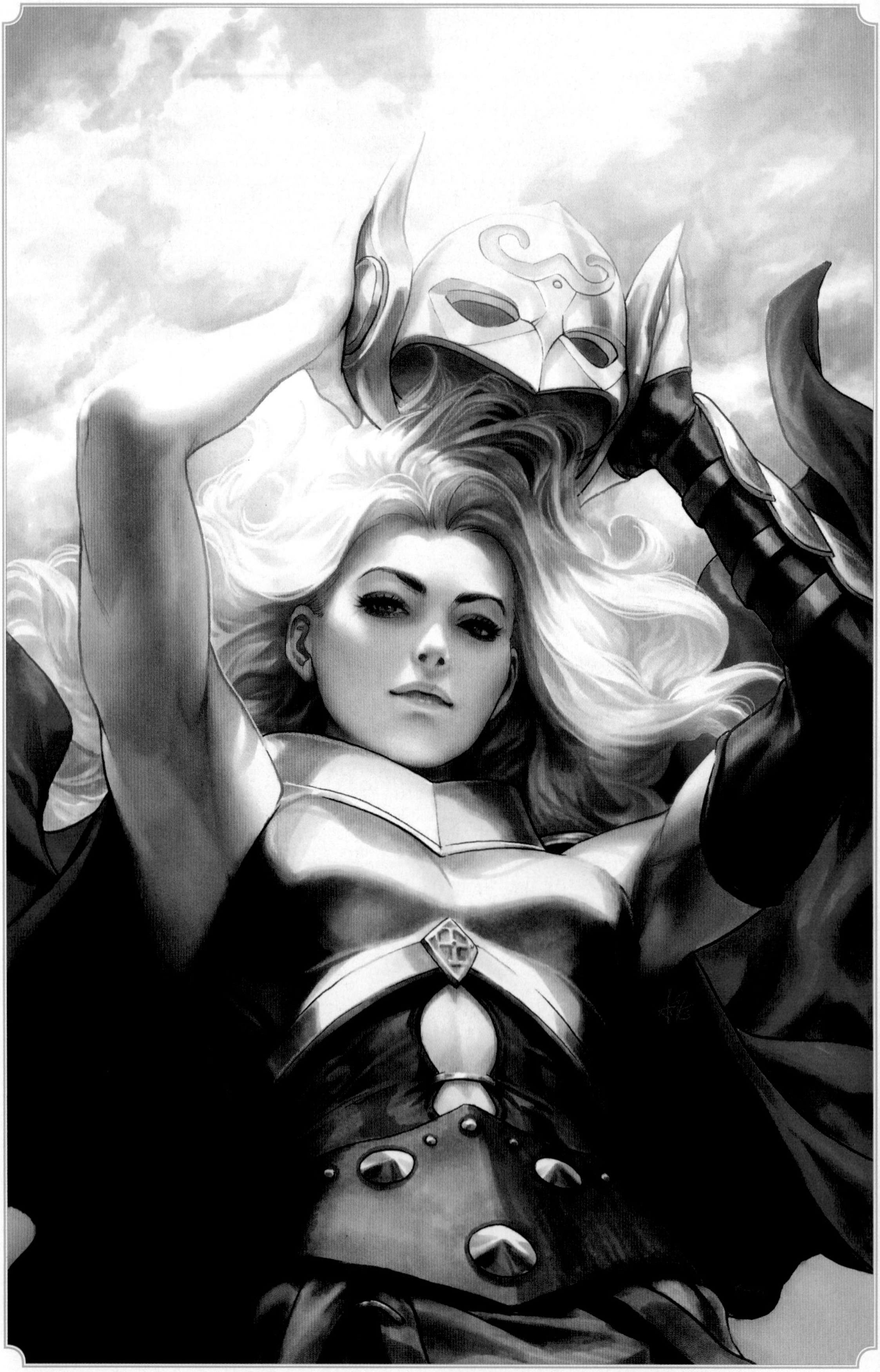

MIGHTY THOR #705 VARIANT
BY **ARTGERM**

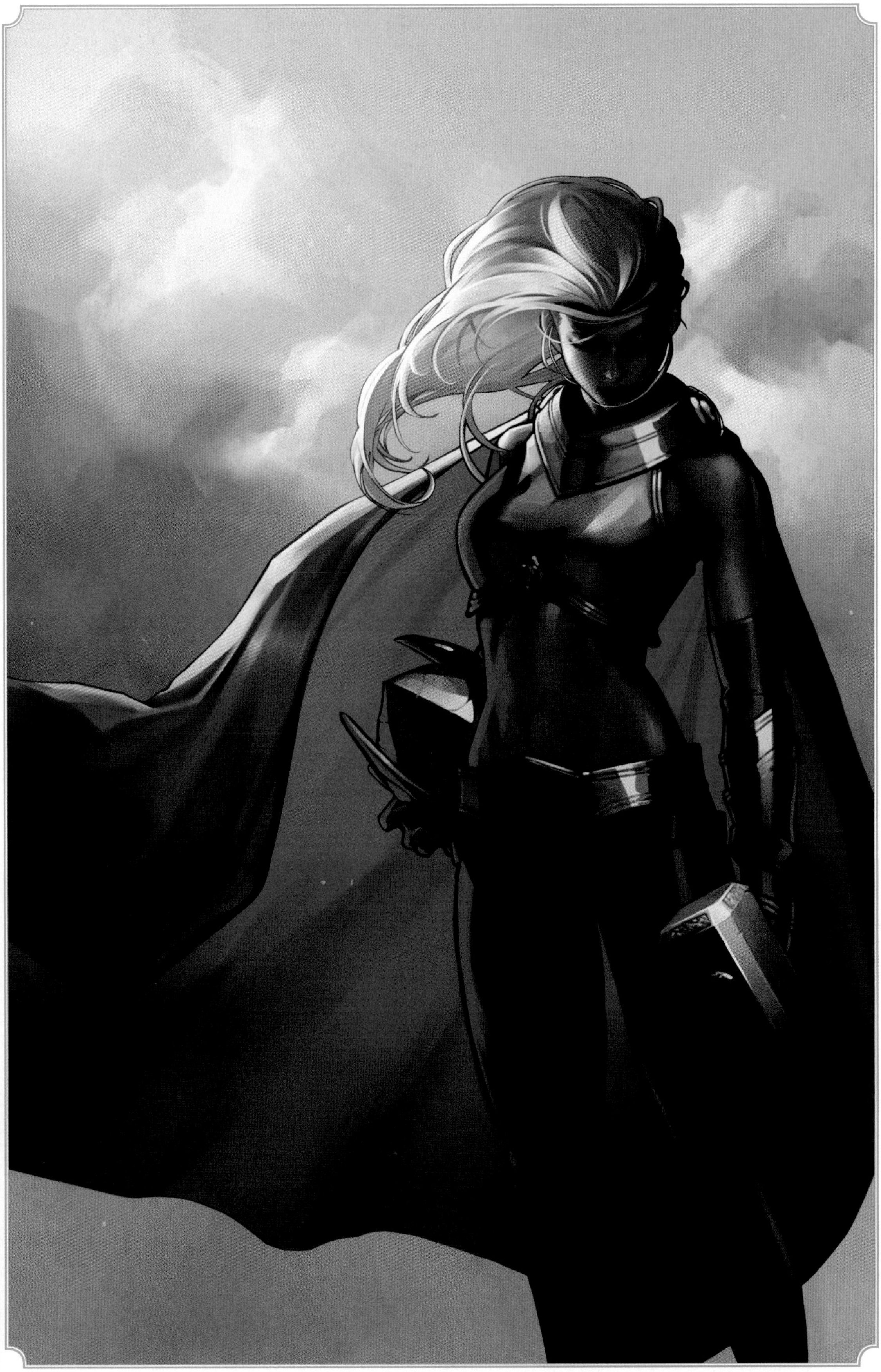

MIGHTY THOR #705 VARIANT
BY **JEE-HYUNG LEE**

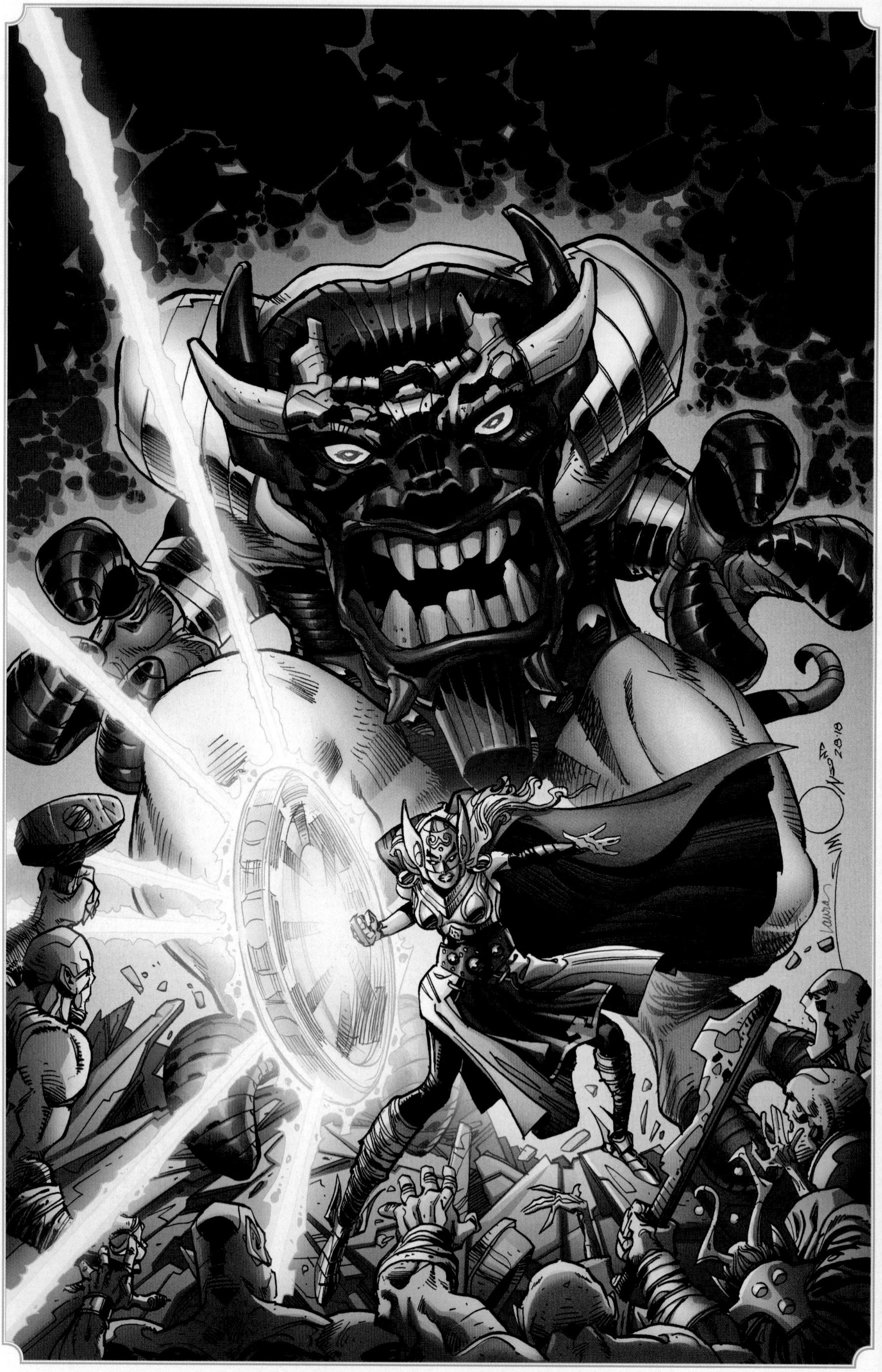

MIGHTY THOR #706 VARIANT
BY **WALTER SIMONSON & LAURA MARTIN**

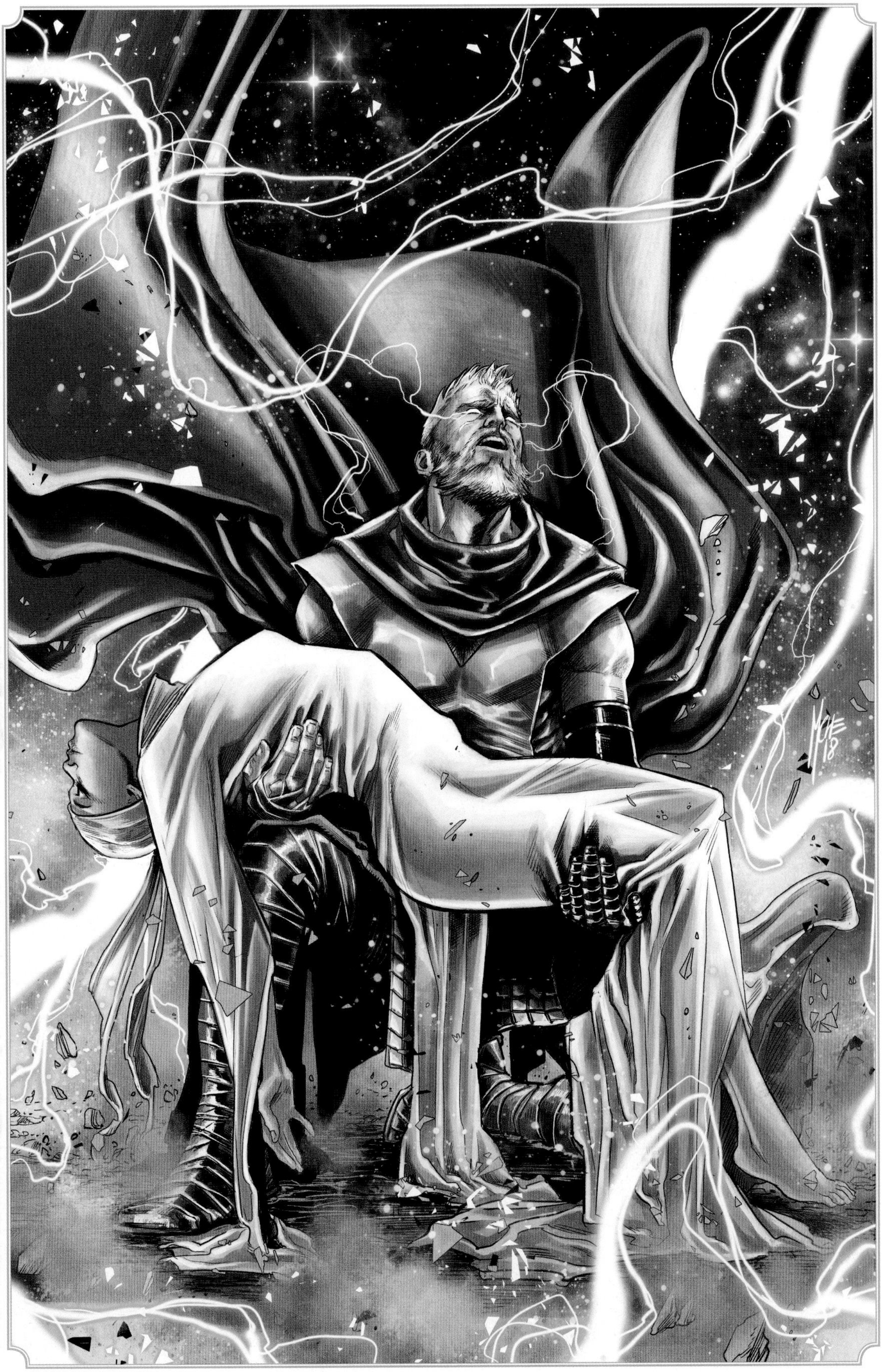

MIGHTY THOR #706 VARIANT
BY **MARCO CHECCHETTO**

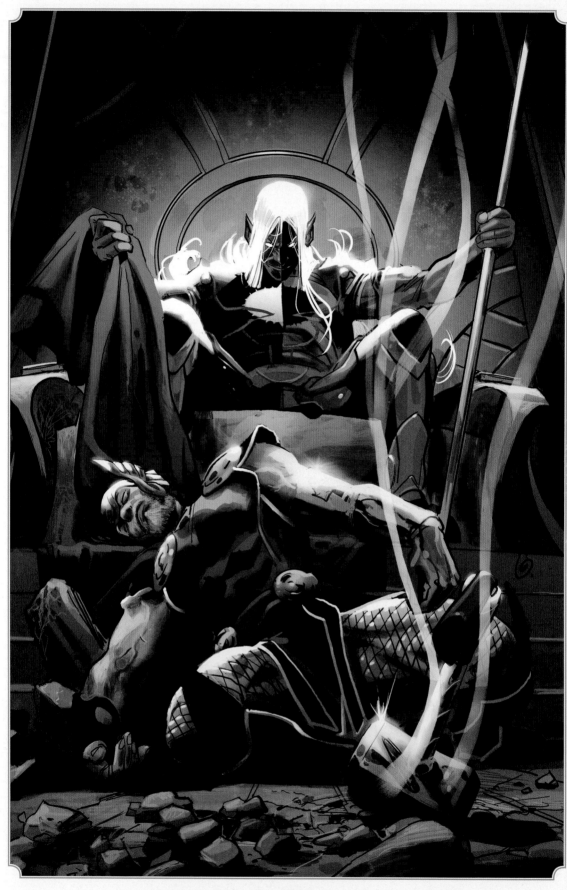

MIGHTY THOR: AT THE GATES OF VALHALLA VARIANT
BY **RON GARNEY & MATT MILLA**